THEGREENGUIDE
Châteaux
of the Loire

Château de Sully-sur-Loire   Photo: © Arnaud Chicurel/hemis.fr

MICHELIN

THEGREENGUIDE **CHÂTEAUX OF THE LOIRE**

Editorial Director   Cynthia Clayton Ochterbeck

Editor   Sophie Friedman
Principal writer   Nick Taylor, Terry Marsh
Production Manager   Natasha George
Cartography   Peter Wrenn
Picture Editor   Yoshimi Kanazawa
Interior Design   Chris Bell
Cover Design   Chris Bell, Christelle Le Déan
Layout   Natasha George

Contact Us   Michelin Travel and Lifestyle North America
                            One Parkway South
                            Greenville, SC 29615
                            USA
                            travel.lifestyle@us.michelin.com

                            Michelin Travel Partner
                            Hannay House
                            39 Clarendon Road
                            Watford, Herts WD17 1JA
                            UK
                            ℰ01923 205240
                            travelpubsales@uk.michelin.com
                            www.viamichelin.co.uk

Special Sales   For information regarding bulk sales,
                            customized editions and premium sales,
                            please contact us at:
                            travel.lifestyle@us.michelin.com

HOW TO USE THIS GUIDE

PLANNING YOUR TRIP

The blue-tabbed PLANNING YOUR TRIP section at the front of the guide gives you **ideas for your trip** and **practical information** to help you organise it. You'll find tours and outdoor activities, a calendar of events, and information on transpotation, shopping, sightseeing, kids' activities and more.

INTRODUCTION

The orange-tabbed INTRODUCTION explores the **Region Today,** including food and drink. The **History** section spans Roman times through the Revolution and World Wars, exploring the development of the region and the châteaux. The **Art and Culture** section covers architecture, art and literature, while **Nature** delves into the landscape, flora and fauna.

DISCOVERING

The green-tabbed DISCOVERING section features Principal Sights by region, highlighting the most interesting local **Sights**, **Walking Tours**, nearby **Excursions**, and detailed **Driving Tours**. Admission prices shown are normally for a single adult.

ADDRESSES

We've selected from the best hotels, restaurants, cafés, shops, nightlife and entertainment to fit all budgets. See the Legend on the cover flap for an explanation of the price categories. See the back of the guide for an index of where to find hotels and restaurants.

Sidebars

Throughout the guide you will find blue, orange and green-coloured text boxes with lively anecdotes, detailed history and background information.

😊 A Bit of Advice 😊

Green advice boxes found in this guide contain practical tips and handy information relevant to your visit or to a sight in the Discovering section.

STAR RATINGS★★★

Michelin has given star ratings for more than 100 years. If you're pressed for time, we recommend you visit the ★★★, or ★★ sights first:

★★★	**Worth a special journey**
★★	**Worth a detour**
★	**Interesting**

MAPS

- 🄫 Principal Sights map
- 🄫 Regional maps
- 🄫 Maps for major cities and villages
- 🄫 Floor plans for major abbeys and cathedrals
- 🄫 Local tour maps

All maps in this guide are oriented north, unless otherwise indicated by a directional arrow. The term "Local Map" refers to a map within the chapter or Tourism Region. A complete list of the maps found in the guide appears at the back of this book.

© Patrick Escudero/hemis.fr

© Laurent Marolleau/age fotostock

PLANNING YOUR TRIP

INTRODUCTION TO CHÂTEAUX OF THE LOIRE

DISCOVERING CHÂTEAUX OF THE LOIRE

CONTENTS

© Arnaud Chicurel/hemis.fr

Welcome to Châteaux of the Loire

Located south/southwest of Paris, the Loire Valley is one of France's most beautiful regions. Its magnificent châteaux, cultural riches and eventful history have earned the Val de Loire between Sully-sur-Loire in the east and Chalonnes, near Angers in the west, a place on the list of UNESCO World Heritage Sites. The area covers a 280km/170mi stretch of the Loire river; rich and fertile land known as "the Garden of France" that offers a wealth of unrivalled attractions, including majestic châteaux and the towns of Amboise, Angers, Blois, Chinon, Saumur and Tours.

THE LOIRET *(pp90–115)*

One of the original 83 *départements* created at the time of the administrative reorganisations of the French Revolution, the Loiret is largely agricultural, with grain production on the plains of the Beauce to the north, horticulture in the Val d'Orléans and livestock in the south. Although known more as the gateway to the Val de Loire, the Loiret has a number of attractions that are well worth discovering before venturing deeper into châteaux country. Orléans Forest, the largest natural forest in France, has walking trails along with opportunities for fishing and water sports.

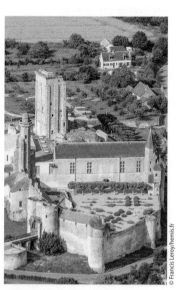

Château du Grand-Pressigny, East Touraine

THE LOIRE BLÉSOISE *(pp116–140)*

The focal point of this region, Blois is renowned for its splendid château, which proudly displays the architectural styles seen throughout the Loire Valley from the Middle Ages to the 17C. The Forest of Russy to the south is a reminder of the appearance of the landscape of the past, while the area's many other magnificent châteaux, led by Chambord, Cheverny, Beauregard, Talcy and Fougères-sur-Bièvre, offer an architectural and historical feast.

THE SOLOGNE *(pp141–154)*

The Sologne is a peaceful, wild and untamed area, abounding with game-filled forests and harbouring almost 3,000 ponds, making this area popular with walkers, anglers and hunters. The Domaine du Ciran in Ménestreau-en-Villette is dedicated to explaining the flora and fauna of Sologne and, like the château de la Ferté-Saint-Aubin, is a must-see. Elsewhere, the Maison des Étangs in Saint-Viâtre provides a superb interpretation of the aquatic life of Sologne.

EAST TOURAINE *(pp155–186)*

The Touraine is a former province of France, with its capital at Tours. Today the area is renowned for its wine production and its celebrated châteaux, notably on the east coast in the town of Chenonceaux, as well as Loches, with its medieval old town, and Amboise, where Leonardo da Vinci spent the last three years of his life (his house can be toured).

WEST TOURAINE *(pp187–223)*

The western part of Touraine has its fair share of stunning châteaux, from the majestic Azay-le-Rideau and the wondrous Château d'Ussé to the stark ruins of Chinon and the breathtaking gardens at Villandry. The main city, Tours, is famous for its many bridges spanning the Loire, but is especially noteworthy for its medieval district, Le Vieux Tours, a place of handsome half-timbered houses. With its excellent TGV links, Tours is a logical starting point for visits to the Loire valley.

THE SAUMUR AND BAUGÉ REGIONS *(pp224–248)*

The historic château town of Saumur lies between the Loire and Thouet rivers, surrounded by extensive vineyards that produce some of the finest wines in France, including Chinon, Bourgueil and Coteaux du Layon. By comparison, Baugé has a fine 15C château; it was here that a major battle against the English was fought in 1421. The popular Opéra de Baugé, modelled on England's Glyndebourne Festival, takes place annually and draws more than 3,000 visitors.

ANJOU AND THE MAUGES COUNTRY *(pp249–274)*

Anjou, an ancient county, duchy and province, centres on the city of Angers in the lower Loire valley. Best known for its castle and the Tapestry of the Apocalypse, Angers can trace its pedigree to Roman times. It occupies both banks of the Maine river, which is spanned by six bridges. Today, the corner of Angers that flanks the river is renowned for its nurseries and market gardens. Several dolmens and menhirs in the countryside of Mauges testify to a prehistoric presence more than 12,000 years ago. The Menhir de Saint-Macaire-en-Mauges is an impressive highlight.

LAVAL AND THE MAYENNE VALLEY *(pp275–288)*

An agreeable mix of nature and tradition reigns in Mayenne, with much to delight lovers of countryside, Romanesque churches, castles and beautiful villages. Flanking the Mayenne river, the main community is the market town of Laval. North of Angers some 17km/10.5mi, the valley boasts the 15C Château du Plessis-Bourré with its vast moat.

THE SARTHE VALLEY AND PERCHE-GOUËT *(pp289–316)*

Straddling the Sarthe river, Le Mans will be forever associated with the famous 24-hour motor races. Historically, however, its significance rests in its well-preserved old town, the *Cité Plantagenet*, where this English dynasty was founded by Henry II of England, son of Geoffrey V of Anjou. It is a delightful part of the city, in which the inspiring architecture is imbued with a great sense of place. The countryside of the Sarthe valley comprises woodland, meadows and fields of cereal; orchards and dairy farms dot the Perche-Gouët.

THE LOIR VALLEY *(pp317–351)*

Everyone is familiar with the Loire (La Loire), France's longest and wildest river, but few people are acquainted with Le Loir, a place of more modest but no less beautiful villages and castles. Le Loir rises in the little village of Fruncé, to the west of Chartres, and along its course runs by numerous troglodytic sites and dwellings, many of which are still used today as homes, shops and restaurants. In Le Loir there is little of the frenetic activity often associated with the attractions of La Loire. In its place comes a rather peaceful approach to life, less dominantly touristy but of great appeal nonetheless.

Flat-bottmed boat on the Loire at sunrise, Chaumont-sur-Loire
© Patrick Escudero/hemis.fr

Michelin Driving Tours

The following is a brief description of possible driving tours in the region covered by this guide.

1 HAUT-ANJOU

170km/102mi starting from Angers
Begin this tour in "Good King René's" city, and discover the surrounding region of Anjou Noir. Hedgerows and sunken paths cut across the landscape, abbeys and châteaux abound. The River Mayenne offers opportunities for pleasant cruises and waterside picnics. Many lovely manor houses and impressive properties line this route. The region is renowned for its mellow, fecund landscapes, and the warm welcome of its people, helped, undoubtedly, by the balmy maritime climate, which does much to support the production of crops and age-old vineyards, and a gentle way of life.

2 LE MANS, SARTHE AND LOIR

240km/144mi starting from Le Mans
Head for the hills, starting from the city of Le Mans, host to the 24-hour motor race since 1923, and famous as the cradle of the Plantagenet dynasty. The rolling landscape sparkles with fine fishing streams; meadows and woods form a patchwork. You may prefer to take your time and spend more than a day on this itinerary. Le Mans is a vibrant, bustling town situated on the Sarthe river, and a vital part of any itinerary. Its inhabitants are called Manceaux and Mancelles, and it is the capital of the Sarthe *département,* which was created during the French Revolution in 1790. In Roman times the province contained the city of Mans, of which a number of ruins are still standing.
The driving tour provides ample opportunity to visit vineyards producing the delightful Jasnières white wine, and takes you by the region's Gallo-Roman wall, which is unique in Europe.

3 LOIR VALLEY AND VENDÔME REGION

170km/102mi starting from Châteaudun
The landscapes along the enchanting Loir Valley are a peaceful and harmonious succession of meadows, woods and vineyards. This natural beauty is dotted with Romanesque churches, romantic ruined castles and houses built in the distinctive white stone of the region. The château at Châteaudun is the northernmost of the châteaux of the Loire (*La Loire*); from there follow the tributary Loir (*Le Loir*) south to Vendôme – a charming, lively town. Continue on to Lavardin, one of the prettiest villages in France, dominated by the ruins of a giant medieval fortress. The route continues to Montoire-sur-le-Loir, then Trôo, where cave dwellings have been carved into the stone cliffs. Visit the Renaissance château in Poncé-sur-le-Loir or the manor of La Possonnière. This itinerary then veers north again, through Mondoubleau, perched on a hillside. In St-Agil, the château is watched over by magnificent lime trees, nearly 300 years old. The Knights Templar established the Commanderie at Arvillé. Return to Châteaudun via Courtalain.

4 ORLÉANS AND SOLOGNE

180km/108mi starting from Orléans
Follow La Loire as it meanders through Sologne. Much of the farmland was once an uninhabitable flood plain. Over time, fields have been recovered for farming; since the 19C, the woodlands have been a favoured hunting ground. Today, wild animals still roam the pine forest, and waterfowl visit the many ponds. Along the riverside, great châteaux welcomed many historic figures. From Orléans, travel to Châteauneuf-sur-Loire, where a museum presents a history of navigation on the river. Then carry on to St-Benoît, site of one of the most beautiful abbeys in France. The château at Sully was rebuilt after the Second World War, and in Gien the brick château is now home to a

hunting museum. Lamotte-Beuvron is famous for its *tarte tatin* (apple upside-down cake). Finish your tour with a relaxing stroll in the gardens of La Source.

5 BLOIS AND THE GREAT CHÂTEAUX OF THE RENAISSANCE

120km/72mi starting from Blois

In the heart of the Centre-Val de Loire region, not far from Paris and easily accessible by road or high-speed train, Blois is the gateway to the kingdom of castles. Here, between the Cher and the Loire, stand some of the most elegant Renaissance châteaux in the world, in such abundance that their grace and beauty are almost overwhelming. Visit the royal palaces of Chambord and Blois (once occupied by King Louis XII); the sumptuous châteaux of the nobility at Beauregard, Chaumont and Cheverny; and the manor house of Villesavin. Blois is of ancient origin, but does not appear in records to any extent until the 6C. In the 9C it became the seat of a powerful countship, and in the 16C, Blois was frequently the location of the French court.

6 VAL DE TOURAINE: A PLACE OF BEAUTY

150km/90mi starting from Tours

This is the land the French dream of when they reflect on all that is good in their country: the roots of history, the fruit of the vine and unequalled *savoir vivre*. Begin in Tours and stop in Vouvray, home to the wine of the same name. Then on to Amboise, where François I held court, and to Clos-Lucé, where Leonardo da Vinci came to live at the King's request. In Montrichard, make time to see a demonstration of birds of prey. Then head for the beautiful Château de Chenonceau, gracefully arcing over the Cher river. A visit to Loches carries the imagination back to the Middle Ages. Return to Tours via the valley of the River Indre and the town of Monbazon.

7 THE MOST BEAUTIFUL CHÂTEAUX IN TOURAINE

130km/78mi starting from Tours

Discovering the Val de Touraine is like opening a jewellery box lined in lush green velvet, fragrant with the scent of summer roses. The jewels on the green field are royal castles. Start out from Tours and drive to the Château de Luynes, perched upon a rocky spur. Then visit Cinq-Mars-la-Pile – the name derives from a slender tower *(pile)* dating from Gallo-Roman times. Langeais presents the severe façade of a feudal fortress, but inside, the decoration is evocative of life at court in ages past. In Bourgeuil, stop and visit a local vintner to taste light-hearted wines; continue on to Chinon to compare them with the slightly more robust red wines made there. Enter the Château d'Ussé quietly, so as not to disturb Sleeping Beauty. The image of Azay-le-Rideau reflected in the waters of the Indre is a model of Renaissance elegance. Villandry is especially loved for the beauty of its carefully restored gardens: the garden of love, the water garden, the herb garden and the kitchen garden.

8 SAUMUR REGION AND LAYON VALLEY

140km/84mi starting from Saumur

This lovely region south of the Loire is a garden of delights – or a vineyard of delights, if you prefer. As you leave the town of Saumur, the sunny hillsides are covered in the vines that produce Anjou wines; the region is also renowned for some excellent cheeses, too. Farther on, encounter a wooded landscape, and culinary pleasures at every stage. Many interesting monuments and sights await your visit: Brissac and its enormous eight-storey château, Doué-la-Fontine, the "City of Roses", and its superb zoo, the medieval ramparts of Montreuil-Bellay, and the royal abbey of Fontevraud.

In the Layon Valley, keep an eye open for the curious *moulins à cavier,* hut-like windmills on conical platforms.

When and Where to Go

WHEN TO GO

CLIMATE

Visitors to the Loire Valley will be impressed by the beauty and diversity of the landscape all year round. When planning your visit, it is worth noting that the weather can be very hot and the various places of interest draw large crowds of tourists at the height of the **summer** (July–August). **Spring** comes early to the Loire Valley, especially in the western Loire, which seems to enjoy its own microclimate that creates a pocket of mild weather conditions. Trees burst into blossom as early as the beginning of April in the Angers region and local plant life thrives in May and June, with green fields and orchards stretching away on either side of the roads. The River Loire is at its most scenic during this period. By July, the river is reduced to a narrow stream in places, winding between golden sandbanks. Tempting as it is to go for a swim, bathers should first check that the river bed is safe, as the sandbanks can be quite treacherous in some places.

In **autumn,** the month of September, which is characteristically mild, heralds the wine harvest, in honour of which are lively traditional harvest processions held throughout the Loire Valley.

WHAT TO PACK

As little as possible. Laundry services are available everywhere. Most personal items can be replaced at reasonable cost. Try to pack everything in one suitcase and a small backpack. Take an extra backpack for new purchases, shopping at the open-air market, carrying a picnic, etc., but if you are flying, check how much carry-on baggage is permitted by airlines. Be sure luggage is clearly labelled. Do not pack medication in checked luggage; keep it with you.

WEATHER FORECAST

Météo-France offers recorded information at national, departmental and local levels. This information is updated three times a day and is valid for up to seven days.

- ♦ **National and departmental forecast:**
  ℘3250 followed by
  1 – for all the information about the *département* for the next 7 days, or
  2 – for information about towns.
- ♦ **Local forecast:** ℘08 92 68 02 followed by the number of the *département* – *see below.*

12-day weather forecasts in English available at www.lachainemeteo.com.

THEMED TOURS

Travel itineraries on specific themes have been mapped out to help you discover the regional architectural heritage and the traditions that make up the cultural heritage of the Loire Valley region. You will find brochures and guides to all these attractions and many more in tourist offices across the region. All the routes in the region are generally very well marked and easy to follow (expect to see plenty of signs posted along the roads directing visitors to the nearest chateau or to places of cultural and historical significance).

HISTORICAL TOURIST ROUTES

The Val de Loire has been on UNESCO's World Heritage list since the end of the year 2000.

To allow tourists to discover France's architectural heritage in a historical context, local authorities have set up a number of routes focusing on local architectural, cultural and traditional themes. These **Routes historiques** are indicated by road signs. Each of them is detailed in a brochure available from tourist information offices. Several interesting itineraries are found in the regions covered in this guide.

◆ **Route historique du Roi René** –
This circuit takes in the most
important châteaux in the Anjou
area, most of which are occupied,
but still open to the public.
Château de Plessis-Bourré *(49460
Écueillé; ℘02 41 32 06 72).*

◆ **Route historique de la Vallée
des Rois** – The route was once
used by the Kings of France, on
the way from Gien to Saumur via
Orléans, Blois and Tours.
Abbaye de Fontevraud *(49590
Fontevraud; ℘02 41 51 30 71,
www.chateaux-france.com/route-
valleerois).* Thematic Michelin map
226 *La Vallée des Rois.*

◆ **Route historique des Dames
de Touraine** – Dedicated to the
great ladies who showed talent
and determination in building,
renovating, embellishing or simply
enjoying their splendid estates,
this route winds its way among the
towns of Amboise, Beauregard,
Montpoupon, Le Grand-Pressigny,
Valençay, Chenonceau, etc.
Château de Montpoupon
*(Céré-la-Ronde, 37460 Montrésor;
℘02 47 94 21 15, www.chateaux-
france.fr/route-dames).*

◆ **Route historique du patrimoine
culturel québécois en France** –
This route links places with French
immigration to Quebec.
Comité Chomedey-de-
Maisonneuve, Centre Culturel
Maisonneuve *(10190 Neuville-sur-
Vannes; ℘03 25 40 68 33, http://
comite.maisonneuve.free.fr).*

◆ **Les routes de Jeanne d'Arc** –
Four itineraries illustrate Joan
of Arc's mission: *Les débuts*
(beginnings), *La campagne de Loire*
(the Loire campaign), *La campagne
du sacre* (the coronation campaign)
and *La capture* (taken prisoner).
Locations in this guide include
the towns of Beaugency, Chinon,

DÉPARTEMENTS IN THE CHÂTEAUX OF THE LOIRE REGION			
Cher	18	Eure-et-Loir	28
Indre	36	Indre-et-Loire	37
Loir-et-Cher	41	Loiret	45
Maine-et-Loire	49	Mayenne	53
Sarthe	72		

Chécy, Gien, Loches, Meung-sur-
Loire and Orléans.
Association des villes Johanniques,
(www.villes-johanniques.fr). The
association has an office in the
town hall at Beaugency.

PARKS AND GARDENS

◆ **Route des Parcs et Jardins** –
The art of the planting and
tending of formal gardens, which
characterise French châteaux
and parks, was born in the Loire
Valley in the early 16C. This tourist
route leads through some of the
most beautiful and ingeniously
designed gardens in the whole
of France, including those dating
from the times of the Renaissance
all the way up to those conceived
and planted in the present
day. Highlights of the driving
tour include the magnificent
Château de **Villandry**, Château
de **Chamerolles**, Château de
Villeprévost, the floral park at
Orléans-la-Source, Château
de **Beauregard**, Château de
Chaumont-sur-Loire, Château
de **Cheverny**, Château de **Valmer**
and the priory of **St-Cosme**. Full
details and ideas for itineraries
can be found on the website of
the Comité des Parcs et Jardins de
France – *www.parcsetjardins.fr.*

What to See and Do

OUTDOOR FUN
CANOEING AND KAYAKING

This mode of exploring local waterways need not be exclusively reserved for seasoned canoeing experts. Sometimes this sport can be a pleasant way to discover secluded spots inaccessible by any other means. The main difference between a canoe and a kayak is that the former is propelled by a single-bladed paddle and the latter by a double-bladed paddle. Canoeing trips of half a day, a whole day or more can be organised for individuals or a group (allowing for brief training and certain safety measures). The most suitable rivers are the Cisse, Conie, Cosson, Huisne, Indre, Le Loir, Sauldre, Thouet, Vienne, the Sarthe and, of course, La Loire. For detailed information, contact the Loisir Accueil section in each *département*, or the:

- **Fédération Française de Canoë-Kayak (FFCK)**, *Base Nautique Olympique et Paralympique 2024, Route de Torcy 77 360 Vaires sur Marne*, ☎*01 45 11 08 50, www.ffck.org.*
- **Comité Régional Canoê-Kayak Centre-Val de Loire – Pôle nautique du Cher**, *5 Prom. de Florence, 37000 Tours*, ☎*02 47 63 13 98, www.ckctours.org/.*
- **Canoë Kayak Club Angers,** *75 av. du lac de Maine, 49000 Angers,* ☎*02 41 72 07 04. http://ckca.fr.*

CYCLING

The **Loire à Vélo** cycling trail features 800km/497mi of signposted routes across the Pays de la Loire and Loire valley as well as the Loire-Anjou-Touraine Regional Nature Park.
For full details of packages, bike hire and practical information, access *www.cycling-loire.com.*
The Loire countryside is fairly flat, so it presents few difficulties to the average cyclist. The Indre valley, the Sologne, the numerous forest tracks and the banks of the Loire, away from the main roads, are particularly pretty. The ever-changing scenery and the rich heritage of the Loire valley add greatly to the pleasure of a cycling tour.
Contact the **Fédération Française de Cyclotourisme** *(12 r. Louis-Bertrand, 94207 Ivry-sur-Seine,* ☎*01 56 20 88 88, https://ffvelo.fr)* for suggested itineraries covering most of France, with information on mileage, difficult routes and sights to see. An IGN map (1:50 000) shows cycle routes around Orléans *(1,000km à Vélo autour d'Orléans)*. Lists of bicycle rental firms are also available from tourist offices. For information about mountain biking *(VTT, meaning "vélo tout terrain")* in the Layon region, apply to the Anjou tourist office in Angers.

FISHING

French surveys reveal that **freshwater fishing** is the second most popular national leisure pastime after football. Swift-flowing or not, the waters of the Loire offer anglers numerous attractive possibilities.
All authorised types of fishing are open to the angler, whether fishing for gudgeon, roach and dace, or trying for pike or the striped mullet that come upstream as far as Amboise in summer. Other options include going after the catfish, tench and carp that lurk in dips in the river bed of the Loire, the Indre and the Loir and in the pools of the Sologne, which also teem with perch.
Trout are to be found in the Creuse, the Sauldre, the streams of Anjou or the tributaries of the Loir, whereas the Berry, Briare, or Orléans canals are home to eels and sometimes freshwater crayfish that can be caught with a net.
A flat-bottomed boat is necessary for **salmon fishing**; professionals have specialist equipment such as nets stretched across the river, held in place by poles fixed in the river bed.
Regulations and open seasons – The rules differ according to

whether the water is classified as first category (contains trout and salmon) or second category (coarse fish). Stricter regulations apply to fish needing special protection, so salmon fishing in particular may be forbidden outright during some years, or permitted for a restricted period only between March and June. Likewise, pike may be tackled only between July and January.

Generally speaking, in the case of first-category rivers, the **fishing season** starts the second Saturday in March and ends the third Sunday in September. As for rivers belonging in the second category, fishing is authorised throughout the year. Regional and national regulations should be observed. Anglers will need either to buy a special holiday fishing permit, valid for two weeks (*Jun–Sept*), or take out annual membership in an officially approved angling association. These officially stamped permits cover fishing with up to four lines on second-category waterways administered by an angling association or one line on all public waterways. Only one line is allowed on first-category waters and a supplementary tax is payable.

On **private property**, where fishing rights belong to the owner of the bank, the owner's permission must be obtained. In the case of certain private lakes that are excluded from the angling legislation, the owner's permission (annual, monthly or daily permit) is the only formality required and can be granted at any time of year.

Minimum size of catch – National regulations state that anglers must return to the water any fish they catch below the minimum permitted length (50cm for pike, 40cm for pike-perch, 23cm for trout, 50cm for salmon, 9cm for crayfish).

Fishing permits (*la carte de pêche*) may be obtained online from the **Fédération Nationale de la Pêche en France**. Their website (*www.federationpeche.fr*) offers a wealth of information as well as updated fishing regulations. Useful brochures and folding maps *Fishing in France (Pêche en France)* are published and distributed by the **Comite National des Peche**, 134 av. Malakoff, 75116 Paris; also available from local angling organisations.

For information about regulations contact the Tourist Information Centres or the offices of the *Eaux et Forêts* (Water and Forest Authority).

Federations for fishing and the protection of rivers:
- **Indre-et-Loire:** 178 r. du Pas-Notre-Dame, 37100 Tours, ☎02 47 05 33 77, www.fedepeche37.fr
- **Loir-et-Cher:** 11 r. Robert-Nau, Vallée Maillard, 41000 Blois, ☎02 54 90 25 60, www.peche41.fr.
- **Loiret:** 49 rte. d'Olivet, 45100 Orléans, ☎02 38 56 62 69, http://federationpeche45.fr
- **Maine-et-Loire:** Montayer, 49320 Brissac Loire Aubance, ☎02 41 87 57 09, www.fedepeche49.fr
- **Mayenne:** 78 r. Émile-Brault, 53000 Laval, ☎02 43 69 12 13, www.fedepeche53.com.
- **Sarthe:** 40 r. Bary, 72100 Le Mans, ☎02 43 85 66 01, www.peche72.fr.

Aquariums and angling centres
- Aquarium de Touraine at Lussault-sur-Loire (Indre-et-Loire)
- Aquarium de Sologne, Aliotis, at Villeherviers (Loir-et-Cher)
- Carrefour des Mauges at St-Florent-le-Vieil (Maine-et-Loire)
- Centre Piscicole at Brissac-Quincé (Maine-et-Loire)
- Observatoire de la Loire at Rochecorbon (Indre-et-Loire)
- Observatoire Fédéral at Champigny-sur-Veude (Indre-et-Loire)

GOLF
The popularity of golf, which took off in the early 1980s, is still steadily increasing. Thousands of golf players

are officially registered in France, indulging in their favourite sport on around 700 golf links.

The *Peugeot Golf Guide*, published by D and G Motte in Switzerland, offers a selection of 1,000 courses in 12 European countries. An entire page is devoted to each site; the guide lists all the necessary information (location on Michelin map, rates, clubhouse, nearby hotels, level of skills required) and provides an opinion about each establishment.

- Fédération Française de Golf, 68 r. Anatole-France, 92300 Levallois-Perret, ✆01 41 49 77 00, www.ffgolf.org.
- Ligue du Centre-Val de Loire, Golf de Marcilly, La Plaine, 45240 Marcilly en Villette, ✆06 66 08 47 79, www.golf-centre.fr.
- Ligue de Golf des Pays de la Loire 9 r. du Couëdic, 44000 Nantes, ✆02 40 08 05 06, www.ligue-golf-paysdelaloire.asso.fr.

HUNTING

The varied terrain of the Loire countryside makes it very popular with hunters for stalking, beating, coursing or shooting. The plains of the Beauce and the meadows of Touraine and Anjou provide plenty of food for partridge, quail, thrush and lark. Hares find cover in the copses and the fields of maize and sugar beet. Wild rabbits and partridge breed in the sterile marshland, whereas pheasants favour wooded countryside. Red deer and roe deer are to be found in the thick woods around Baugé, in the forests of Château-la-Vallière and Loches and around Valençay. Wild boar favour the deep forests of Orléans and Amboise and the grounds of Chambord. The islands and banks of the Loire provide nests for teal and mallard.

The Sologne is a favourite haunt for game: duck, teal and woodcock on the lakes and rivers, pheasant by the roadside, wild boar in the marshy brakes and deer in the woods.

Address all enquiries to:

Fédération Nationale des Chasseurs de France, 13 r. du Général Leclerc, 92136 Issy les Moulineux, ✆01 41 09 65 10, www.chasseurdefrance.com.

During the rutting season, which lasts from mid-September to mid-October, the stags are known to behave in a curious way, and it is interesting to observe them in action. It is possible to do so in Chambord forest – contact the **Office National des Forêts** for details, La Plaine, 29300 Quimperlé, ✆02 98 35 14 88, www.onf.fr.

WALKING

Short-, medium- and long-distance footpath *Topo-Guides* are published by the **Fédération Française de la Randonnée Pédestre (FFRP)**, www.ffrandonnee.fr. These guides provide detailed maps of the paths and offer valuable information to the rambler; they are on sale at the information centre at 64 r. du Dessous des Berges, 75013 Paris, ✆01 44 89 93 90. For further information apply to the **Comité de Randonnée Pédestre d'indre-et-Loire** (Maison des Sports de Touraine, rue de l'Aviation, 37210 Parçay-Meslay; ✆02 47 40 25 26, www.cdrp37.fr).

A network of long-distance footpaths *(sentiers de grande randonnée – GR)* covers the area described in the guide:

- **GR 3** along the Loire valley through the forests of Orléans, Russy and Chinon.
- **GR 3c** running westwards across the Sologne from Gien to Mont-près-Chambord.
- **GR 3d** through the Layon vineyards.
- **GR 31** linking Mont-près-Chambord, on the southeast edge of Boulogne Forest, to Souesmes, south through Sologne forest.
- **GR 32** north-south through Orléans Forest.
- **GR 335**, from the Loir to the Loire, north-south between Lavardin and Vouvray.
- **GR 35** along the Loir valley.

- **GR 36**, the footpath from the English Channel to the Pyrénées route, crossing the region described in this guide between Le Mans and Montreuil-Bellay.
- **GR 46** along the Indre valley.

RIDING AND PONY TREKKING

Not surprisingly, in view of the number of highly reputed local stud farms and the National Riding School at St-Hilaire-St-Florent near Saumur, the Loire region has numerous riding centres that are open to visitors. Some of these centres also serve as an overnight stop for those on pony-trekking holidays.

Guides indicating suitable routes and overnight stops for those travelling on horseback are available from the regional and national riding associations, and details of local equestrian centres can be obtained from the tourist offices.

Other useful contacts include:

- **Comité régional de tourisme équestre des Pays de la Loire**; Les Vaux du Puits, 72150 St. Pierre du Lorouer, ℘06 40 96 01 68, http://crte-paysdelaloire.com (départements of Maine-et-Loire, Mayenne and Sarthe);
- **Comité Régional d'Équitation Centre Val de Loire**; Parc équestre Fédéral, Bâtiment la Colonie, 41600 Lamotte-Beuvron, ℘02 36 38 02 57, www.crecvl. org (départements of Cher, Indre, Indre-et-Loire, Loir-et-Cher and Loiret).

ACTIVITIES FOR KIDS 👥

In this guide, sights of particular interest to children are indicated with a KIDS symbol (👥). Some attractions may offer discount fees for children. 🕭Angers, Blois, Chinon, Loches, Le Mans, le Perche-Sarthois, Saumur, Tours, the Loir valley and Vendôme offer family-oriented activities with the **Entrez dans la cour des Grands** programme, which is designed to encourage children (ages 7–12) to

discover the heritage and history of the region. More details at www. touraineloirevalley.com.

The Châteaux de la Loire Pass gives reduced admission and other advantages at the participating châteaux between Sully-sur-Loire and Nantes. Several options are available depending on the length of your stay and the number of châteaux you wish to visit. Information is available from tourist offices and online at www. touraineloirevalley.com.

SHOPPING
BUSINESS HOURS

Most of the larger shops are open Mondays to Saturdays from 9am to 6.30pm or 7.30pm. Smaller, individual shops may close during the lunch hour. Food shops – grocers, wine merchants and bakeries – are generally open from 7am to 6.30pm or 7.30pm; some open on Sunday mornings. Many food shops close between noon and 2pm and on Mondays. Bakery and pastry shops sometimes close on Wednesdays. Hypermarkets usually stay open non-stop until 9pm or later.

SOUVENIRS

Wine is the obvious choice, and wine tasting (*dégustation*) at roadside "shops" will help you choose from the many excellent wines produced in the Loire valley. Note, however, that *en vrac* means that they sell in larger quantities than you would find in supermarkets, i.e. not by the bottle. **Cheese** – The best of the region's array of different varieties are Ste-Maure-de-Touraine, Valençay, and Selles-sur-Cher goat's cheese. 🕭 If your car boot doesn't get over 50°C in the sun, the local cheeses keep and travel well.

Tempting **confectionery and delicacies** from the region include **Cointreau**, a liqueur from St-Barthélémy d'Anjou; apricot-filled prunes from Tours and the **livre tournois**, a rich creation of pure chocolate; **muscadin**, a delicious mix of cherry, ground chestnut and black chocolate from Langeais; **cotignac**, quince jelly from Orléans sold in round wooden pots; smooth honey from the Gâtinais and **praslines** from Montargis; **moinillons**, shaped like tiny monks, are coloured sweets that come in five different flavours and can be found alongside other souvenirs with a monastic theme at the shop run by the Benedictine community at St-Benoît-sur-Loire. Blois is home to the Poulain chocolate factory. **Quernons d'ardoise**, produced in Angers, are nougat bars covered in slate-coloured chocolate that recalls the city's rooftops. The symbol of the town of Sablé-sur-Sarthe is its **sablés**, pure butter shortbread biscuits that are the ideal accompaniment with a tea-time drink in a local café.

Terrines and **pâtés** are popular souvenirs and can be found in and around the region's many game-filled forests and parks. Some are made from often unexpected ingredients such as bison (at Cerqueux-sous-Passavant) or ostrich.

In Angers, Blois, Tours, Vendôme and Vouvray, pork is king, with a huge variety of preserved and potted meat specialities and pâtés to choose from including *rilles, rillauds, rillons* and *rillettes* – all variations on the theme of porkmeat and fat in differing preparations. Try them at one of the many fine *traiteurs* (delicatessens) in the region.

Markets – The region's best, and biggest, open-air market is held every Sunday morning in Amboise, with up to 150 stalls. The Marché aux veaux in Château-Gontier is among the largest in Europe.

Most towns and villages have a market once a week, but in larger towns they may take place twice a week, or even every day. It is doubtful that anyone knows just how many markets there are, but the excellent website – www.jours-de-marche.fr – lists more than 7,500, and admits to there being a great many more.

For the home – Among non-perishable goods, high-quality handicrafts, such as wicker work from Villaines-les-Rochers and Gien earthenware, are well worth taking home. Cholet is famous for its handkerchiefs, and throughout the Loire Valley you are sure to come across a wealth of antiques shops, flea markets and village fairs where you can pick up a bargain.

SIGHTSEEING
BIRDWATCHING

See the Introduction for information on the Loire valley's bird population.

The French National Association for the Protection of Bird Life – **Ligue pour la Protection des Oiseaux (LPO)** – has its headquarters at 8 r. du Docteur Pujos, CS 90263, 17305 Rochefort Cedex ℘05 46 82 12 34, www.lpo.fr. It is a not-for-profit organisation set up to protect species of wild bird as well as their environment. Its aim is to educate the general public and make people more aware of nature by organising visits, excursions and conferences on the subject of natural reserves.

- **LPO Touraine:** 148 rue Louis Blot, 37540 Saint-Cyr-sur-Loire. ℘02 47 51 81 84; www.lpotouraine.fr
- **LPO Anjou:** 35, rue de la Barre 49000 Angers. ℘02 41 44 44 22; www.lpo-anjou.org
- **LPO Loire-Atlantique:** 5, rue Maison David, 44340 Bouguenais ℘02 51 82 02 97; http://loire-atlantique.lpo.fr

The **Carrefour des Mauges** (a permanent centre whose role is to provide information about the Loire and Mauges environment, Ferme abbatiale des Coteaux, BP 44, 49410 St-Florent-le-Vieil, ℘02 41 71 77 30) stages a number of one-day programmes, including on-the-spot visits, during which you can identify the different bird species, study their behaviour and see them in

Hot air balloon over Château de Beauregard in the Loire Blèsoise

© Parc & Château de Beauregard

their natural habitat (⊙*telescopes and binoculars are supplied by the organisations*).

Other useful addresses:
♦ **Maison de la Nature et de l'Environnement d'Orléans**
  64 rte. d'Olivet, 45100 Orléans
  ℘02 38 56 69 84, www.loiret-nature-environnement.org.
This association is responsible for other sites including the Réserve naturelle de l'île de St-Pryvé-St-Mesmin and the Maison forestière d'Ouzouer-sur-Loire.

♦ **SEPN 41**
  (Société de l'étude et de protection de la nature en Loir-et-Cher) 17 r. Roland-Garros, 41000 Blois; ℘02 54 42 53 71.

⊙ *If you find an injured bird, please contact the LPO who will direct you to the nearest Centre de sauvegarde de la faune sauvage (Wildlife protection centre).*

BUS TOURS
Organised bus tours are available through **Discover France** and include Loire valley castles day trips, or visits to vineyards.

Two-day Châteaux Country tours are available from Paris. Other packages are available, from 2-hour introductory tours to week-long excursions. Online booking available at http://tours.discoverfrance.net.

FROM THE AIR
Weather permitting, there are various ways of getting an aerial view of the Loire valley, from microlights (ULM, or *ultra-légers motorisés*), gliders, helicopters or light aircraft. Trips leave from the airport at Tours-St-Symphorien, flying over Chinon, Chambord, Chenonceau and Azay-le-Rideau, and from Blois-le-Breuil or Orléans aerodrome to fly over Amboise, Cheverny and Beaugency. It is also possible to take a trip in a hot-air balloon (⟲*see below*).

Microlights
♦ **Aérodrome d'Amboise-Dierre:**
  ℘02 47 57 93 91,
  www.ailestourangelles.fr
♦ **Aérodrome de Tours-Sorigny:**
  ℘01 59 75 35 86. http://aeroclubdetouraine.com
♦ **Fédération Française de Ultra-Léger Motorisé:** 96 bis r.Marc-Sangnier, BP 341, 94704 Maison-Alfort Cedex. ℘01 49 81 74 43, www.ffplum.fr

Hot-Air Balloons

Travelling by hot-air balloon adds an Old-World charm to seeing the Loire Valley. Balloons take off from almost anywhere (except towns, of course), usually in the early morning or late evening; landing, on the other hand, greatly depends on the strength and direction of the wind, so the landing spot is sometimes unpredictable. Flights last between 1hr and 1hr 30min, but it is wise to allow three times that amount of time for the flight preparation and the drive back to the starting point in the vehicle that follows the balloon; allow at least a half a day for the entire excursion. Prices vary considerably, from €179 to €285 per person. **France Montgolfières**, 4 bis rue du Saussis, 21140 Semur-en-Auxois; ℘03 80 97 38 61, www.france-balloons.com.

LOCAL INDUSTRIES/CRAFTS

The following workshops or factories are open to the public, offering an insight into local crafts and industry:

- **Chinon** – nuclear power station
- **Gien** – potteries
- **Montrichard** – J M Monmousseau's Champagne-method wine cellars
- **Poncé-sur-le-Loir** – arts and crafts centre (☙see Vendôme)
- **St-Barthélemy-d'Anjou** – Cointreau distillery (☙see Angers)
- **St-Cyr-en-Bourg** – Saumur cooperative wine cellar (☙see Saumur)
- **St-Hilaire-St-Florent** – Bouvet-Ladubay sparkling Saumur wines (☙see Saumur)
- **Saut-aux-Loups** –mushroom beds (☙see Chinon)
- **Turquant** – Troglo des Pommes Tapées (dried apples) (☙see Chinon)
- **Vaas** – Rotrou corn mill (☙see Vendôme)
- **Villaines-les-Rochers** – basketwork cooperative (☙see Azay-le-Rideau)

MILL TOURS

The particular geographical and climatic conditions of Anjou account for the presence of many different mills in the region.

The **Association pour la Sauvegarde des Moulins de l'Anjou** (AMA) provides information and organises visits to local mills.

🛈 For details visit their website moulinsdanjou.blogspot.com or http://sites.google.com/site/moulinsdanjou.

☙See the Introduction for the history and types of mills in Anjou.

RIVER TOURS

River cruising

For cruise information, contact the **Comité départemental de tourisme de l'Anjou**, 1 pl. Kennedy, 49100 Angers, ℘02 41 23 50 50, www.destination-angers.com/.

Small private barges can be taken on the **Loire, Maine, Mayenne, Oudon** and **Sarthe** rivers, as well as on the canalised stretch of the **Cher** and the **Canal de Berry**.

Houseboats can also be hired for one or several nights to explore the Anjou region via its waterways. Day cruises on piloted boats are also available.

River passenger boats

Two types of river passenger boat exist: the *bateau-mouche* and the *coche de plaisance*. They usually leave at set hours (often at 3pm and 5pm) between mid-April and mid-October. Some trips include the passing of locks or an instructive commentary on local birds species or water transport in the Loire region. Discovering the tracks of small animals like beavers and bird spotting add to the pleasure of these relaxing, peaceful cruises.

- Starting from **Briare**, along the canal with the company Les Bateaux Touristiques (℘02 38 37 12 75; www.les-bateaux-touristiques-briare.com); from **Chisseaux**, 1h30 cruise along the

Flat-bottmed boats at the confluence of the Vienne and the Loire, Candes-St-Martin

© Hervé Lenain/hemis.fr

Cher, gliding beneath the arches of the Château de Chenonceau and beyond.

♦ From **Fay-aux-Loges**, along the Orléans canal, Syndicat Mixte de Gestion du canal d'Orléans, 61B route de nestin, 45450 Fay aux Loges 📞02 38 46 82 90.

♦ From **Montrichard**, 1h30 cruise along the Cher aboard the *Léonard-de-Vinci* 📞02 54 75 41 53.

♦ From **Saint-Aignan**, 1h cruise along the Cher aboard the *Tasciaca* 📞02 54 71 40 38.

Along the rivers of **Anjou** and **Maine**:

♦ **L'Hirondelle,** Le Moulin Chenillé-Changé, 49220 Chenillé-Champteuse 📞02 41 95 14 23; www.domaine-moulin.fr.

♦ **Le Duc des Chauvières**, Quai Alsace, 53200 Château-Gontier 📞02 43 70 37 83; www.leducdeschauvieres.com.

SOUND AND LIGHT SHOWS AT THE CHÂTEAUX

These polished evening spectacles *(son et lumière)* developed from an original idea of the magician Jean-Eugène Robert-Houdin *(👆see Blois);* they were inaugurated as a feature of the Loire valley tourist season at Chambord in 1952. By combining characters dressed in period costume with firework displays, illuminated fountains and image projection on huge screens, the *son et lumière* shed quite a different light on some of the Loire Valley's most famous châteaux. Nocturnal illuminations enhance the architecture of the buildings, offering a different scene from that seen during the day. Special effects using film and staging techniques, laser-beam projections and an accompanying soundtrack lend ancient walls a surprisingly different aura. From time to time the theme of the *son et lumière* is changed.

👁 *You will find information about these events in the following chapters: Amboise, Azay-le-Rideau, Blois, Château de Chenonceau and Château de Valençay; it is always advisable to verify dates and times with the local tourist office.*

TOURIST TRAINS

A number of charming old steam trains are operated along parts of the Loire Valley, generally by groups of volunteers, with the result that they usually only run on weekends.

♦ **Pithiviers tourist train** (Loiret): contact the Association Musée des Transports de Pithiviers, 📞02 38 30 48 26, http://amtp-pithiviers.wifeo.com.

♦ **Lac de Rille historical railway** (Indre-et-Loire): AECFM, La

The Art of Drinking Wine

To identify and describe the qualities or defects of a particular wine, both wine buffs and wine experts use an extremely wide yet precise vocabulary. Assessing a wine involves three successive stages, each associated with a particular sense and a certain number of technical terms:

The eye (general impression) – Crystalline (good clarity), limpid (perfectly transparent, no particles in suspension), still (no bubbles), sparkling (effervescent wine) or *mousseux* (lots of fine, Champagne-type bubbles).

Colour and hues – A wine is said to have a nice robe when the colour is sharp and clean; the main terms used to describe the different hues are pale red, ruby, onion skin, garnet (red wine), salmon, amber, partridge-eye pink (rosé wine) and golden-green, golden-yellow and straw (white wine).

The nose – Pleasant smells: floral, fruity, balsamic, spicy, flinty. Unpleasant smells: musty, corked, woody, hydrogen sulphide, cask.

The mouth – Once it has passed the visual and olfactory tests, the wine undergoes a final test in the mouth. It can be described as agreeable (pleasant), aggressive (unpleasant, with a high acidity), full-flavoured (rich and well-balanced), structured (well-constructed, with a high alcohol content), heady (intoxicating), fleshy (producing a strong impact on taste buds), fruity (flavour evoking the freshness and natural taste of grapes), easy to drink, jolly (inducing merriness), round (supple, mellow), lively (light, fresh, with a low alcohol content), etc.

Quality control – French wines fall into various official categories indicating the area of production and therefore the probable quality of the wine. AOC *(Appellation d'Origine Contrôlée)* denotes a wine produced in a strictly delimited area, stated on the label, made with the grape varieties specified for that wine in accordance with local traditional methodology. VDQS *(Vin Délimité de Qualité Supérieure)* is also produced in a legally controlled area, slightly less highly rated than AOC. Vin de pays denotes the highest ranking table wine after AOC and VDQS.

Gitonnière, 37330 Marcilly sur Maulne. &02 47 96 42 91, www.aecfm.fr.

♦ **Thourarsais steam train** (Indre-et-Loire): TVT, 3 pl. de la Gare, 79100 Thouars, &09 60 06 38 39, www.train-vapeur-thouarsais.fr.

♦ **Loir Valley tourist train** (Loir-et-Cher): Thoré-la Rochette Town Hall &02 54 72 95 03, www.ttvl.fr.

♦ **Sarthe steam train:** TRANSVAP, Gare Transvap, 72160 Beillé. &02 43 89 00 37, www.transvap.fr.

♦ **Semur-en-Vallon tourist train:** Compagnie du Chemin de Fer de Semur en Vallon, La Gare, 72390 Semur en Vallon. &02 43 93 67 86, www.lepetittraindesemur.com.

WINE COUNTRY

Like all wine-growers, the *vignerons* from the Loire region welcome visitors to their cellars and storehouses for tastings, explanations of winemaking techniques and selling their wine. The Loire Valley is France's third-largest wine-producing region, and the second-largest region for sparkling wine. Loire wines are commonly regarded as the most popular in the restaurants of France, and include white, red, rosé, sparkling, still, dry and sweet. The most famous are Sancerre, Vouvray, Bourgueil, Jasnières and Chinon. The principal grape varieties are Cabernet Franc, Pineau, Gamay and Chardonnay. Tourist offices and the Maisons du Vin (especially those in Amboise, Angers, Bourgueil, Chinon, Montlouis-sur-Loire, Saumur and Vouvray) can supply details on wine producers, merchants and cooperatives:

Here are a few:

- **Maison des Vins d'Anjou et de Saumur**
  5 bis pl. Kennedy, 49100 Angers, ℘02 41 17 68 20, www.vinsvaldeloire.fr.

- **Comité interprofessionnel des vins du Val de Loire**
  Hôtel des Vins La Godeline
  73 r. Plantagenêt, 49100 Angers
  ℘02 47 60 55 00, www.vinsvaldeloire.fr.

- **La Maison du vin de Saumur**
  7 quai Carnot, 49400 Saumur.
  ℘02 41 38 45 83.

- **Interloire**
  12 r. Étienne-Pallu,
  BP 1921, 37019 Tours Cedex 1
  ℘02 47 60 55 00.

BOOKS

REGIONAL HERITAGE

A Wine and Food Guide to the Loire - Jacqueline Friedrich. Henry Holt (1998).
This is an award-winning guide to the Loire, its wines and cuisine. It covers the 60 or so appellations in the five wine regions of the Loire, describing the history, soil and vintners of each, and rates more than 600 wineries; sections on local cheeses, sausages and fish dishes. This book is comprehensive and entertaining.

Châteaux of the Loire - Thorston Droste, Axel M Mosler (Contributor) - St Martins Press (1997). This over-size book is a collection of lavish photographs of the architecture, interiors, and gardens of the Loire châteaux, including previously unpublished photos illustrating life in the châteaux during the 19C and early 20C. Each château is

Saumurois vineyards

© Philippe Body/hemis.fr

accompanied by a text that describes architectural, historical, and travel details.

Châteaux of the Loire Valley - Jean-Marie Perouse De Montclos, Robert Polidori (Photographer) - Konemann (2007). This is a beautiful book, filled with high-quality photographs, portraying the natural beauty of the region as well as highlighting the architecture of the famous châteaux.

Loire Valley Sketchbook - Fabrice Moreau & Jean-Paul Pigeat - St Martin's Press (2003).
A delightful collection of watercolours, history and travel writing that makes this book the perfect souvenir volume to remember your trip.

Loire - Hubrecht Duijker - The Wine Lover's Touring Guides Series (March 1995).
The author of this book was appointed *Officier de l'Ordre du Mérite Agricole* by the French Government for sharing his wealth of information on local treasures, from little-known villages to Gérard Depardieu's castle. Plenty of practical touring advice for an enjoyable trip, especially if you are interested in wine.

Gardens of the Loire Valley - Marie-Francoise Valery - Garden Art Press (2008). This beautifully illustrated book is one of the most attractive and well-informed books on the gardens of the Loire Valley.

A Little Tour in France - Henry James - Elibron Classics (2005).

A facsimile of the 1900 American edition in which the novelist describes his travels among the towns and châteaux of the Loire before heading further south.

French Impressions: The Loire Valley - George East - La Puce Publications (2011).

The latest in a series by this colourful expat who provides a humorous and bracingly honest account of living and travelling in France. He tackles the culture, history, food and drink of the Loire with a sprinkling of odd characters encountered along the way and some tasty local recipes.

Wine Regions of France - Michelin (2016).

This completely revised edition of the Green Guide for wine lovers features an overview of the history, geography and climate of the wine-growing regions and appraisals of the wines. It includes established wine routes and suggested Michelin Driving Tours.

UNDERSTANDING THE FRENCH

Our Man in Paris: A Foreign Correspondent, France and the French - John Lichfield, Signal Books (2010).

A collection of serious and light-hearted dispatches from the *Independent's* Paris correspondent, who gives a great insight into the country and its people.

Crossing the Loire - Heidi Fuller-Love France Pronde Publications (2004).

Written by a travel journalist living in France, *Crossing the Loire* recounts the trials, tribulations and joys of moving to live in France, including battles with the infamous French bureaucracy. Packed with twisted humour, sticky camembert and plumbing tales to make your hair stand on end.

France on the Brink - Jonathan Fenby - Arcade Publishing (1999).

The author has culled 30 years of experience living in or writing about France into this book, which has met with both high praise and keen criticism. From Brigitte Bardot to the baguette, from the integration or exclusion of foreign cultures to hot political scandals, this portrait of contemporary France is personal, perceptive and instructive.

Savoir-Flair: 211 Tips for Enjoying France and the French - Polly Platt - Distribooks Intl (2000).

Useful communication and travel tips if your French is rusty or outdated. Handy phrases and explanations of cultural particularities that are easily misinterpreted by foreign visitors.

French or Foe? - Polly Platt - Culture Crossings Ltd. (1994).

Explores the cultural hurdles to understanding the French, and outlines the essence of Frenchness.

HISTORY

Recent books covering the most noteworthy episodes in the region's eventful history:

The Virgin Warrior: The Life and Death of Joan of Arc - Larissa Juliet Taylor - Yale (2010). A well-balanced critical biography that attempts to get behind the myths and explore the facts of the remarkable story of the teenage girl who inspired a king and country.

The Valois: Kings of France 1328–1589 - R.J. Knecht, Hambledon Continuum (2006). From Philip VI to Henry III, an account of the dynasty that ruled France through some of the most troubled years of its history from the Middle Ages, the Hundred Years War to the dawning of the modern age.

Martyrs and Murders: The Guise Family and the Making of Europe - Stuart Carroll - Oxford (2011). This book traces the fortunes and intrigues of the House of Guise, one of the most powerful families in 16C Europe, renowned for the muder of its Duke at the Château de Blois in 1588.

Conquest: The English Kingdom of France in the Hundred Years War - Juliet Barker - Abacus (2010).

> The respected historian focuses on the last 40 years of the conflict from Henry V's invasion of France in 1417 by way of Joan of Arc to the English withdrawal from all but Calais in 1453.

A Brief History of France: People, History and Culture – Cecil Jenkins – Constable & Robinson Ltd. (2011).

> The author teases out the roots of French society and culture by examining historical events, individuals, architecture, food and wine in a serious but entertaining style.

FICTION

Five Quarters of the Orange - Joanne Harris, William Morrow & Co (2001).

> The narrator of this novel is writing from the restored Loire farmhouse where she grew up and lives under an assumed identity. The 65-year-old Framboise recounts her life and the terrible memories of the Second World War. The heroine is devoted to deciphering and preserving her mother's notebook of recipes and jottings. The texture, shape and aroma of bread and cakes, fruit and wine, thyme and olive become characters in this compelling and complex story.

CLASSIC FICTION

The following novels are set in the Loire region:

Honoré de Balzac: *Eugénie Grandet, Le Curé de Tours, La Femme de Trente Ans, L'Illustre Gaudissart, Le Lys dans la Vallée*

François Rabelais: *Gargantua and Pantagruel* comprising *Pantagruel, Gargantua, Tiers Livre, Quart Livre.*

Émile Zola: *La Terre (1887).*

Alain-Fournier: *Le Grand Meaulnes (1913).*

FILMS

The following films have historical and cultural associations with the places and people that have played a part in the region:

Le Grand Meaulnes (1913).

> Alain-Fournier's haunting tale of youth, yearning, loss and love in the Sologne has twice been adapted for film. Jean-Gabriel Albicocco's 1967 version is widely considered to be a classic, with a remake by Jean-Daniel Verhaeghe in 2006.

La Princesse de Montpensier (2010).

> Based on the novella by Madame de Lafayette. Set during the Wars of Religion, the story follows the tragic destiny of Marie de Mézières who is forced into a marriage with the Prince de Montpensier yet remains in love with the Duke of Guise. Filmed partly on location at the Château de Blois.

La Reine Margot (1994).

> Lavish costume drama based on events in life of Marguerite de Valois, daughter of Catherine de' Medici. It traces her marriage to Henry of Navarre (later Henri IV), her love affairs and the various plots, political tensions and intrigues of 16C courtly life during the Wars of Religion and the St. Bartholomew's Day massacre of Protestants.

Joan of Arc: the Messenger (1999).

> Luc Besson's spectacular take on the story of the Maid of Orléans from her early visions to battles against the English, her trial and burning at the stake.

Calendar of Events

Regional tourist offices usually list local festivals and fairs on their websites. Most places hold festivities for France's National Day (14 Jul) and organise events on 15 Aug, also a public holiday.

JANUARY
Angers
Film festival (Festival d'Angers)
☎01 42 93 43 47
www.premiersplans.org

FEBRUARY
Tours and around
Festival de la Grange de Meslay
(summer music festival) ☎02 47 20 63 46
www.festival-la-grange-de-meslay.fr

MARCH-APRIL
St-Benoît-sur-Loire
Great Easter Saturday Vigil
☎02 38 35 72 43

APRIL
Le Mans
24-hour motorcycle race
☎02 43 40 24 24
www.lemans.org

Cholet
Harlequin Festival
☎02 72 77 24 24
www.ville-cholet.fr/arlequins
Evening Carnival Parade
☎02 41 62 28 09
www.cholet.fr/carnaval

MAY
Orléans
Joan of Arc Festival
☎02 38 24 05 05
www.orleans-metropole.fr, www.experienceloire.com/joan.htm
Le Mans (Abbaye de l'Épau)
Festival de l'Épau
☎02 43 84 22 29
epau.sarthe.fr/festival-de-lepau
Royal Abbaye of Epau wine fair
☎02 43 84 22 29
Château-Gontier
Horse Show at Château
de la Maroutière
☎02 43 70 46 87
Châteauneuf-sur-Loire
Whitsun Rhododendron Festival
☎02 38 58 41 18 (Sat and Sun)
Saumur
International 3-Day Event
(end of month)
☎05 55 73 83 83
www.ifce.fr/cadre-noir

Le Mans 24-hour race

© Gilles Moussé/Ville du Mans

Tours
Florilège Vocal: Choral Festival
☎02 47 05 82 76
www.florilegevocal.com

St Aubin de Luigné
Anjou Wine Festival
www.anjou-tourisme.com

JUNE
Le Mans
24-hour motor race
☎02 43 40 24 24
www.lemans.org

Lamotte-Beuvron
Game Fair: National Hunting and
Fishing Festival (3rd weekend)
☎01 41 40 31 28 www.gamefair.fr

Sully-sur-Loire
International Festival of
Classical Music
☎02 38 25 43 43
www.festival-sully.com

Orléans
Jazz Festival
☎02 38 24 05 05
www.orleans-metropole.fr

Chaumont-sur-Loire
International Garden Festival
☎02 54 20 99 22
www.domaine-chaumont.fr/en/
international-garden-festival

Anjou
Festival in the historical
sites of Maine-et-Loire
☎02 41 88 14 14
www.festivaldanjou.com

Loches
Jazz Festival (2nd weekend)
☎02 47 38 29 34.

JULY
Doué-la-Fontaine
Rose Show in the amphitheatre
☎02 41 59 20 49

Le Mans
Le Mans Classic, the biggest
vintage car event in the world
☎01 42 59 73 40
The Night of the Chimeras
www.nuitdeschimeres.com

St Lambert du Lattay
Festival of Wine and Andouillette
(2nd weekend)
www.anjou-tourisme.com

Anjou Festival
© Anjou Théâtre

La Ménitré
Old-fashioned costume parade
with examples from the region's
folkloric traditions
☎02 41 45 63 63

Saumur
Military tattoo with mounted,
motorised and armoured divisions
☎02 41 40 20 60

AUGUST
Molineuf
Bric-a-brac fair; with antique
dealers, enthusiasts and buyers
☎02 54 70 05 23

Sablé-sur-Sarthe
Festival of Baroque Music
☎02 43 62 22 22
https://lentracte-sable.fr/festivals

SEPTEMBER
Angers
(Les Accroche-cœurs)
Kiss-Curl Festival and spectacles
in the streets
☎02 41 23 50 00
www.angers.fr/

Montlouis-sur-Loire
Festival Jazz en Touraine
(jazz music festival)
☎02 47 50 72 70
www.jazzentouraine.com

Château-Gontier
  Horse Show at Château
  de la Maroutière
  ☎02 41 21 18 28

Château du Rivau
  Wine and Pumpkin Festival
  ☎02 47 95 77 47
  www.chateaudurivau.com

Saumur
  Horsemanship performance by
  the Cadre Noir
  ☎05 55 73 83 83
  www.cadrenoir.fr

OCTOBER
Le Lion-d'Angers
  International Horse Show:
  demonstrations by the best
  riders in the world representing
  20 nations
  ☎02 41 60 36 22

St-Aignan
  Town fair – stalls, entertainment
  ☎02 38 24 05 05

NOVEMBER
Tours
  "Les Soirées d'automne"
  classical music festival
  ☎02 47 21 65 08

Montrichard
  Touraine primeur wine fair
  (3rd weekend in month)
  ☎02 54 32 05 10

24 DECEMBER
Anjou
  Messes des Naulets (held in a
  different country church every
  year). Groups in traditional Anjou
  costume sing Christmas carols
  in the local dialect
  ☎02 41 23 51 11

St-Benoît-sur-Loire
  Christmas Eve midnight Mass
  (begins 11pm)
  ☎02 38 35 72 43
  www.abbaye-fleury.com

MAIN WINEMAKING EVENTS
Year-round a great many wine fairs
and wine festivals are staged at set
dates to promote the different types
of local *appellations*.

MARCH
Bourgueil Wine Fair, Tours
  ☎02 47 97 92 20

APRIL
Onzain Wine Fair, Onzain
  ☎02 54 51 20 40

MAY
**Annual Saumur Wine
Competition, Saumur**
  ☎02 41 51 16 40

JULY
Vendredis du Vin (Wine Fridays),
Château de Montsoreau
  ☎02 41 67 12 60
  www.chateau-montsoreau.com/
  wordpress
**Wine Harvest Festival,
St-Lambert-du-Lattay**
  ☎02 41 78 49 07
**Saumur-Champigny Festival,
Varrains**
  ☎02 41 87 62 57
**Vintage Wine Festival,
St-Aubin-de-Luigné**
  ☎02 41 78 59 38

AUGUST
**Les Grandes Tablées du Saumur
Champigny, Saumur**
  www.ot-saumur.fr

SEPTEMBER
**Festivini Harvest Festival,
Saumur**
  www.festivini.com
**Harvest festival, Château de
Saumur**
  www.ot-saumur.fr

NOVEMBER
**Touraine primeur wine fair,
Montrichard**
  (3rd weekend in month)
  ☎02 54 32 05 10
**Champigny Biennial,
Montsoreau**
  ☎02 41 51 16 40

Know Before You Go

USEFUL WEBSITES

http://uk.france.fr
The French Government Tourist Office site has practical information and links to more specific guidance, for American or Canadian travellers, for example. The site includes information on everything you need to know about visiting France.

www.visiteurope.com
The European Travel Commission provides useful information on travelling in 30 European countries, and includes links to commercial services, rail schedules, weather reports, etc.

www.ViaMichelin.com
This site has maps, tourist information, travel features, suggestions on hotels and restaurants, and a route planner for numerous locations in Europe. In addition, you can look up weather forecasts, traffic reports and service station location, particularly useful if you will be driving in France.

www.france-travel-guide.net
A practical and developing website for visitors to France, written by a Francophile travel writer. Includes essential information, as well as a wide range of regional and local content.

https://uk.ambafrance.org
https://franceintheus.org
The websites for the French Embassy in the UK and the USA provide a wealth of information and links to other French sites (regions, cities, ministries).

TOURIST OFFICES ABROAD

For information, brochures, maps and assistance in planning a trip to France you should apply to the French Tourist Office in your own country:

Australia
French Tourist Bureau, 25 Bligh Street, Sydney, NSW 2000, Australia
℘(0)292 31 62 77;
http://au.france.fr

Canada
Maison de la France, 1800 av. McGill College, Bureau 1010, Montreal, Quebec H3A 3J6, Canada
℘(514) 288 20 26;
http://ca.france.fr

South Africa
Block C, Morningside Close
222 Rivonia Road, Morningside 2196 – Johannesburg
℘(0)10 205 0201.

UK and Ireland
Lincoln House, 300 High Holborn, London WC1V 7JH. ℘020 7061 66 00;
http://uk.france.fr

USA
825 Third Avenue, New York, NY 10022, USA ℘(212) 838 78 00;
http://us.france.fr

TOURIST OFFICES

Visitors may also contact local tourist offices for more precise information, to receive brochures and maps. The addresses and telephone numbers of tourist offices in the larger towns are listed after the symbol 🄸. Below, the addresses are given for local tourist offices of the departments and regions covered in this guide. The index lists the *département* after each town.

At regional level, address enquiries to:
SEM Régionale du Tourisme des Pays de la Loire
7, rue du Général de Bollardière, CS 80221 44202 Nantes cedex 2
℘02 40 89 89 89
www.enpaysdelaloire.com
Comité Régional du Tourisme du Centre-Val de Loire
(Cher, Eure-et-Loir, Indre, Indre-et-Loire, Loir-et-Cher, Loiret), 37 av. de Paris, 45000 Orléans

℘02 38 79 95 00
www.valdeloire-france.com

For each *département* within the region, address enquires to the **Comité Départemental du Tourisme (CDT):**

- **Anjou (Pays de la Loire Département):** 26 ter rue de Brissac (Bât. O), BP 32147, 49021 Angers Cedex 02 ℘02 41 23 51 51 www.anjou-tourisme.com
- **Eure-et-Loir:** 9 rue du Cardinal Pie, CS40067, 28008 CHARTRES cedex; ℘02 37 84 01 00 www.tourisme28.com
- **Indre:** Centre Colbert, 1 pl. Eugène Rolland, BP 141, 36000 CHÂTEAUROUX ℘02 54 07 36 36 www.berryprovince.com
- **Touraine-Val de Loire (Indre-et-Loire Département):** 78-82 rue Bernard Palissy, 37000 TOURS, ℘02 47 70 37 37 www.touraineloirevalley.com
- **Loir-et-Cher:** 2/4 Rue du Limousin, 41000 BLOIS ℘02 54 57 00 41 www.val-de-loire-41.com
- **Loiret:** 15, rue Eugène Vignat, 45000 ORLEANS, ℘02 38 78 04 04 www.tourismeloiret.com
- **Mayenne (Pays de la Loire Département):** ℘02 43 53 18 18 www.mayenne-tourisme.com
- **Sarthe (Pays de la Loire Département):** 31 r. Edgar Brandt – ZA Montheard, 72000 LE MANS ℘02 72 88 18 81 www.sarthetourisme.com

🛈 **Tourist Information Centres –** The addresses and telephone numbers of the local tourist offices *(Syndicats d'Initiative)* appear in the green "orient panels" of the Principal Sights in the *Discovering* section of this guide. These offices provide information about itineraries with special themes, such as wine tours, history tours and artistic tours.

Eleven cities and areas, labelled *"Villes et Pays d'Art et d'Histoire"* by the Ministry of Culture, are mentioned in this guide (Angers, Blois, Bourges, Chinon, Loches, Loire Touraine, Loire Valley, Le Mans, Saumur, Tours and Vendôme). These cities are particularly active in promoting their architectural and cultural heritage and offer guided tours by highly qualified guides, as well as **activities** 👥 for 6–12-year-old children.

🛈 More information is available from local tourist offices and from www.vpah.culture.fr.

INTERNATIONAL VISITORS

EMBASSIES AND CONSULATES
Australia Embassy
4 rue Jean-Rey, 75015 Paris Cedex.
℘01 40 59 33 00
www.france.embassy.gov.au

Canada Embassy
130, rue du Faubourg Saint-Honoré, Paris 8e, ℘01 44 43 29 02
www.international.gc.ca

Eire Embassy
12 ave Foch, 75116 Paris.
℘01 44 17 67 00
www.embassyofireland.fr

New Zealand Embassy
103, rue de Grenelle, 75007 Paris.
℘01 45 01 43 43
www.mfat.govt.nz

UK Embassy
35 rue du Faubourg St-Honoré, 75008 Paris Cedex 08.
℘01 44 51 31 00
www.gov.uk/world/france

UK Consulate
16 bis, rue d'Anjou, 75008 Paris.
℘01 44 51 31 00
www.gov.uk/world/france

USA Embassy
2 avenue Gabriel, 75008 Paris Cedex.
℘01 43 12 22 22
https://fr.usembassy.gov

DOCUMENTS

Passport – Nationals of countries within the European Union entering France need only a national identity card; in the case of the UK, this means your passport. Nationals of other countries must be in possession of a valid national **passport.**

☺ In case of loss or theft, report to your embassy or consulate and the local police.

☺ You must carry your documents with you at all times; they can be checked anywhere.

Visa – No **entry visa** is required for Canadian, US or Australian citizens travelling as tourists and staying less than 90 days, except for students planning to study in France. If you think you may need a visa, apply to your local French Consulate.

US citizens – General passport information is available by phone toll-free from the Federal Information Center (item 5 on the automated menu), *☎800-688-9889*. US passport forms can be downloaded from http://travel.state.gov.

CUSTOMS REGULATIONS

The UK Customs website (www.gov.uk) contains information on allowances, travel safety tips, and to consult and download documents and guides. At the time of writing, there are no limits on the amount of duty and/or tax paid alcohol and tobacco that you can bring back into the UK as long as they are for your own use or gifts and are transported by you. However, Brexit is likely to affect this, so check www.gov.uk for the latest developments. If you are bringing in alcohol or tobacco goods and UK Customs have reason to suspect they may be for a commercial purpose, an officer may ask you questions and make checks.

HEALTH

It is advisable to take out comprehensive travel insurance cover, as tourists receiving medical treatment in French hospitals or clinics have to pay for it themselves.

Nationals of non-EU countries should check with their insurance companies about policy limitations. Keep all receipts.

British and Irish citizens, if not already in possession of an EHIC (European Health Insurance Card), should apply for one before travelling. Up until the end of 2020, the card entitles UK residents to reduced-cost medical treatment. Apply online at www.ehic.org.uk. The card is not an alternative to travel insurance. It will not cover any private medical healthcare or costs. Details of the healthcare available in France and how to claim reimbursement are published in the leaflet Health Advice for Travellers, available from post offices. All prescription drugs taken into France should be clearly labelled; it is recommended to carry a copy of prescriptions. Again, Brexit is likely to change this programme's coverage, or kill it altogether. Check www.gov.uk for the latest developments.

ACCESSIBILITY ♿

The sights described in this guide that are easily accessible to people of reduced mobility are indicated by the symbol ♿. On French TGV and Corail trains there are wheelchair spaces in 1st-class carriages available to holders of 2nd-class tickets. On Eurostar and Thalys special rates are available for accompanying adults. All airports are equipped to receive physically disabled passengers. Disabled drivers may use the EU blue card for parking entitlements.

Many of France's historic buildings, including museums and hotels, have limited or no wheelchair access. Older hotels tend not to have lifts.

Tourism for All UK (*☎0845 124 9971; www.tourismforall.org.uk*) publishes overseas information guides listing accommodation that they believe to be accessible but haven't inspected in person.

Information about accessibility is available from French disability organisations such as **Association des Paralysés de France** (17 bd. Auguste-Blanqui, 75013 Paris; ✆01 40 78 69 00; www.apf-francehandicap. org). Useful information on transportation, holidaymaking, and sports associations for the disabled is available from the French-language website www.handicap.fr. In the UK; www.disabilityrightsuk.org is a good source of info and support, and the

PETS
Recent regulations make it much easier to travel with pets between the UK and mainland Europe. All animals must be microchipped, vaccinated against rabies (at least 21 days prior to travel) and have the EU Pet Passport. Full details are available from the website of the **Department for Environment, Food and Rural Affairs**, www.gov.uk/take-pet-abroad.

Getting There and Getting Around

BY PLANE
The various international and other independent airlines operate services to **Paris** (Roissy-Charles de Gaulle and Orly airports), **Tours** and **Nantes**. ✆Check before booking direct flights, as it is sometimes cheaper to travel via Paris.

Air France (To make a reservation, get real-time information or ask questions, please contact by phone at: 3654 (€0.34/min incl. taxes + call flat rate), 24 hours a day, seven days a week, from France, or +33 (0)9 69 39 36 54 from abroad; www.airfrance.fr), the national airline, links Paris to Nantes and Tours several times a day.

Contact airline companies and travel agents for details of package tour flights with a rail or coach link-up as well as fly-drive schemes.

Discount flights within Europe offer wide choice, but conditions change often, so check the websites.

BA City Flyer operates from 2 to 4 flights a week to Angers from London City Airport between April and October.

Top discounters include **Ryanair** (www.ryanair.com); **easyJet** (www. easyjet.com; **Flybe** (www.flybe.com) and **Jet2.com** (www.jet2.com). Within France, air travel generally compares unfavourably with rail, both for price and time, especially when you consider transport to and from airports, and check-in times.

PRACTICAL ADVICE
Practical advice for travelling by plane, specifically as regards carrying liquids, gels, creams, aerosols, medicines and food for babies is provided on www. francetourism.com. Some countries impose restrictions on liquids bought in duty-free shops when transferring to a connecting flight. Aéroports de Paris recommends that passengers contact individual airline companies for further information. www.parisaeroport.fr

AIRPORT TRANSFERS

Visitors arriving in **Paris** who wish to reach the city centre or a train station can use public transportation or reserve space on the various airport busses (check hwww.parisaeroport.fr for full info on all bus and train lines). You can reach the Loire Valley by TGV direct from Roissy-Charles-de-Gaulle. From Orly, an Air France bus links to Paris-Montparnasse TGV station. Voyages-SNCF run up to 18 TGV daily from Paris to Angers.

For **Nantes Airport**, the TAN (Nantes Area Transport Company; www.tan.fr) links the centre of Nantes to the airport via the Tan Air Service.

At **Tours Val-de-Loire Airport**, there is a bus shuttle to and from the city centre.

BY FERRY

There are numerous **cross-Channel passenger and car** ferry services from the United Kingdom and Ireland. To choose the most suitable route between your port of arrival and your destination use the Michelin Tourist and Motoring Atlas France, Michelin Map 911 (which gives travel times and mileages) or Michelin maps from the 1:200,000 series.

- **Brittany Ferries**
  ℘0330 159 7000 (UK). www.brittanyferries.com. Services from Portsmouth, Poole and Plymouth to Caen (Ouistreham) from where it is a three-hour drive to Angers.
- **Condor Ferries**
  ℘0345 609 1024. www.condorferries.co.uk. Services from Weymouth, Poole and Portsmouth.
- **DFDS Seaways** operate routes between Dover and Calais, Dover-Dunkerque Portsmouth-Le Havre and Newhaven-Dieppe. ℘(UK) 0871 574 7235 and 0800 917 1201. www.dfds.com.
- **P&O Ferries**
  ℘01304 44 88 88 (UK). www.poferries.com. Service between Dover and Calais.

BY TRAIN

Eurotunnel operates a 35-minute rail trip for passengers with a car through the Channel Tunnel between Folkestone and Calais ℘08443 35 35 35 (in the UK) or 08 10 63 03 04 (in France); www.eurotunnel.com.

Eurostar runs from **London** (St Pancras) to **Paris** (Gare du Nord) in under 3hr (up to 20 times daily). In Paris it links to the high-speed rail network (TGV) which covers most of France. There is fast inter-city service from **Paris** (Gare Montparnasse) to **Vendôme** (45min), **Le Mans** (50min), **Tours** (1h) and **Angers** (1h30) on the TGV. Bookings and information ℘03432 186 186 in the UK, ℘01 70 70 60 88 in France; www.eurostar.com.

Citizens of non-European Economic Area countries must complete a landing card before arriving at Eurostar check-in. These cards can be found at dedicated desks in front of the check-in area and from Eurostar staff. Once you have filled in the card, please hand it to UK immigration staff.

France Rail Pass and **Eurail Pass** are travel passes which may be purchased by residents of countries outside the European Union (⊙See www.raileurope-world.com and www.eurail.com).

If you are a **European resident**, you can buy an individual country pass, if you are not a resident of the country where you plan to use it.

At the SNCF (French railways) site, **www.sncf.fr**, you can book ahead, pay with a credit card, and receive your ticket in the mail at home.

Bookings and information

Oui.sncf (formerly Voyages-SNCF) is SNCF's online travel distributor in France (https://en.oui.sncf).

There are numerous **discounts** available when you purchase your tickets in France, from 25–50 percent below the regular rate. They include discounts for using senior cards and youth cards, and seasonal promotions. There are a limited number of

© Illisphotography/iStock

discount seats available during peak travel times, and the best discounts are available for travel during off-peak periods.

🖉Tickets for rail travel in France must be validated *(composter)* by using the (usually) automatic date-stamping machines at the platform entrance *(failure to do so may result in a fine).* The French railway company SNCF operates a **telephone information, reservation and prepayment service in English** from 7am to 10pm (French time) 🖉08 36 35 35 39.

BY COACH/BUS

Regular coach services operate between **London** and **Paris, Tours** or **Nantes: www.eurolines.com** is the international website with information about travelling all over Europe by coach (bus).

Eurolines (in English), 🖉+49 69 971 944 836.

LOCAL SERVICES

Information about shuttle services operating from the airports is included in the section on travelling by air (⏴see p33).

All towns and cities have internal public transport services, sometimes using trams, but more generally buses. These are primarily to serve the local population and are rarely geared to tourism, so be sure to check timetables if you intend to use public transport; this is, however, an excellent way to gain local experience. Attraction-specific transport often operates between the town or city centre and the attraction, and information about this is given in the relevant section of the guide.

BY CAR

PLANNING YOUR ROUTE

The area covered in this guide is easily reached by main motorways and national roads.

Michelin map 726 indicates the main itineraries as well as alternate routes for avoiding heavy traffic during busy holiday periods, and gives estimated travel times. **Michelin map 723** is a detailed atlas of French motorways, indicating tolls, rest areas and services along the route; it includes a table for calculating distances and times. The latest route-planning service is available on **www.ViaMichelin.com**. Travellers can work out a precise route using such options as shortest route, scenic route, route avoiding toll roads or the Michelin-recommended route. The site also provides tourist information (hotels, restaurants and attractions).

The roads are very busy during the holiday period, particularly at weekends in July and August, and to avoid traffic congestion it is advisable to follow the recommended secondary routes (signposted as *Bison Futé – itinéraires bis*). The motorway network includes rest areas *(aires)* and petrol stations, usually with restaurant and shopping complexes attached, about every 40km/25mi, so that long-distance drivers have no excuse not to stop for a rest every now and then.

IN AND ON THE CAR

It is compulsory for all vehicles to carry a **safety jacket** for each passenger, and a **warning triangle** in line with numerous other European countries that have already implemented this measure. It is advisable to have both. For the vehicle, an international distinguishing sign plate or sticker should be displayed as near as is reasonable to the national registration plate at the rear of the vehicle.

DOCUMENTS
Driving Licence
Travellers from other European Union countries and North America can drive in France with a valid national or home-state **driving licence**. An **international driving licence** is useful because the information on it appears in nine languages.

Registration Papers
For the vehicle, it is necessary to have the registration papers (logbook) and a nationality plate of the approved size.

Insurance
Many motoring organisations offer accident insurance and breakdown service schemes for members. Because French autoroutes are privately owned, European Breakdown Cover service does not extend to breakdowns on the autoroute or its service areas – you must use the emergency telephones, or drive off the autoroute before calling your breakdown service.
In the case of a **breakdown,** a red warning triangle or hazard warning lights are obligatory.

ROAD REGULATIONS
The minimum driving age is 18. Traffic drives on the right. All passengers must wear **seat belts**. Children under the age of 10 must ride in the back seat. Headlights must be switched on in poor visibility and at night; dipped headlights should be used at all times outside built-up areas. Use sidelights only when the vehicle is stationary.
In the case of a **breakdown**, a red warning triangle or hazard warning lights are obligatory, as are **reflective safety jackets**, one for each passenger, and carried within the car. It is

now compulsory to carry an in-car **breathalyser kit**, too; you can be fined if you do not. UK right-hand drive cars must use headlight adaptors.
In the absence of stop signs at intersections, cars must **give way to the right**. Traffic on main roads outside built-up areas (priority indicated by a yellow diamond sign) and on roundabouts has right of way. Vehicles must stop when the lights turn red at road junctions and may filter to the right only when indicated by an amber arrow.
The regulations on **drinking and driving** (limited to 0.50g/l) and **speeding** are strictly enforced – usually by an on-the-spot fine and/or confiscation of the vehicle.
Further regulations – It is obligatory to carry spare lightbulbs; yellow fluorescent jackets in case of breakdown, one for each passenger, and accessible from within the car; and an in-car breathalyser kit. UK right-hand drive cars must use headlight adaptors.

SPEED LIMITS
Although liable to modification, these limits are as follows:
- **Toll motorways** (*autoroutes*) 130kph/80mph (110kph/68mph when raining);
- **Dual carriageways and motorways** without tolls 110kph/68mph (100kph/62mph when raining);
- **Other roads** 90kph/56mph (80kph/50mph when raining) and in towns 50kph/31mph;
- **Outside lane on motorways** during daylight, on level ground and with good visibility – minimum speed limit of 80kph/50mph.

PARKING
In town there are zones where parking is either restricted or subject to a fee; tickets should be obtained from the ticket machines (*horodateurs* – small change necessary) and displayed inside the windscreen on

© Laurent Giraudou/hemis.fr

Cycling along the Mayenne, Coudray

the driver's side; failure to display them may result in a fine, or towing of the vehicle. Other parking areas in town may require you to take a ticket when passing through a barrier. To exit, pay the parking fee (usually there is a machine located by the exit – *sortie*) and insert the paid-up card in another machinethat will lift the exit gate.

In France, most motorway sections are subject to a **toll** *(péage)*. You can pay in cash or with a credit card.

PETROL/GASOLINE

French service stations dispense:

- ◆ *sans plomb98*
  (super unleaded 98)
- ◆ *sans plomb95*
  (super unleaded 95)
- ◆ *diesel/gazole* (diesel), including premium diesel
- ◆ *GPL* (LPG).

Prices are listed on signboards on the motorways, although it is usually cheaper to fill up before joining or after leaving the motorway.
The website www.prix-carburants. gouv.fr collects information on current fuel prices around the country.

CAR RENTAL

There are car rental agencies at airports, railway stations and in all large towns throughout France. European cars have manual transmission; automatic cars are available only if an advance reservation is made. Drivers must be over 21; between ages 21 and 25, drivers are required to pay an extra daily fee; some companies allow drivers under 23 only if the reservation has been made through a travel agent.

Car hire and holders of UK driving licences

In 2015, changes to the UK Driving License came into force which mean that because details of fines, penalty points and restrictions are now only held electronically you are going to have to enable a car hire company to access your online driving record by means of a DVLA-issued pass code. Full details are available at www.gov.uk/view-driving-licence.

Where to Stay and Eat

For Hotel & Restaurant listings, see the **Addresses** *within the Principal Sights in Discovering the Châteaux of the Loire.*

WHERE TO STAY
FINDING A HOTEL

Turn to the **Addresses** within individual Sight descriptions for a selection and prices of typical places to stay (**Stay**) and eat (**Eat**).

The key on the cover flap of this book explains the symbols and abbreviations used in these sections, as well as the coin price ranges. To enhance your stay, hotel selections have been chosen for their location, comfort, value for the money, and in many cases, their charm, but it is not a comprehensive listing.

For an even greater selection, use the red-cover **Michelin Guide France**, with its famously reliable star-rating system and hundreds of establishments all over France.

A guide to good-value, family-run hotels, **Logis et Auberges de France**, is available from the French Tourist Office: www.tourisme.fr. The website gives a list of accommodation for each *département*, as well as links for making reservations, and a list of tourist offices all over France.

Another resource, which publishes a catalogue listing holiday villas, apartments or chalets in each *département* is the **French national family tourism network CléVacances** *(www.clevacances.com)*. For good-value, family-run accommodation, the **Logis** network, is one of the best organisations to contact *(℘01 45 84 83 84; www.logishotels.com)*.

Relais & Châteaux provides information on booking in luxury hotels with character: ℘01 76 49 39

39; within the UK: ℘020 3519 1967; within the US: ℘1 800 735 2478; www.relaischateaux.com.

www.viamichelin.com covers hotels in France, including famous selections from the Michelin Guide as well as lower-priced chains.

ECONOMY CHAIN HOTELS

If you need a place to stop en route, these can be useful, as they are inexpensive and generally located near the main road. Breakfast is available, but there may not be a restaurant; rooms are small, with a TV and bathroom.

Central reservation numbers and websites (online booking is usually available):

- **Akena** ℘0810 220 280; www.hotels-akena.com
- **B&B** ℘08 92 78 29 29; www.hotel-bb.com
- **Best Hôtel** ℘03 28 27 46 69; www.besthotel.fr
- **Campanile**, ℘020 7519 5045 (UK number); www.campanile.com
- **Kyriad**, ℘020 7519 50 45 (UK number); www.kyriad.com
- **Première Classe**, ℘020 7519 5045 (UK number); www.premiereclasse.com
- **www.ihg.com** (International Hotels Group)
- **www.choicehotels.com** (Comfort)
- **www.bestwestern.fr** (Best Western)
- **https://ibis.accor.com** (Ibis Hotels)

COTTAGES, BED AND BREAKFAST

The **Maison des Gîtes de France** lists self-catering cottages or apartments, or bed and breakfast accommodation *(chambres d'hôtes)* at a reasonable price: ℘0826 10 44 44; www.gites-de-france.com.

La Fédération des Stations Vertes BP 71698, 21016 Dijon ℘03 80 54 10 50; www.stationverte.com lists some 600 country and mountain sites ideal for families.

*Chambre d'hôte Troglododo,
Azay-le-Rideau*

© Stéphane Lemaire/hemis.fr

There is also **Bed and Breakfast France**, 12 rue des Tulipes - 85100 Les Sables d'Olonne; www.bedbreak.com. The **Fédération des Logis de France** offers hotel-restaurant packages geared to walking, fishing, biking, skiing, wine-tasting and enjoying nature ✆01 45 84 83 84; www.logishotels.com.

The adventurous can consult **www.gites-refuges.com**, where you can order a guidebook, *Gîtes d'étapes et refuges*, listing some 4,000 shelters for walkers, mountaineers, rock-climbers, skiers, canoe/kayakers, etc.: 74 rue A. Perdreaux, 78140 Vélizy ✆01 34 65 11 89.

HOSTELS, CAMPING

To obtain an International Youth Hostel Federation card (no age requirement; senior card also available) contact the IYHF in your own country. An online booking service (*www.hihostels.com*), lets you reserve rooms up to six months ahead. The two main youth hostel associations (*auberges de jeunesse*) in France are:

- ♦ **Ligue Française pour les Auberges de la Jeunesse**
  67 r. Vergniaud, Bâtiment K, 75013 Paris. ✆01 44 16 78 78. www.auberges-de-jeunesse.com.

- ♦ **Fédération Unie des Auberges de Jeunesse**
  27 r. Pajol, 75018 Paris.
  ✆01 44 89 87 27. www.fuaj.org.

There are numerous officially graded camp sites with varying standards of facilities throughout the Burgundy-Jura region.

The **Michelin Camping France** guide lists a selection of camp sites. The area is very popular with campers in the summer months, so it is wise to reserve in advance.

WHERE TO EAT

A selection of places to eat in the different locations covered in this guide can be found in the **Addresses** throughout *Discovering Châteaux of the Loire*. The key on the cover flap of this book explains the symbols and abbreviations used in these sections, as well as the coin price ranges. Several eating places are highlighted, primarily for their atmosphere, location and regional delicacies; but it is by no means a comprehensive list. Price indicators are for the average cost of a starter, main dish and dessert for one person.

Use the red-cover **Michelin Guide France,** with its well-known star-rating system and hundreds of establishments throughout France, for an even greater choice. If you would like to experience a meal in a highly rated restaurant from The Michelin Guide, be sure to book ahead. In the countryside, restaurants usually serve lunch between noon and 2pm and dinner between 7.30 and 10pm. It is not always easy to find something in between those two mealtimes, as the "non-stop" restaurant is still a rarity in the provinces. However, a hungry traveller can usually get a sandwich (usually a filled baguette) in a café, and ordinary hot dishes may be available in a brasserie.

Restaurants usually charge for meals in two ways: a fixed-price *menu*, with two or three courses and sometimes a small pitcher of wine, or the more expensive *à la carte*, with each course ordered separately.

Cafés generally only serve coffee and other beverages; **brasseries** offer inexpensive, classic French dishes; **relais routiers** offer straightforward, hearty food and are mainly frequented by lorry drivers. These can be found on A roads (*www.relais-routiers.com*); **auberges** and **tables d'hôtes** are usually found in the countryside and can be a good option to both eat and stay. Regional produce is the keynote. Their addresses are often well-kept secrets, so enquire at the local tourist information centre.

In French restaurants and cafés, a service charge is included.

Basic Information

BUSINESS HOURS

Admission to state-owned **museums** and historic monuments is free for travellers with special needs, such as people with disabilities – as well as those accompanying them – but the rules require that you show an identification card. Admission is free in most museums for children under 18 years of age. Admission is sometimes free for all visitors on the first Sunday in every month. Museums and art galleries are often closed on Mondays; municipal museums are generally closed on Mondays.

Most of the larger **stores** are open Mon–Sat 9am–6.30pm/7.30pm. Smaller, individual shops may close during the lunch hour. Food shops – grocers, wine merchants and bakeries – are open from around 7am–7.30pm; some open on Sunday mornings. Open-air food markets usually close on Mondays. Hypermarkets typically stay open until 9pm/10pm.

Banks are usually open from 9am–4.30pm or 5pm and are closed on Mondays or Saturdays; some branches open for limited transactions on Saturdays. Banks close early on the day before a bank holiday.

DISCOUNTS

Almost all attractions offer discounted admission prices for children, seniors, students and (sometimes) family groups; many also offer discounts for advance booking online.

The ages that children's discounts apply to vary, but where these relate to Sights that are noted as specific attractions for children with the 👤👤 symbol, the price and age range for children are shown. Student discounts tend as a rule to be for French students only, on presentation of a student ID card.

ELECTRICITY

The electric current is 220 volts. Circular two-pin plugs are the rule. Adapters and converters (for hairdryers, for example) should be bought before you leave home; they are sold in most airports. If you have a rechargeable device (mobile phone, video camera, portable computer, battery recharger), read the instructions carefully or contact the manufacturer or shop. Sometimes these items only require a plug adapter, in other cases you must use a voltage converter as well or risk ruining your appliance.

EMERGENCIES

If you are driving on an *autoroute,* emergency telephones are placed at regular intervals which will connect you with a service to repair the problem or get you off the autoroute.

EMERGENCY NUMBERS	
Police:	☎17
SAMU (Paramedics):	☎15
Fire (Pompiers):	☎18
European-wide Emergency number:	☎112

MAIL/POST

Main post offices open Monday to Friday 9am to 7pm, Saturday 9am to noon. However, many post offices, especially smaller ones, close at lunchtime between noon and 2pm, and some may close early in the afternoon; in short, opening hours vary widely. Stamps are also available from newsagents and tobacconists *(tabacs)*. Stamp collectors should ask for *timbres de collection* in any post office. France has two different stamps which are used for the standard postal service. The red stamp is the one used for a quicker delivery, and letters should take between 1 and 3 days to arrive. This is the equivalent of the first class service in the UK. The green stamps offer a slower service, between 2 and 3 days, the equivalent of second class deliveries in the UK.
Postage via air mail:
UK: letter (20g) €1.40.
North America: letter (20g) €1.40
Australia and NZ: letter (20g) €1.40
Stamps are also available from newsagents and *bureaux de tabac.* Stamp collectors should ask for *timbres de collection* in any post

office. A useful website for mailing information and prices is www.prixdestimbres.fr.

MONEY
CURRENCY

There are no restrictions on the amount of currency visitors can take into France. Visitors carrying a lot of cash are advised to complete a currency declaration form on arrival, because there are restrictions on currency export.

NOTES AND COINS

The **euro** is the only currency accepted as a means of payment in France, as in the other European countries participating in the monetary union. It is divided into 100 cents or centimes.

BANKS

Bank hours vary from branch to branch, but for typical hours ⓒ*see BUSINESS HOURS above.*
One of the most economical ways to obtain money in France is by using **ATM machines** to get cash directly from your bank account (with a debit card) or to use your credit card to get a cash advance. Be sure to remember your PIN number; you will need it to use cash dispensers and to pay with your card in shops, restaurants, etc. Code pads are numeric; use a telephone pad to translate a letter code into numbers. PIN numbers have 4 digits in France; enquire with the issuing company or bank if the code you usually use is longer.

CREDIT CARDS

Visa is the most widely accepted credit card, followed by MasterCard; other cards, credit and debit (Diners Club, Plus, Cirrus, etc.) are also accepted in some cash machines. American Express is accepted primarily in premium establishments. Most places post signs indicating which cards they accept; if you don't see such a sign, and want to pay with a card, ask before ordering or making a selection.

Cards are widely accepted in shops, hypermarkets, hotels and restaurants, at tollbooths and in petrol stations. Before you leave home, check with the bank that issued your card for emergency replacement procedures. At the same time, inform the bank that you will be using your credit card abroad – it may prevent refusal of your card at cash desks. Carry your card number and its emergency phone numbers separately from your wallet and handbag; leave a copy of this information with someone you can easily reach. If your card is lost or stolen while you are in France, call one of the 24-hour hotlines shown in the box above.

😊 *If your card is lost or stolen* call the appropriate 24h hotlines listed on *www.totallymoney.com/credit-cards/lost-stolen-credit-card*.

Better still: always carry with you the correct number to call for your particular credit cards. You must report any loss or theft of credit cards or traveller's cheques to the local police who will issue you with a certificate (useful proof to show the issuing company).

TRAVELLER'S CHEQUES

It may be a good idea to carry a few traveller's cheques in addition to your credit cards, and to keep them in a safe place in case of emergency. A passport is necessary as identification when cashing traveller's cheques in banks or major hotels. Smaller establishments are not likely to cash them. Commission charges vary and hotels usually charge more than banks for cashing cheques.

PUBLIC HOLIDAYS

🕯️*See the box below for a list of major public holidays in France.* There are other religious and national festivals days, and a number of local saints' days. On all these days, museums and other monuments may be closed or may vary their hours of admission. In addition to the usual school holidays at Christmas and in the spring and

1 January	New Year's Day (*Jour de l'An*)
Mon after Easter Sun	Easter Day and Easter Monday (*Pâques*)
1 May	May Day (*Fête du Travail*)
8 May	VE Day (*Fête de la Libération*)
Thurs 40 days after Easter	Ascension Day (*Ascension*)
7th Sun-Mon after Easter	Whit Sunday and Monday (*Pentecôte*)
14 July	France's National Day (*Fête de la Bastille*)
15 August	Assumption (*Assomption*)
1 November	All Saint's Day (*Toussaint*)
11 November	Armistice Day (*Fête de la Victoire*)
25 December	Christmas Day (*Noël*)

summer, there are long mid-term breaks (10 days to a fortnight) in February and early November.

SMOKING

In France smoking is banned in public places such as offices, universities railway stations, restaurants, cafés, bars, nightclubs and casinos. In 2013 the ban was extended to e-cigarettes.

TELEPHONES
PUBLIC TELEPHONES

Due to the widespread use of mobile phones, the number of **public telephones** in France is decreasing. Those that remain accept pre-paid phone cards (*télécartes*), rather than coins. Some telephone booths accept credit cards (Visa, Mastercard/Eurocard). *Télécartes* (50 or 120 units) can be bought in post offices, branches of France Télécom, *bureaux de tabac* (cafés that sell cigarettes) and newsagents and can be used to make calls in France and abroad. Calls can be received at phone boxes where the blue bell sign is shown; the phone will not ring, so keep your eye on the little message screen.

NATIONAL CALLS

French telephone numbers have ten digits. Paris and Paris region numbers begin with 01; 02 in northwest France; 03 in northeast France; 04 in southeast France and Corsica; 05 in southwest France.

Local directory enquiries
☎ **118 218**

Available online, the website **www.118218.fr** provides business and private phone numbers free-of-charge and includes listings of recommended bars, restaurants, films, exhibitions and other leisure activities.

INTERNATIONAL CALLS

To call France from abroad, dial the country code (+33) + 9-digit number (omit the initial 0). When calling abroad from France, dial 00, then dial the country code followed by the area code and number of your correspondent.

MOBILE/CELL PHONES

While in France, all visitors from other European countries should be able to use their mobile phone as normal. Visitors from other countries need to ensure before departure that their phone and service contract are compatible with the European system (GSM). The three main mobile phone operators in France are SFR, Orange and Bouygues:

Orange www.orange.fr
Bouygues www.bouyguestelecom.fr
SFR www.sfr.fr

A number of service providers now offer the facility to use home-country units rather than paying roaming charges, but make a daily charge for this. If you plan to make regular use of a mobile phone while abroad, this is worth considering.

The EU abolished roaming charges in June 2017, as a result EU citizens won't be charged extra for calls. But for the foreseeable future the application of this decision in practice remains unclear. If necessary, consult your own provider.

TIME

France is 1h ahead of **Greenwich Mean Time (GMT).**

France goes on **Daylight-Saving Time** the last Sunday in March to the last Sunday in October. In France "am" and "pm" are not used but the 24-hour clock is widely applied.

WHEN IT IS NOON IN FRANCE, IT IS	
3am	in Los Angeles
6am	in New York
11am	in Dublin
11am	in London
7pm	in Perth (6pm in summer)
9pm	in Sydney (8pm in summer)
11pm	in Auckland (10pm in summer)

TIPPING

Since a service charge is automatically included in the price of meals and accommodation in France, any additional tipping is up to the visitor, generally small change, and usually not more than 5 percent. Taxi drivers and hairdressers are normally tipped 10–15 percent.

Tour guides and tour drivers should be tipped according to the amount of service given: from €2–5 would not be unusual.

VALUE ADDED TAX

In France a sales tax (TVA or Value Added Tax ranging from 2.1% to 20%) is added to almost all retail goods – it can be worth your while to recover it. VAT refunds are available to visitors from outside the EU only if purchases exceed €175 per store. The system works in large stores that cater to tourists, in luxury stores and other shops advertising "duty free". Show your passport, and the store will complete a form that is to be stamped (at the airport) by customs. The refund is paid into your credit card account.

CONVERSION TABLES

Weights and Measures

1 kilogram (kg)	**2.2 pounds (lb)**	**2.2 pounds**	*To convert kilograms to pounds, multiply by 2.2*
6.35 kilograms	14 pounds	1 stone (st)
0.45 kilograms	16 ounces (oz)	16 ounces
1 metric ton (tn)	**1.1 tons**	**1.1 tons**
1 litre (l)	**2.11 pints (pt)**	**1.76 pints**	*To convert litres to gallons, multiply by 0.26 (US) or 0.22 (UK)*
3.79 litres	1 gallon (gal)	0.83 gallon
4.55 litres	1.20 gallon	1 gallon
1 hectare (ha)	**2.47 acres**	**2.47 acres**	*To convert hectares to acres, multiply by 2.4*
1 sq kilometre (km²)	**0.38 sq. miles (sq mi)**	**0.38 sq. miles**
1 centimetre (cm)	**0.39 inches (in)**	**0.39 inches**	*To convert metres to feet, multiply by 3.28; for kilometres to miles, multiply by 0.6*
1 metre (m)	**3.28 feet (ft) or 39.37 inches or 1.09 yards (yd)**	
1 kilometre (km)	**0.62 miles (mi)**	**0.62 miles**

Clothing

Women	🇪🇺	🇺🇸	🇬🇧
	35	4	2½
	36	5	3½
	37	6	4½
Shoes	38	7	5½
	39	8	6½
	40	9	7½
	41	10	8½
	36	6	8
	38	8	10
Dresses	40	10	12
& suits	42	12	14
	44	14	16
	46	16	18
	36	6	30
	38	8	32
Blouses &	40	10	34
sweaters	42	12	36
	44	14	38
	46	16	40

Men	🇪🇺	🇺🇸	🇬🇧
	40	7½	7
	41	8½	8
	42	9½	9
Shoes	43	10½	10
	44	11½	11
	45	12½	12
	46	13½	13
	46	36	36
	48	38	38
Suits	50	40	40
	52	42	42
	54	44	44
	56	46	48
	37	14½	14½
	38	15	15
Shirts	39	15½	15½
	40	15¾	15¾
	41	16	16
	42	16½	16½

Sizes often vary depending on the designer. These equivalents are given for guidance only.

Speed

KPH	10	30	50	70	80	90	100	110	120	130
MPH	6	19	31	43	50	56	62	68	75	81

Temperature

Celsius (°C)	0°	5°	10°	15°	20°	25°	30°	40°	60°	80°	100°
Fahrenheit (°F)	32°	41°	50°	59°	68°	77°	86°	104°	140°	176°	212°

To convert Celsius into Fahrenheit, multiply °C by 9, divide by 5, and add 32.
To convert Fahrenheit into Celsius, subtract 32 from °F, multiply by 5, and divide by 9.
NB: Conversion factors on this page are approximate.

MENU READER

agneau	lamb	**poivre**	sauce
alose	shad	**fèves**	broad beans
anguilles	eels	**foie**	liver
bavette aux échalottes	sirloin with shallots	**filets de sole**	sole fillets
blanquette de veau	veal in cream sauce	**frites**	French fries
		fromage de chèvre	goat cheese
		fruits de mer	seafood
boudin blanc	chicken sausage	**garbure**	hearty vegetable and meat soup
boudin noir	blood sausage		
brioche	sweet egg-and-butter bread	**haricots**	beans
		homard	lobster
canard	duck	**huître**	oyster
cèpes	wild mushrooms	**jambon**	ham
chapon	capon	**jus de fruits**	fruit juice
charcuterie	pork meats	**langouste/ langoustines**	spiny lobster
chipirones/seiches	squid		
choux	cabbage	**lapin**	rabbit
confits (canard)	(duck) cooked and preserved in fat	**loukinos**	garlic sausage
		magret	duck fillet
coq au vin	chicken in red wine sauce	**marrons**	chestnuts
		menu enfant	children's menu
côtes d'agneau	lamb chops	**mojettes**	white beans
crevettes	shrimp / prawns	**moules**	mussels
crudités	raw vegetable salad	**mouton**	mutton
		noix	walnuts
dorade aux herbes	sea bream with herbs	**nos viandes sont garnies**	our meat dishes are served with vegetables
éclade	mussels cooked over pine needles		
		oie	goose
escargots	snails	**omelette aux morilles**	wild-mushroom omelette
esturgeon	sturgeon		
faux filet au	sirloin with pepper		

Goat cheese - AOC Sainte-Maure-de-Touraine

© Makosh/Shutterstock

palombe	wood pigeon	**sorbet: trois parfums**	sorbet: three flavours
pastis	anise-flavoured liqueur	**steak haché**	minced beef
pêche	peach	**tarte aux pommes**	apple pie
pibales	young eels	**terrine de lapin**	rabbit pâté
poule/poulet	chicken	**tournedos**	fillet steak
poule au pot	chicken stew with vegetables	**tourteau fromager**	sweet cake made with cheese
prune	plum	**tourtière**	flaky pastry with prune filling
pruneau	prune	**tripotcha**	mutton sausage
ravigote	seasoned white sauce	**ttoro**	Basque fish stew
salmis	stew of roast fowl and game	**vin rouge, vin blanc, rosé**	red wine, white wine, rosé wine
saumon grillé	grilled salmon		

well-done, medium, rare, raw = *bien cuit, à point, saignant, cru*

Useful Words and Phrases

Sights

	Translation
abbey	abbaye
belfry	beffroi
bridge	pont
castle	château
cemetery	cimetière
chapel	chapelle
church	église
cloisters	cloître
courtyard	cour
convent	couvent
covered market	halle
fountain	fontaine
garden	jardin
gateway	porte
house	maison
lock (canal)	écluse
market	marché
monastery	monastère
museum	musée
park	parc
port/harbour	port
quay	quai
ramparts	remparts
square	place
statue	statue
street	rue

tower	tour
town hall	mairie
windmill	moulin

Natural Sites

	Translation
beach	plage
beacon	signal
cave	grotte
chasm	abîme
coast, hillside	côte
dam	barrage
forest	forêt
lake	lac
ledge	corniche
pass	col
river	rivière
spring	source
stream	ruisseau
swallow-hole	aven
valley	vallée
viewpoint	belvédère
waterfall	cascade

On the Road

	Translation
car park	parking
driving licence	permis de conduire
east	Est
garage (for repairs)	garage
left	gauche

motorway/highway	autoroute
north	Nord
parking meter	horodateur
petrol/gas	essence
petrol/gas station	station essence
right	droite
south	Sud
toll	péage
traffic lights	feu rouge
tyre	pneu
west	Ouest
wheel clamp	sabot
zebra crossing	passage clouté

Time

	Translation
today	aujourd'hui
tomorrow	demain
yesterday	hier
autumn	automne
spring	printemps
summer	été
winter	hiver
week	semaine
Monday	lundi
Tuesday	mardi
Wednesday	mercredi
Thursday	jeudi
Friday	vendredi
Saturday	samedi
Sunday	dimanche

Numbers

	Translation
0	zéro
1	un
2	deux
3	trois
4	quatre
5	cinq
6	six
7	sept
8	huit
9	neuf
10	dix
11	onze
12	douze
13	treize
14	quatorze
15	quinze
16	seize
17	dix-sept
18	dix-huit
19	dix-neuf
20	vingt
30	trente
40	quarante
50	cinquante
60	soixante
70	soixante-dix
80	quatre-vingt
90	quatre-vingt-dix
100	cent
1,000	mille

Shopping

	Translation
bank	banque
baker's	boulangerie
big	grand
butcher's	boucherie
chemist's	pharmacie
closed	fermé
cough mixture	sirop pour la toux
cough sweets	cachets pour la gorge
entrance	entrée
exit	sortie
fishmonger's	poissonnerie
grocer's	épicerie
newsagent, bookshop	librairie
open	ouvert
post office	poste
push	pousser
pull	tirer
shop	magasin
small	petit
stamps	timbres

Food and Drink

	Translation
beef	bœuf
beer	bière
butter	beurre
bread	pain
breakfast	petit-déjeuner
cheese	fromage
dessert	dessert
dinner	dîner
fish	poisson
fork	fourchette
fruit	fruits
glass	verre
chicken	poulet
ice cream	glace
ice cubes	glaçons
ham	jambon
knife	couteau
lamb	agneau
lunch	déjeuner
lettuce salad	salade
meat	viande
mineral water	eau minérale
mixed salad	salade composée

orange juice	jus d'orange
plate	assiette
pork	porc
restaurant	restaurant
red wine	vin rouge
salt	sel
spoon	cuillère
sugar	sucre
vegetables	légumes
water	de l'eau
white wine	vin blanc
yoghurt	yaourt

Personal Documents and Travel

	Translation
airport	aéroport
credit card	carte de crédit
customs	douane
passport	passeport
platform	voie
railway station	gare
shuttle	navette
suitcase	valise
train ticket	billet de train
plane ticket	billet d'avion
wallet	portefeuille

Clothing

	Translation
coat	manteau
jumper	pull
raincoat	imperméable
shirt	chemise
shoes	chaussures
socks	chaussettes
suit	costume
tights	collants
trousers	pantalon

Useful Phrases

	Translation
goodbye	au revoir
hello/good morning	bonjour
how	comment
excuse me	excusez-moi
thank you	merci
yes/no	oui/non
I am sorry	pardon
why	pourquoi
when	quand
please	s'il vous plaît

Do you speak English?
Parlez-vous anglais?
I don't understand
Je ne comprends pas

Talk slowly
Parlez lentement
Where's...?
Où est...?
When does the ... leave?
A quelle heure part...?
When does the ... arrive?
A quelle heure arrive...?
When does the museum open?
A quelle heure ouvre le musée?
When is the show?
A quelle heure a lieu la représentation?
When is breakfast served?
A quelle heure sert-on le petit-déjeuner?
What does it cost?
Combien cela coûte-t-il?
Where can I buy a newspaper in English?
Où puis-je acheter un journal en anglais?
Where is the nearest petrol/gas station?
Où se trouve la station essence la plus proche?
Where can I change traveller's cheques?
Où puis-je échanger des chèques-voyage?
Where are the toilets?
Où sont les toilettes?
Do you accept credit cards?
Acceptez-vous les cartes de crédit?

Useful to Know

On national and departmental roads, there are often roundabouts just outside the towns, which serve to slow traffic down.

At a French roundabout (**rond point**), you are likely to see signs pointing to the **Centre Ville** (town centre) or to other towns (the French use towns as directional indicators, rather than cardinal points).

You are also likely to see a sign for **Toutes Directions** (all directions – it is often the bypass road to avoid going through the town) or **Autres Directions** (other directions – in other words, a place that isn't indicated on one of the other signs on the roundabout).

Château de Chinon and the vineyards
© Laurent Marolleau/age fotostock

INTRODUCTION TO CHÂTEAUX OF THE LOIRE

The Region Today

POPULATION AND LIFESTYLE

The population of the Loire valley is roughly 2.6 million, with the greatest concentrations being in;

- Tours (136,252)
- Orléans (116,685)
- Angers (152,960)

The population density is in the region of 100 persons per sq km.

The Loire region is a prime tourist destination and wine-producing area, and as a result its inhabitants enjoy a comfortable and prosperous lifestyle based on these principal activities. Some branches of the region's economy (such as industry, tourism and property building) have had problems with providing new jobs in recent years, or even with keeping pre-existing employment. But on the whole, the general economic trend of the Pays de la Loire region is quite similar to the economic situation of the rest of France.

Unemployment issues have persisted since the 1970s, and the Pays de la Loire has an unemployment rate of 5.8%, although a number of attempts have been made since to curb the unemployment rate. As France is the most-visited country in the world, with more some 85.7 million visitors in 2013, tourism is a significant contributor to the French economy, or as much as 7 percent of Gross Domestic Product (GDP). Paris, the capital city, is the third most visited city in the world.

Following the terrorist attacks of 2015 and 2016, it was expected that tourism numbers would fall, and while this was true for a time, the long-term impact was not as severe as had been feared. The number of foreign tourists visiting France rose in the fourth quarter of 2016 and has continued to rise every year since.

RELIGION

In matters of religion, the region is not dissimilar to the rest of France: Catholicism is the primary religion, as nearly all villages' main, or only, church attest. During the Ancien Régime, France had traditionally been considered the Church's eldest daughter, and the King of France always maintained close links to the Pope. Roman Catholicism, however, is no longer considered a state religion as it was before the 1789 Revolution.

ECONOMY AND GOVERNMENT

France is the seventh largest economy in the world in USD exchange-rate terms. With a GDP of $US2.7 trillion (2019 data) and the tenth largest by purchasing power parity, it shows a low poverty rate (7.9 percent) among the large economies, and one of the lowest income inequality rates. The country has some of the world's strongest social services (such as health care, education, retirement systems) and public service sectors (such as public transport and public security). According to World Bank and IMF figures, France is the second largest economy in Europe after Germany.

France is the European Union's leading agricultural producer, accounting for about one third of all agricultural land within the EU: Northern France is characterised by large wheat farms; dairy products, pork, poultry and apple production are concentrated in the western region; beef production is located in central France; while the production of fruits, vegetables and wine ranges from central to southern France.

In 2017, Emmanuel Macron replaced François Hollande as President of France. At the age of just 39, he became the youngest President in the history of France. He ran the election under the banner of En Marche! – La République En Marche! – a centrist political movement he founded in April 2016. Macron has notably advocated in favour of the free market and reducing the public-finances deficit. Politically, he says that he is neither right nor left, and advocates a collective solidarity.

His election marks the first occasion in modern times when France has not been governed by either a right-wing or left-wing government.

New French regions
In 2014, the French Parliament (the National Assembly and the Senate) passed a law that reduced the number of regions in Metropolitan France from 22 to 13. The new regions took effect on 1 January 2016. The Centre-Val de Loire region, however, remains unchanged.

LOCAL GOVERNMENT
According to its constitution, France has three levels of local government: 22 *régions* and four *régions d'outre-mer* or overseas regions (Réunion, Martinique, Guadeloupe and French Guiana); 96 *départements* and four *départements d'outre-mer* (Réunion, Guadeloupe, Martinique and French Guiana). There are 36,679 *communes* (municipalities).

FOOD AND DRINK
Local specialities below are shown with wines best suited to accompany them.

Hors-d'œuvre: various types of potted pork; sausage stuffed with chicken meat *(boudin blanc)*.

Fish: pike, salmon, carp or shad with the famous *beurre blanc* (white butter) sauce; small fried fish from the Loire, rather like whitebait *(friture)*; stuffed bream and casserole of eels simmered in wine with mushrooms, onions and prunes (in Anjou).

Main course: game from Sologne; pork with prunes; veal in a cream sauce made with white wine and brandy; casserole of chicken in a red wine sauce or in a white wine and cream sauce with onions and mushrooms; spit-roasted capon or pullet.

Rillauds, rillons and rillettes: all three words derive from the French 16C term *rille*, meaning small dice of pork. *Rillons*, sometimes referred to as *grillons*, are made with pork meat, both lean and fat, which is cut into small morsels. These are then sautéed in fat until they are golden brown and served cold. To make *rillettes*, take some *rillons*, slice them finely and put them back to cook on a low heat. They are kept in a pot where the fat rises to the surface, ensuring perfect conservation. *Rillettes* can also be made with goose meat. Anjou *rillauds* are chunks of belly of pork cooked in a vegetable stock enhanced with aromatic herbs for several hours. When the sauce has been reduced, some lard can be added for the final stages of cooking. The dish is best served with a glass of Vouvray.

Vegetables: green cabbage with butter; Vineuil asparagus; mushrooms – stuffed or in a cream sauce; lettuce salad with walnut oil dressing.

Cheese: St-Benoît, Vendôme and St-Paulin are made from cows' milk. Chavignol, Valençay, Selles-sur-Cher, Ste-Maure and Crémets d'Anjou are made from goats' milk (the latter are small fresh cream cheeses); Olivet is factory made with a coating of charcoal.

Fruit: plums, prunes and melons from Tours; strawberries from Saumur; apricots and pears from Angers; Reinette apples from Le Mans.

Dessert: macaroons from Cormery; apple pastries; quince and apple jelly *(cotignac)*; preserves from Orléans and pastries from Tours; caramelised upside-down apple tart.

Liqueurs: there are excellent marcs and fruit liqueurs, including the famous Cointreau.

Bottle of Bourgueil
© S. Sauvignier/MICHELIN

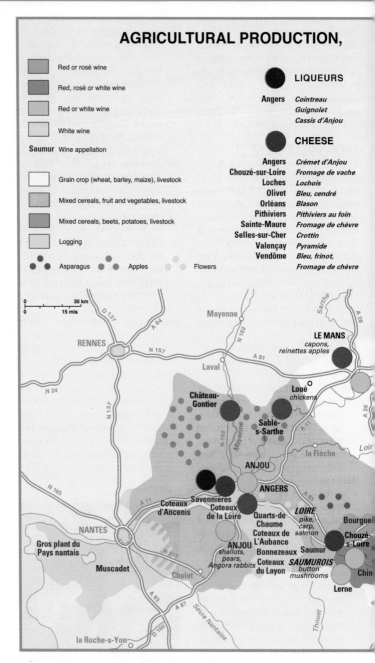

AGRICULTURAL PRODUCTION,

Red or rosé wine

Red, rosé or white wine

Red or white wine

White wine

Saumur Wine appellation

Grain crop (wheat, barley, maize), livestock

Mixed cereals, fruit and vegetables, livestock

Mixed cereals, beets, potatoes, livestock

Logging

Asparagus   Apples   Flowers

LIQUEURS

Angers	Cointreau
	Guignolet
	Cassis d'Anjou

CHEESE

Angers	Crémet d'Anjou
Chouzé-sur-Loire	Fromage de vache
Loches	Lochois
Olivet	Bleu, cendré
Orléans	Blason
Pithiviers	Pithiviers au foin
Sainte-Maure	Fromage de chèvre
Selles-sur-Cher	Crottin
Valençay	Pyramide
Vendôme	Bleu, frinot,
	Fromage de chèvre

Marcs: pure white spirit obtained from pressed grape skins and pips.

WINE

See also "Wine Country" in What to See and Do in the Planning Your Trip section. For a guide to the best years and advice on the best combinations of

SPECIALITIES AND VINEYARDS

CONFECTIONERY

Angers	Quernons d'ardoise
Beaugency	Liquorice
Blois	Chocolate, chocalate buttons
Château-Gontier	Croquets
Cormery	Macaroons
Gâtinais	Honey
Le Mans	Bugattises
Orléans	Apple Jelly
Pithiviers	Pithiviers almond tart
Romorantin-Lanthenay	Liquorice
Sablé-sur-Sarthe	Shortbread
Saint-Benoît-sur-Loire	Moinillons
Sologne	Tarte tatin, palet solognot
Tours	Livre tournois
	Sucres d'orge
	Stuffed prunes
	Muscadines

OTHER SPECIALITIES

Angers	Crêpes, veal chump chop, rilletes, rillons
Blois	Pâtés, rillettes, rillons
Chinon	Fouace bread, eel stew
Jargeau	Smoked pork sausage
Lerné	Fouace
Le Mans	Fricassée de poulet, rillettes, rillons
Orléans	Mustard, vinegar
Tours	Rillettes, rillons
Vendôme	Andouille, poulet à la ficelle, rillettes, rillons
Vouvray	Andouillettes, rillettes, rillons

foods and wines, see the list printed in the Michelin Guide France.
For more in-depth wine-related touring information, consult The Green Guide Wine Regions of France.

Local wines
The vestiges of an early stone winepress were discovered at Cheille, near Azay-le-Rideau, testifying to the existence of winemaking in the Loire valley

In the Temple of Bacchus

Picture the scene: the owner of the vineyard fills the glasses and the ruby-red nectar is held up to the light. The wine should be savoured first for its bouquet and then, after a knowing glance at one's neighbour, tasted in small sips. On emptying the glass, a simple click of the tongue is enough to signal appreciation. The owner, his eyes shining, will say *"ça se laisse boire"*.

Once inside the cellar, all round, projecting from recesses in the rock, are coloured bottle tops – red, yellow, blue and white: full-bodied Sancerre; Vouvray, among the most famous white wines from Touraine and said to "rejoice the heart" (you will notice the motto etched on the glasses there); heady Montlouis from the terraced tufa slopes abutting the river Loire; Chinon with its aftertaste of violets; Bourgueil with its hint of raspberries or wild strawberries; and their Angevin brothers, sparkling Saumur, lively and spirited, white Saumur, dry and sprightly, wines from La Coulée de Serrant and the Layon.

under Roman rule, around AD 100. It is thought that the great St Martin himself ordered vines to be planted on the slopes of Vouvray in the 4C. From then onwards, this activity became firmly established in the area. Over the centuries, Anjou, Touraine and the Orléanais have adopted a number of grape varieties coming from different natural regions, which accounts for the great diversity of the *cépages* (grape varieties). The best-known white wines are Vouvray, a dry, mellow wine tasting of ripe grapes, and Montlouis, known for its delicate, fruity flavour. Both are made from the Chenin Blanc grape, referred to locally as Pineau de la Loire.

The best-known red wine, known as Breton, is made from the Cabernet Franc grape, which originally came from Bordeaux and produces the fine, light wines of Bourgueil and those from Chinon, which have a stronger bouquet; the same grape is used to make a dry rosé, which has charm and nobility. Among the wines of Anjou are the Rouge de Cabernet and the Saumur-Champigny, which have a fine ruby glow and the subtle taste of raspberries. The Cabernet de Saumur is an elegant dry rosé with a good flavour. Another red wine comes from the Breton vines grown on the Loudun slopes. The wines of Sancerre, on the eastern fringe of the châteaux country, are made from the Sauvignon grape and are known for their gunflint flavour. Less famous wines are the *gris*

meuniers from the Orléanais and the *gascon*, which are pale and have a low alcohol content.

The slopes of the Loire produce a dry white and an acid-tasting red which improve with ageing. A light and pleasant white wine is made from the Romorantin grape, which is grown only in the Sologne. The slopes of the Loire produce 15% of the entire Muscadet crop. The Ancenis-Gamay wine, made from Burgundy Gamay vines, is less well known than the Gros Plant from Nantes as it is produced in smaller quantities. This light, dry, fruity wine, a perfect accompaniment to pork and other cold cuts, is produced in a 350ha/865-acre area around Ancenis.

The character of the region is most apparent in the wine cellars, which are often old quarries hollowed out of the limestone slopes at road level. They are therefore easily accessible so that the owner can drive his vehicles straight in. The galleries often extend for several hundred metres. Some open out into chambers where local societies hold their meetings and festivities.

The wine cellars also host meetings of the *confréries vineuses* that preserve the tradition of good wine in the Loire valley and initiate new members *(chevaliers)* to their brotherhoods joyously: Les Sacavins in Angers, Les Bons Entonneurs Rabelaisiens in Chinon, La Chantepleure in Vouvray and La Côterie des Closiers in Montlouis.

History

GALLO-ROMAN ERA AND THE EARLY MIDDLE AGES

52 BCE	Carnutes revolt. Caesar conquers Gaul.
AD 1C–4C	Roman occupation of Gaul.
313	Constantine grants freedom of worship to Christians (Edict of Milan).
372	St Martin, Bishop of Tours (dies at Candes in 397).
573–594	Episcopacy of Gregory of Tours, author of the *History of the Franks*.
7C	Founding of the Benedictine abbey of Fleury, later to be named St-Benoît.
late 8C	Alcuin of York's school for copyists. Theodulf, Bishop of Orleans.
768–814	Charlemagne.
840–877	Charles the Bald.
9C	Vikings invade Angers, St-Benoît and Tours. Rise of Robertian dynasty. The Capets (987–1328)
987–1040	Fulk Nerra, Count of Anjou.
996–1031	Robert II, the Pious.
1010	Foundation of the Benedictine abbey at Solesmes.
1060–1108	Philippe I.
1101	Foundation of Fontevraud Abbey.
1104	First Council of Beaugency.
1137–1180	Louis VII.
1152	Second Council of Beaugency. Eleanor of Aquitaine marries Henry Plantagenet.
1154	Henry Plantagenet becomes King of England as Henry II.
1180–1223	Philippe Auguste.
1189	Death of Henry II Plantagenet at Chinon. Struggle between Capets and Plantagenets.
1199	Richard the Lionheart dies at Châlus and is buried at Fontevraud.
1202	John Lackland loses Anjou. The last of the Angevin kings, he dies in 1216.
1215	Magna Carta.
1226–1270	Louis IX (St Louis).
1285–1314	Philippe IV, the Fair.
1307	Philippe the Fair suppresses the Order of the Knights Templars.

THE VALOIS (1328–1589)

1337–1453	Hundred Years War: 1346 Crécy; 1356 Poitiers; 1415 Agincourt.
1380–1422	Charles VI.
1392	The King goes mad (see *Le Mans*).
1409	Birth of King René at Angers.
1418	The Massacre at Azay-le-Rideau.
1422–1461	Charles VII.
1427	The Dauphin Charles establishes his court at Chinon.
1429	Joan of Arc delivers Orléans, but she is tried and burnt at the stake two years later (see *Chinon*, and *Orléans*).
1453	Battle of Castillon: final defeat of the English on French soil.
1455–1485	Wars of the Roses: Margaret of Anjou leader of Lancastrian cause.
1461–1483	Louis XI.
1476	Unrest among the powerful feudal lords.
1477	The region's first printing press is set up in Angers.
1483	Death of Louis XI at Plessis-lès-Tours.
1483–1498	Charles VIII.
1491	Marriage of Charles VIII and Anne of Brittany at Langeais.
1494–1559	The Campaigns in Italy.
1496	Early manifestations of Italian influence on French art (see *Amboise*).
1498	Death of Charles VIII at Amboise.
1498–1515	Louis XII. He divorces and marries Charles VIII's widow.
1515–1547	François I.

1519 French Renaissance: work on Chambord starts. Da Vinci dies at Le Clos-Lucé.

1539 Struggle against Emperor Charles V. He visits Amboise and Chambord.

1547–1559 Henri II.

1552 The sees of Metz, Toul and Verdun join France. Treaty signed at Chambord.

1559–1560 François II.

1560 Amboise Conspiracy. François II dies at Orléans.

1560–1574 Charles IX.

1562–1598 Wars of Religion.

1562 St-Benoît Abbey is pillaged by the Protestants. Battles at Ponts-de-Cé and Beaugency.

1572 The St Bartholomew's Day Massacre in Paris.

1574–1589 Henri III.

1576 Founding of the Catholic League by Henri, Duke of Guise to combat Calvinism. Meeting of the States-General in Blois.

1588 The assassination of Henri, Duke of Guise and his brother, the Cardinal of Lorraine (⚲see Blois).

THE BOURBONS (1589–1702)

1589–1610 Henri IV.

1589 Vendôme recaptured by Henry IV.

1598 Edict of Nantes. Betrothal of César de Vendôme (⚲see Angers).

1600 Henri IV weds Marie de' Medici.

1602 Maximilien de Béthune buys Sully.

1610–1643 Louis XIII.

1619 Marie de' Medici flees from Blois.

1620 Building of the Jesuits college at La Flèche.

1626 Gaston d'Orléans, brother of Louis XIII, is granted the County of Blois.

1643–1715 Louis XIV.

1648–1653 Civil war against Mazarin. The Fronde.

1651 Anne of Austria, Mazarin and young Louis XIV take refuge in Gien.

1669 Première of Molière's play *Monsieur de Pourceaugnac* at Chambord.

1685 Revocation of the Edict of Nantes by Louis XIV at Fontainebleau.

1715–1774 Louis XV.

1719 Voltaire exiled at Sully.

1756 Foundation of the Royal College of Surgeons at Tours.

1770 The Duke of Choiseul in exile at Chanteloup.

THE REVOLUTION AND FIRST EMPIRE (1789–1815)

1789 Storming of the Bastille.

1792 Proclamation of the Republic.

1793 Execution of Louis XVI. Vendée War. Fighting between the Republican Blues and Royalist Whites (⚲see Cholet and Les Mauges).

1803 Talleyrand purchases Valençay.

1804–1815 First Empire under Napoleon Bonaparte.

1808 Internment of Ferdinand VII, King of Spain, at Valençay.

CONSTITUTIONAL MONARCHY AND THE SECOND REPUBLIC (1815–1852)

1814–1824 Louis XVIII.

1824–1830 Charles X.

1830–1848 July Monarchy: Louis-Philippe.

1832 The first steamboat on the River Loire.

1832–1848 Conquest of Algeria.

1848 Internment of Abd El-Kader at Amboise.

1848–1852 Second Republic. Louis Napoleon-Bonaparte, Prince-President.

THE SECOND EMPIRE (1852–1870)

1852–1870 Napoleon III as Emperor.

1870–1871 Franco-Prussian War.

1870 Proclamation of the Third Republic on 4 September in

Paris. Frederick-Charles of Prussia at Azay-le-Rideau. Defence of Châteaudun. Tours made headquarters of Provisional Government.

1871   Battle of Loigny.

THE THIRD REPUBLIC (1870–1940)

1873   Amédée Bollée completes his first car, L'Obéissante (&see Le Mans).

1908   Wilbur Wright's early trials with his aeroplane.

1914–1918   First World War.

1919   Treaty of Versailles.

1923   The first 24-hour sports car race at Le Mans.

1939–1945   Second World War.

1940   Defence of Saumur. Historic meeting at Montoire.

1945   Reims Armistice.

POST-WAR TIMES

1946   Fourth Republic.

1952   First Son et Lumière performances at Chambord.

1958   The Fifth Republic came into being. On 8 January, Charles de Gaulle became the first President of the new era.

1963   France's first nuclear power station at Avoine, near Chinon.

1972   Founding of the Centre (later called Centre-Val-de-Loire) and Pays de la Loire regions.

1989   Inauguration of the TGV Atlantique (high-speed train).

1993   Opening of the International Vinci Congress Centre in Tours.

1994   The Centre region is renamed Centre-Val de Loire.

1996   Pope John Paul II visits the city of Tours.

1999   The euro is introduced in France to replace the franc.

THE 21ST CENTURY

2000   The Val de Loire (between Sully-sur-Loire and Chalonnes-sur-Loire) is placed on the UNESCO World Heritage List.

2007   Opening of the final section of the A 85 linking Vierzon and Angers.

2009   A grant is given for developing the new Loire Cycle Route in Maine-et-Loire and Loire Atlantique.

2014   Chateau Dunois in Beaugency reopens to the public after being closed 11 years.
The Regional Nature Park of Loire Anjou Touraine initiates sustainable tourism efforts and a 5-year plan.

2015   500th Anniversary of François I's accession to the French throne is celebrated at Château Ambois with the media in attendance.

2015   The single deadliest terrorist attack in French history occurred in Paris, involving multiple shootings and grenade attacks, which killed 90 people.

2016   A 19-tonne cargo truck was deliberately driven into crowds celebrating Bastille Day on the Promenade des Anglais in Nice. More than 80 people were killed.

2017   Emmanuel Macron is elected President of France, representing his "La République En Marche!" centrist political party. He beat the far-right National Front's Marine Le Pen. He appointed Le Havre mayor Édouard Philippe to be Prime Minister. His party wins an overall majority in parliamentary elections.

AN EVENTFUL PAST

ANTIQUITY AND THE EARLY MIDDLE AGES

During the Iron Age the prosperous and powerful people known as the **Cenomanni** occupied a vast territory extending from Brittany to the Beauce and from Normandy to Aquitaine. They minted gold coins and put up a long resistance to both barbarian and Roman invaders.

The Cenomanni reacted strongly to the invasion of Gaul by the Romans, and in 52 BCE the **Carnutes**, who inhabited the country between Chartres and Orléans, gave the signal, at the instigation of the Druids, to raise a revolt against Caesar. It was savagely repressed, but the following year Caesar had to put down another uprising by the Andes, under their leader Dumnacos.

Peace was established under Augustus and a period of stability and prosperity began. Existing towns such as Angers, Le Mans, Tours and Orléans adjusted to the Roman model with a theatre, forum, baths and public buildings. Many agricultural estates (villae) were created or extended as the commercial outlets developed. They reached their peak in the 2C. By the end of the 3C, instability and danger were so rife that cities had been enclosed behind walls.

At the same time Christianity was introduced by St Gatien, the first bishop of Tours; by the end of the 4C it had overcome most opposition under **St Martin**, the greatest bishop of the Gauls, whose tomb later became a place of pilgrimage (St Martin's Day: 11 November).

In the 5C the Loire country suffered waves of invasion; in 451 Bishop Aignan held back the Huns outside Orléans while waiting for help. Franks and Visigoths fought for domination until the Frankish King Clovis was finally victorious in 507. His successors' endless quarrels, recorded by Gregory of Tours, dominated the history of the region in the 6C and 7C while St Martin's Abbey was establishing its reputation.

In 732 the Saracens, who were pushing north from Spain, reached the Loire before they were repulsed by Charles Martel. The order achieved by the Carolingians, which was marked by the activities of **Alcuin** and **Theodulf**, did not last.

In the mid-9C the Vikings came up the river and ravaged the country on both sides, particularly the monasteries (St-Benoît, St-Martin). **Robert**, Count of Blois and Tours, defeated them, but they continued their depredations until 911 when the Treaty of St-Clair-sur-Epte created the Duchy of Normandy. In this period of insecurity, the Robertian dynasty (the forerunner of the Capet dynasty) gained in power to the detriment of the last Carolingian kings.

PRINCELY POWER

The weakness of the last Carolingian kings encouraged the independence of turbulent and ambitious feudal lords. Although Orléans was one of the favourite royal residences and the Orléans region was always Capet territory, Touraine, the county of Blois, Anjou and Maine became independent and rival principalities. This was the age of powerful barons, who raised armies and minted money. From Orléans to Angers every high point was crowned by an imposing castle, the stronghold of the local lord who was continually at war with his neighbours.

The counts of Blois faced a formidable enemy in the counts of Anjou, of whom the most famous was **Fulk Nerra**. He was a first-class tactician; little by little he encircled Eudes II, Count of Blois, and seized part of his territory. His son, Geoffrey Martel, continued the same policy; from his stronghold in Vendôme he wrested from the house of Blois the whole county of Tours. In the 12C the county of Blois was dependent on Champagne, which was then at its peak. At the same period the counts of Anjou reached the height of their power under the **Plantagenets**, a dynasty founded in Le Mans; when Henri, Count of Anjou, became King Henry II of England in 1154 his kingdom stretched from the north of England to the Pyrenées. This formidable new power confronted the modest forces of the kings of France, but they did not quail under the threat of their powerful neighbours and skilfully took advantage of the quarrels that divided the Plantagenets.

In 1202, when King John of England, known as **John Lackland**, lost all his continental possessions to **Philippe Auguste**, the Loire country returned to the French sphere of interest.

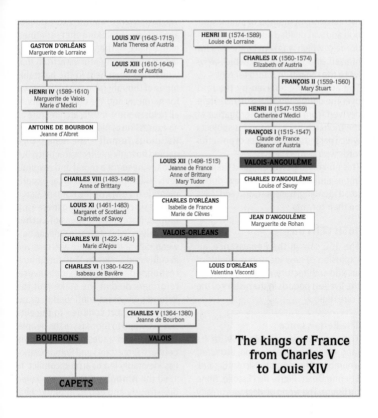

The kings of France
from Charles V
to Louis XIV

In accordance with the wishes of his father Louis VIII, when Louis IX came to the throne he granted Maine and Anjou as an appanage to his brother Charles, who abandoned his French provinces, including Provence, and tried to establish an Angevin kingdom in Naples, Sicily and the Near East, as did his successors. Nonetheless, Good **King René**, the last Duke of Anjou, earned himself a lasting place in popular tradition.

CRADLE OF FEUDALISM

Feudalism flourished in France in the 11C and 12C in the region between the Seine and the Loire under the **Capet** monarchy. The system was based on two elements: the fief and the lord. The **fief** was a beneficium (benefice), usually a grant of land made by a lord to a knight or other man who became his vassal. The numerous conflicts of interest which arose from the system in practice produced a detailed code of behaviour embodying the rights of the parties. During the 12C the services due were defined, such as the maximum number of days to be spent each year in military service or castle watch. Gradually the fiefs became hereditary and the lord retained only overall ownership. In the case of multiple vassalage, liege homage was paid to one lord and this was more binding than homage to any other.

An almost perfect hierarchical pyramid was created descending from the king to the mass of simple knights. The more important vassals had the right of appeal to the king in the event of a serious dispute with their suzerain; it was by this means that King John (John Lackland) was deprived of his French fiefs by Philippe Auguste early in the 13C.

All the inhabitants of an estate were involved in the economic exploitation of the land; the estate had evolved from the Carolingian method of administration and was divided into two parts: the domain, which was kept by the lord for himself, and the holdings, which were let to the tenants in return for rent.

The authority exercised by the lord over the people who lived on his estate derived from the royal prerogative of the monarch to command his subjects which passed into the hands of powerful lords who owned castles.

This unlimited power enabled them to impose military service, various duties (road mending, transport, etc.) and taxes on their tenants.

16TH CENTURY

The 16C saw in the Renaissance, an explosion of new ideas in the fields of art and architecture, resulting in one of the liveliest periods in the history of the Loire region.

The Renaissance

The University of Orléans, with its long-established reputation, attracted a number of **humanists**: Nicolas Béraud, Étienne Dolet, Pierre de l'Estoile, Anne du Bourg. The world of ideas was greatly extended by the invention of **printing** – the first printing press in the Loire valley was set up in Angers in 1477 – which made learning and culture more accessible. By the middle of the century, the **Pléiade** was formed in the Loire valley and attracted the best local talent (see p81).

By choosing Touraine as their favourite place of residence, the kings made a significant contribution to the artistic revival of the region. The chief instigators of the great French Renaissance were **Charles VIII** and even more so **Louis XII** and **François I**, who had all travelled in Italy. These monarchs transformed the Loire Valley into a vast building site where the new aesthetic ideals flourished at Amboise, Blois and especially Chambord. The great lords and financiers followed suit and commissioned the building of elegant houses (Azay-le-Rideau, Chenonceau) while graceful mansions were erected in the towns.

The Renaissance was the expression of a new way of thinking that redefined man's place in the world and presented a radically different view from that which had been held in the past; this mode of thought gave rise to the desire for harmony and the cult of beauty in all fields: poetry, music, architecture as an expression of nature shaped by man. **Religious Tumult** – The Renaissance excited not only intellectual activity, but also the need for a moral and religious revival. Despite several local experiments (e.g. Le Mans), the Roman Church did not succeed in satisfying these aspirations. Naturally the ideas of **Luther** and **Calvin** (who stayed in Orléans between 1528 and 1533) were well received in cultivated circles. In 1540 the Church responded with repression; several reformers died at the stake, but the Reform movement continued to grow; nor was support confined to the elite but extended to the mass of the people, craftsmen and tradesmen. The dispute between Protestants and Roman Catholics inevitably led to armed conflict. In 1560 the **Amboise Conspiracy** failed disastrously and ended in bloodshed. Catherine de' Medici tried to promote conciliation by issuing edicts of tolerance, but in April 1562 the Huguenots rose up, committing numerous acts of vandalism: damaging places of worship and destroying statues, tombs and relics.

The Roman Catholics, under Montpensier and Guise, regained the upper hand and exacted a terrible vengeance, particularly in Angers. From 1563 to 1567 there was relative peace, but in 1568 the armed struggle broke out anew; the Catholic and Protestant armies, the latter under Condé and Coligny, indulged in regular waves of violence. The inhabitants of Orléans suffered their own **massacre of St Bartholomew** with nearly 1 000 deaths. During the last quarter of the century, the Reformed Churches had become much weaker and **Henri III**'s struggle with the Catholic League came to the fore.

In 1576 Touraine, Anjou and Berry were granted to François d'Alençon, the

© Angelo Calvino/age fotostock

Portrait of Catherine de Medici, Chateau de Blois

King's brother and head of the League, as a conciliatory gesture, but the Guises would not compromise and conspired against the King who, seeing no other solution, had them assassinated at Blois in December 1588. The population divided into Royalists and Leaguers, who were powerful in the Loire region. Henri III, who had been forced to withdraw to Tours, allied himself with Henri of Navarre and was marching on Paris when he himself was assassinated on 2 August 1589.

It took Henri IV nearly 10 years to restore peace to the region. The brilliant period in the history of the Loire valley, which coincided with the last years of the Valois dynasty, ended in tragedy.

17C–18C: PEACE RESTORED

The Loire country ceased to be at the centre of political and religious ferment. There were admittedly a few alarms during the minority of Louis XIII and the Fronde uprising, in which the indefatigable conspirator, Gaston d'Orléans, played a significant role. Order was restored under Louis XIV with centralisation under the crown stifling the slightest sign of autonomy: the districts of Orléans and Tours were administered by energetic treasury officials while the towns lost the right to self-government. As far as religious life was concerned, the Roman Catholic Church re-established

itself: a growth in the number of convents and seminaries, the reform of the old monastic foundations and the suppression of sorcery went hand in hand with an improvement in the intellectual level of the clergy. Protestantism struggled to survive, except in Saumur thanks to the Academy, and was dealt a devastating blow by the **Revocation of the Edict of Nantes** in 1685.

A Developing Economy

Human enterprise benefited from the general stability. Agriculture developed slowly: cereals in the Beauce, raw materials for textiles (wool, linen, hemp), market gardening together with fruit growing and winemaking in the Loire Valley, were a considerable source of wealth whereas cattle raising remained weak. Rural crafts played an important role together with urban manufacturing: hemp cloth around Cholet, cheesecloth in the district of Le Mans, sheeting in Touraine and Anjou and bonnets in Orléanais. The silk weavers of Tours earned themselves a good reputation. Nevertheless in the 18C, except for sheets from Laval and Cholet, the textile industry fell into decline. Orléans, the warehouse of the Loire, specialised in sugar refining and the finished product was distributed throughout the kingdom. The Loire, under the control of the community of merchants, was the main axis for trade: wine from Touraine and Anjou, wool from the Berry, iron from the Massif Central, coal from the Forez, wheat from the Beauce, cloth from the Touraine and cargoes from exotic countries – everything travelled by water. On the eve of the Revolution these activities were waning, but the region featured two million inhabitants and several towns: Orléans (2015 pop. 118 030), Angers (pop. 154 463), Tours (pop. 138 150) and Le Mans (pop. 148 484).

THE REVOLUTION
The Touraine and Orléanais regions accepted the Revolution, but Maine and Anjou rose in revolt.

Social Conflict
At first it was social conflict in which the country peasants were opposed to the townspeople and the weavers from the villages. Townspeople, who had been won over by the new ideas, were enthusiastic about the new political order, while peasants became increasingly disillusioned. Religious reform upset parish life and the administrative reforms aroused criticism and discontent because they favoured the townspeople. The national guards in their blue uniforms were increasingly disliked: they were sent out from the towns to impose revolutionary decisions on the populace, if necessary by force. The decree imposing mass conscription in March 1793 was seen as an unacceptable provocation in rural areas and the peasants rose in a body. Les Mauges in particular was immediately in the forefront of the battle.

The Vendée War
The Angevin rebels appointed leaders from among their own class: countrymen like Stofflet and Cathelineau, as well as noblemen like Bonchamps. For four months their armies won several important engagements in support of the Church and the King; they captured Cholet, Saumur and then Angers. The **Convention**, the Republican government of France between September 1792 and November 1795, replied by sending in

several army units. The royalist Whites were severely defeated at Cholet on 17 October by General Kléber and General Marceau and compelled to retreat. As they fled, they were pitilessly massacred and the remnants of the great Catholic and Royal Army were exterminated in the Savenay Marshes beyond Nantes. By way of reprisal against the local population, the Convention appointed General Turreau in January 1794 to clean up the country. From February to May his **infernal columns** converged on the centre, killing women and children and setting fire to villages.

The Chouans
The war was followed by sporadic outbursts of guerrilla activity: daring exploits, ambushes and even assassinations. **Jean Cottereau**, also known as Jean Chouan, was the leading figure who gave his name to the movement. The country people maintained a relentless resistance. At the end of August, a faint peacemaking gesture was made under the authority of **General Hoche**. Charette and Stofflet, who continued the struggle, were arrested and shot in February and March 1796. The insurrection in the Vendée came to an end under the Consulate, a triumvirate including a certain **General Bonaparte** set up in 1799 to provide stronger government than the existing Republican regime with its divided factions. The war left in its wake widespread ruin and an entrenched bitterness that was revealed later in the rigid political attitudes of the people of Maine and Anjou.

FROM WAR TO WAR
October 1870–January 1871
After the fall of the Empire, France recovered its balance under the stimulus of Gambetta, who arrived in Tours by balloon on 9 October, having escaped the Paris siege. The Bavarians, who were victorious at Artenay, had already captured Orléans (11 October), and indicated that they would link up with the **Prussian army** at Versailles via the Beauce. Châteaudun put up a heroic resistance for

10 hours on 18 and 19 October, but was bombarded and set on fire in reprisal. The army of the Loire was formed under the command of **General d'Aurelle de Paladines**; two corps, the 15th and 16th (Chanzy), formed in the Salbris camp, set out from Blois for Orléans. The engagement took place at Marchenoir and then at Coulmiers on 9 November: the French were victorious and General Von der Thann was forced to evacuate Orléans. Meanwhile the 18th and 20th Corps tried to check the advance of the Duke of Mecklenburg on Le Mans and Tours, but they were beaten on 28 November at Beaune-la-Rolande by Prince Frederick-Charles, who had hastened south from Metz. On 2 December the 16th and 17th Corps were defeated at Patay and Loigny, where the Zouaves under Lt Col de Charette, the great-nephew of the famous Vendéen Royalist, fought with distinction. Although cut in two, the first army of the Loire survived. Orléans had to be abandoned while the government retreated to Bordeaux (8 December).

A second Loire army was formed under **General Chanzy**; it resisted every enemy attack, and then retrenched on the Loir. On 19 December the Prussians captured Château-Renault, and two days later arrived in front of Tours but did not besiege the town. The decisive battle was fought between 10 and 12 January on the Auvours plateau east of Le Mans. Chanzy was forced to retreat towards Laval; Tours was occupied and Prince Frederick-Charles took up residence at Azay-le-Rideau. The armistice was signed on 28 January 1871.

1917–1918

The Americans set up their headquarters in Tours, while the first US soldiers disembarked at St-Nazaire and were billeted along the Loire.

1940–1944

On **10 June 1940** the French Government moved to Tours, and Cangé Château, on the southeast edge of the town, became the temporary residence of the President of the Republic. On 13 June the Franco-British Supreme Council met in Tours; at Cangé the Council of Ministers decided to transfer the government to Bordeaux. During that week of tragedy, the bridges over the Loire were machine-gunned and bombarded; floods of refugees choked the roads. The towns were badly damaged. Two thousand cadets from the Cavalry School at Saumur excelled themselves by holding up the German advance for two days along a 25km/15.5mi front (⛵see Saumur). On 24 October 1940 Marshal Pétain met Hitler at **Montoire** (⛵see Montoire-sur-le-Loir), and agreed to his demands; collaboration was born. The Gestapo in Angers unleashed a reign of terror in the region.

The **Resistance** was born in 1941; the information and sabotage networks, the underground forces and the escape agents (the demarcation line followed the River Cher and ran between Tours and Loches) hampered the movements of the occupying forces who responded with torture, deportation and summary execution. In August and September 1944, the American army and the forces of the Resistance achieved control of the area, with heavy losses.

DEVELOPMENT OF THE CHÂTEAUX

THE FIRST CHÂTEAUX (5C–10C)

In the Merovingian period the country was protected by isolated strongholds: some had evolved from Gallo-Roman villas (country estates), which had been fortified; others were built on high ground (Loches, Chinon). Generally they covered a fairly large area and served several purposes: residence of important people, place of worship, place for minting money, agricultural centre and place of refuge for the population. This type of stronghold continued under the Carolingians, but the growing insecurity in the second half of the 9C introduced a wave of fortification in an attempt to counter the Viking threat.

The early castles, which were built in haste, rested on a mound of earth surrounded by a wooden palisade; sometimes a central tower was erected as an observation post. The structure contained very little masonry. Until the 10C castle building was a prerogative of the king, but thereafter the right was usurped by powerful lords; small strongholds proliferated under the designation of towers – the keep had been invented.

THE MOTTE CASTLE (11C)

The motte was a man-made mound of earth on which was erected a square wooden tower, the keep. An earth bank protected by a ditch supported the perimeter fence, which consisted of a wooden palisade and enclosed an area large enough to contain people from the neighbourhood. The **keep** was built either as the last place of refuge or at the weakest point in the perimeter fence; some castles had more than one motte. In several of the Angevin castles built by Fulk Nerra the keep protected a residential building erected at the end of a promontory, as at Langeais, Blois and Loches, which are typical of the Carolingian tradition.

THE STONE CASTLE (12C–13C)

By the 11C some castles had defensive works built of stone. The keep was still the strongest point and took the form of a massive quadrangular structure. The keeps at Loches, Langeais, Montbazon, Chinon (Coudray) and Beaugency are remarkable examples of 11C architecture.

The 12C keep overlooked a courtyard which was enclosed by a stone curtain wall, gradually reinforced by turrets and towers. Within its precincts each castle comprised private apartments, a great hall, one or more chapels, soldiers' barracks, lodgings for the household staff and other buildings such as barns, stables, storerooms, kitchens, etc.

The tendency grew to rearrange the buildings more compactly within a smaller precinct. The keep comprised a storeroom on the ground floor, a great hall on the first and living rooms on the upper floors. The compact shape and the height of the walls made it difficult to besiege and only a few men were needed to defend it.

In the 13C, under the influence of the crusades and improvements in the art of attack, important innovations began to make their presence felt. Castles were designed by experts to be even more compact with multiple defensive features so that no point was unprotected. The **curtain wall** bristled with huge towers and the keep was neatly incorporated into the overall design.

A circular plan was adopted for the towers and keep; the walls were splayed at the base; the depth and width of the moat were greatly increased.

Sometimes a lower outer rampart was built to reinforce the main rampart; the intervening strip of level ground was called the lists. Improvements were made to the arrangements for launching missiles: new types of loophole (in a cross or stirrup shape), stone machicolations, platforms, brattices, etc.

The 13C castle, which was more functional and had a pronounced military character, could be built anywhere, even in open country.

At the same time a desire for indoor comfort began to express itself in tapestries and draperies and furniture (chests and beds), which made the rooms more pleasant to live in than they had been in the past.

THE LATE MEDIEVAL CASTLE

In 14C and 15C castle-building the accent moved from defence to comfort and decoration. The living quarters were more extensive; large windows to let in the light and new rooms (state bedrooms, dressing rooms and lavatories) appeared; decoration became an important feature.

In the military sphere there were no innovations, only minor improvements. The keep merged with the living quarters and was surmounted by a watchtower; sometimes the keep was suppressed altogether and the living quarters took the form of a rectangular block defended by huge corner towers. The entrance was flanked by two semicircular towers and protected by a barbican (a gateway flanked by towers) or by a separate fort.

The top of the curtain wall was raised to the height of the towers which were crowned by a double row of crenellations. In the 15C the towers were capped by pointed, pepper-pot roofs.

OTHER FORTIFIED BUILDINGS

Churches and monasteries, which were places of sanctuary and therefore targets of war, were not excluded from the fortification movement, especially during the Hundred Years War.

The towns and some of the villages also turned their attention to defence and built ramparts round the residential districts. In 1398, 1399 and 1401 Charles VI issued letters and ordinances enjoining the owners of fortresses and citizens to see that their fortifications were in good order.

From the end of the 13C, fortified houses were built in the country districts by the lords of the manor; they had no military significance but are similar in appearance to the smaller **châteaux**.

SIEGE WARFARE

The attackers' first task was to besiege the enemy stronghold. The defences they constructed (moat, stockade, towers, forts or blockhouses) were intended both to prevent a possible sortie by the besieged and to counter an attack from a relief army.

In the great sieges a fortified town grew up in its own right to encircle the site under attack. In order to make a breach in the defences of the besieged place the attackers used mines, slings, battering rams and siege towers. For this they had specialist troops who were experts in siege operations.

The advent of the cannon altered siege technique. Both attackers and defenders used artillery: the firing rate was not very high and the aim was even less accurate. Military architecture was completely transformed; towers were replaced by low thick bastions and curtain walls were built lower but much thicker. This new system of defence was perfected by Vauban.

THE RENAISSANCE CHÂTEAU

In the 16C military elements were abandoned in the search for comfort and aesthetic taste: moats, keeps and turrets appeared only as decorative features, like at Chambord, Azay-le-Rideau and Chenonceau. The spacious attics were lit by great dormer windows in the steep pitched roofs. The windows were very large. The spiral turret stairs were replaced with stairs that rose in straight flights in line with the centre of the main façade beneath coffered ceilings. The gallery – a new feature imported from Italy at the end of the 15C – lent a touch of elegance to the main courtyard.

Whereas the old fortified castle had been built on a hill, the new château was sited in a valley or beside a river where it was reflected in the water. The idea was that the building should blend in with its natural surroundings, although these were shaped and transfigured by human intervention; the gardens, laid out like a jewel casket, were an integral part of the design. Only the chapel continued to be built in the traditional style with ogive vaulting and Flamboyant decoration.

THE COURT IN THE LOIRE VALLEY

A BOURGEOIS COURT

The court resided regularly in the Loire Valley under **Charles VII** whose preference was for Chinon and Loches. These visits ended with the last of the Valois, Henri III. Owing to the straitened circumstances to which the King of France was reduced, Charles VII's court was not particularly glittering; but the arrival of Joan of Arc in 1429 won the castle of Chinon a place in the history books. **Louis XI** disliked pomp and circumstance. He installed his wife, Charlotte of Savoy at Amboise, but he himself rarely went there. He preferred his manor at Plessis-lès-Tours where he lived in fear of an attempt on his life. According to the writer and diplomat Commines, his only interests were hunting and dogs.

The queen's court consisted of 15 ladies-in-waiting, 12 women of the bedchamber and 100 officers in charge of various functions including the saddler, the

Daily Life in the Châteaux

The Medieval Household: In the 10C and 11C life in a castle was thought to be somewhat primitive. The whole family lived, ate and slept in the same room on the first floor of the keep. Furniture was sparse and tableware rudimentary. When the lord was out hunting or fighting his neighbours or off on a crusade, his lady would take over the administration of his affairs.

The Great Hall: The finest room in the castle was the Great Hall, where the lord held audience and dispensed justice, and where feasts and banquets were organised. The earlier loopholes were replaced by windows, fitted with panes and shutters.

The walls were hung with paintings and tapestries; the floor tiles were covered with rush mats or carpets on which one could sit or lie; flowers and greenery were strewn on the floor and, in summer, in the fireplaces.

The Bedchamber: Except in royal or princely households, a married couple slept in the same room. Over the centuries the furnishings grew richer; the bed was set on a dais and surrounded with sumptuous curtains; there were Venetian mirrors, tapestries, costly drapes, benches with backs, a princely chair, a *prie-dieu*, library steps and cushions, a dresser, a table, chests and a cupboard. To entertain the ladies there was an aviary, often with a parrot. Near the bedchamber was a study which was also used for private audiences, a council chamber and an oratory or chapel. A special room was set aside for the guards. In the larger houses there was also a stateroom where the ceremonial clothes were on display.

Food: Food at court was good and the meals gargantuan. When eaten in private, meals were served in the bedchamber or in the Great Hall. Before and after eating, basins and ewers of scented water were provided for the diners to rinse their hands since fingers often took the place of forks. The plates were made of silver.

Bathing and Hygiene: Near the bedchamber or in a separate building was the bathhouse. Until the 14C bathing was the fashion in France. The common people used to go to the public baths once a week; the upper classes often took a daily bath. The bathhouse contained a sort of pool which was filled with warm water and a chamber for the steam bath and massage. A barber or a chambermaid was in attendance, for it was the fashion to be clean shaven. In the absence of a bathhouse, baths were taken in a tub made of wood or bronze or silver. Men and women bathed together without being thought immoral. These habits of cleanliness disappeared from the Renaissance until the Revolution. In the 13C there were 26 public baths in Paris; by the time of Louis XIV's reign there were only two. In other respects medieval castles were well enough provided with conveniences.

Entertainment: Castle life had always had plenty of idle hours and a variety of distractions had developed to fill them. Indoors there was chess, spillikins, dice, draughts and, from the 14C, cards. Outdoors there was tennis, bowls and football, wrestling and archery. Hunting with hounds or hawks and tournaments and jousts were the great sports of the nobles. The women and children had dwarfs to entertain them; at court the jester was free to make fun of people, even the king. There were frequent festivities. Performances of the Mystery Plays, which sometimes lasted for 25 days, were always a great success.

librarian, the doctor, the chaplain, the musicians, the official tasters and a great many butlers and manservants. Charlotte was a deep-thinking woman and a great reader; her library contained over 100 volumes, a vast total for that time. They were works on religious thought, ethics, history, botany and domestic science. A few lighter works, such as the *Tales of Boccaccio*, relieved this solemnity. In fact, compared with that of Charles the Bold, the royal lifestyle seemed homely rather than princely.

A LUXURIOUS COURT

In the late 15C, **Charles VIII** acquired a considerable amount of furniture and numerous other decorative objects in order to embellish the interior of the Château d'Amboise. He installed hundreds of Persian carpets, Turkish woollen pile carpets, Syrian carpets, along with dozens of beds, chests, oak tables and dressers. The rooms and sometimes the courtyards (in the case of prestigious events) were hung with sumptuous tapestries from Flanders and Paris. He also endowed the château with an extensive collection of beautifully crafted silverware, and a great many works of art, mainly from Italy. The Armoury (note the inventory dating back to 1499) contains several sets of armour and outstanding weapons having once belonged to Clovis, Dagobert, St Louis, Philip the Fair, Du Guesclin and Louis XI.

A GALLANT COURT

Louis XII, who was frugal, was the "Bourgeois King" of Blois. But under **François I** (1515–47) the French court became a model of elegance, taste and culture. The Cavalier King invited men of science, poets and artists to his court. Women, who until then had been relegated to the Queen's service, were eased by the King into a more prominent role in public life as focal points of a new kind of society. He expected them to dress perfectly and look beautiful at all times – and gave them the means to do so. The King also ensured that these ladies were treated with courtesy and

© S. Sauvignier/MICHELIN

Salamander (François I) – Nitrusco et Extinguo (I Nourish the Good and Destroy the Bad)

respect. A code of courtesy was established and the court set an example of good manners.

François I divided his time between Amboise and Blois. The festivities he organised were of unprecedented brilliance. Weddings, baptisms and the visits of princes were lavishly celebrated. Sometimes these celebrations took place in the country, as on the occasion when the reconstruction of a siege was organised; a temporary town was built to be defended by the Duke of Alençon while the King led the assault and capture. To increase the sense of realism, the mortars fired huge balls. Hunting, however, took pride of place; 125 people were employed in keeping the hounds while 50 looked after the hawks.

Upon his return from Italy, he had Chambord built and spent the rest of his life there.

THE LAST VALOIS

Under **Henri II** and his sons, Blois remained the habitual seat of the court when it was not at the Louvre palace in Paris. It was **Henri III** who drew up the first code of etiquette and introduced the title His Majesty, taken from the Roman Emperors. The Queen Mother and the Queen had about 100 ladies-in-waiting. Catherine de' Medici also had her famous **Flying Squad** of pretty girls, who kept her informed and assisted her in her intrigues. About 100 pages acted as messengers. In addition there were 76 gentlemen servants, 51 clerks, 23 doctors and 50 chambermaids.

The King's suite included 200 gentlemen-in-waiting and over 1 000 archers and Swiss guards. There was a multitude of servants. Princes of the blood and great lords also had their households. Thus, from the time of François I, the royal entourage numbered about 15,000 people. When the court was on the move, 12,000 horses were needed. By way of comparison, in the 16C only 25 towns in the whole of France had more than 10 000 inhabitants!

QUEENS AND GREAT LADIES

Whether they were queen or the current royal mistress, women at court played an increasingly important political role, while the lively festivities with which they surrounded themselves made a major contribution to the sphere of cultural and artistic influence of the royal court.

Agnès Sorel graced the court of Charles VII at Chinon and at Loches. She gave the King good advice and reminded him of the urgent problems facing the country after the Hundred Years War, while the Queen, Marie d'Anjou, moped in her castle.

Louise of Savoy, mother of François I, was a devout worshipper of St Francis of Paola. This religious devotion, mingled with the superstitions of her astrologer Cornelius Agrippa, was barely enough to keep her insatiable ambition in check. She lived only for the accession of her son to the throne and to this end she upset the plans of **Anne of Brittany** by making him marry Claude, daughter of Louis XII.

The love life of François I featured many women, including Françoise de Châteaubriant and the **Duchess of Étampes**, who ruled his court until his death.

Diane de Poitiers, the famous favourite of Henri II, was a remarkably tough woman. She retained her energy, both physical and mental, well into old age, to the amazement of her contemporaries. She made important decisions of policy, negotiated with the Protestants, traded in Spanish prisoners, distributed honours and magistracies and, to the great humiliation of the Queen, saw to the education of the royal children. Such was her personality that almost every artist of the period painted her portrait.

The foreign beauty of **Mary Stuart**, the hapless wife of young King François II, who died at the age of 17 after a few months' reign, lent an all too brief lustre to the court in the middle of the 16C. She is recalled in a drawing by Clouet and some verses by Ronsard.

A different type altogether was **Marguerite de Valois**, the famous Queen Margot, sister of François II, Charles IX and of Henri III. Her bold eyes, her exuberance and her amorous escapades caused a great deal of concern to her mother, Catherine de' Medici. Her marriage to the future King Henri IV did little to calm her down and was in any case later annulled.

Catherine de' Medici married the Dauphin Henri in 1533 and was a prominent figure at court for 55 years under five different kings. Although eclipsed for a while by the beautiful Diane de Poitiers, she had her revenge on the death of Henri II by taking Chenonceau from her and building the two-storey gallery across the River Cher. With the accession of Charles IX she became regent and tried to uphold the authority of the monarchy during the Wars of Religion by manoeuvring skilfully between the Guises and the Bourbons, making use of diplomacy, marriage alliances and family intrigue.

Art and Culture

ARCHITECTURE AND ART
GOTHIC PERIOD

In addition to the castles built for the dukes of Anjou, such as Saumur, manor houses and mansions were constructed in the 14C for merchants who had grown rich through trade. The 15C saw a proliferation in the lively ornate Gothic style of châteaux built of brick with white stone facings, such as the château at Lassay, of manor houses such as Le Clos-Lucé near Amboise, of town mansions with projecting stair turrets and high dormers, and of half-timbered houses. The finest examples of Gothic houses are to be found in Le Mans, Chinon and Tours.

Gardens

Monastic gardens, such as those belonging to the abbeys in Bourgueil, Marmoutier and Cormery, consisted of an orchard, a vegetable patch with a fish pond and a medicinal herb garden.

In the 15C they were succeeded by square flower beds, created by King René at his manor houses in Anjou and by Louis XI at Plessis-lès-Tours. A fresh note was introduced with shady arbours and fountains where the paths intersected; entertainment was provided by animals at liberty or kept in menageries or aviaries.

RENAISSANCE PERIOD

The Renaissance did not spring into existence at the wave of a magic wand at the end of the Italian campaigns. Before the wars in Italy, Italian artists had been welcomed to the French court and the court of Anjou; Louis XI and King René had employed sculptors and medallion makers such as Francesco Laurana, Niccolo Spinelli and Jean Candida. New blood, however, was imported into local art by the arrival of artists from Naples in 1495 at the behest of Charles VIII.

At Amboise and Chaumont and even at Chenonceau, Azay or Chambord, the châteaux still looked like fortresses but the machicolations assumed a decorative role. Large windows flanked by pilasters appeared in the façades, which were decorated with medallions; the steep roofs were decorated with lofty dormers and carved chimneys. Italian influence is most apparent in the low-relief ornamentation. At Chambord and Le Lude the decor was refined by local masters such as Pierre Trinqueau.

The Italian style is most obvious in the exterior of the François I wing at Blois where Il Boccadoro copied Bramante's invention of the rhythmic façade which featured alternating windows and niches separated by pilasters. Later, as in Beaugency town hall, came semicircular arches and superimposed orders, then the domes and pavilions which mark the birth of Classical architecture.

The Italians created new types of staircases: two spirals intertwined as at Chambord, or straight flights of steps beneath coffered ceilings as at Chenonceau, Azay-le-Rideau and Poncé.

The Renaissance also inspired a number of towns halls – Orléans, Beaugency, Loches – and several private houses – Hôtel Toutin in Orléans, Hôtel Gouin in Tours and Hôtel Pincé in Angers.

Gardens

In his enthusiasm for Neapolitan gardens, Charles VIII brought with him from his kingdom in Sicily a gardener called **Dom Pacello de Mercogliano**, a Neapolitan monk, who laid out the gardens at Amboise and Blois; Louis XII entrusted him with the royal vegetable plot at Château-Gaillard near Amboise. Pacello popularised the use of ornate flower beds bordered with yew and fountains with sculpted basins. The gardens of Chenonceau and Villandry give a good idea of his style.

The extraordinary vegetable garden at Villandry, whose decorative motifs were highly popular during the Renaissance, has retained a number of traditional and monastic features dating from the Middle Ages; the rose trees planted in a symmetrical pattern symbolise the monks, each digging in his own plot.

CLASSICAL PERIOD (17C–18C)

Following the removal of the court to the Paris region (Île-de-France), architecture in the Loire valley fell into decline. Handsome buildings were still constructed but the designers came from Paris. In the more austere climate of the 17C the pompous style of the Sun King displaced the graceful fantasy of the Renaissance and the picturesque asymmetry of medieval buildings. The trend was towards pediments, domes (Cheverny) and the Greek orders (Gaston-d'Orléans wing at Blois). Tower structures were abandoned in favour of rectangular pavilions containing huge rooms with monumental fireplaces decorated with caryatids and painted ceilings with exposed beams; they were covered with steep roofs in the French style.

There was a new wave of château building, but the main legacy of the 18C is in the towns. Great terraces were built in Orléans, Tours and Saumur with long perspectives aligned on the axis of magnificent bridges with level roadways.

ROMANESQUE (11C–12C)

Orléanais

The church in Germigny-des-Prés, which dates from the Carolingian period, and the Benedictine basilica of St-Benoît are particularly fine examples of Romanesque art in the Orléans area. There are two pretty churches in the Cher valley at St-Aignan and Selles.

Touraine

Various influences from Poitou are evident: apses with column buttresses, domed transepts, doorways without pediments. The bell-towers are unusual: square or octagonal with spires surrounded at the base by turrets.

Anjou

Angevin buildings are clustered round Baugé and Saumur. The church in Cunault shows the influence of Poitou in the nave buttressed by high aisles with groined vaulting. The domes roofing the nave of the abbey church at Fontevraud and the absence of aisles are features of the Aquitaine School.

FROM ROMANESQUE TO GOTHIC

The **Plantagenet style**, which is also known as **Angevin**, takes its name from Henry Plantagenet. It is a transitional style which reached the height of its popularity in the early 13C and died out by the end of the century.

Angevin Vaulting

Unlike standard Gothic vaulting in which all the keystones are placed at the same level, Angevin vaulting is domical so that the central keystones are higher than the supporting arches. The best example is the cathedral of St-Maurice in Angers. This type of vaulting evolved to feature an ever finer network of increasingly fragile-looking ribs, which were eventually adorned with sculptures.

The Plantagenet style spread from the Loire valley into the Vendée, Poitou, Saintonge and the Garonne Valley. At the end of the 13C it was introduced into southern Italy by Charles of Anjou.

GOTHIC (12C–15C)

Gothic art is characterised by the use of intersecting vaults and the pointed arch. The triforium, which originally was blind, is pierced by apertures which eventually give way to high windows. The tall, slender columns, which were crowned by capitals supporting the vaulting, were originally cylindrical but later flanked by engaged columns. In the final development the capitals were abandoned and the roof ribs descended directly into the columns.

The **Flamboyant style** follows this pattern; the diagonal ribs are supplemented by other, purely decorative, ribs called liernes and tiercerons.

The Flamboyant style (15C) of architecture is to be found in the façade of La Trinité in Vendôme and of St-Gatien in Tours, in Notre-Dame-de-Cléry and in the Sainte-Chapelle at Châteaudun.

RENAISSANCE AND CLASSICAL STYLES (16C–17C–18C)

Italian influence is strongly evident in the decoration of **Renaissance** churches: basket-handle or round-headed arches, numerous recesses for statues. Interesting examples can be seen at Montrésor, Ussé, Champigny-sur-Veude and La Bourgonnière.

In the **Classical** period (17C–18C) religious architecture was designed to create a majestic effect, with superimposed Greek orders, pediments over doorways, domes and flanking vaulting. The church of Notre-Dame-des-Ardilliers in Saumur has a huge dome whereas the church of St-Vincent in Blois is dominated by a scrolled pediment.

STAINED GLASS

A **stained-glass window** is made of pieces of coloured glass fixed with lead to an iron frame. The perpendicular divisions of a window are called **lights**. Metal oxides were added to the constituent materials of white glass to give a wide range of colours. Details were often drawn in with dark paint and fixed by firing. Varied and surprising effects were obtained by altering the length of firing and by the impurities in the oxides and defects in the glass. The earliest stained-glass windows to have survived date from the 12C (The Ascension in Le Mans Cathedral).

In the 12C–13C the colours were vivid with rich blues and reds predominating; the glass and leading were thick and smoothed down with a plane; the subject matter was naïve and confined to superimposed medallions.

The Cistercians favoured grisaille windows, which were composed of clear-to-greenish glass with foliage designs on a cross-hatched background, giving a greyish effect.

The master-glaziers of the 14C–15C discovered how to make a golden yellow; lighter colours were developed, the leading became less heavy as it was produced using new tools and techniques, the glass was thinner and the windows larger. Gothic canopies appeared over the human figures.

Windows became delicately coloured pictures in the 16C in thick lead frames, often copied from Renaissance canvases with strict attention to detail and perspective; there are fine examples at Champigny-sur-Veude, Montrésor and Sully-sur-Loire.

In the 17C–19C traditional stained glass was often replaced by vitrified enamel or painted glass without lead surrounds. In the cathedral of Orléans there are 17C windows with white diamond panes and gold bands, along with 19C windows portraying Joan of Arc.

The need to restore or replace old stained glass stimulated a revival of the art in the **20C**. Representational or abstract compositions of great variety emerged from the workshops of the painter-glaziers: **Max Ingrand**, **Alfred Manessier**, **Jean Le Moal**, **M Rollo**.

MURAL PAINTING AND FRESCOES

In the Middle Ages the interiors of ecclesiastical buildings were decorated with paintings, motifs or morally and spiritually uplifting scenes. A school of mural painting akin to that in Poitou developed in the Loire region. The surviving works of this school are well preserved owing to the mild climate and low humidity. The paintings are recognisable by their weak matte colours against light backgrounds. The style is livelier and less formalised than in Burgundy or the Massif Central whereas the composition is more sober than in Poitou. Two techniques were used: **fresco work**, which was done with watercolours on fresh plaster thus making it impossible to touch it up later; and **mural painting**, where tempera colours were applied to a dry surface, producing a less durable work of art.

Romanesque Period

The art of fresco work with its Byzantine origins was adopted by the Benedictines of Monte Cassino in Italy, who in turn transmitted the art to the monks of Cluny in Burgundy. The latter used this art form in their abbeys and prio-

17C frescoes, Galerie des Châteaux, Château de Gizeux

ries, from where it spread throughout the country.

Technique

The fresco technique was the one most commonly used, although beards and eyes were often added once the plaster was dry with the result that they have since disappeared. The figures, drawn in red ochre, were sometimes highlighted with touches of black, green and the sky-blue so characteristic of the region.

Subject Matter

The subjects were often inspired by smaller-scale works. The most common theme for the oven vaulting was Christ the King Enthroned, majestic and severe; the reverse of the façade (at the opposite end of the church from the apse) often carried the *Last Judgement*; the walls depicted scenes from the New Testament whereas the Saints and Apostles adorned the pillars. Other subjects portrayed frequently are the Conflict of the Virtues and Vices, and the Labours of the Months.

Good examples of fresco painting are to be found throughout the Loire valley in Areines, Souday, St-Jacques-des-Guérets, Lavardin and best of all in the chapel of St-Gilles at Montoire. There is also a fine work in St-Aignan in the Cher

valley. The crypt of the church in Tavant in the Vienne valley is decorated with lively paintings of high quality.

In Anjou a man called Fulk seems to have supervised the decoration of the cloisters in the abbey of St-Aubin in Angers. His realistic style, although slightly stilted in the drawing, seems to spring from the Poitou School. More characteristic of the Loire valley are the Virgin and Christ the King from Ponginé in the Baugé region.

Gothic Period

It was not until the 15C and the end of the Hundred Years War that new compositions were produced on themes which were to remain in fashion until the mid-16C. These were really more mural paintings than frescoes and new subjects were added to the traditional repertoire; a gigantic *St Christopher* often appeared at the entrance to a church (*see Amboise*), whereas the legend of the Three Living and Three Dead, represented by three proud huntsmen meeting three skeletons, symbolised the brevity and vanity of human life. In the Loire valley such paintings are to be found in Alluyes, Lassay and Villiers. Two compositions with strange iconography adorn the neighbouring churches in Asnières-sur-Vège and Auvers-le-Hamon.

Renaissance

In the 16C paintings in churches became rarer. There are, however, two surviving examples from this period: the Entombment in the church in Jarzé and the paintings in the chapter house of Fontevraud abbey.

SECULAR PAINTING

During the 15C and 16C, the French School asserted itself, first through the work of Jean Fouquet (c. 1420–80), a portrait painter and miniaturist native of Tours who travelled to Italy, and later through the paintings of the Master of Moulins (late 15C), sometimes identified with Jean Perréal (c. 1455–1530).

The Flemish artist Jean Clouet, commissioned by Louis XII and François I, and his son François Clouet (1520–72), who was born in Tours, became famous for their portraits of the Valois.

Last but not least, Leonardo da Vinci (1452–1519) spent the last three years of his life at the court of François I.

TAPESTRIES FROM THE LOIRE WORKSHOPS

Hanging tapestries, which had been in existence since the 8C to exclude draughts or divide up huge rooms, became very popular in the 14C. The weavers worked from cartoons or preparatory sketches using wool woven with silk, gold or silver threads on horizontal (low warp – *basse lisse*) or vertical (high warp – *haute lisse*) looms.

Their value made tapestries ideal for use as investments or diplomatic gifts; as well as those commissioned for châteaux or even specific rooms, some were hung in churches or even in the streets. The most famous is the 14C Apocalypse tapestry (*see Angers*).

The *mille-fleurs* (thousand flowers) tapestries evoked late medieval scenes – showing an idealised life of enticing gardens, tournaments and hunting scenes – against a green, blue or pink background strewn with a variety of flowers, plants and small animals. These are attributed to the Loire Valley workshops (c. 1500). Good examples can be seen in Saumur, Langeais and Angers.

THE RENAISSANCE TO THE 20C

The use of cartoons (full-scale designs, usually in reverse) instead of paintings, and more sophisticated weaving techniques and materials rendered greater detail possible. The number of colours increased and panels were surrounded by wide borders. In the 18C the art of portraiture was introduced into tapestry work.

In the 20C Jean Lurçat, originally a tapestry renovator, advocated the use of natural dyes. Contemporary weavers started to experiment with new techniques in order to create relief and three-dimensional effects.

GEMMAIL

Gemmail is a modern art medium consisting of assembling particles of coloured glass over a light source. The inventor of this art form was **Jean Crotti** (1878–1958). The Malherbe-Navarre brothers, an interior decorator and a physicist, provided the technical expertise; they discovered a bonding agent which did not affect the constituent elements.

RURAL ARCHITECTURE

Mills of Anjou

Very early on, the extensive network of waterways encouraged the construction of a great many watermills of all kinds (barge-mills, bank-mills, mills with hanging wheels). But the region is furthermore exposed for most of the year to strong winds blowing from the southwest to the northwest – a fact which led to the proliferation of various types of windmills as early as the 13C. Some of these have been restored or converted and are still standing today.

The region still features many structures sometimes open to the public during the summer season or on request. They fall into three categories:

Corn Mills

Characteristic of the Anjou landscape, the corn mill consists of a conical stone base called the cellar, surmounted by a wooden cabin bearing the shaft and sails.

ABC OF ARCHITECTURE

Ecclesiastical architecture

LE MANS – Ground plan of St-Julien Cathedral (12C-15C)

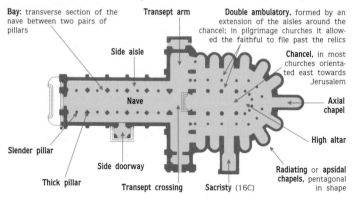

Bay: transverse section of the nave between two pairs of pillars

Transept arm

Double ambulatory, formed by an extension of the aisles around the chancel; in pilgrimage churches it allowed the faithful to file past the relics

Side aisle

Chancel, in most churches orientated east towards Jerusalem

Nave

Axial chapel

High altar

Slender pillar

Side doorway

Thick pillar

Transept crossing

Sacristy (16C)

Radiating or **apsidal chapels,** pentagonal in shape

ST-AIGNAN – Longitudinal section of the collegiate church (11C-12C), transept and chancel

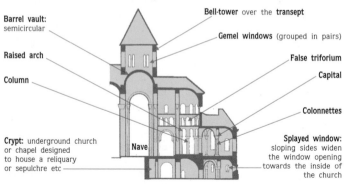

Barrel vault: semicircular

Bell-tower over the **transept**

Raised arch

Gemel windows (grouped in pairs)

Column

False triforium

Capital

Colonnettes

Crypt: underground church or chapel designed to house a reliquary or sepulchre etc

Nave

Splayed window: sloping sides widen the window opening towards the inside of the church

ANGERS – Vaulting of St-Serge Church (early 13C)

This type of domical vaulting is known in France as **Angevin** or **Plantagenet vaulting.** It is curved so that the central keystone is higher than the supporting arches, unlike ordinary Gothic vaulting where they are at the same level. Towards the end of the 12C, Angevin vaulting became lighter, with slimmer, more numerous ribs springing from slender round columns. Early in the 13C, church interiors became higher, beneath soaring lierne vaulting decorated with elegant sculptures.

Quarter or **cell,** in brick

Keystone

Rib

Lierne: auxiliary rib

Capital

Rib vault

Pillar or **column**

© R. Corbel/MICHELIN

ST-BENOÎT-SUR-LOIRE – Basilique Ste-Marie (11C-12C)

Romanesque church. Ground plan with double transept is rare in France; the small, or false, transept crosses the chancel.

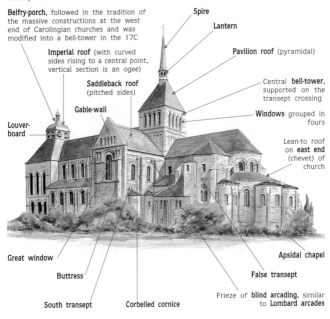

Belfry-porch, followed in the tradition of the massive constructions at the west end of Carolingian churches and was modified into a bell-tower in the 17C

Imperial roof (with curved sides rising to a central point, vertical section is an ogee)

Saddleback roof (pitched sides)

Gable-wall

Louver-board

Spire

Lantern

Pavilion roof (pyramidal)

Central **bell-tower,** supported on the transept crossing

Windows grouped in fours

Lean-to roof on **east end** (chevet) of church

Great window

Buttress

South transept

Corbelled cornice

Apsidal chapel

False transept

Frieze of **blind arcading,** similar to **Lombard arcades**

LE MANS – Chevet of St-Julien Cathedral (13C)

Chevet: French term for the far (usually east) end of the chancel, on the church exterior; the interior far end is known as the **apse**

Gallery

Flying buttress

Tracery: ornamental stone open-work in the upper part of the windows

Pinnacle on the tip of a pier to give it stability

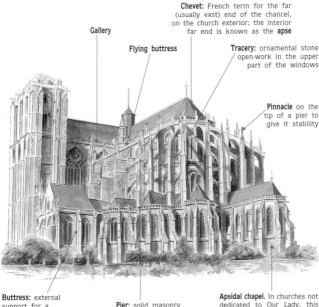

Buttress: external support for a wall, built against it or projecting from it

Pier: solid masonry support structure absorbing the thrust of the arches

Apsidal chapel. In churches not dedicated to Our Lady, this chapel in the main axis of the building is often consecrated to her (Lady Chapel)

© R. Corbel/MICHELIN

TOURS – Façade of St-Gatien Cathedral (13C-16C)

St-Gatien is a fine example of a harmonious combination of styles: Romanesque at the base of the towers, Flamboyant Gothic on the façade, and Renaissance at the top of the bell-towers which are crowned with **lantern-domes**.

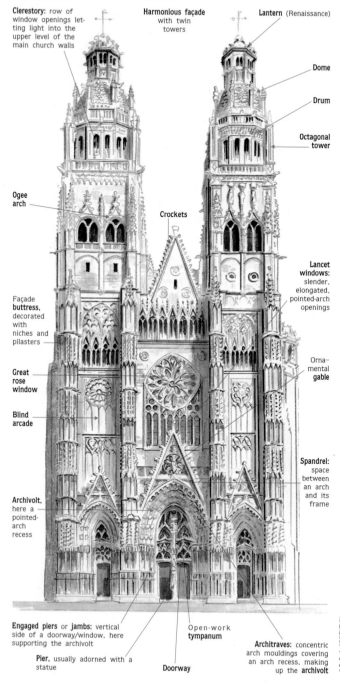

Clerestory: row of window openings letting light into the upper level of the main church walls

Harmonious façade with twin towers

Lantern (Renaissance)

Dome

Drum

Octagonal tower

Ogee arch

Crockets

Lancet windows: slender, elongated, pointed-arch openings

Façade **buttress,** decorated with niches and pilasters

Orna–mental **gable**

Great rose window

Blind arcade

Spandrel: space between an arch and its frame

Archivolt, here a pointed-arch recess

Engaged piers or **jambs:** vertical side of a doorway/window, here supporting the archivolt

Pier, usually adorned with a statue

Open-work **tympanum**

Doorway

Architraves: concentric arch mouldings covering an arch recess, making up the **archivolt**

© R. Corbel/MICHELIN

LORRIS — Organ case (15C) in Notre-Dame Church

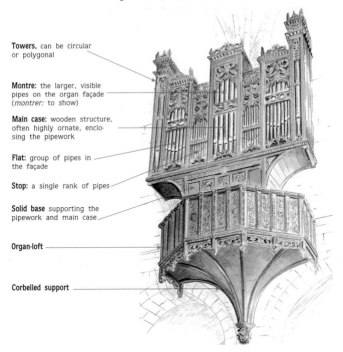

Towers, can be circular or polygonal

Montre: the larger, visible pipes on the organ façade (*montrer:* to show)

Main case: wooden structure, often highly ornate, enclosing the pipework

Flat: group of pipes in the façade

Stop: a single rank of pipes

Solid base supporting the pipework and main case

Organ-loft

Corbelled support

ANGERS — Monumental 19C pulpit in St-Maurice Cathedral

This work by Abbé René Choyer is a pastiche (1855) of 13C Gothic art. As a whole, the pulpit embodies an in-depth knowledge of medieval architecture and sculpture.

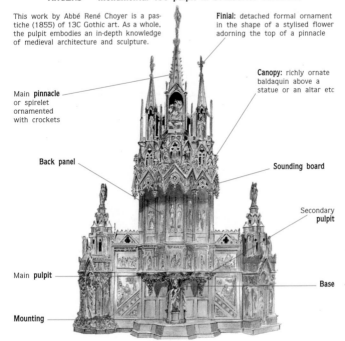

Finial: detached formal ornament in the shape of a stylised flower adorning the top of a pinnacle

Canopy: richly ornate baldaquin above a statue or an altar etc

Main **pinnacle** or spirelet ornamented with crockets

Back panel

Sounding board

Secondary **pulpit**

Main **pulpit**

Base

Mounting

Military architecture

LOCHES – Porte des Cordeliers (11C and 13C fortified gateway)

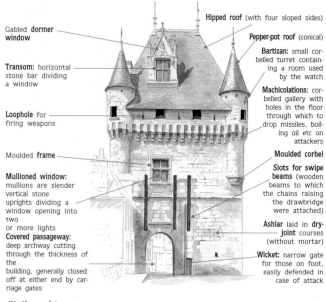

Gabled **dormer window**

Transom: horizontal stone bar dividing a window

Loophole for firing weapons

Moulded **frame**

Mullioned window: mullions are slender vertical stone uprights dividing a window opening into two or more lights

Covered passageway: deep archway cutting through the thickness of the building, generally closed off at either end by carriage gates

Hipped roof (with four sloped sides)

Pepper-pot roof (conical)

Bartizan: small corbelled turret containing a room used by the watch

Machicolations: corbelled gallery with holes in the floor through which to drop missiles, boiling oil etc on attackers

Moulded corbel

Slots for swipe beams (wooden beams to which the chains raising the drawbridge were attached)

Ashlar laid in **dry-joint** courses (without mortar)

Wicket: narrow gate for those on foot, easily defended in case of attack

Civil architecture

BLOIS – Château, François-1er staircase (16C)

The spiral stairway is built inside an octagonal staircase half set into the façade. It opens onto the main courtyard in a series of balconies which form loggias. The king and his court would view all sorts of entertainment from here: the arrival of dignitaries, jousting, hunting or military displays.

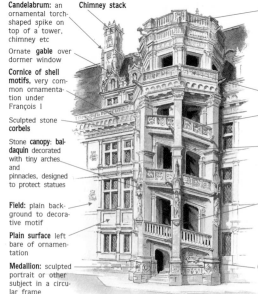

Candelabrum: an ornamental torch-shaped spike on top of a tower, chimney etc

Chimney stack

Ornate **gable** over dormer window

Cornice of shell motifs, very common ornamentation under François I

Sculpted stone **corbels**

Stone canopy: **baldaquin** decorated with tiny arches and pinnacles, designed to protect statues

Field: plain background to decorative motif

Plain surface left bare of ornamentation

Medallion: sculpted portrait or other subject in a circular frame

Gargoyle: drain in the shape of an imaginary and often grotesque animal, through whose mouth rainwater would be projected away from the castle walls

Balustrade

Sculpted **parapet** (filled-in protective wall)

Rampant arch: arch with ends springing from different levels

Sculpted **bracket** (projecting support, smaller than a corbel)

Crowned salamander: decorative motif of François I, sculpted in low relief

© R. Corbel/MICHELIN

SERRANT – Château (16C-17C)

Brown schist, white tufa and grey-blue slate lend great character to this luxurious residence in which Renaissance and Classical styles are harmoniously combined.

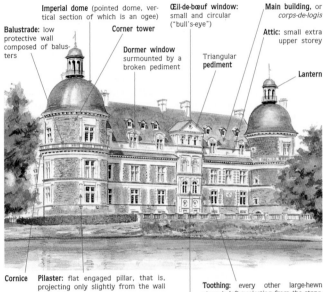

Imperial dome (pointed dome, vertical section of which is an ogee)

Œil-de-bœuf window: small and circular ("bull's-eye")

Main building, or *corps-de-logis*

Balustrade: low protective wall composed of balusters

Corner tower

Dormer window surmounted by a broken pediment

Triangular **pediment**

Attic: small extra upper storey

Lantern

Cornice

Pilaster: flat engaged pillar, that is, projecting only slightly from the wall behind it

Toothing: every other large-hewn stone is left projecting from the stonework framing the windows for a more solid – and more decorative – bond with the adjoining schist walls

Avant-corps: part of a building projecting from the rest of the façade for the entire height of the building, roof included

VILLANDRY — Layout of the Jardins d'Amour (Renaissance style)

The four gardens on the theme of love consist of box borders punctuated by clipped yews and filled with flowers. Each box parterre is laid out in the form of symbolic images: tragic love is represented by sword blades and daggers; unfaithful love by cuckolds' horns, ladies' fans and love letters etc

Monumental fountain in a niche against the wall

Arbour: trellised row of clipped hornbeams

Viewing terrace: commanding a view of the gardens

Mall: tree-lined avenue originally used for games of pall-mall, a precursor of croquet

Espalier wall

Hedge formed by clipped shrubs

Canal

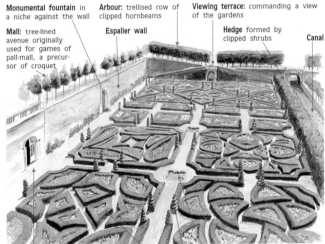

Path covered in *mignonnette* (sand from the Loire which resembles coarse-ground pepper, hence its name)

Box-edged **bed**

Basin

Box edging: low box border (basic element of topiary art)

Topiary: free-standing clipped shrub. Topiary art involves clipping and trimming trees and shrubs to create figurative or geometric shapes verging on sculpture.

The cellar was used for storing grain, flour and spare parts; in some cases, it also housed stables and a shed.

Post Mills
The post mill was a huge wooden structure supporting the sails, the millstone as well as the whole mechanism. Unfortunately, because it was made entirely of wood, its age of glory was short lived, either through lack of maintenance or because the shaft suffered damage.

Tower Mills
By far the most common type of mill, the tower mill – built in stone – has remained comparatively intact over the centuries. The conical roof, with its rotating cap, carries the sails.

21C ARCHITECTURE
Museum buildings in the Loire took the lead in contemporary architecture. In 2007 a new façade, designed by architect Philippe Chiambaretta, for the Centre de creation contemporaine was unveiled, with LED-lit plexiglass slides. In 2016 the ultra-modern Olivier Debré Centre of Contemporary Creation debuts in Tours, designed by the architectural firm of Aires Mateus.

LITERATURE
"LE BEAU PARLER"
Since the Loire Valley was the cradle of France, it is here that old France is recalled in the sayings that have shaped the French language. It is said that the best French is spoken in the Touraine region; though this tendency does not mean that only the most sophisticated, high-brow language is heard. However, the French language has certainly found some of its finest expression in the Loire Valley, where the peace and beauty of the countryside have fostered many leading French writers.

MIDDLE AGES
In the 6C, under the influence of St Martin, Tours became a great seat of learning. Bishop **Gregory of Tours** wrote the first history of the Gauls in his *Historia Francorum*. **Alcuin of York**

founded a famous school of calligraphy at the behest of Charlemagne, while art in the 11C came under the influence of courtly life in the Latin poems of **Baudri de Bourgueil**. At the beginning of the 13C, Orléans witnessed the impact of the popular and lyrical language of the *Romance of the Rose*, a didactic poem by two successive authors – the mannered **Guillaume de Lorris**, who wrote the first 4,000 lines, and the realist **Jean de Meung**, who added the final 18,000. The poem was widely translated and exerted tremendous influence throughout Europe. **Charles d'Orléans** (1391–1465) discovered his poetic gifts in an English prison. He was a patron of the arts and author of several short yet elegant poems; at his court in Blois he organised poetic jousts – **François Villon** won a competition in 1457.

Hitherto a princely pastime, poetry in the hands of Good King René of Anjou became an aristocratic and even mannered work of art. In Angers, Jean Michel, who was a doctor and a man of letters, produced his monumental *Mystery of the Passion*; its 65 000 lines took four days to perform.

RENAISSANCE AND HUMANISM
When the vicissitudes of the Hundred Years War obliged the French court to move from Paris to Touraine, new universities were founded in Orléans (1305) and Angers (1364). They soon attracted a vast body of students and became important centres in the study of European humanism.

Among those who came to study and to teach were Erasmus and William Bude, Melchior Wolmar, a Hellenist from Swabia, and the reformers Calvin and Theodore Beza; **Étienne Dolet**, a native of Orléans, preached his atheist doctrines for which he was hanged and burned in Paris.

François Rabelais (1494–1553), who was born near Chinon, must be about the best-known son of the Touraine. After studying in Angers, he became a learned Benedictine monk and then a famous doctor. In the adventures of

Gargantua and Pantagruel, he expressed his ideas on education, religion and philosophy. He was quite attached to his native country and made it the setting for the Picrocholine war in his books. His comic and realistic style, his extraordinarily rich vocabulary and his universal curiosity made him the foremost prose writer of his period.

THE PLÉIADE

A group of seven poets from the Loire founded a new school (named after a cluster of stars in the Taurus constellation), which was to dominate 16C French poetry; they aimed to develop their language by imitating Horace and the Ancients. Their undoubted leader was **Pierre de Ronsard**, the Prince of Poets from near Vendôme, but it was **Joachim du Bellay** from Anjou who wrote the manifesto of the group, *The Defence and Illustration of the French Language*, which was published in 1549.

The other members of the group were **Jean-Antoine de Baïf** from La Flèche, Jean Dorat, Étienne Jodelle, Marot and Pontus de Tyard, who all held the position of Court Poet; their subjects were nature, women, their native country and its special quality, *la douceur angevine*.

CLASSICISM AND THE AGE OF ENLIGHTENMENT

At the end of the Wars of Religion, when the king and the court returned north to the Paris region (Île-de-France), literature became more serious and philosophical. The **Marquis of Racan** composed verses on the banks of the Loir and the Protestant Academy in Saumur supported the first works of **René Descartes**.

In the following century, **Néricault-Destouches**, from Touraine, followed in Molière's footsteps with his comedies of character; Voltaire stayed at Sully; Rousseau and his companion Thérèse Levasseur lived at Chenonceau; Beaumarchais, who wrote *The Barber of Seville,* settled at Vouvray and visited the Duke of Choiseul in exile at Chanteloup.

ROMANTICISM

The pamphleteer **Paul-Louis Courier** (1772–1825) and the songwriter **Pierre-Jean de Béranger** (1780–1857), both active during the second Bourbon restoration, were sceptical, witty and liberal in politics. **Alfred de Vigny** (1797–1863), a native of Loches who became a soldier and a poet, painted an idyllic picture of Touraine in his novel *Cinq-Mars*.

The greatest literary genius of Touraine was however **Honoré de Balzac** (1799–1850). He was born in Tours and brought up in Vendôme; he loved the Loire Valley and used it as a setting for several of the numerous portraits in his vast work, *The Human Comedy*.

CONTEMPORARY WRITERS

The poet **Charles Péguy**, born in Orléans, wrote about Joan of Arc and his beloved Beauce. **Marcel Proust** also returned to the Beauce in his novel *Remembrance of Things Past*. Another poet, **Max Jacob** (1876–1944), spent many years in work and meditation at the abbey of St-Benoît-sur-Loire.

The Sologne calls to mind the young novelist **Alain-Fournier** and his famous work *Le Grand Meaulnes (The Lost Domain)*. The character of Raboliot the poacher is a picturesque evocation of his native country by the author **Maurice Genevoix** (1890–1980), a member of the Academy. The humourist **Georges Courteline** (1858–1929) was born in Touraine, which was also the retreat of several writers of international reputation: Maeterlinck (Nobel Prize in 1911) at Coudray-Montpensier; Anatole France (Nobel Prize in 1921) at La Béchellerie; Bergson (Nobel Prize in 1927) at La Gaudinière. **René Benjamin** (1885–1948) settled in Touraine, where he wrote *The Prodigious Life of Balzac* and other novels.

Angers was the home of **René Bazin** (1853–1932), who was greatly attached to the traditional virtues and his home ground, and of his great-nephew, **Hervé Bazin** (1911–96), whose violent attacks on conventional values were directly inspired by his native town.

Nature

LANDSCAPES

GEOLOGICAL FORMATION

The Loire region is largely enclosed by the ancient crystalline masses of the Morvan, Armorican Massif and Massif Central and forms part of the Paris Basin. In the Secondary Era the area invaded by the sea was covered by a soft, chalky deposit known as **tufa**, which is now exposed along the valley sides of the Loir, Cher, Indre and Vienne. A later deposit is the limestone of the sterile marshlands *(gâtines)* interspersed with tracts of sands and clays supporting forests and heathlands. Once the sea had retreated, great freshwater lakes deposited more limestone, the surface of which is often broken down into loess or silt. These areas are known as **champagnes** or *champeignes*.

During the Tertiary Era, the folding of the Alpine mountain zone created the Massif Central, and rivers running down from this new watershed were often laden with sandy clays, which, when they were deposited, gave rise to areas such as the Sologne and Orléans forest. Later subsidence in the west permitted the ingress of the **Faluns Sea** as far as Blois, Thouars and Preuilly-sur-Claise, creating a series of shell marl beds *(falunières)* on the borders of Ste-Maure plateau and the hills to the north of the Loire. Rivers originally flowing northwards were attracted in a westerly direction by the sea, thus explaining the great change in the direction of the Loire at Orléans. The sea finally retreated permanently, leaving an undulating countryside with the river network the most important geographical feature. The alluvial silts *(varennes)* deposited by the Loire and its tributaries were to add an extremely fertile light soil composed of coarse sand.

The limestone terraces, which provided shelter, and the naturally fertile soil here attracted early human habitation, of which there are traces from the prehistoric era through the Gallo-Roman period (site of Cherré) to the Middle Ages (Brain-sur-Allonnes). This substratum is immediately reflected in the landscape: **troglodyte dwellings** in the limestone layers, vineyards on the slopes, cereals on the silt plateaux, vegetables in the alluvial silt. The marshy tracts of the Sologne were, for many centuries, untilled since they were unhealthy and unsuitable for any sort of culture.

THE RIVER LOIRE

The longest French river (1,013km/629mi) springs up beneath the Mont Gerbier de Jonc, in the Vivarais region, on the southern edge of the Massif Central mountain range. The flow of the Loire is somewhat erratic: in summer it is reduced to a few meagre streams meandering along the wide, sandy river bed, but in autumn, during the rainy season,

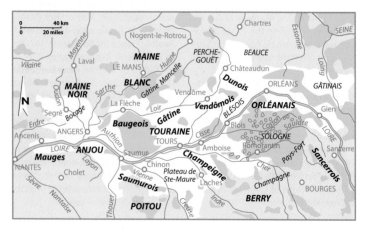

Marshland near La Ferté-Beauharnais, the Sologne

© Patrick Escudero/hemis.fr

or in spring, when the thaw comes, the river is in spate, sometimes causing memorable floods (the worst recorded floods took place in 1846, 1856, 1866, 1910, 1980 and 2018).

Until the end of the 19C, the Loire was a busy waterway in spite of its unpredictable behaviour: flat-bottomed boats rigged with square sails used to sail up and down the river and its tributaries, in particular the Cher, carrying cargo and passengers between Orléans and Nantes (even horse-drawn carriages were placed on rafts).

In 1832 the first steam-powered regular service between Orléans and Nantes was inaugurated, but the development of railways soon struck a decisive blow to boat transport.

LANDSCAPES

The Garden of France

From whatever direction you approach the Loire region – across the immense plains of the Beauce, through the mysterious Berry countryside or the green wooded farmland *(bocage)* of the Gâtine Mancelle – you are always welcomed by the sight of vineyards, white houses and flowers. For many international travellers, this peaceful, fertile countryside is a typically French landscape. But the Garden of France is not simply a sort of Eden laden with fruit and flowers.

The historian Michelet once described it as a "homespun cloak with golden fringes", meaning that the valleys – the

golden fringes – in all their fertility, bordered plateaux whose harshness was tempered only by occasional fine forests.

Northern Berry

This region, lying between the Massif Central and the Loire country, includes the **Pays Fort**, an area of clay soil sloping down towards the Sologne. The melancholy atmosphere of the landscape is described by Alain-Fournier in his novel *Le Grand Meaulnes (The Lost Domain)*. Between the Cher and the Indre is the Champeigne, an area of limestone silt pock-marked with holes *(mardelles)*.

Orléanais and Blésois

Below Gien the valley opens out, the hills are lower and a refreshing breeze makes the leaves tremble on the long lines of poplars and willows. This is the gateway to the Orléanais, which covers the Beauce, the Loire valley (i.e. the Dunois and Vendômois), the Sologne and Blésois (Blois region). In the vicinity of St-Benoît, the valley, commonly known as the **Val**, is a series of meadows; beyond, horticulture predominates with the growing of seedlings and rose-bushes on the alluvial deposits known locally as *layes*. Greenhouses proliferate, some with artificial heating. Orchards and vineyards flourish on the south-facing slopes.

From Orléans to Chaumont along its northern bank, the Loire eats into the

Beauce limestone and then into the flinty chalkland and tufa. On the south the river laps the alluvial sands brought along by its own waters. This area, where asparagus and early vegetables are grown, features large expanses of dense brushwood full of game where the kings of France once used to hunt. The great châteaux then begin: Blois, Chambord, Cheverny, Chaumont and so on.

The **Beauce**, the granary of France, a treeless plain covered with a thin layer (2m maximum) of fertile silt or loess, extends into the area between the Loire and Loir known as the Petite Beauce, where silt gives way to clay in Marchenoir Forest. In the **Sologne** and the **Forest of Orléans**, meagre crops alternate with lakes and woodland.

Touraine

The comfortable opulence of the **Loire valley** will delight the visitor already charmed by the dazzling quality of the light. The blue waters of the Loire, which flow slowly between golden sandbanks, have worn a course through the soft tufa chalk. Channels abandoned by the main river are divided into backwaters *(boires)* or occupied by tributary streams such as the Cher, Indre, Vienne and Cisse.

From Amboise to Tours the flinty chalk soil of the valley slopes is clad with vineyards producing the well-known Vouvray and Montlouis wines. **Troglodyte** houses have been carved out of the white tufa. The **Véron**, lying between the Loire and the Vienne, is a patchwork of small fields and gardens bordered by rows of poplars.

The **Gâtine** of Touraine, between the Loir and Loire, was once a great forest; the area is now under cultivation, although large tracts of heath and woodland have survived (Chandelais and Bercé forests).

The main features of the Touraine Champeigne, where the fields are studded with walnut trees, are the forests of Brouard and Loches and the Montrésor Gâtine. The plateaus of Montrichard and Ste-Maure are similar in many ways to the **Champeigne**.

Anjou

The north bank of the Loire consists of a fertile alluvial plain (**varenne de Bourgueil**) where spring vegetables thrive, surrounded by the famous vineyards planted on warm, dry gravels lying at the foot of the pine-covered hills. Between the Loire and the Authion, lined with willows, green pastures alternate with rich market gardens growing vegetables, flowers and fruit trees. The land below Angers is covered with vineyards, especially the famous Coulée de Serrant vineyard.

The pleasant **Saumurois**, which lies south of the Loire and extends from Fontevraud and Montsoreau to Doué-la-Fontaine and the Layon Valley, has three differing aspects: woods, plains and hillsides – the slopes of which are often clad with vineyards, producing excellent wine including the white wine to which the town of Saumur has given its name. The many caves in the steep, tufa valley sides of the Loire around Chênehutte-les-Tuffeaux are now used for mushroom growing. North of the river lies the sandy **Baugeois**, an area of woods (oak, pine and chestnut) and arable land.

Angers marks the border between the schist countryside of Black Anjou and the sharply contrasting limestone of White Anjou. The countryside is greener, heralding an area of wooded farmland – the Bocage Segréen and **Les Mauges** – which is characterised by a patchwork of small fields surrounded by hedge-topped banks criss-crossed by deep lanes leading to small farmsteads. Around Angers, nursery and market gardens specialise in flowers and seedlings.

Maine

Only the southern part of this region is included in the guide.

The Lower Maine (**Bas-Maine**), otherwise known as Black Maine, is a region of sandstones, granites and schists and wooded farmland. Geographically this area is part of the Breton Armorican massif. The Upper Maine (**Haut-Maine**), covering the Sarthe and Huisne basins, is known as the White Maine because of its limestone soils.

Wheat field of Beauce

© Thierry DUCHAMP/Getty Images

EARTH'S BOUNTY

A well-disposed lie of the land, fertile soil and temperate climate make the Loire valley ideal for the cultivation of trees and market gardens. Fruit and vegetables make a significant contribution to the economy of the Centre-Val de Loire and Pays de la Loire regions, accounting for around 20 percent of domestic production. The cultivation of many of the varieties found in the Loire Valley dates from as early as Roman rule, whereas others introduced to the region during the Renaissance continue to thrive.

FRUIT

Ripening well in the local climate, the succulent fruits of the region are renowned throughout France. The most common are apples, pears and, more recently, blackcurrants. Many have a noble pedigree: Reine-Claude green-gages are named after Claude de France, the wife of François I; Bon-chrétien pears originated from a cutting planted by St Francis of Paola in Louis XI's orchard at Plessis-lès-Tours. They were introduced into Anjou by Jean Bourré, Louis XI's Finance Minister. Rivalling the latter are the following varieties: Monsieur, Williams, a speciality of Anjou; Passe-crassane; and autumn varieties such as Conférence, Doyenné du comice and Beurré Hardy.

Melons were introduced to the region by Charles VIII's Neapolitan gardener. Already in the 16C the variety and quality of the local fruit and vegetables were much praised, namely by Ronsard. The walnut and chestnut trees of the plateaux yield oil and much-prized wood (in the former case) and edible chestnuts (in the latter), often roasted during evening gatherings.

Alongside traditional varieties like the Reinette apple from Le Mans are more prolific varieties better adapted to market demands such as the Granny Smith and Golden Delicious.

EARLY VEGETABLES

A wide variety of vegetables is grown in the Loire Valley. There are two main areas of production: the stretch of valley between Angers and Saumur and the Orléans region. Vegetables cultivated under glass or plastic include tomatoes, cucumbers and lettuces, especially around Orléans. Early vegetables are a speciality in the Loire valley since, in general, they are ready two weeks before those of the Paris region. Asparagus from Vineuil and Contres, potatoes from Saumur, French beans from Touraine, onions and shallots from Anjou and Loiret and artichokes from Angers are dispatched to Rungis, the main Paris market.

One of the region's more unusual crops is mushrooms; over 60 percent of button mushrooms cultivated in France come from the Loire valley. They are grown in the former tufa quarries near Montrichard, Montoire, Montsoreau, Tours and particularly in the Saumur area.

FLOWERS AND NURSERY GARDENS

Pots of geraniums or begonias, borders of nasturtiums and climbing wisteria with its pale mauve clusters adorn the houses. The region of Orléans-la-Source, Olivet and Doué-la-Fontaine is famous for its cultivated flowers – roses, hydrangeas, geraniums and chrysanthemums – which are grown under glass. Tulips, gladioli and lilies are grown (for bulbs) near Soings.

Nursery gardens proliferate on the alluvial soils of the Loire. The lighter soils of Véron, Bourgueil and the Angers district are suitable for the growing of artichokes, onions and garlic for seed stock. The medicinal plants that were cultivated in the Chemillé region during the phylloxera crisis (a severe blight that destroyed many French vineyards in the 19C) are attracting renewed interest.

LIVESTOCK

Dairy stock are generally reared outdoors in the fields, except in winter, when they are kept inside and given corn silage. However, in the case of beef cattle, the animals spend most of the year feeding on pastures in the Maine, Anjou and Touraine valleys.

The main dairy cattle breeds are Prim'Holstein, Normandy and Pie-Noire, whereas the best-known beef breeds are Normandy, Maine-Anjou and especially Charolais. Dairy production is concentrated in Maine, Anjou, the Mayenne Valley, Les Mauges and in the west of the Sarthe Valley. Sheep rearing is confined to the limestone plateaux of the Upper Maine where the black-faced Bleu du Maine and Rouge de l'Ouest prosper.

Pigs can be found everywhere but particularly in Touraine, Maine and Anjou; the production of potted pork specialities – *rillettes* and *rillons* – is centred in Vouvray, Angers, Tours and Le Mans. Recently, in the Sarthe *département* a *label rouge* (red label), guaranteeing the highest quality, was awarded to free-range pigs raised on farms.

The ever-growing demand for the well-known goats' cheeses, in particular the *appellation d'origine contrôlée* (AOC) brands, Selles-sur-Cher and, more recently, Sainte-Maure, have led to an increase in goat keeping. Market days in the west country are colourful occasions: the liveliest are the calf sales in Château-Gontier and the cattle and goat sales in Cholet and Chemillé.

Poultry – Poultry rearing, firmly established in the Loire region, has developed quite considerably; its expansion is linked to the food industry and local co-operatives. This sector has two main characteristics: the high quality of its produce, thanks to many labels, in particular the most prestigious ones recommending the free-range poultry of Loué, and variety: chickens, capons, ducks, guinea fowl, turkeys, geese, quails, pigeons and, generally speaking, all game birds.

FAUNA

The Loire is frequently referred to as the "last untamed river in Europe". During the summer months, along some of its banks, the local climate can tend to resemble more that of African climes. This phenomenon, known as a topoclimate, favours the growth of many tropical plants. The Loire is also inclined to overflow, flooding the surrounding meadows and filling the ditches with water. When it eventually withdraws, leaving the gravel pits and sandbanks to dry out, it creates many natural niches and shelters, the perfect environment for myriad animal and plant species. Consequently, the banks of the Loire are home to many forms of wildlife and especially bird life attracted by the relative peace and calm of the river's waters, which are well stocked with food (water insects, larvae, tiny shellfish and amphibians).

More than 220 species of bird live in, nest in or migrate to the Loire valley every year. To get the most out of bird-watching, without disturbing the birds while respecting their nesting places, you need to identify the particular habitat associated with each species. Along the banks of the Loire, suitable habitats include islets, gravel banks, tributary channels or *boires*, alluvial plains and marshes.

In addition to its healthy bird population, the Loire region is home to developing populations of otter, European beaver, wild boar, polecat, pine marten, snakes, badger, European pond tortoise, and red deer.

ISLETS AND GRAVEL BANKS

The islets, long sandbanks and high grasses found in midstream, provide safe refuges for the **common heron**, the **kingfisher**, the great crested grebe and the **cormorant**, who can rest peacefully, protected from intruders by a stretch of water. The irregular flow of the Loire appears to suit their reproductive pattern, as it offers many open shores suitable for building nests.

Downstream from Montsoreau, the **Île de Parnay** (a protected site closed to the public from April to mid-August) alone is home to more than 750 pairs of birds between March and late June, including **black-headed gulls**, common gulls, Icelandic gulls, **common terns** and little ringed plovers. The **Île de Sandillon**, 15km/10mi upstream of Orléans, is home to 2 500 such pairs.

BOIRES

This name is given to the networks of channels filled with stagnant water that line either side of the Loire, and that flow into the river when it is in spate. These channels, teeming with roach, tench and perch, provide shelter to the bittern, the moorhen, the coot, the garganey, and small perchers like the great reed warbler, which builds its nest 50cm/20in above the water, solidly attached to three or four reeds.

ALLUVIAL PLAINS

Meadows and pastures that can sometimes be flooded after heavy rains offer hospitality either to migratory birds like the whinchat and the gregarious black-tailed godwit, or to more sedentary species such as the corncrake (March to October).

Little ringed plover

Grey heron

© M. Guillou/MICHELIN

Black-tailed godwit

© M. Guillou/MICHELIN

MARSHES AND POOLS

Among the many migratory birds, the **osprey**, which feeds on fish, had practically disappeared from French skies in the 1940s; fortunately, its population is now on the increase. It is an impressive sight to see it skimming over the water while it looks for its prey, then darts forward, claws open, to pounce on a 30–40cm long fish.

The **water rail** is another breed that finds comfort in the long reeds and bulrushes surrounding the marshes.

Château de Chambord
© Arnaud Chicurel/hemis.fr

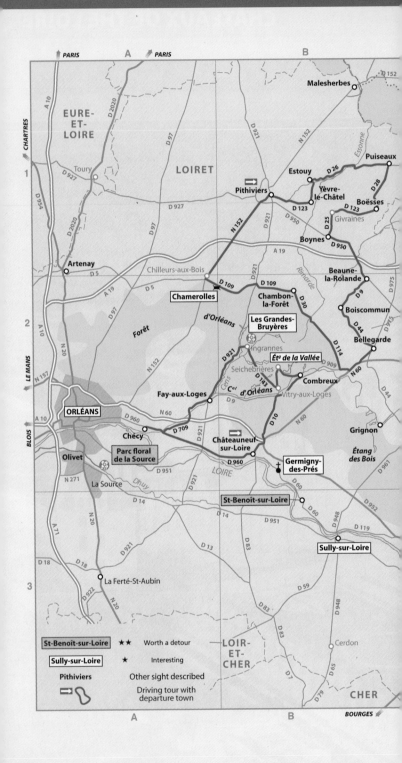

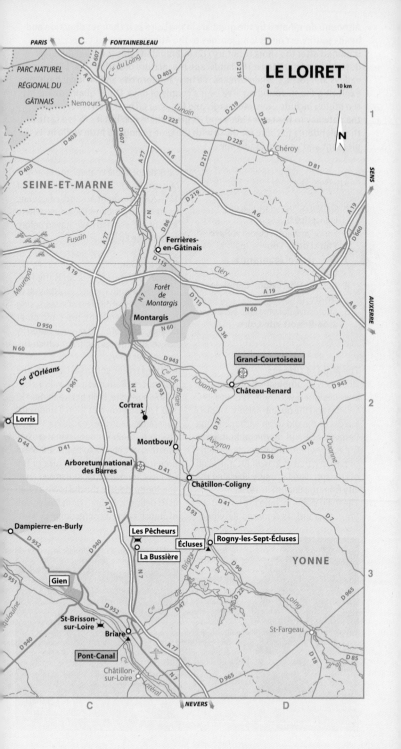

LE LOIRET

THE LOIRET

Although dominated by the great arc in the Loire as it changes direction and heads southwest on its long journey to the Atlantic, the Loiret *département* is named after the short tributary (12km/8mi) that joins the main river just downstream of Orléans. The landscape is a mixture of agricultural plains, river valleys and forests, while Orléans is a busy modern city and an ideal base for exploring the surrounding area over a couple of days. Other quaint towns in the region include Gien, Montargis and Pithiviers. The region is very much the gateway to the Loire Valley and its great châteaux, but it offers a taste of the splendours to come for those with the time to linger a little while in its pleasant and verdant landscapes.

Highlights

1 **Orléans**, former capital of France (p93)
2 Spring flowers in bloom at **Parc Floral de la Source** (p99)
3 The canals of **Montargis** (p104)
4 Gustave Eiffel's **Pont-Canal de Briare** (p109)
5 Impressive Romanesque basilica at **St-Benoît-sur-Loire** (p112)

The Maid of Orléans

Orléans is a combination of wide, airy avenues lined with fine 18C and 19C façades and the quaint, narrow winding streets of the old town with many fine Renaissance and medieval buildings. But everywhere, the one unavoidable presence is that of Joan of Arc, the Maid of Orléans, who famously liberated the city from the English in 1429.

The main sights include the Cathédrale Ste-Croix and its remarkable wood-work décor in the chancel, the Fine Arts Museum and its impressive collection of 16C–20C European art and, of course, the reconstruction of the house where Joan of Arc is said to have stayed before routing the English armies.

Spring blooms

A short distance upstream is the Parc Floral de la Source which, in addition to superb seasonal displays of irises, spring bulbs, rhododendrons, roses and other flowers, also features a popular butterfly house and the spring from which the Loiret river flows.

A little farther southeast stands the magnificent Romanesque basilica of St-Benoît-sur-Loire, built between the 11C and 13C. The town of Gien, famous for its ceramics, and the nearby Pont-Canal de Briare, a 662m aqueduct that crosses over the Loire are not to be missed. Make time for Montargis, the "Venice of the Gâtinais", renowned for its narrow canals and footbridges in the old town as well as its delicious pralines from Mazet, one of France's oldest confectioners.

Rose garden and the château, Parc Floral de la Source

© Hervé Lenain/hemis.fr

Orléans★

Once the capital of France, Orléans is today the capital of the Centre region and an important administrative and university town. In spite of having no castle, Orléans has a lot to offer visitors, such as its cathedral, its old town and Classical façades, its splendid fine arts museum, and its beautiful parks and rose gardens. Along with Tours and Angers, Orléans is one of the three large cities in the Loire valley.

> ▶ **Population:** 118,030.
> ◔ **Michelin Map:** 318: I-4
> 🚩 **Info:** Orléans Val de Loire Tourisme, 2 pl. de l'Etape, 45056 Orléans. ✆02 38 24 05 05. www.tourisme-orleansmetropole.com.
> ▶ **Location:** One hour from Paris by A 10, unless you prefer to idle leisurely through the many back roads of the Île-de-France.
> ⊙ **Don't Miss:** The Fêtes de Jeanne d'Arc in spring.
> ♛ **Kids:** The Maison Jeanne d'Arc.
> ⊘ **Timing:** Allow 1 day for exploring the city.

A BIT OF HISTORY

The Carnutes to Joan of Arc

The Gauls considered the land of the Carnutes to be the centre of their territory, Gaul; each year the Druids held their great assembly there, and it was at Cenabum *(Orléans)* that the signal was given to revolt against Caesar in 52 BCE. A Gallo-Roman city soon rose from the Gaulish ruins. In 451, it was besieged by Attila the Hun, but the inhabitants succeeded in driving off the invaders.

SIEGE OF 1428–1429

The siege was one of the great episodes in the Hundred Years War between France and England for control of France.

The Forces Engaged – From the early 15C the defences of Orléans had been set up to repel English attack. The city wall was divided into six sections, each defended by 50 men. All of the townspeople took part in the defence of the city either by fighting as soldiers or by maintaining the walls and ditches.

During the summer of 1428, the commander of the English army, the **Earl of Salisbury**, had destroyed the French strongholds along the Loire and gained control of the river downstream from Orléans.

The struggle started on 17 October when the English began pounding the city with heavy cannon fire. On the south side of the town, a bridge spanning the Loire was defended at its southern end by the Tourelles Fort, which the English

captured, but Salisbury was killed by a cannon-ball.

Orléans was now cut off from the rest of the French Kingdom. On 8 November most English forces withdrew to Meung-sur-Loire, and the French razed the other suburbs to prevent the English from re-establishing themselves there.

The two sides settled into a war of attrition punctuated by skirmishes outside the gates. The prowess and cunning of Master-Gunner Jean de Montesclerc became legendary: he killed many English soldiers, and would often pretend to die so that when he reappeared, the alarm of the English was redoubled.

However, food grew scarce, and in February 1429 part of the garrison left. It seemed that the English were close to victory. The future **Count of Dunois**, called the Bastard of Orleans, who had defended the city since the siege began, was the only remaining optimist.

The Arrival of Joan of Arc – In April 1429 Jeanne d'Arc persuaded the future **Charles VII** to rescue Orléans. She left Blois with the royal army, crossed the river and approached Orléans along the south bank, intending to take the English by surprise, but the river was too high and the army had to return

Tram in front of the Cathédrale Ste-Croix

© HildaWeges/iStock

to the bridge at Blois. Meanwhile, Joan and several compatriots crossed by boat a few miles upstream and entered the town on 29 April through the Porte de Bourgogne. Greeted by an enthusiastic crowd, she issued her famous ultimatum to the English, that they should surrender to her, the young girl sent by God to drive them out of France.

The people of Orléans rallied and prepared for battle while Joan found herself up against the hostility of the captains and the Governor. On 4 May the royal army, which Dunois had rejoined, attacked the Bastille St-Loup without warning Joan. When she learned of it, she made a sortie, raising her banner, and the French were victorious. On the morning of 6 May, Joan herself led the attack against the Augustins Fort. For a second time her spirited intervention threw the English into confusion. This second victory increased her popularity. Joan went on the offensive again on 7 May against the advice of the Governor who tried to bar her way.

Fighting in the front line outside Les Tourelles, she was wounded in the shoulder by a crossbow bolt. The English thought she was dying. Dunois suggested postponing the attack until the following day, but Joan returned to the attack with her standard raised high. Caught in crossfire, the English garrison in the fort were forced to surrender. On Sunday 8 May the English withdrew

from the last fort. Joan was carried into Orléans in triumph after her victory.

SIGHTS

The town centre owes its stately character to the vast expanse of place du Martroi, to the elegant arcades along rue Royale, to the 18C and 19C façades of the buildings and private mansions. However, the old town nearby offers a striking contrast with its medieval and Renaissance houses lining the lively pedestrianised streets right to the edge of the River Loire.

Hôtel Groslot

Built in 1550 by the bailiff of Orléans, Jacques Groslot, this large Renaissance mansion in red brick was subject to extensive remodelling in the 19C.

It was the King's residence in Orléans: François II, who died here after opening the States-General in 1560, Charles IX, Henri III and Henri IV all stayed here. **Place Ste-Croix**, a symmetrical esplanade, bordered by neo-Classical façades and arcades, was laid out c. 1840 when rue Jeanne-d'Arc was opened up.

Place du Martroi

Adorned with a statue of Joan of Arc, this square marks the symbolic centre of the town. On the west corner of rue Royale stands the old **Pavillon de la Chancellerie**, built in 1759 by the Duke of Orléans to house his archives.

Rue Royale

This broad street, lined with arcades, was opened c. 1755 when the Royal Bridge (**Pont George-V**) was built to replace the old medieval bridge that stood upstream in line with the main street of the old medieval city.

Beyond the house and the two adjoining Renaissance façades on the right, an arch leads to square Jacques-Boucher. Standing alone in the garden is the **Pavillon Colas des Francs**, an elegant Renaissance building, where Boucher's grandson conducted his business; a room on the ground floor houses the archives; another upstairs is the place where the silver was kept.

Quai Fort-des-Tourelles

Located opposite a statue of Joan of Arc standing in a small square are a commemorative cross and an inscription on the low wall beside the Loire. They mark the site of the southern end of the medieval bridge and of the 15C Tourelles Fort, the capture of which by Joan of Arc led to the defeat of the English and the lifting of the siege.

Quai du Châtelet provides a quiet shaded walk beside the river. Early in the 17C, this part of town was one of the busiest: goods bound for Paris were transferred here from river to road, and the six-day voyage downstream to Nantes began.

Rue de Bourgogne

This thoroughfare was the main east-west axis of the old Gallo-Roman city. Now largely pedestrianised, it is ideal for window shopping. There are several old façades, and at No. 261 is a 15C stone house with a half-timbered gable.

Along the street, the **préfecture** is housed in a 17C Benedictine convent. Opposite, in rue Pothier, the façade of the old **Salle des Thèses**, a 15C library, is the only remnant of the University of Orléans, the site where **Jean Calvin**, the religious reformer, studied law in 1528.

Cathédrale Ste-Croix★★

⏲ Nov-Feb daily 9.15am-5pm, Mar-May 9.15am-6pm, Jun-Sept 9.15am-7pm. Night opening some weekends, check website for details. ℘02 38 77 87 50. www.orleans.catholique.fr.

Begun in the 13C, this cathedral was under construction until the 16C, although the building was partly destroyed by the Protestants in 1568. Henri IV, the first Bourbon king, grateful to the town for having supported him, undertook to rebuild the cathedral in the Gothic style. The **west front** has three large doorways with rose windows above them crowned by a gallery with open-work design.

Interior

Splendid early-18C **woodwork★★** adorns the chancel and the stalls. In the **crypt** are traces of the three buildings that predated the present cathedral, and two sarcophagi; one belonged to Bishop Robert de Courtenay (13C) who collected the most precious items in the **treasury**.

North transept and east end

In the north transept is a rose window with the emblem of Louis XIV at the centre. Excavations at the base have revealed the old Gallo-Roman walls and part of a tower. With its flying buttresses

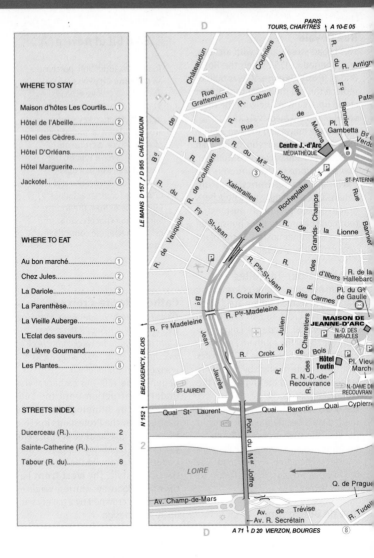

and pinnacles, the **east end** is clearly visible from the gardens of the former episcopal palace, an 18C building that now houses the municipal library.

Campo Santo
To the left of the modern Fine Arts School (École Régionale des Beaux-Arts) is a graceful Renaissance portal; on the north side of this same building is a garden edged with an arcaded gallery.

Musée des Beaux-Arts★★
🕐 Tue–Sat 10am–6pm (Fri 8pm), Sun 1–6pm. €6, free 1st Sun/month. ♿ ☎02 38 79 21 83. www.orleans-metropole.fr.
The collections displayed in this fine arts museum date back to the French Revolution. The paintings, sculptures and objets d'art provide a fascinating insight into European art from the 15C–20C.
The **second floor** is devoted to the Italian, Flemish and Dutch Schools, represented by works by Correggio (Holy Family), Tintoretto (Portrait of a Venetian), Annibale Carracci (Adoration

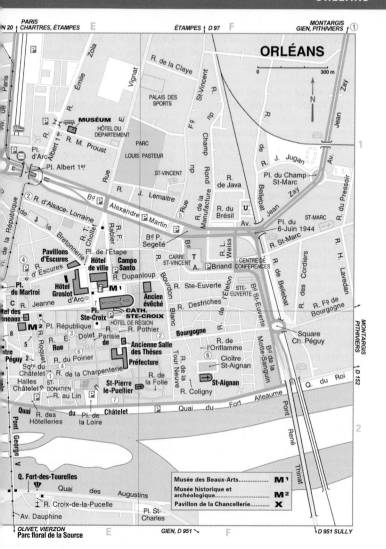

PARIS
CHARTRES, ÉTAMPES
N 20
ÉTAMPES ‡ D 97
MONTARGIS
GIEN, PITHIVIERS

ORLÉANS

0   300 m

N

Musée des Beaux-Arts.................	**M** 1
Musée historique et archéologique..................	**M** 2
Pavillon de la Chancellerie...........	**X**

OLIVET, VIERZON
Parc floral de la Source
GIEN, D 951
D 951 SULLY

of the Shepherds), Van Dyck, Teniers and Ruysdael. On the **first floor**, there are works from the 17C–18C French School. In the **Pastel Gallery**, 18C portraits include works by Perronneau, Quentin La Tour, Chardin *(Self-Portrait with Spectacles)* and Nattier.

The rooms devoted to the 19C offer a wealth of interesting collections covering Neoclassicism, Romanticism, Realism and pre-Impressionism. The modern art section, housed in the basement, concentrates above all on sculpture.

Musée historique et archéologique

🕐 *Apr–Sept Tue–Sun 10am–1pm, 2–6pm; rest of year Tue–Sun 1–6pm.*
🕐 *1 Jan, 1 and 8 May, 14 Jul, 1 and 11 Nov, 25 Dec.* ⊛*€6, free 1st Sun/month.*
𝄢 *02 38 79 25 60.*
www.orleans-metropole.fr.

The Museum of History and Archaeology is housed in an elegant mansion, **Hôtel Cabu** (1550), next to another Renaissance façade.

On the ground floor, the astonishing **Gallo-Roman treasure**★ from

Neuvy-en-Sullias consists of a series of statues, a horse and a wild boar in bronze as well as statuettes of great artistic value.

The first floor is devoted to treasures of the Middle Ages and the Classical period, as well as local ceramic ware. The second floor is occupied by local folklore, pewter ware, gold and silverware and clocks. Another room presents the history of the port of Orléans, describing the various industries associated with river traffic in the 18C–19C.

Centre Charles Péguy

Museum and temporary exhibits Tue-Sat 2pm-6pm (Fri 5pm); document centre Mon-Tue 9am-noon, 2pm-6pm; Free. 02 38 53 20 23. www.charlespeguy.fr.

This centre is housed in the old **Hôtel Euverte-Hatte**, which was built later during the reign of Louis XII. The rectangular windows are framed with Gothic friezes; the Renaissance arcade in the courtyard was added during the reign of François I. The library is devoted to the poet and essayist Péguy (1873-1914), his work and his literary, political and social environment.

Maison de Jeanne d'Arc

Apr–Sept Tue–Sun 10am–1pm, 2–6pm; Oct–Mar Tue–Sun 2–6pm. €6. 02 38 68 32 63. www. jeannedarc.com.fr/maison/maison.htm.

The tall timber-framed façade contrasts with the modernity of the square, place du Général-de-Gaulle, which in 1940 was heavily bombed. The building is a reconstruction of the house of Jacques Boucher, Treasurer to the Duke of Orléans, where Joan stayed in 1429. An audiovisual show *(first floor)* recounts the ending of the siege of Orléans by Joan of Arc on 8 May 1429.

Centre Jeanne-d'Arc

Mon–Thu 9am–noon, 2–6pm, Fri 5pm. Weekends. Free. 02 38 68 32 64. www.jeannedarc.com.fr/centre/centre.htm

The centre's resources include a book library, a film library and microfilm and photographic archives.

Museum of Natural Sciences★

Closed for refurbishment; check website for updates. 02 38 54 61 05. www.orleans-metropole.fr.

The old building housed a museum of natural sciences, with displays of a scientific and cultural interest.

The four upper floors of the museum were devoted to the marine world, aquatic ecosystems (aquarium), reptiles and amphibians, higher vertebrates (diorama on the Sologne region), mineralogy, geology, palaeontology and botany.

EXCURSIONS

Artenay

20km/12.4mi N on N 20.

The entrance to this large town in the Beauce region is marked by a windmill-tower with a revolving roof (19C).

A Beauce farmhouse is the setting for the **Musée du Théâtre forain** (*daily Jul–Aug 2–6pm; 21 Sept–Jun 2–5pm; €3 or free the 1st Sun of the month; 02 38 80 09 73; www.museetheatreforain.fr*), a museum devoted to the life of travelling theatre that toured French towns and villages from the 19C to the 1970s.

La Loire Blésoise★★

From Orléans to Blois – 84km/52mi. Leave Orléans on av. Dauphine (S of the town map); cross the Loiret that flows between wooded banks.

Olivet

The greater part of Olivet is given over to growing flowers, roses and ornamental plants. It is also a pleasant summer resort on the south bank of the Loiret, composed of elegant houses and old watermills, where people come for the fishing and canoeing.

Promenade des moulins

5km/3mi round trip from the bridge along the north bank of the Loiret going W; returning on D 14 going E.

At the far end of the loop, two old mills straddle the river over their mill-races between the wooded banks of the Loiret, while ducks and swans glide up and down on the quiet river.

▶ In Olivet take D 14 E to the park.

Parc Floral de la Source★★

🕐 *Daily late Mar–mid-Sept 10am–7pm; late Sept–early Nov 10am–6pm; mid-Nov–mid-Mar 2–5pm (free admission).* 🕐 *1 Jan, 25 Dec.* ♿. ⬚€6. ✆02 38 49 30 00. www.parcfloraldelasource.com.

This park was laid out in the wooded grounds of a 17C château to host the 1967 Floralies Internationales horticultural exhibition.

As the seasons change, so does the display: in spring, the flower beds are in bloom with tulips, daffodils, then **irises★**, rhododendrons and azaleas; mid-June to mid-July is the period when the rose bushes are at their best; in September the late-flowering rose bushes come into bloom, along with the dahlias.

The **butterfly house** is a popular attraction *(late Mar–mid-Nov)*.

The **Loiret spring★** can be seen bubbling up from the ground. The spring is the resurgence of the part of the river that disappears underground near St-Benoît-sur-Loire. Throughout the year, flocks of cranes and emus and herds of deer frequent the park, while flamingoes stalk the banks of the Loiret.

ADDRESSES

🛏 STAY

⊜⊜ **Hotel Jackotel** – *18 cloître St-Aignan.* ✆02 38 54 48 48. www.jackotel-orleans.fr. *Closed Sun and public holidays at lunch.* 🅿. *61 rooms.* Set near the river in the old town, this hotel resides in the lovely peaceful St-Aignan Cloister, shaded by horse chestnut trees.

⊜⊜ **La Villa Dunois** – *44 Rue du Maréchal Foch, 45000 Orléans.* ✆07 69 36 56 04. www.lavilladunois.fr. *2 rooms.* Situated on the ground floor of a historic house, this B&B offers spacious, stylish rooms with the intimacy and peace of a traditional bed and breakfast. Situated close to the river with free parking, wifi and a beautiful garden that adds to the tranquillity.

⊜⊜ **Hôtel Marguerite** – *14 pl. du Vieux-Marché.* ✆02 38 53 74 32. www.hotel-orleans.fr. *Closed 23 Dec–8 Jan. 25 rooms.* Renovated entrance hall and corridor, increased soundproofing: this centrally located hotel is improving its comfort level. Simple yet spacious rooms.

⊜⊜-⊜⊜⊜ **Hôtel des Cèdres** – *17 r. Mar.-Foch.* ✆02 38 62 22 92. www.hotelcedresorleans.com. *Closed 20 Dec–6 Jan. 32 rooms.* This hotel enjoys a quiet location. The veranda, where breakfast is served, overlooks the garden planted with cedar trees.

⊜⊜ **Hôtel de l'Abeille** – *64 r. d'Alsace-Lorraine.* ✆02 38 53 54 87. https://hotel-abeille.com. *25 rooms.* Located in the town centre, this hotel offers small, nicely spruced-up rooms with personalised colour schemes and selected period furniture. No lift.

⊜⊜ **Hôtel d'Orléans** – *6 r. Adolphe-Crespin.* ✆02 38 53 35 34. www.hoteldorleans.com. *18 rooms.* This establishment consists of two buildings surrounding a courtyard and linked by the breakfast room. The simple yet practical rooms are well kept.

🍴 EAT

⊜⊜ **La Mangeoire** – *28 rue du Poirier, 45000, Orléans.* ✆02 38 68 15 38. lamangeoire-orleans.com. Cheery bistrot with attractive pavement seating and chalkboard menu featuring French classics plus seafood specialities. The friendly chef often emerges to greet patrons and chat about the latest specials.

⊜⊜–⊜⊜⊜ **L'Hibiscus** – *1175 Rue de Bourgogne, 45000 Orléans.* ✆02 38 72 74 11. www.hibiscus-restaurant.com. *Closed Sun and Mon.* Modern twists on French classics served in an artful create way. Clever presentation of well-sourced ingredients and an elegant dining room that makes this a special spot in the heart of the town, just a stone's throw from the river.

La Dariole – *25 r. Étienne-Dolet. ℰ02 38 77 26 67. Closed Sat, Sun and evenings except Tue and Fri.* This half-timbered house sits near the elegant Hôtel Cabu (1550), now home to the Museum of History and Archaeology. The old-fashioned dining room is quite attractive, and in the summer, there is alfresco dining in the back garden. Traditional French fare is served.

L'Eclat des saveurs – *233 r. de Bourgogne. ℰ02 38 53 12 21. http://eclat2saveurs.fr. Closed Sun–Mon lunch. Dinner reservation advised.* &. With its distinctive burgundy front, this restaurant serves traditional cuisine, including the speciality, gastronomic pancakes.

Les Plantes – *44 r. Tudelle. ℰ02 38 56 65 55. www.restaurantdesplantes.fr. Closed Sat lunch, Sun eve, Mon. Reservation advised.* It's not easy to find this small restaurant located on the left bank of the Loire, close to the George V bridge. Inside, the colour scheme, the pictures and the photo prints create a cosy atmosphere. On the menu: cuisine from the Loire valley and fish specialities.

Jane A – *15 rue Croix de Malte, 45000, Orléans. ℰ02 38 42 75 89. Wed-Thu 12-2:30pm, Fri-Sun 7-9:30pm.* Reservations are a must at this crepe hotspot. It's only open a few hours a day, and it remains busy all the time. Sweet and savoury crepes served alongside salads and desserts, plus a decent list of good local wines.

La Parenthèse – *26 pl. du Châtelet. ℰ02 38 62 07 50. www.restaurant-la-parenthese.com. Closed Sun–Mon.* A familiar address in Orléans, this dining establishment offers generous portions, fresh produce and good overall cuisine from a creative team, and has remained popular almost since the day if first opened.

La Chancellerie – *27 pl. du Martroi. ℰ02 38 53 57 54. www.restaurant-lachancellerie.fr. Daily 8am–1am. Closed Sun eve.* In this up-market café-restaurant run by the Lefèvre family, fish and shellfish specialities are accompanied by fine wines. The terrace on Place du Martroi is a favourite meeting place for Orléans residents, and especially the city's business people.

Le Lièvre Gourmand – *28 quai du Châtelet. ℰ02 38 53 66 14. www.lelievregourmand.com. Closed Mon lunch, Tue, and Wed lunch.* Chef Tristan Robreau prepares beautifully presented and inventive dishes of delicious food local to the Loire valley. Enjoy creative dishes in an elegant and yet relaxed environment in this Michelin-starred restaurant.

SHOPPING

Martin Pouret – *11 rue Jeanne d'Arc, Orléans ℰ02 38 62 19 64. www.martin-pouret.com.* Founded in 1797, this is the only establishment in town that still makes wine vinegar in wooden casks according to the authentic Orléans method and Orléans mustard using stone-ground mustard seed, to a recipe dating from 1580.

Café d'Eric – *Les Halles Chatelet, Rue Thiers, 45000 Orléans. ℰ02 38 54 87 36. www.les-cafes-deric-orleans.fr.* Find a large selection of teas and coffees here; the latter is roasted on the premises. Also on hand are speciality groceries and a range of sweet treats.

Les halles Châtelet – *pl. du Châtelet. ℰ02 38 62 85 70. www.orleans-metropole. fr. Open year round.* This large covered market houses butchers, a wine merchant and a coffee merchant, cheesemongers, two delicatessens, a caterer, a shop for ready-prepared dishes, fresh produce, six greengrocers, fishmongers, poulterers, an ice-cream seller and a specialist in Italian cooking, among others.

LEISURE ACTIVITIES

Base de loisirs de l'Île Charlemagne – *R. de la Levée. 45650 St-Jean-le-Blanc. 2km/1mi E. ℰ02 38 51 92 04. www.orleans-metropole.fr.* The outdoor recreation area offers swimming (May–Aug), windsurfing boards, catamarans, sailing dinghies and kayaks for hire. Beach-ball, pony club and mountain bike trails.

ENTERTAINMENT

Boulangerie Patisserie Traiteur Jano – *4 r. du Tabour. ℰ02 38 53 59 25. www.plisson-patissier.fr. Mon–Sat 8am–7.30pm. Closed Sun.* Try original, hand-made macaroons in a rance of inventive flavours, such as: glacé raspberries in Orléans vinegar, rose petal jam, pear and ginger preserve, etc. and the Loiret gourmand, a hazelnut cake with pear and cherry filling smothered in hazelnut cream. Other specialities include delicious pastries, artisanal bread, huge meringues and claypot stews.

Pithiviers

Pithiviers is situated on the border between the Beauce and the Gâtinais regions. Its main economic activities are related to local products – cereals and sugar beet (sugar refinery at Pithiviers-le-Vieil) – but other industries are currently being introduced.

- ▶ **Population:** 9,263
- **Michelin Map:** 318: K-2
- **Info:** 1 mail Ouest, Maison Des Remparts, 45300 Pithiviers. ℘02 38 30 08 77. www.pithiviers.fr.
- **Location:** 43km/27mi NE of Orléans along the N 152, and 100km/63mi S of Paris.
- **Timing:** Allow 1 hour.
- **Don't Miss:** St George's Fair in April if you're a gourmet.
- **Kids:** Transport Museum.

SIGHTS
🚹 Musée des Transports
r. Carnot. Jul–Aug Tue, Sat and Sun, 2.30pm, 4pm and 5.15pm, plus Sun and public holidays year-round. €8.50 (child 4–14, €6.50), including a train ride. ℘02 38 30 48 26.
http://amtp-pithiviers.wifeo.com.
The Transport Museum was founded by volunteer workers in the old terminus of the Tramways à Vapeur du Loiret line. The 0.6m/2ft wide tracks designed by Decauville, who promoted this particular width for French railways, carried passengers and sugar beets from Pithiviers to Toury until 1951. The museum contains several steam locomotives, two electrical tramways and a rail car running on both electricity and oil (1923).

EXCURSIONS
Malesherbes
18km/11.2mi NE along N 152.
Situated along the Essonne valley, this small town is entirely surrounded by woods. The **Buthiers** leisure park lies close to the river, in a forest setting dotted with sandstone boulders.

Atelier-Musée de l'Imprimerie
70 avenue du général Patton, Malesherbes. Sept-Jun Tue-Fri 9am-5.30pm, Sat 2-5.30pm, Sun 10am-5.30pm; Jul-Aug Tue-Fri 10am-6.30pm, Sat 2-6.30pm, Sun 10am-6.30pm; closed Mon, 25 Dec, 1 Jan 1 May. €8 (child 6–18, €4) ℘02 38 33 22 67. http://a-mi.fr.
Largest museum in Europe dedicated to printing and the printed work with historical exhibits and the chance for kids to try letterpress typesetting and other printing tecniques.

Château
Open Jul–Sept; check with tourist office (19/21, place du Martroy. ℘02 38 34 81 94. www.ville-lemalesherbois.fr) for hours, or www.tourismeloiret.com. €1. Privately owned: interior closed to the public.
The 14C round towers are all that remains of the feudal castle rebuilt in the 15C. The courtyard leads to former outbuildings: 14C tithe barns where wheat was stored four floors high; Tour des Redevances; and a pavilion known as Châteaubriand's House in memory of the famous poet who stayed in it.
The 14C dovecote could accommodate 8,000 pigeons.

🚗 DRIVING TOUR

95km/59mi round trip. Allow half a day.

▶ Leave Pithiviers E along D 123.

Yèvre-le-Châtel
Perched on its promontory, Yèvre overlooks the Rimarde, a tributary of the River Essonne. The ramparts date from the 13C. A fortified gate under the elm trees in the main square opens into the outer bailey of the castle.

Château fort
Apr–Oct 2–6pm. €5.
℘02 38 34 25 91. www.yevre-la-ville.fr.
The restored stronghold is diamond-shaped with a round tower at each cor-

Malesherbes

This tolerant man, who became one of Louis XVI's ministers, encouraged the introduction and circulation throughout France of Diderot's *Encyclopédie*. Having retired from public service on the eve of the Revolution, he requested the honour of defending the King before the Convention. He was later guillotined together with his daughter, his son-in-law, as well as one of his granddaughters and her husband the Marquess of Châteaubriand, the eldest brother of the writer.

ner containing hexagonal rooms with ogival vaulting. The northwest and south towers provide a **view** of the Beauce and the Gâtinais. To the south Orléans forest darkens the horizon.

Église St-Lubin

On the south side of the village among the tombstones stands the unfinished stone shell of a huge Gothic church. Its vast size seems to have been dictated by the need for a place of refuge rather than a place of worship.

▶ Drive to Estouy and turn right onto D 26 which follows the River Essonne.

Puiseaux

This busy cereal centre of the Gâtinais region developed round a priory belonging to the Parisian abbey of St-Victor, a famous theological centre in medieval times. The twisted spire of the 13C church can be seen from afar.

▶ Drive S out of Puiseaux along D 948 then turn right onto D 28.

Boësse

This once-fortified village stretches its winding streets on the hillside; the church is preceded by an impressive porch reminiscent of part of a cloister.

▶ Take D 123 on the right to Givraines then turn left onto D 25 to Boynes.

Boynes

Seeing it today, it is difficult to imagine that Boynes remained the world capital of saffron for 300 years (16C–19C). Drastic changes in the agricultural world brought with them the decline of saffron and of wine-growing, but the town's prosperous past is recalled at the **Musée du Safran** (*First and third weekend of the month 2.30–6pm; €5; 02 38 33 14 81*).

Beaune-la-Rolande

Beaune lies on the banks of the River Rolande. Sugar beets and cereals have replaced saffron and vines in this market town.

The 15C–16C **church** features an elegant north side in the Renaissance style: there are pilasters bearing medallions, recesses and doorways with pediments decorated with busts.

Boiscommun

5.5km/3.4mi SW on D 9.

Of the castle only two towers and other ruins remain; they can be seen from the path that now follows the line of the former moat.

The 13C **church** has a Romanesque doorway and a Gothic nave with a majestic elevation. It is relatively easy

Source of Saffron

© S. Sauvignier/MICHELIN

to discern the different periods of construction by looking at the changes in the capitals, the form of the high windows and openings of the triforium.

Bellegarde

The town's colour-washed houses are grouped round a huge square and surrounded by rose nurseries, market gardens and wheat fields.

Château★

Grouped round the old keep, this picturesque ensemble, built in the 14C by Nicolas Braque, Finance Minister to Charles V, stands on a platform surrounded by a moat. The brick **pavilions** with stone dressings that frame the courtyard were built by D'Antin to house the château staff and his guests; from left to right they comprise the Steward's pavilion surmounted by a pinnacle turret, the Captain's massive round brick tower, the kitchen pavilion, the Salamander pavilion, which houses the town hall (**Hôtel de ville**) and contains the **Regency Salon** with wood panelling. On the other side of the gate, the D'Antin Pavilion has a mansard roof. A rose garden has been laid out round the moat.

Church

Note the ornamentation of the central doorway of this Romanesque edifice: wreathed and ringed engaged piers support carved capitals depicting foliage and animals. The nave contains 17C **paintings**: *St Sebastian* by Annibale Carracci and *The Infant Louis XIV as St John the Baptist* by Mignard (right wall) and *The Deposition* by Lebrun (*right chapel*); Louise de la Vallière may have been the model for the two female characters in these pictures.

▶ Drive SW through Bois de la Madeleine then turn right onto D 114.

Chambon-la-Forêt

This lovely flower-decked village lies on the edge of Orléans forest.

▶ Drive out along D 109.

Château de Chamerolles★

🕐 *Early Mar-Apr and Oct-Dec Wed-Mon 1.30-5.30pm; May-Jun and Sept Wed-Mon 10am-6pm; Jul-Aug daily 10am-6pm* 🕐 *Jan, 25 Dec.* ⚙️€8. ☎02 38 39 84 66.
www.chateauchamerolles.fr.
Standing on the edge of Orléans forest, Chamerolles resembles a medieval fortress. The sumptuous Renaissance château and its formal gardens have been restored to their former glory. The Dulac family moved here in the 15C, when **Lancelot du Lac** commissioned the construction of the present château. Acquainted with Louis XII and François I, he designed a medieval stronghold with an elegant, comfortable interior.

Promenade des parfums★

The south wing of the château houses a chronological exhibit of different scents from the 16C up to the present day in a series of rooms decorated with objects related to perfume.

A small bridge spanning the moat allows you to continue an aromatic exploration by visiting the **garden★**. The flower beds have been painstakingly restored to the layout they would have had during the Renaissance, reflecting the threefold purpose of gardens in those days: ornamentation, leisure and utility.

▶ Return to Pithiviers along N 152.

ADDRESSES

🏠 STAY

⊜⊜ **Relais de la Poste** – *10 mail Ouest, 45300 Pithiviers.* ☎02 38 30 40 30. *www. le-relais-de-la-poste.fr. 41 rooms. Restaurant* ⊜⊜. *Wi-Fi.* A former coaching inn, this large hotel in the town centre has good-size wood-panelled rooms furnished in rustic style.

🍴 EAT

⊜⊜ **Le Lancelot** – *12, rue des Déportés,* ☎02 38 32 91 15. *www.restaurantlelancelot. com.* Creative and colourful seasonal food, presented in an attractive setting by conscientious staff.

Montargis

More than 130 bridges and footbridges over a maze of canals have earned Montargis its nickname of the "Venice of the Gâtinais." It invites visitors to stroll among its old half-timbered houses and fine Renaissance residences, discover the ruins of the châteaux, and the gardens at nearby Grand-Courtoiseau.

> ▶ **Population:** 15,192.
> ⚲ **Michelin Map:** 318: N-4
> ⏚ **Info:** 35 r. Renée-de-France, 45202 Montargis, ☏ 02 38 98 00 87. www.tourisme-montargis.fr.
> ⏵ **Location:** 56km/35mi SW of Sens, 60km/38mi west of Joigny.
> ⊗ **Don't Miss:** Old Montargis, and pralines from the Mazet shop.
> ⚰ **Kids:** The Beekeeping museum.
> ⏲ **Timing:** Allow 1–2 hours to discover the town.

WALKING TOUR

THE OLD TOWN

Some streets in the old town enjoy fine views of the Canal de Briare, which has encircled the north and east of Montargis since 1642 and links the river Loing to the Loire. The canals in the town were dug to regulate the water level in a region that was subject to constant danger of flooding. These, and the many bridges and footbridges that now span the channels, give the historic part of the town its unique and charming appeal.

⏵ Take r. du Port, then bd. du Rempart and from the canal bridge, bd. Durzy, to the musée Girodet.

Musée Girodet

2 r. du Fg-de-la-Chaussée. Thu-Sun 2-6pm. ☏ 02 38 98 07 81. www.musee-girodet.fr.
This museum is dedicated to painter **Anne-Louis Girodet-Trioson** (1767–1824), born in Montargis, and favourite pupil of Jacques-Louis David, the pre-eminent neo-Classical artist during the Revolution and First Empire. It is housed in the 19C **Hôtel Durzy** set in pleasant grounds on the banks of the Loing.
The **Girodet collection★** is the main attraction with a score of pictures including portraits (Dr Trioson and Mustapha Sussen), a copy by the artist of his most famous work (in the Louvre) inspired by Chateaubriand's novel, *The Funeral of Atala*, and the charming *Geography Lesson* (1803).

In the first part of the gallery, don't miss the extraordinary *Flood (Déluge)*, a painting that took Francisco de Zurbarán four years to complete. Part of the rich collection of sketches is displayed in a rotating exhibit in the salon Girodet. The painted ceiling featuring the monuments of the region is the work of one of his pupils. The library, with furniture by Romantic sculptor **Henri de Triqueti** (1804–74), houses a large collecion of small Romantic sculptures by Girodet's contemporaries: Feuchère, Barre, Gechter, Pradier, etc. Upstairs are delightful terra-cotta pieces.

Boulevard Durzy

Shady avenue lined with plain trees running between the canal and the jardin Durzy. At the end a tall and elegant metallic humpback footbridge, the work of the Eiffel factories in 1891, completes the perspective. The bridge affords pretty views of two canal locks.

⏵ Take the footbridge over the canal and continue straight on.

Boulevard Belles-Manières

As the channel narrows to the north, footbridges lead to houses built on the levelled towers of the old ramparts.

⏵ Walk back to the beginning of bd. Belles-Manières, turn left into r.

du Moulin-à-Tan, then, with pl. de la République on your left, take r. Raymond-Laforge.

Rue Raymond-Laforge

Old dwellings with wash-houses overlook two canals. Decorative small boats are used as window boxes along the canal banks.

◖ Retrace your steps and take r. de l'Ancien-Palais. At the end of the street, turn right into an alley with a bridge at the end that gives **views** over the canal you have just crossed.

◖ Turn right into r. de la Pêcherie.

Walk through the renovated district where several half-timbered houses remain. From place Jules-Ferry, rue Raymond-Tellier leads, after about 50m, to another impressive **view** of the water channels as far as the Canal de Briare.

◖ Turn left into r. du Loing, then r. du Gén.-Leclerc along the south side of the Église Ste-Madeleine, and turn left into r. du Château.

Musée du Cuir et des Tanneurs

Carr. Henri-Perruchot. ◷*Sat 2.30– 5.30pm.* ⊕€2. *02 38 98 00 87.* Located in the renovated historic Ilot des Tanneurs district, this 16C house displays the craft, methods and tools of tanners from the last century. The first floor features a display of local costumes and headdresses including the fanchon (checkered scarf) for everyday wear, the caline (bonnet) for going out and about in the town, and embroidered headdresses for special occasions.

◖ Return to pl. du 18-Juin-1940 by the pont du Québec.

EXCURSIONS
Ferrières-en-Gâtinais
Best route is along D 315 through the Forest of Montargis (18km/11mi).
The town is a maze of narrow winding streets at the foot of the former Benedictine abbey, an important centre of Carolingian civilisation and monastic life in the Gâtinais.

Ancienne abbaye St-Pierre-et-St-Paul – *Leave your car on the shady esplanade.* The Gothic **church** stands out for its **transept crossing★** (12C), built as a rotunda on eight high columns. A 9C Carolingian edifice built here probably inspired this canopy style. Note the unusual liturgical accessory in the transept arm: a gilded palm leaf adorned with grapes used to exhibit the Holy Sacrament. The 13C chancel is illuminated by five Renaissance stained-glass windows. In the left transept arm is a collection of 14C and 17C statues. From the terrace below the courtyard of the old cloister there are **views** of the southern wall of the church and the chapel.

Château-Renard
17km/10.5mi SE on D 943.
This small town owes its name to a château built in the 10C on the hill overlooking the river Ouanne, and to Count Renard de Sens. It has kept some of its historic half-timbered houses with sculptured features (the finest dates from the 15C on place de la République). On the left bank of the Ouanne, the 17C Château de la Motte *(private)* stands in pretty grounds.
The **church** was erected on the site of the former chapel (11C and 12C) of the château. A fortified doorway between two towers leads to the structure, set among the ruins. A deep well stands in front of the bell-tower façade, which is crowned by a lantern. The nearby terrace, with a 12C oil mill, offers interesting **views** of the town below.
♟♙ Learn all about the fascinatng life of bees at the **Musée vivant de l'Apiculture**, towards Chuelles (D 37; ♿◷*afternoons Apr–Aug by appointment;* ⊕€6, *child 3–14,* €4; *02 38 95 35 56; www.museevivant.com).* Follow the discovery tour and then spot the queen bee in the glass-sided hives. Animated displays and videos show how life is organised inside the hive. The visit concludes with the extraction of the honey and a tasting session.

Jardins du Grand-Courtoiseau★★

18km/11mi E of Montargis, between Château-Renard and Triguères, on D 943. ♿*(in fine weather).* ◐*Mid-Apr–mid-Oct daily 2–6pm.* ✏️€10 *(children under 11, free).* 📞*06 80 24 10 83.*

Situated on the grounds of a former 13C fort, this estate had several owners over time. In the 17C, the small fort was converted to the manor house seen on the premises today.

The 6ha award-winning garden was designed by talented landscape architect Alain Richert. It combines an orchard, kitchen garden, flower garden, Italian garden, garden of exotics and antique garden, among others, around the stately manor house. Fountains, topiary hedges and footpaths grace the grounds.

ADDRESSES

🏨 STAY

📧🛏️ **Hôtel de France** – *54 Place de la Republique, 45200, Montargis.* 📞*02 38 99 09 09. www.leshotelsdorele.com. 19 rooms.* This is the slightly fancier sister hotel to the Hôtel de la Gare (see below). It's smaller, and situated inside a slightly nicer, older building, though the rooms and facilities are relatively bland and basic. It does the job for a clean, comfortable place to rest one's head in a central location, close to the lake.

📧🛏️ **Hôtel de la Gare** – *222 r. Émile-Mengin.* 📞*02 38 07 18 18. www.leshotels dorele.com. 52 rooms (5 rooms* ♿*).* In this modern building near the station, the rooms, although not spacious, are well soundproofed. Comfortable lounge.

📧🛏️ **Hôtel Ibis Montargis** – *2 pl. Victor-Hugo.* 📞*02 38 98 00 68. www.accorhotels. com. 59 rooms.* Rooms are modern and practical and up to the usual standard of this economy chain. The 3rd-floor rooms are ideal for families. Nice restaurant with a retro atmosphere and brasserie cuisine.

📧🛏️ **Hôtel Central** – *2 r. Gudin.* 📞*02 38 85 03 07. www.hotel-montargis.com. 12 rooms.* This hotel In the town centre is set in a former convent, fully restored. The rooms vary in size, but are simple and well kept.

📧🛏️ **Hôtel Le Belvédère** – *192 r. J.-Ferry, 45200 Amilly.* 📞*02 38 85 41 09. www.hotel-belvedere-amilly.com. 24 rooms. Closed 19 Dec–4 Jan.* This family hotel stands within a pleasant flower garden opposite the village school. The small guest rooms are quiet and comfortable and have character.

🍴 EAT

📧🛏️ **L'Orangerie** – *57 r. Jean-Jaurès, Montargis.* 📞*02 38 93 33 83. www.restaurant-orangerie-montargis.com. Closed Sun eve, Mon and Tue.* A memorable dining halt, in a most pleasant setting. Seasonally changing menus, according to availability of local produce. Good wine list.

📧🛏️ **La Gloire** – *74 avenue du Général de Gaulle, 45200 Montargis.* 📞*02 38 85 04 69. www.lagloire-montargis.com.* ♿. A taste of Michelin-starred dining from a chef who respects the traditional cuisine of the region while bringing subtlety and innovation to the table. Good regional wine list, including many wines by the glass.

📧🛏️ **Restaurant sur le Lac** – *Rue du Gué aux Biches Parc de Loisirs, 45120, Chalette-sur-Loing.* 📞*02 38 07 19 20. www. restaurantsurlelac.com.* This charming modern eatery is built overhanging the lake, with a very reasonably priced menu or French classics, and specials such as roast rack of lamb, cod, trout and veal brains, served in an airy and bright dining room by chatty staff. Good regional wines grace the list.

SHOPPING

Praslines Mazet – *pl. Mirabeau. www. mazetconfiseur.com. Open daily.* Famed for gourmet pralines, this confectionery was founded in 1903 and continues to purvey fine chocolates and other delights, such as hand-made candy, varieties of nuts wrapped in rich dark chocolate, and pastries baked fresh on the day. They have a factory and chocolate school, too, just a few streets away.

Châtillon-Coligny

Dotted with old wash-houses, an unusual church and a ruined château, this village hugs the banks of the river Loing and the Canal de Briare. It still bears the scars from the Wars of Religion as an important centre of Protestantism. It is the gateway to the southern reaches of the Gâtinais, a popular terrain for hunting and fishing.

▶ **Population:** 2,004.
Michelin Map: 318: O-5
Info: 2 pl. Coligny. ℘02 18 69 31 14 38. www.tourisme-gatinais-sud.com.
▶ **Location:** 22km/13.6mi SE of Montargis on D 93, and 31km/19.5mi NW of St-Fargeau.
Kids: The Henri Becquerel displays at the museum.
Timing: Allow time for a stroll on the banks of the Loing.

THE TOWN

Château
The marshal of Châtillon (Gaspard I de Coligny) built a luxurious home in the early 16C by the medieval castle and polygonal Romanesque keep (1180–90), an unusual edifice put up by the Count of Sancerre. The Revolution spared only the keep and the cellars. Three monumental terraces and a well attributed to sculptor Jean Goujon are all that remain from the fine Renaissance building. Below lies the **church** (16C and 17C).

Musée de Chatillon-Coligny
⏲Apr-4 Jul and Sep-15 Nov, Fri-Sun 2-5pm; 5 Jul-Aug, Thu-Mon 2-5pm. €4 (children under 12 free). ⏲1 Jan, 1 May, 25 Dec. ℘ 02 38 92 61 39. www.museeprotestant.org.
Set in the former Hôtel-Dieu (15C), the museum features portraits and documents relating to the Coligny and Montmorency families, successive owners of the estate, and the violent history of Protestantism in France. Note the jaw-dropping advert from 1905 vaunting the merits of radium as a cure for hair loss.

EXCURSIONS

Montbouy
6km/3.7mi NW on D 93.
The remains of a Gallo-Roman amphitheatre (1C) can be seen north of the village.

Cortrat
12km/7.5mi NW via Montbouy and Pressigny-les-Pins.
The small country **church** in this hamlet has an 11C **tympanum★** portraying people and animals of the Creation.

Arboretum national des Barres
8km/5mi NW.
⏲11 Apr-Nov 10am-6pm, Tue-Sun. €5 for a guided visit. ℘ 02 38 97 62 21. www.arboretumdesbarres.fr.
At the heart of a vast forest domain, the arboretum harbours 3,000 plant species set in 35ha.

Rogny-les-Sept-Écluses★
10km/6mi S.
Henri IV ordered construction of the Rogny locks in 1605 as part of a vast project to link the Mediterranean to the Atlantic and the English Channel. The canals were opened for navigation in 1642. Six other locks are now open for craft using the Canal de Briare.

La Bussière
10km/6mi NE on D 622.
This village is renowned for the **Château de la Bussière (also called "des Pêcheurs")** (May-Jun and Sept Wed-Mon 10am-12pm and 2-6pm; Apr and Oct, Wed-Mon 2-6pm; Jul-Aug daily 10am-6pm) €9.50, www.chateau-de-la-bussiere), a fortress rebuilt in the 17C on the banks of a pond. It houses a collection of art and artefacts related to fishing.

Lorris★

Lorris is located in the southernmost area of the former Gâtinais region. The small town is famous for the Freedom Charter, which was granted to it in 1122 by Louis VI.

A BIT OF HISTORY

The town was a hunting seat for the Capet kings and a place of residence for Blanche of Castille and her son Louis IX of France. It became the birthplace in 1215 of **Guillaume de Lorris**, who wrote the first part of the *Romance of the Rose (Roman de la Rose)*, a poem of courtly love that influenced Geoffrey Chaucer in his writings

SIGHTS

Église Notre-Dame★

An elegant Romanesque door leads into a well-lit Gothic nave, containing a **gallery** and the early-16C **organ loft★** (*see Architecture in Introduction*), both ornately carved. The late-15C **choir stalls★** are decorated with the Prophets and Sibyls on the cheekpieces and scenes from The Golden Legend, the New Testament and everyday life on the misericords.

A **museum** dedicated to the organ and old musical instruments in general is set up under the eaves.

Musée départemental de la Résistance et de la Déportation

Jun daily 2–6pm; Jul–Aug daily 10am–noon, 2–6pm; rest of year one weekend per month; see website or call for details. Christmas school holidays–3 Jan. €6. 02 38 94 84 19. www.museelorris.fr.

This museum is housed in the old train station. Its collections relate the history of the Second World War and its consequences in this region. The course of events, from the underlying causes of the war until the liberation of France, is illustrated with the aid of documents, dioramas (the exodus of refugees and a reconstruction of a camp of members of the Resistance movement in a forest).

▶ **Population:** 3,077.
Michelin Map: 318: M-4
Info: 1 r. des Halles, 45260 Lorris. 02 38 94 81 42. www.tourisme-lorris.fr.
Location: Lorris is midway between Montargis and Châteauneuf-sur-Loire.
Don't Miss: Resistance and Deportation Museum.
Timing: Allow around 2 hours to explore the town.

Musée Horloger Georges Lemoine

4 r. des Marchés (entry via the Tourist Office). Oct-Apr, Tue-Sat 9.30am-12.30pm and 1.30-5pm; May-Sept Tue-Sat 9.30am-12.30pm and 2-5pm. 02 38 94 85 75. www.musee-horloger-lorris.fr.

The museum displays the working environment of a rural clock and watch-maker in the 1930s–60s. The collection of tools and timepieces is Interesting.

EXCURSIONS

The **Canal d'Orléans**, which had its heyday in the 18C, was finally closed to traffic in 1954. It is currently being dredged and restored with the aim of having 78km/48mi navigable by 2020.

Grignon

5km/3mi W on D 44 then left at Le Coudroy on D 444.

This attractive hamlet has three canal locks. Cross **Vieilles-Maisons** (pretty church with half-timbered porch).

Étang des Bois

5km/3mi SW on D 88.

Oak, beech and chestnut trees stand on the banks of this small lake, which is popular in fine weather (fishing, swimming, and riding in pedal boats).

Briare

This quiet town on the banks of the Loire is the meeting point of two canals that connect the basins of the Seine and Loire. Completed in 1642, 38 years after its conception, the **Briare Canal** was the first canal in Europe to link different canal networks in this way. Along its 57km/36mi path, six locks move the waters from the Loire Lateral Canal to the Loing Canal.

SIGHTS
Pont-Canal★★
The 1890 bridge, inaugurated in 1896, no longer fills an economic role, but a stroll along the towpaths is pleasant.

Musée des Emaux et de la Mosaïque (MEMO)
&♿◷Dec-Feb, Sat-Sun and holidays 2-6pm, Mar, Nov and May-Sept 10am-6pm, Apr and Oct 10am-noon and 2-6pm. ⊛€6 or €10 including a pass to MENO and Musée des deux Marines. ℘02 38 31 20 51. www.emauxdebriare.com.
The museum presents local enamel crafts, the history of the inventor of the

first machine able to produce buttons in industrial quantities, late-19C mosaic work typical of the town, and works of Art Nouveau precursor Eugène Grasset.

Musée des Deux Marines et du Pont-Canal
◷Daily Jun–Sept 10am–12.30pm, 2–6.30pm; Mar–May and Oct–mid-Nov 2–6pm. ⊛€6 (child -7 free) and €10 for a ticket MEMO and Musée des deux Marines. ♿. ℘02 38 31 28 27. www.musee-2-marines.com.
Run by volunteers, this private museum is devoted to the history of two types of inland navigation: on canals, and on the Loire.

- ▶ **Population:** 5 924.
- ◉ **Michelin Map:** 318: N-6
- **Info:** 1 pl. Charles-de-Gaulle, 45250 Briare. ℘02 38 31 24 51. www.terresdeloireet canaux.com
- ▷ **Location:** 80km/50mi SW of Orléans, 10km/6mi SE of Gien by the D 952.

Gien★

Built on a hillside overlooking the north bank of the Loire, this small town with many pretty gardens, is well known for its glazed blue-and-yellow earthenware, or faïence, and for its splendid hunting museum housed in the castle, said to have been built by Charlemagne.

A BIT OF HISTORY
It was here, in 1410, that the Armagnac faction was set up in support of Charles d'Orléans against the Burgundians in the civil war, which led up to the last episode in the Hundred Years War.
The castle was later rebuilt by **Anne de Beaujeu** (1460–1522), the Countess of Gien, who was Louis XI's eldest daugh-

ter. Aged 23 when her father died, she was appointed regent during the minority of her brother Charles VIII (1483–91).

- ▶ **Population:** 15,300
- ◉ **Michelin Map:** 318: M-5
- **Info:** Pl. Jean-Jaurès, 45500 Gien. ℘02 38 67 25 28. www.gien-tourisme.fr.
- ▷ **Location:** 67km/42mi E of Orléans, 45km/28mi S of Montargis.
- **Don't Miss:** Le musée du Cirque et de l'Illusion.
- ◷ **Timing:** 2 hours for the town.

SIGHTS
Château-Musée de Gien★★

May–Sept 10am–6pm; Oct–Apr 1.30–5.30pm. &02 38 67 69 69. www.chateaumuseegien.fr.

Gien **château★** stands on the eastern fringe of Orléans forest and the Sologne, a region abounding in game, making it an ideal setting for a **Hunting Museum**.

The château, which dominates the town, was rebuilt shortly before 1500 with red brick and a slate roof. The decoration is restrained: a pattern of contrasting dark bricks and bands of white stone and a few stair turrets.

The rooms of the château with their beamed ceilings and fine chimney-pieces form an attractive backdrop to the exhibition of fine art inspired by hunting as well as weapons and accessories used in hunting since the prehistoric era. Particularly noteworthy is the collection of some 4,000 blazer buttons decorated with hunting motifs. There is also a collection of hunting horns as well as 500 antlers, given to the museum by the great hunter, Claude Hettier de Boislambert.

Musée de la Faïencerie

78 pl. de la Victoire (access via the quai Lenoir or la rue Paul-Bert).
Mon–Sat 10am–6pm Sun and public holidays. &02 38 05 21 05.

An old paste store has been converted into this **Faïence Museum**; some of the large pieces were made for the Universal Exhibition in 1900. There is also a display of the current production and a shop where factory pieces can be purchased at reduced prices.

EXCURSIONS
St-Brisson-sur-Loire

6km/3.7mi SE along D 951.

Here in the borderlands between Berry and the Orléans region stand the remains of a 12C hilltop **château** deprived of its original keep and crenellated south wall. The east wing and the staircase tower were restored in the 19C.

Dampierre-en-Burly

13km/8mi NW along D 952.

The flat-tiled roofs of Dampierre present an attractive spectacle to anyone approaching from the west on D 952 from Ouzouer-sur-Loire. As the road crosses the tree-lined lake by a causeway, the ruins of a château loom into sight. Beyond what remains of the towers and curtain wall of the castle rises the church tower. In the square by the church stands one of the château gatehouses, an elegant early-17C building, in brick and stone, decorated with bossed pilasters beneath a pyramidal roof.

Musée du Cirque et de l'Illusion

Outside Dampierre-en-Burly, on D 952, on the right. Jul–Aug 10am–6pm; Sept–Jun 10am–12.30pm, 1.30–6pm. Jan. €8 (child 4–13, €5.50). &02 38 35 67 50. www.museeducirqueetdelillusion.com.

Learn the surprising history of the circus and discover the tricks of master magicians. Interesting artefacts, models and displays are on hand to fascinate and intrigue visitors.

Centre Nucléaire de Production d'électricité CNPE

3km/S of Dampierre-en-Burly. Centrale nucléaire de Dampierre-en-Burly, BP 18, 45570 Ouzouer-sur-Loire. Free guided tours for groups only at 3pm Mon–Fri. Information centre open Mon–Fri and 1st Sat of month 2–5.30pm. Public holidays. Proof of identity must be shown. &02 38 29 70 04. www.edf.fr/groupe-edf.

Learn the workings of the Dampierre nuclear power station, which was commissioned in 1980. Its four cooling towers rise 165m above the banks of the Loire, and it houses four 900 MW pressurised water reactors.

The **Henri-Becquerel information centre** is named after the local scientist who helped to discover radioactivity. The family lived 30km/18.6mi from the site of the plant at Châtillon-Coligny.

Sully-sur-Loire★

The Château de Sully commanded one of the Loire crossings. Its history is dominated by four great names: Maurice de Sully, Bishop of Paris who commissioned the building of Notre-Dame; Joan of Arc; statesman duc de Sully and Voltaire. Today, an agreeable charm pervades the mellow stones of the castle reflecting in the still waters of the moat and bathed in the soft light of the Loire Valley.

▶ **Population:** 5,541.
⏱ **Michelin Map:** 318: L-5
▤ **Info:** pl. du Général-de-Gaulle, BP 12, 45600 Sully-sur-Loire. ℘02 38 36 23 70. www.sully-loire-sologne.fr.
▶ **Location:** On the left bank of the Loire at an important crossroads between Gien and Orléans.
▣ **Don't Miss:** International music festival in June.

A BIT OF HISTORY

In 1429, Sully belonged to Georges de la Trémoille, a favourite of Charles VII. The King was living in the castle when Joan of Arc defeated the English at Patay. Joan hastened to Sully and eventually persuaded the indolent monarch to be crowned at Reims. She returned to the castle in 1430, and there felt the jealousy of La Trémoille gaining influence over the King. She was detained, but escaped to continue the struggle. **Maximilien de Béthune**, the Lord of Rosny, bought the château in 1602. Henri IV made him Duc de Sully. Sully had begun to serve his King at age 12. He was a great soldier, the best artilleryman of his time and a consummate administrator. A glutton for work, Sully rose at 3am and kept four secretaries busy writing his memoirs.

CHÂTEAU★

⏱ Jul–Aug 10am–6pm; Apr–Jun and Sept Tue–Sun 10am–6pm; Feb–Mar and Oct–Dec Tue–Sun 10am–noon, 2–5pm. €8. ℘02 38 36 36 86. www.chateausully.fr.

This imposing feudal fortress dates largely from before 1360. The keep was built (late 14C) by Guy de la Trémoille. The huge main hall was the part of the seigneurial residence used during the Middle Ages for dispensing justice and holding feasts. An iron door concealed in the panelling leads to the old exercise room from which the guards operated the drawbridge and the trapdoor. Now called the **oratory**, this room was also the Duke's treasury in the 17C.

The upper half of the keep has a fine **timber roof**, surviving from the 14C. The **petit château** houses the Duke's apartments, notably his bedchamber and its coffered ceiling adorned with mottoes and motifs related to his title of Grand Master of the Artillery.

ADDRESSES

🛏 STAY

🍽 **Hostellerie du Château –** 4 r.de Paris, 45600 St-Père-sur-Loire. ℘02 38 36 24 44. www.hostellerie-du-chateau.fr. ♿ ℙ. 42 rooms. On the river-bank opposite the town, this modern hotel has pleasant, well-maintained rooms. Restaurant and brasserie (🍽🍽).

🍽🍽 **La Closeraie –** 14 r. Porte-Berry. ℘02 38 05 10 90. www.hotel-la-closeraie.com. 11 rooms. Play the piano or relax in the library. Simple, tastefully decorated rooms. Dining room.

🍴 EAT

🍽 **Auberge du Faisan Doré –** 5 rte de Sully, 45600 St-Florent, 10km/6mi SE on D 951 then D 63. ℘02 38 36 93 83. The food based on fresh produce is popular with regulars at this charming auberge.

🍽🍽 **La Bonne Etoile –** 1 rue de la Poste, 45460 Les Bordes, 6km/3.5mi NE on D 948 then D 961. ℘02 38 35 52 15. www.restaurant-labonneetoile.fr. Closed Sun eve, and Mon. Traditional cuisine with fresh market produce, near Orléans forest.

St-Benoît-sur-Loire★

The basilica of St-Benoît-sur-Loire is one of the most famous Romanesque buildings in France. Visitors are enthralled by its harmonious proportions and its elaborate carvings steeped in golden light.

A BIT OF HISTORY

Foundation (7C) – According to Celtic tradition, St-Benoît-sur-Loire was the place local Carnute druids assembled. In 645 or 651 Benedictine monks led by an abbot from Orléans came to this spot and founded a monastery. Around 672 the **Abbot of Fleury** ordered that the body of **St Benedict**, the father of western monasticism who died in 547, be transported from the burial site in Italy to the banks of the Loire, where it attracted great crowds.

Theodulf, **Odo**, **Abbo and Gauzlin** – Charlemagne gave Fleury abbey to his adviser and friend, **Theodulf** (&see box), the Bishop of Orléans, who founded two monastic schools. In 930, **Odo**, a monk from Touraine, became abbot of Cluny; he reopened the abbey school, to which students flocked; the French king extended patronage.

The late 10C was dominated by **Abbo**, a scholar and teacher who entered Fleury as a child, studied in Paris and Reims and returned c. 975 to Fleury as Head of Studies. He added to the **library** and enlarged the area of study. During his tenure as abbot (from 988), the abbey was at the forefront of western intellectual life. Abbo commissioned a monk called Aimoin to write a History of the Franks, which became the official chronicle expounding the ideology of the Capet monarchy. In 1004 Abbo was assassinated.

The reign of Abbot **Gauzlin**, the future Archbishop of Bourges, early in the 11C is marked by the production of the so-called Gaignières **Evangelistary**, an illuminated manuscript – gold and silver lettering on purple parchment – the work of a Lombard painter, and by the construction of the porch belfry.

▶ **Population:** 2,094.
🕭 **Michelin Map:** 318: K-5
🅱 **Info:** 55 r. Orléanaise, 45730 St-Benoît-sur-Loire. ℘02 38 35 79 00. www.tourisme-valdesully.fr.
🅾 **Location:** At the intersection of the meridian of Paris and the Loire, between Gien and Orléans; access St-Benoît by taking D 60, which hugs the curve of the river.
🕓 **Timing:** Spend half a day at St-Benoît, allowing 45min for the basilica.

The present church was built between 1067 and 1108; the nave was not completed until the end of the 12C.

Middle Ages to the present – In the 15C St-Benoît passed *in commendam*, meaning the revenues of the abbey were granted by the monarch to commendatory abbots, often laymen, who were simply beneficiaries and took no active part in the religious life of the community. The monks did not always make such abbots welcome. Under François I they refused to receive Cardinal Duprat and shut themselves up in the tower of the porch. The King came with an armed force to make them submit. During the Wars of Religion (1562–98) one of these abbots, Odet de Châtillon-Coligny, the brother of the Protestant leader Admiral Coligny, was himself converted to Protestantism. In 1562, St-Benoît was looted by Condé's Huguenot troops. The treasure was melted down, the library was sold and its precious manuscripts are now to be found in Berne, Rome, Leyden, Oxford and Moscow.

The celebrated Congregation of St-Maur, introduced to St-Benoît in 1627 by Cardinal de Richelieu, restored its spiritual and intellectual life.

During the Revolution, the abbey was closed, its archives transferred to Orlé-

Theodulf, a dignitary at Charlemagne's court

Theodulf was a Goth, probably originally from Spain or the Ancient Roman province of Gallia Narbonensis (modern southwest France). This brilliant theologian, scholar and poet, well-versed in the culture of Classical Antiquity, came to Neustria after 782 and joined Charlemagne's erudite circle. After a long time spent journeying round the south of France as the emperor's *missus dominicus,* he was made Bishop of Orléans, then Abbot of Micy and of St-Benoît-sur-Loire.

Theodulf had a villa not far from Fleury; all that now remains is the oratory, or church of Germigny-des-Prés (&see Excursion). The villa was sumptuously decorated, with murals depicting the Earth and the World, marble floors and superb mosaics in the oratory that date from about 806. On Charlemagne's death, Theodulf fell into disgrace, accused of plotting against Louis the Pious. He was deposed in 818, exiled and finally died in an Angers prison in 821.

ans. In the First Empire the monastic buildings were destroyed and the church fell into disrepair. In 1835 it was registered as a historical monument, and restored from 1836 to 1923. Monastic life was revived in 1944.

BASILICA★★

⏱ *Daily 6.30am–10pm.* ✎ *Guided tours Mar–Oct Sun and public holidays 3.15pm.* ☎ *01 80 52 33 55. www.abbaye-fleury.com.*

This imposing basilica was built between 1067 and 1218. The towers were originally much taller.

Belfry-porch★★

A fine example of Romanesque art, the belfry originally stood by itself. Look closely at the richly decorated Corinthian capitals with their abaci and corbels carved in golden stone from the Nevers region. Stylised plants and acanthus leaves alternate with fantastic animals, scenes from the Apocalypse, and events in the Life of Christ and the Virgin Mary.

Nave

This was rebuilt in the early-Gothic style during the 12C. It is suffused with light thanks to its white stonework and high vaulting. The organ was added c. 1700.

Transept

Completed in 1108; the dome carries the central bell-tower. Under the dome are the stalls dated 1413 and the remains

of a choir screen in carved wood presented in 1635 by Richelieu, when he was Commendatory Abbot of St-Benoît. In the north transept is the 14C alabaster statue of Notre-Dame-de-Fleury.

Chancel★★

The long Romanesque chancel was built between 1065 and 1108; note the décor of blind arcades with sculpted capitals forming a triforium. The ambulatory with radiating chapels is typical of a church built for crowds and processions. The floor is paved with a Roman mosaic transported from Italy in 1531 by Cardinal

Stalls, Basilica of St-Benoît-sur-Loire

© Franck Guiziou/hemis.fr

Duprat; it is similar to the style popular in the eastern part of the Roman Empire.

Crypt★

This masterpiece of the late 11C has kept its original appearance. Large round columns form a double ambulatory with radiating chapels round the large central pillar. The crypt contains the modern shrine of St Benedict, whose remains have been venerated here since the 8C.

EXCURSION
Oratoire Carolingien de Germigny-des-Prés★
5.5km/3mi NW.

The little church in Germigny is a rare example of Carolingian art; it is one of the oldest in France and can be compared with the Carolingian octagon in the cathedral at Aachen, Germany. The original church, with a ground plan in the form of a Greek cross reminiscent of Echmiadzin Cathedral in Armenia, among other places, had four very similar apses.

ADDRESSES

🏠 STAY

🛏️ **Chambre et Table d'hôte Cervina** – *28 rte. de Châteauneuf, 45110 Germigny-des-Prés. ℘02 38 58 21 15. www.kopp.fr. 5 rooms.* 🅿️. Dine with the host family *(in winter)* in this 19C house. Kitchen for guests' use.

🛏️ **Chambre d'hôte Ferme de la Borde** – *6-8 chemin de la Borde. ℘02 38 35 70 53. www.fermedelaborde.com. 5 rooms.* ♿🅿️. Eat at the host's table at this working farm. Nice rooms.

🛏️ **Hôtel du Labrador** – *7 pl. de l'Abbaye. ℘02 38 35 74 38. www.hotel-du-labrador.com. Closed early Jan. 24 rooms.* 🅿️. The hotel comprises several buildings facing the basilica, a tea room, renovated rooms and a garden.

🍴 EAT

🍽️ **Le Grand St-Benoît** – *7 pl. St-André. ℘02 38 35 11 92. www.restaurant-grand-saint-benoit.com. Closed Sun eve, Mon except holidays.* Enjoy this beamed dining room and terrace situated in the village centre.

Châteauneuf-sur-Loire

The town owes its name to the former fortified castle in which Charles IV, the Fair, died in 1328. On its site a small-scale imitation of the château of Versailles was erected. Only the 17C rotunda and gallery, the outbuildings and the pavilions in the forecourt, some of which are used as the town hall, remain today.

A BIT OF HISTORY

Louis Phelypeaux de la Vrillière, Secretary of State to Louis XIV, built a smaller version of Versailles palace here. After the Revolution the château was sold to an architect from Orléans who had it demolished.

Today a pleasant promenade begins from the former château's park and extends along the river to the charming **Canal of Orléans**. Built between 1677 and 1692, the canal (the Loire Reach sec-

▶ **Population:** 8,018.
🎬 **Michelin Map:** 318: K-4
ℹ️ **Info:** 3 pl. Aristide-Briand, 45110 Châteauneuf-sur-Loire. ℘02 38 58 44 79. www.valdeloire-foretdorleans.com.
📍 **Location:** 25km/15.5mi E of Orléans.
🕐 **Timing:** Allow 1–2 hours to explore the town.
👪 **Kids:** Étang de la Vallée, W of Combreaux.

tion) was the scene of intense shipping activity, mainly the transport of timber and coal, for 250 years. A portion of the canal remains open today to navigation.

VISIT

Château grounds

The park is bordered by a moat; the western section is filled with water and spanned by a stone footbridge.

Musée de la Marine de Loire

1 pl. Aristide-Briand. ○Apr-Oct 10am-6pm (closed 1-2pm on weekends) Nov-Mar 2-6pm. ○1 Jan, 1 May, 25 Dec. ☞€5. ♿☏02 38 46 84 46. www.musee-marinedeloire.fr.
The museum has collections that testify to the importance of the Loire over the ages, including carpentry tools, garments, jewellery and faïence.

🚗 DRIVING TOUR

64km/40mi round trip. Allow 3h.

Pays de la Forêt d'Orléans

The Forest of Orléans is the largest national forest in France, stretching over 60km/37mi between Gien and Orléans.

▶ Leave Châteauneuf to the NE on D 10. In Vitry-aux-Loges, take D 9 to Combreux.

Combreux

13km/8mi NE along D 10 and D 9.
The town clusters on the south bank of the Orléans Canal. On the north side of the town and the canal stands an eye-catching **château** (19C).

♟ Étang de la Vallée★

2km/1mi W of Combreux.
The reservoir feeding the Orléans Canal is on the eastern fringe of Orléans forest in a wild setting where there are facilities for water sports and picnics.

Arboretum des Grandes Bruyères★

○21 Mar-1 Nov, Mon-Sat 10am-noon and 2-6pm; Sun and public holidays 10am-6pm (ring the bell at the entrance). ○Apr 12 ☞€10 (child 6–12, €5). ☏ 02 38 57 28 24. www. arboretumdesgrandesbruyeres.fr.
This 5ha park was laid out in 1972 with plants from different climates in the northern and southern hemispheres. To preserve the ecosystem, no herbicides, fertilisers or chemicals are used in the maintenance of the species on display. Dogwood, magnolias, old roses and heather form the core of the four main collections. After the French-style garden, visitors enter the informal English park with its grass paths winding between copses, a lake, a maze, a rose garden and an organic vegetable garden.

▶ Take D 921 S to Fay-aux-Loges.

Faye-aux-Loges

9km/5.5mi NW on D 11.
This village on the banks of the canal has a stoutly built 11C–13C **church** *aux lignes dépouillées* (bare in style). Behind it, the presbytery occupies a fortified house.

Chécy

15km/9mi W along N 960.
The church of St-Pierre-St-Germain, with its 12C belfry-porch, offered hospitality to Joan of Arc on the eve of the Orléans siege. Behind it, the small **Musée de la Tonnellerie** (○*open Jul–Oct Thu–Sat 2–5.30pm; ☏02 38 86 95 93; www. checy.fr)* and a restored farmhouse evoke bygone days when local people were wine-growers.

ADDRESSES

🛏 STAY

☞☞ **Chambre d'hôte Les Saules** – *18 r. des Jardins-du-Coulouis, 45460 Bray-en-Val. ☏02 38 29 08 90. Closed 15 days in Mar and 15 days in Oct.* 🅿 ⚞. *4 rooms.* This converted former cottage is set in 3ha of grounds. Billiards, a piano and library are at guests' disposal. Breakfast is quite consistent.

☞☞☞ **Chambre d'hôte La Ferme du Grand Chesnoy** – *Lieu-dit Grand-Chesnoy, 45260 Chailly-en-Gâtinais. ☏02 38 96 27 67. Closed Dec–Mar.* 🅿 ⚞. *4 rooms.* The rooms are set in a tower dating from 1896 and are decorated in a rustic style. Kitchen and dining room are available.

Lying between the Sologne and the Touraine, the Loire Blésoise is home to some of the region's most spectacular châteaux, all located within a relatively small area around the main town of Blois. Perched high in the town centre, Blois' château gives an insight into 15C to 17C French history, and is complemented by the palatial contours of the nearby Château de Chambord, the largest and most impressive of the Loire's royal residences.

Highlights

Courtly Life

Standing on the northern bank of the Loire, the Château de Blois impresses with its unique combination of medieval, Renaissance and Classical architecture. Although surrounded by a busy modern town, it gives a glimpse of courtly life through the ages. By contrast, Chambord rises seemingly from nowhere in the midst of the nearby forest, a symbol of François I's taste for

splendour echoed only in the following century by Louis XIV's grandiose dreams for Versailles. The Forest of Russy, south of Blois, and the Chambord estate offer opportunities for walking, cycling and other outdoor pursuits. Travelling downriver from Orléans, Meung-sur-Loire and Beaugency are delightful stopovers with their attractive old towns and historic civic buildings, while the Château de Talcy, inland north of the Loire, is a delightful Renaissance manor house.

Portraits and Tintin

The Château de Beauregard, south of Blois on the edge of the Forest of Russy, is unique for its fascinating portrait gallery that features more than 300 historical figures of all the kings of France from 1328 to 1643 along with their queens, courtiers and foreign contemporaries, including Elizabeth I. The spacious park and curious Jardin des Portraits in the kitchen garden are also not to be missed. Cheverny, a gem of 17C Classical architecture, will be familiar to admirers of Tintin as the inspiration for Marlinspike Hall (Château de Moulinsart in the original French) in the *Adventures of Tintin* series.

Galerie des Illustres, Château de Beauregard

© Parc & Château de Beauregard

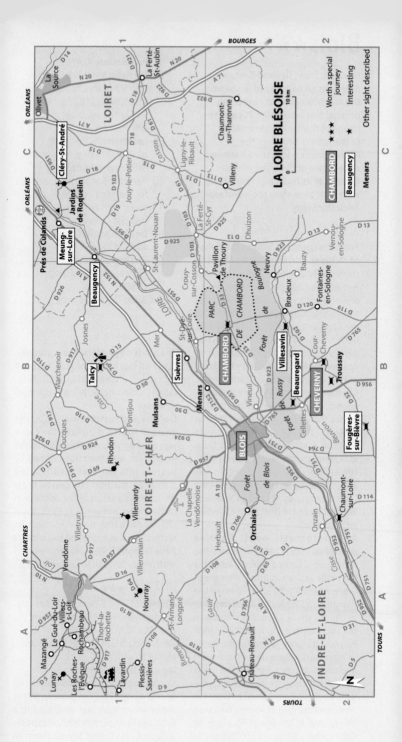

LA LOIRE BLÉSOISE

CHAMBORD ★★★
Beaugency ★★
Menars ★

★★★ Worth a special journey
★★ Interesting
★ Other sight described

0 ————— 10 km

Blois★★★

Louis XII, François I and Gaston d'Orléans all had a hand in shaping the magnificent royal castle (the original was built in the 9C) into the image of their era. The terracing of the houses produces the characteristic tricoloured harmony of the town of Blois, the white façades of its buildings contrasting with their blue-slate roofs and red-brick chimneys.

A BIT OF HISTORY

From the counts of Blois to the dukes of Orléans – In the Middle Ages the counts of Blois were powerful lords with two estates: Champagne and the region of Blois and Chartres. One of the counts of Blois married the daughter of William the Conqueror and their son, Stephen, became King of England in 1135. In this period the House of Blois reached its peak under Thibaud IV. After his death in 1152, attention was concentrated on Champagne, and the Loire area was abandoned together with England, where the Plantagenets took over in 1154. In 1392 the last count, Guy de Châtillon, sold the county to Louis, Duke of Orléans and brother of Charles VI. Fifteen years later Louis d'Orléans was assassinated in Paris on the orders of the Duke of Burgundy. His widow, Valentina Visconti, retired to Blois, where she died inconsolable.

An aristocratic poet: Charles d'Orléans (1391–1465) – Charles, the eldest son of Louis d'Orléans, inherited the castle and spent some of his youth there. At the age of 15 he married the daughter of Charles VI, who later died in childbirth. At 20 he married again but soon departed to fight the English. He proved a poor general at the Battle of Agincourt, where he was wounded and taken prisoner, but his poetic gift helped him to survive 25 years of captivity in England. He returned to France in 1440, and being once more a widower, he married, at the age of 50, Marie de Clèves, who was then 14. The Château de Blois was his favourite residence.

> **Population:** 47,486.
> **Michelin Map:** 318: E-F 6
> **Info**: 23 pl. du Château, 41043 Blois. ✆02 54 90 41 41. www.blois chambord.com.
> **Location:** On the north bank of the Loire, between Orléans and Tours.
> **Parking:** See the map for the town's parking areas; two are fairly near the château.
> **Don't Miss:** The château, and Old Blois.
> **Timing:** 2 hours to visit the château, plus 2 hours for Old Blois.
> **Kids:** The magic museum.

The golden age of the Renaissance – **Louis XII** was born at Blois in 1462 and succeeded Charles VIII in 1498. Blois, rather than Amboise, became the royal residence.

Decline and restoration – After the death of Gaston d'Orléans, the castle was abandoned, wrecked during the Revolution, and then transformed by decrees into barracks, which saved it from destruction but caused great damage. As a result of the outrage of many writers and artists in 1840, it was classified as a Historical Monument. Its restoration was entrusted to architect **Félix Duban** (1798-1870), who worked with great attention to historical detail.

CHÂTEAU★★★

Daily Jul–Aug 9.15am–7pm; Apr–Jun and Sep–early Nov 9.15am–6.30pm; Nov–Mar 10.15am–5pm. 1 Jan, 25 Dec (doors close at 4pm 24 and 31 Dec). €10.50. ✆02 54 90 33 33. www.chateaudeblois.fr.

Containing more than 560 rooms and 35,000 works of art, the château, where many an intrigue was plotted and a famous crime perpetrated, illustrates a Flamboyant Gothic style influenced by the fantasy and inventiveness of the

The Duke of Guise's Assassination

The historical interest of the château reached its peak under King **Henri III**. In 1588 **Henri de Guise**, the Lieutenant-General of the kingdom and all-powerful head of the League in Paris, supported by the King of Spain, forced Henri III to call a second meeting of the States-General, which was then the equivalent of Parliament. Five hundred deputies, nearly all supporters of the Duke of Guise, attended. Guise expected them to depose the King. The latter, feeling himself to be on the brink of the abyss, could think of no other means than murder to get rid of his rival.

It is the morning of 23 December 1588. Of the 45 impoverished noblemen who are Henri III's men of action, 20 have been chosen to deal with the Duke. Eight are waiting in the Chambre du Roi (King's Chamber), with daggers hidden under their cloaks, sitting on chests and seeming innocently to be swapping yarns. The 12 others, armed with swords, are in the Cabinet Vieux (Old Cabinet). Two priests are in the oratory of the Cabinet Neuf (New Cabinet), where the King is making them pray for the success of his enterprise.

The Duke of Guise is in the Salle du Conseil (Council Chamber) with various dignitaries. Henri III's secretary tells Guise that the King would like to see him in the Old Cabinet. To reach this room Guise has to go through the King's chamber as, only two days previously, the door between the council chamber and the old cabinet had been walled up. The Duke enters the King's chamber and is greeted by the men there as if nothing were amiss. He turns left towards the old cabinet but, as he opens the door leading into the corridor outside it, he sees men waiting for him with swords drawn in the narrow passage. He tries to retreat but is stopped by eight men, who are now clearly assassins, in the King's chamber. They fall upon their victim, seizing him firmly by his arms and legs and trapping his sword in his cloak. The Duke, who is an exceptionally strong man, manages to strike down four of his assailants and wound a fifth with his comfit box. He gives his murderers a run for their money for the entire length of the King's chamber, but with the odds so heavily stacked against him, his valiant efforts are in vain. He finally collapses, riddled with stab wounds, by the King's bed.

Henri III emerges from behind the wall hanging where he has been hiding and ventures up to the corpse of his rival. According to some accounts, he slapped his face, marvelling at the dead man's size and commenting that he seemed almost bigger now than he did when alive.

Afterwards, Henri III is reported to have gone down to his mother, Catherine de' Medici, and told her joyfully, "My comrade is no more, the King of Paris is dead!" His conscience apparently clear, Henri goes to hear Mass in the chapel of St-Calais as an act of thanksgiving.

The next day, the Duke of Guise's brother, the Cardinal de Lorraine, imprisoned immediately after the murder, was also assassinated. His body was placed with the body of Guise somewhere in the château; speculation surrounds the precise location of the room where the bodies were kept. Finally, they were burned and the ashes thrown into the Loire river.

Eight months later Henri III himself succumbed to the dagger of Jacques Clément.

Outdoor staircase, Aile François-I, Château de Blois

Italian Renaissance. The four wings of the successive buildings that make up the castle form a remarkable example of the evolution of 15C–17C French architecture. There's also a sound and light show, every night from April to September, see page 136.

Place du Château

This vast esplanade was once the farmyard of the castle. Slightly below, the terraced gardens offer a wide **view** of the bridge spanning the Loire beyond the rooftops and place Louis XII at the foot of the retaining wall; the spires of the church of St-Nicolas *(right)* and the cathedral with its Renaissance tower.

The **façade** on the esplanade has two main parts: the pointed gable of the Salle des États-Généraux, relic of the former feudal castle (13C), on the right and then the brick and stone structure erected by Louis XII. In keeping with the whimsy that characterises buildings from the Middle Ages, this one has a random, asymmetrical arrangement of window openings.

The great Flamboyant **gateway** is surmounted by an alcove containing an **equestrian statue★** of Louis XII, a modern copy (made in 1857 by Seurre) of the original. The window consoles are adorned with spirited carvings. The coarse humour of the period is some-times displayed with great candour (1st and 4th windows left of the gateway).

Inner Courtyard

Cross the courtyard to reach the delightful terrace (affording a good **view** of the church of St-Nicolas and the Loire), on which stands the 13C **Tour du Foix**, a tower that formed part of the medieval fortified wall.

Chapelle St-Calais

This was the private chapel of the king, rebuilt by Louis XII on the site of an older version; only the Gothic choir remains.

Galerie Charles-d'Orléans

Although named after Charles d'Orléans, this gallery probably dates from the Louis XII period. Until alterations were made in the 19C, the gallery was twice its present length and connected the two wings at either end of the courtyard. Note the unusual basket-handle arches.

Aile Louis-XII

The corridor or gallery serving the various rooms in the wing marks a step forward in the quest for greater comfort and convenience. Originally rooms opened into one another. At each end of the wing, a spiral staircase gave access to the different floors. The decoration is richer and Italianate panels of arabesques adorn the pillars.

Aile François-I

The building extends between the 17C Gaston-d'Orléans wing and the 13C Salle des États-Généraux. Only 14 years passed between work finishing on the Louis-XII wing and beginning on the François I wing, but in this time an important milestone had been passed, heralding the triumphant arrival of the Italian decorative style.

French originality persisted in the general composition. The windows were made to echo the internal arrangement of the rooms, without regard for symmetry; they could be close together in some places and far apart in others; their mullions might be double or single; and pilasters might flank the window openings or occupy the middle of the opening.

A magnificent **staircase★★** was added to the façade. Since Mansart demolished part of the wing to make room for the Gaston d'Orléans buildings, the staircase is no longer in the centre of the façade. It climbs spirally in an octagonal well, three faces of which are recessed into the building.

Salle des États-Généraux

The Chamber of the States-General is the oldest (13C) part of the château, the feudal hall of the old castle of the counts of Blois. From 1576 to 1588 the States-General, the French Parliament, convened in this hall. The twin barrel vaults are supported by a central row of columns.

Royal Apartments and Museums

Inside the Gaston-d'Orléans wing, a projecting gallery runs round the base of the cupola crowning the grand staircase, sumptuously decorated on all but the lower level with trophies, garlands and masks. Many plans displayed on the ground floor illustrate the various alterations of the château.

Apartments in the François-I Wing

The François-I staircase leads up to the Royal apartments on the **first floor,** where a succession of rooms containing fireplaces, tapestries, busts, portraits and furniture can be seen. The interior decoration was restored by Felix Duban aound 1861.

The most interesting room on the first floor is the **apartment of Catherine de' Medici★**. It still has its 237 carved wood panels concealing secret cupboards that may have been used to hide poisons, jewels or State papers, or may simply have been made to cater for the then prevalent taste for having wall cupboards in Italian-style rooms. They were opened by pressing a pedal concealed in the skirting board.

The **second floor** was the scene of the **murder of the Duke of Guise** (&see box p119). The rooms have been altered and the old cabinet demolished to make way for the Gaston-d'Orléans wing. It is therefore rather difficult to follow the phases of the assassination.

▷ Redescend to the first floor by the grand staircase.

Aile Gaston-d'Orléans

The unfinished work is a fine example of the Classical style. Carried out 1635-38 by François Mansart for Duke Gaston of Orleans, brother of Louis XIII, it contrasts with the rest of the building. To be fairly judged, it must be seen from outside.

Musée des Beaux-Arts★

Same hours as château.

The main interest of this Fine Arts Museum lies in the 16C and 17C paintings and portraits. The **portrait gallery** contains paintings from the Château de St-Germain-Beaupré (Creuse département) and Château de Beauregard, and an outstanding collection of 50 terracotta **medallions** by Jean-Baptiste Nini. The Guise Gallery houses several works on the theme of the events of 1588, such as *Meeting of the Duke of Guise* and *Henri III* by Pierre-Charles Comte. The wrought-iron and locksmithing gallery displays the Frank collection, which

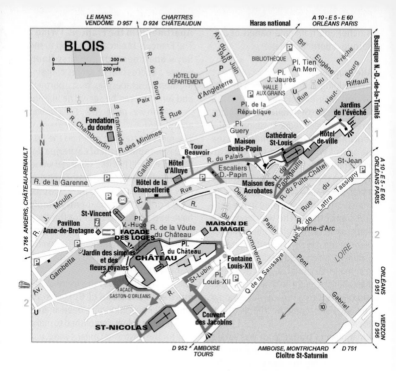

includes the fire-pan destined for the Count of Chambord, executed by local ironsmith Louis Delcros.

WALKING TOUR

OLD BLOIS★

Follow route on map. Allow at least 2h.
Every street corner of this fascinating town has something to offer the visitor prepared to stroll in the old districts.

Pavillon Anne-de-Bretagne

This graceful little building of stone and brick, crowned by a high slate roof, once the belvedere of the Royal Gardens, is now the **tourist office**. Note the cable mouldings that emphasise the corners, and the open-work sculptured stone balustrade with the initials of Louis XII and Anne of Brittany, his wife.
On the right along avenue Jean-Laigret, the pavilion extends into a long half-timbered wing, also built under Louis XII, which was later used as an **orangery** (*now a restaurant*).

Walk along place Victor-Hugo, which is lined on the north by the 17C **church of St-Vincent** built in the style known as Jesuit, and on the south by the beautiful **Façade des Loges** of the château.

Jardin des Simples et des Fleurs Royales

This small terraced garden is all that remains of the vast château gardens. From near the balustrade, a fine **view★** unfolds (*left*) over the Pavillon Anne-de-Bretagne, the church of St-Vincent and place Victor-Hugo; on the right rises the Façade des Loges (François-I wing of the château) and the end pavilion of the Gaston-d'Orléans wing. Down below, a modern garden (1992) is a delightful tribute to Renaissance gardens.

Façade des Loges★

The interior part of François I's initial construction backed on to the medieval rampart wall and had no outside view. This troubled the King, so he added a second building with many openings against the outside of the ramparts. Following the King's wish to copy the most recent Roman buildings, the architect drew inspiration from the Vatican palace; however, the addition of bartizans adds a somewhat medieval note to the overall effect. The top storey is underlined by fine gargoyles.

Église St-Nicolas★

This fine 12C and 13C church formed part of the Benedictine abbey of St-Laumer whose monastic buildings stretch down to the river bank. It features a vast chancel and ambulatory with aspidial chapels and delicately sculpted capitals. In the left of the chancel is a retable dedictaed to St Mary of Egypt.

Couvent des Jacobins
r. Anne-de-Bretagne.

As early back as the 15C–16C, these convent buildings already housed the **Muséum Diocésain Art Religieux** *(first floor; &, ∞free; ℘02 54 78 17 14)* devoted to religious art collections on the first floor and on the second floor, beneath a timber roof shaped as an inverted hull, the **Muséum d'Histoire naturelle** 👥 *(&, ○Wed and Sat 10am–noon, 2–6pm, Sun 2pm–6pm; during school holidays, also open Tue; ○1 Jan, 1 May, 1 Nov, 25 Dec; ∞€5, under 12 years free; ℘02 54 90 21 00; www.blois.fr)*, where mounted animals vividly portray the wildlife of the region.

Fontaine Louis XII

This Flamboyant Gothic fountain is a copy of the monument erected during the reign of Louis XII. The weather-worn original is kept in the Château.

👥 Maison de la magie Robert-Houdin★

&○*Early Apr–Aug and mid-Oct–1 Nov daily 10am–12.30pm, 2–6.30pm; 1–mid-Sept and 21-30 Dec (except 25), Mon–Fri 2–6.30pm, Sat–Sun 10am–12.30pm, 2–6.30pm. ∞€11 (child 6–17, €6.50). ℘02 54 90 33 33. www. maisondelamagie.fr.*

Dedicated to the great **Robert-Houdin**, the museum is set up in a 19C *hôtel particulier*, an attractive mansion made with tufa and painted bricks facing the châ-

☺ **A Bit of Advice** ☺

Guided **Heritage Tours** of the town can be reserved at the tourist office *(℘02 54 90 41 41; www. bloischambord.com)* or at the château *(℘02 54 90 33 33; www. chateaudeblois.fr)*. An audioguide is available in 4 languages. Trails are marked with bronze nails in 5 languages.

teau. It focuses on the history of magic, and serves as a national centre for the art of illusionism *(open to professional conjurers and researchers only)*.

The journey of discovery depicts the history of conjuring, illustrating the chronological developments in this fascinating world. Walk through a giant kaleidoscope and a room of optical illusions and Georges Méliès space, who paved the way for special effects in the film industry.

The **Cabinet fantastique Robert-Houdin** *(second floor)* displays exhibits relating to the world of magic.

On the top floor the **Hallucinoscope** presents "The Secret Garden of Robert Houdin", a dream world in which visitors might experience a dizzying floating sensation *(hand rails provided)*.

The **Théâtre des Magiciens★** (340 seats set up under the château esplanade) has been especially designed for high-class conjuring acts and offers a 20min show of dazzling expertise, performed by some of the world's leading illusionists.

Hôtel de la Chancellerie

At the corner of rue Chemonton and rue du Lion, this late-16C mansion is one of the largest in Blois. In the courtyard notice the superb staircase.

Hôtel d'Alluye
8 r. St-Honoré.

This fine private mansion was built in 1508 for **Florimond Robertet**, treasurer successively to Charles VIII, Louis XII and François I. When accompanying Charles VIII on his expedition to Naples, the financier took a liking to Italian art.

Behind the façade of the mansion with its delicate Gothic Renaissance sculptures, a large courtyard opens up with Renaissance Italianate **galleries★**.

Tour Beauvoir

🕐*Group visits only.*

This square keep (11C) belonged to a separate fief from the château and was later incorporated into the town's fortifications. The cells were used until 1945. From the terrace there is a fine **view★** of Blois and the surrounding area.

Old half-timbered façades line rue Beauvoir (Nos. 3, 15 and 21), surrounding a 15C stone house (No. 19).

Escalier Denis-Papin – This steep staircase offers fine views to the south. At the top stands a statue of **Denis Papin** (1647–1712) recognised (posthumously) as the father of the steam engine.

Maison des Acrobates

3 pl. St-Louis.

This is a typical medieval house, with its half-timbered façade, two corbelled storeys, posts carved with acrobats and jugglers, and foliage ornamentation.

Cathédrale St-Louis

The cathedral was almost entirely destroyed by a storm in 1678. It was rebuilt in the Gothic style and features contemporary stained-glass windows in the nave that contrast with the highly decorative 19C windows in the chancel. Evoking a Carolingian church, the vast 10C **St-Solenne crypt** *(access to the right of the choir)*, enlarged in the 11C, now houses the tombs of the bishops of Blois.

Hôtel de Ville and Jardins de l'Évêché

Access through the gate to the left of the cathedral.

Situated behind the cathedral, the town hall lies in the former bishop's palace, built in the early 18C by the father of the architect of place de la Concorde in Paris. Farther east, the gardens of the bishop's palace form a terrace overlooking the Loire, with a lovely **view★** *(🅟 stand near the statue of Joan of Arc)* over the river, its wooded slopes and the roofs of the

town; to the south is the pinnacle of the church of St-Saturnin and on the north bank, the pure spires of the church of St-Nicolas.

Hôtel de Villebresme (maison Denis-Papin) is a Gothic house perched at the top of rue Pierre-de-Blois; **Rue des Papegaults** features attractive Renassiance houses at nos.15, 13, 10, 8 and 4; while no. 7 **Rue du Puits-Châtel** is worth seeing for its Renaissance arcaded courtyard.

ADDITIONAL SIGHTS
Fondation du doute★

r. Franciade. 🚻🕐*Feb–Mid Apr and mid-Nov–20 Dec, Fri–Sun 2–6.30pm; mid-Apr–Jun and early Sept–early Nov Wed–Sun 2–6.30pm; Jul–Aug Tue–Sun 2–6.30pm.* ∞€7.50. 𝄢*02 54 55 37 40. www.fondationdudoute.fr.*

The collections are presented in the former Couvent des Minimes. True to the spirit of Fluxus (from Latin for flow, flux) set forth since the 1960s by the founders, whose main point is "no one knows what it is", the Foundation strives to remind us of this concept through its collections of avant-garde or experimental art, such as Benjamin Vautier's 300 writing tables, Daniel Spoerri's **astro-gastronomic trap tables★** and Wolf Vostell's monumental installation **Fandango★** (1974), as well as works by Ben and Gino Di Maggio. Some 50 international artists fostered the Fluxus movement, including Marcel Duchamp, Joseph Beuys, John Cage, Robert Filliou, Nam June Paik and Yoko Ono.

Mur des Mots

On the corner of rue Franciade and rue de la Paix, one of the walls of the Conservatoire is covered with graffiti stating axioms and proverbs.

EXCURSIONS
Orchaise

9km/5.6mi W on D 766.

Situated near the church, the **Priory Botanical Gardens** (🚻🕐*open daily 3–7pm: 20 Apr–9 Jun and early Oct; at other times call to arrange entry* ∞€7; 𝄢*06 80 18 75 56; www.orchaise.eu),* covering an area of 3ha, boast a superb collection of rhododendrons, azaleas, camellias and peonies, as well as evergreen plants.

Ménars

6km/3.5mi NE along D 50.
Amid well-kept gardens, this village shows off its Classical façade on the right bank of the Loire. The Marquis de Pompadour bought the château in 1760. After his death four years later, it passed to his brother, the Marquis de Marigny, who improved the castle and converted the gardens to the French style.

Mulsans

14km/8.7mi NE along D 50.
This small farming village on the edge of the Beauce, has the traditional walled-in farmyards that are characteristic of this region. The charming **church** has Flamboyant windows and a fine Romanesque bell-tower decorated with blind arcades and twin round-arched window openings. A Renaissance gallery is supported by carved wooden columns extending the full width of the nave and incorporating a porch, known as a *caquetoire*, where people would talk after Mass.

Suèvres★

11km/7mi NE along N 152.
The ancient Gallo-Roman city of Sodobrium hides its picturesque façades below the noisy main road on the north bank of the Loire. The St-Christophe church beside the road is entered via a huge porch *(caquetoire)*. The stonework is decorated with fishbone and chevron patterns characteristic of the Merovingian period.
The houses at No. 9 and No. 14 bis in rue Pierre-Pouteau date from the 15C. Turn right into a picturesque cul-de-sac, rue des Moulins, running beside the stream spanned by several footbridges.
The washing place occupies the corner of rue St-Simon; on either side of the street are traces of an old fortified gate. Farther on through the trees *(left)* the two-storey Romanesque tower of **Église St-Lubin** has a fine south door (15C).

ADDRESSES

🛏 STAY

🍴🛏 **Hôtel Anne de Bretagne** – *31 av. du docteur Jean Laigret.* ✆*02 54 78 05 38. www.hotelannedebretagne.com. Closed 23 Nov–7 Dec. 29 rooms.* This small family hotel is located near the castle and the terraced Jardin du Roi.

🍴🛏– 🍴🛏🛏 **Chambre d'hôte les Salamandres** – *1 r. de St-Dyé, 41350 Montlivault. 10km/6mi SE of Blois.* ✆*006 52 14 76 06. www.salamandres.fr. 5 rooms.* ♿🅿. This former wine-producing building has been tastefully restored in rustic and contemporary styles. The bedrooms are housed in the former barns.

🍴🛏🛏 **Chambre d'hôte La Villa Médicis** – *1 r. Médicis, Macé, 41000 St-Denis-sur-Loire. 4km/2.5mi NE of Blois on N 152 towards Orléans.* ✆*02 54 74 46 38 (tourist office). 4 rooms.* 🅿🍴. *Restaurant* 🍴🛏🛏. *Reservation required in winter.* Marie de Medici came to take the waters at the springs in the park. This 19C villa was built as a hotel for spa patrons.

🍴🛏🛏 **Hôtel Ibis** – *3 r. Porte-Côté, in the town centre.* ✆*02 54 74 01 17. www. ibis.com. 56 rooms.* Central location, with some adjoining, all well soundproofed, rooms.

🍴🛏🛏 **Hôtel le Monarque** – *61 r. Porte-Chartraine.* ✆*02 54 78 02 35. www. hotel-lemonarque.com. Closed 22 Dec–Jan. 29 rooms. Restaurant* 🍴🛏. Housed in a 19C building, the hotel features well-kept rooms, all of which are air-conditioned.

🍴🛏🛏🛏 **Chambre d'hôtes Le Plessis** – *195 r. Albert-1er.* ✆*02 54 43 80 08. www.leplessisblois.com. 5 rooms.* 🅿🍴. This accommodation offers a reading room and serves a brunch-style breakfast in the 18C main house. Nicely appointed rooms reside in the old wine-press building. Swimming pool on-site.

🍴🛏🛏🛏 **Chambre d'hôtes Le Clos Pasquier** – *10-12 impasse de l'Orée du Bois.* ✆*02 54 58 84 08. www.leclospasquier.fr. 4 rooms.* 🅿. Once Catherine de Medicis' hunting lodge, this tranquil B&B is situated at the forest's edge. Of special note are the huge breakfasts.

♈ EAT

La Trouvaille – *5-7 rue de la Chaîne.* ♿ *℘02 54 74 77 96. www.brasseriela trouvaille.com. Closed Mon eve.* Set on the bank of the Loire, this brasserie offers a beautiful view of Blois. Dishes like shrimp and vegetable tartar, Piperade Basquaise, and oxtail Parmentier are guided by the market and the seasons.

Les Banquettes Rouges – *16 r. des Trois-Marchands. ℘02 54 78 74 92. www. lesbanquettesrouges.com. Closed Sun–Mon.* This pretty little restaurant has a red façade. Warm furnishings, bistro chairs and red benches. The food is good.

Hôtel Restaurant Côté Loire – *2 pl. de la Greve. ℘02 54 78 07 86. www. coteloire.com.* The charm of this country inn derives from the original 16C beams, varnished wooden tables and a set blackboard menu prepared from seasonal market produce. 9 guest rooms (♈♈).

L'Embarcadère – *16 quai Ulysse Besnard. ℘02 54 78 31 41. www. lembarcadere.fr.* Edging the Loire, this restaurant serves local cuisine. Dine on the terrace or th deck on fish, fried smelt, and other gourmet dishes.

Au Rendez-vous des Pêcheurs – *27 r. du Foix. ℘02 54 74 67 48. www.rendez vousdespecheurs.com. Closed Sun, Mon.* This provincial-style bistro in the old part of Blois prominently features fish. Stained-glass windows filter the light in the quiet dining room.

Restaurant la Vieille Tour – *7 r. Nationale, 41120 Cellettes. ℘02 54 74 67 15. www.restaurant-la-vieille-tour-blois.com. Closed Sun eve, Mon eve and Weds.* This gourmet restaurant is situated halfway between Blois and Cheverny. Dine on the likes of foie gras or scampi finished with desserts such as praline chantilly or seasonal fruits.

Le Médicis – *2 allée François-1er. ℘02 54 43 94 04. www.le-medicis.com.* This house dating from 1900 offers good contemporary cuisine in a luxurious dining room/veranda (moulded ceilings, Second Empire furniture). Ten modernised guest rooms (♈♈♈; Wi-Fi).

Restaurant l'Orangerie du château – *1, avenue Jean-Laigret, Blois. ℘02 54 78 05 36. www.orangerie-du-chateau.fr.* This Michelin-starred restaurant

with a beautiful terrace overlooking the chateau offers innovative and refined cuisine, with a nod in the direction of the Renaissance. A good wine list, but especially covering the Loire valley wines.

Assa Restaurant – *189 quai Ulysse Besnard, Blois. ℘02 54 78 09 01. www.assarestaurant.com. Open Wed–Sun except Thu lunch and Sun eve.* Another Michelin-starred restaurant, this serving 'Cuisine du Marché', chosen and invented on a daily basis to ensure the freshest of dishes. Excellent wine list.

NIGHTLIFE

Rond-point de la Résistance – There are three cafés near this roundabout by the river. It is more pleasant to go late in the evening, to avoid car exhaust fumes: L'Époque, Le Maryland and Le Colonial Café.

Nearby are tobacconists and newsagents that stay open late.

Rue Foulerie – In this narrow street on the edge of the old part of town you will find a disco, a piano bar and a couple of pubs.

SHOPPING

Rue du Commerce – Rue du Commerce and the adjacent streets (rue Rebrousse-Pénil, rue St-Martin) in this pleasant pedestrian-only district offer all kinds of shopping.

SON ET LUMIÈRE

Enormous projectors combine photographs with special sound and lighting effects at the chateau to give a lively show about the history of Blois. 👥 *Performances (45min): Apr and Sept 10pm; May–Aug 10.30pm. €11 (child 6–17, €6.50) – tickets can be purchased which include entry to the chateau and/or the Maison de la Magie, and/or the Fondation du Doute, from €20-33. ℘02 54 90 33 33. www.chateaudeblois.fr.*

ℹ INFORMATION

Tours – Discovery tours *(2h)*. Information at the tourist office or on www.vpah. culture.fr.

Château de Chambord★★★

The writer Henry James elegantly summed up this great castle: "Chambord is truly royal – royal in its great scale, its grand air, its indifference to common considerations." The largest by far of the Loire châteaux, Chambord is built on a scale that foreshadowed the château at Versailles. It looms into sight suddenly, and as the view of its white mass gradually expands on approaching, its detail becomes ever clearer. At sunset especially, it makes a striking impression on the viewer. The magnificent building also owes its impact to its fine architectural unity and sumptuous Renaissance decoration, dating from the period when this style was at its most splendid.

A BIT OF HISTORY

Grandiose creation of François I (16C) – The counts of Blois had built a small castle in this isolated corner of the forest of Boulogne, which was excellent hunting country.

As a young man François I liked to hunt in the forest, and in 1518 he ordered the old castle to be razed to make room for a sumptuous palace. Several designs were put forward and no doubt Leonardo da Vinci, the King's guest at Le Clos-Lucé, drew up a plan that was made into a model by Le Boccador. As work progressed, the original plans were altered and large sums of money were swallowed up, but the King refused to cut corners. Even when the Treasury was empty and there was no money to pay the ransom for his two sons in Spain, work went on. It suffered only one interruption, from 1524 to 1525, during the Italian campaign, which resulted in the defeat of Pavia. In his enthusiasm the King even proposed in 1527 to divert the course of the Loire so that it should flow before the château, but in view of the enormity of this task, a smaller river, the Cosson, was chosen instead.

- 🕭 **Michelin Map:** 318: G-6.
- ℹ **Info**: ℘02 54 50 40 00. www.chambord.org/en. 🕓Daily Apr–Oct 9am–6pm; Nov–Mar 9am–5pm. 🕓1 Jan, 30 Nov, 25 Dec. ⊛€14.50. ➴Guided tours in English daily Jul–Sept 11.15am. €5. 🅿 600m from chateau €6.
- ▶ **Location:** An hour-and-a-half drive SW of Paris, the château is situated between Beaugency and Blois. It sits back from the Loire, off the south bank, at the end of a long avenue. Visitors enter through the Porte Royale. Brochures with a detailed map of the château are available from the reception desk.
- ⊘ **Don't Miss:** The great staircase, the roof terrace, tapestries in the State Rooms.
- 🕓 **Timing:** Allow a full day to enjoy Chambord, alloting at least 2 hours for the castle. Stay to see the castle's floodlights at nightfall.
- ⚇ **Kids:** Boating on the canal.

By 1537 the major construction work was completed. Only the interior decoration remained to be done. In 1538 the King commissioned a pavilion linked to the keep by a two-storey building, and a second symmetrical wing to be added to the west side. The whole complex measured 117m by 156m.

In 1539 the King was able to receive **Charles V** at Chambord. In 1545 the royal pavilion was finished, but François I, who until then had lived in the northeast tower, died two years later.

Henri II continued his father's work by building the west wing and the chapel tower while the curtain wall was completed. At his death in 1559, the château was still unfinished.

Louis XIV and Molière – François II and Charles IX came frequently to hunt in the forest. Henri III and Henri IV hardly put in an appearance at Chambord, but Louis XIII reforged the royal link. Louis XIV stayed at Chambord nine times between 1660 and 1685.

Molière wrote *Monsieur de Pourceaugnac* at Chambord in a matter of a few days. During the première the King did not seem at all amused. Lully, who had written the music and was playing the role of an apothecary, had an inspiration: he jumped feet first from the stage on the harpsichord and fell through it. The King burst out laughing and the play was saved. *Le Bourgeois gentilhomme* caused Molière renewed anguish. The King was icy at the first performance. The courtiers who were made fun of in the play were ready to be sarcastic. But after the second performance the King expressed his pleasure and the whole court changed their criticism into praise.

The Affair of the White Flag (1871–73) – In 1871, Henri, Count of Chambord and, since the fall of Charles X in 1830, legitimate heir to the French throne, was close to achieving his goal. It was the year when, following the disruption of the Franco-Prussian War, the French elected a monarchist assembly in favour of restoring the monarchy. However, the monarchists were divided into two groups: the legitimists who supported the traditional conception of absolute monarchy, and the Orléanists, more modern in their outlook, who upheld the principles of 1789. Eventually both parties agreed on the name of the heir: **Henri V**, the last of the Bourbon line.

As he had lived in exile for 40 years, Henri was not well-informed of the realities of French politics when he returned to his native soil. He went to live at Chambord, where, on 5 July

Maréchal de Saxe (18C)

Louis XV presented the estate, with a revenue of 40,000 *livres,* to the Maréchal de Saxe as a reward for his victory over the Dutch and English at the Battle of Fontenoy in 1745. The extravagant, proud and violent Maréchal entertained a lively, exciting lifestyle. To satisfy his taste for arms, he made room to accommodate two regiments of cavalry composed of Tartars, Wallachians and natives of Martinique. These unconventional troops rode high-spirited horses from the Ukraine that were trained to assemble at the sound of a trumpet. The Maréchal imposed iron discipline on his entourage. If the slightest offence was committed, the culprits would be hanged from the branches of an old elm. More by terror than by courtship, Maurice de Saxe won the favours of a well-known actress, Mme Favart, and compelled her to remain at Chambord. He re-erected Molière's stage for her amusement. Monsieur Favart played the triple role of director, author and consenting husband.

The Maréchal died at 54, some said in a duel with the Prince de Conti, whose wife he had seduced. Others ascribed his death to a neglected chill. Vainglorious even in death, Maurice de Saxe had given orders that the six cannon he had placed in the main courtyard of the château should be fired every quarter of an hour for 16 days as a sign of mourning.

Double Staircase attributed to Leonardo da Vinci

© Patrick Escudero/hemis.fr

1871, he proclaimed his convictions in a manifesto that ended with these words: "Henri V will not give up the white flag of Henri IV". The effect of this declaration on public opinion was a disaster: the Royalists lost the elections. The Count of Chambord stubbornly refused to reconsider the matter and returned to Austria. Two years later in October 1873 a final attempt to compromise – a tricolour flag dotted with fleur-de-lis – failed. The National Assembly accepted the situation and voted for the Republic. Henri did not accede to the throne, and died in 1883. The Château de Chambord, which had witnessed the final hours of the monarchy, was handed down to his nephew, the Duke of Parma. In 1932 his descendants sold it to the State for about 11 million francs.

VISIT

Although the ground plan of Chambord is feudal (a central **keep** with four towers, which qualifies as a château in its own right, set in an enclosed precinct) the architecture is Renaissance and makes no reference to war. Indeed, the château is a royal palace built for pleasure. During the construction two wings were added, one containing the royal apartments and the other the chapel. Chambord is the personal creation of François I. The name of the architect has

not been recorded, but the architecture seems to have been inspired by the spirit of Leonardo da Vinci, who had been staying at the French court and died in the spring of 1519 just as work on the château began.

Double Staircase★★★
The famous double staircase, undoubtedly conceived by Leonardo da Vinci, stands at the intersection of the cross formed by the four guard-rooms. The two flights of steps spiral round each other from the ground floor to the roof terrace. The stonework at the centre and round the outside is pierced by many openings so that you can see from one flight to the other.

State Apartments
These rooms on the ground floor and first floor contain a superb collection of French and Flemish tapestries.
François I's rooms were in the north tower on the **first floor**. In the King's Bedchamber the bedspread and hangings are made of gold embroidered velvet (16C Italian). In François I's dressing room the salamander, the King's emblem, and the letter F alternate in the coffers of the barrel-vaulted ceiling. The Queen's Bedchamber in the Tour François-Ier is hung with Paris tapestries relating the History of Con-

stantine, after cartoons by Rubens. The King's Suite which follows is decorated with tapestries and historic portraits. The Royal or State Bedchamber has the original Regency style panelling fitted in 1748 for the Maréchal; the room next door, at the exact centre of the building, gives a remarkable view of the park. The Dauphin's Suite in the East Tower, contains many mementoes of the Count of Chambord.

Salles de la Chasse et de la Nature

Three rooms (second floor of the keep) are devoted to the importance of the Château's location to François I as a keen huntsman. Hunting was the favourite medieval sport, and princes were brought up to it from their earliest days. Some 50 works on the hunting art on display include the remarkable Diana and her nymphs (a joint work by Rubens and Jean Bruegel) and scenes such as the Salon de Chasse and the Chambre des chasseurs by Mark Dion, a contemporary artist.

The château estate was richly stocked with game and lent itself to hawking. At one time there were more than 300 falcons.

A gallery leads to the rectangular chapel★, which occupies the West Tower. The initials of François I, Henri II, Louis XIV and the Count of Chambord testify to its different stages of construction and decoration.

The Château in Numbers

The Château de Chambord is a jewel of the Renaissance, comprising 440 rooms, 365 fireplaces, 13 main flights of stairs and 70 backstairs. Some 1,800 workmen toiled for 28 years at the site (1st phase: the keep and royal wing), François I stayed for just 72 days, the Count of Chambord 3 days and the Maréchal de Saxe 10 years. 2,000 people could be accommodated in the Château.

Terraces★★★

The terraces, a direct inspiration from castles such as Méhun-sur-Yèvre and Saumur, are unique: they consist of a maze of **lanterns★,** chimneys, stairs and dormer windows, all intricately carved and decorated with a mosaic of inset slates cut in various shapes – lozenges, circles and squares – in imitation of Italian marble. It was here that the court spent most of its time watching the start and return of the hunts, military reviews and exercises, tournaments and festivals. The thousands of nooks and crannies of the terrace invited the confidences, intrigues and assignations that played a great part in the life of that glittering society.

Salle des Carrosses

On the ground floor of the royal wing, the last automobiles ordered by the Count in 1873, in anticipation of his entry into Paris, are displayed.

The Park

Since 1948 the park has been a national hunt reserve covering 5,500ha of which 4,500ha are taken up by forest; it is enclosed by a wall, the longest in France, 32km/20mi long and pierced by five gates at the end of six beautiful drives.

🏛️ Écuries du Maréchal de Saxe

A display of **horsemanship** (℘02 54 50 40 00; www.chambord.org) is held from time to time in the ruins of the former stables belonging to the Maréchal de Saxe. It retraces the history of the château from the Renaissance period to the days of the Comte de Chambord.

EXCURSION

Château de Villesavin★

11km/7mi S by D112 and D 102; turn right at Bracieux. 🚻🕐Daily Mar–May 10am–noon, 2–7pm (except Thu in Mar); Jun–Sept 10am–7pm; Oct–mid-Nov 10am–noon, 2–6pm (except Thu in Nov). ⊛€9.50. ℘02 54 46 42 88. www.chateau-de-villesavin.fr.

Villesavin derives from Villa Savini, the name of a Roman villa, which stood

Pigeons as a Status Symbol

The right to keep pigeons – held essentially by large landowners – was one of the privileges that disappeared with the Revolution. The size of the dovecote depended on the size of the estate: there was one pigeon-hole containing a couple of birds for each acre of land. In the Middle Ages, dovecotes were built to attract pigeons and doves for two reasons: not only did the birds provide meat, but their droppings were also highly prized as a fertilizer – though it was so rich in nitrates that it could be used only in the rainy season, when it would be naturally diluted. It is thought that the practice of keeping pigeons was brought back by the Crusaders from the Middle East where the land has always been fertilized with pigeon manure.

beside the Roman road that passed through Ponts-d'Arian (Hadrian's Bridges).

The château was built between 1527 and 1537 by Jean Le Breton, Lord of Villandry and superintendent of works at Chambord. It is a charming Renaissance building with certain Classical tendencies and consists of a central block flanked by symmetrical pavilions.

A perfect quadrilateral, the **courtyard** is adorned in the centre with a 16C basin of white Carrara marble.

Highlights of the interior include two Renaissance kitchens; rooms appointed with 18C and 19C furnishings, especially the oval office and music room with a backgammon table; and a **museum★** devoted to wedding traditions from 1850-1950 with 1,500 objects.

Left of the château stands a large 16C **dovecote** with 1,500 pigeon-holes.

ADDRESSES

🛏 STAY

🍴🍴–🍴🍴🍴 **Chambre d'hôte la Giraudière** – *256 r. de la Giraudière, 41250 Mont-Près-Chambord.* ☎02 54 70 84 83. *3 rms.* 🅿. Not far from the forest of Boulogne, this chambre d'hôte provides a rural, wooded setting. Pretty flower garden (picnicking possible) with swimming pool .

🍷 EAT

🍴 **La Bigoudène** – *r. de la Mairie, 41250 Bracieux.* ☎02 54 78 43 37. *www.creperie-labigoudene.fr. Closed Tue eve, Wed eve, and Sun.* This family-run business pampers their patrons with delicious crêpes and salads. Bookings strongly advised in season.

🍴🍴–🍴🍴🍴 **Chez Jacques** – *11 pl. de la Halle, 41250 Bracieux.* ☎02 54 46 03 84. A very agreeable table that combines the quality and seasonal products of the land with attentive service. Savour the likes of a gourmet salad and dishes such as lamb with garlic cream sauce. The dining room is small, so booking ahead is advised.

🍴🍴🍴 **Auberge du Bon Terroir** – *20 r. du 8-Mai, 41500 Muides-sur-Loire.* ☎02 54 87 59 24. *www.auberge-bon-terroir.fr. Closed Sun dinner, Mon–Tue.* Enjoy traditional cuisine and Loire valley specialities inside or on the terrace under a shady lime tree. The sweetbreads with morels is a speciality of the house.

LEISURE ACTIVITIES

Boating – Take a boat trip or electric boat on the canal at the foot of the chateau, and enjoy a unique perspective. ☎02 54 50 40 00. www.chambord.org.

Cycling – ☎02 54 50 40 00. Apr–early Nov 10am–7pm. Discover the chateau's park on a bike (€8, child €4.50), or 4-seater Rosalie (€22).

Horse-Drawn Carriage Rides – *45min Mar–Sept. €12 (child 5–17, €8), or €23 with visit to the château.* ☎02 54 50 50 40. *On-board commentary on the château and grounds.*

Château de Talcy★

This austere-looking château on the borders of the Loire valley and the Beauce region stands well off the beaten track. Once inside the courtyard, visitors discover a charming Renaissance manor house.

VISIT

The keep, part of which dates from the 15C, has a double doorway (postern and carriage gate), two corner turrets and a crenellated sentry walk that looks medieval, although it dates from 1520. The first courtyard holds a graceful gallery and an attractive well. In the second courtyard, a large 16C **dove-cote** has some 1,500 pigeon-holes in a good state of preservation. Fine furniture (17C–18C) and Gothic **tapestries** adorn the guard-room, office, kitchen, bedrooms and salons, which are roofed with French-style ceilings (with decorated exposed beams).

- **Michelin Map:** 318: F-5
- **Info:** 18 r. du Château, 41370 Talcy. ℘02 54 81 03 01. www.chateau-talcy.fr. *2 Jan–Mar and Oct–Dec daily except Tue 10am–12.30pm, 2–5pm; Apr and Sept daily 10am–12.30pm, 2–5pm; May–Aug daily 9.30am–12.30pm, 2–6pm. 1 Jan, 1 May, 25 Dec.* €6.
- **Location:** Between Beaugency (18km/11mi to the E) and Vendôme (36km/22.4mi to the W).
- **Timing:** Allow 1h30 for the Château.

Beaugency★

Beaugency certainly recalls the Middle Ages; it was an important town in the 11C–13C. Due to its proximity to the Loire, the town was commerically important when trade was conducted on the river. It is best to enter the town from the south, crossing the River Loire by the age-old multi-arched bridge, offering an attractive view. The oldest parts of the bridge date from the 14C, but an earlier bridge used as a toll was already in existence in the 12C.

A BIT OF HISTORY

The two councils of Beaugency (12C) – Both councils were called to deal with the marital problems of Philippe I and Louis VII. While visiting **Fulk IV** in Tours, Philippe seduced his host's wife, the Countess Bertrade, and shortly afterwards repudiated Queen Bertha. The King thought that he would easily obtain the annulment of his marriage

- **Population:** 7,753.
- **Michelin Map:** 318: G-5
- **Info:** Tourist office: 3 pl. Dr. Hyvernaud, 45190 Beaugency. ℘02 38 44 32 28. www.entre-orleans-et-chambord.com.
- **Location:** Beaugency is 20km/12mi S of Orléans, and 29km/18mi N of Blois, and the right bank of the Loire.
- **Parking:** There are areas to park (fee) on the river front.
- **Don't Miss:** The medieval houses in the centre.
- **Timing:** A leisurely half-day, or whizz around the town in an hour.
- **Kids:** Check with the tourist office for activities including walks, water sports and horse riding during the summer months.

by raising a vague claim of consanguinity, but Pope Urban II refused to comply with his request. The King persisted and was excommunicated, and so he was unable to join the First Crusade (1099). Eventually the excommunication was lifted by the **Council of Beaugency** in 1104 and four years later the King died at peace with the church.

Far more important was the **Council of 1152**, which annulled the marriage of Louis VII and **Eleanor of Aquitaine**. The beautiful and seductive Eleanor had married Louis in 1137. For 10 years the royal couple lived in perfect harmony. In 1147 they set out on the Second Crusade, but once in Palestine their relationship took a turn for the worse. Divorce became inevitable and on 20 March 1152 the Council of Beaugency officially dissolved the union of Louis and Eleanor for prohibited kinship. Eleanor was not without suitors; she married **Henry Plantagenet**, the future King of England, so that her dowry, a large part of southwest France, passed on to the English crown.

●✦ WALKING TOUR

Known as the "Princess de la Loire", the Medieval centre and riverside are listed on the UNESCO World Heritage list.

Petit Mail
This tree-lined avenue overlooks the Loire and commands fine views of the valley. The **porte Tavers** (12C) is a vestige from the town's defensive walls.

▶ r. de la Porte-Tavers leads to pl. St-Firmin .

Clocher St-Firmin
A street used to run under this tower, which is the sole remaining feature of a 15C church destroyed during the Revolution. You can hear the chimes of the Angelus bell at 8am, noon and 7pm.

▶ Cross pl. St-Firmin into the short rue de la Sirènes.

Maison de Templiers
Note the Romanesque windows in this 12C house at the corner of rue du Puits-de-l'Ange and rue du Traîneau.

▶ Follow r. du Traîneauback to pl. du Dr-Hyvernaud and on the left, r. des Chevaliers.

Clock Tower
This tower was originally the Exchange Tower. In the 12C it became one of the main gateways in the town wall.

▶ Take r. du Change back to pl. du Dr-Hyvernaud, at the foot of the hôtel de ville, on your left.

Hôtel de Ville
●✦*Reserve at the tourist office for guided tours of historic Beaugency (included are the 17C embroidered tapestries in the Hôtel de ville's reception hall).* ⊚€6.
The Council Chamber on the first floor is hung with eight beautiful pieces of **embroidery★**, executed with remarkable skill. Four of them, depicting the four continents known at that time, are 17C.

▶ Take r. du Pouët-de-Chaumont to the delightful r. du Pont. Turn right and stroll along the Rû, the flower-lined brook that flows into the Loire. Turn right, walk under the **voûte St-Georges**, otherwise known as the "porte de la Barrière" as the only gateway into the town, the château and the abbey church.

Château de Beaugency
The medieval fortress was converted into a typical 15C residence by Dunois, Lord of Beaugency, one of Joan of Arc's followers. It is now a private chateau, but the exterior can be viewed from r. du Pont.

▶ Take r. du Traîneau back to pl. du Dr-Hyvernaud and, on the left, r. des Chevaliers.

Église Notre-Dame★

This restored 12C Romanesque abbey church was damaged by fire during the Wars of Religion. In the chancel, the windows and main arcades are separated by gemelled arches. Next to the church are the 18C buildings of the former abbey of Notre-Dame. At night, old street lights illuminate the charming **place Dunois**, in front of the church and the keep, and **place St-Firmin.**

Tour César★

This rectangular 36m tower, supported by buttresses, is a good example of 11C military architecture. The interior, which covered five floors, is a ruin.

Donjon★

This keep is another fine example of 11C military architecture. At this period, keeps were rectangular and buttressed; later they became circular.

Tour du Diable

At the bottom of the narrow rue de l'Abbaye stands the Devil's Tower, which was part of the fortifications defending the bridgehead; in the Middle Ages the Loire flowed at its foot.

○ Cross place de la Motte, the town's old river harbour. Before going up rue de l'évêché – where offloaded goods were carried to the town centre – note the pretty street to your left, r. Ravelin, previously r. des Pêcheurs. Pl. St-Firmin, r. de la Porte-Tavers lead you back to the tree-lined Petit Mail.

ADDRESSES

🛏 STAY

○○🍴 **Chambre d'hôte Le Clos de Pont-Pierre** – *115 r. des Eaux-Bleues, 45190 Tavers. 2km/1mi SW towards Blois* ✆*02 38 44 56 85. www.clos-de-pontpierre.com.* 🅿 ✒. *4 rooms.* Though near the road, this old farmhouse has a **swimming pool** set in a huge garden. The simple rooms overlook the countryside.

○○🍴 **Hôtel de la Sologne** – *6 place Saint-Firmin, 45190 Beaugency.* ✆*02 38 44 50 27.* 🅿. *15 rooms.* Located in a tree-lined square close to the abbey church; a peaceful place in spite of being in the centre of town.

🍴 EAT

○○🍴–○○🍴🍴 **Le Petit Bateau** – *54 r. du Pont.* ✆*02 38 44 56 38. www.restaurant-lepetitbateau.fr. Closed Mon, Tue.* A gastronomic restaurant, in two rustic dining rooms, where the chef serves delicious traditional cuisine.

Meung-sur-Loire★

This fortified village stretches from the Loire, which laps at the roots of the tall trees lining the avenue up the slope, to the main road (N 152) on the plateau.
From the old market a narrow and twisting street, rue Porte-d'Amont, climbs up to an archway; little lanes skirt Les Mauves, a stream with many channels that runs between the houses.

▸ **Population:** 6,264.
◉ **Michelin Map:** 318: H-5
🗐 **Info:** Office de Tourisme Val des Mauves, 1 r. Emmanuel Troulet, 45130 Meung-sur-Loire. ✆02 38 44 32 28. www.entre-orleans-et-chambord.com.
○ **Location:** 14km/8.7mi from Orléans, via the N 152.
🕐 **Timing:** Allow around 2 hours.
🏛 **Don't Miss:** The Château.
🧍🧒 **Kids:** The Jardins de Roquelin and Arboretum des Prés de Culands.

A BIT OF HISTORY

The town erected a statue of its most famous son, Jean de Meung. In about 1280 he added 18,000 lines to the *Romance of the Rose (Roman de la Rose)*, which had been written some 40 years earlier by Guillaume de Lorris. The allegorical narrative was the greatest literary achievement of a period in which readers certainly had to have stamina.

SIGHTS

Collégiale St-Liphard★

This rather austere collegaite church (11C–13C) features a bold bell-tower with a stone spire and a triple apse.

Château de Meung-sur-Loire★

Mid-Feb-Mar Sat–Sun 2–6pm; Apr and Oct Tue-Sat 1-6pm Sun 10am-6pm May–Jun and Sept Tue–Sun 10am–6pm; Jul–Aug daily 10am–7pm; for other times, please check website. €9.50. 02 38 44 36 47. www.chateau-de-meung.com.

This old building reflects a curious mixture of styles, having partly retained its medieval aspect, for instance, in the entrance façade (12C–13C). Until the 18C the château belonged to the bishops of Orléans, who administered justice.

Musée Van-Oeveren

Le Clos de Bel Air, rte. d'Orléans, 45130 Meung-sur-Loire. Jul–Aug Tue–Sun 2–6pm; rest of year by appointment. €8. 02 38 45 35 82. www.musee-escrime.com.

This museum is dedicated to fencing, duelling and weaponry set in the Château de Bel Air (17C).

Centre Culturel La Monnaye

Musée municipal, 22 r. des Remparts. Wed and Fri 2.30–6.30pm, Sat 9.30am–12.30pm, plus Apr-Oct Sun 3–6pm. Public holidays, 2 wks in Aug and Christmas holidays. Free. 02 38 22 53 36. www.meung-sur-loire.com.

On the site of a former mint where copper coins, *liards*, were minted in the 17C. The museum displays a collection of rare works and texts including books by François Villon, Jehan de Meun, etc. One of the highlights is an illustrated facsimile of the *Roman de la Rose* which is kept in New York. Other rooms are given over to the collection of archaeological items, fossils and coins put together by François Quatrehomme. Visitors can discover the work of another local artist Gaston Couté (1880–1911), poet and songwriter who made his name in the taverns of Montmartre

EXCURSIONS

Jardins de Roquelin

Towards Cléry-St-André, cross the bridge and head immediately left, follow the signs (500m). Late-Apr–early Oct Wed-Mon 10am–6pm. €6, (under 18 free). 06 70 95 37 70. www.lesjardinsderoquelin.com.

The 1ha garden at this working nursery features old roses, a vegetable garden, aquatic plants, medieval style trellises and a "jardin à l'anglaise."

Arboretum des Prés de Culands

Towards Orléans, beyond the Nivelle Mill. 25 Apr-early Oct Wed-Mon 2-6pm. 06 70 95 37 70. www.jardinarboretumdilex.com.

This romantic site, famous for its display of holly, is criss-crossed by canals that form tiny islands planted with maple trees, oaks and alders.

ADDRESSES

STAY

Chambre d'hôte La Mouche Abeille – *Impasse du la Mouche. 02 38 44 34 36. www.chambres-hotes-loire.com.* 3 rooms. On the banks of the Loire, this 18C place has an orchard, vegetable garden and a pond. Tastefully decorated rooms.

La Feuillaie - Chambres et Tables d'hôtes – *4 rue Basse, 45130 Saint Ay. 06 16 75 71 27. www.lafeuillaie.com.* 5 rooms. Only 5km from Meung-sur-Loire, this 18C house with comfortable rooms is set within a large park that is quiet and tranquil.

Basilique de Cléry-St-André★

The present Notre-Dame de Cléry is a church dating from the 15C with the exception of the 14C square tower that abuts the north side of the basilica. It remains the only part of the original structure to have escaped destruction by the English.

A BIT OF HISTORY

In 1280, labourers set up a statue of the Virgin Mary they had found in a chapel that was to become the present-day **church**. Worship of it spread throughout the district, and the chapel, too small to accommodate the pilgrims, was transformed into a church served by a college of canons. In 1428, the church was destroyed by the English commander Salisbury during his march on Orléans. Charles VII and Dunois supplied the first funds for rebuilding, but the great benefactor of Cléry was **Louis XI**. During the siege of Dieppe, while still only the Dauphin, he vowed to give his weight in silver to Notre-Dame de Cléry if he were victorious. His prayer was answered and he kept his vow. When he became King, Louis XI dedicated himself to the Virgin Mary and in doing so strengthened his

- **Michelin Map:** 318: H-5
- **Info:** Office de Tourisme, 1, rue Emmanuel Troulet. ✆02 38 44 32 28. www.entre-orleans-et-chambord.com.
- **Location:** 13km/8mi from Orléans via the D 951, on the Loire's left bank.
- **Timing:** Allow 30–45min.

attachment to Cléry. He was buried there at his request and the building was completed by his son, Charles VIII.

VISIT

✆02 38 45 70 05. www.clery-saint-andre.com. Enter through the transept. The rather austere interior is suffused with light and conveys great elegance.

Tomb of Louis XI

The tomb is on the north side of the nave and is aligned with the altar dedicated to Our Lady. The marble statue of the King is the work of an Orléans sculptor, Bour-

Stained-glass windows and the vaults of the chancel, Basilique de Cléry-St-André

din (1622). The original bronze statue was melted down by the Huguenots.

Funerary vault of Louis XI – Louis XI's bones and those of his wife, Charlotte de Savoie, are still in the vault, which opens onto the nave near the tomb. The two skulls, sawn open for embalming, are in a glass case.

Tanguy de Châtel, who was killed during a siege while saving the life of Louis XI, is buried under a flagstone alongside the royal vault. Further to the right, another stone covers the urn containing the heart of Charles VIII.

Chapelle St-Jacques★

The church dean, Gilles de Pontbriand, and his brother built this chapel, dedicated to St James, to serve as their tomb. The vaulting is decorated with girdles and pilgrims' purses, for Cléry is on the pilgrimage route to St James' shrine in Santiago de Compostela, Spain. The walls are studded with ermines' tails and bridges (the arms of the Pontbriands). The Breton-style wooden grille was donated by Louis XIII in 1622.

Chapelle de Dunois

Dunois and his family are buried here. The church at Cléry was already finished when this chapel was added (1464), hence the construction of the vaulting was complicated by the presence of a buttress. In the **stalls**, the seats are carved with human masks and the initials of the donor, Henri II, and his mistress, Diana de Poitiers.

EXCURSION

Orléans Wine Routew

A signposted route lined by vines and fruit trees between Saint-Hilaire, Saint-Mesmin and Cléry-Saint-André takes in the Orlénas-Cléry winegrowing region.

Château de Beauregard★

The château stands in a vast park overlooking the Beuvron valley.

VISIT

The building has kept its Renaissance appearance despite 17C additions and the 20C roof extension.

Cabinet des Grelots★

This charming little room, was fitted out towards the middle of the 16C for Jean du Thier, Secretary of State to Henri II and then Lord of Beauregard. His coat of arms decorates the coffered ceiling; the bells reappear as a decorative motif on the oak panelling lining the room that conceals the cupboards where the château archives are kept.

Galerie des Illustres★★

The long room has retained its splendid old Delft tiling depicting an army on the march. The ceiling was covered in 1624 with a rich blue paint made from ground lapis lazuli. The most interesting feature of the gallery is the collection of more than 327 **historical portraits** arranged in bays, each devoted to a different reign making a complete succession of monarchs from the first Valois, Philippe VI, to Louis XIII.

- **Michelin Map:** 318: F-6
- **Info:** 12 r. de la Fontaine, 41120 Cellettes. *Apr–Sept daily 10.30am–6.30pm; Feb–mid-Mar and Oct–early Nov Mon–Fri 1.30am–6pm, Sat–Sun 10.30am–6pm.* €12.50. *02 54 70 41 65. www.beauregard-loire.com.*
- **Location:** 9km/6mi from Blois on D765, 7km/4.3mi from Cour-Chevernny.
- **Timing:** Allow 1–2 hours.

Château de Cheverny

© imageBROKER/hemis.fr

Château de Cheverny★★★

Standing on the edge of Sologne Forest, not far from the châteaux of Blois and Chambord, Cheverny owes its beauty to the harmonious proportions of its symmetric design, and to its sumptuous interior decoration.

VISIT

Crowned by a splendid slate roof, the Classical façade is built of attractive white stone from the Bourré quarries (28km/17mi SW). The château is surrounded by a lovely 100ha park.

Château

Construction work was carried out uninterrupted between 1604 and 1634; consequently, the château displays a rare unity of style, both in the architecture and the decoration. The symmetric design and harmonious grandeur of the façade are characteristic features of the period of Louis XIII. At first-floor level there are oval niches housing the busts of Roman emperors, whereas the Hurault coat of arms above the main doorway is surrounded by two concentric collars, one symbolising the Order of the Holy Ghost, the other, the Order of St Michael.

Dining room

To the right of the hall, the dining room is hung with a fine 17C Flemish tapestry. The room has retained its French-style

- 🕭 **Michelin Map:** 318: F-7
- 🛈 **Info:** 🕐 *Daily Jan–Mar and Nov–Dec 10am–5pm; Apr–Sept 9.15am–6.30pm.* ✆€12.50 *(chateau and gardens).* ✆02 54 79 96 29. *www.chateau-cheverny.fr.*
- 🔗 **Location:** 17km/10.5mi S of Blois via the D 765.
- 🕘 **Timing:** Allow 1–2 hours to visit the château, but if the weather is good, consider taking a walk or a picnic in the gardens.
- 👫 **Kids:** The exhibit about the adventures of Tintin and Captain Haddock.

painted ceiling and small murals depicting the story of Don Quixote; both are by Jean Mosnier (1600–56), a native of Blois.

Private Apartments

Access to the west wing is via the splendid main staircase with its straight flights of steps and rich sculptural decoration. The private apartments consist of eight rooms, all magnificently furnished.

Armoury★

The ceiling, the wainscots and the shutters were painted by Mosnier. A collection of arms and armour from the 15C to the 17C is displayed on the walls. The superb 17C tapestry **l'Enlèvement d'Hélène★★**, is distinguished by its striking colours.

King's Bedchamber★★
The King's Bedchamber is the most splendid room in the château. The ceiling is in the Italian style, gilded and painted by Mosnier. The walls are hung with tapestries from the Paris workshops (1640) after Simon Vouet.

Grand Salon★★
Back to the ground floor.
The Grand Salon is decorated with 17C and 18C furniture and paintings. The ceiling is entirely covered, as is the wall panelling, with painted decoration enhanced with gilding. The paintings on either side of the mirror include a portrait of Cosimo de' Medici by Titian, another of Jeanne d'Aragon from the School of Raphaël and on the chimney-piece, a portrait by Mignard of Marie-Johanne de Saumery, Countess of Cheverny.

Gallery, Petit Salon, Library
The **Gallery** is furnished with magnificent Régence chairs and contains several paintings, including three splendid **portraits★★ by François Clouet**, a portrait of Jeanne d'Albret by Miguel Oñate and a Self-Portrait by Rigaud. The **Petit Salon** is hung with 16C, 17C and 18C pictures.

Tapestry Room
The smaller salon is hung with five 17C Flemish tapestries after cartoons by Teniers. Both rooms contain Louis XIV and Louis XV period furnishings, including a Louis XV Chinese lacquered commode and a magnificent Louis XV **clock★★** decorated with bronzes by Caffieri.

The Park
👥 Visitors of all ages will enjoy a tour of the grounds aboard an electric car or a boat trip. Fans of Tintin and Captain Haddock will delight in the permanent exhibition displayed in the château's former smithy.

Outbuildings
There are **kennels★** for about 90 hounds, cross-breeds from English foxhounds and the French Poitou race, and the **Trophy Room** displays 2,000 deer antlers.

L'Orangerie
Some 200m from the northern steps, on the way out of the château grounds, stands a magnificent early-18C orangery, now entirely restored.

👥 Les secrets de Moulinsart
Near the castle's entrance gate, the **old forge** holds a permanent exhibit about the adventures of Tintin wherein Cheverny is revisited by Hergé.

EXCURSION
Château de Troussay
3.5km/2mi W skirting the Cheverny park as far as D 52; turn left and take the first fork on the right.
♿ – ⏱Daily Apr-Sept 11am–6pm.
💶€8 (park and museum, €6). 📞02 54 44 29 07. www.chateaudetroussay.com.
This, the smallest of the Renaissance châteaux of the Loire, was refurbished in the late 19C by the historian Louis de la Saussaye.
Note particularly the stone carving of a **porcupine**, the emblem of Louis XII, on the rear façade taken from the Hurault de Cheverny mansion in Blois and the beautiful **chapel door★** carved with delicate scrollwork. The tiles on the ground floor date from the reign of Louis XII, the Renaissance windows came from the Guise mansion in Blois and the grisaille on the ceiling in the small salon are attributed to **Jean Mosnier**.
The château, which is lived in (and offers B&B accommodation), is furnished with fine pieces dating from the 16C to the 18C. The outbuildings round the courtyard house a small **museum** evoking past domestic and agricultural life in the Sologne.

© Evannovostro/Shutterstock

Château de Fougères-sur-Bièvre★

In the charming village of Fougères, surrounded by nursery gardens and fields of asparagus, stands the austere north façade of the feudal-looking château of Pierre de Refuge, Chancellor to Louis XI.

Michelin Map: 318: F-7

Info: 2 Jan–early May and mid-Sept–Dec daily except Tue 10am–12.30pm, 2–5pm; early May–early Sept daily 9.30am–12.30pm, 2–6.30pm. 1 Jan, 1 May, 1 and 11 Nov, 25 Dec. €6. 02 54 20 27 18. www.fougeres-sur-bievre.fr.

Location: 21km/13mi S of Blois, on the D 52 between Pontlevoy and Cheverny.

Timing: Allow 1 hour to explore the château.

VISIT

It is easy to imagine the original moats, drawbridge and arrow slits – replaced in the 16C by windows – and the keep's battlements, which disappeared when the roof was added.

The present building was begun in 1450 with the construction of the two wings giving onto the courtyard, dedicated to Jeanne de Faverois, the wife of Jean de Refuge. In 1470, Pierre de Refuge was granted royal permission to fortify his castle and shortly afterwards, he erected the north wing, whose defensive features were aimed to impress, playing a purely symbolic role in times of peace. However, when completed by his grandson, Jean de Villebresmes, the château acquired a certain grace: the east wing in the main court has a gallery of arcades with lovely dormer windows; the attractive turreted staircase in the northwest corner has windows flanked by pilasters with Renaissance motifs; the large windows added in the 18C to the south wing made it ideal as a spinning mill in the 19C. The size of the rooms seen from within is impressive; so are the wooden roof-frame of the main building that is shaped like a ship's hull, and the conical roof-frame of the towers.

The Medieval-themed garden, east of the château, features herbs and plants that were used for dyes and traditional medicines. The garden enjoys pretty views of the nearby **Église St-Éloi,** just behind the château. Note the quarter-sphere vault and finely carved choir stalls in the early 12C chancel and the Villebresmes coat of arms on the vaulted roof of the family chapel.

Bordered by the Loire to the north and the Cher to the south, the Sologne is a largely unspoilt region of forests, lakes and farmland where time seems to have stood still in its sleepy red-brick and half-timbered villages. It offers the perfect combination of nature, picturesque hamlets, a couple of remarkable châteaux, a range of outdoor activities, wildlife spotting and some truly delicious local specialities with goats' cheese and the famous tarte tatin.

Country Life

The best way to appreciate the Sologne is a walking tour from the Domaine du Ciran in Ménestrau-en-Villette, especially early in the morning or at dusk, which are the best times to spot deer, wild boar, foxes and pine martens. The visitor centre provides explanations of local history, flora and fauna. The region also features two noteworthy châteaux. Valençay, once home to Napoleon's wily minister Talleyrand, is best viewed during one of the candlelit tours in summer complete with carriage rides in the park, hunting horns and other attractions. La Ferté Saint-Aubin has a superbly restored estate that offers a wealth of family attractions, including working stables and an Orient Express railway station on the grounds, equipped with its own steam engine and carriage.

Ambitions of François I

Romorantin-Lathenay is the main town in the Sologne. In 1517 François I had great intentions for the locality. He asked Leonardo da Vinci to start drawing up grandiose plans for a magnificent palace and town centre. Sadly, the project came to nothing as the King's famous guest was to die at Amboise in

Highlights

1 Driving tour through the **Sologne** woods in autumn (p144)

2 The **Domaine du Ciran** nature trail, particularly at dawn or dusk (p145)

3 Tasting home-made madeleines in the kitchens of **La Ferté-Saint-Aubin** château (p149)

4 A unique combination of architectural styles at **Selles-sur-Cher** (p152)

5 Automobile Museum at **Château de Valençay** (p154)

1519. The main attraction today is the local history museum, the Musée de Sologne.

Visitors seeking a lasting impression of the Sologne should read Alain-Fournier's classic novel *Le Grand Meaulnes*. Indeed, no other work better captures the atmosphere of the region's flat expanses as early morning mists linger over still ponds and bird calls are the only sounds to break the silence.

Mill of the River Sauldre, Romorantin-Lanthenay

© Jean-Marc Charles/age fotostock

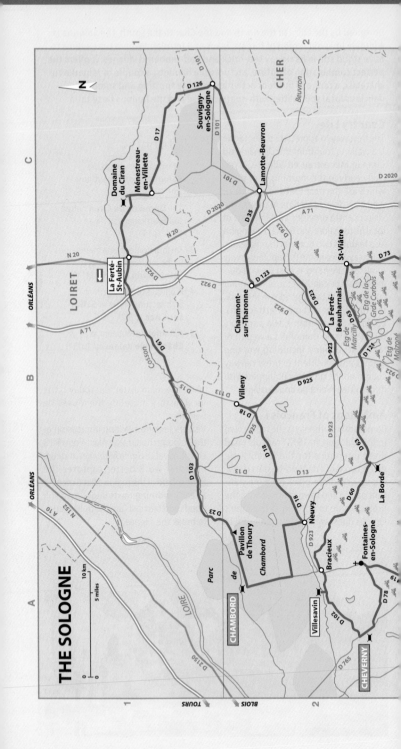

THE SOLOGNE

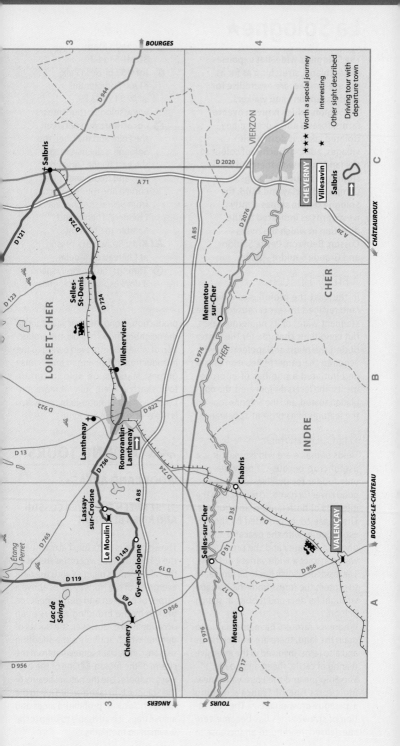

BOURGES

VIERZON

Salbris

D 944

D 121

D 724

D 2020

A 71

A 85

D 2076

CHÂTEAUROUX

D 123

Selles-St-Denis

D 724

Villeherviers

LOIR-ET-CHER

CHER

CHER

D 922

Lanthenay

D 922

D 976

Romorantin-
Lanthenay

D 756

Mennetou-
sur-Cher

D 13

A 85

D 724

Lassay-
sur-Croisne

Chabris

INDRE

Le Moulin

D 143

Gy-en-Sologne

Selles-sur-Cher

D 35

D 4

BOUGES-LE-CHÂTEAU

Étang
Perret

D 765

D 119

D 19

D 956

D 57

VALENÇAY

Lac de
Soings

D 63

Chémery

D 976

Meusnes

D 956

D 956

D 17

ANGERS

TOURS

★★★ Worth a special journey

★ Interesting

○ Other sight described

Driving tour with
departure town

CHEVERNY

Villesavin

Salbris

143

La Sologne★

The Sologne's wide, flat expanses of heathland, stretching as far as the eye can see, are a paradise for hunters, anglers and walkers. The region, which is given over to farms, forests and a great many isolated lakes, is dotted with villages, adding touches of colour to the landscape with their red-brick, stone and timber buildings. Composed of clay and sand, the Sologne terrain slopes gently westwards as indicated by the direction in which the rivers – Cosson, Beuvron, Petite Sauldre and Grande Sauldre – flow.

A BIT OF HISTORY

In the past the region was a wasteland ravaged by fevers caused by the stagnant water of its numerous lakes, but conditions changed for the better during the reign of Napoleon III, who acquired the Lamotte Beuvron estate and initiated a number of improvements. The fevers disappeared, the population soared, and the Sologne took on the features of its present appearance.

THE COUNTRYSIDE

Fields of maize are widespread; it is a useful crop because it provides not only fodder for the livestock but also good cover for game, so reconciling the interests of both farmers and hunters. The dense cover provided by the forest, together with the peaceful atmosphere of the area and the presence of water, attract a wide variety of fauna. The resident wildlife has to be regulated to protect the forest from the damage wrought by deer and rabbits in search of food.

Wherever farmers have been able to drain the land, there are fruit orchards and also farms involved in the intensive rearing of cattle, sheep and goats. The Sologne and the Loire valley near Blois form one of France's leading asparagus-growing areas. The cultivation of strawberries has become very specialised, leading to an increase in production. Along the Cher valley and in the neighbourhood of Blois, the production of wine has improved owing to the introduction of Sauvignon and Gamay grapes. Markets are held in certain towns such as Gien, Sully, Romorantin-Lanthenay and Lamotte-Beuvron, which is the centre of the Sologne.

- **Michelin Map:** 318: H-5 to J-7
- **Info**: 32 pl. de la Paix, 41200 Romorantin. 02 54 76 43 89. www.sologne-tourisme.fr.
- **Location:** Lying between the Loire and the Cher, the Sologne is deliniated to the east by the Sancerre hills and to the west by a curved line running north from Selles-sur-Cher via Chémery, Thenay and Sambin to Cheverny.
- **Kids:** Strawberry season at Château du Moulin.
- **Timing:** You can easily spend 3 days exploring Sologne.

🚗 DRIVING TOURS

WOODLAND AREAS★

1 BETWEEN THE RIVER COSSON AND RIVER BEUVRON

The Sologne is at its most attractive in the early autumn, when the russet of the falling leaves mingles with the dark evergreen of the Norway pines above a carpet of bracken and purple heather, broken by the brooding waters of an occasional lake. However, the bursts of gunfire, which announce the shooting season, can detract somewhat from the charm of the region. One of the best ways to appreciate the natural beauty of the Sologne is to take a walk. Due to the many enclosures, prohibited areas and animal traps, it is advisable to keep to the waymarked footpaths.

Deer in the Sologne forest

La Ferté-Saint-Aubin★
See LA FERTÉ-SAINT-AUBIN

▶ Drive NW out of La Ferté along D 61 towards Ligny-le-Ribault. D 61 then becomes D 103; in Couy-sur-Cosson, turn left onto D 33.

The **Pavillon de Thoury** marks the entrance to the Chambord estate. Walkers and visitors are welcome along footpaths. An observation area is available for keen picture hunters wishing to catch a glimpse of deer and wild boar on the move.

Château de Chambord★★★
See CHÂTEAU DE CHAMBORD

▶ Follow D 112 S, turn left at the Chambord intersection, then right at King Stanislas crossroads onto the forest road to Neuvy.

Neuvy
Apply to the town hall to visit.
04 70 44 31 36.
Neuvy is located on the southern edge of Boulogne forest on the north bank of the River Beuvron. The village church stands on its own in a graveyard near a half-timbered farmhouse with brick infill on the opposite bank. It was partially rebuilt in 1525. The rood beam supports 15C statues.

Villeny
The **Maison du cerf** reveals all the secrets of the stag, the "king" of the forests of the Sologne (open mid-Jun–mid-Sept daily except Mon and public holidays 10am-12.30pm, 1.30–6.30pm, open all year for group visits, call ahead to book; €5; 02 54 98 23 10; www.lamaisonducerf.e-monsite.com).

▶ Head S to La Marolle and D 925. At Neung, take D 923.

La Ferté-Beauharnais
The village has retained several old houses (Maison du Carroir, Cour à l'Écu, Relais du Dauphin) worth a detour.

▶ Drive E along D 922 then turn left onto D 123.

Chaumont-sur-Tharonne
The line of the old ramparts can be traced in the layout of the town, which is situated round its 15C–16C church on a bluff in the centre of the Sologne.

Lamotte-Beuvron
Soon after Napoleon III acquired the château, this simple hamlet got its own railway station and promptly became the rendezvous point of hunters in the Sologne region.

Souvigny-en-Sologne
The 12C–16C church, preceded by a vast timber porch (known as a *caquetoir* or gossip place), is surrounded by timber-framed houses.
The immediate surroundings are criss-crossed by 80km/50mi of marked

footpaths *(detailed map available in local shops)*.

Ménestreau-en-Villette
7km/4.3mi E from La Ferté-St-Aubin.
In this Sologne village, the **Domaine du Ciran** (Conservatoire de la Faune Sauvage de Sologne ⅄ ◷ *daily Nov–Mar 10am–noon, 2–5pm; Apr–Jun and Sept–Oct 10am–noon, 2–6pm; Jul–Aug 10am–12.30pm, 2–7pm; ⊜€5; ℘02 38 76 90 93; www.domaineduciran.com*) is devoted to the Sologne region, its flora and its fauna.
Here you get an insight into the natural resources of the area, thanks to a discovery trail featuring around 20 display cases framed with wood. Observation points have been set up all along, providing opportunities for photographing deer, wild boar, foxes, martens and roe deer, especially at sunrise or sunset.

🗎 The Domaine du Ciran is criss-crossed by discovery trails. For a closer look at the natural environment, take advantage of walking tours, which last several days, and witness the astonishing variety of the Sologne flora and fauna. *Don't forget your camera, binoculars and sturdy shoes.*

LAKES AND MOORS★

② ROUND TRIP FROM ROMORANTIN-LANTHENAY

Romorantin-Lanthenay
See ROMORANTIN-LANTHENAY

▷ Drive E out of Romorantin along D 724.

Villeherviers
The village is set among asparagus fields in the broad valley of the Sauldre. There is Plantagenet vaulting in the 13C church.

Selles-St-Denis
This village lies on the north bank of the Sauldre. The chapel, which dates from the 12C and 15C and has side chapels

and an apse in the Flamboyant style, is decorated with 14C murals of the Life of St Genoulph to whom it is dedicated.

Salbris
On the south bank of the Sauldre, Salbris is a busy crossroads and a good centre for excursions into the forest.
The stone and brick **church of St-Georges** was built in the 15C and 16C. The transept chapels have coats of arms of the donors on the keystones of the vault and attractive pendant sculptures representing the Three Wise Men and the Virgin and Child and the symbols of the Evangelists.

▷ Drive N out of Salbris along N 20, turn left onto D 121 then right 10km/6.2mi farther on towards St-Viâtre on D 73.

St-Viâtre
This smart little town was formerly a place of pilgrimage containing the relics of St Viâtre, a hermit who retired here in the 6C.
At the chancel step stands a remarkable carved wood desk (18C) of surprising size. In the south transept are four **painted panels★** dating from the early 16C.
👤👤 **Maison des Étangs** – The site occupies two houses and presents the ecology, fauna and fish life in the Sologne, as well as a display of traditional crafts (⅄ ◷ *Apr–Oct daily 10am–noon, 2–6pm; Nov–Mar Wed, Sat–Sun and public holidays 2–6pm; ◷1 Jan, 25 Dec; ⊜€5, child 6–16, €3; ℘02 54 88 23 00; www.maison-des-etangs.com*).
Reposoir St-Viâtre – This small 15C brick building sits at the north entrance.

▷ Continue W along D 63 to Vernou-en-Sologne.

South of the village stands the beautiful **Château de La Borde** (⊶ *closed to the public)*. Note the slate inlays underlining the openings.

▷ Drive to Bracieux along D 60 via Bauzy.

Bracieux

This smart village lies on the border of the Sologne and the region round Blois. The houses are grouped round the 16C market on the south bank of the Beuvron, which is spanned by a bridge.

Château de Villesavin★

2km/1mi from Bracieux along D 102.
See CHAMBORD: Excursion

Château de Cheverny★★★

See CHÂTEAU DE CHEVERNY

▶ Drive out of Cheverny along D 765 then turn left onto D 78.

Fontaines-en-Sologne

The **church**, which largely dates from the 12C, was fortified in the 17C. Beside the church there are half-timbered houses with roofs of small flat tiles, commonly found in the region.

▶ Take D 119 S along Perret Lake then along Soings-en-Sologne Lake.

Lac de Soings

The water level of the lake is liable to change abruptly without any apparent reason; in the past, this tendency gave rise to many local legends.

▶ Continue along D 119. Just before Rougeiu take D 63 right.

Château de Chémery

Apr–Sept daily 11am–6pm; Jan–Feb with reservation. 8€. 02 54 71 82 77. www.chateaudechemery.fr.
The château (15C and 16C) is a mixture of medieval and Renaissance architecture. It was built on the site of a 12C fortress. In the grounds is a dovecote with spaces for 1,200 birds.

▶ In Rougeou, turn left onto D 143.

Gy-en-Sologne

In this village, take time to visit a typical Sologne cottage here: the **locature de La Straize** (*Apr–mid-Sept Sat–Sun and holidays 10am–11.30am, 3–6pm; weekdays by reservation; call ahead*

for all visits and for entry fee; 02 54 83 81 03; http://lastraize.pagesperso-orange.fr) dates from the 16C.

Lassay-sur-Croisne

Lassay is a village in the Sologne, a region of woodland and vast lakes. A cluster of old houses, crowned with long slate roofs, add a colourful touch to the urban landscape thanks to their stone and brick architecture.

Église St-Denis

This charming little 15C church has a beautiful rose window and a slender spire. In the left transept, above the recumbent figure of Philippe du Moulin, there is an attractive early 16C **fresco** depicting St Christopher.

Château de Selles Sur Cher★

1 place du Château – 41130 Selles sur Cher. Early Apr-Jun 10am-noon, 2-6pm; Jul-August daily 10am-7pm; Sept-mid-Nov daily10am-noon, 2-6 pm; mid-Nov-Palm Sunday, Wed-Sun, 1.30-5.30pm.
1 Jan, 25 Dec; 8, child 6–16, €5 02 54 97 76 50. www.chateau-selles-sur-cher.com.
This vast medieval chateau has features that date back to the 13th century, but has been restored and filled with attractions that cater to a broad demographic, from kids to history enthusiasts. Wine is also produced on the estate and can be tasted and purchased. The oldest section of the chateau is the gate and tower, including the tower of the coq, which was constructed in the 13th century. Note the defensive holes in the wall to the east of the tower, and the latrines visible on the northwest side. The medieval chateau is situated on the west, and there are extensive parklands surrounding the estate. Originally, the entrance to the west was defended by a moat and a drawbridge, which has been made into a bridge. Picnics are permitted on the grounds.

ADDRESSES

🛏 STAY

🍴🛏 **Chambre d'hôte Le Petit Clos** – 6 r. de la Folie. 41600 Chaumont-sur-Tharonne. ☏02 54 88 28 17. www. lepetitclos.com. 5 rooms. 🅿. This brick-built house at the heart of the village has an enclosed garden. The bedroom furniture, adorned in colourful fabrics, was made by the inn's owner.

🍴🛏 **Domaine de Valaudran** – Av. de Romorantin-Lanthenay, 41300 Salbris. ☏02 54 97 20 00. www.hotelvaludran.com. Closed 25 Dec–1 Jan. 31 rooms. This fine brick house with its own park is a good place to relax and find peace and quiet. Follow the tree-lined drive to the house, where the rooms have views over the countryside. Pool on-site.

🍴🛏 **Hôtel Restaurant Le Parc Sologne** – 8 av. d'Orléans, 41300 Salbris. ☏02 54 97 18 53. www.hotelleparcsologne. com. Closed mid-Dec–early Jan. 26 rooms. 🅿. Restaurant: dinner only. An elegant old-Sologne style hotel in a rural setting, with a rustic restaurant. In warmer season, dine on the terrace.

🍴🛏 **Hôtel Tatin** – 5 av. de Vierzon, 41600 Lamotte-Beuvron. ☏02 54 88 00 03. www.hotel-tatin.fr. Closed 15–30 Mar. 14 rooms. Restaurant: dinner only. This family-run bourgeoise hôtel has a garden terrace and well-outfitted rooms. The Tatin sisters invented their famous apple tarte here (the era's oven is installed in the bar).

🍴🛏 **Château de Beauharnais** – 172 r. du Prince Eugène, La Ferté-Beauharnais. ☏02 54 83 72 18. www. chateaudebeauharnais.com. 3 rooms. 🅿. The B&B-style rooms are furnished in a stately château that was once the residence of the Beauharnais. It possesses a huge park where you can enjoy pleasant walks.

🍴🛏 **Le Manoir de Contres** – 23 r. des combattants en Afn, 141000 Contres. ☏02 54 78 45 39. www.manoir decontres.com. Closed 25 Dec–13 Feb. 8 rooms. 🅿. Though in town, the refurbished 19C manor house is surrounded by a 1ha park. The comfortable rooms are spacious and equipped with a modern bathroom. The restaurant (🍴🛏) serves traditional fare in a pleasant atmosphere.

🍴 EAT

🍴 **Les Copains d'Abord** – 52 av. d'Orléans, 41300 Salbris. ☏02 54 97 24 24. www.auxcopains.com. Locals know this bistro with its happy, convivial atmosphere. Good traditional cooking and weekend jazz.

🍴 **Chez Jacques** – 11 pl. de la Halle, 41250 Bracieux. ☏02 54 46 03 84. &. Pretty spot next to the marketplace (every Sat). Best for eating outdoors on fine days. Traditional cuisine, excellent welcome.

🍴🛏 **Le Relais de Sologne** – 63 pl. 8 mai, 45240 Ménestreau-en-Villette. ☏02 38 76 97 40. www.le-relais-de-sologne.com. Closed Sun eve, Mon eve, Tue eve, Wed. In the heart of the village, this traditional restaurant features a rustic dining room and terrace. Don't miss the nearby Domaine du Ciran nature conservation centre 2km/1.2mi away.

🍴🛏 **Auberge du Prieuré** – 5 rte de Romorantin, 41230 Lassay-sur-Croisne. ☏06 61 25 96 04. Closed Sun eve, Mon–Tue. &.🅿. This restaurant has a lovely setting opposite a Gothic church. Simple and refined décor with exposed beams and carved wooden mantelpiece.

SHOPPING

Bergeries de Sologne – Feme de Jaugeny, 41250 Fontaines. ☏02 54 46 45 61. Call for opening hours and details about visitor centre and tastings (Feb–mid-Nov). Small holding specialising in raising sheep and chickens. The "discovery and gastronomy" days include tours of the farm, sheepdog displays and sheep shearing. Shorter programmes also available. Preserved meat dishes are available for sale.

Fresnel Pascal –54 av. de l'Hôtel-de-Ville, 41600 Lamotte-Beuvron. ☏02 54 88 08 81. Since the Sologne is hunting country, this butcher naturally decided to make his own wild boar sausage. He also makes other award-winning produce such as game pâtés and terrines, black pudding with wild mushrooms, sausages, foie gras as well as the local rillettes and rillons potted meat specialities. Meat-lovers should stop by and ask the staff what is fresh and special that day.

La Ferté-Saint-Aubin★

The old district has a few typical local houses: low, timber-framed constructions with brick infill and large roofs of flat tiles. A splendid château stands among greenery, on the banks of the River Cosson.

VISIT

Château★

⏱ *Feb school holidays 2–6pm; Mar and Sept weekends 2-6pm; Apr school holidays 10am-6pm; May-Jun, weekends and holidays 10am-6pm; Jul-Aug daily 10am-7pm; Dec weekends and holidays 2-6pm.* ⬛ *€9.50 for park and chateau, €7.50 under 25s; €14.50 including "Poison treasure hunt".* ☎ *02 38 76 52 72. www.chateau-ferte.com.*

This impressive edifice is built in brick relieved with courses of stone. To the left is the Little Château with its 16C diamond-patterned brickwork and to the right, the mid-17C château, with a Classical façade topped by sculpted dormers.

Inside, the Dining Hall and the Grand Salon have 18C furnishings and portraits including one of the Marquis de la Carte attributed to Largillière. One room is devoted to the memory of **Maréchal de la Ferté**, who distinguished himself

- ▶ **Population:** 7,127
- **Michelin Map:** 318: I-5
- **Info:** r. des Jardins, 45240 La Ferté-St-Aubin. ☎02 38 64 67 93. www.otsilafertesaintaubin.fr.
- **Location:** On the N 20, 15km/9mi S of Orléans.
- **Kids:** Escape game.
- **Timing:** Allow 1 hour.

in battle. The Château is renowned for its working stables and tack room. In the fully functioning kitchens, **madeleines** are baked and can be sampled.

It's also possible to stay on the grounds or rent a number of cottage in the estate. Hunting trips also offered, or escape games and themed treasure hunts for all visitors. See website for full activities on offer.

The Park

Walk in the English-style park with its network of islets.

ADDRESSES

STAY

Chambre d'hôtes Bambous et Pamplemousses – 4 rue de la Poste, 45240 La Ferté-St-Aubin. ☎06 73 61 66 17. http://bambous-pamplemousses.com. 2 rooms. This pretty historic house is clean and comfortable, with friendly staff who will help arrange visits in the local area. Restaurant and two rooms with private bathrooms on first floor.

EAT

L'Orée des Chênes – 921 route de Marcilly-en-Villette, 45240 La Ferté-St-Aubin. ☎02 38 64 84 00. www.loreedeschenes.com. Elegant hotel and restaurant in large grounds that offers high-class cuisine served indoors or outside during the warmer months. A good place for a special occasion.

Château de la Ferté-Saint-Aubin
© MarekUsz/iStock

Romorantin-Lanthenay

The point where the River Sauldre divides into several arms is the site of the former capital of the Sologne, with its pine forests, moorlands, numerous lakes, and gastronomic specialities including pumpkin pâté.

SIGHTS

Old Houses★

On the corner of rue de la Résistance and rue du Milieu stands the **chancellerie**, a corbelled Renaissance house, of brick and half-timber construction, where the royal seals were kept when the King resided in town. The corner post features a coat of arms and a musician playing the bagpipes.

Standing at the junction of rue du Milieu and rue de la Pierre is the **Maison du Carroir doré** with its remarkable carved corner posts showing the Annunciation and St George killing the Dragon.

View from the bridges★

From the north branch of the river there is a **view** of the **Château royal** opposite the Sologne museum complex, which dates from the 15C and 16C and now houses the sub-Prefecture. Along the narrow southern branch of the river is a row of half-timbered houses.

▶ **Population:** 17,615.

⚙ **Michelin Map:** 318: H-7

ℹ **Info:** pl. de la Paix, 41200 Romorantin-Lanthenay. ☎02 54 76 43 89. www. sologne-tourisme.fr.

◖ **Location:** 40km/25mi SE of Blois; almost all the routes of Sologne converge on Romorantin.

⊚ **Don't Miss:** The Old Town.

🕐 **Timing:** Allow 1–2 hours to explore the town.

Square Ferdinand-Buisson

This is a pleasant public garden with tall trees and footbridges over the Sauldre river. There are beautiful views of the banks, especially of the mill.

Chapelle St-Roch

☞ *Closed to the public.*

Situated on the edge of the St-Roch suburb, this graceful chapel features a façade framed by small towers: the attractive semi-circular windows are typical of the Renaissance

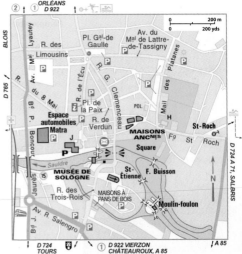

Église St-Étienne
Above the transept crossing of the church rises a Romanesque tower with finely executed sculptures.

ADDITIONAL SIGHTS
Espace automobiles Matra
7 r. des Capucins. ♿🕐*Daily Mon–Fri 9am–noon, 2–6pm; Sat–Sun and public holidays 10am–noon, 2–6pm.* 🕐*1 Jan, 1 May, 25 Dec.* ☞*€7.* 📞*02 54 94 55 58. www.museematra.com.*

Housed in disused factory premises, this Motor Racing Museum presents an exhibition of Matra cars, including the Formula 1 car that won the world championship in 1969. A series of display cases retrace the technical developments in racing car construction. Established in 1968, Matra is the biggest employer in the town.

Musée de Sologne★
Quai de l'Île-Marin. 🕐*Closed until further notice; check website for details.* 📞*02 54 95 33 66. www.museedesologne.com.*

In the old quarter of Romorantin-Lanthenay, spanning the river, the museum is housed in three buildings.

The **Moulin du Chapitre**, whose exterior still reveals traces of its former activity as a 19C flour mill, consists of exhibit areas laid out over four floors: the history, flora and fauna of the Sologne region; life in the châteaux and the rural community.

The **Moulin de la Ville** presents the history of Romorantin, focusing on Leonardo da Vinci's plans to build a new city and royal residence. The **Jacquemart Tower**, the oldest building in town, houses temporary exhibits.

EXCURSIONS
Lanthenay
4km/2.5mi N.

The Chapelle St-Aignan contains a painting of the Virgin Mary between St John the Baptist and St Sebastian, dating from 1523 and attributed to Timoteo Viti from Urbino who influenced Raphael.

Mennetou-sur-Cher
20km/12.4mi SE along D 922 and N 76.

This medieval town is enclosed within its original ramparts, which were built in the 13C. On the side of town towards Vierzon, En-Bas gateway can boast that Joan of Arc once passed through its portal; it features pointed supporting arches, and its guard-room contains the original fireplace complete with hood.

Old houses – Grande-Rue, the steep and winding main street, leads from Bonne-Nouvelle gateway to that of En-Haut, past Mennetou's old houses. They embody a variety of architectural styles, dating from the 13C to 16C.

ADDRESSES

🛏 STAY
🍽🍽 **Chambre d'hôte La Petite Maison** – *Nocfond, 41320 Langon.* 📞*02 54 98 16 21. 4 rooms.* 🅿🚪. Small establishment in a lovely rural setting. Visit Langon's 16C church.

🍽🍽🍽 **Hôtel La Pyramide** – *r. de la Pyramide.* 📞*02 54 76 26 34. https://hotel-la-pyramide.fr. 66 rooms. Restaurant🍽🍽.* This modern building is near a cultural complex. Functional rooms, which are all identical, in a modern style. Traditional meals are served in the simple dining room or on the terrace behind the restaurant.

🍴 EAT
🍽🍽 **Auberge Le Lanthenay** – *9 r. Notre Dame du Lieu. 2.5km/1.5mi by D 922.* 📞*02 54 98 35 94. www.hotel-restaurant-le-lanthenay.fr. Closed Sun eve, Mon.* The auberge is a pleasant place to spend the night *(10 rooms 🍽🍽)* in a picturesque hamlet where you'll discover good cuisine combined with quiet surroundings. The dining room is more intimate than the veranda. *Book in advance.*

Selles-sur-Cher

There are two good reasons to savour the charms of Selles-sur-Cher: its delicious goats' cheese with a hint of hazelnut, and a château that, on one side, presents the face of an austere fortress and on the other, a gracious Italian Renaissance residence. The town straddles both banks of a loop in the River Cher.

▶ **Population:** 4,715.
⏱ **Michelin Map:** 318: G-8
ℹ **Info:** 26 r. de Sion, 41130 Selles-sur-Cher. ✆02 54 95 25 44. www.sudvaldeloire.fr.
▶ **Location:** 16km/10mi SW of Romorantin and 15km/9mi E of St-Aignan on the D 976 or the more scenic D 17.
👁 **Don't Miss:** The decorative elements in the church St-Eusice.
🕐 **Timing:** Allow 1–2 hours to explore the town.

THE TOWN
Église St-Eusice
Built in the 12C and 15C, torched by Coligny in 1562, this church was partly restored in the 17C and 19C. The façade, almost entirely Romanesque, includes columns and capitals from an earlier church. The **end of the chancel** is finely constructed with two Romanesque friezes: one, under the windows, illustrates scenes from the New Testament with naively sculpted figures; the other, higher and more elegant, relates incidents from the saint's life.

By the north wall, the bas-reliefs represent work in different months of the year; higher up *(to the right)* is a Visitation, sheltered by the transept chapel. The late 13C north wall is broken by a doorway with sculpted capitals and a garland of wild rose flowers and leaves. The crypt houses the 6C tomb of Saint Eusice.

Château
The remains of the stout 13C fortress stand opposite two 17C buildings joined by a long wall. Four bridges span the wide moat.

EXCURSION
Meusnes
6.5km/4mi SW on D 956 towards Valençay, then right on D 17.
The **church** is pure Romanesque style. In the transept, a triumphal arch is surmounted by three arcades. The statues are 15C and 16C.

The town hall houses the small **musée de la Pierre à Fusil**, which recounts the history of the local gunflint industry over three centuries (♿ ✆02 54 40 43 31).

ADDRESSES

🛏 STAY

🍴🍴🍴 **Courjumelle** – *1 sq. du Centenaire, 41130 Selles-sur-Cher.* ✆02 54 97 46 00. www.courjumelle.com. 🅿. *2 gîtes.* This charming guesthouse sits just outside Selles-sur-Cher. The ground floor gives way to a flower garden and a small swimming pool. The rooms are very comfortable and decorated in good taste by the owners with a flair for antiques.

🍽 EAT

🍴🍴 **Le Pont de la Saudre** – *2 r. Nationale, rte. de Tours, 41130 Billy.* ♿🅿. ✆02 54 96 21 65. www.lepontdesauldre.fr. This traditional restaurant with a bright décor serves local specialities, including goat cheeses from the region. Meals are served outside in nice weather.

SHOPPING

La Fromagerie Sarl – *2 r. du Dr-Massacré.* ✆02 54 88 57 60. Open daily except Mon 9am–12.30pm, 3–7pm, Sun 9.30am–noon, closed first week Jan. Here you'll find a full selection of regional goats' cheese including Selles-sur-Cher, Pyramides de Valençay, Pouligny-Saint-Pierre, an unusual blue cheese and a selection of Loire wines.

© Lionel Lourdel/Photononstop

Château de Valençay

Château de Valençay★★★

Geographically speaking, Valençay is in the Berry region, but the château can be included with those in the Loire valley because of the period of its construction and its huge size, in which it resembles Chambord. A *Son et Lumière* show enhances the château's beautiful setting.

A BIT OF HISTORY

A Financier's Château – Valençay was built c.1540 by Jacques d'Estampes, the owner of the existing castle. He had married the daughter of a financier, who brought him a large dowry, and he wanted a residence worthy of his new fortune. The 12C castle was demolished, and in its place rose the present sumptuous building.

Born in Paris into aristocracy, and educated for the church (a deformed foot prevented his military service), **Charles-Maurice de Talleyrand-Périgord** (1754–1838) began his career under King Louis XVI as the Bishop of Autun. He was serving as the Minister of Foreign Affairs when he bought Valençay in 1803 at the request of Napoleon, so that he would have somewhere to receive important foreign visitors. Talleyrand managed his career so skilfully that he did not finally retire until 1834.

Michelin Map: 318: G-9

Info: Tourist Office: 2 av. de la Résistance, 36600 Valencay. ℘02 54 00 04 42. www.valencay-tourisme.fr. **Chateau:** Mar–Apr 10.30am–6pm; May and Sept 10am–6pm; Jun 9.30am–6.30pm; Jul–Aug 9.30am–7pm; Oct–mid-Nov 10.30am–5pm; Dec 11-Jan 3 11am-5pm. 1 Jan, 25 Dec. €14. ℘02 54 00 10 66. www.chateau-valencay.fr.

Location: 56km/35mi south of Blois and 23km/14mi southeast of St-Aignan.

Kids: The animal park and Napoléon's vast maze.

Don't Miss: The park; wine and cheese tasting.

Timing: Getting the most out of your visit will take at least 3 hours.

VISIT

The **entrance pavilion** is a huge building, designed like a keep, but for show rather than defence, with many windows, harmless turrets and fancy machicolations. The **west wing** was added in the 17C and altered in the 18C. At roof level mansard windows alternate with small circular apertures. The visit of the ground floor includes the great Louis XVI vestibule; the gallery devoted to the Talleyrand-Périgord family; the Grand Salon and the Blue Salon, which contain many works of art and sumptuous **Empire furniture★★** including the famous Congress of Vienna table; and the apartments of the Duchess of Dino. On the first floor, the bedroom of Prince Talleyrand is followed by the room occupied by Ferdinand VII, King of Spain, when he was confined to Valençay by Napoleon from 1808 to 1814; the apartments of the Duke of Dino and those of Mme de Bénévent (portrait of the princess by Élisabeth Vigée-Lebrun); the great gallery (with a Diana by Houdon) and the great staircase.

Le Petit Théâtre – Opened to the public in 2012, this 90-seat theatre was built in 1810 for the amusement of the Princes of Spain. With its trompe l'oeil decoration and faux marble, it depicts a remarkable unity of First Empire style.

Park

Black swans, ducks and peacocks strut freely in the formal French gardens near the château. Under the great trees in the park, deer, llamas, camels and kangaroos are kept in vast enclosures.

Musée de l'Automobile de Valençay

12 Av. de la Résistance. ♿ ○*Daily Apr– Sept 10am–12.30pm, 2–6pm.* ○*Nov– Mar.* ☞*€6.* ℘*02 54 00 07 74. www.musee-auto-valencay.fr.*

The Car Museum contains the collection of the Guignard brothers, the grandsons of a coachbuilder from Vatan (Indre). More than 60 perfectly maintained vintage cars, the earliest dating from 1898, help convey the colourful history of the automobile.

The 1908 Renault limousine was used by presidents Poincaré and Millerand. There are also old Michelin maps and guides predating 1914. Car parts and posters round out the collection. Tem-

porary exhibitions are also installed each year.

EXCURSION
Chabris

14km/8.7mi NE along D 4.

This ancient Roman town lying on the south bank of the Cher is renowned for its wines and its goats' cheese.

Église

The church is dedicated to St Phalier, a 5C anchorite who died in Chabris and was at the origin of a pilgrimage. Two naive panels in the chancel illustrate the life and miracles of St Phalier. The 11C **crypt** contains the saint's sarcophagus.

ADDRESSES

🛏 STAY

🍴 **Hotel Le Grand Chêne** – *Le Grand-Chêne, 41130 Gièvres (A 85, exit Romorantin).* ℘*02 54 98 61 70. www.hotel-legrandchene.com. 21 rooms.* ♿🅿. Closed to the RN 76, but thankfully not too noisy, this hotel offers rooms with bathrooms and contemporary furnishings.

🍴🍴 **Logis Hotel le Relais du Moulin** – *94 r. Nationale, 36600 Valençay.* ℘*02 54 00 38 00. www.logishotels.com. 54 rooms.* 🅿. *Restaurant*🍴🍴. Functional, well soundproofed rooms at this bright, clean, modern hotel. The restaurant serves traditional cuisine.

🍽 EAT

🍴🍴🍴 **Auberge St-Fiacre** – *5 r. de la Fontaine, 36600 Veuil (6km S of Valençay on D 15 and minor road).* ℘*02 54 40 32 78. www.aubergesaintfiacre.com. Closed Sun eve, Mon and Tue (except Jul–Aug open Tue).* This low-built 17C house in the centre of the village has a terrace under the horse chestnut trees beside a stream.

LEISURE ACTIVITIES

The **château** hosts a number of live shows to illustrate the life of Talleyrand.

🚹🚺 Enjoy getting lost in the **Grand Labyrinthe de Napoléon**, a maze covering more than 2,000 sq m.

The eastern part of the Touraine region boasts some of the Loire valley's finest châteaux at Amboise, Chenonceaux and Chaumont. Farther inland stands the medieval stronghold town of Loches, while Montrésor, Montpoupon and Montrichard are home to other châteaux lying off the beaten track that are well worth discovering. Here the history of the French monarchy in the Loire valley really comes to life as witnessed by the marks left by kings, queens and court favourites in the form of stunning châteaux and charming towns.

Queens and Favourites

Many of the châteaux in the region are dominated by the role that women have played in their lives. Diane de Poitiers, mistress of Henri II, was the chatelaine of Chenonceau before being given her marching orders by Catherine de' Medici upon the King's death in 1559. The favourite moved a short distance up the Loire to Chaumont, while the queen settled in and set about reshaping Chenonceau.

The medieval castle and town of Loches are remembered for Agnès Sorel, mistress of Charles VII, whose tomb lies in the collegiate church. Despite forensic work on her remains when they were returned to the church, there are still questions as to the circumstances of the royal mistress' death, and an exhibit explains how the enquiry was carried out.

The château also bears witness to the passage of Joan of Arc, who came to urge the King to go to Reims for his coronation during the struggle to rid France of the English armies in 1429.

Leonardo da Vinci

The main town in the region is Amboise, renowned for its imposing hilltop château where Charles VIII met an untimely end. Château Clos-Lucé is the nearby manor house in which Leonardo da Vinci spent the last years of his life; it features an exhibit of models of his famous machines, including the first helicopter, automobile and parachute. The displays are always popular with children.

In addition to the fine views it affords of the Loire, the Château de Chaumont hosts an international garden festival every year that draws crowds of landscape gardeners, architects, designers

Château Clos-Lucé

© Hervé Lenain/hemis.fr

and enthusiasts from all over the world. In addition, Montrichard and St-Aignan are pleasant small towns situated on the banks of the Cher river, with some fine medieval buildings, Romanesque churches and, of course, châteaux of their own.

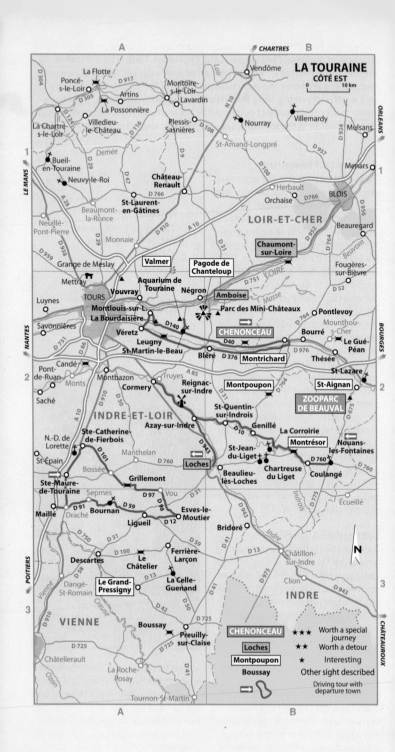

LA TOURAINE
CÔTÉ EST

0   10 km

Amboise★★

East of Tours, the town of Amboise lies on the south bank of the Loire below the remains of its castle; it is best seen from the bridge or the river's north bank. The rock spur dominating the town, on which the château stands, has been fortified since Gallo-Roman times. From the terrace overlooking the river, a fine view of the Loire valley and blue-slate roofs of the town unfolds.

A BIT OF HISTORY

Charles VIII's taste for luxury – The golden age of Amboise was the 15C, when the château was enlarged and embellished by Louis XI and Charles VIII, who spent his childhood in the old castle. Work began in 1492 and for the five following years two ranges of buildings were added to the older structure. Hundreds of workmen laboured continuously, often by candlelight, to meet the King's demands.

In the meantime, the King visited Italy, where he was dazzled by the high artistic standards and extravagant lifestyle. He returned to France laden with furniture, works of art and fabrics. He recruited scholars, architects, sculptors,

▶ **Population:** 13,119.
◔ **Michelin Map:** 317: O-4
▯ **Info**: Tourist Office Val d'Amboise, quai du Général-de-Gaulle, 37402 Amboise. ✆02 47 57 09 28. www.amboise-valdeloire.com.
◐ **Location:** On the south bank of the Loire, 10km/6mi from Chenonceau, and 26km/16mi E of Tours.
🅿 **Parking:** There are a number of pay car parks overlooking the Loire on the quai Général-de-Gaulle, and parking in pl. St Denis.
⊛ **Don't Miss:** The views of Amboise and the Loire from the terrace and towers of the château or views of the château from l'île d'or.
◷ **Timing:** Allow half a day.
👥 **Kids:** The *Son et Lumière* shows in the château, Parc des Mini-Châteaux, the models of Leonardo da Vinci's inventions at Le Clos-Lucé, the Touraine Aquarium.

The Amboise Conspiracy (1560)

This conspiracy was one of the bloodier episodes in the château's history. During the turbulent years leading up to the Wars of Religion, a Protestant aristocrat known as **La Renaudie** gathered a body of reformists around him in Brittany. They were dispatched to Blois in small groups to request of the young king, François II, the freedom to practise their religion. While they were there, they intended to also try to lay hands on the Guises, the deadly enemies of the Huguenots.

The plot was uncovered, and the court promptly moved from Blois, which was indefensible, to Amboise, where the King signed an edict of pacification in an attempt to calm things down. The conspirators persisted, however, and on 17 March they were arrested and killed as quickly as they arrived. La Renaudie also perished. The conspiracy was harshly suppressed; some of the conspirators were hanged from the balcony of the château, some from the battlements; others were thrown into the Loire in sacks, whereas the noblemen were beheaded and quartered. In 1563, a truce was followed by an Act of Toleration, signed at Amboise, which brought an end to the first War of Religion. The country settled down to four years of peace.

Son et Lumière

Entitled "The Amboise Prophecy", this *son et lumière*, entirely written, staged and acted out by local volunteers, features around 400 jugglers, horsemen, fire-eaters and extras, assisted by some highly sophisticated technology (fireworks, fountains, huge images projected onto the surroundings). The show evokes the building of the château, the arrival of Louise of Savoy, the childhood and adolescence of François I, the Italian campaign, as well as daily life and festivities at Amboise to honour the King and his court. *Performances are held Wed and Sat from 4 July to Aug 29 at 10.30pm (10pm in August). €22. ℘02 47 57 14 47. www.renaissance-amboise.com.*

decorators, gardeners, tailors, and even a poultry breeder who had invented the incubator. Thus the year 1496 marked the beginning of Italian influence over French art, although there is little to attest to these changes at Amboise, since the new building was by then well advanced. Impressed by Italian gardens, Charles VIII, on his return, instructed Pacello to design an ornamental garden on the terrace at Amboise.

Among the architects whom he employed were Fra Giocondo, and Il Boccadoro, a leading figure in the introduction of Renaissance ideas to France. He had worked at Blois and Chambord and on the Hôtel de Ville in Paris.

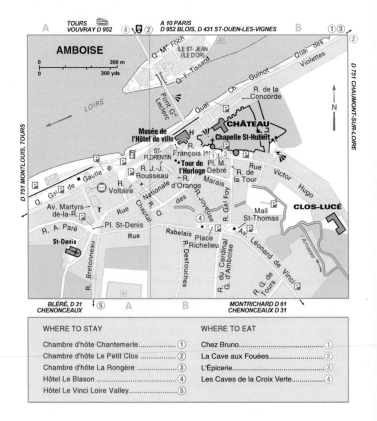

WHERE TO STAY	
Chambre d'hôte Chantemerle	(1)
Chambre d'hôte Le Petit Clos	(2)
Chambre d'hôte La Rongère	(3)
Hôtel Le Blason	(4)
Hôtel Le Vinci Loire Valley	(5)

WHERE TO EAT	
Chez Bruno	(1)
La Cave aux Fouées	(2)
L'Épicerie	(3)
Les Caves de la Croix Verte	(4)

Château Royal d'Amboise and the Loire

The Destruction of the Château –
Together with Blois, Amboise passed to Gaston d'Orléans, Louis XIII's brother and a conspirator. During one of his many rebellions, the château was captured by Royalist troops; the outer fortifications were razed in 1631. It reverted to the crown and was used as a prison where Fouquet, his financial adviser, and the Duke of Lauzun were incarcerated by Louis XIV. Later Napoleon granted the château to Roger Ducos, a former member of the Directory.
As there were no subsidies for its upkeep, the new owner had a large part of it demolished.

VISIT
Château Royal d'Amboise★★
🕐*Daily: Jan and mid-Nov–24 Dec 9am–12.30pm, 2–4.45pm; Feb 9am–12.30pm, 1.30–5pm; Mar 9am–5.30pm; Apr–Jun 9am–6.30pm; Jul–Aug 9am–7pm; Sept–Oct 9am–6pm; 26–31 Dec 9am–4.45pm.* 🕐*1 Jan, 25 Dec.* 🎫*€13.10.* 📞*02 47 57 00 98. www.chateau-amboise.com.*

Terrace
The château is entered via a ramp that opens onto the terrace overlooking the river. From here a magnificent **view★★** of the Loire and of the town's pointed roofs and walls unfolds. The silhouette of the 15C **Tour de l'Horloge** can be seen rising above the rooftops not far

from the old ramparts, and to the west that of the **church of St-Denis**.
In the time of Charles VIII, festivals were held in this enclosed courtyard: tapestries adorned the walls, and a sky-blue awning decorated with sun, moon and stars, gave protection from the weather.

Chapelle St-Hubert
Curiously set astride the fortified town walls, this jewel of Flamboyant Gothic architecture dating from 1491 is all that remains of the buildings that once lined the ramparts. The transept houses the tomb thought to contain the body of the great artist **Leonardo da Vinci**, who died at Amboise.

> "The Wars of Religion have left here the ineffaceable stain which they left wherever they passed. An imaginative visitor at Amboise today may fancy that the traces of blood are mixed with the red rust on the crossed iron bars of the grim-looking balcony, to which the heads of the Huguenots executed on the discovery of the conspiracy of La Renaudie are rumoured to have been suspended. There was room on the stout balustrade – an admirable piece of work – for a ghastly array."
>
> **Henry James**
> *A Little Tour in France*

Royal Apartments

The Royal Apartments are the only part of the château to have escaped demolition. The Gothic wing, overlooking the ramparts above the Loire, was built by Charles VIII.

The **Salle des Gardes nobles**, or guardroom, is roofed with vaulting supported on a single column, forming a Gothic palm-tree of ribs. A spiral staircase leads up to the **Salle des Tambourineurs** (named after the drummers who accompanied the King on royal visits), where Charles VIII withdrew from the public gaze. The room features some interesting pieces of furniture (Cardinal Georges d'Amboise's pulpit) and a fine Brussels tapestry (16C) on the wall, **Homage to Alexander the Great**. Leading on from the Salle des Tambourineurs is the **Salle du Conseil**, also known as the Salle des États (Hall of State). This room features a double stone vault supported by a line of columns down the centre of the room, liberally adorned with motifs of the Kingdom of France and the Duchy of Brittany, the fleur-de-lis and ermine. The second wing was built at the beginning of the 16C and furnished in early French Renaissance style. Note the Gothic piece with a distinctive linen-fold motif, wine-waiter's sideboard, carved extendable tables and chests in walnut.

In **Henri II's bedchamber** *trompe-l'œil* decoration is echoed in the furniture and wall hangings.

Tour des Minimes (or Cavalière)★★

This round tower adjoining the Logis Royal is famous for its wide ramp that horsemen could ride up, ensuring easy access for the provisioning of supplies from the outbuildings in the gardens. The ramp spirals round an empty core that provides air and light.

From the top there is a sweeping **view**★★ of the Loire valley, the Gothic wing of the château and, to the left, the balcony from which several of the conspirators of 1560 were hanged.

Gardens

These pleasant gardens, redesigned in the 19C under Louis-Philippe, lie within the rampart walls, where parts of the château once stood.

Souterrains

Guided tours (1h; in French only) by reservation: Apr–Jun Sat–Sun 5pm; Jul–Aug daily 5pm; Sept Sat–Sun 5pm. *Heritage Days.* €4.20 supplement. Guided tours ("Les coulisses de l'histoire") cross the ramparts from the Tour Garçonnet (15C) and go through underground passages leading to the Minimes cavalry tower.

Inside the Tour des Minimes

© Bertrand Rieger/hemis.fr

Leonardo da Vinci's studio, Château du Clos-Lucé

© Andrea Pistolesi/hemis.fr

Château du Clos-Lucé★★ (Leonardo da Vinci's House)

⏱ *Daily: Jan 10am–6pm; Feb–Jun 9am–7pm; Jul–Aug 9am–8pm; Sept–Oct 9am–7pm; Nov–Dec 9am–6pm.* ⏱ *1 Jan, 2 May, 25 Dec.* 🎫 *Apr–mid-Nov €17; mid-Nov–Mar €14.* ℘ *02 47 57 00 73. www.vinci-closluce.com.*

This manor house was acquired by Charles VIII in 1490. François I also resided in it; he invited **Leonardo da Vinci** to Amboise in 1516 and lodged him here. The great artist and scholar organised court festivities, and lived in this house until his death in 1519 at the age of 67.

The wooden gallery in the courtyard gives a good view of the manor's main façade. On the first floor is Da Vinci's studio, and the bedroom in which he is believed to have worked on his project for draining the Sologne and his design for a palace at **Romorantin** for Louise of Savoy. The basement houses Leonardo's **fabulous machines**, a collection of models based on the designs of this polymath, who was a painter, sculptor, musician, poet, architect, engineer and scholar all in one. His ideas were four centuries ahead of his time.

ADDITIONAL SIGHTS

Musée de l'Hôtel de Ville

Entrance on r. François-1er. ⏱ *Mon–Thu, 8.45am–12pm, 1.30-5.30pm; Fri 8.45am–12pm, 1.30-4.30pm; Sat 9am–12pm.* ⏱ *Public holidays except 14 Jul and 15 Aug. Guided tours available on request.* ℘ *02 47 23 47 42. www.ville-amboise.fr.*

The former town hall was built early in the 16C for Pierre Morin, treasurer to the King of France. It now houses a museum with examples of the royal signature, a 14C carving of the Virgin Mary, Aubusson tapestries, portraits of the Duke of Choiseul, and six rare 18C gouaches of the Château de Chanteloup depicting it at the height of its splendour.

Tour de l'Horloge

The clock tower, also known as the Amboise belfry, was built in the 15C at the expense of the inhabitants on the site of a town gateway called L'Amasse. It spans a busy pedestrian street.

EXCURSIONS

👪 Parc des Mini-Châteaux

S of town, along the Chenonceaux road (D 81). ♿ ⏱ *Daily Apr–Jun and Sept–Oct 10am–6.30pm; Jul–Aug 9.30am–7pm, otherwise closed.* 🎫 *€14, or €22 for combined ticket with aquarium (child 4–12, €10.50).* ℘ *02 47 23 44 57. www.parcminichateaux.com.*

Pagode de Chanteloup

© La Pagode de Chanteloup

(149 steps), there are fine views of the Loire valley, the Forest of Amboise and as far as Tours.

🧑‍🧒 Grand Aquarium de Touraine

8km/5mi W on D 751. After Lussault-sur-Loire, take the D 283 and follow the signs.

♿🕐*Daily Mar 10.30am-6pm (closed Mon-Tue); Apr–Jun 10.30am-6.30pm; Jul-Aug 10am-7pm, Sept-Dec 10.30am-6pm (closed some weekends and holidays, check website for full details).* 🕐*25 Dec, Jan-Feb and 1 wk and Mon–Tue in Nov.* ⊜€14, €22 combined ticket with Mini-Châteaux (child 4–12, €10.50). ✆*02 47 23 44 57.*
www.grandaquariumdetouraine.com.
The aquarium keeps 70 species of mostly European freshwater fish in open-air ponds with reconstituted natural environments. The main advantage of this approach is to allow the fish to develop at the natural rhythm of the seasons.

Négron

3.5km/2.2mi. Cross the river at Pont du Général Leclerc and turn left, following the D 952.

Standing below N 152, this village has a charming square overlooked by the church and a Gothic house with a Renaissance front.

Grounds of Château de Valmer

12km/7.5mi NW of Amboise via the D 751. 🕐*Early Jan–Apr wine tours available by reservation only, Mon–Fri 10am–noon, 2–4pm; May–Jun and Sept Wed–Sun and public holidays 10am–6pm; Jul–Aug Tue-Sun 10am-6pm.* ⊜€10. ✆*02 47 52 93 12.*
www.chateaudevalmer.com.
Wine tastings available year round by appointment.
The park and **gardens★** of Valmer castle occupy a remarkable position on a hillside overlooking the River Brenne. The castle was destroyed by fire in 1948. The Italian-style terraced gardens with statues and fountains, the vast kitchen garden with its varieties of forgotten vegetables and the park enclosed

This 2ha park is home to 44 scale models (scale 1:25) of great châteaux and smaller manor houses of the Loire valley, displayed in a setting commensurate with their size (bonsai trees, miniature TGV railway and boats on the river, etc.). By night, fibre-optical illuminations lend a fairytale atmosphere.

Pagode de Chanteloup★

3km/1.8mi S on D 31 towards Bléré.
🕐*Daily: Mar-May and Sept 10am–6pm; Jun-Aug 10am-7pm; Oct 2-6pm; early Nov 2–5pm.* 👥*Guided tours Wed, Sat–Sun Jul–Sept at 3.30pm.* ⊜€10. ✆*02 47 57 20 97.*
www.pagode-chanteloup.com.
At the edge of the Forest of Amboise, the pagoda is all that remains of the replica of Versailles that was built here by the Duke of Choiseul, minister of Louis XV. When the Duke was exiled to his estates by the King's mistress, Mme du Barry, Choiseul transformed Chanteloup into a haven of intellectual and artistic life and ordered the construction of the pagoda (1775–78) by architect Louis-Denis Le Camus. This folly was in keeping with the decorative fashion of the age for all things Chinese.

With its wide half-moon lake *(boats for hire, €5/h)*, the **setting★** and the paths that fan out across the park give an idea of the grandeur of the sumptuous country residence built by the exiled Duke of Choiseul. From the top of the pagoda by a wall have remained as they were in the 17C. A chapel hewn into the cliffside has retained two 16C stained-glass windows.

The estate produces fine Vouvray AOC and Touraine rosé wine and organises tastings all year round upon appointment. Planted with hydrangeas, the moat provides welcome shade in summer. *To get down, take the 15C spiral staircase hidden by the large clipped yew tree on the terrace in the Italian garden.*

ADDRESSES

🛏 STAY

😊😊 **Chambre d'hôte le Petit Clos** – *7 r. Balzac. ✆02 47 57 43 52. Closed 15 Oct–15 Mar except by reservation.* 🍽 *3 rooms.* 🅿. On the northern bank of the Loire, this B&B provides three rooms with a separate entrance.

😊😊 **Hôtel le Blason** – *11 pl. Richelieu. ✆02 47 23 22 41. www.leblason.fr. Closed 5 Jan–5 Feb. 27 rooms.* 🅿. *Restaurant* 😊😊. This 15C building near the town centre has retained its original walls. The hotel offers rooms with exposed beams, some of which are attic rooms (shower only). The breakfast is of a high standard.

😊😊 **Chateau de Nazelles** – *116, rue Tue-La-Soif, 37530 Nazelles-Negron. www.chateau-nazelles.com ✆06 22 33 55 18.* 🅿. *4 rooms.* Charming, historic country house converted into a guesthouse with outdoor swimming pool and lush, green gardens. The interior mixes clean lines and contemporary styles with the historic bones of the buildings.

😊😊😊 **Hôtel Le Vinci Loire Valley** – *12 av. E. Gounin. 1km/0.6mi S. ✆02 47 57 10 90. www.vinciloirevalley.com. 26 rooms.* 🅿♿. In the suburbs, this Best Western hotel is in a pleasant, contemporary syle. Comfortable, well-equipped rooms.

😊😊😊 **Le Clos d'Amboise** – *27 Rue Rabelais, 37400 Amboise. ✆02 47 30 10 20. www.leclosdamboise.com.* 🅿. *11 rooms.* Well-presented four-star hotel in a former country house with good facilities including sauna and pool, and a historic air.

🍴 EAT

😊 **L'Épicerie** – *46 pl. Michel-Debré. ✆02 47 57 08 94. www.lepicerie-amboise.com.* 🅿. This well-placed restaurant near the castle has a good reputation for the standard of cooking.

😊😊 **Les Caves de la Croix Verte** – *20 rte. d'Amboise. 37530 Pocé-sur-Cisse. 3.5km/2.2mi NE. ✆02 47 57 39 98. www.cavesdelacroixverte.com. Open Fri evenings, Sat lunch and dinner and Sun lunch.* Located in a troglodytic cave, this place serves good meat dishes, *fois gras* and smoked salmon.

😊😊😊 **L'ecluse** – *Rue Racine, 37400 Amboise. ✆02 47 79 94 91, www.ecluse-amboise.fr. Closed Sun, Mon.* Creative and artfully presented dishes served in a minimal yet historic dining room. Excellent use of local vegetables and other seasonal produce.

😊😊😊 **La Cave aux Fouées** – *476 quai des Violettes. ✆02 47 30 56 80. www.lacaveauxfouees.com.* 🅿♿. At this original place in a huge troglodytic cave, sample *rillettes* and other regional specialities, accompanied by *fouées*, flat bread rolls cooked in a wood-fired oven. On Saturday there is a DJ and live music.

TAKING A BREAK

Bigot – *M.-Debré. ✆02 47 57 04 46. https://maison-bigot-amboise.com. Open daily 9am-7pm. Closed Mon morning.* Founded in 1913, this charming pâtisserie near the château offers beautiful cakes, tempting pastries and luscious chocolates handmade according to family recipes.

EVENTS

Festivals – Brass-bands festival, mid-Jun; "Les Courants" contemporary music festival on l'île d'Or, late Jun-early Jul; classical music festival at Église St-Denis Jul-Aug; Fête de la Saint-Hubert 1st Sun Nov at the Château; European Festival of Renaissance Music at Le Clos-Lucé the last weekend in Sept.

Exhibition – "L'univers de la creation" at Le Clos-Lucé first 2 weeks in May.

Market – Jul–Aug: crafts, regional produce, open-air shows.

Wine – Weekends from Easter to 15 August in the Château tunnel. Fête du touraine primeur festival 3rd Fri in Nov.

Château-Renault

On a tongue of land between the River Brenne and the River Gault, at the point where they meet, the château was founded in 1066 by Renault, son of Geoffroi de Château-Gontier. The main street runs in a large curve down to the river bank. Shaded terraces laid out beneath the castle keep offer fine views of the two rivers and their valleys.

▶ **Population:** 5 176.
◔ **Michelin Map:** 317: O-3
▤ **Info:** Office du tourisme, 32 pl. Jean-Jaurès 37110. ℘02 47 56 22 22. www.chateau-renault-tourisme.fr.
◐ **Location:** Between Tours (28km/17mi to the S) and Vendôme (25km/15.5mi N).
▣ **Parking:** Parking areas along the river Gault to the S and W of the château.
◉ **Don't Miss:** The view of the town from the terraces.
◔ **Timing:** Allow 2 hours for the town and surroundings.

VISIT
Musée du Cuir et de la Tannerie
105 terr, r. de la République. ◷*Open May–Sept Tue–Sun 2–6pm.* ◉€6. ℘*02 47 56 03 59. www.museeducuir.org.* Housed inside an old tannery, this **Leather and Tanning Museum** displays the various stages of traditional leather manufacture with, among many other things, a collection of old currying machinery.

Château
The town hall occupies this 17C castle. It belonged to the owners of the château in Châteaudun and then to two illustrious sailors: the Marquis de Château-Renault under Louis XIV and, under Louis XVI, the Count of Estaing, who died by the guillotine in 1793.
A 14C gate, surmounted by a hoarding (to enable the defenders to protect the entrance) leads onto the terraces shaded by lime trees, from which there is an attractive **view★** over the town.
The top of the 12C keep *(donjon)* has been demolished.

EXCURSION
St-Laurent-en-Gâtines
9km/5.6mi W.
At the roadside stands a massive brick and stone edifice. Known for many years as **La Grand' Maison** (Great House), it was once the residence of the abbots of Marmoutier, who owned the land of St-Laurent-en-Gâtines. The building was constructed in the 15C and converted into a church in the 19C. A spire was added to the polygonal tower that housed the stairs; two large Flamboyant windows were inserted on one side.

ADDRESSES

◉ **STAY AND** ◉/**EAT**

◍◍ **Chambre d'hôte La Maréchalerie –** *Hameau le Sentier, 37110 Monthodon. 7km/4.3mi W of Château-Renault by D 54.* ℘*02 47 29 61 66. www.lamarechalerie.fr.* ◰. *5 rooms and 2 gites. Evening meal◍ (Sat only).* This former blacksmith's workshop is full of character with its half-timbering and exposed beams. The five rooms each have different furnishings, but are of equal comfort with private bathrooms.

Château de Chaumont-sur-Loire

Château de Chaumont -sur-Loire★

Overlooking the town and the river, the Château de Chaumont is as well sited as Amboise on the south bank of the Loire. The feudal austerity of the structure is softened by its Renaissance influence, its elegant stair tower and its sumptuous Council Room.

A BIT OF HISTORY

The original fortress of Chaumont was demolished twice; it was rebuilt between 1445 and 1510 by Pierre d'Amboise, Charles I d'Amboise (the eldest of Pierre's 17 children) and Charles II, his grandson.

In 1560, Catherine de' Medici, the widow of Henri II, acquired the castle purely as a means of exacting revenge against Diane de Poitiers, the mistress of the late King. The Queen forced her rival to give up her favourite residence at Chenonceau in exchange for Chaumont. Catherine's stay at Chaumont and the existence there of a room connected by a staircase with the top of a tower have given rise to plenty of speculation. The room has been said to be the study of the Queen's astrologer, and the tower the observatory from which Catherine consulted the stars.

Since 1938 Chaumont has belonged to the French State.

Michelin Map: 318: E-7

Info (Chateau): ♿ ⏱*Daily Jan and mid-Nov– Dec 10.15am–5.30pm; Feb–Mar and end Oct–mid-Nov 10am–6pm; Apr and 1–late Oct 10am–7pm; May–Aug 10am–8pm; Sept 10am–7.30pm. ⏱1 Jan, 25 Dec. €19 (Apr–Oct); €14 rest of year. ☎02 54 20 99 22. www.domaine-chaumont.fr.*

Location: 20km/12mi N of Amboise and 17km/10mi S of Blois.

Parking: By the entrance for disabled visitors. *From the traffic lights in Chaumont, follow signs for Montrichard, and turn right at the first crossroads.*

Timing: Allow 1–2 hours to visit the château.

VISIT

Since its acquisition by the Centre region in 2007, the Domain of Chaumont-sur-Loire has developed both in terms of visitor numbers and the growth in its national and international reputation, which makes it a prime location on the Loire valley.

Les Bulbes Fertiles,
International Garden Festival

© Patrick Escudero/hemis.fr

International Garden Festival

Every year, 30 landscape gardeners create individual plant displays in 30 separate plots, many influenced by Pop Art. Visitors enter a plant kingdom, which is neither a landscape garden nor a botanical park, but rather a unique site that pays tribute to the beauty of nature. This annual festival aims to introduce new creations and unusual combinations of plants and flowers. *Open late Apr–early Nov daily.* ⊜€15 (festival and historical park only).

appearance. The two other façades, despite their feudal aspect, reflect the influence of the Renaissance. At ground-floor level, a frieze bears the interlaced C's of Charles de Chaumont-Amboise, alternating with the rebus of the castle: a volcano or *chaud mont* (Chaumont).

Apartments

Note the room of the two rivals, Catherine de' Medici and Diane de Poitiers, and also Ruggieri's study and the Council Room, which is paved with 17C Spanish majolica tiles bought in Palermo, Sicily, by the Prince of Broglie. These apartments contain 16C and 17C tapestries, fine furniture and a collection of the terra-cotta medallions made by Nini, an 18C Italian artist who set up his workshop in the stables.

The size and luxurious fittings of the **stables★** indicate the importance of horses in the lives of princely families. Built in 1877 by the Prince de Broglie and fitted with electric lighting in 1906, they include stalls for the horses, boxes for thoroughbreds, a kitchen, harness room, horse-drawn carriages and a second courtyard in which there is a small riding centre.

Centre d'arts et de nature

The estate functions as a designated cultural centre dedicated to exploring nature, culture, artistic creation and landscape design.

Each year *(Mar–early Nov)*, around a dozen visual artists, photographers and lanscape are commissioned to create works that celebrate the environment of the château and grounds. The works are on view throughout the château, grounds and Goualoup Park.

The site boasts a three-fold identity: a major historic and heritage site – the Château; new trends in global landscape design – the International Garden Festival (⊜*see panel above*); and in contemporary design – the Centre of Arts and Nature, as well as special commissions created on site.

Park★

A 10min walk uphill will bring you to the castle. This pleasant stroll is an opportunity to admire the fine landscaped gardens designed by Henri Duchêne at the end of the 19C. The paths wind their way through cedar, lime and redwood.

The Buildings★★★

The outer west façade, which is the oldest, has an austere and military

ADDRESSES

♈/ EAT

⊜⊜ **La Madeleine de Proust** – *33 r. du Mar. Leclerc, 41150 Chaumont-sur-Loire. ☎02 54 20 94 80. Closed Wed and Sun eve, Tue.* Small, charming restaurant serving traditional French dishes. Try the fish or the duck.

Montrichard★

From the river bank and bridge over the Cher, a good view unfolds of this town clustered around the church below the crumbling keep. The north bank above the town is pitted with quarries that have now been transformed into dwellings, caves for growing mushrooms and cellars for storing renowned sparkling wines. In many ways Monrichard is just a laid-back market town, but one that also happens to have a full complement of medieval and Renaissance buildings, plus a hilltop fortress.

▸ **Population:** 3,371.
⊙ **Michelin Map** 318: E-7
▯ **Info:** Office de Tourisme du Cher, 25, rue Nationale Montrichard. ℘02 54 71 66 34. www.montrichardvaldecher.fr.
▷ **Location:** 35km/29mi S of Blois, 45km/28mi E of Tours.
⊛ **Don't Miss:** The view from top of the keep.
⊙ **Timing:** 1–2 hours.
⊖ **Kids:** Bourré, and the underground village.

◥◣ WALKING TOUR

⊖ Donjon★
⊙Tue-Sun Jul–Aug 10am–6pm; Apr–Jun 10am–noon, 2–5pm. ⊛€5. ℘02 54 32 57 15.
The square keep, which stands on the edge of the plateau above the River Cher, is enclosed by the remains of its curtain wall and by a complex system of ramparts that protected the entrance. It was built c. 1010 by Fulk Nerra, reinforced with a second wall in 1109 and then with a third in 1250. Despite having been reduced in height by 4m on the orders of Henri IV in 1589 for having fallen into the hands of the Catholic League at one stage, the keep still evokes its distant past. The **museums** retrace the archaeological history of the town and the surrounding area.

Église Ste-Croix
Originally the castle chapel, the church stands below the keep at the top of the steps known as Grands Degrés Ste-Croix. The façade is decorated with elegant Romanesque arches; the arches of the porch are ornamented with a twisted torus. The doorway is also Romanesque. **Jeanne de France**, the daughter of Louis XI, and her young cousin, the Duke of Orléans, were married in this chapel in 1476.

Old houses
Hôtel d'Effiat in rue Porte-au-Roi, which was built in the late 15C–early 16C, has Gothic décor with a few Renaissance elements. In the 16C it was the residence of Jacques de Beaune-Semblançay, Treasurer to Anne of Brittany and then to Louise of Savoy. The mansion has retained the name of its last owner, the Marquis d'Effiat, who at his death (1719) presented it to the town to be converted into an old peoples' home. On the corner of rue du Pont stands the **Maison de l'Ave Maria** (16C), which has three gables and finely carved beams. Opposite are the Petits Degrés Ste-Croix, which lead to troglodyte dwellings. Farther on, at the corner of rue du Prêche, stands the 11C stone façade of the **Maison du Prêche** (Sermon House).

Caves Monmousseau
⊙Apr–Jun and Sept-Oct daily 10am–12.30pm, 1.30–6pm; Jul–Aug daily 10am–6.30pm; Nov–Mar 10am–noon, 2–5.30pm. ⊛€3.50. ◥◣Guided tour €4.50. ℘02 54 32 35 15. www.monmousseau.com.
These cellars (15km/9mi of underground galleries) are particularly interesting as they present age-old methods alongside modern, more sophisticated techniques, known as the **Dom Pérignon method**.

Château de Montpoupon

© Philippe Michel/age fotostock

Église de Nanteuil

On the road to Amboise (D 115).
This church is a tall Gothic building with a Flamboyant doorway; the apses are Romanesque decorated with carved capitals. The high, narrow nave features Angevin vaulting. Above the entrance porch, a chapel built by Louis XI can be entered up interior or exterior steps.

EXCURSIONS
Bourré

3km/2mi E.
Digging underground galleries appears to have been practiced widely here since Roman Antiquity. The local stone tufa (*tuffeau*, also called *pierre de Bourré*) has often been used to construct the châteaux. Yet, these quarries were gradually abandoned and later used as wine cellars or mushroom beds. Among the latter, the most fascinating is the **Caves champignonnières des Roches et la ville souterraine★** 👤👤 (👁👁*guided tours daily: Apr–Sept 10am, 11am, 2pm, 3pm, 4pm, 5pm; rest of year 11am, 3pm and 4pm; closed 25 Dec, 1 Jan.* 👁€12, *ticket includes the quarry and the Ville souterraine; ℘02 54 32 95 33; www.le-champignon.com*). Discover the strange and silent kingdom of mushrooms, lit by the glow of torchlights, where the oyster, button, shiitake and pied-bleu varieties thrive in darkness. The course is nearly 1km and integrates the reconstruction of a lively **underground village** square complete with a church, town hall and school.

👤👤 La Magnanerie

4 chemin de la Croix-Bardin. 👁👁*Guided tours (75min) only: Apr–mid-Jul and Sept–early Nov 11.30am, 2.30pm, 4pm; mid-Jul–Aug also at 3.30pm, 4.30pm and 5.30pm.* 👁€8 (child 13-17, €6.50, child 6-12, €5, under 6 years free). ℘02 54 75 50 79. www.magnanerie-troglo.fr. This troglodyte site gets its name from its role as a silkworm farm. Featured is a display of a typical troglodyte dwelling, with an explanation of how the tufa stone was quarried. The terrace commands fine views of the Cher valley.

Thésée

10km/6mi E along D 176.
West of the village stand the remains of the Gallo-Roman settlement of Tasciaca beside the Roman road from Bourges to Tours. During the 1C–3C, it prospered from the making and selling of ceramic ware. Known as Les Maselles, the settlement extended over the area of modern Thésée and Pouillé.

Musée archéologique

👁👁*Guided tours only (45min–1h) at 11.15am and 4pm: Jul–Aug daily except Mon–Tue. Other times, tours can be arranged for groups – call to arrange.* 👁€3.50. ℘02 54 71 40 20. www.tasciaca.com.
This museum is housed in the town hall, an 18C wine-grower's property situated in the middle of a splendid park. Its archaeological collection consists of objects excavated from the sanctuary (*fanum*) and from the numerous potteries unearthed on either side of the river.

Château du Gué-Péan

13km/8mi E along D 176 then D 21.
🕐*Jul–Aug and 19-20 Sept, daily except Tue, 10.30am-6pm.* 👁€6.50.

℘02 54 71 37 10. www.guepean.com.
The château is isolated in a quiet
wooded valley; a picnic area has been
set up in the grounds. It was built as a
country house in the 16C and 17C, but
the plan is that of a feudal castle: three
ranges of buildings round a closed
courtyard with a huge round tower at
each corner, surrounded by a dry moat
and reached by a stone bridge.

Château de Montpoupon★

12km/7.4mi S along D 764. ⏰*Daily:*
Feb–Mar and Nov Sat–Sun school and
public holidays 10am–1pm, 2–5pm;
Apr–Sept daily 10am–7pm; Oct daily
10am–6pm. ⏰*Dec–Jan, 5-26 Jul.* ﹩€*10.*
℘02 47 94 21 15. www.montpoupon.com.
Only the towers remain of the original
13C fortress on this site. The main building, which has mullioned windows and
Gothic-style gables, was built in the
15C, whereas the **fortified gatehouse**
is early 16C. The **outbuildings★** house
a hunt museum with art and artefacts
illustrating the region's centuries-old
tradition of hunting with hounds.

Pontlevoy

This small town in the agricultural
region north of Montrichard boasts a
number of charming old houses with
stone dressings. Some 30 panels, decorated with advertisements for Poulain
chocolate, illustrate life in Pontlevoy in
the early days of motor cars.

Abbey★

The old abbey was founded in 1034
when, legend has it, Gelduin de Chaumont established a Benedictine community here as a token of gratitude for
his surviving a shipwreck.
The main interest of the old abbey lies
in the 14C–15C Gothic chapel and its
elegant 18C buildings, including the
refectory, the remarkable staircase
leading to the upper floor, and the fine
façade decorated with embla.
Today, the buildings house the European
American Center (Eur-AM; *www.euram-
center.com*), dedicated to the exchange
of ideas among European and American
scholars.

ADDRESSES

🛏 STAY AND 🍴 EAT

⊖⊜ – ⊖⊜🍽 **La Ferme des Bords** – *rte.
de Chaumont-sur-Loire, 8 Les Bordes, 41400
Pontlevoy. ℘06 81 01 85 58. www.la-ferme-
des-bordes.net. 5 rooms (1 triple, 2 family
suites). Table d'hôtes by reservation €35
per person.* Relax on this working cereal
farm close to the château. Rooms occupy
a separate building and are simply yet
comfortably furnished.

⊖⊜🍽 **Le Bellevue** – *24 quai de la
République. ℘02 54 32 06 17. www.
hotel-le-bellevue41.com. Closed Dec 24–25.
30 rooms.* 🅿. Most rooms in this hotel
offer a panoramic view of the Cher. The
restaurant (⊖⊜🍽) has bay windows
facing out on the valley, and serves
traditional cuisine.

⊖⊜🍽🍽 **Château de Chissay** – *1–3
Place Paul Boncour, 41400 Chissay-en-
Touraine (4km/2½mi W by D 176). ℘02 54
32 32 01. www.chateaudechissay.com. 32
rooms and 2 suites.* 🅿. This former royal
residence, close to Chenonceau castle is a
perfect base for exploring the Loire valley.
The elegant restaurant (⊖⊜🍽) serves
contemporary cuisine based around local
produce and seafood.

LEISURE ACTIVITIES

**Hot-air Ballooning – France
Montgolfières** – *10 Chemin de Bordebure,
41400 Saint-Julien-de-Chédon. ℘03 80 97
38 61. www.franceballoons.com. Apr–Sept,
call for hours and fees.* Dawn and dusk
flights take off from Chenonceau, Amboise
and Loches. Snacks and refreshments are
included.

Distillerie Giradot-Fraise-Or – *62 rte.
de Tours, 41400 Chissay-en-Touraine.*
🎧*Guided tours from Easter–Sept daily
3–6pm (time of last tour). ℘02 54 32 32 05.
www.distillerie-girardot.fr.* This family-
run distillery dating from the early 20C
produces liqueurs and brandies that can
be tasted. In fine weather the tour includes
the tufa cellars and an explanation of
distilling techniques.

EVENTS

Montrichard – *14 Jul:* Medieval Day.
Pontlevoy – *Jul–Aug:* Classical music
festival. Call for info. *℘02 54 71 60 77
(2–6pm), www.festivaldepontlevoy.com.*

Château de Chenonceau★★★

The magnificent Château de Chenonceau (its town of residence, Chenonceaux, is written with an "x") stretches across the River Cher in a harmonious natural setting of water, greenery, gardens and trees. To this perfection is added the elegance of the château's architecture, interior décor and exquisite furnishings. A superb avenue of plane trees leads to the château, creating a grand entryway. Tourists with a fanciful imagination can try to envision the arrival of Charles IX, among mermaids, nymphs and satyrs.

A BIT OF HISTORY

A château shaped by women – The first château was built 1513–1521 by **Thomas Bohier**, Treasury Superintendent under François I. His acquisition of Chenonceau and the château's frequent change of ownership thereafter make an eventful tale. For 400 years the main protagonists were women; royal wives, mistresses and queens.

Katherine Briçonnet, the soul of an architect – In 1512, Chenonceau was put up for sale, whereupon Bohier bought it for 12,400 livres. He immediately demolished all the old buildings except the keep. Often away, he could not supervise construction of his new residence. His wife Katherine took charge and was the creative spirit behind the project. The new building was completed in 1521, but Bohler died in 1524 and Katherine in 1526.

Diane de Poitiers, the everlasting beauty – When Henri II came to the throne in 1547, he gave Chenonceau to Diane de Poitiers, the widow of Louis de Brézé. Some 20 years older than Henri, she was still radiantly attractive. Her influence over him humiliated the rejected Queen. An able manager, Diane set out to exploit her estate and position, taking an interest in agriculture, the sale of wine, her income from taxes and anything else that brought in money.

Michelin Map: 317: P-5.

Info: Office de Tourisme Chenonceaux Bléré, 8 rue Jean Jacques Rousseau – 37150 Bléré. 02 47 23 94 45. www.autourdechenonceaux.fr. **Chateau:** *Daily: Jan-Mar 9.30am–4.30pm; Apr–May 9am–5.30pm; Jun 9am–6pm; Jul–Aug 9am–7.30pm; Sept 9am–6.30pm; Oct 9am–5.30pm, Nov-Dec 9.30am-4.30pm. €15 (child 7–18, €12, under 7 free). With audioguide €19 (child 7–18, €14) 08 20 20 90 90. www.chenonceau.com.*

Location: 14km/8.7mi S of Amboise, 32km/19.8mi E of Tours.

Don't Miss: The nighttime illuminations.

Timing: Allow at least 2 hours to tour the château and another hour to enjoy the gardens. The driving tour takes close to 2hrs.

Kids: Garden maze, Wax Museum, donkey park.

She created a beautiful garden and had a bridge built linking the château with the south bank of the Cher.

When Henri II was killed in a tournament in 1559, Diane found herself face to face with Catherine de' Medici, who was now regent. While her husband was alive, the Queen had been patient, but now she wanted vengeance. Knowing that Diane was attached to Chenonceau, she forced her to give up the property in exchange for Chaumont. After a brief resistance, Diane gave in and retired to Anet Château, where she died seven years later.

Château de Chenonceau with the Garden of Diane de Poitiers

Catherine de' Medici, lady of leisure – Catherine satisfied her thirst for magnificence on a grand scale at Chenonceau. She had a park laid out, built a two-storey gallery on the bridge and added extensive outbuildings. She held one splendid feast after another. She put on a huge party for the arrival of François II and Mary Stuart, and a more sumptuous one for Charles IX, with banquets, dances, fancy-dress balls, fireworks and even a naval battle on the Cher.

Louise de Lorraine, the inconsolable widow – Catherine bequeathed the chateau to her daughter-in-law, Louise de Lorraine, wife of Henri III. After the King's assassination, Louise retired there, and according to royal custom, put on white mourning, which she continued to wear until the end of her life, earning the nickname the White Queen or White Lady. From Louise de Lorraine, Chenonceau passed to her niece, Françoise de Lorraine, wife of César de Vendôme, the son of Henri IV and Gabrielle d'Estrées, who had stayed at the château in 1598.

Madame Dupin, the literary spirit – In 1733 it became the property of Dupin, the farmer-general who was the tax collector. Madame Dupin held a salon that was attended by all the famous names of the time. **Jean-Jacques Rousseau** was her son's tutor; it was for the benefit of this boy that he wrote his treatise on education, *Émile*. In his *Confessions*

the philosopher writes warmly of those happy days, "We had a good time in that beautiful place, we ate well, I became as fat as a monk".

Madame Dupin grew into old age encircled by the affection of the villagers, with the result that the château survived the Revolution unscathed. At her request she was buried in the park.

VISIT

Expect long lines at the ticket booth in high season. It's best to arrive midday or late in the day to avoid crowds.

There is now a free app available that allows visitors to access information about the château as they make their way around. Look out for signs at the ticket office to download and access the app, or find links to download it on the website, *www.chenonceau.com*.

As you walk towards the castle and pass between two sphinxes, the outbuildings erected after the plans of Philibert Delorme can be seen on the right. After crossing a bridge, the path reaches a terrace surrounded by a moat. To the left is Diane de Poitiers' Italian garden; to the right, that of Catherine de' Medici, bounded by the great trees in the park. On the terrace stands the **keep** of the former 15C Château des Marques.

Château★★★

This rectangular mansion has turrets at the corners. It stands on two piers from the old mill, which rest on the bed of the

Cher. Catherine de' Medici's two-storey gallery stretches across the bridge over the river. This structure has a classical simplicity contrasting with the ornate appearance given to the older section that now looks like an annexe.

Ground floor

The four main rooms lead off the hall, which features ribbed vaults with keystones aligned along a zigzag axis. The old guard-room *(left)* is paved with majolica tiles and adorned with 16C Flemish tapestries; in the chapel is a 16C marble low-relief sculpture of a Virgin and Child; the fireplace in **Diane de Poitiers' bedroom** was designed by Jean Goujon; note the touching Virgin and Child believed to be the work of Murillo. Pictures by Jordaens and Tintoretto and a 16C Brussels tapestry hang in Catherine de' Medici's **Green Cabinet★★**. The 16C ceiling is lined with fine layers of pewter decorated in green. The small adjacent room overlooking the River Cher was Catherine de' Medici's library; it has retained its splendid coffered ceiling in carved oak, dating from 1525. The **Great Gallery★** overlooking the Cher is 60m long and has black and white chequered paving. During the First World War the gallery was converted into a military hospital and from 1940 to 1942 the demarcation line ran right through the middle. At the end of the gallery, a drawbridge, raised every evening, leads to the wooded area on the south bank of the Cher and to Madame Dupin's grave. Note the remarkable Renaissance fireplace in **François I's Bedchamber★★**, which contains paintings by Van Loo

(Three Graces) and Il Primaticcio *(Diane de Poitiers as the Huntress Diana)*, and a handsome 15C Italian piece of furniture inlaid in ivory and mother-of-pearl.

First floor

This is reached by a straight staircase, which at the time it was built was an innovation in France. From the vestibule, with its Oudenaarde tapestries depicting hunting scenes, walk through to Gabrielle d'Estrées' Bedchamber, then the Royal or **Five Queens' Bedchamber★**, then Catherine de' Medici's Bedchamber and finally to that of César de Vendôme.

Second floor

The bedchamber of Louise de Lorraine, has an impressive funeral décor. The furniture is covered with black velvet, the curtains are made of black damask and the ceiling is decorated with crowns of thorns and cable motifs painted in white over a black background.

Kitchens★

Set up in two hollow piers of the château, resting on the very bed of the river, the kitchen quarters comprises several rooms: the butlery, the pantry, a larder for storing meat, the actual kitchen where royal meals were prepared and the refectory for staff members. From the bridge giving access to the kitchens, take a look at the mini-harbour through which supplies were delivered to the castle and which Diane de Poitiers is said to have used as a swimming pool.

Gardens★★

The gardens stretch along the banks of the Cher. Picnic areas border the moat. **Garden of Diane de Poitiers** – The layout includes intersecting straight and diagonal paths, eight triangular lawns and a décor of grey-leaved cotton lavender.

The design has remained unchanged since the garden was first planted. Diane de Poitiers decided to create this magnificent garden in 1551. The ground level was raised and a walled terrace built to protect against flooding from the Cher.

© Dominique Couineau/Château de Chenonceau

In the centre rises a fountain that sends a jet of water 6m into the air. Flowers (roses, lilies, violets) and vegetables (onions, leeks, cabbages and artichokes – new to France in the 16C), fruit trees and strawberries are used to create geometric designs. Today, in spring and autumn, the flower beds are planted with more than 30,000 blooms.

Garden of Catherine de' Medici – Covering 5,500 sq m, five lawns bordered with lavender and rose trees encircle a round pond. Box shrubs clipped into spheres line the paths. Twice a year, the flower beds are relaid with 10,000 new plants.

At Chenonceau, Catherine de' Medici staged sumptuous royal festivities and dedicated much of her time to improving the gardens.

Green Garden – Laid out in front of the orangery by Bernard Palissy for Catherine d' Medici, the rolling lawn is bordered with tall trees.

Maze – 1ha of clipped yew hedges 1.3m tall delineate the circular maze that recalls those of the era of Catherine d' Medici. There are five entrances but only two paths to the central gazebo.

Kitchen garden – Set behind the 16C farm, the kitchen garden also produces flowers (meticulously labelled) that make up the 150 bouquets decorating the château every week.

🚗 DRIVING TOUR

CHER VALLEY
Round trip of 60km/37mi.
Allow 1h45.

▶ Leave Chenonceaux eastwards (towards Montrichard), cross the Cher and take N 76 W towards Tours.

Bléré
At the entrance to Bléré stands an elegant monument with particularly fine Italian-style sculpted decoration: this is the funerary chapel (1526) of Guillaume de Saigne, Treasurer of the Royal Artillery under François I.

▶ Beyond Bléré, continue along N 76 to Azay-sur-Cher.

Château de Leugny
🕐 Jul–Aug Tue–Sun 10am–noon, 2–6pm. ⊗€2.50. ☎02 47 50 41 10.
This elegant château on the Cher was built by André Portier, a pupil of Gabriel, for his own use. It is furnished in the Louis XVI style.

▶ Rejoin N 76 towards Tours.

Véretz
This little town tucked between the Cher and the hillside makes a charming picture from the north bank of the river: the houses and church lead the eye west to

the tree-lined paths and terraces of the Château de Véretz.

Among those who once strolled in the château grounds were the Abbé de Rancé (1626–1700), who reformed the Trappist Order, the Abbé d'Effiat and Madame de Sévigné, the Princesse de Conti, and the Abbé de Grécourt, who wrote light verse; Voltaire stayed at the château in his youth. In the village square stands a monument to **Paul-Louis Courier** (1772–1825), an officer under the Empire who bought the Chavonnière estate with its large house on the Véretz plateau in 1816 and settled there with his young wife. From his country retreat he began to harass the government with wittily caustic pamphlets, such as "A petty village tyrant under the Restoration". Despite his talent, his quarrelsome temperament made him unpopular, and on 10 April 1825 he was assassinated in Larçay Forest under mysterious circumstances.

▶ Take D 85 N across the River Cher to Montlouis.

Montlouis-sur-Loire

Montlouis is built in terraces up a hillside of tufa that is riddled with caves. Its vineyards on the south-facing plateau between the Loire and the Cher produce a heady, fruity white wine made from the famous Pinot de la Loire grape. At **Maison de la Loire** *(60 quai A.-Baillet;* ⏱*Tue-Sat 2–5pm;* ⏱*Mondays, public holidays;* ⊜*€3;* ℘*02 47 50 97 52; www. maisondelaloire37.fr)* exhibits focus on the fauna and flora of the Loire region.

▶ Exit Montlouis towards Amboise then turn right toward La Bourdaisière.

Château de la Bourdaisière

⏱*(Park and gardens only) Apr and Oct 11am-6pm, May-Sept 10am–7pm.* ⊜*€7.50.* ℘*02 47 45 16 31. www.labourdaisiere.com.*

Now operating as an elegant hotel, the château (⚬─) is no longer open for tours. Visitors may still wander the public areas, the gardens and the **kitchen garden★**,

which features more than 400 varieties of tomato. Or you can book a room at the hotel, which is open mid-March to mid-November, and over Christmas.

▶ Return to Chenonceaux on D 40.

ADDRESSES

🛏 STAY

⊜⊜⊜ **Chambre d'hôte La Marmittière** – *22 Vallée de Mesvres, 37150 Civray-de-Touraine. 4km/2.5mi W of Chenonceaux.* ℘*06 88 83 82 48. http://marmittiere.perso. libertysurf.fr. 3 rooms.* 🅿🚭. A delightful B&B owned by a wine producer; the décor features stone.

⊜⊜⊜ **Le Prieuré de la Chaise** – *8 r. du Prieuré, lieu-dit la Chaise, 41400 St-Georges-sur-Cher. 2km/1mi S of St Georges-sur-Cher.* ℘*02 54 32 59 77.* 🅿. *5 rooms.* It is almost impossible to resist the charm of this 16C priory, set amidst vineyards. The rooms are adorned with antiques. **Swimming pool** 🏊. Continental breakfast.

⊜⊜⊜ **Hôtel La Roseraie** – *7 r. Bretonneau, 37150 Chenonceaux.* ℘*02 47 23 90 09. www. hotel-chenonceau.com. Closed mid-Nov –mid-Mar. 22 rooms. Restaurant* ⊜⊜⊜ *(closed Tue).* Long building near the castle covered with ivy. The spacious rooms are air-conditioned. Meals served on the terrace in summer. **Heated pool** 🏊 on the premises.

🍴 EAT

⊜⊜ **La Renaudiere** – *24 r. du Dr-Bretonneau.* ℘*02 47 23 90 04. www. renaudiere.com. Closed Wed eve, Sat lunch, Sun.* This restaurant serves traditional cuisine that incorporates fresh produce. The terrace overlooks a pretty meadow. The hotel of the same name has rooms (⊜⊜⊜) for overnight guests *(late Feb– early Nov)*.

⊜⊜⊜ **L'Orangerie** – *Château de Chenonceaux.* ℘*02 47 23 91 97. www. chenonceau.com. Closed mid-Nov–mid-Mar.* ♿🅿. Set in the heart of the château, the restaurant serves traditional cuisine on the terrace or in the superb dining room. Afternoon tea service is available (*3–5pm*).

St-Aignan★

St-Aignan stands on the south bank of the Cher at the heart of a region of woods and vineyards. Coteaux du Cher is the wine produced in Seigy and Couffy. Both the church and the Renaissance château are interesting, and the nearby zoo boasts some rare white tigers.

SIGHTS

Château

The château courtyard affords a pleasant view of the roofs of the town, a few made of slate but most of them are tiled. The château consists of two buildings at right angles, mostly built in the 16C and backing on to the remains of the medieval fortifications on the east side of the courtyard. The elegant Renaissance dwelling has pilasters flanking the windows, carved dormer gables and a handsome stair in an octagonal turret terminating in a lantern. The terrace overlooks the turbulent Cher passing under the bridge.

Maison de la Prévôté

r. Constant-Ragot. ⏱*Wed–Fri 3–6pm, Sat–Sun and public holidays 10am–noon, 2–6pm.* ☞*Free.* ☏*02 54 71 22 23. www.ville-saintaignan.com.*
The 15C building is used for hosting temporary exhibitions. Rue Constant-Ragot contains two Gothic houses and provides the best view of the chevet of the church. A stroll in the narrow streets and neighbouring square will reveal some 15C carved stone or half-timbered houses.

ADDITIONAL SIGHT

Église St-Aignan★

The collegiate church is a Romanesque building dating from the 11C and 12C with an impressive tower over the transept. A spacious tower-porch with delicately carved capitals leads into the high, radiant nave; the capitals are finely carved into acanthus leaves and fantastic animals; the chancel and ambulatory have historiated capitals showing the

▶ **Population:** 2,988.
⏱ **Michelin Map:** 318: F-8
ℹ **Info:** 60 r. Constant-Ragot, 41110 St-Aignan-sur-Cher. ☏02 54 75 22 85. www.sudvaldeloire.fr.
▶ **Location:** 17km/10.5mi E of Montrichard and 40km/25mi W of Blois.
◉ **Don't Miss:** View of town from the bridge or from the north bank on the road (D 675) N of Noyers-sur-Cher.
⏱ **Timing:** Allow 1 hour to have a look around the town.
👥 **Kids:** ZooParc de Beauval.

Flight into Egypt *(north ambulatory)*, the Sacrifice of Isaac and King David (south side).

Lower church★★

Entrance in north transept.
Formerly known as the Church of St John or Church of the Grottoes, this church was probably the early Romanesque church used as a stable or store during the Revolution. It is similar in plan to the chancel and decorated with **frescoes** (12C–15C): St John the Evangelist (15C) in the central chapel of the ambulatory; the Legend of St Giles in the south chapel. A great Christ in Majesty in a double mandorla (1200) fills the open vaulting of the chancel and spreads his blessing through the mediation of St Peter and St James to the Sick who are prostrate; the vault over the transept crossing shows the figure of Christ in Judgement resting on a rainbow.

EXCURSIONS

Chapelle St-Lazare

2km/1mi NE on the north bank of the River Cher.
The chapel of St-Lazare, standing near the road, was once part of a leper house; note the gabled belfry.

👥 ZooParc de Beauval★★★

4km/2.5mi S along D 675.

♿🕐*Daily from 9am; closing times vary.* 🎫*€32 (child 3–10, €25) – online booking discount.* ℘*02 54 75 50 00. www.zoobeauval.com.*

A haven for some 5,700 animals and countless plants, this 26ha zoo-park is built on undulating woodland. The following are hightlights of a visit.

Begin at the 2,000 sq m **glass aviary★**, housing several hundred exotic birds (including tiny humming birds) free to flutter about in the lush environment of an equatorial forest complete with waterfalls and streams. Outside, there are about 2,000 more birds to be seen, including more than 400 parrots, some very rare.

The **African savanna** section is home to herbivores such as giraffe, rhinoceros, zebra, antelope and ostrich. The section devoted to **wild beasts★★** (big cats) includes rare white tiger with blue eyes, Sumatra tiger, black panther, puma and hyena.

In the **equatorial environment★★** visitors can closely observe **gorillas**, specifically Asato, a magnficent 250kg gorilla and the head of a large family. Rare **manatee** swim in their own pool. A landscape of rocks, meadows and a lake hosts several **elephants**. Opposite these pachyderms, admire the **okapi**, a member of the giraffe family. In the **mini-farm**, goats approach visitors, demanding biscuits.

Discover koalas in the **Australian** section, as well as an aquarium with fish and colourful corals.

Since 2012, Beauval has been the only zoo in France to host **pandas**; see these adorable animals in the pagoda-filled section devoted to **China★★**.

Numerous species of monkey and lemur inhabit the huge **tropical great apes habitat★**, including small monkeys from the Congolese basin and the Guinean heights, orangutan and various gibbon. It also contains a **vivarium** (with around 100 snakes) and an aqua-terrarium in which turtles and crocodiles are raised.

👁 **Shows** – Several times a day *(Mar–mid-Nov)*, the underwater antics of sea-lions amuse spectators in the amphitheatre. Flight demonstrations showcase birds of prey, some withwingspans of nearly 3m. *Find the schedule at zoo entrance and online.*

ADDRESSES

🛏 STAY

⊖🍴 **Chambre d'hôte Le Sousmont** – *66 r. Maurice-Berteaux.* ℘*02 54 75 24 35. www.lesousmont.fr.* 🚭. *4 rooms.* This 19C house is set in delightful grounds with views of the château de St-Aignan. Pleasant rooms include one in a chalet in the garden. Reading lounge and attractive breakfast room.

⊖🍴 **Les Hotels de Beauval** – *4 km/2.5mi on D 675.* ℘*02 54 75 60 00. https://leshotelsdebeauval.com.* 🅿. *112 rooms. Restaurant (⊖🍴).* Indonesian style villas sit amid a tropical garden. Find comfort and relaxation in a décor recalling Java and Bali: teak furniture and pictures of Ubud. Restaurant, heated **Swimming pool** 🏊 (Apr–Oct), outdoor bar.

⊖🍴 **Hostellerie Le Clos du Cher** – *2 r. Paul-Boncour, 41110 Noyers.sur-Cher. 1km/0.6mi on D 675.* ℘*02 54 75 00 03. www.closducher.fr. Closed Jan and Sun eve Oct–Mar.* 🅿. *10 rooms. Restaurant(⊖🍴).* Set in woodland grounds, this 19C manor features classical style rooms and offers occasional theme weekends (wine tastings, St Valentine's day, etc.). Family atmosphere and traditional cuisine.

🍴 EAT

⊖🍴 **Le Crêpiot** – *36 r. Constant-Ragot.* ℘*02 54 75 21 39. Closed Mon. Weekend reservations required.* This place is a gril, salad bar and creperie combined into one. Enjoy a meal amid wooden beams, chequered tablecloths and red booths.

⊖🍴 **Le Mange-Grenouille** – *10 r. Paul Boncour.* ℘*02 54 71 74 91. www. lemangegrenouille.fr. Closed Sat lunch, Sun eve, Mon.* Serving traditional cuisine, this baroque-styled restaurant is housed in a former coaching inn, and focuses on local and seasonal produce. There are two internal dining rooms and a shady terrace outdoors.

© Philippe Michel/age fotostock

Montrésor★

With its Renaissance château and Gothic church, this interesting village is reflected in the River Indrois. The town's old market is a timber-framed construction. A handsome 16C house with a watchtower in the main street now serves as the town hall. Montrésor has been named one of *Les plus beaux villages de France* (the most beautiful French villages), an association which includes 153 outstanding villages selected for their beautiful settings, fine buildings and lovely surroundings.

VISIT

Château★

🕐 *Mar–Jun 10am–6pm; Jul-Aug 10am–7pm, Sept-mid-Nov 10am–6pm. Closed mid-Nov-Feb.* ☞€9, children 8-12, €5. ✆02 47 92 60 04. *https://chateaudemontresor.com.*

The curtain wall with its ruined towers belongs to the fortress built by Fulk Nerra in the 11C; within it at the centre of a charming, romantic park stands the residence built in the early 16C by **Imbert de Bastarnay**, Lord of Montrésor from 1493, adviser to several kings of France and grandfather to Diane de Poitiers. This building has mullioned windows on the south front facing the river, gabled dormers and two machicolated towers. In 1849 the château was restored by Count Xavier Branicki, a Polish émigré who accompanied Prince

▶ **Population:** 374.
🖑 **Michelin Map:** 317: Q-6
🛈 **Info:** Office du tourisme Val d'Indrois-Montrésor, 43 Grande-Rue, 37460 Montrésor. ✆02 47 92 70 71. www.loches-valdeloire.com.
◖ **Location:** 25km/15.5mi E of Loches and 23km/14mi S of Montrichard.
🕐 **Timing:** Allow 1 hour to explore the château; up to half a day for the valley.
🚹 **Kids:** Water sports at Chemillé-sur-Indrois.

The Treasure of Montrésor

There are many theories as to origins of the name of Montrésor. The most endearing is that of a knight and his equerry who saw a lizard covered in gold dust scuttling over the rocks. Intrigued, they began searching the hillside and discovered a magnificent treasure trove. However, the true story is more mundane: one of the early lords of the manor was treasurer to the cathedral chapter in Tours, and the place was named, quite naturally, *mons thesauri*, or Treasurer's Mount, which, in time, became Montrésor.

Napoleon to Constantinople during the Crimean War. Inside, be sure to see the dining room filled with trophies, the intimate **salon★** with 16C paintings, the small **staircase in colimaçon★** and the **library★**.

Church

The (1519–41) Gothic-style church was originally a collegiate foundation set up by Imbert de Bastarnay. Only the doorway is Renaissance in style.

EXCURSIONS

La Corroirie

5 km/3mi on D 760 towards Loches.
🖉 *06 80 43 38 75. www.corroirie.com.*
In the valley hollow, on the right, behind a screen of trees, you can see the outline of some of the remains of the Abbaye du Liget, fortified in the 15C. To the west, the main gate and square tower with its drawbridge and machicolations can clearly be made out. Today a refurbished wing of the main tower operates as a historic bed-and-breakfast.

Chartreuse du Liget

🖉 *06 48 16 23 92.*
http://lachartreuseduliget.com.
Alongside the road, on the eastern edge of Loches Forest, stands the great wall of the **charter house**.
The elegant 18C **gateway★** is flanked by numerous outbuildings indicating the size and wealth of the abbey before the Revolution.
The abbey was founded in the 12C by Henry II of England in expiation, it is said, for the murder of Thomas à Becket, Archbishop of Canterbury. Today, the building is available as a historic gite.

Chapelle St-Jean-du-Liget

Return to the Loches road and 1km/ 0.5mi E turn left.
🗊 *Obtain key from Loches tourist office.*
🖉 *02 47 92 60 02.*
Standing alone in the middle of a field is a round 12C building where the first charter house monks probably lived.

🚗 DRIVING TOUR

VALLÉE DE L'INDROIS★

FROM NOUANS-LES-FONTAINES TO AZAY-SUR-INDRE

33km/20mi along D 760 and D 10. Allow 2h.

The River Indrois winds its picturesque way westwards across the Montrésor marshland to join the Indre. Its course is lined by willows, alders and poplars and lush green meadows. The sunny slopes are planted with fruit trees, in orchards or espaliers, and a few vines.

Nouans-les-Fontaines

This village has a 13C church that harbours a masterpiece of Primitive art: the **Deposition★★**, or *Pietà of Nouans*, by Jean Fouquet. The vast painting on wood is one of the finest late-15C French masterpieces.

Coulangé

At the entrance of this pleasant hamlet stands the bell-tower of the old parish church (12C). On the opposite river bank are the remains of the fortifications of the Benedictine abbey of Villeloin. Farther on, the road (D 10) offers scenic views of the lake at **Chemillé-sur-Indrois** and the countryside east of Genillé (👥 swimming, fishing, pedalos).

Genillé

The houses climb up from the river to the late-15C château with its corner towers and dovecote. The church presents a striking belfry with a stone spire and, inside, a 16C Gothic chancel.

St-Quentin-sur-Indrois

The town occupies one of the best sites in the valley.
East of the village the road (D 10) offers a fine view south of Loches Forest before joining the valley of the River Indre at Azay-sur-Indre.

Azay-sur-Indre

🕭 *See LOCHES: Excursions*

© Philippe Michel/age fotostock

Château de Loches

Loches★★

Loches is a small town on the south bank of the Indre; the old town, huddled on the slopes of a bluff above the river, still resembles a medieval fortified town, with two of its original three defensive walls remarkably well preserved.
Loches was the birthplace of the Romantic poet Alfred de Vigny (1797–1863), whose mother's family had been closely involved with the town's history since the Renaissance. The poet left the town when he was only an infant.

- ▶ **Population:** 7,129.
- **Michelin Map:** 317: O-6
- **Info:** pl. de la Marne, 37600 Loches. ☎02 47 91 82 82. www.loches-valdeloire.com.
- **Location:** 44km/27.3mi SW of Tours, 36km/22.3mi south of Amboise.
- **Timing:** Plan a day to visit the town and the château, then allow an hour or two for sights outside the town.

👣 WALKING TOUR

MEDIEVAL TOWN★★

Allow 3h. 🅿 *Park in the Mail Droulin.*
Loches remains largely as it was in the 15C and at the time of the Renaissance, except for the shops and the numerous stalls that enliven the lower part of the town on market days.

Porte Royale★

The Royal Gate (11C) had powerful defences; it was flanked by two towers in the 13C.

▶ Go through the gateway; turn left onto r. Lansyer to reach the museum.

Maison Lansyer

🕐*Daily 10am–12.30pm, 2–6pm May–early Nov.* ⊗€5. ☎02 47 59 48 21. *https://www.loches-valdeloire.com.*
This house was the family home of the artist **Emmanuel Lansyer** (1835–93), a pupil of Gustave Courbet and a friend of the poet José-Maria de Heredia. Lansyer was influenced by the landscape painters of the Barbizon School.

Collégiale St-Ours★

In 1802 the old collegiate church of Notre-Dame became the parish church dedicated to St Ours, a local apostle in the 5C.
The alabaster recumbent **figure of Agnès Sorel**★ is of special interest. During the Revolution, soldiers took the favourite of Charles VII for a saint,

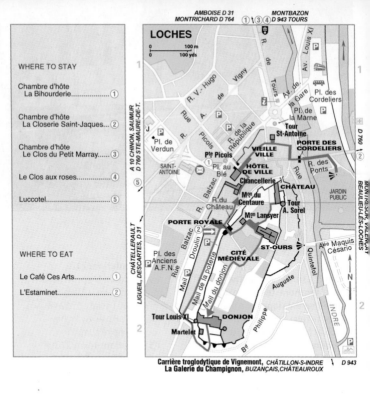

AMBOISE D 31
MONTRICHARD D 764 ① ③ ④ D 943 TOURS
MONTBAZON

LOCHES

WHERE TO STAY

Chambre d'hôte
La Bihourderie.................. ①

Chambre d'hôte
La Closerie Saint-Jaques... ②

Chambre d'hôte
Le Clos du Petit Marray...... ③

Le Clos aux roses.............. ④

Luccotel............................ ⑤

WHERE TO EAT

Le Café Ces Arts................ ①

L'Estaminet...................... ②

Carrière troglodytique de Vignemont, *CHÂTILLON-S-INDRE* \ *D 943*
La Galerie du Champignon, *BUZANÇAIS, CHÂTEAUROUX*

---

destroyed her statue, desecrated her grave and scattered her remains. The monument was restored in Paris under the Empire and was moved to the château in 1970. It was returned to the church only in 2005 following scientific research that determined that Agnès died from mercury poisoning, although whether murder or self-medication remains a mystery. An exhibit in the château explains the forensic work in some detail.

▷ As you come out of the church, the castle is on your right.

CHÂTEAU★★

🕙*Daily Apr–Sept 9am–7pm; Oct–Mar 9.30am–5pm.* 🕙*1 Jan, 25 Dec. Château and donjon* ⌖€10.50. ✆*02 47 19 18 08.* www.chateau-loches.fr.
The tour starts from the **Tour Agnès Sorel**, a tower dating from the 13C traditionally referred to as the Beautiful Agnès Tower.

Royal Apartments

From the terrace, which commands a fine view of Loches and the Indre Valley, it is clear that the château was built at two different periods. The Vieux Logis (14C), the older, taller building, is heavily fortified with four turrets linked by a sentry walk at the base of the roof. It was enlarged under Charles VIII and Louis XII by the addition of the more recent Nouveau Logis, in the Flamboyant Gothic style.

One room contains a **triptych★** from the 15C School of Jean Fouquet, which originally came from the church of St-Antoine, with panels evoking the Crucifixion, the Carrying of the Cross and the Deposition.

The tour ends with Anne of Brittany's **oratory**, a tiny room decorated with finely worked motifs of the ermine of Brittany and the girdle of St Francis.

▷ Head for the keep through the streets of the medieval town.

A Thousand-year-old Fortress

Loches is built on a natural strong point, which has been occupied since at least the 6C when Gregory of Tours made reference to a fortress commanding a monastery and a small town. From the 10C to the 13C, Loches was under the sway of the counts of Anjou, who altered the fortress by building a residential palace and a moated keep at the tip of the promontory. Henry II of England reinforced the defences. On his death in 1189, his son Richard the Lionheart took possession of the land before leaving on crusade with Philippe Auguste.

In the Holy Land Philippe Auguste, an artful schemer, abandoned Richard and hurried back to France (1191), where he plotted with John Lackland, Richard's brother, who agreed to give up the fortress (1193). When Richard was finally ransomed – he had been held captive in Austria – he hastened to Loches and seized the castle in less than three hours (1194), an exploit that was celebrated in all the chronicles of the day. When Richard died, Philippe Auguste recaptured the castle by way of revenge, but much less impressively: the siege lasted a whole year (1205). Loches was given to Dreu V de Mello, son of the victorious besiegers' leader, and repurchased by Louis IX in 1249.

Loches took on the role of royal residence for a succession of monarchs. In 1429, after her victory at Orléans, Joan of Arc rejoined Charles VII at Loches and insisted that he should set out for Reims.

Donjon★★

🕐 *Same hours as château.*

This keep was built in the 11C by Fulk Nerra to defend the fortified town from the south. It is a solid square construction which, together with the Ronde and Martelet towers, form an imposing defensive system.

Tour ronde

Like the Martelet, it was built in the 15C to complete the fortifications. To the left, in the entrance pavilion, Philippe de Commines' cell presents an iron collar weighing 16kg and the reconstitution of one of Louis XI's famous cages.

Martelet

The most impressive dungeons, occupying several floors below ground, are to be found in this building. The first was that of **Ludovico Sforza**, Duke of Milan, nicknamed the Moor, who was taken prisoner by Louis XII.

For four years he paid for his treachery. On the day of his release, the sunlight was so bright and the excitement of freedom so great that he fell down dead. Ludovico, who was Leonardo da Vinci's patron, covered the walls of his prison with paintings and inscriptions. As you exit the Martelet, walk back to the Porte Royale and turn right onto rue du Château for a stroll through the old town, which developed at the foot of the fortress.

OLD TOWN★

Located inside the second perimeter wall, the old town is criss-crossed with narrow streets lined with old houses built of tufa. A leisurely walk will take you past the **chancellerie**, dating from the Henry II period (mid-16C), embellished with fluted columns, pilasters and wrought-iron balconies; nearby, the **Maison du Centaure** owes its name to the low-relief sculpture on the façade that depicts the centaur Nessus abducting Deianira; proceed to the 15C **Porte Picois**, also with machicolations. This tower stands next to the **hôtel de ville★**, an elegant Renaissance building with flower-decked balconies. From there, head for the 16C **Tour St-Antoine**, one of the rare belfries to be found in central France and continue to the late-15C **Porte des Cordeliers★**; this and the Porte Picois are the only two remaining gates of the town's original four.

EXCURSIONS

Carrière troglodytique de Vignemont★

Closed until November 2020.
55 ter r. des Roches, S towards
Châteauroux (wear warm clothing).
&♿🕐*Daily Easter–Oct 10am–noon,*
2–6pm (Jul–Aug 10am–7pm); rest of
year by appointment. ☞€14 *or* €11 *for*
children. Groups of 10-19 adults €12
or €10 *for children.* 📞02 47 91 54 54.
www.carriere-de-vignemont.fr.
🅿*Parking available near La Citadelle*
campground.

750 metres of galleries arranged
underground in a former quarry. The
museum explains the history of tufa,
its geological formation, its extraction,
its use in constructions across the Loire
Valley, and the different uses of the
underground caves of the region, from
troglodyte dwellings to underground
refuges, wine cellars and mushroom
beds. It's all there is to know about the
extraction and use of the famous white
limestone that brightens up the castles
and villages of the Loire valley.

Beaulieu-lès-Loches

1km/0.6mi E along the east bank
of the River Indre.

This old village contains the ruins of a
famous abbey founded in 1004 by Fulk
Nerra, who was buried there.

Bridoré

14km/8.7mi SE via N 143 and D 241.
🐾*Guided tours only, by arrangement.*
☞ €7. 📞02 47 94 72 63.

The **castle**, which belonged to Marshal
Boucicaut in the 14C, was altered in the
15C by Imbert de Bastarnay, Secretary
to Louis XI. It is an imposing, well-preserved complex, bordered by towers,
caponnières and a deep dry moat.

🚗 DRIVING TOUR

Moulins de l'Indre★
27km/16.7mi NW via N 143 and D 17.
Allow 1h.

From Chambourg-sur-Indre to Esvres
the road (D 17) follows a pretty route
beside the Indre. which meanders lazily
past a windmill here or a boat there
moored in the reeds.

Azay-sur-Indre

Azay stands in a pleasant setting at the
confluence of the Indre and the Indrois.
Adjoining it is the park of the château
that once belonged to La Fayette.

Reignac-sur-Indre

Visible from the bridge spanning the
Indre (on the road to Cigogné) is Reignac
windmill, standing on a small lake set in
lush, verdant surroundings.

▷ Take D 58 towards N 143 until you
reach the locality named Le Café Brûlé.

Cormery

Cormery, which is famous for its macaroons, sits prettily beside the Indre with
inns on either bank. Near the bridge,
half-hidden under the weeping willows is an old mill; downstream the river
feeds the old washing place.
The Benedictine **abbey**, founded in 791,
was suppressed 1,000 years later during
the Revolution. The scale of the abbey
in its heyday can be measured from
the model that shows the edifice as
it was in the 14C and 15C and the different ruins that remain in the village.
The rue de l'Abbaye passes under a
tall ruined tower, **tour St-Paul,** an 11C
belfry that marked the entrance to the
church. The nearby prior's lodge, **logis
du prieur** (15C), is reached by a graceful curved staircase. The small street to
the left leads to the ruins of the cloister
and the arches of the **refectory** (13C).

Église N.-D.-du-Fougeray

Overlooking the valley, this Romaneque
church (12C) features a majestic triple
apse supported by buttress columns.

▷ Cross the Indre and follow N 143
towards Tours for 1km/0.6mi then bear
left onto D 17 to Esvres.

ADDRESSES

🛏 STAY

🍽🍲 **Le Clos aux roses** – *2 r. du Lavoir, 37310 Chédigny. ℘02 47 92 20 29. www.le closauxroses.fr. 5 rooms.* 🅿. This beautifully renovated hotel offers simply decorated rooms. The restaurant (🍽🍲🍲; *closed Tue-Wed, plus Sun-Mon dinner*) draws regional gourmets.

🍽🍲 **Chambre d'hôte La Bihourderie** – *37310 Azay-sur-Indre. 11km/7mi N of Loches. ℘02 47 92 58 58. www.labihourderie.com. 5 rooms. Evening meal (Mon–Tue, Thu–Fri only)* 🍽🍲. In spite of its proximity to a main road, this B&B is very quiet. Regional cuisine based on seasonal produce.

🍽🍲 **Chambre d'hôte Le Clos du Petit Marray** – *37310 Chambourg-sur-Indre. 5km/3mi N of Loches on N 143 towards Tours. ℘02 47 92 50 67. www.petit-marray.fr. 2 rooms.* 🚭🅿. An imposing country property set in a large garden, with a small lake. The rooms are spacious and attractively decorated.

🍽–🍽🍲🍲 **Luccotel** – *12–14 r. des Lézards. ℘02 47 91 30 30. www.luccotel. com. 69 rooms.* 🅿. *Restaurant* 🍽🍲. This functional hotel offers copious meals.

🍽🍲🍲🍲 **Chambre d'hôte La Closerie Saint-Jacques** – *37 r. Balzac , 37600 Loches. ℘02 47 91 63 12. https://closeriesaintjacques. com. 3 rooms.* Refinement reigns at this 17C post office at the foot of the castle walls. Library stocked with regional books. Garden.

🍽 EAT

🍽 **Estaminet** –*14 r. de l'Abbaye, 37600 Beaulieu-lès-Loches. ℘02 47 59 35 47.* Set in a shaded nook close by the abbey, this spot serves traditional cuisine in a relaxed atmosphere.

🍽 **Le Café Ces Arts** –*4 pl. au Blé, 37600 Loches. ℘02 47 59 00 04. Closed Mon.* ♿. This traditional café/brasserie is perfect for a market-day break. Simple, well-prepared dishes at reasonable prices.

Ste-Maure-de-Touraine

This small town occupies a knoll commanding the Manse valley. The settlement, which is Roman in origin, developed in the 6C round the tombs of St Britta and St Maurus, and then round the keep built by Fulk Nerra. The Rohan-Montbazon family were the overlords from 1492 to the Revolution. The town is known for its busy poultry markets and its local goats' milk cheeses.

▶ **Population:** 4 342.
⏱ **Michelin Map:** 317: M-6
ℹ **Info:** 77 ave. Général de Gaulle. ℘02 47 65 40 12. www.sainte-maure- de-touraine.fr.
▶ **Location:** On N 10 between Tours and Chatellerault to the S.

CHURCH
The church is 11C, but its original appearance was altered when it was restored in 1866. A chapel to the right of the chancel has a 16C white-marble statue of the Virgin Mary by the Italian School.

🚗 DRIVING TOUR

Plateau de Ste-Maure
This plateau is dissected by the green valleys of two rivers – the Manse and the Esves – and bordered by three others –

the Indre, the Vienne and the Creuse. It is composed of limestone which is easily eroded by running water.

▶ Leave Ste-Maure on D 59 going SE.

Maison du souvenir (Maillé)
On the right upon entering the village. ♿ ⏱*Mon–Sat 10.30am–1pm, 2–6pm; Sun 2–6pm.* ⏱*1 Jan, 25 Dec.* 🎫€6.40. ℘02 47 65 24 89. *www.maisondusouvenir.fr.*
On 25 August 1944, just as Paris was enjoying liberation, 124 residents of

Maillé, mostly women, children and old people, were massacred by the German army. The village was pillaged and put to the torch.

The Maison du Souvenir, which is also a research centre, displays objects, films, photographs and documents from the period in a moving and sombre tribute to the children of the martyred village.

▶ Follow D 91 via Draché to Sepmes, then D 59 on the right.

At **Bournan**, the Romanesque church has a beautiful apse and tower over the side chapel.

Ligueil is a small town built of white stone; there are a few old houses. The decorated wooden washing place lies on the edge of the town on the road to Loches (D 31).

Esves-le-Moutier

The village, on the south bank of the Esves, takes its name from a priory that was surrounded by a fortified wall.

Château de Grillemont

The huge white château stands half way up a slope overlooking an attractive **valley★** of meadows round a lake; the slopes are capped by oak and pine woods. The large round towers of the castle with their pepper-pot roofs were built in the reign of Charles VII for Lescoet, the governor of Loches castle; in 1765 the 15C curtain wall was replaced by magnificent Classical buildings.

▶ Drive to Bossée and follow D 101.

Ste-Catherine-de-Fierbois

The spirit of Joan of Arc hovers over this village, which lies grouped round its church, east of the main road (N 10). On 23 April 1429, following directions given by Joan of Arc, a sword marked with five crosses was found on this site. It was supposed to have been placed there by **Charles Martel** after his victory over the Saracens at Poitiers in 732.

▶ N 10 leads back to Ste-Maure.

Descartes

It was in Descartes, which used to be called La Haye, that **René Descartes** (1590–1650), the famous French philosopher, physicist and mathematician, was baptised, although the family home was in the neighbouring town of Châtellerault. Descartes' work gave birth to an intellectual revolution, one of whose first fruits was analytical geometry.

A BIT OF HISTORY

A Remarkable Individual – At the age of eight Descartes was sent to the Jesuit College of Henri IV in La Flèche, where he received a semi-military education, before joining the army under the Prince of Nassau. While pursuing his military career, he travelled widely in Europe, devoting most of his time to study, and the pursuit of his life's mission as it was

▶ **Population:** 3,772.
 Michelin Map: 317: N-7
 Info: Pl. Blaise-Pascal, 37160 Descartes. ℘02 47 92 42 00. www.ville-descartes.fr.
▶ **Location:** 58km/36mi S of Tours, and 50km/ 31mi E of Chinon.
 Timing: Allow 1 hour.

revealed to him on 10 November 1619. In 1629 he returned to Holland, where he stayed for 20 years, studying at various universities and writing and publishing some of his most famous works.

Cartesian Thought – His *Discourse on Method* (1637), published four years after Galileo's condemnation by the Inquisition, met with a different reception and was destined to confound the sceptics;

it marked the beginning of modern thought and scientific rationalism.

In it, Descartes broke with scholasticism and founded a way of thinking based entirely on reasoned methodology and the systematic application of doubt. His method included the questioning of one's own existence, which he resolved in the following way, "I who doubt, I who am deceived, at least while I doubt, I must exist, and as doubting is thinking, it is indubitable that while I think, I am."

VISIT
Musée René Descartes
29 r. Descartes. &Apr–May and Sept–Oct daily except Tue 2–6pm, Jun–Aug 10am–noon, 2–6pm. €5 ℘02 47 59 79 19. www.ville-descartes.fr.
This museum is housed in Descartes' childhood home. Documents illustrating his life and works are on display.

EXCURSIONS
Château du Châtelier
10km/6mi E along D 100.
Standing on a rocky outcrop, this austere castle has preserved some of its medieval fortifications and, to the east of its rampart, an imposing round keep with large window openings.

Ferrière-Larçon
16km/10mi E along D 100.
Emerging from among the tiled roofs along the valley, the church is architecturally interesting with its narrow Romanesque nave (12C) and tall, open Gothic chancel (13C). Rising above in the centre is a fine Romanesque bell-tower sorrounded by four smaller corner bell turrets.

Le Grand-Pressigny

Le Grand-Pressigny stands in an attractive location facing the confluence of the River Claise and River Aigronne. It was once protected by its hilltop castle. The site is well known in the field of prehistory on account of its many flint workshops where large numbers of blades were made at the end of the Neolithic Era.

CHÂTEAU★

Jan–Mar and Oct–Dec 10am–noon, 2–5pm, Sun 10am–5pm; Apr–Jun and Sept daily 10am–6pm; Jul–Aug daily 10am–7pm. €6. ℘02 47 94 90 20. www.prehistoiregrandpressigny.fr.
The castle, which provides a setting for the Prehistory Museum, has retained characteristics of the medieval fortress of Guillaume de Pressigny: ramparts flanked by towers, fortified gateway, keep and late-12C underground gallery. Amid the carefully tended gardens stands the 16C seigneurial home; the elegant Renaissance gallery opens

▶ **Population:** 979.
Michelin Map: 317: N-7
Info: Place Savoie-Villars, 37350 Le Grand-Pressigny. ℘02 47 94 96 82. www.loches-valdeloire.com.
Location: 70km/44mi S of Tours.
Don't Miss: Musée de la Préhistoire in the castle.
Timing: Allow 1–2 hours.

through a portico onto the Court of Honour, laid out as French gardens.
The **Musée de la Préhistoire★** traces the different stages of prehistoric evolution made in major sites in the Touraine. There are special facilities for the blind. The 16C coach house, containing a section on palaeontology, displays fossils from the Touraine, in particular those found in deposits from the Faluns Sea to the north and south of the Loire.

EXCURSION
La Celle-Guenand
8.5km/5.3mi NE along D 13.
La Celle-Guenand has a harmoniously proportioned church with a sober Romanesque façade. The covings in the façade's central doorway have been finely carved with masks and imaginary figures.

Preuilly-sur-Claise

Preuilly, which has retained numerous interesting old houses and the former abbey church beneath the ruins of its fortress, rises in terraces on the north bank of the Claise amid woodland, green meadows and vineyards. The town was once considered to be the leading barony of the Touraine region, held by such illustrious families as those of Amboise, La Rochefoucauld, César de Vendôme, Gallifet and Breteuil. Five churches and a collegiate church were barely enough to accommodate the town's worshippers in its heyday.

ÉGLISE ST-PIERRE
This old Benedictine abbey church (c. 1000) is a Romanesque building in which traces of the architectural styles of the Poitou and Touraine regions are evident. Architect Phidias Vestier carried out some excellent repair work in 1846, but the church was subsequently subjected to shoddy restoration in 1873, the year when the tower was built. Near the church, one of the 17C mansions has been turned into a hospice (previously Hôtel de la Rallière).

ADDRESSES

⬦/ EAT

⬠⬠⬠⬠ **La Promenade** – *11 r. du Savoureulx.* ✆*02 47 94 93 52. www. restaurantdallaislapromenade.com. Closed Sun eve, Mon–Tue (but open Tue evening Jul–Aug).* Classical French cuisine that depends on fresh local cheeses, oils, seafood and produce. Try the excellent carrot bouillon, grilled baby leeks or in season, lièvre (hare) à la royale.

▶ **Population:** 1,056.
◉ **Michelin Map:** 317: O-7
▤ **Info:** Grande-Rue, 37290.
✆02 47 94 59 43. www. lochessudtouraine.com.
▶ **Location:** To the SE of Descartes (24km/15mi) and 35km/22mi S of Loches.
◷ **Timing:** Allow 30min to visit the church.

EXCURSION
Boussay
5.3km/3.3mi along D 725.
The château in Boussay combines such diverse elements as 15C machicolated towers, a wing in the Baroque style of Mansart, the architect who designed much of the château at Versailles, and an 18C façade. It stands in fine gardens in the French style.

ADDRESSES

⬦/EAT

⬠⬠⬠ **Restaurant la Claise** – *4 Avenue Léon Berthier.* ✆*02 47 92 08 50, Tue-Sun noon-1.30pm, 8-11pm.* Classic French and modern European cuisine served in a traditional stationmasters home. Fresh, local produce and the chance to dine outside in the summer months.

The western region of Touraine encapsulates the richness and variety of the Loire valley. It is home to the largest city, Tours, and some of the most stunning châteaux at Villandry, Azay-le-Rideau and Chinon. Its fertile green valleys have rightly earned it the title of the "Garden of France", and its important role in the country's history and culture is dominated by the presence of such towering figures as Joan of Arc and Honoré de Balzac. It is worth spending a few days in the region to take in all the magnificent attractions it has to offer.

Garden of France

You may choose to follow in the footsteps of Henry James during his Little Tour in France and use Tours as a base for excursions in the region, but the city itself, standing astride the Loire and boasting a mixture of classical art and artisan crafts, is a lovely place to spend a couple of days. Home to 30 street markets, from the Tuesday produce market to the annual Foire à l'ail et au basilic (garlic and basil fair), the town is a gastronomic destination in its own right. The historic district around Place Plumereau, the Cathédrale St-Gatien and the Fine Arts museum has been magnificently restored: visitors can enjoy a stroll along winding streets, past half-timbered houses and shops before resting outside a café to soak up the atmosphere and take in the view. The rich soils of the surrounding countryside have been cultivated for millennia, and the region offers a vast array of fresh fruit and vegetables throughout the seasons. The history of the French monarchy in the Loire valley is best witnessed at nearby Langeais, the favourite château of Louis XI, and the now ruined fortress of Chinon, a Plantagenet stronghold and scene of the famous meeting between Joan of Arc and Charles VII during France's struggle against England in the Hundred Years War.

Renaissance treasures

With Villandry and Azay-le-Rideau, the region boasts two of the most beautiful châteaux of the Loire valley. Villandry is famous throughout the world for

Highlights

1 Walking around the old quarter of **Tours** (p192)

2 The **Villandry** gardens (p202)

3 Richly furnished apartments of **Château de Langeais** (p204)

4 Charming, romantic **Azay-le-Rideau** (p209)

5 **Chinon**, both the town and the impressive château (p214)

Château de Langeais

© Arnaud Chicurel/hemis.fr

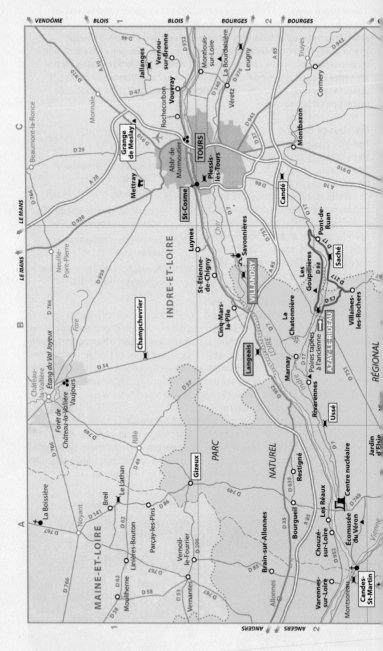

its spectacular gardens, the result of a lifetime's work by Joachim Carvallo, a Spaniard who set about restoring them to their original Renaissance splendour after buying the run-down estate in the early 20C. Many connoisseurs admire Azay-le-Rideau as the perfect embodiment of French Renaissance architecture. Built by a rich financier, it suffered a similar fate to that of Chenonceau as its

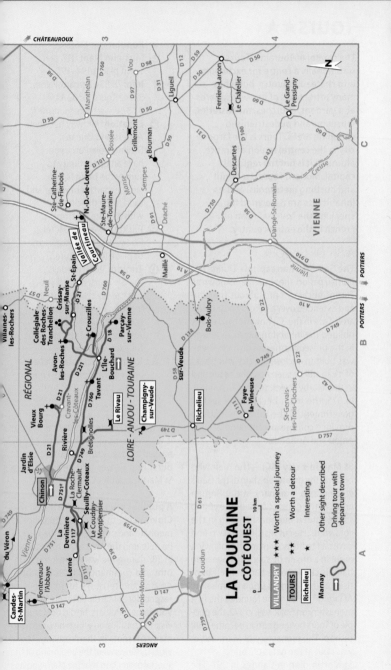

splendours attracted the jealous gaze of the King – François I in the case of Azay-le-Rideau – who took the first opportunity to confiscate it for his own pleasure. After some intensive châteaux visiting and sightseeing, explore Vouvray, east of Tours, and Bourgueil, south-west of Tours, where some of the region's finest wines are made.

Tours★★

The capital of Touraine, Tours is traditionally a centre for excursions into châteaux country, but it has many attractions of its own: squares and gardens, churches, monasteries, museums and pedestrianised shopping areas. Tours is the largest city in the central region of France, although it is not the regional capital. Modern Tours is a bright and bustling metropolis, and its inhabitants are renowned for speaking the "purest" form of French in the entire country.

▶ **Population:** 136,252.

⊙ **Michelin Map:** 317: N-4 Town plan, p194–195

Info: 78-82 r. Bernard-Palissy, 37042 Tours. ℘02 47 70 37 37. www.tours-tourisme.fr.

◗ **Location:** Midway between Angers and Orléans. Driving from Paris, you have an opportunity to survey the bridges, the large expanses of water and sand, then the city itself, with its slate rooftops.

P **Parking:** Near the Hôtel Gouin, pl. de la Résistance or pl. de la Préfecture.

🕔 **Timing:** Take two days to visit Tours, more if you use the town as a central location for excursions into the countryside. Allow at least one day for exploring the city

👪 **Kids:** Caves at Savonnières and a boat trip on the Loire.

A BIT OF HISTORY

The Gallo-Roman capital – During the Roman period, the settlement known as Turons became a prosperous free city and extended over a densely populated area. Late in the 3C, however, invasions obliged the inhabitants to take refuge in the present cathedral district. A wall was built to enclose the city and traces of it can still be seen near the castle and in the nearby street, rue des Ursulines. In 375, the town became the seat of government of the third Lyonnaise, a province comprising Touraine, Maine, Anjou and Armorica.

St Martin's city (4C) – The man who became the greatest bishop of the Gauls started as a legionary in the Roman army. At the gates of Amiens the young soldier met a beggar shivering in the cold wind. He cut his cloak in two and gave half to the poor man. The following night in a dream he saw Christ wearing half his cloak, so he had himself baptised and embarked upon his mission. At Ligugé in Poitou he founded the first monastery on Gallic soil. In 372, the people of Tours begged him to become their bishop. The monastery of Marmoutier was built at the gates of Tours.

St Martin died in Candes in 397. The monks of Ligugé and Marmoutier quarrelled over his body; while the men of Poitou slept, the men of Tours transferred the saint's body to a boat and rowed hard upstream for home. Along the way, a miracle occurred: although it was November, as the saint's body passed by, trees turned green, plants burst into flower and birds sang – a St Martin's summer.

A popular pilgrimage – In 496 or 498 **Clovis** came to St-Martin's Basilica to meditate and promised to be baptised if he defeated the Alemanni. He returned in 507 during the war against the Visigoths and commanded his army not to despoil the territory of Tours out of respect for St Martin. After his victory at Vouillé, near Poitiers, he did not forget to visit the basilica on which he bestowed many presents in thanksgiving. These visits by Clovis were the beginning of the special protection that the Merovingians granted to the sanctuary.

For many years pilgrims had been flocking to Tours for cure or counsel. Besides the ordinary pilgrims in search of the supernatural, kings, princes and pow-

The Loire and Pont Wilson

Gregory of Tours

In 563, a young deacon in poor health, who was heir to a noble Gallo-Roman family in the Arverne (later Auvergne), visited St Martin's tomb. His name was Gregory. He was cured and settled in Tours. Owing to his piety and probity, coupled with the renown of several of his relatives (he was the great-nephew of St Nizier of Lyon), he was elected bishop in 573. Gregory of Tours produced many written works, especially the *History of the Franks*, which has been the main source of information about the Merovingian period. He also wrote eight *Books of Miracles* and the *Lives of the Fathers*. Under his enlightened direction, the town developed and an abbey grew up round St-Martin's Basilica. Gregory died in 594.

erful lords came seeking absolution for their many crimes and abuses. The sanctuary was also a place of asylum, an inviolable refuge for both the persecuted and the criminal. The popularity of the cult of St Martin brought the abbey great wealth; its estates, the result of many donations, extended as far as Berry and Bordelais.

From the early Capets to Louis XI – The Viking invasions reached Tours in 853: the cathedral, the abbeys and the churches were set on fire and destroyed. The relics of St Martin were removed and hidden in the Auvergne. In 903, after further attacks, the abbey was surrounded by a wall and a new town grew up to the west of the old city; it was called Châteauneuf or Martinopolis.

The Robertians, in charge of St-Martin's Abbey, held immense temporal power and the opportunity to pursue ecclesiastical careers; abbots, bishops and archbishops were appointed from among the 200 canons attached to the abbey. The nickname **Capet**, by which King Hugh was known at the end of the 10C, comes from an allusion to the *cappa*

(cloak) of St Martin, thus proving that the success of the new royal dynasty owed much to the famous monastery. In 997, a huge fire destroyed Châteauneuf and St Martin's Abbey, which had to be completely rebuilt.

The rivalry in the 11C between the houses of Blois and Anjou, whose domains met in Touraine, ended with victory for the Angevins. When Pope Alexander III held a great council in Tours in 1163, Touraine belonged to the Plantagenets, but in 1205 **Philippe Auguste** captured the town, which then remained French.

The 13C was a period of peace and prosperity; the **denier tournois**, the money minted in Tours, was adopted as the official currency in preference to the denier parisis.

In 1308, Tours played host to the États Généraux (French Parliament). Less welcome events soon followed; the arrival of the **Black Death** (1351) and the beginning of the Hundred Years War forced the citizens to build a new wall in 1356, enclosing Tours and Châteauneuf. In 1429 Joan of Arc stayed in Tours while her armour was being made. Charles

Place Plumereau

© Laurent Marolleau/age fotostock

VII settled in Tours in 1444 and on 28 May he signed the Treaty of Tours with Henry VI of England.

Under **Louis XI** Tours was very much in favour; the city acted as the capital of the kingdom and a mayor was appointed in 1462. The King liked the region and lived at the Château de Plessis-lès-Tours (🕭see p199). Once again life became pleasant and the presence of the court attracted a number of artists of which the most famous was **Jean Fouquet** (born in Tours c. 1420). The abbey once again enjoyed royal favour and recovered some of its former prestige. Louis XI died in 1483 at Plessis, whereupon the court moved to Amboise.

Silk weaving and Wars of Religion – Louis XI had promoted the weaving of silk and cloth of gold in Lyon, but the project had not met with much enthusiasm, so the weavers and their looms were moved to Touraine.

In this world of craftsmen, intellectuals and artists, the **Reformation** found its first supporters and Tours, like Lyon and Nîmes, became one of the most active centres of the new religion. In 1562 the Calvinists caused great disorder, particularly in St-Martin's Abbey. The Roman Catholics were merciless in their revenge; 10 years before Paris, Tours had its own St Bartholomew's Day Massacre, with 200-300 Huguenots being drowned in the Loire. In May 1589 Henri III and the Parliament retreated from Paris to Tours, which once again resumed its role as royal capital.

In the latter half of the 18C, extensive town planning by royal decree opened up a wide road on a north-south axis along which Tours was to develop in the future.

Wars – Owing to its communications facilities, Tours was chosen in 1870 as the seat of the **Government for the National Defence**, but three months later, in the face of the Prussian advance, the government withdrew to Bordeaux. In June 1940 the same chain of events took place, but at greater speed. The town was bombed and burned for three days. In 1944 the bombings resumed. In all, between 1940 and 1944, 1 543 buildings were destroyed and 7,960 damaged; the town centre and the districts on the banks of the Loire were the most badly hit.

🐾 WALKING TOURS

1 THE OLD TOWN★★★

The vast restoration work begun about 1970 around place Plumereau, and the building of the Faculté des Lettres beside the Loire, have brought the old quarter to life; its narrow streets, often pedestrian precincts, have attracted shops and craftspeople, and the whole quarter near the university has become one of the liveliest parts of town.

Place Plumereau★
This picturesque and animated square, once the hat market, is lined with fine

15C timber-framed houses alternating with stone façades. Pavement cafés and restaurants overflow onto the square. On the corner of rue du Change and rue de la Monnaie, there is a lovely house featuring two slate-roofed gables and posts decorated with sculptures.

◖ Continue to the corner of rue de la Rôtisserie where there is an old façade with wooden lattice-work.

To the north of the square a vaulted passageway opens on to the attractive **place St-Pierre-le-Puellier**, with its pleasant gardens.

Rue du Grand-Marché
This is one of the most interesting streets in old Tours, with a great number of half-timbered façades embellished with bricks or slates.

Rue Bretonneau
At No. 33 stands a 16C hôtel with pretty Renaissance carved foliage; the northern wing was added towards 1875.

Rue Briçonnet★
This charming street is bordered by houses showing a rich variety of local styles, from the Romanesque façade to the 18C mansion. Off the narrow rue du Poirier, No. 35 has a Romanesque façade, No. 31 a late-13C Gothic façade; opposite, at No 32, stands a Renaissance house with lovely wooden statuettes. Not far away, an elegant staircase tower marks the entrance to place St-Pierre-le-Puellier.
Farther north, on the left, No. 23 has a Classical façade. No. 16 is the **Maison de Tristan,** a remarkable stone and brick construction with a late-15C pierced gable: it is used as the premises of a modern languages centre, the Centre d'Études de Langues Vivantes.

Rue Paul-Louis-Courier
In the inner courtyard, above the doorway of the 15C–16C Hôtel Binet (No. 10) is an elegant wooden gallery served by two spiral staircases.

Place de Châteauneuf
There is a fine view of the **Tour Charlemagne** and the remains of the **Ancienne basilique St-Martin**, built in the 11C and 13C over the tomb of the Bishop of Tours after the Vikings had destroyed the 5C sanctuary.
Opposite, the 14C ducal residence, **Logis des ducs de Touraine,** houses a centre for military servicemen, the Maison des Combattants, while the late-15C church of **St-Denis** has been converted into a music centre. Further along rue des Halles stands the **Tour de l'Horloge**, a clock tower marking the façade of the basilica which was crowned with a dome in the 19C.

Musée St-Martin
◷ Mid-Mar–mid-Nov Wed–Sun 10am–1pm. 2–5.30pm. ⊜€2.
℘02 47 64 48 87. www.mba.tours.fr.
This museum in rue Rapin is housed in the 13C Chapel of St-Jean, once an outbuilding of St Martin's cloisters. Texts and engravings and remains from the basilicas built in succession over the saint's tomb are displayed, including carved marble items from the one built in about 470, and murals and mosaics from the 11C Romanesque basilica.

Nouvelle Basilique St-Martin
7 rue Baleschoux. ℘02 47 05 63 87. www.basiliquesaintmartin.fr.
Built between 1886 and 1924 in the neo-Byzantine style, the new basilica is the work of local architect Victor Laloux (1850–1937). The crypt holds the tomb of St Martin and is still a popular pilgrimage site, particularly on 11 November and the following Sunday.

◖ Return to pl. Plumereau along r. du Change.

② CATHEDRAL DISTRICT★★

This peaceful district has retained a few fine mansions and the Archbishop's Palace nestling round the cathedral.

TOURS

WHERE TO STAY

Cathédrale St-Gatien★★

Work on the cathedral started in the mid-13C and was completed in the 16C. It demonstrates the complete evolution of the French Gothic style; the chevet typifies the early phase, the transept and nave the development of the style and the Flamboyant west front belongs to the final phase (*see Architecture in the Introduction*). The first traces of the Renaissance are visible in the tops of the towers.

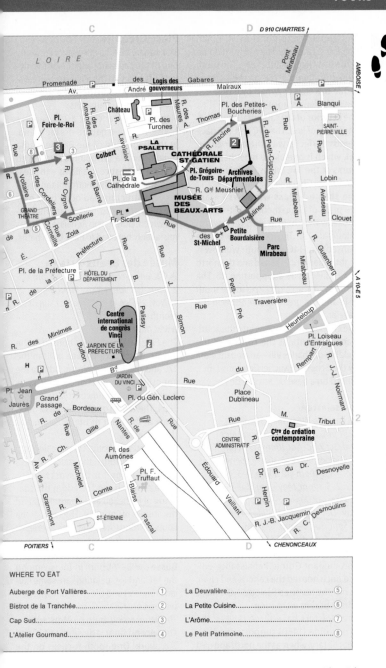

Despite the mixture of styles, the soaring **west front** is a harmonious entity. A slight asymmetry of detail ensures that the façade is not monotonous. The foundations of the towers are a Gallo-Roman wall and solid buttresses indicate that the bases are Romanesque. The rich Flamboyant decoration was added to the west front in the 15C. The buttresses, which rise to the base of the belfries, were decorated at the same period with niches and crocketed pinnacles.

The upper section of the 15C north tower is surmounted by a lantern dome in the early Renaissance style. The south belfry, built in the 16C on the Romanesque tower, is crowned by a dome in the early Renaissance style.

The **interior** of the cathedral has a striking purity of line. The 14C and 15C nave blends perfectly with the older **chancel**, which is one of the most beautiful works of the 13C and is reminiscent of the Sainte-Chapelle in Paris.

The **stained-glass windows★★** are the pride of the cathedral of St-Gatien. Those in the chancel with their warm colours are 13C. The rose windows in the transept are 14C; the south window is slightly diamond-shaped and the north one is divided by a supporting rib. The windows in the third chapel in the south aisle and the great rose window in the nave are 15C.

The chapel, which opens into the south transept, contains the **tomb★** of the children of Charles VIII – an elegant work by the School of Michel Colombe (16C), placed on a base by Jerome de Fiesole.

La Psalette★

⊙ *Jan–Feb Wed–Sat 9.30am–12.30pm, 2–5pm, Sun 2–5pm; Mar and Oct Wed–Sat 10am–12.30pm, 2–5.30pm, Sun 2–5.30pm; Apr and Sept Mon–Sat 10am–12.30pm, 2–5.30pm, Sun 2–5.30pm; May–Aug Mon–Sat 9.30am–12.30pm, 2–6pm, Sun 2–6pm; Nov–Dec Wed–Sat 9.30am–12.30pm, 2–5pm, Sun 2–5pm.* ⊙ *1 Jan, 1 May, 25 Dec.* ⊚€4. ℘ *02 47 47 05 19. www.cloitre-de-la-psalette.fr.*

This elegant Gothic-Renaissance edifice once housed the canons and choir, hence the name La Psalette – the place where psalms were sung.

The cloisters have three ranges: the west range (1460) supports the first-floor library, whereas the north and east ranges (1508–24) are almost completely covered by terraces. A Renaissance spiral staircase leads to the scriptorium (1520) next to the library, a fine room with ogive vaulting and an exhibit of the 13C–14C frescoes from the church in Beaumont-Village.

Place Grégoire-de-Tours★

This square offers a fine view of the east end of the cathedral and the Gothic flying buttresses; to the left is the medieval gable of the **Archbishop's Palace** (now the Musée des Beaux-Arts).

Note, in rue Manceau, a 15C canon's house with two gabled dormers and, at the beginning of rue Racine, a tufa building with a 15C pointed roof, which housed the Justice des Bains – the seat of jurisdiction of the metropolitan chapter. This structure had been built over the ruins of a Gallo-Roman amphitheatre which, during the Renaissance, was mistakenly believed to have been baths.

Musée des Beaux-Arts★★

&⊙ *Daily except Tue 9am–12.45pm, 2–6pm.* ⊙ *1 Jan, 1 May, 14 Jul, 1 and 11 Nov, 25 Dec.* ⊚€6 *(free first Sun of month).* ℘ *02 47 05 68 73. www. mba.tours.fr.*

The Fine Arts Museum is housed in the old **Archbishop's Palace** built in the 17C and 18C. Before going in, admire the imposing cedar of Lebanon, which was planted in the main courtyard around 1804. The formal garden permits a good **view** of the front of the museum and the cathedral.

Decorated with Louis XVI panelling and silks made in Tours, the rooms make a perfect setting for the works of art, some of which used to adorn the châteaux of Richelieu and Chanteloup and the abbeys of Touraine. The walls of the Louis XIII room are hung with a series of highly colourful anonymous paintings executed after engravings by **Abraham Bosse** (1602–76), born in Tours. Among the 14C and 15C paintings are some Italian Primitives and the museum's masterpieces, *Christ in the Garden of Olives* and *The Resurrection*, both by **Mantegna**.

The **second floor** is devoted to 19C and 20C work. One room focuses on the contemporary painter Olivier Debré. A display of **ceramics** by Avisseau (19C), from the Touraine, includes plates decorated with motifs in relief in the style of Bernard Palissy. Note the splendid collections of Langeais faïence, highly valued throughout 19C Europe: the fine texture of the local clay, combined with kaolin, makes it possible to produce a variety of shapes. The platinum glaze is an unusual finishing touch.

Jardin des archives départementales d'Indre-et-Loire

Access by an arched passage through buildings at the corner of rue du Petit-Cupidon and rue des Ursulines.
This spot contains the best-preserved part of the Gallo-Roman walls and the ancient city of Caesarodunum with one of its defence towers and, carved out of the wall, the southern postern, which would have been the entrance to a Roman road.

▶ Cross over r. des Ursulines into **Parc Mirabeau** to see its statues.

Petite Bourdaisière et chapelle St-Michel

2 r. du Petit-Pré. &.⏱*Jul–late-Sept daily except Wed and Sun 10am–noon, 3–6pm.* ⏱*Public holidays.* ✆*02 47 64 14 30.*
This small 15C townhouse and the chapelle St-Michel constituted the buildings of the Ursulines convent in the 17C. A museum presents the life and work of Marie de l'Incarnation Guyart, an ursuline nun who worked as a missionary in Canada where she founded the first Ursulines convent in Quebec in 1639.

▶ Turn right at the end of r. des Ursulines. From **pl. François-Sicard** you have fine views of the cathedral.

3 ST-JULIEN DISTRICT★

The streets near the bridge over the Loire suffered considerable bomb damage in the Second World War, but behind the regular modern façades in rue Nationale some charming squares have survived.

▲▲ Musée du Compagnonnage★★
Entrance through a porch, 8 r. Nationale, and over a footbridge.

&.⏱*9am–12.30pm, 2–6pm: mid-Jun–mid-Sept daily; rest of year Wed–Mon.* ⏱*Public holidays.* ✆€5.80 (under 12 years free). ✆02 47 21 62 20. www.museecompagnonnage.fr.*
The Trade Guild Museum is housed in the Guest Room (11C) and the monks' dormitory (16C) above the chapter house of the abbey of St-Julien. It traces the history, customs and skills of trade guilds that provided training for their members and protected their interests. Both current and obsolete trades (weavers, ropemakers, woodturners, etc.) are represented through their tools, historical documents and the many masterpieces that the companions (derived from *com pani* and meaning someone with whom one shares one's bread) had to produce to receive their official title.

Église St-Julien
The 11C belfry-porch is set back from the street in front of the 13C church. The sombre Gothic interior is lit through stained-glass windows (1960) executed by Max Ingrand and Le Chevalier.

Hôtel Goüin★
25 r. du Commerce.
This mansion is a fine example of living accommodation during the Renaissance. It was burnt out in June 1940, but the **south façade★**, with its sculpted Renaissance ornamental foliage, and the north façade, with its fine staircase tower, were spared.

Hôtel Beaune-Semblançay★
Entrance through a porch, 28 r. Nationale.
The Renaissance mansion belonged to the unfortunate Minister of Finance who was hanged in the reign of François I. The only parts to have escaped destruction are the façade of an arcaded gallery decorated with pilasters (standing alone) and a finely sculpted fountain.

In rue Jules-Favre stands the sober and elegant façade of the **Palais du Commerce**, which was built in the 18C for the merchants of Tours.

Rue Colbert

Before Wilson Bridge was built, this street, together with its extension rue du Commerce, was the main axis of the city. The half-timbered house at no. 41 bears the sign *À la Pucelle armée* (The Armed Maiden); Joan of Arc's armour is believed to have been made by the craftsman living here in April 1429. Rue Colbert and rue de la Scellerie, which is reached via rue du Cygne, are home to several antique dealers.

Place Foire-le-Roi

This was the site of the free fairs established by François I; it was also the stage for the mystery plays that were performed when the kings visited Tours. The north side is lined by 15C gabled houses. The Renaissance mansion (No. 8) belonged to Philibert Babou de la Bourdaisière. On the west side, a side street leads into the narrow and winding passage du Cœur-Navré (Broken-Heart Passage), which accesses rue Colbert.

ADDITIONAL SIGHTS

Château

25 av. André-Malraux. ℘*02 47 21 61 95. https://chateau.tours.fr.*

A tree-lined walk beside the Loire skirts the heterogeneous buildings of the castle, reminders of past ages. The **Tour de Guise**, with machicolations and a pepper-pot roof, was part of the 13C fortress; the tower owes its name to the young Duke of Guise, who was imprisoned in the castle after the assassination of his father and then escaped.

The **Logis des Gouverneurs** on the quay is a 15C building with gable dormers. At its base and running towards the Tour de Guise is the Gallo-Roman wall, composed of courses of brick alternating with small stones, typical of the period. On the second floor, a permanent exhibit on **Urban Development** (Wed and Sat 2–6pm; free) contains archaeological and historical documents as well as models and audiovisual presentations that explain the history of Tours and the development of its cityscape.

Centre International de congrès Vinci

26-28 blvd. Heurteloup.
⚲ *No public access.*

Standing beside the railway and coach stations, this huge exposition hall was designed by architect Jean Nouvel (1993). It is distinctive for its prominent glass bow. The three auditoriums seem to be suspended in space and can seat 350, 700 and 2,000 people respectively.

Centre de création contemporaine

55 r. Marcel Tribut. ♿ Wed–Sun *11am–6pm (9pm on Thursday and 7pm on Saturday).* 1 Jan, 25 Dec. €7. ℘*02 47 66 50 00. www.cccod.fr.*

Temporary exhibitions of contemporary art have been held here since 1985.

Jardins Historiques

Follow signs for parcs et jardins de la ville de Tours. 1–3 r. des Minimes. Daily. ℘*02 47 70 37 37.*

Within the city, several public gardens are the ideal spot for a quiet stroll.

Jardin Botanique – On the city's western edge, Tours' oldest garden (5.8ha) comprises an arboretum, a water lily and lotus pond, a Mediterranean garden, a historical garden, a small zoo and play areas. The orangery and greenhouses (*greenhouses open daily 2–5pm*) separate the garden from the propagation houses.

Jardin des Prébendes d'Oé – This garden (5ha) was created by Eugène Bühler in 1874 and features fine ornamental trees planted by species groups.

Jardin de la Préfecture – Situated close to the Vinci exposition centre, this pleasant garden (1ha) presents a mixture of styles.

Demeure de Ronsard au Prieuré de St-Cosme★

3km/2mi W via quai du Pont-Neuf and av. Proudhon, then along the riverside embankment.
♿ Jan–Mar and Nov–Dec daily except Tue 10am–12.30pm, 2–5pm; Apr–May and Sept–Oct daily

Demeure de Ronsard
au Prieuré de St-Cosme

10am–6pm; Jun–Aug daily 10am–7pm. 1 Jan, 25 Dec. €6. 02 47 37 32 70. www.prieure-ronsard.fr.

A haven of peace set amid well-tended gardens, the priory is the perfect place for a leisurely stroll.

The St-Cosme community was founded in 1092, and welcomed pilgrims along the route to Santiago de Compostela. The priory was decommissioned in the 18C. The poet **Pierre de Ronsard** (1524–85) began living at the priory in 1565, where he received Catherine de Medici and her son, King Charles IX. Ronsard died here in 1585 and was buried in the church.

The **Prior's Lodging**, where Ronsard lived and died, is a charming little 15C house; in Ronsard's time an outside staircase led to the first floor of the residence, which had only one large room on each level. This staircase was pulled down in the 17C.

The gardens boast more than 200 varieties of roses, peonies and irises as well as an orchard, a vegetable garden and a pergola. New for 2020, an adult treasure hunt (*available all year, no extra cost, reservation not necessary*) and a "five-senses tour" of the herbarium for adults and kids (€8.50, under 7 years old €2.50. *Reservation required on 02 47 37 32 70*).

Château de Plessis-lès-Tours

1km/0.6mi from the Prieuré de St-Cosme along av. du Prieuré.
⌐ *Closed to the public.*

This modest brick building is only a small part of the château built by Louis XI in the 15C. He died in the castle in 1483 after 22 years of rule.

EXCURSIONS

Grange de Meslay★

10km/6mi NE via N 10 and road to the right. Apr–Oct Sat–Sun and public holidays 3–6pm. €4.
02 47 29 19 29. www.meslay.com.

This former **fortified tithe farm** belonging to Marmoutier abbey has a beautiful porch, the remains of a perimeter wall and a remarkable barn. The barn is a very good example of 13C secular architecture. The rounded main door is set in a pointed gable and the 15C timber roof is supported by four rows of oak heartwood pillars.

Montbazon Fortress

9km/5.6mi S along N 10. 12-14 rue du Château Apr–Jun and Sept weekends and holidays 10am-6pm; July-Aug daily 10am-7pm. €12. 02 47 34 34 10. www.forteressedemontbazon.com

The fortress of Montbazon and its 10C dungeon have dominated the town of Montbazon for more than a thousand years. The site is brought to life by reconstructions of life in the Middle Ages, including combat, jousts and underground passages. Visitors can try weaving, calligraphy and stone carving.

Dolmen de Mettray

10km/6.2mi NW along N 138 turning right onto D 76 to Mettray.

In a spinney in St-Antoine-du-Rocher to the north of Mettray on the right bank of the Choisille (*signposted*) stands the dolmen of the Fairy Grotto, one of the most skilfully constructed megalithic monuments in France.

Luynes
7km/4.3mi W along N 152 then right.
From the road running along the Loire embankment, there is a pretty view of this charming little town built in tiers up the hillside. Luynes still has numerous cellars hollowed out of the rock face, and a timber-frame covered market hall, the **halles**, dating from the 15C, with a high roof of flat tiles.

Vernou-sur-Brenne
15km/10mi NE of Tours.
Vernou's attractive old houses are surrounded by Vouvray vineyards against a hillside riddled with caves.

Vouvray
4km/2.5mi W of Vernou by D 46.
At the heart of the famous vineyard is the village of Vouvray, which is set on the south-facing slopes of the hills that overlook the north bank of the Loire upstream from Tours. There are one or two old cliffside dwellings in the village.
Vouvray boasts a statue of Gaudissart, the famous travelling salesman whom Balzac described in one of his novels. **Honoré de Balzac** was born in Tours and often came to visit friends.
Still or sparkling white **Vouvray wines** are some of the finest of Touraine. Many wine producers and merchants have cellars (*caves*) open to the public.

On approaching **Rochecorbon**, a small town at the foot of a bluff riddled with dwellings hewn in the rock, note the **lantern**, a watchtower on the top of the hill. Farther on, at the end of a long wall (*right*) stands an imposing 13C doorway, part of the **Abbaye de Marmoutier**, which was founded by St Martin in 372 and fortified in the 13C and 14C.

Château de Jallanges
19.5km/12mi NE of Tours or 3.7km/2.3mi N of Vernou-sur-Brenne.
www.jallanges.com.
This grand brick-and-stone edifice comes into sight on a small ridge rising out of a sea of vineyards. It is Renaissance, with a 17C chapel and a superb park. It is now operated as a bed and breakfast and conference centre.

Domaine de Candé★
20km/12.4mi S of Tours, on N 10 and D 87 at Monts. ◐*Jul–Aug daily 10.30am–7pm; Apr–Jun and Sept Wed–Sun 10.30am–12.30pm, 1.30–6pm; Oct Wed–Sun 10.30am-12.30pm, 1.30-5pm. Nov-Mar open by appointment, call for details.* ◎€7. ℘*02 47 34 03 70. www.domainecande.fr.*
The **château** hosted the most talked-about wedding of the age between Wallis Simpson and the Duke of Windsor. Fifteen rooms are open to the public, including the music room where the duke and duchess exchanged vows. In the library, admire the **Skinner organ★★**. Fern Bedaux's Art Deco bathroom features modern conveniences including heated a towel rail and a system to fill and empty the bath in less than a minute.
Covering 200ha, the **grounds** are a rich reserve for local plants and wildlife. Around 60 deer wander freely and many species of birds nest in the superb trees that include sequoia, ginkgo biloba, cedars and plane trees.

Savonnières
This pleasant city is home to a church with a beautiful Romanesque portal decorated with animals and doves.

♨♿ Grottes Pétrifiantes
W of town, on the road to Villandry. ☛*Visit by guided tour (1hr) only, daily Feb–Mar and Oct–mid-Nov 10am–noon, 2–6pm; Apr–Jun and Sept 10am–7pm; Jul-Aug 9.30am-7.30pm; mid–end Nov 2–6pm.* ◎€7.40 (child 5-16, €5.30). ℘*02 47 50 00 09. www.grottes-savonnieres.com.*

The caves were used as quarries in the 12C and then partially flooded with water. The continuing infiltration of water saturated with limestone is slowly creating stalactites, pools and curtains.

ADDRESSES

🛌 STAY

🍽 **Chambre d'hôte le Moulin Hodoux** – *Le Moulin Hodoux, 37230 Luynes, 14km/8.7mi W. ℘02 47 55 76 27. www.moulin-hodoux.com. 5 rooms.* Close to the Château de Luynes this former 18C water mill enjoys a favourable rural setting.

🍽 **Hotel l'Adresse** – *12 r. de la Rotisserie. ℘02 47 20 85 76. www.hotel-ladresse.com. 17 rooms. Wi-Fi.* A place of 18C charm, but with modern décor and service. A quiet oasis in the Plumereau district.

🍽 **Hotel Castel Fleuri** – *10 r. Groison. ℘02 47 54 50 99. www.castel-fleuri-tours.com. 15 rooms.* 🅿. This hotel is in a quiet part of town that has a little bit of everything. Functional rooms.

🍽 **Hotel du Théâtre** – *57 r. Scellerie. ℘02 47 05 31 29. www.hoteldutheatre tours.com. 14 rooms. No pets.* This 15C house offers small rooms that are cosy and well kept. Quiet courtyard.

🍽🍽🍽 **Château du Vau** – *Near a golf course. 37510 Ballan-Miré, 10km/6mi SW. ℘02 47 67 84 04. www.chateau-du-vau.com. 5 rooms.* A stony road leads to this 18C château amid an immense park. Rooms are refined. Pool. Enjoy an unusual stay in one of their tree houses.

🍴 EAT

🍽🍽 **L'Atelier Gourmand** – *37 r. Etienne-Marcel. ℘02 47 38 59 87. www.latelier gourmand.fr.* Classic cuisine served in a rustic dining room with beams and a fireplace. Pleasant terrace.

🍽🍽 **Bistrot de la Tranchée** – *103 av. Tranchée. http://bistrot.charles-barrier.fr. ℘02 47 41 09 08.* Handsome wood façade and an open kitchen help make this bistro popular. Gourmet fare and daily specials.

🍽🍽 **La Petite Cuisine** – *24 r. Berthelot. ℘02 47 61 30 92. www.lapetitecuisine.eu. Closed Sat, Sun.* A small kitchen serving 12 guests at a single communal table. Regional, Lebanese, maritime, and other flavours.

🍽🍽 **Le Petit Patrimoine** – *58 r. Colbert. ℘02 47 66 05 81. www.lepetitpatrimoine.fr. Closed Sun, Mon.* Hearty and simple fare served in a rustic setting.

🍽🍽 **Maison Colbert** – *26 r.Colbert. ℘02 47 05 99 81. www.maisoncolbert.fr. Closed Sun, Mon.* Authentic local dishes, steaks, fish and baked goods at this small but welcoming spot.

🍽🍽–🍽🍽🍽 **Auberge de Port Vallières** – *195 quai des Bateliers, 37230 Fondettes. ℘02 47 42 24 04. www.auberge-de-port-vallieres.fr. Closed Sun eve, Mon except public holidays.* Patrons enjoy regional dishes in the chic, modern dining room.

🍽🍽🍽 **La Deuvalière** – *18 r. de la Monnaie. ℘02 47 64 01 57. www. restaurant-ladeuvaliere.com. Closed Sat–Sun.* A tasteful blend of a 15C stone house and modern styles; contemporary takes on traditional cuisine.

SHOPPING

La Chocolatière – *2-4 r. de la Scellerie . ℘02 47 05 66 75. www.la-chocolatiere.com.* The pavé de Tours chocolate cake is the speciality at this luxury pâtisserie in a stylish setting of mirrors, wood panels and antiques.

La Balade gourmande – *26 pl. du Grand Marché. ℘09.52.61.76.22. www.labalade gourmande.com. Open Tue–Sat 10am–7pm.* This gourmet shop is not to be missed for local products and regional specialities.

SPORT AND LEISURE

👫 **Boat trips on the Loire** – *56 quai de la Loire, 37210 Rochecorbon. ℘06 37 49 92 61. Call for times during season. www. naviloire.com. €10.50 (children under 12, €7).* Loire cruises on board the *Saint-Martin-de-Tours* explore the heritage, nature and crafts of the Loire valley.

© vlad155/iStock

Gardens and Château de Villandry★★★

Villandry was one of the last great Renaissance châteaux to be built on the Loire; it has unusual features for Touraine, like rectangular pavilions (instead of round towers) as well as the layout of the esplanade and its moat. Villandry's international fame is based not so much on its château as on its gardens, which are among the most remarkable in France.

VISIT
Gardens★★★
The gardens at Villandry are the most complete example in France of the formal Renaissance style adopted under the influence of the Italian gardeners brought to France by Charles VIII.

The **Promenade dans les Bois** is an itinerary leading to the belvedere and, from there, to the greenhouses, offering views all along. The tour continues south to the water garden, the **maze**, the herb and kitchen gardens.

Terraces are laid out one above the other: at the highest level is the new **Sun Garden**, overlooking the whole estate, a kind of "cloister" of greenery, with limes, lindens and hornbeam in three sections; the water garden has a fine sheet of water acting as a reservoir; the **flower garden** displays geometric

- 🕭 **Michelin Map:** 317: M-4
- 🗎 **Info:** 3 rue Principale, 37510 Villandry. ☎02 47 50 02 09. www.chateauvillandry.fr. *The chateau and gardens are open every day including public holidays from 9am, but closing times vary, check website for details.* ⊗€12 (chateau and gardens), €7.50 (gardens only), reduced mid-Nov– Mar €9/€5.
- ▶ **Location:** 32.6km/2mi NE of Chinon.
- 👪 **Kids:** Play area, maze.
- 🕓 **Timing:** Allow 1 hour to walk through the gardens before taking a 2 hour guided tour of the château.

designs outlined in box, one representing allegories of Love, the other symbolising Music; further designs are based on the Maltese, Languedoc and Basque crosses. At the lowest level the ornamental **kitchen garden** is a multi-coloured chequerboard of vegetables and fruit trees arranged in nine squares and enclosed by clipped hedges of box and yew.

Between it and the church, a herb garden has been laid out; as was the case in the Middle Ages, it is devoted to aromatic herbs and medicinal plants.

Château★★

Nothing remains of the early fortress except the keep, a square tower incorporated in the present structure that was built in the 16C by Jean Le Breton, Secretary of State to François I.

Joachim Carvallo, a Spaniard, furnished the château with an interesting collection of furniture and paintings. The grand staircase leads to the first floor, where you will see a brightly coloured Empire-style bedroom; at the end of the corridor, Madame Carvallo's bedroom commands a view of the gardens. *Return to the staircase.* The other wing houses the picture gallery, which contains a great deal of Spanish religious painting; note, however, a striking work by Goya depicting a severed head, as well as two 16C Italian paintings on wood *(St Paul and St John)* in lively colours and a portrait of the Infanta by the Velasquez School.

At the end of the gallery is the room with the 13C **Mudéjar ceiling★** from Toledo; the coffers are painted and gilded with typical Moorish motifs, an unexpected sight under northern skies.

ADDRESSES

🏠 STAY

⊜⊜🗒 **Le Chat courant** – *Villandry (7km along the Cher River to access an island facing Château Villandry).* ☎06 37 83 21 78. *www.le-chat-courant.com. 3 rooms.* 🅿️🍴. Here you'll find small, pleasant guest rooms in a typical local house dating from the 19C that is well-maintained. Beautiful garden and pool.

⊜⊜🗒 **Le Petit Villandry** – *21 Rue de la Mairie, 37510 Villandry.* ☎02 47 50 04 47. *www.petitvillandry.com. 2 rooms.* 🍴. *2-nights minimum.* In the village centre, not far from the château, this fine guesthouse is an oasis of calm. Its garden has

Villandry's kitchen garden

The arrival of new vegetables from the Americas revolutionised kitchen gardens during the Renaissance. The garden at Villandry was re-created in the early 20C by Joachim Carvallo (1869–1936) using 16C documents. He combined geometric designs of the monastic tradition with the style of Italian monastic gardens. Nearby, interesting gardens include La Bourdaisière with 400 varieties of tomato; Valmer, forgotten fruit and vegetables; Montriou has marrows, pumpkins and other cucurbitaceae; and the château du Rivau evokes the world of François Rabelais with Gargantua's kitchen garden.

a view overlooking the château gardens. Breakfast on the patio, if good weather.

⊜⊜🗒 **Les Mazeraies** – *R. des Mazeraies, 37510 Savonnières (5km E of Villandry).* ☎06 24 89 19 26. *www.les mazeraies.com. Rooms and gites.* A quiet retreat within large grounds. Comfortable bedrooms with bathrooms are well-maintained. Breakfast on a private terrace.

🍴 EAT

⊜⊜ **La Doulce Terrasse** – ☎02 47 50 02 10. *The château's restaurant and tearoom open 9am–6pm.* Charming spot for traditional food with an original touch.

⊜⊜ **L'Étape Gourmande "La Giraudière"** – *(1km S of Villandry by D121 toward Druye).* ☎02 47 50 08 60. *www.letapegourmande.com. Closed mid-Nov–Mar. Reservation recommended.* ♿🅿️. A former convent-farmhouse, la Giraudière restaurant is today renowned for featuring local flavours. A gite on the premises has 3 bedrooms (⊜⊜⊜🗒).

SHOPPING

Château shops – *Same hours as château.* Books, plants, tools and accessories for the house and garden for sale on-site.

Château de Langeais★★

The town's white houses nestle beneath the high walls of the château. Facing the château there is a lovely Renaissance house decorated with pilasters; the church's tower is also Renaissance.

A BIT OF HISTORY

At the end of the 10C, the Count of Anjou built a donjon, the ruins of which still stand in the gardens; it is thought be the oldest surviving castle keep in France. The château itself was built by **Louis XI** from 1465 to 1469 as a stronghold on the road from Nantes, the route most likely to be taken by an invading Breton army. This threat vanished after the marriage of Charles VIII and Anne of Brittany was celebrated at Langeais itself in 1491.

VISIT

The château was built in one go, a rare event. It has not been altered since, also a rarity. It is one of the most interesting in the Loire valley, owing to the patient efforts of Jacques Siegfried, the last owner, who refurnished it in the style of the 15C and who bequeathed it to the Institut de France.

On the town side, it resembles a feudal fortress: high walls, round towers, a crenellated and machicolated sentry walk and a drawbridge spanning the moat.

Apartments★★★

The apartments exude an atmosphere much more alive than in many old castles. They also convey an accurate picture of aristocratic life in the 15C. The guard room, converted into a dining room, has a monumental chimney-piece, the hood of which represents a castle with battlements manned by small figures.

On the first-floor, in the Crucifixion room, note an early four-poster bed and a 17C panel from Brussels. On the second floor, in Charles VIII's bedchamber, stands a curious 17C clock with only one hand as well as two 16C tapestries. The great hall has a chestnut timber roof in

- ▶ **Population:** 4,299.
- **Michelin Map:** 317: L-5
- **Info: Tourist office**, 19 r. Thiers, 37130 Langeais. ✆02 47 96 58 22.
  Chateau: ⏱*Daily: Feb–Mar 9.30am–5.30pm; Apr–Jun and Sept–mid-Nov 9.30am–6.30pm; Jul–Aug 9am–7pm; mid-Nov–Jan 10am–5pm (except 25 Dec, 2–5pm). ⊜€10.50 (child 10–17, €5.20). ✆02 47 96 72 60. www.chateau-de-langeais.com.*
- ▶ **Location:** Situated along the Loire, between Tours (30km/19mi to the E) and Saumur (N 152) (43km/27mi to the W).
- ⏱ **Timing:** Allow 1–2 hours. The grounds are a delight.

the form of a ship's hull; 15 wax figures re-create the scene of Charles VIII and Anne of Brittany.

Donjon

Medieval scaffolding has been reconstructed to show siege techniques. It also gives great views of the château and the town.

Parc de l'an mil

This tree-lined park is perfect for a leisurely stroll. Kids will love the play areas and treehouse.

Some of the ruins of the chapelle Saint-Sauveur (11C) can still be seen. From the terrace, there are fine **views** of the Loire, the bridge in Langeais and, farther afield, the Forest of Chinon.

EXCURSIONS

Cinq-Mars-la-Pile

5km/3mi E on N 152.

The place name is derived from a brick-built monument in the shape of a slender tower that dominates the ridge east of the village. The structure is topped by four small pyramids.

Château

♿🕐 *Jul–mid-Sept Wed–Mon 11am–8pm; Apr–Jun and mid-Sept–Oct Sat–Sun and holidays 11am–6pm.* ☞€6. 𝄞*02 47 96 40 49. www.chateau-cinq-mars.com.*
Two 13C round towers on the hillside mark the site of the medieval castle in which the Marquis of Cinq-Mars was born. He was the favourite of Louis XIII, but was convicted of conspiring against Richelieu and was beheaded in Lyon in 1642, at the age of 22.
The **park★** is particularly lovely: a garden, a maze, and dense woodland.

St-Étienne-de-Chigny

7.5km/4.7mi NE on N 152; fork left onto D 76 and left again onto D 126 towards Vieux Bourg.
Set back from the village, which lies on the Loire embankment, the Vieux Bourg nestles in the Bresme Valley, filled with old houses with steep gables.

Château de Champchevrier★

12km/7.4mi N on D 15 then D 34; turn right when leaving Cléré-les-Pins.
Located within a wooded area in which wolves roamed for many years, the château stands on the site of an old stronghold that played a defensive role in the area for many centuries. It is surrounded by a late-17C moat.
The present building, dating from the 16C, was modified in the 17C and 18C; it has been occupied by the same family since 1728. The interior is enhanced by superb **Regency furniture**. The series of **tapestries★** was executed by the Manufacture Royale d'Amiens after cartoons by Simon Vouet. The wood panelling of the wide staircase and its polychrome coffers were taken from the **Château de Richelieu** (🔾*see RICHELIEU*), demolished in 1805.

Three Weddings and a Funeral

In 1490, Anne de Bretagne, who was barely 14, was married by proxy to Maximilian of Austria. However, the marriage was annulled a year later so that Anne could marry the King of France, Charles VIII. Brittany was thus united with France and the wedding contract stipulated that if the King died, she should marry his successor … which is exactly what she did six years later when Louis XII succeeded Charles VIII.

ADDRESSES

🛏 STAY

⊜🛏 **Chambre d'hôte La Meulière** – *10 r. du Breuil, 37130 Cinq-Mars-la-Pile.* 𝄞*02 47 96 53 63. lameuliere.free.fr. 3 rooms.* 🅿🚭. This 19C house is quiet despite being close to the station. The colourful rooms are well sound-proofed and pleasantly furnished. Attractive breakfast room and garden.

⊜🛏🛏 **L'Ange est rêveur** – *5 pl. Pierre-de-Brosse (at foot of the château).* 𝄞*02 47 96 55 97. www.langeaisreveur.fr. 5 rooms.* This B&B, which also sells décor items, offers a simple combination of refinement and friendliness.

⊜🛏🛏🛏 **Domaine du Château de Hommes** – *rte. de Gizeux, 37340 Hommes.* 𝄞*02 47 24 95 13. 5 rooms.* 🅿*Wi-Fi.* Small 15C château set in the countryside. The pleasantly furnished rooms are in the old barn. 175ha park, jacuzzi, **heated pool** 🏊 *(May–Sept)*, walking, fishing, biking.

🍽 EAT

⊜🛏 **Au coin des Halles** – *9 r. Gambetta, 37130 Langeais.* 𝄞*02 47 96 37 25. www. aucoindeshalles.com. Closed Wed, Thu, Sun night.* This restaurant, half bistro, half gastronomic, serves cuisine based on local produce such as mullet and zander from the River Loire, shoulder of lamb, and farm poultry.

Bourgueil

Bourgueil enjoys a fortunate location in a fertile region between the Loire and the Authion at the eastern end of the Anjou valley, where vines and woodland abound. French poet **Pierre de Ronsard** was a frequent visitor, and it was here that he met the Marie mentioned in his romantic ballads. Nowadays the little town's renown derives from the full-bodied red wines yielded by the ancient Breton vines found only in that area.

▶ **Population:** 4,027.
◔ **Michelin Map:** 317: J-5.
🚹 **Info:** pl. de l'Église, 37140 Bourgueil. ℘02 47 97 91 39. www.tourainenature.com.
◗ **Location:** A crossroads on the D 35 and D 10 between Langeais (22km/14mi to the E) and Saumur (30km/19mi to the W).

SIGHTS
Church
The large Gothic chancel of this parish church is roofed with ribbed vaulting. Its width contrasts with the narrow and simple 11C Romanesque nave.

Market
Backing on to the old town hall is the elegant covered marketplace *(halles)* with stone arcades.

Saint Pierre Abbey & Museum of art and folk traditions
E of town on the road to Restigné.
🔹 *Guided tours only, Apr–Jun and Sept weekends 2-6pm; Jul–Aug Tue-Fri 2-7pm, Sat-Sun 10am-7pm.* ⊙ *1 Jan, 25 Dec.* 🎟€5.90. ℘07 81 52 09 18. *www.touraineloirevalley.co.uk.*
The abbey was founded at the end of the 10C by the Benedictines and was one of the richest in Anjou. Its vineyards stretched over the entire hillside In the 13C and 14C it was fortified and surrounded by a moat. The building by the roadside containing the **cellar** and **granary** dates from the same period. Another (18C) building has a monumental **staircase★**.

EXCURSIONS
Moulin bleu
2km/1mi N.
This windmill has a wooden cabin perched on top of a cone made of ashlar-work supported by a vaulted substructure, so that the top can pivot to bring the sails into the wind. The tannin obtained from grinding the bark of the chestnut tree was used in the tanneries in Bourgueil.

Restigné
5km/3mi E.
The wine-growing village lies just off the main road clustered round the church. The façade is decorated with a diaper pattern and the lintel of the south doorway is carved with fantastic beasts and Daniel in the lion's den. The Romanesque nave is roofed with early-16C timberwork; the beams are decorated with the faces of monsters.

Les Réaux
4km/2.5mi S.
This **château** (🔒 *closed to the public*), dates from the late 15C, and is surrounded by a moat. It's closed to the public but from the outside you can glimpse the entrance pavilion, which is flanked by two machicolated towers; the defensive features have been subordinated to the decorative ones: chequerwork in brick and stone; gracefully carved ornamentation in the shell-shaped dormer windows; the salamander above the entrance; and soldiers for weather vanes.

Chouzé-sur-Loire
7km/4.3mi SW.
The attractive village on the north bank of the Loire was once a busy port; the deserted dockside where the mooring rings are rusting and the **Musée des Mariniers** (Nautical Museum) (♿ ⊙ *mid-Jun–mid-Sept Thu–Sun*

and public holidays 2–6pm; €4; https://marinierschouzesurloire.fr. 02 47 95 18 47) recall the past.

Varennes-sur-Loire
15km/9mi SW.
The old river port on the Loire offers a fine view of Montsoreau Château. The towpath is a pleasant place for a walk.

Brain-sur-Allonnes
10km/6mi W.
Excavations in a 14C house have uncovered the medieval site of the **Chevalerie de Sacé** (reopens early 2021, then Apr–Oct Tue–Sun 2–6pm; €6; 02 41 52 87 40; www.ot-saumur.fr).
Some beautiful faïence tiles are displayed in the adjoining **museum**.

Château d'Ussé★

The château stands with its back to a cliff on the edge of Chinon forest, its terraced gardens overlooking the Indre. Its impressive bulk and fortified towers contrast sharply with the white stone and myriad roofs, turrets, dormers and chimneys rising against a green background. Tradition has it that when Charles Perrault, the famous French writer of fairy tales, was looking for a setting for *Sleeping Beauty*, he chose Ussé as his model.

A BIT OF HISTORY
Ussé is a very old fortress; in the 15C it became the property of a great family from Touraine, the Bueils, who had distinguished themselves in the Hundred Years War (1337–1453). In 1485, Antoine de Bueil sold Ussé to the Espinays, a Breton family who had been chamberlains and cupbearers to the Duke of Brittany and to Louis XI and Charles VIII.
The château frequently changed hands. Among its owners was Vauban's son-in-law, Louis Bernin de Valentinay; the great engineer paid frequent visits to Ussé. Voltaire and Châteaubriand were guests at the château. The estate has belonged to the Blacas family since the late 19C.

Exterior
On the walk up towards the château, a lovely kaleidoscope of roofs and turrets can be glimpsed through the leaves of the stately cedars of Lebanon, said to have been planted by the great French author Chateaubriand.

- **Michelin Map:** 317: K-5
- **Info:** Daily: mid-Feb–Mar and Oct 10am–6pm; Apr–Sept 10am–7pm. €14. 02 47 95 54 05. www.chateaudusse.fr.
- **Location:** 41km/25mi SW of Tours and 14km/8.7mi NE of Chinon on the left bank of the Indre.
- **Don't Miss:** Ussé's annual exhibition of historic costumes.
- **Timing:** Allow 2 hours to explore the château.

The outside walls (15C) have a military appearance, whereas the buildings overlooking the courtyard carry an elegant Renaissance touch.
Chapel★ – Standing on its own in the park, the chapel was built from 1520 to 1538 in the pure Renaissance style. The decorative initials C and L refer to the first names of Charles d'Espinay, who built the chapel, and his wife Lucrèce de Pons.
Caves – Behind the chapel, three limestone quarries have been converted into showrooms for exhibits on the local viviculture and the exploitation of tufa.

Interior
Salle des Gardes – In a corner of the building, the guard room boasts a 17C trompe-l'œil ceiling and a collection of Asian weapons.

Château d'Ussé
© Arnaud Chicurel/hemis.fr

Salon Vauban – The old chapel, which has been converted into a salon, has a fine set of furniture, including a Mazarin desk fashioned from lemon-tree wood and 400-year-old Brussels tapestries.

Grande Galerie – Linking the east and west wings of the château, the Great Gallery is hung with **Flemish tapestries★** depicting lively, realistic country scenes inspired by the work of Teniers. Beyond the room devoted to hunting trophies, the wide 17C staircase (fine wrought-iron banister) leads to the rooms on the first floor: the library and the King's apartment. In the antechamber a splendid 16C Italian cabinet has 49 drawers with ebony marquetry inside, inlaid with ivory and mother-of-pearl.

Chambre du Roi – As in all large stately residences, one bedroom was set aside for the king in the event of his paying a visit to the château. This particular room was never occupied by the sovereign.

Salle de Jeux★ – The top of the *donjon* (keep) houses an extremely interesting recreation room with china dinner services, toy trains and miniature furniture items from dolls' houses.

Wall Walk – Dotted along the wall walk, several display cabinets illustrate the story of Sleeping Beauty and other popular childhood characters.

EXCURSION
Rivarennes
5km/3mi from Rigny-Ussé.
Lying on the banks of the River Indre, Rivarennes once boasted some 60 ovens producing the famous dried pears.

La Poire Tapée à l'Ancienne
14 r. de Quinçay, 2km E of Rivarennes via D 17. ◑*Open daily 10am–noon, 2–6pm.* ℘*02 47 95 45 19. www.poirestapees.com.*
This troglodytic cave contains an old oven where pears are still dried today. Its owners will tell you the story of this regional speciality and how it is made.

Dried Pears, a Speciality of Rivarennes

The recipe is virtually identical to that used for making dried apples: the pears are peeled whole, then left to dry in a bread oven for four days. During this process, they lose 70 percent of their weight. They are then beaten flat with a spatula in order to remove the remaining air, and kept dried or preserved in glass jars. These dried pears provide a perfect accompaniment to game or meat dishes served with gravy, in which case they are simply made to swell by soaking in a good Chinon wine.

ADDRESSES

🏨 STAY

🛏️🍽️ **Chambre d'hôte La Buronnière** –
2 rte. des Sicots, 37190 Rivarennes.
𝄞02 47 95 47 61. www.chambre-hote-la-buronniere.com. 4 rooms. 🅿️🍽️. Bedrooms
in this former wine-grower's house
combine modern décor with an old
building. Local cooking is served at a
communal dining table (🛏️🍽️).

🛏️🍽️ **Hôtel Le Clos d'Ussé** –
*7 r. Principale, 37420 Rigny-Ussé (at foot
of the château). 𝄞02 47 95 55 47. www.*
*leclosdusse.fr. 4 rooms and 1 suite of 3
rooms.* 🅿️. *Wi-Fi.* This fine residence in
local stone is listed in "La Loire cycling
guide".

🛏️🍽️🍽️ **Domaine de la Juranvillerie** –
*15 r. des Fougères, 37420 Rigny-Ussé. 𝄞02
47 95 57 85. www.lajuranvillerie.com.
3 rooms, 1 cottages.* 🅿️🛏️. *Restaurant*
(🛏️🍽️🍽️) On the edge of the Chinon
forest, this pleasant ensemble of 17C
stone buildings includes gardens and a
natural swimming pool. Medieval meals
(🛏️🍽️🍽️) are served, and the breakfast
room has a huge fireplace.

Château d'Azay-le-Rideau★★★

A luxuriant setting on the banks of
the Indre provides the backdrop for
the Château d'Azay-le-Rideau, one of
the gems of the Renaissance. Similar
to Chenonceau, but less grandiose,
it conveys an unforgettable
impression of elegance especially
since its lines and dimensions suit
the site so perfectly.

A BIT OF HISTORY

Tragic past (15C) – The Château is
named after one of its lords, Ridel or
Rideau d'Azay, who was knighted by
Philippe Auguste, and built a strong
castle. The most tragic incident in its
history was a massacre that occurred in
1418. When Charles VII was Dauphin, he
was insulted by the Burgundian guard
as he passed through Azay. Instant
reprisals followed. The town was seized
and burnt, and the captain and his 350
soldiers were executed. Until the 18C,
Azay was called Azay-le-Brûlé (Azay
the Burnt).

A financier's creation (16C) – When
it rose from its ruins, Azay became
the property of **Gilles Berthelot**, one
of the great financiers of the time. He

- 🚭 **Michelin Map:** 317: L-5
- ℹ️ **Info:** Tourist office:
  4 r. du Château,
  37190 Azay-Le-Rideau.
  𝄞02 47 45 44 40.
  www.azay-chinon-valdeloire.com.
  Chateau: 🕐*Daily:
  Jan–Mar and Oct–Dec
  10am–5.15pm; Apr–Jun
  and Sept 9.30am–6pm;
  Jul–Aug 9.30am–7pm.*
  🕐*1 Jan, 1 May, 25 Dec.*
  💶*€11.50, free first Sun of
  month (Nov–Mar).*
  𝄞02 47 45 42 04.
  www.azay-le-rideau.fr.
- ▶ **Location:** Almost midway
  between Tours and
  Chinon, via the D 751.
- 🅿️ **Parking:** On-site parking,
  as well as pay car parks
  in the town centre.
- 👁️ **Don't Miss:** A walk around
  the water to get the best
  view of the château.
- 🕐 **Timing:** You should
  spend around 1 hour
  exploring the château
  and its grounds, but up
  to half a day to make
  the most of the town.

Château d'Azay-le-Rideau

© Pascal Ducept/hemis.fr

had the present delightful mansion built between 1518 and 1527. His wife, **Philippa Lesbahy**, directed the work, as Katherine Briçonnet had directed that of Chenonceau. François I confiscated Azay and gave it to one of his companions in arms from the Italian campaigns, **Antoine Raffin**.

In 1870, when Prince Frederick-Charles of Prussia was staying in the château, one of the chandeliers crashed down on to the table. The Prince thought that his life was being threatened and Azay barely escaped further retribution. In 1905 the château was bought by the French State for 200,000 francs.

VISIT

Though Gothic in outline, Azay is forward-looking in its bright appearance and the handsome design of its façades. The medieval defences are purely symbolic and testify only to the high rank of the owners.

Exterior

Partly built over the Indre, Azay-le-Rideau is surrounded by water, and consists of two main wings set at right angles. The reflections in the water add to the quality of the site and, together with the rows of houses and gardens along the River Indre, make excellent subjects for photographs.

Parc à l'anglaise – Extending over 8ha around the castle, the park was created for the Marquis of Biencourt in 1810 following extensive drainage.Two "mirrors" of water *(south and west)* reflect the image of the castle. Planted with cedar, bald cypress, redwood and other trees, the park provides an unforgetable view of grand structure.

Église St-Symphorien – This curious 11C church on the castle grounds was rebuilt in the 12C and enlarged in the 16C. On its gabled façade sculptures of Christ and saints in the niches date from the original edifice.

Interior

The interior is lavishly decorated and furnished with some pieces of outstanding beauty: late-15C oak canopy throne, fine brocade bed dating from the late 17C, credence tables, cabinets, etc.

Grand staircase★ – The château's most striking feature is the main staircase with its three storeys of twin bays forming loggias opening onto the courtyard and its elaborately decorated pediment.

Les combles★ – The attic has a magnificent 18C interior carved of oak cut from the Royal Forest of Chinon. Its ceiling, made of cedar, was a haven for bats.

Chambre Renaissance★★ – Recently restored in great detail by the Centre of National Monuments, this room is unique in France. Its walls and floor were completely covered with woven reed matting, which provided insulation from the cold. The bed, the fabrics, upholstery and artworks were all based on paintings of the period. Be sure to also see the adjoining wardrobe.

Chambre du roi – The king's chamber was preceded by a traditional ante-room where subjects were kept waiting a length of time suitable with their rank. The chamber has an exquisite 19C cabinet made of dark pear-tree wood.

Tapestries★ – A splendid collection of 16C and 17C are exhibited on the walls: *verdures* (landscapes dominated by flower and plant motifs) from Antwerp and Tournai; lovely compositions woven in Oudenaarde (scenes from the Old Testament) and Brussels (Story of Psyche series); the fine Tenture de Renaud et Armide, executed in the Parisian workshops of the Faubourg St-Marcel after cartoons by Simon Vouet; and superb 17C hunting scenes, which have retained their beautiful colours.

Ground Floor– In the grand salon, the dishes are still those of the Biencourt family, the last owners, in the 19C, of the castle. Next door is the billiard room. You can also visit the kitchens. The library has engravings of the various states of the castle in the 19C.

EXCURSIONS
⚫⚲ Vallée troglodytique des Goupillières
3km/1.8mi via ID 84, rte. d'Artannes. ⏰Daily: Mar 2-5pm; Apr–Jun and Sept 10am–6pm; Jul–Aug 10am–7pm; Oct 11am–5.30pm. ⚬€6.90 (child 5–17, €5). ☏02 47 45 46 89. www.troglodytedesgoupillieres.fr.
A remarkable series of troglodyte farms shows what country life used to be like in this valley. Explore the stables, wells, bread ovens, grain stores and medieval refuge. Then get close to the farm

animals, including black pigs, poultry, goats, donkeys, horses and others.

Marnay
6km/3.7mi NW on D 57, then D 120.

⚫⚲ Musée Maurice-Dufresne★
♿⏰Daily: Apr–Jun and Sept Wed-Sun 10am-7pm; Jul–Aug daily 10am-7pm. ⚬€12 (child 10–17, €7; 18–25 €9.50). ☏02 47 45 36 18. www.musee-dufresne.com.
Set up in a former paper mill, this museum is devoted to locomotion. The exhibits were painstakingly gathered over 30 years, restored and painted in their original bold colours. They take the visitor on an unexpected and unusual tour through the ages: American, German and French military vehicles from the First and Second World Wars, converted into farming machinery; gypsy caravans from the turn of the 19C; the first French machine used for making draught beer; a Blériot monoplane, identical to the one that crossed the Channel in July 1909.
Each presentation portrays the history of mankind: a small Bauche tractor found in an attic, entirely dismantled to avoid being requisitioned; a Hanomag mine extractor-excavator, which helped to erect the Wall of the Atlantic; or one of the several hundred Fordson tanks that landed in Arromanches on 6 June 1944.

🚗 DRIVING TOUR

BALZAC'S LANDSCAPES
26km/16mi round tour of the valley of the Indre E of Azay-le-Rideau. About 2h.

▶ Leave Azay heading S by the bridge over the Indre, which offers an attractive view of the château through the trees of the park. Bear left immediately onto D 17 and then right onto D 57.

Villaines-les-Rochers
Wickerwork has always been the mainstay of this village. The black and yel-

low water-willow and green rushes are cut in winter and steeped in water until May when they are stripped and woven. This craft was traditionally handed down from father to son who worked in troglodyte workshops (several such dwellings can be seen).

The **coopérative Vannerie de Villaines** (& 𝒫02 47 45 43 03; www.vannerie.com), which was founded in 1849 by the parish priest, numbers about 80 families; several basketwork workshops have been set up where young craftspeople are trained. The workshops can be visited and the work is for sale.

▶ Rejoin D 17 via D 217, which runs beside the River Villaine.

Saché

Saché won a degree of renown through its association with novelist **Honoré de Balzac** (1799-1850), who stayed there on several occasions. A more recent famous resident was the American sculptor, **Alexander Calder** (1898–1976), who created mobiles and stabiles in abstract forms; one of his mobiles is displayed in the main square of Saché, which bears his name.

Château de Saché

The 16C and 18C château is set in a pleasant park. In the last century it belonged to M de Margonne, a friend of **Balzac**. The writer loved to escape to Saché from the bustle of Paris (he came here every year from 1828 to 1838).

In the tranquil setting of the château he wrote easily, and one of his novels, *Le Lys dans la Vallée*, is set in the Indre Valley between Saché and Pont-de-Ruan. Balzac also found plenty of material locally for characters and places that appeared in his *Scènes de la Vie de Province*. The room where Balzac worked remains today exactly as it was during his lifetime.

Today, the chateau houses the **Musée Balzac** (🕑 *daily: Apr–Jun and Sept 10am–6pm; Jul–Aug 10am–7pm; Oct–Mar 10am–12.30pm, 2–5pm (closed Tue).* 🕑*1 Jan, 25 Dec.* ⊛€6. 𝒫02 47 26 86 50. www.musee-balzac.fr), which displays

furniture reminiscent of the 19C, when Balzac was there, along with other collections that Balzac kept at the chateau. It became a museum dedicated to the writer in 1951, and continues to be developed in his memory as new rooms are opened and more memorabilia displayed.

Throughout each year, the museum organises themed visits and events, a programme for which can be downloaded from their website.

Pont-de-Ruan

Do not miss the beautiful scene as the road crosses the Indre of the two windmills, each on an island, set among trees. The site is described at length by Balzac in his novel *Le Lys dans la Vallée*.

▶ Return to Azay on D 84.

ADDRESSES

🍽 STAY

⊜⊜🍴 **Chambre d'hôte Troglododo** – *9 chemin des Caves.* 𝒫02 47 45 31 25. www.troglododo.fr. 5 rooms. 🅿. A really original place to stay offering 5 rooms, 4 of which are troglodytic – located inside caves; all are tastefully furnished with chic contemporary furniture. The gardens and terraces offer good views over the Indre valley.

⊜⊜🍴 **Hôtel de Biencourt** – *7 r. de Balzac.* 𝒫02 47 45 20 75. www.hotel biencourt.fr. Closed mid-Nov–late Mar. 17 rooms. &. Close to the château, this 18C house has décor evoking its past life as a school. Rustic or Directoire-style furniture, garden, breakfast on the patio in nice weather.

⊜⊜🍴 **Hôtel des Châteaux** – *2 rte. de Villandry.* 𝒫02 47 45 68 00. www.hoteldes chateaux.com. Closed Nov–mid-Mar. 27 rooms. &🅿. An ideal stopping-off point as you explore the châteaux, this hotel has comfy and calming rooms, many with a view over the park and the Chinon valley. The restaurant (La Rose Des Vents ⊜⊜🍴) serves traditional food.

Mobiles and Stabiles

Having studied mechanical engineering, American **Alexander Calder** (1898-1976) turned to art, enrolling in a course in New York. He was a skilled draughtsman, able to capture a subject in a few swift strokes. Before long he had moved into making wire sculptures, initially of figurative, and later abstract, subjects. From the early 1930s, he began producing abstract constructions that moved either by means of a motor or when touched. In 1932 Marcel Duchamp, a fellow member of the Abstraction-Création group in Paris in which Calder became involved at this time, coined the name "mobiles" for these inventions, whereupon artist Jean Arp came up with the term "stabiles" for Calder's non-moving sculptures.

Calder is best known for the mobiles he made of tin shapes, which were usually suspended or balanced in such a way as to move in response to draughts of air or even their own weight. Calder referred to them as his four-dimensional drawings and made no secret of the fact that his abstract geometrical creations were influenced in part by Mondrian. Calder's reputation rests on the fact that he was one of the first artists to include movement in sculptural art. Although he might be regarded as a precursor of Kinetic art, Calder was far more concerned with exploring free movement, rather than the more controlled motion produced by Kinetic artists. Most of Calder's works are on show in the US, but others are displayed at the Tate Modern Art Galley in London and the Pompidou Centre in Paris.

♥/EAT

La Crédence – 15/17 Rue Balzac, 37190 Azay-le-Rideau. ℘09 81 04 67 77. *Closed Sun eve, Mon.* Plenty of vegetarian options at this cafe-restaurant in a historic stone cottage. Fresh, tasty dishes made from locally sourced ingredients and ample room on the terrace makes it a popular though tranquil spot to enjoy lunch or an early dinner during the summer months.

Auberge Pom'Poire – 21 Route de Vallères. ℘02 47 45 83 00. www.aubergepompoire.fr. Highly creative dishes crafted from local produce and presented with style and elegance, and the occasional dollop of humour. Chef Bastien Gillet's table is a representative palette of the flavours of the Loire Valley – seafood direct from the ocean, meat from local farms, fruit and vegetables plucked from the Loire Valley vegetable gardens. Auberge Pom'Poire also has six equally colourful rooms upstairs at reasonable prices.

L'Aigle d'Or – 10 av. Adélaïde-Riché. ℘02 47 45 24 58. https://laigle-dor.com. *Closed Sun eve through Tue.* This pretty stone house sits a few yards from the château making it a top choice after the splendour of Château Azay-Le-Rideau. The dining room, decorated in white and pastel tones, is elegant. Tasty, traditional Michelin Bib Gourmand cuisine from chef Simon Desiles; reservations advised.

Auberge du XIIe Siècle – 1 r. Château, 37190 Saché. 6.5km/4mi E of Azay-le Rideau on D 17. ℘02 47 26 88 77. *Closed Sun eve, Mon, Tue lunch. https://auberge12emesiecle.eatbu.com. Reservation advised.* This old half-timbered inn in the village centre is famous for its Assiette Michelin cuisine. The exposed beams and stone walls, together with the fireplace, enhance its two dining rooms.

Chinon★★

Chinon lies at the heart of a well-known wine region, surrounded by the fertile Véron and beautiful Chinon Forest. The road approaching Chinon from the south gives the best **view**★★ of the spectacular setting of the town and castle. The well-preserved old houses of this medieval town are strung along the banks of the Vienne beneath the crumbling walls of its gigantic ruined fortress. An annual **medieval market** plunges visitors into the lively atmosphere of the late Middle Ages.

A BIT OF HISTORY

François Rabelais – (1494–1553) was born near Chinon at La Devinière, and grew up in Chinon in his parents' house in rue de la Lamproie. He was the author of the spirited adventures of Pantagruel and his father Gargantua. Written in the manner of a burlesque farce, his books were intended for the budding bourgeoisie: they denounced priggishness and ignorance and praised a moral society based on free, honest citizenship.

From the Plantagenets to the Valois – Chinon was originally a Gallo-Roman camp and then a fortress belonging to the counts of Blois. In the 11C it passed

USEFUL INFORMATION
TOURS OF THE TOWN
Information at the tourist office or online at www.vpah.culture.fr.

FESTIVALS IN CHINON
There are several fairs and other events organised in Chinon, don't miss them if you're in town. In April visit the Salon des Vins (wine fair); in late June and on 15 August, there are horse races. In July the town is the venue of a Festival of Musical Comedy. An old-fashioned market is held on the 3rd Saturday in August.

- ▶ **Population:** 8,476.
- **Michelin Map:** 317: k 5-6
- **Info:** 1 Rue Rabelais, 37500 Chinon. ✆02 47 93 17 85. www.azay-chinon-valdeloire.com.
- **Location:** Chinon is 22km/13.6mi NW of Richelieu and 10km/6mi SW of Château d'Ussé.
- **Parking:** It isn't easy to get around town by car in the summer months, so leave your car in the large car park above the town, on the road from Azay, and take the lift down to the centre (*see Chateau de Chinon info on p217*). There are two small parking areas near the entrance to the château. Or park along quai Danton to absorb the sweeping panorama.
- **Timing:** Allow 45min for the Old Chinon walking tour, 1 hour for the castle, 1 hour for the museums and 1 day for the driving tours.
- **Kids:** The River Museum.

to their enemies, the counts of Anjou, one of whom, **Henry Plantagenet**, built the major part of the present castle. In 1154 he became King of England, but Chinon remained one of his favourite residences; he died there on 6 July 1189. **John Lackland**, the youngest son of Henry II, inherited the Plantagenet kingdom on the death of his elder brother Richard the Lionheart, who was killed at Châlus in 1199. His deceitful character and underhand plotting earned him many enemies. First he quarrelled with his nephew, Arthur of Brittany, who sought refuge at the French court. Then he abducted Isabelle d'Angoulême, the fiancée of the Count of La Marche, and married her at Chinon on 30 August 1200. Discontented with the behaviour of their overlord, the knights of Poitou

© Pascal Ducept/hemis.fr

appealed to the royal court in Paris. John refused to attend the hearing, at which he was condemned to forfeit his French fiefs. One by one, Philippe Auguste recaptured all the English strongholds in France; in 1205, Chinon passed to the French crown. After the truce of October 1206, John was forced to give up.

The Court of the King of Bourges (early 15C) – With the accession of **Charles VII**, Chinon moved into the limelight. France was in a terrible predicament. Henry VI, King of England, was also King of Paris; Charles VII was only King of Bourges when he set up his little court at Chinon in 1427. The following year he called a meeting of the States-General of the central and southern provinces, which had remained faithful to him. They voted 400,000 livres for organising the defence of Orléans besieged by the English (*see ORLÉANS*). Then, in 1429, Joan of Arc appeared on the scene.

 WALKING TOUR

OLD CHINON★★
Formerly surrounded by high walls that earned it the name Ville-Fort (Fortified Town), the old city (Le Vieux Chinon) with its pointed roofs and winding streets lies tucked between the banks of the River Vienne and the castle bluff. Numerous medieval houses show off

picturesque details: half-timbered houses with carved corbels, stone gables with corner turrets, mullioned windows and sculpted doorways. One of the many pleasant activities Chinon has to offer is a walk along the banks of the Vienne, particularly near the English-style landscape garden, the **Jardin anglais**, where flourishing palm trees are a testimony to the mild climate of the Loire valley.

▷ Start from r. Haute-St-Maurice. The 12C–18C **Église St-Maurice** stands on the main street of the old town.

Palais du Bailliage
73 r. Haute-St-Maurice.
Walk round onto rue Jacques-Cœur to admire the southern façade of this building that houses the Bailiff's Court and the Hôtellerie Gargantua.

Grand Carroi★★
Despite its small size, which hardly merited such a grand name (*carroi* means crossroads), this spot was the centre of town in the Middle Ages, where rue Haute-St-Maurice intersected rue du Grand-Carroi.
The broad stone doorway of No. 48, the 17C **Hôtel du Gouvernement** (Government House), opens into an attractive courtyard lined with elegant arcades; another half-timbered house, No. 45, is decorated with statues serving as columns; No. 44, the **Hôtel des États-**

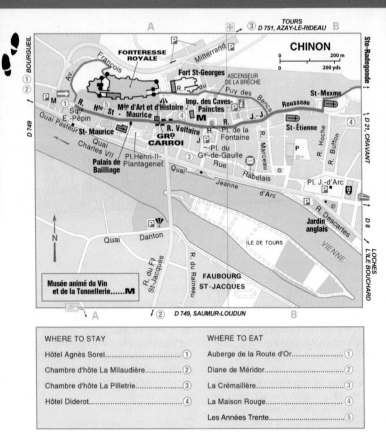

WHERE TO STAY		WHERE TO EAT	
Hôtel Agnès Sorel	(1)	Auberge de la Route d'Or	(1)
Chambre d'hôte La Milaudière	(2)	Diane de Méridor	(2)
Chambre d'hôte La Pilletrie	(3)	La Crémaillère	(3)
Hôtel Diderot	(4)	La Maison Rouge	(4)
		Les Années Trente	(5)

Généraux (States-General House), is a handsome 15C–16C brick building, which houses the Museum of Old Chinon; No. 38, called the **Maison rouge** (Red House – 14C), is half-timbered with brick and an overhanging storey.

Carroi-musée

44 r. Haute-St-Maurice. ◷*Daily mid-Jun–mid-Sept Wed–Mon 2.30–6.30pm.* ✆€3. ✆02 47 93 18 12. *www.chinon-vienne-loire.fr.*
The museum, devoted to the history of the town, is housed in the Hôtel des États-Généraux, where Richard the Lionheart is said to have died in 1199 after being wounded at the siege of Châlus in the Limousin. It was also the place where the French Parliament met in 1428 at the behest of Charles VII to provide money to continue waging war against the English.

Hôtel Torterue de Langardière

The classical façade of this 18C mansion is enhanced by wrought-iron balconies. Farther on, rue Jeanne-d'Arc starts its steep climb up to the castle; a plaque marks the **well** where, according to tradition, Joan of Arc is said to have placed her foot on dismounting from her horse.

Impasse des Caves-Painctes

♿ ☛*Guided tours (90min) Jul–Aug.* ✆02 47 93 30 44. *www.chinon.com.*
This narrow alley leading up the hillside takes you to the **Caves Painctes** (Painted Cellars), where Pantagruel drained many a glass of cool wine according to his creator Rabelais, who was known to patronise the establishment on frequent occasions. The paintings have since disappeared, but these old quarries have always been dedicated to the Sacred Bottle; the annual cer-

emony of the **Bons Entonneurs Rab-elaisiens** (Wine-Growers' Brotherhood) is held here .

👥 Musée Animé du Vin et de la Tonellerie

12 r. Voltaire. 🕐*Mid-Mar–mid-Nov daily 10am–10pm.* 💶*€4.50 (child 7–12, €4).* 📞*02 47 93 25 63.*
The museum features life-size animated models of Rabelais and his fellow revellers who explain all about working in the vineyards, wine-making and how barrels are made.

Rue Jean-Jacques-Rousseau
Several striking medieval houses can be seen, especially Nos. 71 and 73 at the crossroads with rue du Puy-des-Bancs.

Église St-Étienne
A finely sculpted Flamboyant Gothic doorway bears the arms of Philippe de Commynes (1480), governor of Chinon.

Collégiale St-Mexme
Only the nave and narthex remain of this 10C–11C church.

Chapelle Sainte-Radegonde
Access on foot up the steep path NE of the church of St-Mexme.
🕐*Guided tours May–late Sept Sat–Sun and public holidays 3–6pm; Jul–Aug daily except Tue.* 📞*02 47 93 18 12. www.ville-chinon.com.*
In the 6C, a pious hermit had his cell built in the cave. Radegund, the wife of King Clotair I, came to consult the hermit about her intention to leave the court and found the convent of the Holy Cross (Ste-Croix) in Poitiers.
Also of interest to visitors are the cave dwelling adjoining the chapel and the **Musée des Arts et Traditions populaires**.

CHATEAU DE CHINON: FORTRESSE ROYALE★★
🕐*Daily: Jan–Feb and Nov–Dec 9.30am–5pm; Mar–Apr and Sept–Oct 9.30am–6pm; May–Aug 9.30am–7pm.* 🕐*1 Jan, 25 Dec.* 💶*€10.50.* 📞*02 47 93 13 45. www.forteressechinon.fr.*

ℹ️ *It is best to approach the château by route de Tours (D 751, ave. François Mitterrand), which skirts the massive walls on the north side.* 🅿️ *There is a large car park NE of the chateau on the D 751, from where a narrow street (r. du Chateau) leads down to the entrance.*
Built on a spur overlooking the Vienne, this vast fortress dates mostly from the reign of Henry II (12C). Abandoned by the court after the 15C and bought in the 17C by Cardinal de Richelieu, the castle was dismantled little by little until Prosper Mérimée undertook to preserve it. In the 21C, six years of extensive restoration with a budget of 17 million euros have resulted in the fortress visitors see today.

Fort St-Georges – The fort, since dismantled, was built in 1160 to protect the castle's vulnerable side. Henry II wanted to administer his vast land holdings from Chinon and expanded the stronghold to most of its current mass. Today a newish building (2010) houses an exhibit on the castle's history and a gift shop.

Fort du Coudray – West of the gardens another bridge crosses the moat to the Fort du Coudray on the point of the rock spur. The keep *(right)* was built early in the 13C; the Templars were imprisoned here by Philip the Fair in 1308, and it was they who carved the graffiti on the north wall of the present entrance.

Château du Milieu – The entrance to the Middle Castle is across the moat and through the 14C Tour de l'Horloge (Clock Tower), which is unusually shallow. A bell, the Marie Javelle, dated 1399, sounds the hour from the lantern at the top of the tower.

Royal Apartments★★ – Joan of Arc was received in the great hall on the first floor, of which only the fireplace remains. The guard room on the ground floor displays a large model of the castle as it was in the 15C.

Joan of Arc at Chinon

Escorted by six men-at-arms, Joan travelled from Lorraine to Chinon, arriving on 6 March 1429, without encountering any of the armed bands that were ravaging the country. The people took this safe passage as a clear sign of divine protection. Waiting to be received by Charles VII, Joan spent two days at an inn, fasting and praying. When the 18-year-old peasant girl was finally admitted to the palace, an attempt was made to put her out of countenance.

The great hall was lit by 50 torches and 300 courtiers in rich apparel were assembled there. The King was hiding among the crowd, while a courtier wore his robes. Joan ventured forward, immediately recognised the real King and went straight up to him. "Gentle Dauphin," she said – for Charles, not having been crowned, was only the Dauphin to her – "my name is Jehanne la Pucelle (Joan the Maid). The King of Heaven sends word by me that you will be anointed and crowned in the city of Reims, and you will be the Lieutenant of the King of Heaven, who is the King of France." Charles was consumed with doubts about his birthright as a result of the scandalous behaviour of his mother, Isabella of Bavaria. When Joan said to him, "I tell you in the name of Our Lord Christ that you are the heir of France and the true son of the King", he was reassured and almost believed in the courageous girl's mission.

His advisers were more stubborn, however. Joan was made to appear before the court at Poitiers. A tribunal of doctors and midwives was set up to decide whether she was inspired by God or the devil. The simplicity and swiftness of her responses, her piety and her confidence in her heavenly mission convinced even the most sceptical, and she was declared to be truly a "Messenger of God". She returned to Chinon, where she was given troops and equipment. She left on 20 April 1429 to fulfill her miraculous and tragic destiny.

EXCURSIONS

Le Jardin d'Elsie

1–5 rte. de Huismes. Guided tours on request. 02 47 98 07 58. www.elsiederaedt.com.
On the northwestern edge of the town, the garden features almost 1,000 plants, bushes and trees in the grounds of a 19C house. The main atraction is the rose garden (over 300 varieties), at their best between mid-May and early summer.

Centre Nucléaire de Production d'Électricité de Chinon

12km/7.4mi NW towards Borgueil. Mon–Fri 9am–noon, 2–5pm. Free. 02 47 98 60 60. http://edf.fr. Proof of identity must be shown.
France's first nuclear power station, EDF1, was opened at Avoine in 1963. The site's current four 900MW generators provide 40 percent of the power used in the Loire valley, Brittany and Centre region.

Écomusée du Véron

10km/6.2mi NW towards Candes-St-Martin. 80 rte. de Candes, 37420 Savigny-en-Véron. Mid-Apr– May and Oct–early Nov Mon–Fri 10am–12.30pm, 2–6pm, Sat–Sun and public holidays 2–6pm; Jun–Sept Mon– Fri 10am–12.30pm, 2–6pm, Sat–Sun and public holidays 2–7pm. Mid-Nov to mid-Apr open by appointment to groups 1 May, 1 Nov, 23 Dec–7 Jan. €5 (under 18, €2.50). 02 47 58 09 05. www.ecomusee-veron.fr.
The presqu'île du Véron lies at the confluence of the Loire and Vienne rivers. The ecomuseum presents the different aspects of 19C rural life: working among the vineyards, raising cattle and goats, beekeeping, etc. Displayed are the tools and implements winegrowers used, a collection of headdresses and other items. Visitors also learn about the the influence of river flooding on local life. The visit concludes with an encounter with the farm animals.

Chinon, a great wine at the heart of the Val de Loire

The area entitled to carry the Chinon appellation covers 2,000ha embracing 19 winemaking localities. Red Chinon is made with a single grape variety, Cabernet-Franc. Graced with a subtle bouquet of violets and wild strawberries, Chinon is definitely a wine for laying down, sometimes for many years. But, depending on the *terroir*, some bottles may be imbided young, as early as Easter. Generally speaking, Chinon is a perfect accompaniment to red meat, poultry and game and can round off a meal nicely when served with a mild cheese. The serving temperature should be between 14°C and 16°C for reds and between 8°C and 12°C for rosés and whites, of which there are far fewer varieties. *For further information, apply to the Syndicat des Vins de Chinon, impasse des Caves-Painctes,* 🖉*02 47 93 30 44.*

🚗 DRIVING TOURS

1 RABELAIS COUNTRY★
25km/15.5mi round-trip. 🚶*Leave by* ③ *on the town map.*

▷ The road runs through a tunnel of tall plane trees to St-Lazare; turn right onto D 751, an old Roman road; after 3km/2mi turn left onto D 759; then right onto D 224 and continue along D 117.

Musée Rabelais
4 r. de la Devinière, Seuilly, SW of Chinon. 🕐*Jul–Aug daily 10am–7pm; Apr–Jun and Sept daily 10am–12.30pm, 2–6pm; Oct–Mar Wed–Mon 10am– 12.30pm, 2–5pm.* 🕐*1 Jan, 25 Dec.* ✍€6. 🖉*02 47 95 91 18. www.musee-rabelais.fr.*
This farmhouse was the birthplace of **François Rabelais** (1494–1553), son of a Chinon lawyer, who became a monk after a studious childhood, fell in love with Ancient Greek and studied the humanists. He transferred to the secular clergy, studied medicine at Montpellier and became a famous doctor.
With the publication of *Pantagruel* in 1532, Rabelais, the distinguished Hellenist, revealed the humorous side of his character by choosing burlesque farce and every kind of comedy to express his philosophy. At La Devinière visitors can see Rabelais' room and a small museum illustrating his life and work.

▷ Rejoin D 117 and turn right.

On the opposite side of the valley stands the beautiful **Château du Coudray-Montpensier** (15C) with its numerous roofs, restored in the 1930s. Next comes **Seuilly-Côteaux**, a long straggling street of troglodyte houses. It was in the abbey at Seuilly that Rabelais was educated.

Lerné
In Rabelais' book this was the village from which the bakers *(fouaciers)* of a special sort of bread set out to sell their goods *(fouaces)* in Chinon's market.

▷ Return to Chinon along D 224 through Seuilly-Bourg.

2 VALLÉE DE LA VIENNE★
60km/38mi round-trip. About 3h.

▷ Leave Chinon to the E on r. Diderot and D 21 (🚶*see map, p216*).

The road follows the chalky hillside through the well-known vineyards of Cravant-les-Coteaux.

Vieux Bourg de Cravant
1km/0.5mi N of Cravant-les-Coteaux. Not used for worship since 1863, the **church** in this old town boasts a nave that is a rare example of the Carolingian style (early 10C), built of characteristically small stones (🕐*daily 9am–7pm;* 🖉*06 07 04 43 34*).

▶ Follow D 21 to Panzoult and then take D 221 to Crouzilles.

Crouzilles

Built in the 12C, the **church** was covered with Angevin vaulting in the 13C.

▶ Take D 760 W to L'Île-Bouchard.

L'Île-Bouchard

see L'ÎLE-BOUCHARD

▶ Take D 18 E to Parçay-sur-Vienne.

Parçay-sur-Vienne

This 12C **church** has a fine Romanesque doorway flanked by blind arcades. It is decorated with carved archivolts representing bearded faces (33 in total), foliated scrolls and palmettes, and the ensemble is surmounted by a motif resembling fish scales.

▶ Return to L'Île-Bouchard and take D 760 W on the Vienne's south bank.

Tavant

The Romanesque **church** here is of special interest because of the 12C **frescoes★** that adorn the vaulting, apse and crypt.

About 3km/2mi farther on, beyond Sazilly, the road (D 760) passes the **Château de Brétignolles** *(left)*, a Louis XII-style building with turrets.

▶ Turn left onto D 749.

Rivière

The church of Notre-Dame (11C–12C), close to the banks of the Vienne, is the oldest church dedicated to the Virgin Mary in Touraine. An early pilgrimage site was established in the 3C. Famous pilgrims incude Saint Martin and Joan of Arc, who stopped here on her way to Chinon. Under the triple arcaded porch note the Romanesque frieze on the right showing the resurrection of Lazarus. Inside, the Neo-Gothic friezes are 19C. The layout is unusual: two side staircases

lead to the raised chancel and a semi-interred crypt with three small chapels housing the statue of Notre-Dame de Rivière and 16C tomb effigies of the lords of Basché.

Château et jardins du Rivau★

🕐 *Daily May–Sept 10am–7pm; Apr and Oct 10am–6pm.* ●●€11. *𝄞02 47 95 77 47. www.chateaudurivau.com.*

Erected in the 13C and fortified in the 15C, the Château is a building of great distinction. Joan of Arc found horses for her soldiers here on her way to the siege of Orléans. It is circled by a dry moat and defended by a drawbridge. **Gardens★** themed on fairy tales and other literature include **Gargantua's kitchen garden** and **Petit Poucet's Path**.

▶ Return to Chinon along D 749.

ADDRESSES

🛏 STAY

◒◓ **Maison d'hôte la Milaudière** – *5 r. St Martin, 37500 Ligré. 8km/5mi SW. 𝄞02 47 98 37 53. www.milaudiere.com. 7 rooms.* ♿️ 🅿️ 🍽. Tastefully decorated rooms in a former farm with historical trappings such as four-poster beds and tapestries.

◒◓◔ **Chambre d'hôte La Pilleterie** – *8 rte de Chinon, 37420 Huismes. 6km/3.7mi N of Chinon on D 16. http://lapilletrie. com. 𝄞02 47 95 58 07. 2 rooms.* 🅿️. This property in the heart of the country is a delight if you want peace and quiet. Pleasant, rustic-style rooms and a tranquil garden.

◒◓◔ **Hôtel Agnès Sorel** – *4 quai Pasteur. 𝄞02 47 93 04 37. www.hotel-agnes-sorel.com. 10 rooms.* ♿️. Not far from the town centre, this hotel on the banks of the Vienne is almost like home.

◒◓◔ **Hotel Diderot** – *4 r. Buffon. 𝄞02 47 93 18 87. www.hoteldiderot.com. 26 rooms.* 🅿️. This 18C building features simple rooms furnished with antiques.

♈ EAT

⊜⊜ **La Part Des Anges** – *5 rue Rabelais, 37500 Chinon. ℘02 47 93 99 93. www. lapartdesanges-chinon.com. Closed Mon-Tue.* Expert traditional French dishes, all strickly made with primarily organic and locally sourced ingredients by the chef-owner.

⊜⊜ **La Maison Rouge** – *38 r. Voltaire. ℘02 47 98 43 65.* This half-timbered restaurant in the medieval quarter is the place to indulge in regional specialities.

⊜⊜⊜ **Auberge de la Route d'Or** – *2 pl. de l'Eglise, 37500 Candes-St-Martin. 16km/10mi NW. ℘02 47 95 19 01. Closed Mon-Tue.* This little auberge is located within 17C walls, and serves cuisine inspired by local produce.

⊜⊜⊜ **Les Années Trente** – *78 r. Haute-St-Maurice. ℘02 47 93 37 18. www.lesannees30.com. Open Thu lunch to Sun eve.* Located in a 14C building, the restaurant serves cuisine with fresh produce amid paintings and photos from the 1930s.

Richelieu★

Lying on the southern limits of Touraine, bordering on Poitou, Richelieu is a quiet town that comes to life on market days. It is a rare example of Classical town planning, the project of one man: the statesman and churchman Cardinal de Richelieu, who was eager to lodge his court near his château, then under construction. The building of the town itself started in 1631 at a time when Versailles was still only an idea.

A BIT OF HISTORY

In 1621, when **Armand du Plessis** (1585–1642) bought the property of Richelieu, it consisted of a village and manor on the banks of the Mable. Ten years later the estate was raised to the status of a duchy. On becoming Cardinal and First Minister of France, Richelieu commissioned Jacques Le Mercier, the architect of the Sorbonne and the Palais-Royal in Paris, to prepare plans for a château and a walled town. The project was considered to be a marvel of urban planning.

Determined not to have his creation outstripped in grandeur, Richelieu created a small principality around his masterpiece and jealously razed in whole or in part many other châteaux in the vicinity. An enormous park was once the setting for a marvellous palace filled with great works of art. Two vast courtyards surrounded by outbuildings stood in front

- ▶ **Population:** 1,635.
- **Michelin Map:** 317: K-6
- **Info:** 7 pl. du Marché, 37120 Richelieu. ℘02 47 58 13 62.
- ▶ **Location:** 20km/12.4mi S of Chinon.
- ◔ **Timing:** Allow 2 hours for the town and 1 hour for the château grounds.

of the château, which was protected by moats, bastions and watchtowers. The gardens were dotted with copies of Antique statues and artificial grottoes that concealed the then-popular water tricks (fountains or jets that would spring up unexpectedly, soaking unwary visitors). It was in these gardens that the first poplar trees from Italy were planted. After the Revolution the descendants of Richelieu ceded the château to a certain Boutron who demolished it for the sale of the building materials.

THE TOWN★

The walled town, which Richelieu planned at the gates of his château, was in itself a fine example of the Louis XIII style designed by Jacques Le Mercier. The town embodies the sense of order, balance and symmetry that characterised the 17C, or Grand Siècle, in France. The rectangular ground plan was surrounded by ramparts and a moat. The impressive entrance gates are flanked by rusticated and pedimented gatehouses surmounted by high French roofs.

Grande-Rue

The main street crosses Richelieu from north to south. In addition to the gateways note the Louis XIII-style *hôtels* with the decorative elements in white tufa stone, especially No. 17, Hôtel du Sénéchal, which has retained its elegant courtyard with busts of Roman emperors.

Place du Marché

In the southern square, opposite the church, stands the 17C covered market, its slate roof supported by a fine chestnut timber frame.

Hôtel de Ville

Early-Apr–Sept Wed–Mon 10am–12.30pm, 2–6pm; rest of the year Mon–Fri (except Tue pm) 10am–noon, 2–5pm. www.ville-richelieu.fr. 3€. 02 47 58 10 13.

This former law court houses a **museum**, which contains documents and works of art pertaining to both the Richelieu family and the château.

Parc du château

Daily Apr–Sept 8am–8pm; Oct–Mar 9am–6pm. 02 47 58 10 13. www.parc-richelieu.fr.

A magnificent statue of Richelieu by Ramey stands at the southern end of the main street in front of the park, which is criss-crossed by straight avenues of chestnut and plane trees.

Of the many splendid buildings once to be found here, there remains a domed pavilion (part of the outbuildings), which houses a small **museum** containing historical documents on Richelieu.

EXCURSIONS

Champigny-sur-Veude★

6km/3.7mi N along D 749.

Champigny lies in the green valley of the Veude. The collegiate chapel is a remarkable instance of Renaissance art at its height; it was part of a château built from 1508 to 1543 by Louis I and Louis II de Bourbon-Montpensier.

Sainte-Chapelle★

Jul–Sept daily 2pm–6pm (except Tue in Sept); May–Jun Thu–Sun 2–6pm. 02 47 95 71 46. 6€ or 10€ with entry to the Chateau.

The Sainte-Chapelle, which owed its name to the portion of the True Cross that was kept there, was saved by the intervention of Pope Urban VIII.

The 11 **stained-glass windows★★** (16C) are the chapel's most precious jewel, forming a remarkable example of Renaissance glasswork. They comprise 34 portraits of the Bourbon-Montpensier House; above are scenes from the Passion.

Faye-la-Vineuse

7km/4.3mi S along D 749 and D 757.

Faye-la-Vineuse stands on a rise once covered in vineyards overlooking the valley formed by a tributary of the Veude. During the Middle Ages it was a prosperous walled city of five parishes and 11,000 inhabitants.

ADDRESSES

STAY

Hôtel Le Puits Doré – 24 pl. du Marché. 02 47 58 16 02. www.lepuitsdore.fr. 25 rooms. . Located on Market Square, this hotel has nicely decorated rooms, all of them different. The restaurant offers a varied, traditional menu that changes with the seasons.

Le Ragois – 13 Grande-Rue. 02 47 81 22 27. 2 rooms. In the town centre, Le Ragois retains the charm of an old 19C mansion. Quiet guest rooms, attractively furnished, and with fine bathrooms.

EAT

Auberge Le Cardinal – 3 rue des écluses. 02 47 58 18 57. Good traditional cuisine served in a country dining room with a menu that features French classics like veal, duck and rillets.

L'Île-Bouchard

The ancient settlement of L'Île-Bouchard, once a port on the River Vienne, derives its name from the midstream island where, in the 9C, the first known lord, Bouchard I, is said to have built a fortress that was destroyed in the 17C.

SIGHT

Prieuré St-Léonard

The priory church stood on the lower slopes of the valley. There are few vestiges of the original edifice: the 11C Romanesque apse in white tufa, an ambulatory and radiating chapels.

🚗 DRIVING TOUR

VALLÉE DE LA MANSE★
27km/16.7mi. About 2h.

The **River Manse** flows west through quiet picturesque countryside away from the main roads to join the Vienne at L'Île-Bouchard.

▶ Leave L'Île-Bouchard to the N along the D 757.

Avon-les-Roches
The 12C–13C **church** has a stone spire over the right transept. The arches of the porch and the door are decorated with archivolts and delicately carved capitals; an inscription in the porch *(left)* tells of the death of Charles the Bold.

▶ Take the road E towards Crissay; after 1km/0.6mi turn left.

Collégiale des Roches-Tranchelion
The ruins of this Gothic collegiate church (1527) can be seen from some way off. Car drivers can take the steep earthen road that leads up to the church. These ruins perched on a hill overlooking the surrounding countryside bear witness to past greatness. Little remains of the church vaulting, but the elegant façade is still standing, decorated with delicate

- ▶ **Population:** 1,678.
- **Michelin Map:** 317: L-6
- **Info:** Office de Tourisme du Bouchardais, 18 pl. Bouchard, 37220 L'Île-Bouchard. ℰ02 47 58 67 75. www.bouchardais-valdeloire.com.
- ▶ **Location:** Midway between Chinon (15km/9mi to the W) and Ste-Maure-de-Touraine.
- **Timing:** Allow 1 hour to explore the town.

carving; note the seated figure above the great window under the triumphal arch, and the Renaissance decoration of pilasters and medallions representing the local feudal lords.

Crissay-sur-Manse
The ruins of the partly troglodytic 15C castle *(left)*, the stone spire of the village church *(right)* and the several 15C houses with square turrets make up a charming scene.

St-Épain
The village **church** (12C, 13C and 15C) is capped by a 13C square tower. Adjoining it is a **fortified gate**, all that remains of the 15C curtain wall. On the other side of the main street stands a house with a watch turret where the road bends southeast to Ste-Maure. This road leads up the lush Manse valley.

▶ After passing under the railway, bear left.

Vallée de Courtineau★
This small scenic road winds between the stream hidden amid the trees and the cliff dotted with dwellings hewn out of the rock. The Chapelle **Notre-Dame-de-Lorette**, a small 15C oratory, has been carved into the cliff face beside a small dwelling of the same period.

This region is renowned for its many vineyards that produce some of France's finest wines, including the Chinon, Borgueil, Côteaux du Layon and Saumur *appellations*. Most of the Saumurois and Baugeois is taken up by the Loire-Anjou-Touraine Regional Nature Park, one of 49 such entities in France which have been set up to coordinate economic, environmental and social initiatives to improve the quality of life within the parks' boundaries.

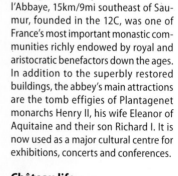

Highlights

The Art of Horsemanship

Alongside its imposing château, Saumur is best known for the Cadre noir equestrian academy, now part of the National Riding School. A unique establishment, it is recognised as one of the world's finest practitioners of classical equitation, and gives regular performances throughout the year. Fontevraud l'Abbaye, 15km/9mi southeast of Saumur, founded in the 12C, was one of France's most important monastic communities richly endowed by royal and aristocratic benefactors down the ages. In addition to the superbly restored buildings, the abbey's main attractions are the tomb effigies of Plantagenet monarchs Henry II, his wife Eleanor of Aquitaine and their son Richard I. It is now used as a major cultural centre for exhibitions, concerts and conferences.

Château life

The Château de Brézé and Château d'Oiron are two of the lesser known Renaissance châteaux of the Loire, but both are architectural gems. The Château de Brissac, one of the tallest in France, combines elements of the original medieval fortress with the more ornate Renaissance structure. It has been in the same family since the early 16C; every year it hosts the Festival de la Vallée de la Loire. The estate also includes a 28ha vineyard that produces red and rosé AOC Anjou wines. Overnight guests are welcome as the château has *chambre d'hôte* accommodation with dinner: a truly splendid way to experience life in one of the Loire valley's most prestigious monuments.

Twisted spires

The Bauge region is known for its prevalence of curious church spires. Their origin is a highly controversial subject: according to water diviners, the spires follow the path of underground water running beneath the churches; according to poets, they are like windmills facing the wind; sailors think they were built by inexperienced shipwrights; whereas joiners believe that the timber used for building them was still green and became warped with time.

Château d'Oiron

© Otto Werner/age fotostock

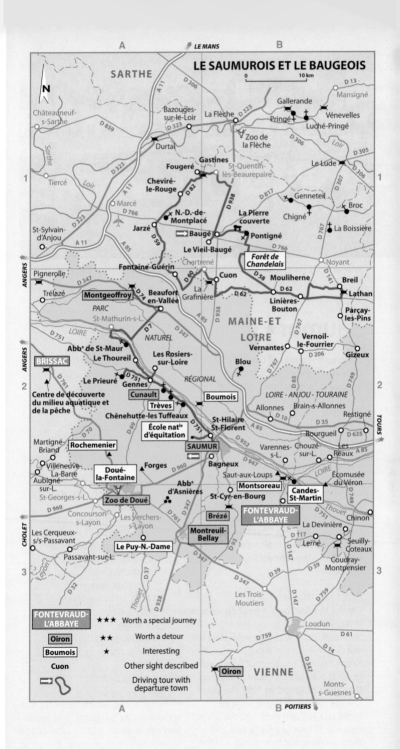

LE SAUMUROIS ET LE BAUGEOIS

0   10 km

A / LE MANS / B

SARTHE

Châteauneuf-s-Sarthe

D 859

Bazouges-sur-le-Loir

La Flèche

Zoo de la Flèche

Durtal

Tiercé

Marcé

Fougeré

Gastines

St-Quentin-lès-Beaurepaire

Cheviré-le-Rouge

N.-D.-de-Montplacé

Jarzé

Baugé

Le Vieil-Baugé

Chartrené

La Pierre couverte

Pontigné

Forêt de Chandelais

Fontaine-Guérin

Cuon

Mouliherne

La Grafinière

Linières-Bouton

Gallerande

Pringé

Luché-Pringé

Vénevelles

Mansigné

Le Lude

Genneteil

Chigné

Broc

La Boissière

Breil

Lathan

Parçay-les-Pins

St-Sylvain-d'Anjou

Pignerolle

Trélazé

ANGERS

Montgeoffroy

PARC

St-Mathurin-s-L.

Beaufort en-Vallée

NATUREL

Abb⁰ de St-Maur

Le Thoureil

Les Rosiers-sur-Loire

Vernoil-le-Fourrier

Vernantes

Blou

Gizeux

BRISSAC

Le Prieuré

Gennes

Cunault

Trèves

Chênehutte-les-Tuffeaux

Boumois

RÉGIONAL

LOIRE - ANJOU - TOURAINE

Allonnes

Brain-s-Allonnes

Restigné

Bourgueil

Les Réaux

ANGERS

Centre de découverte du milieu aquatique et de la pêche

Martigné-Briand

Rochemenier

École nat¹⁰ d'équitation

St-Hilaire St-Florent

SAUMUR

Varennes-s-L.

Chouzé-sur-L.

TOURS

Villeneuve-La-Barre

Aubligné-sur-L.

St-Georges-s-L.

Doué-la-Fontaine

Forges

Bagneux

Saut-aux-Loups

Montsoreau

Candes-St-Martin

Écomusée du Véron

Chinon

Zoo de Doué

Abb⁰ d'Asnières

St-Cyr-en-Bourg

Montreuil-Bellay

Brézé

FONTEVRAUD-L'ABBAYE

La Devinière

Lerné

Seuilly-Coteaux

Concourson-s-Layon

Les Verchers-s-Layon

Les Cerqueux-s/s-Passavant

Le Puy-N.-Dame

Passavant-sur-L.

Coudray-Montpensier

Les Trois-Moutiers

Loudun

FONTEVRAUD-L'ABBAYE

★★★ Worth a special journey

★★ Worth a detour

★ Interesting

Oiron

Boumois

Cuon

Other sight described

Driving tour with departure town

Oiron

VIENNE

Monts-s-Guesnes

A / B POITIERS

225

Saumur by the Loire – Château de Saumur, Église St-Pierre and Hôtel de Ville

Saumur★★

Lying on the banks of the Loire, beneath its imposing fortress, Saumur is famous for its national riding school, its wines (especially sparkling wines), its medal makers and its mushrooms (almost half of France's total production). Art lovers will note that Saumur served as the model for the castle featured in the *Les Très Riches Heures du Duc de Berry*, a Book of Hours considered to be the most magnificent illuminated manuscript of the 15C, now kept at the Musée Condé in Chantilly, north of Paris. The town is also the setting for Balzac's great novel *Eugénie Grandet*.

A BIT OF HISTORY

Charles the Bald built a fortified monastery in the 9C to house the relics of St Florent, but it was not long before it was destroyed by the Vikings. In the 11C Saumur was the subject of numerous conflicts between the Count of Blois and the Count of Anjou. In 1203 the town was captured by Philippe Auguste. In the late 16C and early 17C, the town enjoyed its true heyday. It was one of the great centres of Protestantism. Henri III gave it as a stronghold to the King

▶ **Population:** 27,486.
◔ **Michelin Map:** 317: I-5.
▤ **Info:** 8 bis quai Carnot, 49415 Saumur. ℘02 41 40 20 60. www.ot-saumur.fr.
◑ **Location:** Saumur lies 65km/40mi SE of Angers, 32km/20min NE of Chinon, 1h40 from Paris by TGV.
◔ **Don't Miss:** Every year a tattoo using horses and motor transport is given by the **Cadre noir** on the vast place du Chardonnet. Repeat performances are given in the Riding School of the National Equitation Centre in Terrefort.
👥 **Kids:** Le trésor des Ducs d'Anjou *son-et-lumière* show.
◑ **Timing:** Allow 1 day for the town and the château; half a day for excursions.

of Navarre, the future Henri IV, who appointed as Governor **Duplessis-Mornay**, a great soldier, scholar and fervent Reformer, who was known by the Roman Catholics as the Huguenot

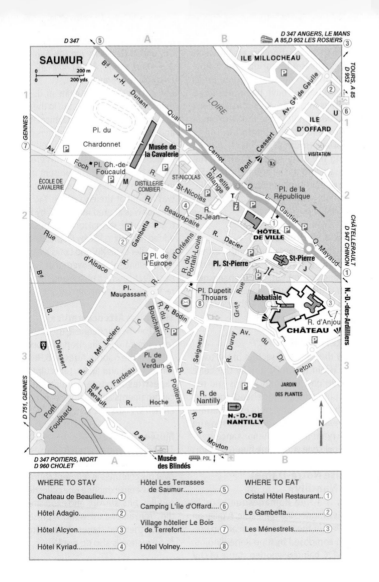

WHERE TO STAY		WHERE TO EAT
Château de Beaulieu.......①	Hôtel Les Terrasses de Saumur.................⑤	Cristal Hôtel Restaurant..①
Hôtel Adagio.................②	Camping L'Île d'Offard....⑥	Le Gambetta.................②
Hôtel Alcyon.................③	Village hôtelier Le Bois de Terrefort.................⑦	Les Ménestrels.............③
Hôtel Kyriad.................④	Hôtel Volney..................⑧	

Pope. In 1611 a general assembly of the Protestant churches was held there to consolidate their organisation following the assassination of Henri IV in 1610 and the retirement of the Duc du Sully. Louis XIII grew alarmed at the Protestant danger and ordered the town walls to be demolished in 1623. The Revocation of the Edict of Nantes in 1685 dealt Saumur a fatal blow; many of the inhabitants emigrated and the Protestant church was demolished.

École d'application de l'arme blindée et de la cavalerie (EAABC) – It is interesting to note the mementoes of officers who served in the cavalry of the African Army between 1830 and 1962: Bugeaud, Gallifet, Charles de Foucault, who was an officer before he became a recluse, Lyautey, Henry de Bournazel and Leclerc de Hauteclocque.

OLD TOWN★

The narrow twisting streets between the castle and the bridge still follow their original course; in some areas the old houses have been preserved whereas in others, new constructions have been built in the medieval style or are resolutely modern but full of surprises (south of St Peter's church). Along the main shopping street, rue St-Jean, and in the square, **place St-Pierre**, half-timbered houses and 18C mansions with wrought-iron balconies stand side by side.

Église St-Pierre

The church is Plantagenet Gothic except for the west front, which collapsed in the 17C and was rebuilt. The Romanesque door in the south transept leads into the interior, which is hung with two series of 16C **tapestries★**.

Hôtel de Ville★

Only the left-hand section of the town hall is old (16C). Originally the Loire flowed past the foundations and the building was a bridgehead and part of the town walls, hence its military appearance. The façade facing the courtyard is Gothic Renaissance transitional style with some fine sculpture.

Église Notre-Dame-de-Nantilly★

This is a fine Romanesque church. Louis XI added the right aisle. A pillar on the left in the same aisle bears an epitaph composed by King René d'Anjou. The 12C painted wooden statue of Our Lady of Nantilly was placed in the apse on the right of the chancel. The organ case dates from 1690.

Dating from the 15C and 16C are fine **tapestries★★** except for eight in the nave that were made at Aubusson in the 17C.

SIGHTS
Château★★

ⓒJul–Aug daily 10am–6.30pm; Apr–mid-Jun and mid-Sept–early Nov Tue–Sun and public holidays 10am–1pm, 2–5.30pm; mid-end Jun and 1–mid-Sept daily 10am–6.30pm; early–mid-Nov and 23 Dec–early Jan Tue–Sun 2–5.30pm. ⚙€7. ℘02 41 40 24 40. www.chateau-saumur.fr.

Compact and solid, the château, despite being a fortress, is decorated in the style of a country house with machicolations and balustrades at the windows overlooking the courtyard.

A succession of fortresses was erected on the promontory. The present building, which succeeded Louis IX's castle, was rebuilt at the end of the 14C. The interior was altered in the 15C by René d'Anjou and external fortifications were added in the late 16C by Duplessis-Mornay. Under Louis XIV and Louis XV, it was the residence of the Governor of Saumur but later became a prison and then barracks. Two museums are on-site.

Musée des Arts décoratifs★★

Based on the Lair bequest, this museum features a fine collection of works of art from the Middle Ages and Renaissance: wood and alabaster sculptures, **tapestries**, furniture, paintings, liturgical ornaments and a large collection of French 17C and 18C porcelain.

Musée du Cheval★

The former abbey church houses this museum devoted to equestrian history over the centuries in different countries. The museum exhibits a rare collection of saddles, bits, stirrups and exquisite bridles from around the world. A presentation on the main stages of the château's construction is also on display.

Musée de la Cavalerie

ⓒMon 10am–6pm, Tue–Fri 10am–noon, 2–6pm, Sat–Sun and public holidays 2–6pm. ⚙€8. ℘02 41 83 69 23. www.musee-cavalerie.fr.

In 1763, the Carabiniers Regiment, a top-notch corps recruited from the best horsemen in the army, was sent to Saumur. The present central building was constructed between 1767 and 1770 as their barracks.

This museum's rich display of souvenirs, created in 1936 from Barbet de Vaux collections, traces the heroic deeds of the

French Cavalry and the Armoured Corps since the 18C.

Musée des Blindés★★

Via bd. Louis-Renault; follow the signposts. 1043 rte de Fontevraud.
♿ ⏱*Jul–Aug daily 9.30am–6.30pm; Apr–Jun and Sept daily 10am–6pm; Jan–Mar and Oct–Dec Mon–Fri 10am–5pm, Sat–Sun and public holidays 11am–6pm.* ⏱*1 Jan, 25 Dec.* ✆€10. ☏*02 41 83 69 95. www.museedesblindes.fr.*

This museum devoted to tanks houses more than 100 vehicles (tanks, armoured vehicles, artillery equipment), many of which are still in working order, from a dozen or more countries. The most prestigious exhibits are the **St-Chamond** and the **Schneider** (the first French tanks), the Renault FT 17 (French tank used in the last stages of the First World War), the Somua S 35, the B1bis (issued to the 2nd Armoured Division under General de Gaulle in 1940) and German tanks dating from the French Campaign until the fall of Berlin (Panzers III and IV, Panther, Tiger), the Comet A 34 (the British tank used in the Normandy landing), the Churchill A 22, the Sherman M 4 and AMX 13 and 30.

Église Notre-Dame-des-Ardilliers★

On the eastern edge of the city, quai du Jagueneau, D 947. ⏱*Daily (except Sun morning) 8.30am–noon, 2–6.30pm.*
This 17C church edifice is one of the most popular places of pilgrimage in France. Devotion to Our Lady of Ardilliers began to develop in the reign of François I thanks to a miraculous statue a farm labourer was supposed to have discovered on this spot in the previous century. It was to reach its height in the 17C when pilgrims exceeded 10,000 a year.

EXCURSIONS

Bagneux

S of Saumur.
Bagneux, which lies at the heart of the oldest inhabited region of Anjou, is an old village on the banks of the Thouet. The engines displayed in the **Musée du Moteur** (*18 r. Alphonse-Caillaud; second street on the left after Fouchard bridge;* ⏱*early Apr–end Oct Tue–Sat 2–6pm;* ⏱*public holidays;* ✆€7; ☏*02 41 50 26 10; www.museedumoteur.fr*) have been collected by mechanics enthusiasts, most of whom attended the Saumur Industrial School and wish to preserve and restore old and contemporary engines.

▷ Return to r. du Pont-Fouchard for a short distance. Beyond the town hall, bear left onto r. du Dolmen.

Le Grand Dolmen

56 r. du Dolmen. ♿ ⏱*Jul–Aug daily 9am–7pm; Sept–Jun Thu–Tue 9am–6pm.* ✆€4. ☏*02 41 50 23 02. http://ledolmendebagneux.com.*
The Great Dolmen, situated in the centre of the village, is one of the most remarkable in Europe. It consists of 16 standing stones forming a passage and supporting a roof composed of four capstones.

St-Cyr-en-Bourg

8km/5mi S on D 93.
A visit to the **Cave des vignerons de Saumur** (⏱*May–Sept Mon–Sat 9.30am–7pm, Sun and public holidays 10.30am–1pm and 3–7pm; Oct–Apr Mon–Sat 9.30am–12.30pm, 2–6.30pm;* ☛*guided tours of the wine cellars at 11am, 3pm, 4pm, 5pm.* ✆€5. ☏*02 41 53 06 18; www.robertetmarcel.com*) is a good way of learning more about the whole winemaking process, from the grape to the finished product, in a series of underground galleries.

Château de Montsoreau★

13km/8mi E on the D 947. ♿ ⏱*Mar and Oct Sat–Sun noon–6pm; Apr Wed–Mon noon–7pm; May–Jun Wed–Mon 10am–7pm; Jul–late Sept daily 10am–7pm; late Sept Wed–Mon noon–6pm; rest of year Wed–Mon noon–6pm.* ✆€10.20. ☏*02 41 67 12 60. www.chateau-montsoreau.com.*
Montsoreau is famed for its château, which overlooks the confluence of the Loire and the Vienne. The château was rebuilt in the 15C by a member of the Chambes family. The river front, which

Parc Naturel Régional Loire-Anjou-Touraine

Maison du Parc, 15 av. de la Loire,
49730 Montsoreau. ☎02 41 38 38 88.
www.parc-loire-anjou-touraine.fr.

Parcs naturels régionaux are zones set aside for both protection and development. Unlike nature reserves or national parks, these zones are inhabited, and measures are taken to stimulate environmentally friendly economic activities that respect the traditions and customs of the region.

Château de Montsoreau at the confluence of the Loire and the Vienne, Parc naturel régional Loire-Anjou-Touraine

The parks are run by a committee comprising local politicians, landowners and community groups. Stakeholders draw up a charter and ensure that its provisions and aims are correctly applied and respected. The Loire-Anjou-Touraine Regional Nature Park was set up in 1996 and covers 136 towns and villages across the departments of Indre-et-Loire (Centre region) and Maine-et-Loire (Pays-de-la-Loire region), and spreads over 235,000 ha. The park straddles the Loire and its Indre, Vienne and Thouet affluents, while the landscape encompasses valleys, farmland and hedgerows, woodland and open heaths.

Planning your visit | The Information Centre, which doubles as the Montsoreau tourist office, has been built to high environmental quality standards and is specially designed to welcome visitors with access requirements; it has interactive displays, films and booklets available.

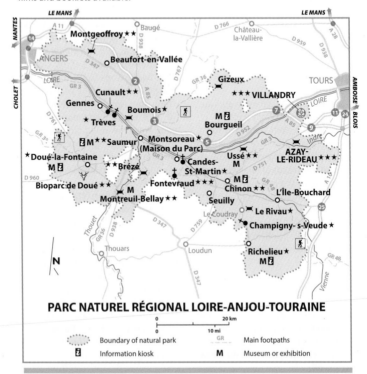

PARC NATUREL RÉGIONAL LOIRE-ANJOU-TOURAINE

Boundary of natural park	Main footpaths
Information kiosk	Museum or exhibition

was once at the water's edge, is an impressive example of military architecture. The façade giving onto the courtyard features far more gentle contours and presents two staircase turrets. From the bridge over the Loire west of Montsoreau, there is a fine view upstream of Montsoreau and Candes and downstream of Saumur Château, which is just visible. The road (D 947) is bordered by troglodyte dwellings and white Renaissance houses.

👥 Champignonnière du Saut aux Loups

At Saut aux Loups, just beyond Montsoreau on the Maumenière hillside, galleries (♿ ⏱ *mid-Feb–early-Nov 10am–6pm/7pm in Jul–Aug;* ⬡€7, child 4–18, €5.50; ℘02 41 51 70 30; www.troglosautauxloups.com) display the different stages of mushroom cultivation and exhibit some of the rarer varieties such as Japanese shitake, which is increasingly popular in France's restaurants and health shops.

If in season, try the delicious *galipettes*, harvested at full maturity and baked in a bread oven. The terrace offers fine **views** of the Loire.

Candes-St-Martin★

14km/8.7m E on the D 947.

The village of Candes stands on the south bank of the Vienne at its confluence with the Loire. The church was built on the spot where St Martin died in 397, and it was from here that his body was taken on its miraculous journey up the Loire to Tours.

Collégiale★

The church was built in the 12C and 13C and fortified in the 15C. The roadside façade mixes military architecture and decorative features. Inside, the vaulted roof is supported by finely tapering pillars that create an impression of lightness. Outside, the path to the right of the church leads to the top of a hill (*15min walk round trip*) with fine views of the river. There is a pleasant walk from rue St-Martin, below the church, to rue du Bas (riverbank and paved path).

Château de Boumois★

7km/4.3mi NW, on the north bank of the Loire. ⏱*Late Jun–early Sept Mon–Thu 10am–noon, 2–6pm.* ⬡€7.

Boumois was the birthplace in 1760 of **Aristide Dupetit-Thouars**. This highly experienced naval officer took part in the French expedition to Egypt. In the course of the Battle of the Nile, Dupetit-Thouars preferred to die a hero's death on the quarterdeck of his ship, the *Tonnant*, rather than haul down his flag.

The apparently feudal exterior of the 16C château conceals an elegant residence in the Flamboyant and Renaissance styles. The driveway leads to the main entrance; on the left stands a 17C dovecote still with its rotating ladder and nesting places for 1,800 birds.

The house itself, which is late 15C, is flanked by two huge machicolated towers. The entrance to the stair turret in the inner courtyard is closed by a door with detailed Renaissance motifs and the original and wrought-iron lock.

The Great Hall contains a marble effigy of Marguerite de Valois, a full-length portrait of Elizabeth I of England and an Indian screen from Coromandel. In the Flamboyant chapel is a Virgin and Child by Salviati and a 15C Burgundian sculpture of the Holy Family.

Blou

16km/10mi N of Saumur via D 347.

The Romanesque **church** (⏱*Easter–Oct 8am–7pm; rest of year, key available at the café opposite the church Mon–Sat*) with its massive buttresses has curious 11C diapering on its north transept.

Vernantes

20km/12mi N of Saumur on D 347.

A 12C tower marks the site of the **church**, of which only the chancel is still standing. The nave, destroyed by lightning in the 19C, has been replaced by a simple porch.

Vernoil-le-Fourrier

23km/14mi N of Saumur via D 347

The **church** has a massive bell-tower. Enter the priory yard (*right*) to see the solid octagonal turret and mullioned windows of the old prior's lodging.

Gizeux

33km/20mi NE of Saumur via D 347
East of the village of Gizeux, along a tree-lined avenue, stands an impos-ing château of the Angers area, which was the fief of the Du Bellay, princes of Yvetot, from 1330 to 1661 and which has been occupied by the same family since 1786.

♿ Château de Gizeux★

By guided tour (45min) daily Jul–Aug 9.30am–7pm; Apr–Jun and Sept–Oct 10.30am–6pm. €9.50. 02 47 96 45 18.
www.chateaudegizeux.com.
The central building, flanked by two perpendicular wings, was erected on the site of the old fortress in 1560. All that remains of the former building is the machicolated tower in the front of the Court of Honour.
The interior boasts a fine set of Louis XV furniture. **Salle François-Ier** is deco-rated with paintings on wood executed by Italian artists. The **Galerie des Châ-teaux★** features 17C frescoes depicting royal châteaux (Chambord, Vincennes, Fontainebleau, Versailles).

Parçay-les-Pins

6km/3.7mi N along D 15 and D 86.
This small village is the home of the **Musée Jules-Desbois** (*mid- Jun–mid-Sept Tue–Sun 10.30am–12.30pm, 2.30–6pm; Apr–mid-Jun and mid-Sept–1 Nov Sat–Sun and public holidays 2.30–6pm; €6; 02 41 82 28 80*). Born in Parçay-les-Pins, sculptor **Jules Desbois** (1851-1935) became a friend of and assis-tant to the sculptor Auguste Rodin. He studied at the École des Beaux-Arts in Paris. Over his life time he worked in wood, marble, terra-cotta, bronze and other materials; he later turned to pewter for several decorative art pieces. Many of Desbois' powerful, sensual fig-ures (*Leda and the Swan*) and busts are displayed to full advantage in this former farmhouse that has been renovated to accommodate the museum collection.

🚗 DRIVING TOUR

FROM SAUMUR TO ANGERS

48km/30mi. About 3h30.

La Loire Angevine

▷ Leave Saumur along D 751.

St-Hilaire-St-Florent

2km/1mi NW.
This village consists of one long street straggling at the foot of the hill beside the River Thouet. It is in fact a suburb of Saumur, which is given over mainly to the production of a famous sparkling white wine made by the Champagne method. It is also known for its national school of riding as well as a mushroom museum.

Caves Bouvet-Ladubay

♿ *Jun–Sept Mon–Fri 8.30am–7pm, Sat–Sun 9am–7pm; Oct–May Mon–Fri 8.30am–12.30pm, 2–6pm, Sat–Sun and public holidays 10am–12.30pm, 2.30–6pm; 24–31 Dec 8.30am–4pm. 1-5 Jan, 25 Dec. €5. 02 41 83 83 83. www.bouvet-ladubay.fr.*
From its premises in galleries hollowed out of the tufa rock, this leading pro-ducer of Saumur Brut unveils the stages involved in the production of its wines, from the initial fermentation to the sophisticated design of its bottles. There is an outstanding collection of labels.

Centre d'Art Contemporain Bouvet-Ladubay

02 41 83 83 83.
www.bouvet-ladubay.fr.
This modern art gallery at Bouvet-Ladubay consists of nine rooms exhib-iting works by contemporary artists. There is also a section on journalism. A delightful little theatre founded in the late 19C to entertain staff has been reopened.

♿ École nationale d'équitation★

♿ *Mid-Feb–early Nov Mon 2–5.30pm, Tue–Fri 9.30am–12.30pm, 2–5.30pm, Sat 9.30am–12.30pm.*
Guided tours (1h): hours vary,

check website for details. ⌨€8 (child 16 years, €6). ⊘Public holidays. ✆02 41 53 50 60. www.ifce.fr/cadre-noir.

Opened in 1972, this riding school comes under the auspices of the French Ministry for Youth and Sport. One of the vocations of the school is to maintain the level of French horsemanship and further its renown.

The large modern complex consists of several units, each comprising a granary where food is stored, a sizable dressage arena that can seat 1,200 spectators, and stables for 400 horses with harness rooms and showers.

The **Cadre noir** (Black Squad) has been based here since 1984. A fundamental part of the school, the squad is involved in all of its projects and presents its traditional repeat performances of *Manège* (dressage) and *Sauteurs en liberté* (jumps) in France and all over the world.

♟ Musée du Champignon

♿⊘Daily Apr–Sept 10am–7pm; Feb–Mar and Oct–Nov 10am–6pm. ⌨€9 (child 6-18, €7). ✆02 41 50 31 55. www.musee-du-champignon.com.

Large areas of the old tufa quarries that pit the hillsides around Saumur are used for the cultivation of mushrooms, which need humidity and a constant temperature. Mushrooms have been grown in the quarries since the time of Napoleon I, but production has escalated to industrial scale yielding some 12t per year. The museum is a thriving mushroom bed that explains the various options open to growers; the oldest method of growing in mushroom beds is gradually being replaced by more modern techniques using wooden crates, plastic bags, bales of straw and tree trunks.

♟ Pierre et Lumière

On the way out of St-Hilaire-St-Florent. ⊘Feb–Mar and Oct–Nov 10am–6pm, Apr–Sept 10am–7pm. ⌨€9 (child 6-18, €7). ✆02 41 50 70 04. www.pierre-et-lumiere.com.

This former underground quarry houses remarkable sculptures by Philippe Cormand. They are scale models of buildings and villages of the region carved in intricate detail out of the rock walls. Tours cathedral is a particular highlight. Each of the 20 sculptures are bathed in changing coloured lights.

Chênehutte-les-Tuffeaux

The village **church** stands beside the road on the north side of the village. It is an attractive Romanesque building with a handsome doorway in the same style; the arch stones are carved.

Trèves-Cunault★

A 15C crenellated keep is all that remains of the old castle. Tucked in beside it is the little **church★** of Trèves, once the castle chapel. It has a beautiful interior with great arches supporting the broad Romanesque nave; the chancel arch frames the rood beam on which there is a Crucifix.

Église Notre-Dame de Cunault★★

Cunault abbey was founded in 847 by monks from Noirmoutier; in 862 they had to take refuge farther away in Tournus in Burgundy, where they deposited the relics of St Philibert. Cunault therefore became a rich Benedictine priory dependent on Tournus abbey.

The monastic church is a Romanesque structure dating from the 11C to the 13C.

Columns, Église Notre-Dame de Cunault

© Christian Guy/hemis.fr

Cunault Church was built in the regular Benedictine style to provide for the liturgical ceremonies (seven per day) and for the crowds that attended the pilgrimage on 8 September.

Gennes

Among the wooded hills hereabouts are numerous megaliths, including the **Madeleine dolmen** south of the Doué road. Discoveries including an aqueduct, baths, an amphitheatre and the figure of a nymph point to the former existence of a Gallo-Roman shrine dedicated to a water cult.

Amphithéâtre

◷ Jun–Sept Wed–Sun 9am–7pm.
𝄞 02 41 51 81 30.
Discovered as long ago as 1837 and still being excavated, this structure is assumed to have served as the local amphitheatre between the 1C and 3C. It is set on a terraced slope cut into on the northeast by a podium and has an elliptical arena. On the north side, the boundary wall is built of sandstone, tufa and brick paralleled by a paved drainage corridor.

Église St-Eusèbe

This church, overlooking the Loire, has kept only its transept, its tower from the 12C and on the north side, a small 11C doorway. From the tower there is a vast **panorama** over Gennes and the Loire valley from the Avoine nuclear power station to Longue and Beaufort.

▶ 6.5km/4mi W of Gennes on D 751, turn left beyond Le Sale-Village.

Le Prieuré

The hamlet clusters around this priory whose church (12C and 13C) has a square Romanesque tower and a painted wooden altar (17C).

Les Rosiers-sur-Loire

1km/0.6mi N of Gennes.
Linked to Gennes by a suspension bridge, this village has a church whose Renaissance tower was built by the Angers architect Jean de l'Espine; the staircase turret flanking it is pierced by pilastered windows.

▶ Cross back over the bridge; turn right immediately onto D 132 along the south bank.

Le Thoureil

This quiet, spruce village was formerly an active river port for the handling of apples. Inside the church, on either side of the chancel there are two wooden reliquary shrines dating from the late 16C, which originally belonged to the abbey of St-Maur-de-Glanfeuil (◐ see below); they are adorned with statuettes of Benedictine monks and saints who were popular locally.

Abbaye de St-Maur-de-Glanfeuil

This ruined Benedictine abbey is believed to be named after St Maurus, a hermit who came from Angers and founded a monastery in the 6C on the site of the Roman villa of Glanfeuil on the Loire.

▶ Cross the river via D 55. In St-Mathurin, turn right onto D 952 and left onto D 7.

Beaufort-en-Vallée

Beaufort nestles amid the rich plains of the Anjou valley. In the 18C–19C it was one of the largest manufacturers of sailcloth in France. The town is dominated by the ruins of the **château**, built in the 14C by Guillaume Roger, Count of Beaufort and father of Pope Gregory XI. The Tour Jeanne de Laval was rebuilt in the 15C by King René.
From the top of the bluff on which the ruins stand there is a fine **view** of the surrounding country. An unusual collection of disparate objects and artefacts make up the 19C cabinet of curiosities that is the **Musée Joseph-Denais** (5 pl. Notre-Dame; ◷ mid-Jun–mid-Sept Tue–Sun 10.30am–12.30pm, 2.30pm–6pm; rest of the year call for hours; ⊕ €5; 𝄞 06 23 88 24 56 . www.damm49.fr).

▶ Follow N 147, then turn right onto the D 74.

Château de Montgeoffroy★

Rte de Seiches, 49630 Mazé.

🔧 *Guided tours only (in French; tours in English by arrangement) Apr–Jun and Sept–mid-Nov Wed–Sun 10am–noon, 2–5pm; Jul–Aug daily 10am–6pm.* 🎫*€11.* 📞*06 42 33 68 07. www.chateaudemontgeoffroy.com.*

This elegant château, overlooking the Authion valley, has a harmonious Louis XV façade. The two round towers attached to the wings, the curvilinear moat defining the courtyard and the chapel to the right are the only remains of the original 16C building.

The Montgeoffroy estate came into the possession of Erasme de Contades in 1676; the buildings owe their appearance to his grandson, the famous Marshal who commanded the German army in the Seven Years War and who was Governor of Alsace for 25 years.

The château has remained in the family; furnishings and décor are original.

In the **stables** is a collection of horse-drawn vehicles. The **Harness Room** fitted out in Norway spruce contains a collection of saddles, stirrups, bridles, whips and riding crops.

▶ N 147 leads to Angers.

ADDRESSES

🛌 STAY

🛏 **Camping l'Ile d'Offard** – *R. de Verden (access via town centre).* ♿ 📞*02 41 40 30 00. www.saumur-camping.com. Open mid-Mar –Oct. Reservations advised.* Occupying a large part of the island, the four-star camping site has 242 places.

🛏 **Hotel Volney** – *1 r. Volney.* 📞*02 41 51 25 41. www.levolney.com. Closed 23 Dec–6 Jan. 14 rooms.* A central location, modest but stylish rooms, a nice reception and regular room service: it's a small, pleasant hotel perfect for discovering "the pearl of Anjou" without breaking the bank.

🛏 **Hotel Alcyon** – *2 r. de Rouen.* 📞*02 41 67 51 25. www.alcyon-saumur.com. 13 rooms.* ♿📱. Close to the station and just 10 minutes on foot from the centre. Some rooms have a view of the chateau.

🛏 **Village hôtelier Le Bois de Terrefort** – *av. de l'École-Nationale-d'Équitation, 49400 St-Hilaire-St-Florent. 2km/1.5mi W of Saumur on D 751.* 📞*02 44 27 67 56. www.villagehotelier.com.* ♿📱. *14 units.* Near the national riding school, in a peaceful country setting, this village hotel with a **swimming pool** 🏊 and bar offers simple, functional cottages.

🛏🍽 **Château de Beaulieu** – *98 rte. de Montsoreau (2km from Saumur centre via D 947).* 📞*02 41 50 83 52. www.chateaude beaulieu.fr. 5 rooms.* Situated in a tranquil park planted with trees and with a heated **swimming pool** 🏊, this 18C château has elegant rooms appointed with antique furniture. A luxurious setting and all amenities.

🛏🍽 **Hotel Adagio** – *94 av. du Gén-de-Gaulle.* 📞*02 41 67 45 30. www.hotel adagio.com. 39 rooms.* ♿📱. This Best Western property is located on the Ile de la Loire, faces the château. Some of the contemporary-style rooms have river views.

🛏🍽 **Hotel Kyriad** – *23 r. Daillé.* 📞*08 92 23 48 13. www.kyriad-saumur-centre.fr. 29 rooms.* A central location, but in an area of calm. Basic but adequately decorated rooms.

🛏🍽 **Hotel les Terrasses de Saumur** – *2 r. des Lilas, 49400 St-Hilaire-St-Florent.* 📞*02 41 67 28 48. www. lesterrassesdesaumur.fr. 20 rooms.* ♿📱. *Restaurant Bistronomique (*🍽🍽*) closed Mon–Tue afternoons.* The hotel overlooks the château, and offers tasteful rooms and a **swimming pool** 🏊.

🍴 EAT

🍽🍽 **Cristal Hôtel Restaurant** – *10 bis pl. de la République.* 📞*02 41 51 09 54. www.cristal-hotel.fr.* Good food, relaxed atmosphere and impeccable décor explain the success of this restaurant with its perfect riverfront location. 22 rooms (🛏🛏🍽) for overnight guests.

⊜⊜⊜ **L'Essentiel** – *11–13 r. Raspail.* ✆*02 41 67 71 10. www.restaurant-lessentiel-saumur.fr. Closed Sun, Mon.* Loire wines and contemporary food served in a former 14C chapel.

⊜⊜⊜ **Le Gambetta** – *12 r. Gambetta. ✆02 41 67 66 66. www.restaurantle gambetta.com. Closed Sun, Mon.* This country house near the riding school offers two dining rooms serving gourmet cuisine that is beautifully presented.

NIGHTLIFE

Bar le Général – *67 avenue du General de Gaulle. ✆02 41 67 31 77.* Traditional French bar with local's propping up the counter, and plenty of seats outside if it's sunny. Basic decor but authentic to the core.

Place St-Pierre – Several of the 18C half-timbered buildings of St Pierre house cafés with shady terraces in this lovely square.

Pub House – *64 avenue du General de Gaulle. ✆02 41 40 08 95.* Lively Irish-style pub that is reknowned for its pizzas and beer. Simple decor is offset by warm staff and genuine attention to the quality of their food.

SHOPPING

Girardeau – *53 r. St-Nicolas. ✆02 41 51 30 33. www.girardeau-traiteur.com. Closed 3 weeks in Feb and 2 weeks in Aug plus afternoons on public holidays.* Ideally located for stocking up on regional products: pig's trotters (award winning speciality), *foie gras*, *boudin noir* (European champion for *boudin blanc* with truffles), and fine wine as well.

La Duchesse Anne – *22 r. Franklin-Roosevelt. ✆02 41 51 07 50. www. laduchesseanne.fr. Open Mon 2.30–7pm, Tue–Fri 9am–7pm, Sat 8.30am–7.30pm, Sun and public holidays 8.30am–1pm* The creations of this master chocolatier are often inspired by the history of Saumur.

LEISURE ACTIVITIES

Maison des Vins Anjou-Saumur – *7 Quai Carnot. ✆02 41 38 45 83. Phone for opening times. Closed mid-Jan–mid-Feb, 1–8 May and 1 Nov.* Located next to the tourist office, this is a good place to learn about the wines of Saumur.

Distillerie Combier – *48 r. Beaurepaire. ✆02 41 40 23 00. www.combier.fr. Phone for opening times.* The oldest distillery in the Loire valley; taste the liqueur of your choice and take home a bottle of absinthe, guignolet, pastis d'antan or fruit brandy.

La Cave des Vignerons de Saumur – *14 rte. de Saumoussay. 49260 St-Cyr-en-Bourg.* ⏱*May–Sept Mon–Sat 9.30am–7pm, Sun and public holidays 10.30am–1pm and 3–7pm; Oct–Apr Mon–Sat 9.30am–12.30pm, 2–6.30pm;* 👣*guided tours of the wine cellars:* ⊜€5. *✆02 41 53 06 18; www.robertetmarcel.com.* This cooperative brings together 300 winegrowers making it the ideal halt for discovering the wines of Saumur: wine storehouses and cellars (10km/6mi of galleries in the old tufa quarries) and a tasting session. Wines on sale all bear the AOC label and Les Pouches (white), La Mouraude (red) and Les Poyeux (saumur-champigny) are highly recommended.

EVENTS

Easter – International equestrian vaulting competition.

Apr–Oct – Series of equestrian exhibitions, gala evening performances and guided tours of the Cadre noir and National Riding School.

May – Journées Nationales du Livre et du Vin (books and wine festival); international 3-day event competition.

June – International military music festival; international carriage driving competition.

July – Carrousel de Saumur; Loire en fête, the military and equestrian tattoo.

August – Les Grandes Tablées du saumur-champigny, a huge outdoor feast for thousands of diners.

September – Grande Semaine de Saumur (major equestrian show with carriage driving, dressage, shows). Grape harvesting at the château and organic market (last Sun of month).

November – Salon international de Saumur "Ar(t) Cheval", annual gathering of contemporary art on the theme of horses.

Cloître Ste-Marie, Fontevraud-l'Abbaye

Fontevraud-l'Abbaye★★★

Fontevraud Abbey stands on the borders of Anjou, Touraine and Poitou. Despite the ravages of history, it remains the largest group of monastic buildings in France, having retained many features typical of Anjou architecture.

A BIT OF HISTORY

An aristocratic Order – The success of the new Order was immediate and soon took on an aristocratic character. The **Plantagenets** showered it with wealth. The tomb effigies of Henry II, his wife Eleanor of Aquitaine and their son Richard the Lionheart lie in the nave. The abbey became a refuge for repudiated queens and daughters of royal or highly placed families who, voluntarily or under compulsion, retired from the secular world. There were 36 abbesses, half of whom were of royal blood, including five from the House of Bourbon, between 1115 and 1789.

Violation of the abbey – The Huguenots desecrated the abbey in 1561; in 1792 the Order was suppressed by the Revolutionaries who completely destroyed the monks' priory. In 1804 Napoleon converted the remaining buildings into a prison, which closed only in 1963.

▶ **Population:** 1 575.
⏱ **Michelin Map:** 317: J-5
ℹ **Info:** pl. St-Michel, 49590 Fontevraud-l'Abbaye. ℘02 41 51 79 45. www.ot-saumur.fr.
◖ **Location:** Between Saumur (15km/9mi to the NW) and Chinon (18km/11mi to the E).
◷ **Timing:** Allow 2 hours.

☺ Touring Tip ☺

Every evening in August, the abbey organises Les Rencontres Imaginaires, an open-air *son-et-lumière* performance involving artists as well as professional and amateur actors.

Cultural vocation – In 1975 the abbey embarked on a new vocation as a venue for cultural events, the **Centre culturel de l'Ouest**, which hosts concerts, shows, workshops and exhibits. A hotel and restaurant are on-site.

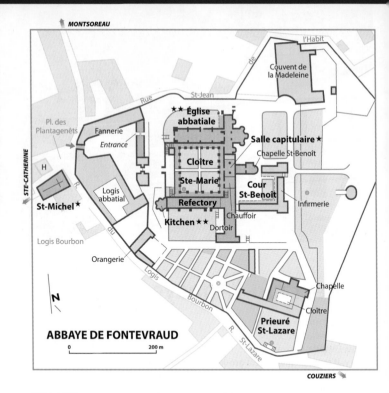

MONTSOREAU

l'Habit

Couvent de
la Madeleine

Rue St-Jean

**★★ Église
abbatiale**

Pl. des
Plantagenêts

Fannerie

Entrance

Salle capitulaire ★

Chapelle St-Benoît

H

Cloître

Ste-Marie

**Cour
St-Benoît**

Infirmerie

Logis
abbatial

Refectory

STE-CATHERINE

St-Michel ★

Kitchen ★★

Chauffoir

Dortoir

Logis Bourbon

Orangerie

Logis Bourbon

Chapelle

Cloître

N

**Prieuré
St-Lazare**

ABBAYE DE FONTEVRAUD

0   200 m

R. St-Lazare

COUZIERS

VILLAGE
Église St-Michel★
Although the church was enlarged
and remodelled in the 13C and 15C, an
inner arcade remains from the original
Romanesque building.

ABBEY★★★
⏱Daily mid-Jan–Mar 9.30am–6pm;
Apr–Oct 9.30am–7pm. €11.
📞02 41 51 73 52. www.fontevraud.fr.
Guided tour on request.
Among the buildings around the
entrance court, most of which date from
the 19C, are, on the left, the vast 18C

Foundation of the Abbey (1101)
The monastic order at Fontevraud was founded by **Robert d'Arbrissel**
(c. 1045–1117), who had been a hermit in Mayenne forest before being
appointed by Urban II to preach in the west of France. He soon gained a
large group of disciples of both sexes and chose this place to found a double
community. From the beginning the abbey was unique among religious houses
in that it had five separate buildings accommodating priests and lay brothers
(St-Jean-de-l'Habit), contemplative nuns (Ste-Marie), lepers (St-Lazare),
invalids (St-Benoît) and lay sisters (Ste-Marie-Madeleine). Each body led its
own life, with its own church and cloister, chapter house, refectory, kitchen
and dormitory. Robert d'Arbrissel had ordained that the whole community be
directed by an abbess chosen from among widows; she was later designated
as Head and General of the Order and this female supremacy was to be
maintained right up to the French Revolution.

stables (*fannerie*) and on the right, the 17C and 18C abbess' house.

Abbey Church★★

This now-restored 12C abbey church was divided into storeys at the time when it served as a prison.

The vast nave is roofed by a series of domes, characteristic of churches in the southwest of France. Fontevraud is the northernmost example of these domed churches, explained by the important links between Anjou and Aquitaine during the Plantagenet reign.

The building houses 13C polychrome **recumbent figures★** of the Plantagenets, representing Henry II, Count of Anjou and King of England, his wife Eleanor of Aquitaine, who died at Fontevraud in 1204, their son Richard the Lionheart and lastly Isabella of Angoulême, second wife of their son, King John of England.

Cloître Ste-Marie

The cloisters in the nuns' convent have Renaissance vaulting except on the south side, which is Gothic inspired.

A richly carved doorway in the east gallery, paved with the Bourbon coat of arms, opens to the **chapter house★**, which has 16C murals representing some of the abbesses.

Refectory

This large hall with its Romanesque walls is roofed with Gothic vaulting that replaced a timber ceiling in 1515.

Romanesque Kitchen★★

This is the only Romanesque **kitchen** in France to have survived the centuries. In many respects it resembles the abbot's kitchen at Glastonbury.

This most intriguing building is roofed with overlapping lozenge-shaped stones and topped by numerous chimneys, added in 1904 during restoration by the architect Magne. Originally, the building was free-standing, built on an octagonal plan and capped by an octagonal hood.

Romanesque kitchen

© Stéphane Lemaire/hemis.fr

Prieuré St-Lazare

This priory houses a hostelry, but it also provides access to the chapel and its splendid 18C **spiral staircase**; in summer the small cloisters are used as a restaurant.

ADDRESSES

🍽 STAY

😊😊😊 **Domaine de Mestré** – *1km/0.6mi N of Fontevraud on D 947.* ℰ*02 41 51 72 32. www.domaine-de-mestre.com. Closed 2 Jan-2 Feb. 13 rooms. Evening meal* 😊😊😊. Spend a night at the old royal abbey farm amid a park planted with centuries-old cedar and lime trees.

😊😊😊 **Fontevraud Hôtel** – *In the abbey.* ℰ*02 46 46 10 10. 54 rooms.* The hotel enlivens the old priory of St-Lazare's sumptuous setting and includes a gourmet restaurant.

🍴 EAT

😊😊 **L'Abbaye Le Délice** – *8 av. des Roches.* ℰ*02 41 51 71 04. www.restaurant-ledelice-fontevraud-abbaye.fr. Closed 29 Jun-9 Jul, 1-9 Dec, Tue eve, Wed.* This restaurant on Fontevraud's main street is entered through the café. Dishes incorporate local produce.

Château de Brézé

© Arnaud Chicurel/hemis.fr

Château de Brézé★★

The castle's imposing outline towers above one of the oldest vineyards of the Loire Valley. Apart from that, little seems to distinguish this château from its neighbours. But closer examination reveals intriguing openings in the moat, the only outward signs of underground galleries and the most extensive underground fortress discovered to date.

A BIT OF HISTORY

The lords of Brézé built the original fortress in the 11C. Their descendants erected the Renaissance living quarters. The Grand Condé, a leader of the uprising known as the "Fronde", which took place at the beginning of Louis XIV's reign, found refuge inside the castle with his whole army. In 1682, he exchanged the property against the Galissonnière estate belonging to the Dreux, who subsequently took the name of Dreux-Brézé. Their descendants still live in the château.

VISIT
Château
Beyond the moat stands the elegant Renaissance edifice remodelled in 1824 by Hodé. Surrounding the courtyard are the main building, the gallery and the gatehouse flanked by two large round

- ⓖ **Michelin Map:** 317: I-5
- ⓘ **Info:** ☎02 41 51 60 15. www.chateaudebreze.com. *Daily: Jul–Aug 10am–6.30pm; Apr–Jun and Sept 10am–6pm; Oct–Dec and Feb–Mar 10am–5.30pm. ✆€11.80. Guided tours (✆€14.90–€17.90) at 10.15am and 3.30pm for the chateau, and an hour later for the underground areas.*
- ▶ **Location:** 10km/6mi S of Saumur.
- ⊙ **Don't Miss:** The underground rooms.
- ⏱ **Timing:** Allow 2–4 hours.
- 👪 **Kids:** The caves.

towers; a terrace makes up the fourth side. From the rooftop, the panoramic view reveals the different stages of construction of the castle.

👪 Ensemble troglodytique★★
Sturdy shoes and warm clothes advised. A discreet door opening onto the main courtyard gives access to a gallery dug in the 15C that leads to a vast **underground network** steeped in mystery.

Its complexity is due to its various uses through the centuries: stone quarry for the construction of the castle, cellars for storing the wine production, etc.

Roche de Brézé★

Located beneath the castle, these underground living quarters were mentioned in the 9C. The area was originally accessed through a well-guarded narrow corridor with a bend in it.

A corridor leads from this area to the underground watch-path with loopholes opening into the moat. The path ends in the moat via a drawbridge spanning a pit.

Underground bakery★

Reached by a staircase hewn of the rock, the bakery has a big fireplace and an impressive baking oven. The heat from the ovens made the bread dough stored in the room above rise more quickly, and enabled silk-worm breeding to take place in the adjacent room.

Winepress and cellars

The vast winepress cellar was used in the making of the famous Brézé white wines. The harvest fell directly into the wine press from a well dug into the rock, which opened in the middle of the vineyards. The grape juice then flowed directly into the vats, along channels running at ground level.

Parc

The 20ha space is perfect for a quiet stroll. Built in 1550 by the entrance to the château, the **dovecote★** can accommodate up to 3,700 birds.

Montreuil-Bellay★

Occupying a charming site beside the Thouet on the border of the Poitou and Anjou regions, the little town of Montreuil-Bellay has retained its authentic medieval character.

CHÂTEAU★★

 Guided tour (1hr) only Jul–Aug daily 10am–12pm, 2–6.30pm; Apr–Jun, Sep Wed–Mon 10.30am-12pm, 2–6pm; Oct-Nov 10am-12pm, 2-5.30pm. €12, gardens only €6.50. 02 41 52 33 06. www.chateau-de-montreuil-bellay.fr.
In front of the castle stretches the picturesque place des Ormeaux (parking space). Imposing walls, pleasant gardens and remarkable furnishings are the main features of Montreuil Château.

Beyond the barbican, inside the fortified gateway, stands the graceful residence built by the Harcourt family in the 15C. The **medieval kitchen** with its central fireplace was slightly altered in the 15C; still in perfect condition, it holds a set of

- ▶ **Population:** 4,275.
-   **Michelin Map:** 317: I-6
- 🗓 **Info:** pl. du Concorde, 49260 Montreuil-Bellay. 02 41 40 20 60. www.ot-saumur.fr.
- ▶ **Location:** 15km/9mi S of Saumur (N 147) and 10km/6mi SE of Doué-la-Fontaine.
- 🔍 **Don't Miss:** The medieval kitchen in the château.
- 🕐 **Timing:** Allow 2 hours.

copper pans and a kitchen range with seven fire boxes fuelled by charcoal.
The 15C **canons' lodge** has four staircase turrets with conical roofs serving four separate sets of rooms, each consisting of living rooms over a storeroom (one was converted into a steam room). The **château neuf** was built in the 15C, and features a beautiful staircase turret decorated with mullioned windows protected by delicately carved mock balustrades. The small **oratory** decorated with frescoes is late 15C.

Recalcitrant Vassals

In 1025, **Fulk Nerra**, Count of Anjou, gave this stronghold to his vassal Berlay (distorted into Bellay), who made it into a powerful fortress. A century later, safe behind their stout walls, his successors plotted against their overlord. In 1151, one of them, Giraud, held out for a year before he capitulated to Geoffrey Plantagenet, who razed the keep he had just taken with the aid of an early incendiary bomb. When the Plantagenets acceded to the throne of England and thus became the main enemy of the King of France, the Berlays (who later became the Du Bellays) pledged allegiance to their immediate overlord; Philippe Auguste thereupon besieged their castle and demolished it.

Visitors see the bedchamber of the **Duchess of Longueville**, Prince Condé's sister, who was one of the main instigators behind the Fronde uprising and was exiled by Louis XIV to Montreuil, where she lived in luxurious style. In the Grand Salon are a Brussels tapestry and a German marquetry cupboard; in the music salon is a superb bureau inlaid with copper and tortoiseshell by Boulle (1642–1732).

In the vaulted **cellar** the brotherhood of the Sacavins held its meetings; it was founded in 1904 by the then owner of the castle, Georges de Grandmaison, to advertise Anjou wine. The winepress, into which the grapes were poured directly from the courtyard through a trapdoor, was still in use at the beginning of the last century.

THE TOWN

▷ As you come out of the château, turn right onto r. du Marché, then follow r. du Tertre.

Les Nobis

Deep in the vegetation beside the Thouet are the ruins of the church of St-Pierre, which was burnt down by the Huguenots in the 16C. Nearby are two wings of some 17C cloisters.

▷ Walk up the St-Pierre steps and turn right.

Maison Dovalle
69 r. Dovalle.
The façade of this 16C house was altered in the 18C. The building is named after the Romantic poet **Charles Dovalle** (1807–29), whose collected works, *Le Sylphe*, were published posthumously.

▷ Continue along rue Dovalle to reach *(on the left)* long stretches of the medieval wall; a path then leads to the **Porte St-Jean**, a 15C gate flanked by two large rusticated towers. Proceed along rue Nationale, the town's high street; at the other end stands the Porte Nouvelle.

EXCURSIONS

Ancienne abbaye d'Asnières
7.5km/5mi NW along D 761 then right to Cizay. Open Tue, Thu-Fri, 9am-12pm.
On the northern edge of Cizay forest are the evocative ruins of what was once an important monastery founded in the 12C. It has recently reopened to the public after rennovations.

Le Puy-Notre-Dame
7km/4.3mi W along D 77.
The **collegiate church★**, built in the 13C, is a remarkable example of Angevin architecture. The tall, narrow nave and aisles lend majesty to the interior. The carved stalls beyond the high altar date from the 16C.

Château d'Oiron ★★

The magnificent Renaissance Château d'Oiron is set in the heart of a forest of cedar trees. Since 1993, it has successfully achieved a surprising marriage of old and modern art. This unexpected encounter between past and present brings to life the many changing artistic trends over the centuries. It is a daring exchange but one of wonder and curiosity.

- **Michelin Map:** 322: F-3
- **Info: Chateau:** ⓖⓞDaily: Jun–Sept 10.30am–6.30pm; Oct–May 10.30am–5.30pm. ⓞ1 Jan, 1 May, 1 and 11 Nov, 25 Dec. ⓢ€8 (under 25 years, €6.50). ℘05 49 96 51 25. www.chateau-oiron.fr.
- **Location:** 45km/28mi S of Saumur, between Thouars and Loudun, Oiron is a small village set in the country.
- **Timing:** Allow at least 2 hours.

VISIT

Exterior

Preceded by two 17C pavilions, the château is composed of a central block (17C) with a steep Mansard roof, flanked by two square pavilions crowned by a balustrade. The courtyard is delineated by two wings (16C and 17C). On the left, the upper section of the **galerie à arcades** features sculpted marble medallions of Roman emperors.

Interior

From the period of the Gouffier family, Oiron has retained its **cabinet des Muses** (King's pavilion), adorned with a Diana the huntress and her nymphs, and its majestic **galerie peinte★★** (Renaissance wing), whose walls feature remarkable scenes inspired by incidents from the Trojan War and the The Aeneid. The Louis XIII ceiling commissioned by Louis Gouffier comprises 1,670 painted panels of animals, birds and weaponry. The main body of the château, the **corps central**, was altered by La Feuillade, who married Charlotte Gouffier in 1667; it features a fine Renaissance staircase, inspired by the one at Azay-le-Rideau. The encounter with modern art begins with the **chambre du Coquatrix** (1993), by Joan Fontcuberta, portraying a discovery of this imaginary animal in the cellars of the château. The **cabinet de curiosités de Claude Gouffier** (1995), by Guillaume Bijl, evokes the passion of the château's first owner for nature's most fantastic creations, echoed by Thomas Grünfeld (1992) whose **cabinet des Monstres** is a hotch-potch of weird creatures put together from various parts of stuffed animals.

In the **couloir des Illusions**, Félice Varini projects abstract lines onto the walls as part of a clever game of optical effects. The **galerie des Chevaux** presents charcoal sketches by Georg Ettl on the remains of the original plasterwork to evoke the portraits that used to hang here of Henri II's finest horses.

La collégiale★

The Renaissance façade consists of twin doors and a large arch surmounted by a pediment bearing the Gouffier coat of arms. In the transept, note the tombs of the Gouffier family, the work of Tuscan sculptors who brought their skills to Tours. In the left transept arm is the tomb effigy of Philippine de Montmorency, second wife Guillaume Gouffier, who died in 1516; nearby is the mausoleum of her son, Admiral Bonnivet, killed at the battle of Pavia in 1525.

Doué-la-Fontaine★

Doué and its outskirts are built on a chalk plateau riddled with caves. The town's flower show takes place each year *(mid-Jul)* in the arena and at a large park where late-18C stables belonging to Baron Foullon have been converted into an open-air museum of old-fashioned shops.

THE TOWN

Alongside its troglodyte dwellings (*rue des Perrières and rue d'Anjou*), Doué has retained some of its **old houses** with towers and outside stairs. On the Saumur road, a **fine windmill** is the only one remaining out of the hundreds that once stood on the hills in the region.

The **Arènes**, or disused open-air quarries were converted into arenas in the 15C, and are used for performances and flower shows.

The **musée aux Anciens Commerces**
👥 *(Ecuries Foullon, towards St-Georges-sur-Layon;* ◷*Feb-Mar and Oct, Wed-Fri 2-6pm, Sat-Sun 10am-12pm, 2-6pm; Apr-Sep 10am-12pm, 2-7pm; Nov-Dec Fri-Sun 10am-12pm, 1pm-5pm;* ◷ *Mon, Dec 24-25.* ⊜€8, child 6–16, €5.50; ℘02 41 52 91 58; www.anciens-commerces.fr)* is a private museum, created in 1992, and set in the stables (the only remaining parts of the château) of Baron Foullon; two reconstituted streets with 20 shops from bygone days tell the story of shopkeeping from 1850–1950 including a recreated apothecary's, milliner's and hardware shop.

EXCURSIONS

👥 Bioparc Zoo de Doué★

103 rte de Cholet. ◷*Feb–Mar 10am–6pm; Apr–Jun and Sept 9am–7pm; Jul–Aug 9am–7.30pm; Oct–Nov 10am–6.30pm, Dec 11am-4pm;* ◷ *Dec 25, Jan 1.* ⊜€22.50 (child 3–10, €17.50). ℘02 41 59 18 58. www.bioparc-zoo.fr.
The zoo is on the western edge of Doué, in a troglodyte **setting★**. The old quarries make an unusual habitat for the many animals that live here, more or less at liberty.

▶ **Population:** 7,891.
⚬ **Michelin Map:** 317: H-5 Local map see Vallée du Layon.
ℹ **Info:** 30 pl. des Fontaines, 49700 Doué-La-Fontaine. ℘02 41 40 20 60. www.ot-saumur.fr.
◉ **Location:** 20km/12.4mi SW of Saumur.
◷ **Timing:** Doué is a fascinating place; allow half a day.
👥 **Kids:** Biopark.

Les Chemins de la rose★

Parc de Courcilpleu, D 960, rte de Cholet. ◷*Mar-Nov daily 10am–6pm (7pm May-Aug, 5pm Nov);* ◷ *weekends Aug-Sep.* ⊜€7.50. ℘02 41 59 95 95. www.lescheminsdelarose.com.
This 4ha garden is planted with more than 1,300 varieties of old and modern roses from all over the world.

👥 Village troglodytique Rochemenier

14 rue du musée, 49700 Louresse-Rochemenier. ◷*Feb–Apr and Sep–Nov Tue–Sun 10am–5pm; May–Aug daily 9.30am–6pm.* ⊜€7, €8.50 with audio guide, from €17 with escape game. ℘02 41 59 18 15. www.troglodyte.fr.
The underground village of Rochemenier was dug out of the marly deposit, and extends over a wide area.

👥 Maisons troglodytes de Forges

3.5km/2mi N on D 214. ◷*Apr-Jun and Sep-Nov weekends only, tours leave at 10am, 2pm, 4pm; Jul-Aug, 10am-6pm* ◷*Tue.* ⊜€6 (child 6–15, €4). ℘02 41 59 00 32. www.maisonstroglo.com.
Excavations in 1979 revealed this example of rural architecture that was formerly unappreciated.

Château de Brissac★

The château is set in a fine park shaded by magnificent **cedar trees★**. The building is unusual both because it is exceptionally tall (48m), and because it comprises two juxtaposed buildings, one of which was intended to replace the other.

BIT OF HISTORY

Built c.1455 by Pierre de Brézé, Minister to Charles VII and then to Louis XI, the château was bought by René de Cossé in 1502 and has remained in the family ever since. René's grandson, **Charles de Cossé**, Count of Brissac, was one of the leaders of the League, the Catholic party that supported the Guises in the 16C. In 1594, as Governor of Paris, he handed the keys of the city to Henri IV, who had arrived newly converted to Roman Catholicism at the city gates. In gratitude the King raised him to the status of duke. The new duke began to rebuild his house but work was brought to a halt by his death in 1621 and the château has been left unaltered ever since.

VISIT

The main façade is flanked by two towers with conical roofs, ringed by elegantly sculpted machicolations. Inside, the **ceilings** are still adorned with their original 17C paintings; the walls are hung with superb **tapestries**. The **Louis XIII staircase** leads to the guard-room on the first floor, as well as to the bedchamber where Louis XIII and his mother, Marie de' Medici, were at least temporarily reconciled after the Battle of Les Ponts-de-Cé in 1620. Opened in 1890 by the Marquise de Brissac, the exquisite 170-seat **theatre**, restored in the 1983, is rich with sconces, red fabrics and a glittering chandelier.

EXCURSION

Centre de découverte du milieu aquatique et de la pêche
Take D 748 S of Brissac-Quincé and follow the signposted route.
This fish-breeding centre, located on a lovely site on the banks of the **Étang**

- ⚹ **Michelin Map:** 317: G-4
- ℹ **Info Tourist office:** 7 pl. Kennedy, 49051 Angers. ℘02 41 23 50 00. www.tourisme.destination-angers.com.
  Chateau: *Guided tour (75min) only: Apr–Jun and Sept daily except Tue 10am–noon, 2–5pm; Jul–Aug daily 10am–5pm; Oct daily except Tue 10.30–11.30am, 2–4.30pm. ≈€12. ℘02 41 91 22 21. www.chateau-brissac.fr.*
- ▶ **Location:** 15km/9mi S of Angers, in the direction of Doué-la-Fontaine.
- ◉ **Don't Miss:** The luxuriously gilded theatre.
- ◔ **Timing:** Allow 1h30.
- ♟ **Kids:** The discovery tour and special events at Christmas and Easter.

Interior, Château de Brissac
© Kris Ubach/age fotostock

de Montayer, enlightens visitors on the river and local efforts to protect its ecosystem. Besides viewing fish typical of the Loire Basin, visitors can watch the various stages involved in the breeding of pike, from the hatching of eggs to the growing of young fry in basins.
🡅 A botanical trail reveals the flora characteristic of shores and wetlands.

Baugé

Baugé, a peaceful town with noble dwellings, is the capital and market town of the surrounding region, a countryside of heaths, forests and vast clearings. There is a good view of the town's ruined walls from rue Foulques-Nerra to the west.

A BIT OF HISTORY

Founded in 1000 by **Fulk Nerra**, Baugé became a favourite residence of Yolanda of Aragon, Queen of Sicily, and her son, King René, in the 15C. Yolanda was a faithful supporter of Charles VII and Joan of Arc. In the battle of Le Vieil-Baugé (1421), Sir Guérin de Fontaines distinguished himself at the head of the Angevins and Scottish mercenaries who succeeded in repulsing the English from Anjou.

SIGHTS

Château

&⟐Feb Wed-Sun, 2-6pm; Apr–mid-Jun and Sept–early Nov daily 2–6pm; mid-Jun–Aug daily 10.30am–12.30pm, 1.30–6pm. ⟐€7.50 ℘02 41 84 00 74. www.chateau-bauge.fr.

This 15C hunting castle now serves as a museum, with collections of weapons, porcelain and old coins. A video show as well as exhibits trace Baugé's history and life at the château. The art of jousting, falconry and wild-boar hunting are conjured up in the great hall, and a reconstruction of King René's bedchamber is open to the public.

In 1455 King René himself supervised the building of the turrets, dormer windows and the oratory as well as the bartizan on the rear façade, where the master masons are portrayed.

An ogee-arched doorway gives access to the **spiral staircase**, which terminates with a magnificent **palm tree vault**, decorated with the Anjou-Sicily coat of arms and other emblems: angels, tau crosses (T-shaped), symbols of the cross of Christ and stars which, in the Apocalypse, represent the souls of the blessed in eternity.

▶ **Population:** 6,459.
⟐ **Michelin Map:** 317: I-3
▤ **Info:** pl. de l'Europe, 49150 Baugé. ℘02 41 89 18 07. www.tourisme-bauge.com.
◖ **Location:** Located at the crossroads of the roads to Angers, Saumur, Tours and others, Baugé sits on the right bank of the Couasnon River and borders the lovely Chandelais forest.
▣ **Parking:** Available at pl. de l'Europe, near the château.
⬡ **Don't Miss:** The finely crafted cross of Anjou, set with precious stones.
◷ **Timing:** Allow 1 hour to see the château and the quiet streets of the town.

Chapelle des Filles-du-Cœur-de-Marie

Formerly part of an 18C hospice, the chapel houses the **Cross of Anjou★★**. With two transoms (the upper one carried the inscription), it is also known as the Cross of Jerusalem, and was venerated as a piece of the Cross of Christ by the dukes of Anjou.

At the end of the 15C, after the Battle of Nancy in which René II, Duke of Lorraine, a descendant of the dukes of Anjou, defeated Charles the Bold, the Lorraine troops adopted the Cross of Anjou as their own symbol in order to recognize one another in battle. It became known henceforward as the Cross of Lorraine. It is supposed to be made from a piece of the True Cross, brought back from the Holy Land after the crusade in 1241.

A marvel of the goldsmith's craft, set with precious stones and fine pearls, the cross was created at the end of the 14C for Louis, first Duke of Anjou, by his brother Charles V's Parisian goldsmith.

≗ Hôtel-Dieu

r. Anne-de-Melun. ⟐Same hours as château. www.chateau-bauge.fr.

Part of the vast hospital building is open to the public.

The Hôtel-Dieu was founded in 1639 by Marthe de la Beausse, helped by Princess Anne de Melun and the Hospitaller Sisters from La Flèche.

The highlight is the **apothecary★**, which is unchanged since it was set up in 1675. Among the Louis XIII walnut and oak surrounds are more than 650 painted boxes, Nevers earthenware pots and 16C Italian-Moorish jars containing crayfish eyes, powdered beetle, stag horns, and other medicines of the day.

🚗 DRIVING TOUR

BAUGEOIS REGION
82km/51mi. About 3h.

▶ Leave Baugé on D 141 E along the Couasnon valley.

Dolmen de la Pierre couverte
Leave the car at the side of the road 3.5km/2mi from Baugé. Some steps on the left lead to the dolmen standing in a forest clearing.

▶ Return to the car and take D 141 towards Pontigné.

Pontigné
The **church** (St Denis) is crowned by an unusual twisting spiral bell-tower. Inside, Angevin vaulting covers the nave whereas the capitals of the transept present monstrous heads and water-lily leaf motifs. The charming central apse is supported by a complex network of radiating tori.

▶ Take the road behind the church; turn right onto D 766, which offers a fine view of the orchards in the valley. Bear left and then turn right towards Bocé.

Forêt de Chandelais★
This is a magnificent state-owned forest, covering 800ha. The splendid fully grown oak and beech trees are replanted every 210 years.

▶ Follow the forest road to the central crossroads before turning right towards Bocé. Turn left on reaching D 58.

Mouliherne
Mouliherne stands on a rock on the north bank of the Riverolle, at the heart of the Baugé region. The quiet, peaceful atmosphere of the area makes it ideal for bicycle rides.

The **church** is all that remains of a fortress belonging to the counts of Anjou; built on a mound, it has a beautiful square 13C bell-tower with splayed windows and a twisting spire typical of the Baugé region.

Linières-Bouton
5km/3mi E on D 62.
This quiet village lies just off the main road. The church has a fine **chancel** built in the Plantagenet style.

▶ Turn left onto D 767 then follow a road to the right which leads to Breil.

Breil
🚶 The path to Breil through Baugeois Woods makes a pleasant walk.

The semicircular apse and the tall stone spire of the **church** are characteristically Romanesque exterior features; note the Plantagenet vaulting in the chancel.

Park and château de Lathan
♿🕐*Apr–Oct Wed–Mon 10am–6pm.* ☞€3. ☎02 41 82 64 98.
Opposite the church stands a double formal park dating from the 17C. It features charming arbours, a long sweep of green lawn adorned with clipped yews and a double avenue of lime trees. There is a delightful view along the ornamental canal to an elegant 18C gazebo.

▶ Follow D 62 until you reach D 938 then turn right.

Cuon
Behind the church with the curious conical spire is a handsome 15C manor house. Opposite the church an old inn still bears the inscription *"Au Soleil*

d'Or" (The Golden Sun) where travellers on foot or on horseback could find lodging.

◐ From Cuon, take the road to Chartrené.

The wooded park on the left marks the site of the Château de la Grafinière.

◐ Beyond Chartrené turn left onto D 60. After 4.5km/3mi follow D 211 to the right, crossing heaths and woodlands, to reach Fontaine-Guérin.

Fontaine-Guérin

The belfry of the heavily restored Romanesque **church** is crowned by a twisting spire. The road D 211 towards St-Georges-du-Bois leads to an artificial **lake** ♁♁ with facilities for swimming, sailboarding and picnicking.

◐ From St-Georges-du-Bois, follow D 59 to Jarzé.

Jarzé-en-Baugeois

The countryside around Jarzé is divided among pasture, crops and woodland. The castle was built in 1500, burnt down in 1794 and restored in the 19C. The **church** was first a collegiate church built in the Flamboyant Gothic style on the foundations of an 11C building. The seigneurial chapel is covered with lierne and tierceron vaulting.

◐ 2.5km/1.2mi on D 82 towards La Flèche; take the first turn on the right.

Chapelle Notre-Dame-de-Montplacé

♥~Guided tours Jul–Aug Sun pm. Call in advance. ℘02 41 89 18 07. The chapel, standing in splendid isolation on its bluff, can be seen from afar.

◐ Follow D 82, the road to La Flèche.

Cheviré-le-Rouge

Set the middle of the village, the **Église St-Médard** is of note for its 11C spire. The chancel vaulting (12C) is a remarkable example of the Plantagenet style.

◐ Continue along D 82 towards La Flèche.

Jardins du château de Gastine

The gardens, designed by Louis Benech, make a majestic backdrop to the château (16C–18C) with a box terrace planted with yews, roses, lavender and Japanese anemones; ponds and fountains; clipped hornbeam hedges; and beds of dwarf bamboo.

◐ Go back along D 82 to drive into Fougeré.

Fougeré

Fougeré takes its name from the French word for fern, *fougère*, but is better known for its twisted spire. The **Église St-Étienne** (11C) features a beautiful chevet, and the 13C chancel is pure Plantagenet style. Note the engouled beams with monsters' heads and, outside *(place de la Mairie)*, the graffiti (11C–12C).

◐ Leave Fougeré on D 138 and drive to St-Quentin-lès-Beaurepaire. Turn right towards Vaulandry. At the junction with D 938, turn right towards Baugé. From Baugé, follow signs for Le Vieil-Baugé

Le Vieil-Baugé

The old village crowns a hilltop overlooking the Couasnon valley. It was the site of the battle in 1421, in which the French forces, aided by Scots, were victorious over the English.

Notice the slender twisted spire of **Église St-Symphorien**, which leans as a result of the distortion of the internal wooden framework. The nave is partially 11C and the handsome **chancel**★ is 13C with Angevin vaulting.

The 15C **Manoir de Clairefontaine** has exquisite 17C-18C furnishings *(♥~guided tours only at varying hours; usually 2pm and 3.30pm, but see website for details; ☞€8; ℘06 07 17 46 32; www.manoirdeclairefontaine.com).*

ANJOU AND THE MAUGES COUNTRY

The delightful pace of life enjoyed in the region is perfectly encapsulated in the expression *Douceur Angevine*, the gentler side of living, with its beautiful countryside, historic and vibrant towns, rich cultural and artistic treasures, clement weather, outstanding food and wine and limitless opportunities for leisure pursuits. The ancient province of Anjou is the birthplace of the Plantagenet dynasty whose princes, at different times, reigned in England, Hungary, Naples, Provence and Jerusalem. The region is still important today as a major hub of economic and industrial activities, services and education, with approximately 43,000 students enrolled at the University of Angers.

Tapestry Masterpiece

If you see only one thing in Angers then it has to be the Tapestry of the Apocalypse, a medieval work of art of unrivalled finesse that puts the Bayeux Tapestry into the shade in terms of its sheer scale and breathtaking beauty. Around the historical district of the castle, the town is a bustling modern business centre.

Outside Angers, the region boasts some of the Loire's more striking noble residences such as the Châteaux de Plessis-Macé, rebuilt in the 15C after the ravages of the Hundred Years War on the ruins of the original 11C fortress, and the Château de Serrant, a superb moated Renaissance and 17C edifice that is renowned for its magnificent library containing more than 12,000 books.

Points South

Anjou's famous *art de vivre* is best appreciated in the countryside on a driving tour through the Vallée du Layon, a landscape of vineyards, orchards and windmills, and in the excellent Côteaux-du-Layon sweet white wines.

Highlights

1 **Angers**, city of tapestry (p252)
2 Anjou theatre festival at **Château du Plessis-Macé** (p266)
3 The library at **Château de Serrant** (p268)
4 A drive through the vineyards of the **Vallée du Layon** (p268)
5 Musée du Textile, **Cholet** (p270)

Les Mauges, the southernmost part of Anjou, and the town of Cholet tell a dark chapter in the history of France and the terrible events of the Vendée War during the Revolution. Some stained-glass windows in the region's churches evoke the many massacres that were perpetrated as Revolutionary troops (Blues) fought Royalist insurgents (Whites).

On a lighter note, the region counts the largest concentration of troglodyte dwellings in Europe; many homes have been carved out in disused tufa quarries.

Tapestry of the Apocalypse, Château d'Angers

© Marc Dozier/hemis.fr

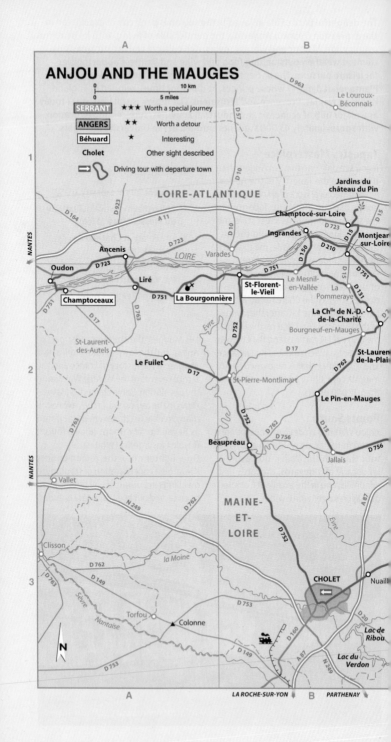

ANJOU AND THE MAUGES

0		10 km
0	5 miles	

SERRANT	★★★	Worth a special journey
ANGERS	★★	Worth a detour
Béhuard	★	Interesting
Cholet		Other sight described
⟹		Driving tour with departure town

LOIRE-ATLANTIQUE

Le Louroux-Béconnais

Jardins du château du Pin

Champtocé-sur-Loire

Ingrandes

Montjear-sur-Loire

Varades

LOIRE

Ancenis

Oudon

Liré

St-Florent-le-Vieil

Le Mesnil-en-Vallée

La Pommeraye

Champtoceaux

La Bourgonnière

La Chlle de N.-D.-de-la-Charité

Bourgneuf-en-Mauges

St-Laurent-des-Autels

St-Laurent-de-la-Plaine

Le Fuilet

St-Pierre-Montlimart

Le Pin-en-Mauges

Beaupréau

Jallais

NANTES

Vallet

MAINE-ET-LOIRE

Clisson

la Moine

CHOLET

Nuaill

Torfou

Colonne

Lac de Ribou

Lac du Verdon

N

LA ROCHE-SUR-YON   PARTHENAY

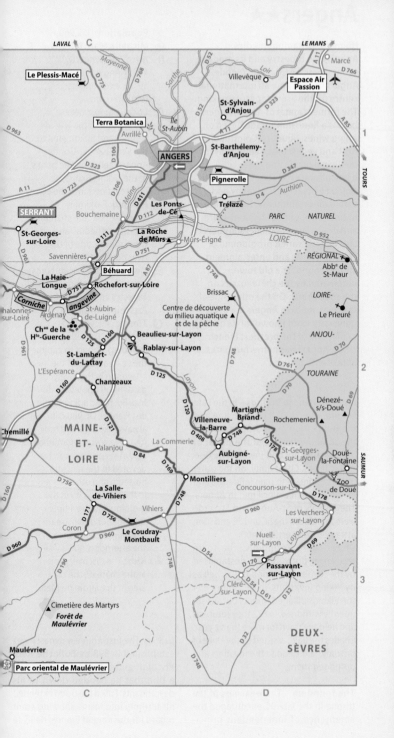

LAVAL **C** LE MANS

Mayenne

Marcé

D 775

D 768

D 52

Villevêque

D 766

A 11

Le Plessis-Macé

Sarthe

Loir

St-Sylvain-
d'Anjou

Espace Air
Passion

D 963

Terra Botanica

Île
St-Aubin

D 323

Avrillé

A 11

St-Barthélemy-
d'Anjou

D 106

ANGERS

Maine

D 723

A 11

D 106

D 347

Authion

Pignerolle

D 411

Bouchemaine

Les Ponts-
de-Cé

D 112

Trélazé

D 4

PARC   NATUREL

SERRANT

D 111

La Roche
de Mûrs

Mûrs-Érigné

LOIRE

D 952

St-Georges-
sur-Loire

D 751

RÉGIONAL

Savennières

D 961

Béhuard

D 748

Abb⁰ de
St-Maur

La Haie-
Longue

D 751

Rochefort-sur-Loire

D 87

Brissac

LOIRE-
ANJOU

Corniche

angevine

St-Aubin-
de-Luigné

Centre de découverte
du milieu aquatique
et de la pêche

Le Prieuré

halonnes-
sur-Loire

Ardenay

Ch⁰ᵘ de la
Hᵗᵉ-Guerche

D 125

D 160

Beaulieu-sur-Layon

ANJOU

D 748

D 70

St-Lambert-
du-Lattay

Rablay-sur-Layon

TOURAINE

L'Espérance

D 125

Layon

D 761

D 70

D 160

Chanzeaux

D 120

Martigné-
Briand

Dénezé-
s/s-Doué

D 169

MAINE-

D 121

Villeneuve-
la-Barre

Rochemenier

Chemillé

Valanjou

La Commerie

D 408

D 748

D 178

St-Georges-
sur-Layon

Doué-
la-Fontaine

ET-
LOIRE

D 84

D 169

Aubigné-
sur-Layon

Zoo
de Doué

D 756

Montilliers

Concourson-sur-L

D 178

D 160

La Salle-
de-Vihiers

D 748

Les Verchers-
sur-Layon

D 171

D 756

Vihiers

D 960

Layon

D 69

Coron

D 960

Le Coudray-
Montbault

Nueil-
sur-Layon

D 196

D 748

D 54

D 170

Passavant-
sur-Layon

D 960

Cléré-
sur-Layon

D 54

D 61

D 32

Cimetière des Martyrs

Forêt de
Maulévrier

DEUX-

D 32

SÈVRES

Maulévrier

D 748

Parc oriental de Maulévrier

C **D**

SAUMUR

TOURS

251

Angers★★

Home to the famous medieval Apocalypse tapestry and its modern counterpart, Le Chant du Monde, Angers has become an international centre for the art of tapestry making. The former capital of Anjou, Angers boasts a flourishing trade based on Anjou wines, liqueurs (Cointreau), fruit and vegetables, seeds, flowers, medicinal plants and other horticultural products. The fantastic Anjou Festival, with its many and varied entertainments, takes place in June throughout Maine-et-Loire and draws large audiences. Angers also offers a varied programme of cultural events and entertainment all year round. The old town, dominated by the château, sits on the south bank. On the other side of the river, modern Angers is a lively university town known for its quality of life. One of the prettiest French cities, Angers has numerous parks, ablaze with flowers.

A BIT OF HISTORY

From Romans to Vikings – In the Late Empire, the city fell into decline and the population level dropped under the combined effect of the threat of impoverishment and invasion by Germanic tribes. Christianity, on the other hand, continued to gain influence, and in 453 a church council met in Angers. The abbeys of St-Aubin and St-Serge were founded in the 6C and 7C and soon attracted new settlements.

Under the Carolingians the town recovered, but was soon destabilised by the revolts of the nobility as well as by Viking invasions. In December 854 the Vikings pillaged Angers but subsequently withdrew. In 872 they returned and held the town for more than a year. Charles the Bald, assisted by the Duke of Brittany, laid siege to the invaders and dislodged them.

The founders – The weakness of the throne in the late 9C encouraged the emergence of independent princi-

- ▸ **Population:** 152,960.
- **Michelin Map:** 317: F-4
- **Info:** 7 pl. Kennedy, 49051 Angers. ℘02 41 23 50 00. www.angers-tourisme.com.
- **Location:** Just over 60km/37mi to the NW of Saumur and 50km/31mi to the S of Château-Gontier, Angers stands on the banks of the Maine, 8km/5mi before it flows into the Loire.
- **Parking:** Parking is available near the château and the cathedral, and on the opposite side of the river near quai Monge.
- **Don't Miss:** The Jean-Lurçat Museum of Contemporary Tapestry and the Fine Arts museum district.
- **Timing:** Allow a half day to visit the old town, including 2 hours to explore the château. Spend the afternoon in the lovely gardens off Boulevard du Mal. Foch, including Jardin des Plantes. Or, you can always take a guided tour (see *Practical Information box*). A second day can be devoted to the tapestry museum and other sights in the modern city in the morning and the 4 hour driving tour downstream to Champtoceaux in the afternoon.
- **Kids:** The discovery tour at the château, the play area at the Jardin du Mail.

palities. The first Angevin dynasty was established in 898 by **Fulk the Red**, Viscount and then Count of Angers, a title that he handed down to his descendants. Fulk II the Good extended his territory into Maine showing scant regard for the King of France, delicate

Fulk the Terrible

Fulk III Nerra (987–1040) was the most formidable of a line of feudal masters. Hot-blooded and aggressive, he was always waging war to extend his territory; he obtained Saintonge, annexed Les Mauges, extended his boundaries to Blois and Châteaudun, captured Langeais and Tours (he was expelled from the latter by Robert the Pious), intervened in the Vendômois, took Saumur, etc. Ambitious, predatory, covetous, brutal and criminally violent, Fulk Nerra (the Black – owing to his very dark complexion) was typical of the great feudal lord in the year 1000. Every so often he would have sudden fits of Christian humility and penitence when he would shower gifts on churches and abbeys or take up the pilgrim's staff and depart for Jerusalem. He also built many fortresses along the Loire.

Louis IV of Outre-Mer, whom he openly despised.

Fulk Nerra and his successors – The rise of the Angevin dynasty to the height of its power in the 11C and 12C was due to its members' exceptional political skill, uninhibited by any scruples; remarkable ability in warfare; and keen eye for alliances through marriage.

Fulk III Nerra's son Geoffrey II (1040–60) continued his father's work consolidating the conquest of Maine and Touraine. The succession was divided between his two nephews who lost no time in quarrelling. **Fulk IV the Morose** finally gained the upper hand over Geoffrey III, at the cost of the Saintonge, Maine and Gâtinais, which he was too lazy to try to recover. In 1092 his second wife, the young and beautiful Bertrade de Monfort, was seduced, abducted and married by King Philip I.

For this scandalous behaviour, the King was excommunicated (🕯 see BEAUGENCY). The family's fortunes were salvaged by Geoffrey IV Martel, killed in 1106, and most of all by **Fulk V the Younger** (1109–31), who took advantage of Anglo-French rivalry and made judicious marriage alliances. He recovered Maine through his own marriage in 1109; later on, with the family's approval, he married his two daughters to the kings of France and England. His greatest success was the marriage in 1128 of his son Geoffrey to Mathilda of England, heir to Henry I and widow of the German Emperor Henry V. His ulti-

mate achievement concerned himself: in 1129, by then a widower, he married Melisand, daughter of Baldwin II and heir to the kingdom of Jerusalem.

Geoffrey V (1131–51), known as Plantagenet because he wore a sprig of broom (genêt) in his hair, ruled with a rod of iron over Greater Anjou (Anjou, Touraine and Maine), and tried to exercise his wife's rights over Normandy (annexed in 1144), and England, where Stephen of Blois had been King since 1135.

Plantagenets and Capets – In 1152 **Henry Plantagenet**, son of Geoffrey and Mathilda, married Eleanor of Aquitaine, whom Louis VII had recently divorced. He already held Anjou, Maine, Touraine and Normandy; by his marriage he acquired Poitou, Périgord, the Limoges and Angoulême regions, Saintonge, Gascony and suzerainty of the Auvergne and the County of Toulouse. In 1153 he forced Stephen of Blois to recognise him as his heir, and the following year succeeded him on the throne of England. He was then more powerful than his Capet rival. Henry II of England spent most of his time in France, often at Angers.

Successive Anjou dynasties (13C–15C) – During the regency of Blanche of Castille, Anjou was again lost as a result of the barons' revolt when Pierre de Dreux surrendered the province to Henry III. Taking advantage of a truce in 1231, Blanche and her son Louis began to build the fortress of Angers.

Anjou returned to the Capet sphere of influence, and in 1246 St Louis gave it, together with Maine, to his younger brother Charles as an apanage. In 1258 it was confirmed as a French possession by the Treaty of Paris. In 1360 Anjou was raised to a duchy by John the Good for his son Louis. From the 13C to the 15C Anjou was governed by the direct line of Capet princes and then by the Valois. The beginning and end of this period were marked by two outstanding personalities, Charles I and King René.

Charles of Anjou – Charles was an unusual character: deeply religious and wildly ambitious. At the request of the Pope, he conquered Sicily and the Kingdom of Naples and established his influence over the Italian peninsula. Intoxicated with success, he dreamt of adding the Holy Land, Egypt and Constantinople to his conquests, but on Easter Monday 1282, the Sicilians revolted and massacred 6 000 Frenchmen, half of whom were Angevins.

Good King René – The last of the dukes was Good King René, titular monarch of Sicily. He had one of the most cultivated minds of his day, having mastered Latin, Greek, Italian, Hebrew and Catalan. He also painted and wrote poetry, played and composed music and was knowledgeable about mathematics, geology and law. He was an easygoing, informal ruler who liked to talk to his subjects; he organised popular festivities and revived the old games of the age of chivalry. He loved flower gardens and introduced the carnation and the Provins rose. At the age of 12 he married Isabelle de Lorraine and was devoted to her for 33 years until her death, shortly after which, at the age of 47, he married Jeanne de Laval, who was only 21. Towards the end of his life, René accepted the annexation of Anjou by Louis XI philosophically. As he was also Count of Provence, he left Angers and ended his days in Aix-en-Provence at the age of 72 (1480).

Henri IV to the present – The Wars of Religion took on a bitter twist at Angers, where there was a strongly entrenched Calvinist church; a dispute on 14 October 1560 brought death to numerous townspeople. Thereafter, confrontations grew more frequent, and in 1572 the town had its own St Barthlomew's Day Massacre. It was at the Château d'Angers in 1598 that Henri IV finally brought the fomenting discontent of the Catholic League to an end by promising his son **César** (&see VENDÔME) to Françoise de Lorraine, daughter of the Duc de Mercœur, the leader of the Catholic party. The promise of marriage was signed on 5 April, when the future bride and groom were six and three years old. A week later the Edict of Nantes came into force; the Protestants had obtained freedom of worship.

In 1652, although held by the forces of the Fronde, Angers had to submit to Mazarin; in 1657 the town lost its right to elect local magistrates. After his arrest in Nantes, Louis XIV's Finance Minister, **Fouquet**, spent three weeks in the château in the governor's apartments, guarded by d'Artagnan. By then the town numbered 25,000 inhabitants and was only slightly industrialised.

At the outbreak of the Revolution in 1789, Angers declared enthusiastically for the reformers. The cathedral was sacked and turned into a Temple of Reason. In 1793 the defection of the Girondin administration allowed the Royalist Vendée party to capture the town between 20 June and 4 July. The Republicans lost no time in retaking it and the Terror claimed many victims.

In the early 19C Angers dozed until awakened by the arrival of the railway line from Paris to Nantes: the station was opened in 1849 by Louis Napoleon. Modern development had begun and, apart from a lull early in the 20C, it has continued to expand in recent decades.

CHÂTEAU★★★

⊙Daily: Jan–Apr and Sept–Dec 10am–5.30pm; May–Aug 9.30am –6.30pm. ⊙1 Jan, 1 May, 25 Dec. ⊸€9.50. ✆02 41 86 48 77. www.chateau-angers.fr.

The **fortress**, which incorporates the former Plantagenet fief, was built by St Louis between 1228 and 1238. It is a fine specimen of feudal architecture in dark schist alternating with courses of white stone. The castle moats are now laid out as splendid gardens.

The towers were originally one or two storeys taller and crowned with pepperpot roofs and machicolations. They were reduced to the level of the curtain walls under Henri III during the Wars of Religion. The original order had been to demolish the fortress entirely, but the governor simply removed the tops of the towers and laid down terraces. From the top of the highest tower, **Tour du Moulin**, on the north corner, there are **views★** over the town, the cathedral towers and St-Aubin, the banks of the Maine and the gardens laid out at the foot of the castle, and in the castle precincts, the series of towers on the curtain wall, the sophisticated design of the gardens, the **chapel** and the **Logis royal** (Royal Apartments), residence of the dukes of Anjou in the 15C.

Follow the **rampart walk** along the east side to a **medieval garden** laid out with lavender, daisies and hollyhocks growing in profusion near a vine like those which King René loved to plant.

Apocalypse Tapestry★★★

🕐 *Open same hours as the château.*

Housed in a gallery especially designed to ensure maximum preservation conditions, this legendary tapestry is the oldest, apart from the Bayeux Tapestry, to survive until the present. It was commissioned for Duke Louis I of Anjou and probably made in Paris at the workshops of Robert Poinçon between 1373 and 1383, after cartoons by Hennequin of Bruges, based on an illuminated manuscript belonging to King Charles V. It was subsequently hung in the courtyard of the bishop's palace in Arles to celebrate the marriage of Louis II of Anjou to Yolande of Aragon in 1400.

Donated to Angers Cathedral by Good King René (d. 1480), it was often displayed during religious festivities up to the late 18C, when it fell into oblivion.

However, Joubert, one of the cathedral canons, had it restored between 1843 and 1870.

Originally 133m long and 6m high, it consisted of six sections of equal size, each featuring a main character seated under a canopy, eyes turned towards two rows of seven pictures, whose alternating red and blue backgrounds form a chequered design.

Chapel and Royal Apartments

These 15C buildings stand inside the rampart wall. In the vast and well-lit chapel, note the finely sculpted Gothic leaves of the door, the small separate ducal chapel with its fireplace and on a keystone, a representation of the Anjou cross. The adjoining staircase, the work of King René, leads to the upper floor of the Royal apartments (**Logis royal**).

Other tapestries – The Royal Apartments house a collection of beautiful 15C and 16C tapestries, including the four hangings of the late-15C **Passion tapestry★★**, which are wonderfully rich in colour, and several **mille-fleurs tapestries★★**. Among the latter is the tapestry entitled **Angels Carrying the Instruments of the Passion**, which is unusual in that it has a religious theme, the admirable 16C **Lady at the Organ** and a fragment showing **Penthesilea**, the Queen of the Amazons, from a hanging of the Nine Heroines, women with chivalrous virtues.

WALKING TOUR

OLD TOWN★

Allow a half day.

Walking through the streets of the old town is like visiting an open-air museum. If the weather is nice, you can enjoy a pleasant break for a picnic lunch in the Jardin des Plantes.

▶ Start from the château entrance and take the narrow r. St-Aignan.

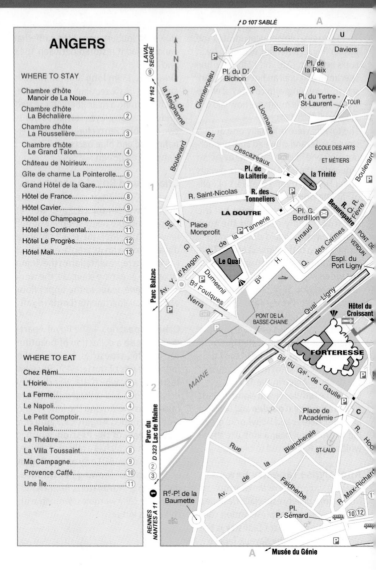

ANGERS

WHERE TO STAY

Chambre d'hôte
  Manoir de La Noue...............①
Chambre d'hôte
  La Béchalière.......................②
Chambre d'hôte
  La Rousselière....................③
Chambre d'hôte
  Le Grand Talon....................④
Château de Noirieux...............⑤
Gîte de charme La Pointerolle....⑥
Grand Hôtel de la Gare............⑦
Hôtel de France.....................⑧
Hôtel Cavier.........................⑨
Hôtel de Champagne..............⑩
Hôtel Le Continental...............⑪
Hôtel Le Progrès....................⑫
Hôtel Mail............................⑬

WHERE TO EAT

Chez Rémi...........................①
L'Hoirie..............................②
La Ferme.............................③
Le Napoli............................④
Le Petit Comptoir..................⑤
Le Relais.............................⑥
Le Théâtre..........................⑦
La Villa Toussaint.................⑧
Ma Campagne......................⑨
Provence Caffé.....................⑩
Une Île...............................⑪

Hôtel du Croissant

This 15C mansion, with mullion windows and ogee arches, housed the registrar of the Order of the Crescent (Ordre du Croissant), a military and religious chivalrous order founded by King René. The blazon on the façade bears the coat of arms of St Maurice, patron of the order, a 4C Christian legionary put to death because he refused to kill his fellow Christians. Opposite stand some interesting half-timbered houses.

▷ Continue to Montée St-Maurice, a long flight of steps that leads to the cathedral square.

Cathédrale St-Maurice★

4 r. St-Christophe. ◷*Daily 8am–7pm.*
℘*02 41 87 58 45.*
The cathedral is a fine 12C and 13C edifice. The Calvary standing to the left of the façade is the work of David d'Angers.
Façade – The front is surmounted by three towers, the central tower having been added in the 16C. The **gateway★**

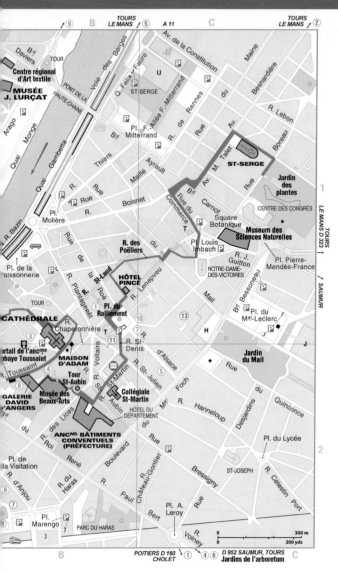

was damaged by the Protestants and the Revolutionaries, and in the 18C by the canons, who removed the central pier and the lintel to make way for processions. Above at the third-storey level are eight niches containing roughly carved, bearded figures in 16C military uniforms: St Maurice and his companions.

Interior – The single nave is roofed with one of the earliest examples of Gothic vaulting that originated in Anjou in the mid-12C. This transitional style, known as Angevin or Plantagenet vaulting, has the characteristic feature of keystones of the diagonal (ogive) arches that are at least 3m above the keys of the transverse and stringer arches, giving a more rounded or domical form. In Gothic vaulting all the keys are at roughly the same level. The vaulting of St-Maurice covers the widest nave built at that time and measuring 16.4m across, whereas the usual width was 9–12m; the capitals in the nave and the brackets supporting the gallery with its wrought-iron balustrade feature remarkable carved decoration.

Details of the façade, Maison d'Adam

© Franck Guiziou/hemis.fr

The chancel, finished in the late 12C, has the same Angevin vaulting as the transept. Its **13C stained glass★★** has particularly vivid blues and reds.

The church is majestically furnished: 18C great organ **(a)** supported by colossal telamones, monumental 19C pulpit **(b)** (&see illustration in the Introduction), high altar **(c)** surmounted by marble columns supporting a canopy of gilded wood (18C), 18C carved stalls **(d)** in front of which is a marble statue of St Cecilia **(e)** by David d'Angers. The walls are hung with tapestries, mostly from Aubusson.

▷ Walk past the Bishop's Palace (Évêché) to reach r. de l'Oisellerie.

At Nos. 5 and 7, two lovely half-timbered houses date from the 16C.

▷ Take the first road on the right.

Maison d'Adam★

This 16C half-timbered house has posts decorated with numerous carved figures. It owes its name to the apple tree, which appears to hold up the corner turret and which was flanked by statues of Adam and Eve until the Revolution.

▷ Continue along r. Toussaint.

No. 37 has a Classical doorway, once the entrance to the **abbey of Toussaint** (All Saints); it leads to an elegant courtyard flanked by a turret on a squinch.

▷ Walk back and follow r. du Musée.

Galerie David-d'Angers★

33 bis r. Toussaint. ○*Tue–Sun 10am–6pm.* ✆€4. ✆02 41 05 38 00. *www.musees.angers.fr.*
The gallery in this restored 13C abbey church houses the vast majority of

---

ST. MAURICE CATHEDRAL

0 — 30 m
0 — 30 yds

N

BISHOPRIC

CHOIR

f g

h

d

e

i

TRANSEPT

c

★★ Stained Glass

NAVE

b

Pl. Freppel

R. du Chanoine-Urseau

a

Chapelle N.-D.-de-Pitié

★Gateway

Pl. du Parvis-St-Maurice

plaster casts donated by the sculptor **David d'Angers** (1788–1856) to his native town. The well-displayed collection comprises monumental statues (King René, Gutenberg, Jean Bart, Larrey), funerary monuments (e.g. of General Bonchamps whose tomb is in the church of **St-Florent-le-Vieil**), busts of famous authors and medallions in bronze depicting contemporary figures.

Musée des Beaux-Arts★★

&Tue–Sun 10am–6pm.€6. 02 41 05 38 00. www.musees.angers.fr.

The late-15C residence **Logis Barrault** housing the **Fine Arts Museum** was built by Olivier Barrault, the King's Secretary, Treasurer to the Brittany States and Mayor of Angers. In the 17C it was taken over by the seminary, whose pupils included **Talleyrand** (see VALENÇAY), the future Bishop of Autun. The Fine Arts Museum was revamped in 2004 and it's still looking good. Five years of renovation and expansion enabled the remarkable collections to be displayed as they deserve. On the first floor are collections belonging to the Archaeological Museum, evoking the history of Anjou from the 12C to the 14C, including the 16C terra-cotta **Virgin of Tremblay**. The second floor is devoted to paintings: lovely Primitive works, two remarkable small portraits of Charles IX as a young man and Catherine de' Medici after Clouet; 17C paintings and above all, works of the 18C and 19C French School. There are also canvases by the local painters Lenepveu and Bodinier, and pastels (separate room) by Alexis Axilette, who was born in Durtal.

Tour St-Aubin

This tower is the belfry (12C) of the former St-Aubin monastery, a wealthy Benedictine abbey founded in the 6C. It takes its name from St Aubin, Bishop of Angers (538–550), who was buried here.

Monastery Buildings★

pl. Michel-Debré. Mon–Fri 8.45am–5.45pm. No charge. 02 41 81 49 49. www.maine-et-loire.fr. Must show personal identification.

The abbey buildings, extensively restored in the 17C and 18C, presently house local government offices.

On the left side of the courtyard is a glazed-in **Romanesque arcade★★**, part of the cloisters, with sculptures of remarkably refined craftsmanship. The door with sculpted arch mouldings led to the chapter house; the arcades support a gallery from which those monks who had no voice in the chapter could listen to the proceedings.

Take r. St-Martin.

Collégiale St-Martin

23 r. St-Martin. Feb-Apr daily 2-6pm; May-Jan daily 1-7pm; Tue–Sun 1pm–6pm. Mondays, 1 Jan, 1 and 8 May, 1 and 11 Nov, 25 Dec. €4. 02 41 81 16 00. www.collegiale-saint-martin.fr.

The first church was built on this site in the 5C, outside the city walls. The nave is one of the few remaining examples in France of Carolingian architecture on a large scale. Vaulting was added to the transept crossing by Fulk Nerra (11C), and the Angevine Gothic chancel was added in the 12C, doubling the length of the church. Forty religious artefacts illustrate terra-cotta techniques of the Angevine and Le Mans schools (17C). A permanent exhibit tells the history of the collegiate church.

Take r. St-Denis to reach pl. du Ralliement.

Place du Ralliement

This lively square is the centre of town. Its shops are dominated by the monumental façade of the theatre, embellished with columns and statues.

Musée Pincé★

32 bis r. Lenepveu. Recently reopened to the public after 15 years of rennovations. Sat-Sun 10am-6pm, Mon-Sun 10am-6pm during vacations. 02 41 05 38 00. Free during 2020. www.musees.angers.fr.

This elegant Renaissance mansion, built for a mayor of Angers and bequeathed to the town in 1861, houses the **musée Turpin de Crissé** (1772–1859). A painter born in Angers and chamberlin to Empress Joséphine, he donated to the town a magnificent collection of exotic artefacts that are on display, including Greek and Etruscan vases, ceramics, and Japanese masks and prints.

▶ In r. Lenepveu, take the first left, r. de l'Espine.

Quartier St-Laud

The small rue St-Laud is the axis of a pleasant pedestrian and shopping district where a number of very old façades can be admired: particularly fine examples include No. 21 rue St-Laud (15C) and No. 9 rue des Poëliers (16C).

▶ Turn right into r. J.-Guitton to the Muséum des sciences naturelles or walk diagonally across pl. Louis-Imbach into r. St-Étienne and r. du Commerce. Cross bd. Carnot.

Muséum des Sciences Naturelles

43 r. Jules-Guitton. ⏱*Tue–Sun 10am–6pm.* 🕐*1 Jan, 1 May, 1 and 11 Nov, 25 Dec.* 💶€4. ☎*02 41 05 48 50. www.angers.fr/museum.*
Two charming historic buildings in the town centre house this treasure trove of a museum, which includes some 700 stuffed animals, 50,000 fossils, 200,000 shells and 2,500 birds.

▶ Take r. St-Étienne and r. du Commerce, then cross bd. Carnot to reach the church of St-Serge.

Église St-Serge★

Pl. du Chanoine-Bachelot.
Until 1802 this was the church of the Benedictine abbey of the same name founded in the 7C.
The 13C **chancel**★★ is remarkably wide, elegant and well lit, a perfect example of the Angevin style, with its lierne vaulting descending in feathered clusters onto slender columns. In contrast, the 15C nave seems narrower because of its massive pillars. The high windows

at the end are filled with graceful 15C stained glass.

GARDENS★
👥 Jardin des Plantes

Located behind the Centre des Congrès and opposite the old conventual buildings (18C) of St-Serge abbey church, this botanical garden is home to some rare species of tree (such as the *Davidia*, or handkerchief tree). There is a pool in the lower part of the garden. Parrots can be heard squawking in the aviary.

👥 Jardin du Mail

bd. de la Résistance-et-de-la-Déportation, opposite the hôtel de ville.
A neo-Classical garden centred on a large fountain and pond. A large play area has a roundabout for children. The garden is at its best in summer.

Parc de l'Arboretum, le jardin des collections★

7 r. du Château-d'Orgement. ♿
🕐*Normally open 8am–dusk, but call for hours.* 💶*Free.* ☎*02 41 22 53 00.*
Southwest of the town centre, this innovative garden is sheltered by the great trees of the Gaston-Allard arboretum (7ha of oak, conifer and shrubs). A superb drive lined with varities of oak leads to the house of the botanist and the park's founder, Gaston Allard (1838–1918). The garden of the senses combines perfume, touch and sight with a range of unusual flowers and fruits including the rare paper mulberry, which gives orange fruit in summer.
An oculus in the wall allows visitors to peep into the superb **National Hydrangea Collection** (*visits by appointment*).

Parc de Balzac★

Cross the Maine on pont de la Basse-Chaîne and park in the Yolande-d'Aragon car park or Farcy-Balzac car park.
🕐*daily 7.30am–8pm; rest of the year call or see website for hours.*
💶*Free.* ☎*02 41 22 53 00. www.angers.fr.*
This 50ha park links the nearby town centre with the Parc de la Maine lei-

sure complex. Along the banks of the Maine, the **floodplains** are typical of the marshlands that lie between here and the Atlantic coast, with hedgerows, poplar trees, donkeys and cattle herds. The plains are criss-crossed by raised paths. Slightly set back but still prone to flooding, the **theme areas★** show off more of the gardener's art with flower-rich fields, seedbeds and bird-filled trees. Deeper in the park, the 120 **family allotments★**, with their pink and blue huts, produce fruit and vegetables and are separated by great climbing roses. Conclude your visit with the fascinating **chênaie**, an avenue of 1,100 hybrid oaks and trees from America, China and the rest of the world, whose variety can be seen in the shape of the leaves and the acorns.

👥 Parc St-Nicolas

Les Combes entrance, bd. Lavoisier.
🕐*daily 8am–6pm.* ✎*Free.*
Four semi-natural parks form a sort of necklace of greenery along the St-Nicolas pond. They alternate carefully tended walks on the banks with more untamed vegetation on the steeper slopes in the former slate quarries. This unusual park covers 112ha in the centre of the town. It also features an animal park that is popular with children.

👥 Parc de la Maine

Access via the riverside road, follow signs for Nantes.
Some 200ha of woods and lawns surround the Lac de Maine. The leisure complex (swimming, windsurfing, canoeing, bikes, walking, tennis, golf driving range, etc.) is a popular attraction with locals at weekends.

NORTH BANK OF THE RIVER MAINE

Musée Jean-Lurçat et de la Tapisserie contemporaine★★

♿🕐*Tue–Sun 10am–6pm.* ✎€6. ✆*02 41 24 18 45. www.musees-angers.fr.*
This stunning Museum of Contemporary Tapestry is housed in the **hôpital St-Jean★**, a hospital founded in 1174 by Étienne de Marçay, Seneschal to the

Plantagenet King Henry I, which provided treatment and care for the sick until 1854. The vast hospital ward features Angevin vaulting resting on slender columns; to the right of the entrance is the 17C **dispensary★** with glazed earthenware jars and trivets on wooden shelves. In the central recess stands a splendid pewter vessel (1720) that once contained treacle, an antidote to snake bites. The room is hung with Lurçat's series of tapestries called the **Chant du Monde★★** (Song of the World). **Jean Lurçat** (1892–1966), who was largely responsible for reviving the art of tapestry, had discovered the Apocalypse Tapestry in 1938, and had been profoundly impressed by it, declaring it to be one of the masterpieces of Western art. Nineteen years later he began work on the tapestry series displayed here, his masterpiece. It is coarsely woven and characterised by an almost total lack of perspective and deliberate restriction of the range of colours.

A short distance away, the **Centre régional d'Art textile** (3 blvd. Daviers) houses workshops for about 20 warp-weavers, and organises tours and courses in the art of tapestry. The weavers here produce remarkable creations, displayed at national and international exhibits, that can be bought or hired.

La Doutre★

This district has preserved some fine half-timbered houses: on the **place de la Laiterie**, in rue Beaurepaire, which runs from the square to the bridge (particularly at No. 67, the house dated 1582 of apothecary Simon Poisson, adorned with statues), and along rue des Tonneliers. Note also the **Église de La Trinité** (12C), with its 16C bell-tower, and the **Abbaye du Ronceray,** founded in the 11C with its present buildings dating from the 17C. At No. 23 boulevard Descazeaux, don't miss the **hôtel des Pénitentes**, an elegant mansion with towers and Renaissance dormer windows. Used successively as a refuge, prison and hospice, it owes its name to the community of women who lived here in the 17C and 18C.

Le Quai

The town's strikingly modern cultural centre (2007) comprises three creative structures: the **NTA** (Nouveau Théâtre d'Angers), which stages drama; the **CNDC** (Centre national de danse contemporaine), a school of modern dance; and **Open-Arts**, which focuses on the circus, visual and street art in addition to music. The **Angers Nantes Opera** also stages some of their productions here.

The ground floor forum hosts temporary exhibits. The roof terrace offers superb **views** of the castle, town and river Maine.

ADDITIONAL SIGHT

Musée du Génie

106 r. Eblé. & ⏱*Mar–Dec Wed–Fri 1.30–6pm, Sat-Sun 2-6pm.* ⊚*free.* ☎*02 41 24 83 16. www.musee-du-genie-angers.fr.*

The collections present the expertise of firemen from Antiquity to the present day. Engravings, maps, paintings, models, uniforms and arms tell the firefighting story along with films and interactive displays. An unusual way of finding out more about the history of France.

EXCURSIONS

👥 Espace Air Passion★

Aéroport d'Angers-Loire, Marcé. 25km/15.5mi NE via A 11, Exit 12 (Seiches-sur-le-Loir).

& ⏱*Nov-Apr Sat-Sun 2-6pm, May-Sep Tue–Sat 2–6pm, Sun 3–7pm.* ⊚€*6 (child 7–18, €3).* ☎*02 41 33 04 10. www.musee-aviation-angers.fr.*

This aircraft museum illustrates the early days of flying with a display of old aeroplanes such as René Garnier's biplane, the Cri-cri air car (smallest twin-engine plane in the world) and the starck (the ancestor of microlights).

St-Barthélemy-d'Anjou

Take the Le Mans road, E on the town map; then turn right onto bd. de la Romanerie.

Carré Cointreau

& 🚂*By guided tour only, by prior request, from Apr-Dec* ⊚€*10.* ☎*02 41 31 50 50. www.carre-cointreau.fr.*

The distillery was founded in 1849 by the Cointreau brothers, who invented the orange-flavoured liqueur. Various attempts to fake it are on display here, as is the firm's own publicity material.

Château de Pignerolle★

6km/3.7mi E on D 61 (just past St-Barthélemy-d'Anjou).

This château is a replica of the Petit Trianon in Versailles. It was built in the 18C for Marcel Avril, the King's equerry and master of the Riding Academy of Angers. During WWII the castle served successively as the seat of the Polish government in exile, the headquarters of the German admiral Doenitz, and after the Liberation of France, the quarters for American units under General Patton.

Musée-château de Villevêque

44 r. du Gén.-de-Gaulle, 49140 Villevêque. & ⏱*Apr-Sep, Tue–Sun 2–6pm.* ⏱*1 May.* ⊚€*4.* ☎*02 41 76 88 07. www.musees.angers.fr.*

This former residence of the bishops of Angers has a rich collection of 12C-16C European art and a library of great importance. Daniel Duclaux, a wealthy industrialist and art lover, bequeathed them to the city of Angers.

Les Ponts-de-Cé

7km/4.3mi S on N 160.

This is a straggling town about 3km/2mi long; its main street spans a canal and several arms of the Loire, affording views from its four bridges. The history of the town includes many bloody episodes in French history. Under Charles IX 800 camp-followers were thrown into the Loire; when the château was taken from the Huguenots in 1562, any surviving defenders were treated to a similar fate.

Trélazé

7km/4.3mi E on the road to Saumur.

Trélazé is famous for its slate, which has been quarried since the 12C. When the Loire was still a commercial highway, the blue-grey slates were transported upstream by boat to roof the châteaux, manor houses and modest residences that lined the banks of the river.

A slate museum, the **Musée de l'Ardoise** (⟨symbols⟩*Tue-Fri 9am-12pm, 2-5.30pm; €5; 02 41 69 04 71; www. lemuseedelardoise.fr*), set up near a disused quarry, focuses on old and new extraction techniques and miners' lives.

St-Sylvain-d'Anjou

9km/5.6mi NE on the Le Mans road.
Archaeologists and master carpenters have worked closely together to reconstruct as faithfully as possible a medieval **motte-and-bailey**. At the end of the 10C and during the 11C and 12C, these wooden strongholds built on a steep man-made earthen mound (*motte*) with a lower courtyard (the bailey or ward), were a common defensive feature.

L'île St-Aubin

Drive N towards the Hospital then follow the signs. In spring and autumn access only by boat, bike or on foot.
On the edge of Angers, this island, covering 600ha, is a protected natural site. A signposted trail explains local flora and fauna. The boat crossing and stop at the traditional *guinguette* outdoor café are worth the trip alone.

⟨symbols⟩ Terra Botanica★

rte. de Cantenay-Epinard, 4km/2.5mi N of Angers. ⟨symbols⟩*Jun and Sept Thu–Fri 10am–6pm, Sat–Sun 10am–7pm; Jul –Aug daily 10am–7pm; mid-Apr–May call or go online.* €21 (child 3–17, €15). 02 41 25 00 00. www.terrabotanica.fr.
This botanical theme park provides a fun way of learning about nature and plant life: gardens, water areas and hothouses with 40 rides and attractions.

La Roche de Mûrs

10km/6mi from Angers on D 160, then towards Nantes, and r. de la Roche-de-Mûrs.
This promontory overlooks the Louet and offers good **views★** of the Loire Valley. The site commemorates the loss of a Republican battalion during the Revolu-

tion. In July 1793, following a season of relentless conflicts in the Vendée War, 12,000 rebels pushed the soldiers into the void and to their destruction. A monument to those who "died for the Republic" was erected to mark the centenary of the French Revolution.

⟨symbol⟩ DRIVING TOUR

LA LOIRE MAUGEOISE★

▷ Leave Angers by bd. du Bon-Pasteur then D 111, dir. Bouchemaine.

Beyond the riverside settlement of La Pointe the road leaves the Loire to wind through vineyards to Épiré, before dropping into the valley of a stream that joins the Loire at Savennières.

Béhuard★

Béhuard Island has formed around a rock on which a little church stands. A short path leads down to the Loire and a sandy beach. In the pagan era there was a shrine on the island dedicated to a marine goddess, which was replaced in the 5C by a small oratory where prayers were said for sailors in peril.

Rochefort-sur-Loire

Rochefort lies in a rural setting on the Louet. The neighbouring slopes produce the famous **Quarts de Chaume**, a distinctive and heady white wine. Several old houses, with turrets or bartizans stand on the square beneath D 751.

Corniche Angevine★

From Rochefort to Chalonnes the road (D 751) along the south bank of the Loire twists and turns through many tight bends cut into the cliff face.

La Haie-Longue

In a bend in the road at the entrance to La Haie-Longue is a chapel dedicated to **Our Lady of Loretto**, the patron saint of aviators. Legend has it that her house was carried by the breeze from Nazareth to the Dalmatian coast and thence to Loretto on the Italian coast, where it is venerated as a holy house.

Montjean-sur-Loire
The narrow streets of Montjean are confined on a rocky promontory overlooking the Loire. From the terrace near the church, there is a broad view of the Loire Valley and of villages with slate roofs mined from the local quarries.

▶ From Montjean to St-Florent take D 210.

The **road★** along the river embankment provides views over the Loire and of the slopes rising to the south of the Thau, once a tributary of the Loire.

Ingrandes
In the 17C and 18C, Ingrandes was a major port. Its position just south of the Breton border made it an important centre for smuggling salt. Anjou was subject to the salt tax, unpopular since salt was the only means of preserving food, leading to an illicit trade in the untaxed commodity.

▶ 6km/3.7mi E of Ingrandes on N 23.

Champtocé-sur-Loire
On the northeast side of the town stand the ruins of the castle of **Gilles de Rais** (1404–40), a Maréchal de France by the age of 25 and the faithful companion of Joan of Arc whom he attempted to rescue from prison in Rouen.

St-Florent-le-Vieil★
The bridge over the Loire affords a good view of the town and its hilltop church. The **Musée d'Histoire locale et des Guerres de Vendée** (◔Sat–Sun 2.30-6.30pm; ◎€3.50; ℘02 41 72 50 03; www.osezmauges.fr) housed in the 17C Sacré-Cœur Chapel, contains documents, costumes, uniforms and weapons mostly relating to the Vendée War and its leaders.

▶ West of St-Florent-le-Vieil the road (D 751) winds through gentle hills.

Chapelle de la Bourgonnière★
S on D 751, between Le Marillais and Bouzillé. ○━The chapel is private

property, but may be visited by appointment. ℘02 40 98 10 18.
Towers, turrets and buttresses adorn the edifice, which is decorated with shells, the initials LC and T-shaped crosses: all symbols of the Hospital Brothers of St Anthony.

Liré
This village in the Loire valley owes its fame to **Joachim du Bellay**, the poet, who was born not far from here.
The **Musée Joachim-du-Bellay** (◔ mid-Feb–Jun Tue-Fri 2-5.30pm; Jul–Aug Tue–Fri 10.30am–12.30pm, 2–6pm, Sun 2.30–6pm; Sep-Oct Tue-Fri 2-5.30pm; ◎€5; ℘02 40 09 04 13; www.musee-joachimdubellay.com) occupies a 16C house (restored) in the middle of the town. Mementoes of the poet are displayed on the first floor; the ground floor is devoted to local customs.

Ancenis
The town fortifications and the castle ramparts, now in ruins, once commanded the valley.

Oudon
The dominant feature of this village is the **medieval keep**, completed in 1415. From the tower's top a view of the valley unfolds.

Champtoceaux★
This village perches on a memorable **site★** overlooking the Loire valley. Behind the church, the **promenade de Champalud★★** has splendid views.

ADDRESSES

🍴 STAY

🛏 **La Petite Charnasserie,** – 60 Rue de la Charnasserie, 49100 Angers. ℘06 84 01 86 05. https://la-petite-charnasserie.business. site. A converted farmhouse B&B amid verdant loveliness. Simple, tidy rooms.

🛏🛏 **Chambre d'hôte Manoir de La Noue** – La Noue, 49190 Denée. ℘06 82 37 73 50. 4 rooms. Spacious quarters open onto a 19C-style country garden.

⊜⊟ **Grand Hôtel de la Gare** – *5 pl. de la Gare.* ℘*02 41 88 40 69. www.grandhotel delagare-angers.com. 52 rooms.* Across from the railway station, this big hotel has modern rooms and is a comfortable, convenient location to spend the night.

⊜⊟ **Logis Domaine du Moulin Cavier** – *La Croix-Cadeau, 49240 Avrillé. 8km/5mi NW of Angers.* ℘*02 41 42 30 45. www. hotelmoulincavier.com. 48 rooms.* ♿⃤. Modern rooms in a restored 18C windmill, which houses the restaurant (⊜⊟). Terrace, **pool** ⌇.

⊜⊟ **Hôtel de Champagne** – *34 av. Denis -Papin.* ℘*02 41 25 78 78. www.hotelde champagne.com. 29 rooms.* Opposite the train station, this hotel offers tastefully decorated rooms.

⊜⊟ **Hôtel le Continental** – *14 r. Louis-de-Romain.* ℘*02 41 86 94 94. www.hotel lecontinental.com. 25 rooms.* A central location in an old building with sound-proofing.

⊜⊟ **Hôtel du Mail** – *8 r. des Ursules.* ℘*02 41 25 05 25. www.hoteldumail.fr.* ⃤ *7€/day. 25 rooms.* The thick walls of this former convent keep out the noise from the nearby downtown.

⊜⊟ **Hôtel le Progrès** – *26 r. Denis-Papin.* ℘*02 41 88 10 14. www.hotelleprogres.com. 41 rooms.* Near the train station, this hotel has modern rooms. Breakfast is buffet-style.

⊜⊟ **Chambre d'hôte la Rousselière** – *49170 La Possonnière. 18km/11mi SW by D 111.* ℘*02 41 39 13 21. www.anjou-et-loire.com/rousseliere.* ⃠. *5 rooms. Closed mid-Nov–mid-Dec. Evening meal* (⊜⊟). Refined rooms with antique furnishings, set in large grounds with a **swimming pool** ⌇. Billiards, fishing. Friendly hosts.

⊜⊟⊟ **Gîte de Charme La Pointerolle** – *chemin des Landes, 49800 Trélazé.* ℘*06 47 03 38 20.* ⃤. Near Château de Pignerolle, this charming gîte sleeps 2 people in a haven of vegetation. Attractive pond in the garden. Bikes available.

⊜⊟⊟ **Hôtel de France** – *8 pl. de la Gare.* ℘*02 41 88 49 42. www.hoteldefrance-angers.com. 55 rooms.* ⃤♿. A luxury hotel with cosy rooms.

⊜⊟⊟ **Hôtel d'Anjou** – *1 Boulevard du Maréchal Foch, 49100 Angers.* ℘*02 41 21 12 11. www.hoteldanjou.fr. 53 rooms.* ⃤. This elegant hotel is a perfect base

from which to explore Angers. Each of the rooms has individual style with historical furniture, not that far from the original design of 1865. From the outside, the hotel doesn't endear itself, but the interior is tastefully opulent and plush, and with delightful idiosyncrasies like the suntrap terrace and the elegant stained glass that backs the reception desk. The integral restaurant (La Salamandre ⊜⊟⊟) has entertained musicians and artists alike.

⊜⊟⊟⊟ **Château de Noirieux** – *26 rte. du Moulin 49125 Briollay. 17km/10.5mi NE of Angers.* ℘*02 41 42 50 05. www. chateaudenoirieux.com. 19 rooms.* Elegant château overlooking the Loir, set in large grounds that are ideal for a stroll. Superbly decorated rooms and high-end cuisine in its restaurant (⊜⊟⊟⊟).

♈/EAT

⊜⊟ **Le Napoli** – *15 r. Toussaint.* ℘*02 41 87 68 09. Closed Sun.* Often considered the best pizza restaurant in Angers. Reservations recommended.

⊜⊟ **Chez Rémi** – *5 r. des Deux Haies.* ℘*02 41 24 95 44. Closed Sat lunch and all day Sun-Mon.* Inventive cuisine using fresh local market produce. Good value; reservations recommended.

⊜⊟ **Brasserie du Théâtre** – *7 pl. du Ralliement -* ℘*02 41 24 15 15.* Easy to find opposite the theatre; fresh cuisine and featuring outdoor dining, under awnings if the weather is not in your favour.

⊜⊟ **La Ferme** – *2 pl. Freppel.* ℘*02 41 87 09 90. www.restaurant-laferme.com. Closed Sun-Mon. Reservations required.* Traditional cooking from chef Bruno Besnard, and situated close to the cathedral.

⊜⊟ **Le Petit Comptoir** – *40 r. David d'Angers.* ℘*02 41 43 32 00. Closed Sun, Mon.* Lively bistro atmosphere at this crowded restaurant serving good fare at affordable prices.

⊜⊟ **Provence Caffé** – *9 pl. du Ralliement.* ℘*02 41 87 44 15. www.provence-caffe.com. Closed Sun, Mon. Reservations required.* Adjacent to Hotel St Julien, Provence Caffe specialises in fish and traditional French dishes.

⊜⊟ **Chez Pont-Pont** – *13 Promenade du Bout du Monde.* ℘*02 41 17 40 03.* Classic dishes in a diner-style environment that's relaxed and fun. Good cocktails and the occassional karaoke night for those who want to take the stage.

⊖⊖⊜ **Ma Campagne** – *14 prom. de Reculée. ℘02 41 48 38 06. www.restaurant-macampagne.fr. Closed Sun eve, Tue eve Wed eve, Mon.* Rustic décor, good food and views of the river Maine.

⊖⊖⊜ **L'Hoirie** – *2 r. Henri-Faris, 49070 Beaucouzé.* ♿🅿 *℘02 41 72 06 09. www. restaurant-lhoirie.com. Closed Sun eve, Mon.* Situated west of Angers, this restaurant emphasises fish dishes and fresh market produce in modern rooms. A little out of the way, but great food if you can make the trip.

⊖⊖⊜ **Le Relais** – *9 r. de la Gare. ℘02 41 88 42 51. Closed Sat, Sun.* Red banquettes and wall murals, appetising cuisine, excellent wine list.

⊖⊖⊜ **Une Presqu'Ile** – *9 r. Max-Richard. ℘02 41 19 14 48. www.une-ile.fr. Closed Sun, Mon.* Refined cuisine and an emphasis on regional wines in this upmarket space.

Château du Plessis-Macé★

Almost hidden amid its lush greenery, this château is protected by a wide moat. Begun in the 11C by a certain Macé, the château became the property in the mid-15C of Louis de Beaumont, the Chamberlain and favourite of Louis XI, who had it rebuilt into a residence fit to accommodate his royal master. A theatre festival is held here each June and July.

VISIT

From the outside, Le Plessis still has the appearance of a fortress with its tower-studded wall and rectangular keep, stripped of all fortifications except the battlements. Once you enter the great courtyard, you notice that the building is similar to a country residence: decorative elements in white-tufa stone enhance the dark grey of the schist; the imposing ruined keep towers over the west side of the enclosure. To the right are the out-buildings housing the stables and guard room. To the left are the chapel, an unusual staircase turret that gets larger as it goes up, and the main residential wing surmounted by pointed gables.

In the corner with the main wing is a charming **hanging gallery★**, from

⚲ **Michelin Map:** 317: E-3

ℹ **Info: Tourist office:** 7 pl. du Prés-Kennedy, BP15157 49051 Angers. ℘02 41 23 50 00. www.tourisme. destination-angers.com/.
Chateau: ♿ ⏰ *Mid-Apr–May and Sept–Oct, Wed, Sat–Sun 2–6.30pm; early Jul–Aug Mon-Fri, Sat-Sun, 10.30am-6.30pm* ⊜€6.50. 🔊 *Guided tours (30min)* ⊜€8.50. *℘02 41 32 67 93. www.chateau-plessis-mace.fr.*

▶ **Location:** 15km/9mi NW of Angers.

⏱ **Timing:** Allow 1 hour.

which the ladies would watch jousting tournaments and other entertainments. A second balcony, opposite, in the out-buildings, was reserved for the servants. The tour includes the dining room, the large banqueting hall, several bed-rooms, one of which was the King's, and the **chapel**, which still features rare 15C Gothic **panelling★** forming two levels of galleries, the first reserved for the lord and his squires, the second for the servants.

Library, Château de Serrant

© Château de Serrant

Château de Serrant★

Although built over a period of three centuries, 16C to 18C, this sumptuous moated mansion has great unity of style and perfection of detail. Its massive domed towers and the contrast between the dark schist and the white tufa give it considerable character. Today, it is classed as a Monument historique.

A BIT OF HISTORY

The **Château de Serrant** was begun in 1546 by Charles de Brie supposedly after drawings by Philibert Delorme, the architect responsible for the construction of the magnificent Palais de Fontainebleau, near Paris.

The castle was bought by Hercule de Rohan, Duke of Montbazon, in 1596, and sold in 1636 to Guillaume Bautru, whose granddaughter married the Marquis of Vaubrun, Lieutenant-General of the King's army. On the death of her husband, the Marchioness continued construction work until 1705. She commissioned Jules Hardouin-Mansart to build the beautiful chapel in memory of her husband, and Coysevox to design the mausoleum.

During the 18C, the property was acquired by Antoine Walsh, a member of the Irish nobility who followed James II into exile in France and became a shipowner in Nantes.

- **Michelin Map:** 317: E-4
- **Info:** *Guided tours (whole castle) daily 9.45am–6pm.* €10 (€5.50 for children) *or €12 (guided tour).* &02 41 39 13 01. www. chateau-serrant.net.
- **Location:** The château is off the D723 20km/10mi W of Angers, and located just before Saint-Georges-sur-Loire.
- **Don't Miss:** The furniture in the château is extremely elegant and very well preserved.
- **Timing:** Take the guided tour of the château before going to the abbey at St-George.

VISIT

In addition to the superb Renaissance staircase surmounted by coffered vaulting, the whole interior is very attractive. The **apartments★★★** are magnificently furnished; this exceptional collection of furniture was added to the list of Historic Monuments. Sumptuous Flemish and Brussels tapestries hang in the reception rooms, which contain rare pieces of furniture such as the unique ebony cabinet by Pierre Gole (17C) adorning the Grand Salon. Note also 17C, 18C and early-19C furniture by prestigious cabinet-makers (Saunier, JE de Saint-Georges) and Empire-style furniture by Jacob, upholstered with Beauvais tapestry, commissioned for Napoleon and Josephine's visit.

There are fine paintings representing the French and Italian schools, a bust of the Empress Marie-Louise by Canova, and two terra-cotta nymphs by Coysevox in the sumptuous **Grand Salon★★**.

The **library★★★** houses some 12,000 volumes. Some of the books are marked with the Trémoille seal showing four Ts and symbolising the main estates owned by the family: Trémoille, Thouars, Talmont and Tarente.

Opening onto the main courtyard, the **chapel★★**, built by Jules Hardouin-Mansart, contains the white-marble funeral monument of the Marquis de Vaubrun killed at the battle of Altenheim (1673).

EXCURSIONS
St-Georges-sur-Loire
2km/1mi W by D 723.

St-Georges, on the north bank of the Loire, is situated not far from the vineyards, the **Coulée de Serrant** and the Roche aux Moines, where some of Anjou's finest white wines are produced. The **abbey** (○*by request;* ☎*02 41 72 14 80*) was founded in 1158 by the Augustinian Order. The building (1684) contains a grand staircase with a wrought-iron banister and a chapter house with original wainscoting.

Jardins du Château du Pin
At Champtocé-sur-Loire, 8km/5mi W on D 723. Upon entering Champtocé, turn right and follow the signs. &○*May-Sep, Sun 2-7pm, visits by appointment rest of week.* ☞€5. ☎*06 11 68 61 81. www.jardinsduchateaudupin.com. Plant Day celebrated last weekend in May and last weekend in Sept.*

The gardens around this 12C–15C château cover 14 different levels and 5ha. Highlights include a collection of citrus, avocado, banana and oleander trees. Perennials, irises, lavender and yellow roses surround ponds. The 700-year old chestnut walk, kitchen garden and elegant 18C chapel with its working clock (16C) complete the bucolic scene.

Vallée du Layon

The Layon River flows into the Loire downstream of Angers. The region is pretty with vineyards, fields of crops interspersed with fruit trees (walnut, peach, plum), hillsides crowned with windmills and wine-growing villages with graveyards in which dark green cypress trees grow.

- ⚲ **Michelin Map:** 317: E-4–H-6
- ▯ **Info:** Loire Layon Aubance, pl. de l'Hôtel-de-Ville, 49290 Chalonnes-sur-Loire. ☎02 41 78 26 21. www.loire-layon-aubance-tourisme.com.
- ⊛ **Don't Miss:** The delicious mellow white wines of the Layon vineyards produced by the chenin, a variety of grape often known as pineau. Bonnezeaux and Quarts de Chaume are well-known wines from this area.

🚗 DRIVING TOUR

THE VINEYARDS
60km/37mi. Allow 3h.

▷ Begin in Passavant-sur-Layon along the D 170.

Passavant-sur-Layon
This pretty village on the edge of a lake is enhanced by the ruins of its castle.

▷ Take D 170 to Nueil-sur-Layon; go right after the church onto D 77; after the bridge over the Layon bear left onto D 69 towards Doué-la-Fontaine.

The landscape at this point is typical of the Poitou: hedgerows, sunken roads and farmsteads roofed with tiles. Vineyards are grouped on the exposed slopes. Note at Nueil the slate roofs, more typical of northern France.

▶ Beyond Les Verchers-sur-Layon, bear left onto D 178 towards Concouron. The road runs parallel with the Layon River through fertile countryside. In St-Georges-sur-Layon head N towards Brigné, turning left onto D 83 to Martigné-Briand.

Martigné-Briand

This wine-growing village lies clustered round a château built in the early 16C.

▶ Take D 748 SW towards Aubigné, turning right to Villeneuve-la-Barre.

Aubigné-sur-Layon

This delightful village still has several elegant old town houses. Near the 11C church stands an old fortified gateway where the remains of the portcullis and drawbridge can still be seen.

▶ Leave Aubigné on D 408 to Faveraye-Mâchelles and turn right onto D 120. After crossing D 24 bear left onto D 125.

Rablay-sur-Layon

This pretty little wine-growing village occupies a well-sheltered site. In Grande-Rue there is a brick and half-timbered tithe house (15C) with an overhanging upper storey. A building dating from the 17C now houses artists' studios.

▶ The road (D 54) crosses the Layon, then skirts a cirque with vine-clad slopes; from the plateau there is a broad view of the valley.

🚶 A disused railway line converted into a footpath follows the Layon, offering strolls in pastoral surroundings.

Beaulieu-sur-Layon

This wine-growing village amid the Layon vineyards has attractive mansard-roofed houses.
The main road drops into the valley, past the steep sides riddled with caves and quarries. At Pont-Barré there is a view of the narrow course of the Layon and a ruined medieval bridge, scene of a bloody struggle on 19 September 1793 (♿see CHOLET).

▶ Drive to D 160 and follow it S.

St-Lambert-du-Lattay

Wine-growing and cooperage tools, illustrations, a collection of presses and commentaries embody the living memory of a people who have always been engaged in the cultivation of the grape at the **Musée de la Vigne et du Vin d'Anjou** (♿🕐*Apr–Jun Wed–Sun and public holidays 2.30–6.30pm; Jul–Aug 10.30am–12.30pm, 2.30–6.30pm; Sept–early Nov Sat–Sun and public holidays 2.30–6.30pm; for visit and wine tasting only: mid-Apr–early Nov 2 Sun per month at 3.30pm, but Jul–Aug Wed–Fri and Sun 3.30pm;*✏€6; *☎02 41 78 42 75; www.musee-vigne-vin-anjou.fr).* The room entitled *L'Imaginaire du Vin* appeals to visitors' senses of sight, smell and taste in a display on wine that emphasises bouquet and flavour.

▶ Before entering St-Aubin-de-Luigné turn left onto D 106; soon after turn right.

Château de la Haute-Guerche

♿🕐*Jul–Sep 9am–noon, 1–5pm; rest of the year by appointment. ☎02 41 78 41 48. www.anjouhauteguerche.com.*
This castle was built in the reign of Charles VII and burned down in the Vendée Wars; all that can now be seen from the valley are its ruined towers.

▶ Return to St-Aubin then drive to Chaudefonds and on to Ardenay to the **Corniche Angevine★** (♿see ANGERS: La Loire Maugeoise) back to Angers.

Cholet

Cholet is a thriving industrial town, with a long-standing tradition as a textile centre. Surrounded by the pastures of Les Mauges, it is also an important cattle market. There is scarcely a building in Cholet that dates from before the Revolution since the town suffered sorely in the Vendée War (☉see box opposite).

SIGHTS

Musée d'Art et d'Histoire★

27 av. de l'Abreuvoir. ♿☉*Wed–Sat and public holidays 10am–noon, 2–6pm, Sun 2–6pm (also Mon in Jul–Aug).* ☉*1 Jan, 1 May, 25 Dec.* ☜€4. ℘*02 72 77 23 22.* *www.cholet.fr/musee-art-histoire.php.* Housed in a building opposite the Hôtel de Ville, the Art and History Museum consists of two separate galleries.

The **History Gallery** evokes Cholet in 1793, as well as the Vendée wars (1793–96, 1815, 1832) and the sequence of events that ravaged the city.

The **Art Gallery** has a strong 18C collection with works by the local artist Pierre-Charles Trémolières (1703–39).

Musée du Textile

R. du Dr-Roux. ♿☉*Wed–Sat and public holidays 10am–noon, 2–6pm, Sun 2–6pm (also Mon in Jul–Aug).* ☉*1 Jan, 1 May, 25 Dec.* ☜€2.50 ℘*02 72 77 22 50. www.museedutextile.com.*

- ▶ **Population:** 53,800.
- ⚲ **Michelin Map:** 317: D-6
- 🈺 **Info:** 14 av. Maudet, 49306 Cholet. ℘02 41 49 80 00. www.ot-cholet.fr.
- ▶ **Location:** 70km/44mi SW of Angers and from Nantes (to the SE); 120km/74.5mi NW of Poitiers.
- 🅿 **Parking:** Mainly on-street parking in the town centre.
- ☺ **Don't Miss:** The Textile Museum, and the Parc oriental de Maulévrier.
- ◐ **Timing:** Allow 1–2 hours to explore the town, but a whole day for the locality.
- ♟ **Kids:** The watersports at Lac de Ribou.

This museum has been set up in an old bleaching house by the River Sauvageau, a remarkable piece of 19C industrial heritage. The visit begins in an unusual modern building, modelled on Crystal Palace in London. This demonstration room houses four looms still in working order, the oldest dating from 1910. Next comes the steam-engine room, in which the furnace and enormous machinery generated the energy for the entire factory. Rooms following trace the history of textiles, in particular the famous **white Cholet** (☉see box p273).

Alexandre Marcel (1860–1928)

The Parisian architect Alexandre Marcel restored many old buildings before gaining recognition for his thermal baths (*Grands Thermes*) in Châtelguyon, private mansions in Paris and Cholet, and a magnificent palace for the Maharajah of Kapurthala. His love of the Orient resulted in La Pagode (*now a cinema*) in rue Babylone in Paris and acclaimed buildings for several international exhibitions. He designed the Round the World Panorama (*Panorama du Tour du Monde*) hall for the French shipping company Messageries Maritimes, and the Cambodian Pavilion, in which he reproduced parts of the Temple of Angkor Wat for the Universal Exhibition in 1900.

Thanks to these constructions, he was brought to the notice of King Leopold II of Belgium, who asked him to rebuild, in Laeken Park (Brussels), the Japanese Tower and Chinese Pavilion, which would have otherwise been demolished.

The Vendée War (1793–96)

At the beginning of the peasant insurrection, the town was captured by the Royalist Whites (15 March 1793), who then regrouped before marching victoriously on Saumur and Angers. On 17 October, Cholet was captured by Kléber after a bloody battle in which 40,000 Whites faced 25,000 Blues; the victor described it as a "battle between lions and tigers"; the dead numbered 10,000. Between 60,000 and 80,000 Whites – panic-stricken men, women and children – crossed the Loire. In an episode that became a byword for brutality in French annals, the survivors were massacred in their thousands, shot down or drowned in the Loire. General Westermann wrote a chilling account of events to the Convention: "There is no more Vendée; it has died under our sword of liberty …. I have had the children crushed under horses' feet and the women massacred. I have not a single prisoner with which to reproach myself."

On 10 March 1794, after vicious hand-to-hand fighting in the streets, Jean-Nicolas Stofflet won Cholet back for the Whites, but a few days later the "infernal columns" under General Turreau put Cholet to fire and the sword. On 18 March Stofflet returned once more, but was soon driven out by General Cordellier, leaving the town of Cholet in ruins.

EXCURSIONS

🏃‍♂️ Lac de Ribou
3.5km/2mi SE
This vast reservoir encircled by hills provides facilities for a variety of **water sports** including windsurfing, rowing, sailing, etc. as well as fishing (*CISPA, Port de Ribou*). The gently sloping, grassy shores are suitable for other sports such as archery, golf and riding. ⚠ There is also a camp site.

Lac du Verdon
5km/3.1mi SE
This lake lies immediately downstream from the Lac de Ribou and covers an area of 280ha. One end of the lake stretches into the hills. The lake has become a nature reserve for **migratory birds**, which flock here in thousands.

Maulévrier
13km/8mi SE along the D 20
The name Maulévrier is believed to date from the Merovingian period and means bad greyhound (*mauvais lévrier*).
Fulk Nerra built the first castle here in 1036 and set up a barony which, under Louis XIV, was passed on to Colbert's brother, whose descendants owned it until 1895.

A monument in the park honours J-N **Stofflet**, who defended the town in 1794 for the Royalists (⚟*see box above*). The castle, which was partly destroyed during the Revolution, was rebuilt to its original plan in the 19C. At the end of the century, a manufacturer from Cholet called upon the architect **Alexandre Marcel** to restore it and lay out an Oriental-style park in the grounds. Today Maulévrier is well known for its greyhound races.

Parc Oriental de Maulévrier★
🕐*Mar, Oct-Nov, Mon-Fri 2-6pm, Sat-Sun, 1.30-6.30pm; Apr-Jun, Sep, Mon-Fri 1.30-6.30pm, Sat-Sun 10.30am-7pm; Jul-Aug, 10.30am-7pm. Night garden open in May-Sep, see website for hours* ⚟€8, €10 night garden. 📞02 41 55 50 14. www.parc-oriental.com.
The terraces of Colbert Castle overlook the Oriental park's 28ha. It was laid out by Alexandre Marcel between 1899 and 1910. Designed to resemble a Japanese garden, it was laid out around a peaceful lake to represent the changing seasons and the progression of living things.
🚶 A path with Japanese lanterns leads around the lake through exotic species of shrubs and trees (Japanese maples,

magnolia stellata, cryptomerias, flowering cherries and aucubas) to a pagoda and garden with a spring. Beyond the shadowy lanes of conifers are a bonsai exhibit and a Raku earthenware workshop.

👁 *The best time of year to visit the park is mid-April to mid-May and mid-October to mid-November.*

Forêt de Maulévrier

The **Cimetière des Martyrs** in the Maine-et-Loire is surrounded by a forest of tall oak trees. During the Vendée War, Stofflet used the inaccessibility of this cemetery to conceal his headquarters where the wounded were brought for treatment.

On 25 March 1794, however, the Blues penetrated the forest and massacred 1,200 of the Whites; two days later the latter took their revenge with a second massacre. The commemorative chapel standing alone in the forest is now a peaceful place.

Château du Coudray-Montbault

The moated 16C château with its two massive round towers of brick and stone and green lozenge decoration was built on the ruins of a 13C castle.

🚗 DRIVING TOUR

LES MAUGES
123km/76mi. Allow about 1 day.

The southern part of Anjou, on the borders of the Vendée and Poitou, which is known as Les Mauges, is a peaceful, somewhat secluded region. Les Mauges is a mixture of woodland and pasture used for cattle rearing, where the Durham-Mancelle breed is fattened before being sold in its thousands at the markets in Chemillé and Cholet.

The straight main roads, which were laid down during the Revolution and under the Empire for political reasons, are superimposed on a network of deep lanes well-suited to the ambushes that played a prominent part in the Vendée War. The windmills still crowning the

hillsides were often used by the Royalist Whites to send signals.

▶ Drive NW out of Cholet on D 752.

Beaupréau

Beaupréau is a small town built on a steep slope on the north bank of the River Èvre. In 1793 it was the headquarters of the Whites; their leader, D'Elbée, owned a manor at St-Martin, on the east side of the town, which now houses the public library. The 15C **château** overlooking the River Evre (good view from the south bank) is now a clinic.

▶ Continue along D 752 then turn left onto D 17.

Le Fuilet

Le Fuilet and neighbouring hamlets (Les Challonges, Bellevue, Les Recoins and others) stand on excellent clay soil that has given rise to brickworks and potteries producing ornamental, horticultural and artistic articles (🕐 *open to the public during working hours*).

▶ Retrace your steps and drive along D 17 to St-Laurent-de-la-Plaine.

St-Florent-le-Veil

The Angevine chapter in the Vendée insurrection began here during the Revolution. It was here that Royalist commander Jacques Cathelineau died on 14 July and the Marquis de Bonchamps, mortally wounded, freed 5,000 Republican prisoners held in the church.

Église abbatiale

The historic stained-glass windows in the chancel portray the insurrection of 12 March 1793, the death of Cathelineau, the prisoners on the field of martyrs, the farewell of Robin the curate and the peace of St-Florent.

▶ Follow D 751 to Mesnil-en-Vallée. Around 1km/0.6mi after the village, turn right to Pommeraye, then take D 131. Before reaching St-Laurent-de-la-Plaine, stop by the chapel on the left.

Cholet Handkerchiefs

Weaving is a long-established industry in Cholet, where hemp and flax have been cultivated and spun since the 11C. In the 16C, the handkerchief was introduced into France from Italy. In the 17C, as the practice of bleaching cloth became ever more widespread, local manufacturers came up with a whiteness for which Cholet was to become famous, by spreading their cloth out to bleach in the sun on green meadows where the damp clay soil prevented it drying out too much. In the 18C, Cholet cloth was part of the cargo of manufactured goods that the shipowners of Nantes and La Rochelle traded on the coasts of Africa in exchange for slaves. The slaves were then sold in the West Indies, where rum bought with the profits was imported into France, in the notorious trade triangle.

Despite the devastation wrought on the town during the revolutionary wars, Cholet was not destroyed; it re-established its crafts and tenaciously fostered its textile industry throughout the 19C. Cholet table and bed linen is now renowned for its high quality and as well known as the traditional red Cholet handkerchief, which is holding its own against stiff competition from abroad and from the disposable handkerchief industry. Many French department stores traditionally hold cut-price sales of table and bed linen in January – *le mois du blanc:* the "white sale" is an idea that originated in Cholet!

Chapelle Notre-Dame-de-la-Charité

Two fine stained-glass windows illustrate Cathelineau's pilgrimage to the chapel, and the apparition of the Virgin in an oak tree at this ancient place of worship. A cross marks the spot of the tree that was destroyed by the Revolutionary "Blues" on 29 August 1791. Half the population of St-Laurent-de-la-Plaine died in the prisons of Angers and on the Avrillé field of martyrs.

St-Laurent-de-la-Plaine

A museum of traditional crafts, the **Musée des Métiers★** ♣♦(◎*Mar–May Sun and public holidays 2.30–6.30pm, plus half-term weeks in Apr; Jun and Sept–Oct Tue–Fri and Sun 2.30–6.30pm; Jul–Aug Tue–Fri 10am–1pm, 2.30–6.30pm, Sat–Sun and public holidays 2.30–6.30pm;*⊛€6, child 6–15, €4; ℘02 41 78 24 08; www.musee-metiers.fr), is housed in a complex of several buildings, among them the 18C vicarage: one of the only two houses in the village to survive the ravages of the Republicans in 1794. About 70 trades are illustrated with implements collected from all over France. In addition to the traditional exhibition rooms (lace), a number of **workshops** have been reconstructed.

▷ Take D17 E to Bourgneuf-en-Mauges, then turn left on D 762.

Le Pin-en-Mauges

The statue of local hero , Jacques Cathelineau, dominates the centre of the village. Behind it, the neo-Gothic church of St-Pavin (1893) houses a remarkable collection of 15 historic **stained-glass windows★**, the work of Jean Clamens (1896–99). The scenes show the entire story of the Vendée War, its generals, mainly Cathelineau, known as the "Saint of Anjou". In the north transept, his tomb (parts of his remains lie in St-Florent-le-Vieil) is the work of Choletais Biron, who portrays him sword in hand. The small **musée Cathelineau** is open upon appointment – ℘02 41 75 38 31 (Beaupréau tourist office).

▷ Leave the village S and take D 15 to Jallais, then D 756.

Chemillé

This town is an important centre for stock-rearing and for the production of medicinal plants (demonstration garden with some 300 species of plants in the grounds of the town hall). In place du Château there is a 13C doorway with honeycomb decoration

▶ At the N end of the town, take D 160 towards Angers. After l'Espérance, turn right.

Chanzeaux

As you continue along the lush Vallée de l'Hyrôme, making a slight detour into the the Loir-Layon country, first note the 16C château as you take the wide bend just before the village. The church, burnt down in 1794 and rebuilt in the 19C, backs onto a 13C bell-tower. On 9 April 1795, 10 women and 18 men, including a priest, took refuge in this tower and held out for 5 hours before it was torched. In the church at the foot of the tower, a stained-glass window by Jean Clamens portrays the tragic event, another in the series of massacres in Chanzeaux which saw over half its population (700 victims) killed during the Revolution. Several stained-glass windows (1955) illustrate the main events of the Vendée War.

▶ Leave by the S, follow D 121 to Valanjou, then D 84. After la Commerie, turn right and take D 169 to Montilliers.

Montilliers

The church (1900) was rebuilt around the 11C chancel and bell-tower. It features stained-glass windows including the "massacre of the Moulin de la Reine" by Jean Clamens, in which the "Blues" spared the lives of only two children.

▶ Leave the village by the S on D 748, drive through Vihiers and take D 960 towards Cholet for about 3km/2mi. Turn right on D 756 towards Chemillé.

La Salle-de-Vihiers

You are now back in Les Mauges. The historic stained-glass windows can be seen in the south transept of the church of St-Martin (late 19C) . In 1794, 30 women and children from the village were gunned down by one of General Turreau's infamous roving firing squads, the *colonnes infernales*.

▶ Head S on D 171 to Coron, then turn right on D 960 to Cholet.

ADDRESSES

🛏 STAY

Chambre d'hôte Parfum d'Ici et d'ailleurs – *La Foy Moreau, 49450 La Renaudière.* ℘*02 41 30 85 20. www. lafoymoreau.com. 4 rooms.* 🅿. This converted farmhouse has an agricultural feel. Rooms are decorated in styles from rustic to Spanish. Home-raised meat served for the *table d'hôte* dinners (🍽).

Chambre d'hôte Le Clos du Marais – *6 chemin du Marais, 49120 Chemillé.* ℘*02 41 30 67 23 or 06 23 83 27 93. www.closdumarais.com. 5 rooms.* 🅿. This large house on the hills of Chemillé sports a rich décor. The rooms occupy the mezzanine floor.

Park Hôtel – *4 av. Anatole-Manceau.* ℘*02 41 62 65 45. www. qualys-park-hotel.fr. 54 rooms.* ♿🅿. Find streamlined, functional, sound-proof rooms at this modern hotel in the centre of Cholet. Breakfast buffet.

San Benedetto Hôtel – *26 bd Gustave-Richard.* ℘*02 41 62 07 20. www. sanbenedetto-hotel.com. 50 rooms.* ♿🅿. This Best Western hotel exudes modern design throughout. Bold-coloured rooms have techy gadgets.

🍴 EAT

La Grange – *64 r. de St-Antoine.* ℘*02 41 62 09 83. www.lagrangecholet.fr. Closed Wed eve, Sun eve, Mon.* Exposed beams and fireplace grace this former farmhouse. Contemporary cuisine.

L'Ourdissoir – *40 r. St-Bonaventure.* ℘*02 41 58 55 18. https://lourdissoir.com. Closed Sun, Mon.* This restaurant in the heart of Cholet has two rustic dining rooms, one a former weaving workshop.

Le Pouce Pied – *1 r. du Lait-de-Beurre.* ℘*02 41 58 50 03. Closed 2 wks Aug, Sat lunch, Sun eve, Mon.* This small restaurant is slightly away from the town centre. Flavourful food.

LEISURE ACTIVITIES

Centre d'Initiation aux Sports de Plein-Air (CISPA) – *37 Allée de la Roche du Ribale.* ℘*02 41 49 80 60. www.cholet-sports-loisirs. fr/cispa.* The centre sits in a green valley next to an artificial lake. Equipment hire for sailing, wind-surfing, canoeing and kayaking.

Sandwiched between Normandy and the Loire valley, the sleepy rural *département* of Mayenne has a seductive low-key charm. Its classic *bocage* landscapes hold much to discover among the undulating fields and hedgerows, including châteaux dating from the 11C, richly frescoed Romanesque churches and the charming ancient towns of Laval and Château-Gontier-sur-Mayenne straddling the River Mayenne as it winds its way south to join the Loire at Angers.

Working Rural Idyll

Green fields provide pasture for dairy cows. Laval might be an unshowy sort of provincial town, but the quaysides make for pleasant strolling, punctuated by a café pause along the Mayenne to take in the imposing 11C château looming above. Don't miss its excellent museum that pays tribute to a local lad made good, the painter Henri Rousseau.

Detour off to the east, and you are in the region known as the Alpes Mancelles – scarcely Alpine, but it is at least verdant and hilly, with pretty villages, orchards and fields of grazing sheep forming a backdrop to a foray underground into the Grottes de Saulges.

Back on the banks of the Mayenne, the delightful old town of Château-Gontier is dominated by the bell-tower of the Romanesque church of St-Jean-Baptiste.

Chasing Châteaux

Château-hounds should take in a trip to Segré, with its bustling quaysides and old stone bridge on the Oudon, where you will find the Château de la

Highlights

1 Old **Laval** and its Château (p277)
2 Impressive cave paintings at the **Grottes de Saulges** (p279)
3 **Château-Gontier-sur-Mayenne** old town (p280)
4 **Château de Plessis-Bourré**, and its fully working drawbridge (p284)
5 Segré and the sumptious **Château de la Lorie** (p286)

Lorie 's richly decorated interior. Also on the Oudon, the white stone château at medieval Craon is worth visiting as well. The stand-out star of the region, however, is to be found at Le Plessis-Bourré, where the magnificent moated 15C château is the stuff of fantasy, offering a unique insight into the life of a Renaissance lord of the manor. No surprise then, that its fairy-tale turrets and fully working drawbridge have been the setting for numerous films.

Vieux Château and the lock on the Mayenne, Laval

© Franck Guiziou/hemis.fr

LAVAL AND THE VALLEY OF THE MAYENNE

0   10 km
0   5 miles

ANGERS   ★★   Worth a detour

LAVAL   ★   Interesting

Daon   Other sight described

Driving tour with departure town

N

CAEN   ALENÇON

N 12

D 23   D 34

N 12

Mayenne

D 35

MAYENNE

N 162

D 32   Évron

Montsûrs

D 31

RENNES

Vitré

D 857

N 157

D 178

D 57

A 81

Abb⁰ de Clermont

LAVAL

A 81

D 57

LE MANS

ILLE-ET-VILAINE

D 178

D 32

D 771

Trappe du Port-du-Salut   Parné-s-Roc

Entrammes

Grotte de Rochefort
Grotte à Margot
St-Cénéré

Saulges

D 127   D 11

D 25

Cossé-le-Vivien

Mayenne

N 162

D 21

D 24

St-Aignan-sur-Roë

Oudon

Craon

D 22

D 28

D 309

Château-Gontier

RENNES

D 11

D 771

Renazé

La Maroutière

St-Denis-d'Anjou

Refuge de l'Arche

St-Ouen

Chemazé

D 20

Vaux

L'Escoublère

Varennes-Bourreau

D 6   D 771

Mortiercrolles

Daon

D 22

Miré

D 768

Sarthe

D 859

Pouancé

D 775

Domaine de la Petite Couère

D 25

D 923

La Jaille-Yvon

Marigné

D 78

La Mine-Bleue

Nyoiseau

Chambellay

Chenillé-Changé

D 878

Menhir de Pierre Frite

Segré

Le Bois-Montbourcher

D 181

Le Bourg-d'Iré

La Lorie

Haras national du Lion d'Angers

D 6

D 923

Raguin

D 73

Le Lion-d'Angers

D 770

La Hamonnière

Montriou

La Motte-Glain

D 163

D 770

D 187   D 191

Grez-Neuville

D 768

Le Plessis-Bourré

D 74

LE MANS

Candé

D 57

Le Plessis-Macé

D 775

Le Sautret

Terra Botanica

Loir

D 52   D 323

A 11

SAUMUR

MAINE-ET-LOIRE

D 963

Montreuil-Juigné

Île St-Aubin

LOIRE-ATLANTIQUE

D 923

A 11

D 723

Champtocé-sur-Loire

A 11

D 723

ANGERS

St-Barthélemy-d'Anjou

Pignerolle

D 347

Ancenis

D 723   D 10

Ingrandes

Varades

LOIRE

D 210   D 15

Montjean-sur-L.

SERRANT

St-Georges-sur-L.

Les Ponts-de-Cé

D 106

Loire

D 111

Trélazé

D 952

NANTES

D 751

D 751

St-Florent-le-Vieil

D 752

La Bourgonnière

D 131

La Ch.
de Charité

D 762

Savennières

Béhuard

Corniche angevine

Chalonnes-sur-Loire

A 87

Mûrs-Érigné

Brissac

D 748   D 761

POITIERS

CHOLET

A   B

Laval★

Laval has neither jungles nor tigers, but the artist Henri "Douanier" Rousseau is still the star of the Museum of Naïve Art in the old château. His work is an inspiration to travel, one which the famous navigator Alain Gerbault would not deny. The timbered houses of his charming native town lead down to the quaysides of the Mayenne, just the spot for a boat trip.

▶ **Population:** 49,848
◔ **Michelin Map:** 310-E6
🗎 **Info:** 84 avenue Robert Buron. ℘02 43 49 46 46. www.laval-tourisme.com.
◖ **Location:** 32km/20mi S of Mayenne on N 162. Le Mans lies 86km/54mi to the E on D 57.
👥 **Kids:** Learn all about milk at Lactopole.
🕐 **Timing:** Allow 1 hour to explore Old Town on foot.

OLD TOWN★

The core of the medieval town climbs above the right bank of the Mayenne and huddles against the château. The modern town sprawls north of the walls and along the opposite bank.

Place de La Trémoille

The square is named after Prince Antoine-Phillipe de Talmont, Duke of La Trémoille. Its highlight is the Renaissance façade of the **Château-Neuf**, the seat of the Counts of Laval since the 16C. Until 2001, it housed the palais de justice (law courts); today it is renovated as a cultural centre.

Vieux Château★

pl. de la Trémoille. 🕐 *Jun–Sept Tue–Sat 9.30am–noon, 1.30–6.30pm, Sun 2–4pm; Oct–May Tue–Sat 9.30am–noon, 1.30–5.30pm, Sun 2–6pm.* 🕐*Public holidays except 14 Jul and 15 Aug.* ⊛€3. ℘02 53 74 12 30.
Climb the ramparts for a superb **view**★ of the roofscape of the old town, and spot the statue of **Béatrix de Gavre**, a Baroness of Laval who helped develop the town's weaving trade in the 14C, the golden age for linen weaving throughout the region. Nowadays, the mills produce cotton and synthetic textiles. Although its crypt and keep date back to the 12C and 13C, the château was built mainly between the 13C and 15C; its rooms are hung with paintings by French and foreign artists.
Amazingly, the **keep** still has its original roofing, as well as the **hourd**★★, a wooden gallery jutting from the wall to help defend the bridge and base of the ramparts, which are 2m thick to support its weight.

Musée d'Art Naïf et des Arts Singuliers (MANAS)★

The studio of **Henri Rousseau** (1844–1910) nicknamed the "Douanier" or customs officer, is re-created here using memorabilia and a couple of his works. A native of Laval, the naïve artist used to measure up his subjects like a tailor before painting them. The writer **Alfred Jarry**, who also hailed from Laval, is featured in one of his works.

QUAYSIDE★

The best **views**★ of Laval are to be had from the quaysides of the Mayenne. Seen from the humpbacked **Pont Vieux** bridge, the old town is a knot of slate roofs and narrow streets of timbered houses beneath the castle keep.

Jardin de la Perrine★

The terraced gardens offer rose beds, lawns, flowery parterres, water features and mature trees such as cedars of Lebanon, as well as fine views of the Mayenne, lower town and castle keep. The **Espace Alain Gerbault** (🕐*Jun–Sept Tue–Sun 1.30–6.30pm; ℘02 43 56 81 49; www.patrimoine.laval.fr) celebrates the life of the little-known Lavallois navigator who crossed the Atlantic in 1923 in a single-masted cutter and lived out his life in Polynesia.

Centre de Culture scientifique, technique et industriel (CCSTI)

◷Tue–Fri 10am–noon, 1.30–6pm, Sat 10am–noon, 2.–5.30pm, Sun 2–6pm. ◷Mondays and public holidays. ⌖€2. ℰ02 43 49 47 81. www.ccsti-laval.org.

Housed in an imposing building (the metal sculptures flanking the central staircase are by Gardet), this institution aims to spark dialogue and exposure to the sciences and developing technologies through exhibitions and cultural events.

ADDITIONAL SIGHTS

Église Notre-Dame-des-Cordeliers★

◷Daily except Sun 8am–7pm.

Built between 1397 and 1407 for a Franciscan brotherhood, this church – the former convent chapel – houses a remarkable collection of seven altar-pieces in limestone and marble by the Lavallois architect Pierre Corbineau. The Corbineau family made Laval into a renowned centre for the production of Baroque altarpieces in the 17C.

♣♣ La Cité du Lait, Lactopole André-Besnier★★

r. Adolphe-Beck (towards Tours). ⌖⌖⌖Guided tour only Jul–Aug daily 3pm; school holidays Mon–Fri 3pm; rest of the year by reservation. ⌖€10 (child 6–12, €2; 12–18, €6.50; under 6 free). ℰ02 43 59 51 90. www.lactopole.com.

This dairy museum offers a fascinating modern interpretation covering all visitors could ever want to know about milk, dairy products and the people who have produced them.

EXCURSIONS

Abbaye de Clairmont

16km/10mi W on D57, then right onto D 115 at la Chapelle-du-Chene. ◷Daily 9am until dusk. €6. Guided tours on request for parties of four or more . ℰ02 43 02 11 96. www.abbaye-de-clairmont.com.

The ruined abbey sits in a rustic site. The layout of the six windows of the chancel and the rectangular chapels in the transept conform to Cistercian style.

Entrammes

13km/8mi S of Laval on N 162.

Taken from the Latin inter amnes meaning 'between rivers', this small town does indeed sit at a ford on the confluence of several waterways. During restoration work on the church, remnants of a Gallo-Roman era **thermal bath** came to light.

Trappe du Port-du-Salut

13km/8mi S of Laval on N 162.

Monks made the famous Port-Salut cheese on this site until 1959. Nowadays the monastic community makes a living from a small dam visible across the Mayenne, producing electricity.

Parné-sur-Roc

14km/8.5mi S of Laval on N 162, then D 21.

This little village perched on a rocky outcrop boasts an 11C church which is home to interesting 15C and 16C murals.

ADDRESSES

🛏 STAY

⌖⌖ **Hôtel Marin** – 102 av. R Buron ℰ02 43 53 09 68. www.marin-hotel.fr. 26 rooms. 🅿. The badges on the walls speak of an ancient building, but the rooms are modern.

🍴 EAT

⌖⌖ **L'Esprit Cuisine** – 8 r. Mazagran. 53810. ♿ ℰ02 43 56 78 51. www.lesprit cuisine.fr. Closed Sun, Mon. Contemporary dishes based on fresh local ingredients. Open kitchen.

Saulges

Surrounded by the *bocage* landscapes of the mayennais, this enchanting town will delight lovers of both nature and history with its bright landscapes dominating the Erve valley, the church built over a Merovingian cemetery, the mysterious legends of its 20 prehistoric caves, and a well whose waters have magical properties.

▶ **Population:** 312.
◉ **Michelin Map:** 310 G-7
▤ **Info:** 4 pl. Jacques-Favrot, 53340 Saulges. ✆02 43 58 42 28. www.saulges.fr.
◐ **Location:** 40km/24.5mi SE of Laval.
◔ **Timing:** Allow half a day for the caves and Saulges.
▲▲ **Kids:** Rock climbing and exploring caves.

THE TOWN
Église St-Pierre
Opposite the parish church on the village square. In the **chapelle St-Sérénède** (16C), the relics of the eponymous saint who spread the gospel throughout the region in the 7C are venerated. Descend a few steps into the little **chapelle St-Pierre,** a rare vestige of the Merovingian era built by Saint Cénéré in the mid-7C.

ADDITIONAL SIGHTS
Oratoire St-Cénéré
1km/0.6mi W. Leave Saulges itoward Vaiges, go left along a gently sloping lane as far as the car park.
A footbridge straddling the river leads to the hermitage, which occupies a tree-shaded spot at the foot of the rocks. Every year pilgrims flock here to pray to the saint and drink from the miraculous spring that he is said to have caused to gush forth. The River Erve broadens to form a small lake popular with anglers.

▲▲ Grottes de Saulges – le Musée de Préhistoire
Entrance to the caves is north of the village. ❧ *Guided tours: mid-Mar–Jun and Sept–mid-Nov Mon–Fri 2–4pm, Sat–Sun and public holidays 10.30am–5pm; Jul–Aug daily 10.30am–6pm.* ▧*1 cave €6.50 (children €4.50), 2 caves €11 (children €7), museum €5 (children €3.50) or €6 for guided tour (children €4).* ✆02 43 90 51 30. www.grottes-musee-de-saulges.com.
The first prehistoric decorations were discovered here in 2005. Inside are rock formations and a wealth of bone fragments and flint tools that attest to human occupation during the paleolithic era. The **Grotte at Margot** has narrow passageways and decorations, while the **Grotte de Rochefort** contains a small underground lake.

Moulin de Thévalles
5min from the Grottes de Saulges. ◔*May–Sept daily (closed Sun and Mon mornings) 10am–noon and 2–6pm.* ▧*€5.* ✆02 43 98 66 70. www.moulin-de-thevalles.com.
This historic water-powered gristmill is one of the few still functioning in France. Its milling mechanisms are distributed throughout four levels, allowing visitors watch spelt kernels being ground into flour.

ADDRESSES

🏨 STAY
🛏🛏🛏 **Hôtel Ermitage** – *r. des Deux-Églises.* ✆02 43 64 66 00. www.hotel-ermitage.fr. ▣. Adjoining the Église St-Pierre, this hotel has a gym, **pool** ⊿ and garden. Spacious rooms are situated in the modern wing. Restaurant on-site.

LEISURE ACTIVITIES
Ateliers préhistoriques – www.grottes-musee-de-saulges.com. *May–Jun and Sept–Oct.* Workshops cover prehistoric jewellery, make-up and stone-age cave art.

Site d'escalade (rock climbing) – www.escaladeenmayenne.fr.

Château-Gontier

On the border between Brittany and the Maine region, Château-Gontier is a striking old town, the capital of the Mayenne country and founded in the 11C. Sitting at the edge of the Mayenne River, the town offers an excellent base from which to follow the river until Angers. The town was a centre of Royalist resistance to the French Revolution.

A BIT OF HISTORY

It was **Fulk Nerra**, Count of Anjou, who constructed a castle on the rocky spur overlooking the river and put it in the keeping of one Gontier, an officer in his army. The surrounding area belonged to the Benedictines of the abbey of St-Aubin at Angers, and it was they who built the 11C priory of St-Jean-Baptiste by the castle.

The Royalist leader and friend of Cadoudal (leader of the Royalist rebels known as the *Chouans*), **Pierre-Mathurin Mercier** was born the son of an innkeeper in rue Trouvée.

Château-Gontier is divided into the upper town on the west bank and the suburb around St-Julien Hospital on the east bank. The quays recall days when Château-Gontier was a port on the canalised Mayenne.

●🐾 WALKING TOUR
Allow 2h.

UPPER TOWN

▷ Start from pl. St-Jean.

Jardin du Bout du Monde

These pretty gardens laid out in the grounds of the old priory are a pleasant place for a stroll and afford glimpses of the river and the far bank.

Viewpoint

From under the elm trees on the terrace built on the old ramparts a fine view of the far bank of the river unfolds.

▶ **Population:** 11,745.
🖒 **Michelin Map:** 310: E-8
🛈 **Info:** Office de Tourisme, pl. Andre-Counord. ℰ02 43 70 42 74. www.sudmayenne.com
▶ **Location:** 31km/19.2mi S of Laval, 51km/31.6mi N of Angers.
👁 **Don't Miss:** The Romanesque interior of St. Jean Baptiste church; the international riding competition at Le Lion-d'Angers.
🕐 **Timing:** Itineraries for walking, cycling or riding are available from the tourist office.
👫 **Kids:** Refuge de l'Arche and Haras national du Lion d'Angers.

Église St-Jean-Baptiste★

The church is built in flint and red sandstone. The **interior★** reflects a remarkably forceful yet pure Romanesque style. The nave has modern stained glass and irregularly spaced columns supporting impressive arcades, whereas the crossing is roofed by an unusual dome. Although there are remains of 13C and 14C frescoes in the nave, those in the transepts date from the 12C.

▷ The walk down to pl. St-Just gives a glimpse of the steep rise known as montée du Vieux-Collège. Walk along montée St-Just to Grande-Rue.

At the corner of Grande-Rue and rue de la Harelle, there is a fine 15C timber-framed house and opposite, the old salt store built in tufa and with a turret dating from the 16C.

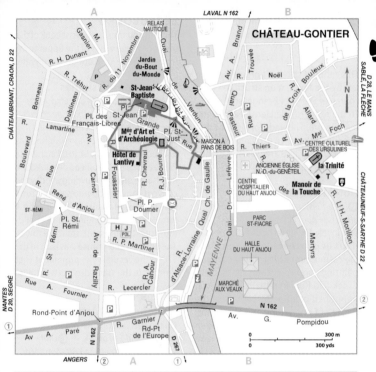

CHÂTEAU-GONTIER

LAVAL N 162

CHÂTEAUBRIANT, CRAON, D 22

NANTES D 20, SEGRÉ

ANGERS

D 28, LE MANS SABLÉ, LA FLÈCHE

CHÂTEAUNEUF-S-SARTHE D 22

Jardin du-Bout-du-Monde

St-Jean Baptiste

Mée d'Art et d'Archéologie

Hôtel de Lantivy

MAISON À PANS DE BOIS

CENTRE CULTUREL DES URSULINES

ANCIENNE ÉGLISE N.-D.-du-GENÊTEIL

la Trinité

Manoir de la Touche

CENTRE HOSPITALIER DU HAUT ANJOU

PARC ST-FIACRE

HALLE DU HAUT ANJOU

MARCHÉ AUX VEAUX

N 162

Av. G. Pompidou

Rond-Point d'Anjou

Garnier Rd-Pt de l'Europe

300 m
300 yds

WHERE TO STAY		WHERE TO EAT	
Chambre d'hôte Le Chêne Vert.................①		Aquarelle..①	
Hôtel Le Parc...②		L'Amphitryon...②	

St-Julien Hospital by the Mayenne

▶ Go up Grande-Rue and turn left onto r. de Thionville, then turn right onto r. d'Enfer.

This cobbled street is bordered on the left by the foundation structure of the church of St-Jean-l'Évangéliste.
To the right, rue de Lierru leads to rue Jean-Bourré, a reminder of the fame that this son of the town acquired as Financial Secretary and Treasurer of France during the reign of Louis XI.

Hôtel Fouquet
🕐 *By request at the tourism office (see above).*
This lovely 17C hotel houses the **musée d'Art et d'Archéologie**, an archaeological museum with a number of good paintings and sculptures. Its Ancient Greek and Roman remains include an unfinished painting by Le Brun of the Battle of Constantine and Maxentius; 17C Dutch pictures; a fine wooden statue of St Martha (15C French) and a 14C marble Virgin Mary. Local artists are represented by engravings by Tancrède Abraham and watercolours by Louis Rénier (19C).

▶ Go up r. du Musée (note the building on the corner with r. Bruchemotte that has an elegant turret) and onto r. Chevreul.

Hôtel de Lantivy
This town house (No. 26) has a particularly interesting 16C façade.

▶ Take r. René-Homo to the left, then on the right r. Fouassier and r. de l'Allemandier to pl. St-Jean.

😊 Touring Tip 😊

For information on hiring a houseboat to travel through the countryside at a leisurely pace, contact Tourisme fluvial *(Les Canalous, 1602 Paray-le-Monial; ✆07 63 78 37 23; www.anjou-navigation.fr).*

LE FAUBOURG
This large quarter on the east bank of the river offers fine views of the upper town from the Pierre-de-Coubertin quayside.

Couvent des Ursulines
Pl. André-Counord. 💬*Guided visits; enquire at the tourist office (see above). www.patrimoine.chateaugontier.fr.*
The Ursuline convent was established as a school for girls in 1634; local architects Pierre and Gilles Corbineau designed the handsome group of buildings. Today the convent complex operates as a cultural centre. The **Manoir de la Touche★** functioned as the original school building; note its handsome staircase tower. The **Église de La Trinité** was built in the 17C in the Jesuit style, popular at that time. Note the stained-glass windows.

EXCURSIONS
👪 Refuge de l'Arche
On the outskirts of town along D 267; rte. De Ménil-St-Fort. 🚭♿🕐*Daily: Jan–Feb and Nov–Dec 1.30–6pm; Mar and Oct 10am–6pm; Apr and Sept 10am–7pm; May–Aug 9.30am–7pm.* 🕐*1 Jan, 25 Dec.* 💳€12 (child 4–11, €8). *✆02 43 07 24 38. www.refuge-arche.org.*
Halfway between a zoo and a veterinary clinic, this 10ha sanctuary is committed to the shelter, care and protection of sick, wounded and abandoned animals (not including domestic pets such as cats or dogs). It has around 800 house guests, fed and cared for mainly by volunteer workers.
👪 A playground outfitted with slides, cable-cars and other recreational facilities has been set up for children.

🚗 DRIVING TOUR

VALLÉE DE LA MAYENNE★
71km/44mi. Allow one day.

The quiet Mayenne follows a picturesque and winding course between steep wooded banks as it flows south to join the Loire. The river was made navigable in the 19C when 39 locks were built between Laval and Angers and it is now ideal for pleasure craft. The route passes through the villages of low redstone houses with slate roofs that crown the top of the slopes.

Daon
The village and its 16C manor house are superbly sited on a slope above the Mayenne. Daon was the birthplace of Abbé Bernier, who negotiated the peace between the Chouans and the Republicans.

▶ In Daon take D 213 E, turn left then left again.

A long avenue of lime and plane trees leads straight to the attractive 16C moated **Manoir de l'Escoublère**.

▶ Beyond Daon, turn right off D 22 onto D 190 to Marigné.

Chenillé-Changé
This attractive village in the Segréen region boasts a fortified **watermill** (©Apr–Oct Mon–Sat 2.30–5pm; ⌖€4; ℘0241951423; www.domaine-moulin.fr), dating from the turn of the 19C. The white streaks of flour on the schist walls are evidence of its use even today. The old houses and a river boat centre with small barges moored along the shady banks of the Mayenne, all add to the peace and beauty of the scene. Take the road across the river to Chambellay and turn right onto D 187.

La Jaille-Yvon
The village is perched on the cliff above the river. The east end of the church permits a view of the fields and meadows.

▶ Take D 189 W and turn left onto N 162 going S.

Shortly after the turning to Chambellay the imposing 15C–17C buildings of the **Château du Bois-Montbourcher** come into sight (left), surrounded by lawns and woods on the edge of a vast lake.

Le Lion-d'Angers
The town occupies a picturesque site on the west bank of the River Oudon just north of the confluence with the Mayenne. It is a horse breeding centre; the horse racing and competitions held here are famous throughout Anjou.

♟♙ Haras national du Lion d'Angers★
1km/0.6mi E of Le Lion-d'Angers. ♿©Daily 10am–6pm. ℘02 41 53 50 50. www.ifce.fr/haras-nationaux.
In 1974 the premises of the national stud farm, which were too cramped in Angers' city centre, were transferred to the **Isle-Briand estate**, where many horses are now stabled in an ultramodern facility.
The visit of the farm includes the barns, the harness room, the forge (with oak flooring, more comfortable for the horses' hooves) and the riding school.

Grez-Neuville
This picturesque village in the heart of the Maine basin slopes gently to the banks of the Mayenne, its slate-roofed bell-tower reflected in the water. It is the departure point for **river cruises** along the Mayenne and Oudon.
The road down the east bank (D 191) sometimes overhangs the river; it passes (left) **Château du Sautret**, an impressive building with a dry moat.

▶ In Feneu take D 768 S across the river to Montreuil-Juigné then follow N 162 to Angers.

♟♙ Parc et Jardin du Château de Montriou
©Jul–Aug Tue–Sun 2–6pm; May–Jun and Sept–Oct by request. ℘02 41 93 30 11.
Montriou is known for its amazing collection of cucurbitaceae – that's to say marrows, courgettes, pumpkins, gourds and colocynths – which hang like spectacular vegetable stalactites from the pergolas.

▶ Rejoin the D 786 and head towards Feneu. In Feneu take D 768 S across the river to Montreuil-Juigné then follow N 162 to Angers.

ADDRESSES

🛏 STAY

⊝⊝🍴 **Chambre d'hôte le Chêne Vert** – *rte. de Nantes.* ℘*02 43 07 90 48. www. hotel-chateau-gontier.fr. 5 rooms.* ♿🅿. Rooms in this magnificent 18C château are charmingly decorated. Heated pool.

⊝⊝🍴 **Parc Hôtel et Spa** – *46 ave. Joffre, 53200 Château-Gontier. 21 rooms.* ℘*02 43 07 28 41. www.parchotel.fr.* 🅿. This stately manor house has modern amenities, including a pool (open from Jun–Sept) and a spa.

🍴 EAT

⊝⊝🍴 **Aquarelle** – *2 r. Félix-Marchand, 53200 St Fort.* ℘*02 43 70 15 44. www. restaurant-laquarelle.com.* This welcoming house serves up superb cuisine and glorious views of the Mayenne.

⊝⊝🍴 **L'Amphitryon** – *2 rte. Daon, 53200 Coudray. 7km /4mi SE by D 22.* ℘*02 43 70 46 46. www.lamphitryon53.fr. Closed Sun–Tue lunch.* Opposite the church, and five minutes from Chateau-Gontier-sur-Mayenne, L'Amphitryon serves traditional cuisine in pleasant contemporary rooms.

EVENTS

Horse show – *3rd weekend Oct; www. mondialdulion.com.* ℘*02 41 60 36 22.* The annual "Mondial du Lion" is a riding competition among amateur riders from around 20 nations.

Château du Plessis-Bourré★★

Le Plessis-Bourré stands at the far end of a vista of meadowland dotted with copses. This white building beneath blue-grey slate roofs gives a strong idea of what seigneurial life in the 15C would have been like.

A BIT OF HISTORY

Born in Château-Gontier, **Jean Bourré** (1424–1506) first entered royal service under Dauphin Louis, the son of Charles VII, whom he served faithfully.

When Louis XI assumed the crown in 1461, Bourré was given the post of Financial Secretary and Treasurer of France. In addition to building several châteaux, he bought the estate of Plessis-le-Vent. In 1468 work began on the ew château, inspired by the château at Langeais, which he had supervised during its construction.

Le Plessis, built in a single go, boasts magnificent unity of style.

⚙ **Michelin Map:** 317: F-3

🛈 **Info Tourist office:** 7 pl. Kennedy, 49051 Angers. ℘02 41 23 50 00. www.tourisme. destination-angers.com. **Chateau:** ✂🕐Feb-Mar, Oct-Nov 2-6pm, closed Mon; Apr–Jun and Sept daily except Mon and Tue morning 10am–6pm; Jul–Aug daily 10am–6pm. ⊕€9.50 (guided tour €11 at 11.30am, 3pm, 4.30pm). ℘02 41 32 06 72. www.plessis-bourre.com.

▶ **Location:** 17km/10.5mi NE of Angers.

🕐 **Timing:** Allow 1h30 for the château and surroundings.

VISIT

On the outside, Le Plessis, enclosed by a wide moat spanned by a long bridge with many arches, is plainly a fortress protected by a gatehouse with a double drawbridge and four flanking towers. The largest of the towers is

Salon Louis XVI, Château du Plessis-Bourré

© Château du Plessis-Bourré

battlemented and served as a keep. A 3m-wide platform at the base of the wall provided for artillery crossfire. To the left of the gatehouse the chapel's slender spire rises above the roof.

Inside of the entrance archway, Le Plessis has been converted into a country mansion with a spacious courtyard, low wings, an arcaded gallery, turret staircases and high dormer windows.

On the ground floor are the richly furnished and decorated **State Apartments**. The wing built at right angles houses the Parliament Hall, a vast dining hall with a superb monumental fireplace. A spiral staircase leads to the splendid guard-room, which has a coffered wooden **ceiling★★★**.

There are also humorous scenes with a moral message, depicting for example the unskilled barber at work on a client, the presumptuous man trying to wring an eel's neck, and a woman sewing up a chicken's crop. The crude realism of some of the scenes, accompanied by lines of verse, and their outstandingly fresh and graphic quality make them striking and evocative.

The castle grounds have been laid out as a park, a pleasant place for a walk.

EXCURSION

Manoir de la Hamonnière

9km/5.6mi N via Écuillé. ⟜⟜*Guided tours (30min) by appointment.* ✆*02 41 42 03 45.*

The architecture of this manor house, which was built between 1420 and 1575, shows the evolution of the Renaissance style. The buildings laid out around the courtyard consist of a plain residential block *(right)* with a stair turret, a Henri III section *(left)* with a window bay framed by pilasters and capitals following the Classical progression of the orders, and at a right angle, a low wing with two twisted columns supporting a dormer window.

To the rear stands the keep, probably the last addition made in the 16C, with a staircase turret and round-arched windows, contrasting with the other architectural features.

ADDRESSES

⌑/EAT

⊖⊜ **Les Tonnelles au Bord du Loir** – *13 r. du Port, 49140 Villevêque.* ✆*02 41 32 38 70. www.lestonnelles.fr.* Charming restaurant where light, fresh cuisine is served in a pleasant dining room overlooking the river.

Segré

The schist houses of Segré cascade down the slope to the river, which is bordered by quays and spanned by attractive bridges. The town is the capital of the Segréen, a region of woods and meadows devoted to mixed farming and known for its high-grade iron ore.

CHÂTEAU DE LA LORIE★

E along D 863. ♿🕐*Daily except Tue Jul–late Sept 10am–noon, 2.30–6pm.* ⊛€9. ℰ02 41 92 10 04. *www.chateaudelalorie.fr.*

La Lorie is an imposing 18C château approached via a long avenue of trees. A dry moat surrounds a square court-yard bordered on three sides by ranges of buildings with white-tufa tiles; the château's imposing dimensions are due to the addition of the two wings and the symmetrical outbuildings (late 18C).

Highlights inside are the Great Gallery decorated with beautiful Chinese vases, the late-18C Marble Salon, the adjoin-ing chapel and 18C woodwork in the Dining Hall. The Great Salon is lavishly decorated with Sablé marble; it was designed by Jean-Sébastien Leysner in 1779.

EXCURSIONS
Château de Raguin

8.5km/5mi S on D 923 then left on D 183 at St Gemmes-d'Andigné.

Around 1600 Guy du Bellay, son of Pierre du Bellay, built this glorious Renaissance pile on the site of the old 15C château. A brigadier of the King's armies, Pierre du Bellay had a taste for splendour, and for his son Antoine's marriage in 1648, he had the walls and ceilings of the first-floor salon and the "Lovers' Bedroom" panelled and painted.

La Mine Bleue

12km/7.5mi W on D775 towards Rennes, turn off to Bel-Air and follow D 219 to la Gâtelière. ℰ02 41 94 39 69. *www.laminebleue.com.*

For 30 years, slate – the "black gold" of Anjou – was mined in the region. After

- ▶ **Population:** 7,340.
- ♿ **Michelin Map:** 317: D-2
- 🏛 **Info:** 5 r. David-d'Angers. ℰ02 41 92 24 94. www.anjoubleu.com.
- ▶ **Location:** Between Laval and Angers.
- 👁 **Don't miss:** The sumptuous Château de la Lorie.

the mine closed it was intelligently rein-terpreted as a tourist site.

After a 130m descent underground, the former miners' train takes visitors to the galleries at the heart of the mine, where the guide brings to life the miners' daily toils *(in French).*

🚗 DRIVING TOUR

CHER VALLEY
21km/13mi. Allow 45min.

▶ Leave Segré to the S on D 923 towards Candé. After the level crossing, turn right onto D 181.

Le Bourg-d'Iré
8km/5mi W on D 181, then after the Verzée valley, right on D 29. After Noyant-la Gravoyère continue to Nyoiseau on D 775 towards Segré then take first left.

The route follows a small valley dotted with ponds, notably those at St-Blaise and la Corbinière, site of a leisure park.

Nyoiseau

This village (meaning "little nest") perched on the heights of the Oudon valley is home to a ruined benedictine nun's convent, now a farm and town hall. North of Nyoiseau, **Domaine de la Petite Couère**★ 🚶🚶 (ℰ02 41 61 06 31 or 02 41 92 22 51; *www.lapetitecouere.fr* ⊛€12) is a 82ha leisure park with out-door activities for all the family, includ-ing a tractor museum, a reconstructed early 20C village, and walking trails.

© Wojtek Buss/age fotostock

Château de la Motte-Glain

Pouancé

Sitting within its protective ring of lakes, Pouancé hugs the border between Anjou and Brittany. In the Middle Ages the town played an important economic role owing to its iron foundries that were supplied with ore from the Segré Basin.

CHÂTEAU

🔎 *Guided tours (1h) depart from the tourist office mid-Jun–mid-Sept Wed, Thu, Sat 3pm. ℘02 41 92 45 86. www.anjoubleu.com.*

The N 171 skirts the town, passing at the foot of the ruined castle (13C–15C), whose towers and curtain wall of dark schist are reinforced by a firing caponier linked to the keep by a postern.

EXCURSIONS
Menhir de Pierre Frite

5km/3mi S on D 878 to la Prévière, then D 6 left and look for sign the right.

This 6m-high standing stone is tucked away in the heart of woodland.

Château de la Motte-Glain

17km/11mi S. ⊙Daily except Tue mid-Jun–mid-Sept 2.30–6.30pm (closed Tue). ⊛€7.50. ℘06 80 95 26 43. https://lamotteglain.com.

Originally built in red-stone, this château was reconstructed in granite and limestone in the late 15C by **Pierre de Rohan-Guéménée**, Counsellor to Louis XI and later one of the commanding officers of the armies of Charles VIII

and Louis XII in Italy. A reminder of the château's location on the Mont St-Michel–Compostela pilgrimage route is given by the scallops and pilgrim's staff motifs decorating the courtyard façade. The gatehouse is flanked by two round towers. Renaissance fireplaces and 15C–16C furniture embellish the interior, together with hunting trophies, most of them of African origin.

ADDRESSES

⧙ EAT

⊜ **Ferme-Auberge Théâtre de l'Herberie** – *1km/.06mi W of Pouancé on D 771 towards Châteaubriant, then D 3 towards Rennes. ℘02 41 92 62 82.*
This former stable block now houses a remarkable set-up combining horse and sheep breeding, cultivation of vegetables, flowers and aromatic herbs, regional cuisine and evenings of theatre. Dining is available with or without a show.

▸ **Population:** 3,177.
🜚 **Michelin Map:** 317: B-2
⧉ **Info:** 2 bis r. Porte-Angevine, 49420 Pouancé. ℘02 41 92 45 86.
◗ **Location:** SW of Château-Gontier (40km/25mi) and 23km/14mi W of Segré.
◔ **Timing:** Allow 1 hour for the castle tour.

Craon

Surrounded by woodland and pastures devoted to arable farming and cattle rearing, Craon (pronounced *Cran*) is a quiet Angevin town on the River Oudon. It is famous for its horse racing *(Aug and Sept)*. The riverside château, one of the finest examples of Louis XVI architecture, is bordered by an English-style park. A few fine old timber-framed houses line the narrow streets of the old town, in particular the Grande-Rue.

▶ **Population:** 4,679.
Michelin Map: 310: D-7
Info: 7 Place du Pilori, 53400 Craon. ℘02 43 06 10 14.
Location: Craon is 30km/19mi S of Laval and 19km/12mi W of Château-Gontier.
Timing: Allow half an hour for the château, then an hour or so to explore the village.

CHÂTEAU DE CRAON★

Guided tours (60min) Jul–Aug Sun–Fri 2-6pm. €5 (château). Grounds and gardens open all year. ℘02 43 06 11 02. www.chateaudecraon.fr.

Built in the local white tufa, this elegant château (now a hotel) has a curvilinear pediment and windows embellished with festoons characteristic of the Louis XVI period. Several 18C rooms with fine woodwork and Louis XVI furnishings are on show.

Many of the trees in the **park** can be identified with the aid of descriptive labels. There is a kitchen garden with its 19C greenhouses, a laundry building where clothes were steamed over wood-ash and an underground ice house.

EXCURSIONS
Cossé-le-Vivien

12km/7.4mi N via N 171.

In 1962 the painter and ceramicist **Robert Tatin** (1902–83) gave free rein to his architectural fantasies around the old farmhouse called La Frénouse. The **Musée Robert-Tatin★** (*Feb–Mar and Oct–Dec daily except Tue 1.30–5.30pm; Apr–Jun and Sept daily except Tue 10am–6pm; Jun–Aug daily 10am–7pm; Jan, 24-25 Dec; €6 museum; €7.50 house and museum; ℘02 43 98 80 89; www.musee-robert-tatin.fr*) is approached along an avenue lined with statues leading to the Giants' Gate and the figure of a dragon. Then come three major coloured structures representing

Our Lady of the Whole World, the Moon Gate and the Sun Gate, which stand reflected in a pool shaped like a cross and lined by representations of the 12 months of the year.

Here the visitor enters the fantastic world of this self-taught artist, whose naïve and visionary creations draw on Oriental, Pre-Colombian and even Celtic sources.

Renazé

10km/6mi SW.

An important centre of slate production in the early 20C, Renazé made quality fine-grained slates until 1975. Now the former slate workers, known as 'perreyeurs' demonstrate their skills in the Musée de l'Ardoise.

Château de Mortiercrolles

11km/7mi SE on D 25 and a track to the left beyond St-Quentin-des-Anges. Mid-Jul–Aug daily noon–6pm (guided tours at 3pm and 4.30pm). €4; €8 tour; ℘06 77 61 66 62.

This beautiful moated château was built in the late 15C by Pierre de Rohan, Marshal of Gié. It is guarded by a remarkable **gatehouse★** with alternating courses of brick and stone and fine machicolations in tufa.

In the courtyard, the main apartment building (*right*) sprouts superb dormer gables. To the rear lies an elegant chapel of brick with stone courses: note the pretty Renaissance side door and the piscina ornamented with shells.

Running southwest from Le Mans towards Angers, the Sarthe valley traces an undulating line between the varying curves of Normandy's hills and the straight lines of Loire valley vineyards. Even if the high-octane thrills of Le Mans' famous car races leave you indifferent, its splendid Gallo-Roman walls, Gothic Cathédrale St-Julien and Renaissance mansions within the restored old town make the city a very special place. Follow the Sarthe as it meanders between woodlands, orchards and fields, calling at ancient towns of medieval dwellings, where you're never far from a Renaissance château.

Much More than Motoring

Synonymous with car racing, Le Mans is an unmissable pit-stop in this region. Petrolhead pilgrims have flocked to Le Mans in June for the 24-hour race ever since daredevil racers strapped on leather helmets and goggles in 1923. But there is far more than high-speed excitement to this ancient walled city, as its attractive medieval centre of half-timbered houses and arcaded alleyways attests. Its centrepiece, Cathédrale St-Julien, rivals any of France's great Gothic monuments.

Southwest of Le Mans lies Sablé-sur-Sarthe, the main port and jumping off point for exploring the Sarthe valley. It has plenty to detain you with its château and 18C mansions, and a lively medieval market on Sundays. Whether you choose to move on by boat, by car, or on foot by striding out on a network of walking trails designed to suit hikers of all abilities, make sure to visit the Benedictine abbey at Solesmes to hear Gregorian plainchant, then admire the Gothic murals in the church at Asnières-sur-Vègre.

La Venise de l'Ouest

Northeast of Le Mans, the canals and waterways of La Ferté-Bernard have earned the town the nickname of "Little Venice of the West": hiring a canoe or electric-powered boat is a fun way to get around its 15C and 16C houses, market hall and the splendid flamboyant Gothic church of Notre-Dame-des-Marais.

The Perche-Gouët region to the east makes for a particularly satisfying driving tour of interesting churches and small châteaux. While in the area, visit Brou, which has preserved a market square straight out of the Middle Ages.

Highlights

1 **Vieux Mans** and the legendary race track (p293)

2 **Sablé-sur-Sarthe**'s delicious shortbread biscuits (p305)

3 A service at the Benedictine monastery of **Solesmes** (p306)

4 Architectural wealth of **La Ferté-Bernard** (p311)

5 A tour of the deep lanes of **le Perche-Gouët** (p312)

Cathédrale St-Julien, Le Mans

© Gilles Moussé/Ville du Mans

THE SARTHE VALLEY AND PERCHE-GOUËT

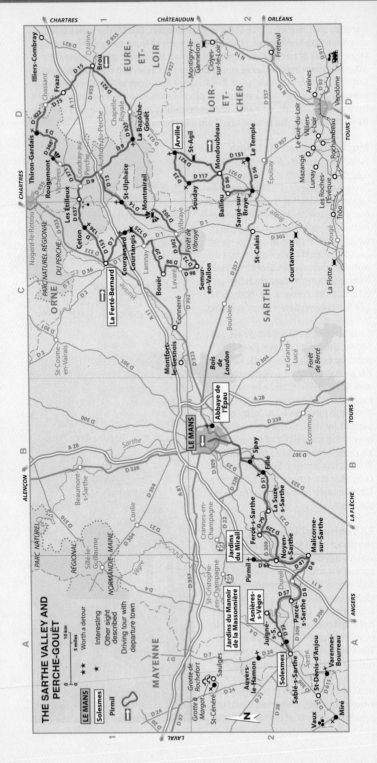

River Sarthe at Le Mans

© Gilles Moussé/Ville du Mans

Le Mans★★

Located 54min southwest of Paris by the high-speed TGV train, Le Mans stands on the banks of the Sarthe at its confluence with the Huisne. It is a thriving provincial capital renowned for good food: potted pork *(rillettes)* and poultry accompanied by sparkling cider and the famous local Reinette apple, as well as for its 24-hour motor race.

A BIT OF HISTORY

The Plantagenet Dynasty

When **Geoffrey Plantagenet**, Count of Anjou, married Matilda, the grand-daughter of William the Conqueror, he added Normandy and Maine to his estates. Geoffrey often resided at Le Mans, and on his death in 1151 he was buried here.

His son, who in 1154 became **Henry II** of England, was the founder of the Coëffort Hospital. It was to Le Mans, his birthplace, that he retired in his old age only to be expelled by one of his rebellious sons **Richard the Lionheart**, then in alliance with the French King.

While on the Third Crusade, Richard married **Queen Berengaria of Navarre**. During her widowhood, Philippe Auguste gave to her the county of Maine, which he had reconquered from Richard's younger brother, John Lackland. Berengaria founded Épau abbey *(see Excursions)*, where she was buried.

- ▶ **Population:** 143,325.
- ⚭ **Michelin Map:** 310: K 6-7
- ▤ **Info:** 16 r. de l'Étoile, 72000 Le Mans, ℘02 43 28 17 22. www.lemans-tourisme.com/en.
- ◗ **Location:** 190km/118mi SW of Paris.
- ℗ **Parking:** There is plenty of parking available around pl. des Jacobins.
- ⊘ **Don't Miss:** A stroll through the old town, along its narrow streets and river embankments.
- ◷ **Timing:** Spend 1 hour in the old town and 1 hour in the Cathédrale St-Julien before taking the 3 hour driving tour through the countryside of the Sarthe valley.
- ♟ **Kids:** Musée Vert – Musée d'Histoire naturelle.

Birthplace of the French Motor-Car Industry

In the second half of the 19C, **Amédée Bollée** (1844–1917), a local bell-founder, began to take an interest in the incipient motor-car industry. His first car (*L'Obéissante*) was completed in 1873. Later he built the *Mancelle*, the first car to have the engine placed in front under a bonnet and to have a transmission shaft. The Austrian emperor, Franz-Joseph, went for a ride in the Mancelle.

Bollée's son Amédée (1867–1926) devoted himself mainly to racing cars; they were fitted with **Michelin** tyres and reached 100kph/62mph. After the First World War, he began to produce an early form of piston rings, which became the main line of manufacture in his factory.

On 27 June 1906, the first prize on the Sarthe circuit was won by Szisz driving a Renault fitted with Michelin detachable rims.

In 1908 his brother, Léon Bollée, invited **Wilbur Wright** to attempt one of his first flights in an aeroplane at Les Hunaudières. When asked how the aircraft had performed, Wright replied, "Like a bird". In 1936, Louis Renault set up his first decentralised factory south of Le Mans in the Arnage plain.

The Drama of 5 August 1392

In the summer of 1392, **Charles VI** of France launched a campaign against the Duke of Brittany, who supported the English.

On 5 August the King left Le Mans with his troops and rode westwards. Suddenly, as they approached a leper house, an old man, hideously disfigured and with his clothes in tatters, blocked the King's path and cried "Don't go any farther, noble King, you have been betrayed."

Charles was deeply affected by this incident, but continued on his way. A little later, when they were pausing to rest under the hot sun, a soldier let his lance fall against a helmet causing a strident clang in the silence. Charles jumped. Gripped by a sudden surge of fury and believing he was being attacked, he drew his sword and shouted out that he was being delivered to his enemies. He killed four men, gave his horse free rein and galloped wildly about for some while without anyone being able to intervene. Finally he wore himself out and one of his knights was able to mount behind and bring the horse under control. They laid the King in a

Maison du Pilier Rouge

wagon and tied him down; then they took him back to Le Mans, convinced that he was about to die.

This terrible onset of madness in the middle of the Hundred Years War had serious consequences. Deprived of its ruler and prey to princely rivalries, the kingdom grew weak. From time to time Charles VI would regain his senses only to lapse back into madness.

Henry V of England was quick to take advantage of the situation: in 1420 he imposed the famous Treaty of Troyes by which Charles VI disinherited his son and recognised Henry as his heir.

Charles VI finally died in 1422, 30 years later. LeMans was under English rule until 1448.

 WALKING TOUR

OLD TOWN★★
Allow 1h.
The old town *(Le Vieux Mans)* is built on a hill overlooking the Sarthe. Restaurants and craft shops enliven the pretty, winding streets, intersected by stepped alleys and lined with 15C half-timbered houses, Renaissance town houses and 18C hotels graced by wrought-iron balconies. Clearly visible from all along the quays of the Sarthe, the well-restored **Gallo-Roman ramparts★** in their typically pinkish hues, are a truly unique landmark.

The overall impression of elegance is created by the alternating layers of brickwork and black and white ashlar arranged in geometrical patterns. This military construction, interrupted by 11 towers, is one of the longest in France.

▷ Start from pl. des Jacobins at the bottom of the cathedral steps.

Cathédrale St-Julien★★
See opposite page.

Place and Quinconces des Jacobins
The square, place des Jacobins, which is famous for its view of the cathedral, was laid out on the site of a former Dominican convent. At the entrance to the tunnel through the old town stands a monument to Wilbur Wright by Paul Landowski.

▷ Go up the steps and follow the itinerary indicated on the town map.

Place St-Michel
Standing in the cathedral precincts is the Renaissance house where **Paul Scarron** (1610–1660) lived while he was a member of the cathedral chapter. His best known novel *Le Roman comique* (The Comic Novel) (*see Musée de Tesse*) tells of the humourous adventures of itinerant actors in Le Mans and the area.

Maison de la Reine-Bérengère★
9 r. de la Reine-Bérengère.
This elegant house was built around 1460 for an alderman of Le Mans, over two centuries after the death of its namesake Queen Berengaria, wife of Richard the Lionheart. The decoration consists of an accolade above the door, beams supported on brackets and sections of carved woodwork on the façade.
Musée de la Reine Bérengère – The maison is now the Museum of History and Ethnography (*Jun–Sept daily 2–6pm, Sat-Sun 10am–12.30pm, 2-6pm; Jun-Sept daily 10am–12.30pm, 2-6pm. €5, Sun €2.50. 02 43 47 38 80. www.lemans-tourisme.com*). A Renaissance room contains regional furniture.
Statuettes, altarpieces, chafing-dishes and other glazed pottery *(1st floor)* of the Sarthe region (Ligron, Malicorne, Bonnétable and Prevelles) is displayed On the second floor are paintings by 19C artists from the Sarthe region.

Maison des Deux-Amis
18–20 r. de la Reine-Bérengère.
The two friends *(deux amis)* are shown supporting a coat of arms. This mansion was built in the 15C and two centuries later was home to the poet and painter Nicolas Denizot.
On the opposite side of rue Wilbur-Wright, which was cut through the hillside to relieve traffic congestion, is

the **Maison du Pilier rouge** (Red Pillar House), a half-timbered house featuring a corner pillar decorated with a dead man's head.

Opposite, at the beginning of Grande-Rue stands *(right)* the **Maison du Pilier vert** (Green Pillar House). The coloured pillars are thought by some to be a rudimentary street recognition system.

▷ Return to the Maison du Pilier Rouge and turn right onto the street of the same name that leads to pl. du Hallai, then continue along r. du Hallai to pl. St-Pierre lined with half-timbered houses.

Hôtel de Ville

The town hall was built in 1760, within the walls of the palace of the counts of Maine. Take the steps to rue Rostov-sur-le-Don from which there is a view of the old town's southeast ramparts; on one side of the steps is a 14C tower and on the other the old collegiate church of **St-Pierre-la-Cour** *(now an exhibition and concert hall)*.

Hôtel de Vignolles

This 16C mansion with tall French-style mansard roofs stands at the beginning of rue de l'Écrevisse on the right.

Maison d'Adam et Ève

No. 71 Grande-Rue.

This superb Renaissance mansion was the home of Jean de l'Épine, an astrologer and physician. At the corner of rue St-Honoré, a column shaft is decorated with three keys, the sign of a locksmith. The street is lined with half-timbered houses. The picturesque Cour d'Assé opens opposite rue St-Honoré. From here onwards Grande-Rue runs downhill between elegant Classical mansions.

▷ Bear right onto the less patrician rue St-Pavin-de-la-Cité. Continue along the street and after a vaulted passageway turn left onto rue Bouquet.

The Hôtel de Vaux at No. 12 is a late-16C mansion.

▷ Farther on to the left there is a view of the Great Postern steps, part of the Gallo-Roman ramparts. Walk back along rue de Vaux. Cross rue Wilbur-Wright and climb the steps turning left onto rue des Chanoines.

Maison de la Tourelle

In front of the cathedral.

This Renaissance mansion is named after the corbelled turret, which it features on the corner of the Pans-de-Gorron stepped alley.

Hôtel du Grabatoire

On the other side of the steps, opposite the Romanesque doorway of the cathedral, this 16C mansion stands on the site of what was originally the infirmary for sick canons.

On its right stands the Maison du Pèlerin (Pilgrim's House) decorated with cockleshells, the symbol adopted by pilgrims on their way to Santiago de Compostela.

CATHÉDRALE ST-JULIEN★★

This magnificent cathedral, dedicated to St Julian, the first Bishop of Le Mans, makes an impressive spectacle seen from place des Jacobins, where its Gothic **chevet★★★** rises in a succession of tiers supported by an amazingly intricate system of Y-shaped, two-tiered flying buttresses. The present building comprises a Romanesque nave, Gothic chancel and Rayonnant or High Gothic transept flanked by a tower.

Exterior

The south porch overlooking the charming place St-Michel has a superb 12C **doorway★★**. At the right corner of the west front is a pink-veined sandstone menhir.

Tradition has it that visitors should place their thumb in one of the holes to claim that they have truly visited Le Mans. Among the other scenes on the arch mouldings are the Annunciation, Visitation, Nativity, Presentation in the Temple, Massacre of the Innocents, Baptism of Christ and the Wedding at Cana.

The west front, built in an archaic Romanesque style, overlooks place du Cardinal-Grente, its sides lined with Renaissance mansions. Clearly visible is the original 11C gable that was embedded in the gable added the following century when the new vaulting was being built.

Interior

&. ⏱Daily Jun–Sept 8am–7pm; rest of the year 9am–noon, 2–5pm. ✆02 43 28 28 98. www.cathedraledumans.fr.

The Romanesque main building rests on great 11C round arches that were reinforced in the following century by pointed arches. The convex or Plantagenet-style vaulting springs from splendid capitals with particularly finely worked detail. In the side aisles are eight Romanesque stained-glass windows; the most famous one represents the Ascension (**1**). The great window of the west front, heavily restored in the 19C, depicts the Legend of St Julian.

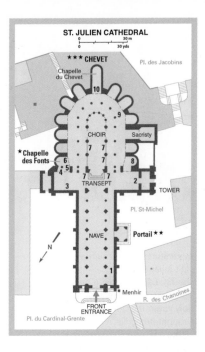

ST. JULIEN CATHEDRAL
★★★ CHEVET
Chapelle du Chevet
Pl. des Jacobins
CHOIR
Sacristy
★Chapelle des Fonts
TRANSEPT
TOWER
Pl. St-Michel
NAVE
Portail ★★
Menhir
R. des Chanoines
FRONT ENTRANCE
Pl. du Cardinal-Grente

Transept

The 14C–15C transept, with its boldly soaring elevation pierced by immense stained-glass windows, has an ethereal quality in striking contrast to the nave. The south arm is dominated by the 16C organ-loft (**2**), whereas the north arm is suffused with light transmitted through the beautiful 15C stained glass. Three 16C tapestry hangings (**3**) illustrate the Legend of St Julian.

At the entrance to the baptismal chapel (Chapelle des Fonts), which opens into the north arm of the transept, are two remarkable Renaissance **tombs**★★ opposite one another. The tomb on the left (**4**), that of Charles IV of Anjou, Count of Maine, the brother of King René, is the work of Francesco Laurana. On the right, the magnificent monument (**5**) to the memory of Guillaume du Bellay, cousin to the poet, shows the figure holding a sword and a book and reclining on one elbow in the Antique manner on a sarcophagus that is adorned with an attractive frieze of aquatic divinities. A third tomb (**6**), that of Cardinal Grente, was erected in 1965.

Chancel

The lofty Gothic chancel (13C), encircled by a double ambulatory with a circlet of chapels, is one of the finest in France.

The massed ranks of the tall upward-sweeping columns support lancet arches showing Norman influence. In the high windows of the chancel and first ambulatory and in the low windows of the chapels, the 13C **stained glass**★★ is a blaze of colour dominated by vivid blues and reds.

Hanging above the 16C choir stalls is the famous series of **tapestries (7)** of the same period depicting the lives of St Gervase and St Protase.

Chancel precincts – In the first chapel on the right is a moving 17C terra-cotta Entombment (**8**). The sacristy door beyond used to be part of the 17C rood screen. The 16C woodwork in the sacristy originally formed the high backs of the choir stalls. The 14C Canons' Door-

Cathédrale St-Julien

© Alain Szczuczynski/Ville du Mans

way features a tympanum with an effigy of St Julian **(9)**.

The 13C **Lady Chapel** *(Chapelle Notre-Dame-du-Chevet)* is dedicated to the Holy Virgin; it is closed by a delicate 17C wrought-iron grille. A remarkable series of late-14C **mural paintings★** on the chapel vaulting was restored in recent years. Forty-seven musicians and singers portrayed as angels declare their faith to Mary; they are suffused with light and compose a magnificent tableau in which colour and perspective blend.

Among the 27 musical instruments depicted in the fresco, note the *échiquier* (also spelt *eschiquier*), a rare occurrence indeed. Up to then, this instrument featuring a stringed keyboard, the ancestor of the piano, had never been represented in art, although mention of it was made in the account books belonging to King John II the Good as far back as 1360. The stained-glass windows date from the 13C; they depict the Tree of Jesse **(10)** and the story of Adam and Eve.

ADDITIONAL SIGHTS
♣♣ Le Carré Plantagenêt
r. Claude Blondeau. ⏰*Tue–Sun 10am–6pm.* ✆*€5, Sun €2.50 (under 18 years free)* ✆*02 43 47 46 45.* *www.lemans-tourisme.com.*
This museum of Archaeology and History opened in 2009 right by the Plantagenet city. It runs through the city's history from prehistoric times to the 15C using collections of more than 1,000 artefacts.

Two circuits are laid out in a fun and educational manner with modern interpretation.

Pont Yssoir
This bridge affords a fine view of the cathedral, the old town, the Gallo-Roman fortified wall with its geometric decoration and a riverside walk past traces of medieval fortifications.

Église Notre-Dame-du-Pré
Close to the bridge on the north bank.
In a square planted with magnolia trees stands the old abbey church of the Benedictine convent of St Julian in the Fields (St-Julien-du-Pré).

Jardin d'horticulture
r. de l'Éventail.
This horticultural garden (5ha) with its rock garden and cascading stream was designed in 1851 by the landscape gardener responsible for the Bois de Boulogne and the parks of Montsouris and Buttes-Chaumont in Paris.

Église Notre-Dame de la Couture★
22 r. Berthelot.
This church, now in the centre of the town, was originally the abbey church of the monastery of St-Pierre-de-la-Couture. The façade is 13C. The wide

single nave, built in the late 12C in the Plantagenet style, is lit by elegant twinned windows surmounted by oculi. The enchanting white-marble **Virgin★★** (1571), on the pillar directly opposite the pulpit, is by Germain Pilon.

The 10C crypt, altered in 1838, has pre-Romanesque or Gallo-Roman columns and capitals; an inverted Antique capital serves as a base for one of the pillars.

Église Ste-Jeanne-d'Arc★

18 Avenue Jean Jaurès. &⃝*May–Sept Sun 3–6pm, other days by request.* ✆*02 43 84 69 55.*

This church was founded c. 1180 by Henry II of England in atonement, it is said, for the murder of his former Chancellor, Archbishop **Thomas à Becket**. The 12C great hall or ward for the sick is now the parish church.

The plain façade, pierced by an arched doorway, crowned by twinned windows, opens into a vast room divided into three naves of equal height. The elevation is elegant with slender columns topped by finely carved capitals, supporting Plantagenet vaulting.

Église de la Visitation

pl. de la République.

Built according to a nun's design, this former 18C convent chapel sits in the bustling centre of Le Mans. Note the classical Corinthian columns of its portico and the rocaille-style door.

Musée de Tessé★

2 av. de Paderborn. &⃝*Tue–Fri 9am–noon, 2–6pm, Sat–Sun and school holidays 10am–12.30pm, 2–6pm.* ⊛€5, *Sun €2.50.* ✆*02 43 47 38 51. www.lemans.fr.*

This museum, housed in the bishop's palace built in the 19C on the site of the Tessé family mansion, contains fine collections of 19C paintings and archaeology. In the basement the **Egyptian collections** are displayed, including a reconstruction of the tombs of Nefertari (Ramses II's first wife) and of Sennefer (mayor of Thebes), and a mummy dating from 750 BC. On the ground floor, a small room *(left)* contains a superb

enamelled copper plaque, called the **Plantagenet enamel★**, a unique piece depicting Geoffrey Plantagenet, Count of Anjou and Maine from 1129 to 1151, Duke of Normandy in 1144 and father of Henry II of England. Italian paintings include a series of 14C–15C altarpieces with gold backgrounds. In the Renaissance Room there are two panels by the Master of Vivoin, part of an altarpiece (c. 1470) from Vivoin Priory (Sarthe). The 18C Room displays a superb bookcase by Bernard van Risenburgh.

On the first floor the Northern School of painting is represented by Van Utrecht, Kalf *(Still Life with Armour)*, bambocciate (scenes of street life) and landscapes. A whole room is devoted to *The Comic Novel* by Scarron; a portrait of the author is exhibited alongside paintings by Coulom and engravings by Oudry and Pater.

♣♟ Musée Vert – Musée d'Histoire naturelle

204 av. Jean-Jaurès. &⃝*Mon–Fri 9am–noon, 2–6pm, Sun 2–6pm.* ⊛€5, *Sun €2.50 (under 18 years free).* ✆*02 43 47 39 94. www.lemans.fr.*

This interesting museum houses a number of collections devoted to mineralogy, palaeontology, entomology, botany and ornithology. Two rooms are reserved for children.

MOTOR-RACING CIRCUITS

To the S of Le Mans between N 138 and D 139. www.lemans.org.

In 1923, Gustave Singher and Georges Durand launched the first Le Mans endurance test, which was to become a sporting event of universal interest and an ideal testing ground for car manufacturers.

Le Mans 24-hour Race

The difficulties of the circuit and the duration of the race are a severe test of the quality of the machine and of the endurance of the drivers. The track has been greatly improved since the tragic accident in 1955 when 83 spectators died and 100 were injured. Whether seen from the stands or from the fields or pine woods that surround the track, the

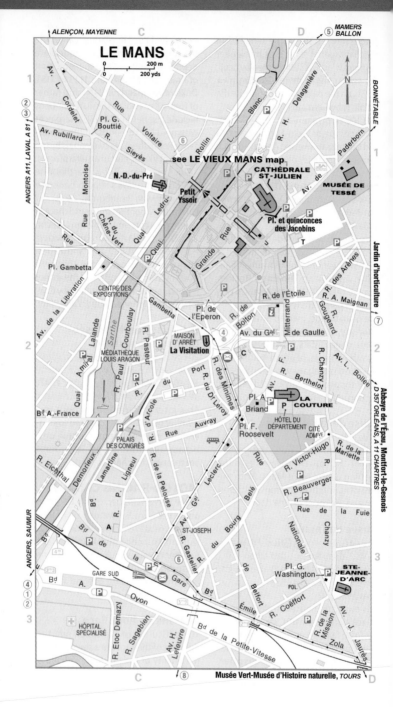

LE MANS

see LE VIEUX MANS map

Ancien hôtel
de Rouxelin d'Arcy....**B**

Maison de la-Reine-
Bérengère (musée)...**M**

Maison
de la Tourelle..........**N¹**

Maison
de Scarron..............**N²**

Maison
des Deux-Amis........**N³**

INDEX OF STREETS

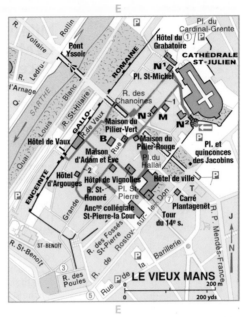

race is an unforgettable experience: the roaring of the engines, the whining of the vehicles hurtling up the Hunaudières section at more than 350kph/200mph, the smell of petrol mingled with the resin of the pine trees, the glare of the headlights at night, the emotion and excitement of the motor car enthusiasts. Every year there is also a Le Mans 24-hour motorcycle race and a Le Mans 24-hour truck race. A Grand Prix de France motorcycle race is held here regularly.

Circuit des 24 Heures

The 24-hour circuit (13.6km/8.5mi long) begins at the Tertre Rouge bend *(virage)* on N 138. The racetrack, which is about

10m wide, is marked in kilometres. The double bend on the private road and the Mulsanne and Arnage hairpin bends are the most exciting hazards on the 24-hour course. In 1972, the course was laid out to give a better view.

▶ From the main entrance to the track on D 139, a tunnel leads to the Bugatti circuit and the museum.

Circuit Bugatti

⟁ ⏰ *Call for hours.* ☎ *02 43 40 80 00. www.lemans.org. Shop open all year 10am–6pm (Apr–Sept until 7pm).*
Apart from being used by its school for racing drivers, the track is also a perma-

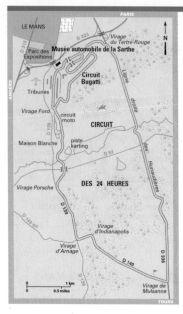

Milestones in the Le Mans 24-hour Race

1923 – The first 24-hour race in 1923 was won by Lagache and Léonard from Chenard and Walcker; they covered 2,209.536km/1,372.942mi at an average speed of 92.064kph/57.205mph; the fastest circuit time was achieved by Clément in a Bentley at 107.328kph/66.691mph.

1971 – In 1971, when the track was 13.469km/8.360mi long, Helmut Marko and Gijs Van Lennep covered 5,335.313km/3,315.2011mi in a Porsche 917 at an average speed of 222.304kph/138.133mph; Siffert drove the fastest lap, also in a Porsche 917, at an average speed of 243.905kph/151.555mph.

1991 – The circuit was redesigned and granted new facilities, making it the first racing track of its kind in the world. Mazda came first (unprecedented victory of a Japanese firm and a rotary engine).

1993 – Peugeot's historic hat-trick: three cars on the starting line, three cars on the finishing line, and three cars winning laurels. Moreover, they succeeded in setting a new track record on the longer circuit (13.6km/8.451mi) covering 5,100km/3,168.993mi at an average speed of 213.358kph/132.575mph.

1998 – The Scot Alan McNish and the two Frenchmen Laurent Aïello and Stéphane Ortelli celebrate Porsche's 16th triumphant appearance; their GT1 performed 351 laps (4,723.78km/ 2,935.22mi) at an average speed of 199.32kph/123.852mph.

2000 – The drivers Biela, Kristensen and Pirro won the 68th race. Three Audi R8s took the first three places, the first one having gone round the track 368 times!

2008 – Audi wins their 9th consecutive victory.

2009 – Peugeot's third win and a double for the 908 HDI-FAP cars, which took the first two places.

Racing at 24 Heures du Mans

© Gilles Moussé/Ville du Mans

Abbaye de l'Épau

© Gilles Moussé/Ville du Mans

nent testing ground for teams of racing car drivers and motorcyclists who use it for private trials.

👤👥 Musée des 24 Heures du Mans – circuit de la Sarthe★★

9 pl. Luigi-Chinetti. ♿🕐*May–Sept daily 10am–7pm; Oct–Apr daily 10am–6pm.* 🚻 *Museum: €9.50 (child 10–18, €7); Circuit: €5/€4.50; Combined: €12.50/ €10.50.* 📞*02 43 72 72 24. www.lemans-musee24h.com.*

Rebuilt in 1991, the Motor Museum displays **110 vehicles** and covers over a century of automotive history in an extremely modern and instructive setting. The section on racing cars, in particular those that won the Le Mans 24-hour race, presents a superb collection of outstanding automobiles.

All of the following were **winning cars**: a 1924 Bentley, a 1949 Ferrari, a 1974 Matra, a 1983 Rondeau, a 1988 Jaguar, a 1991 Mazda and a 1992 Peugeot.

EXCURSIONS

Abbaye de l'Épau★

4km/2.5mi E via av. Léon-Bollée. 🕐*Jul-Aug daily 10am–7pm; Sept-Nov, Feb-Jun Wed–Mon, 11am–6pm; Dec-Jan Wed–Mon 11am–8pm.* 🚻*€5.50.* 🕐*1 Jan, 25 Dec.* 📞*02 43 84 22 29. http://epau.sarthe.com.*

In 1229, a Cistercian abbey was founded on the south bank of the Huisne by **Queen Berengaria**, the widow of Richard the Lionheart, who spent her last days here.

On the left is the **church**, which was built in the 13C and 14C and remodelled in the 15C. The church was designed to the traditional Cistercian layout: a square east end with three chapels facing east in each arm of the transept.

L'Arche de la Nature

Near the Abbaye de l'Épau. 🌿🕐*Apr–Oct daily 2–8pm; Nov–Mar 9am–5.30pm, but the hours of individual attractions vary; so, check the website for details.* 🚻*€3.* 📞*02 43 50 38 45. www.arche-nature.fr.*

This natural site comes to life in season with activities on the theme of "rivers", "woodlands", etc. On offer are visits to the Maison de l'Eau, to a model farm, rides in horse-drawn carts, hikes, sports grounds and outdoor games.

Montfort-le-Gesnois

20km/12.4mi E of Le Mans along av. Léon-Bollée and N 23; after 16km/10mi bear left onto D 83.

Not far from **Connerré**, a small commercial town renowned for *rillettes* (potted meat made from pork or goose), Montfort lies in a peaceful site that grew around the Roman **bridge** over the River Huisne.

Jardins du Manoir de la Massonnière★

In St-Christophe-en-Champagne, 35km/22mi W via A 11 (exit Le Mans Sud) then D 22. 🕐*Jun–Sept Fri–Sun 2–6pm.* 📞*02 43 88 44 62.*

Surrounding an attractive manor house, these gardens, inspired by Impressionist painting, display an array of fragrant trees and bushes. Numerous topiaries are trimmed to resemble chess pieces and other shapes.

Jardins du Mirail★

23km/14mi W in Crannes-en-Champagne. 🏃🕐*Jun–mid-Sept Wed–Sun 1–7pm.* ⊜€5. ☎02 43 88 05 50.
Laid out in 1987, these gardens enfold a 16C château tucked against a hillside. It's an elegant outlook over greenery sheltering perennials and a hundred varieties of roses.

🚗 DRIVING TOUR

73km/45mi. About 3h.

SARTHE VALLEY

The Sarthe meanders peacefully southwest through the beautiful Maine countryside. The river is navigable between Le Mans and the confluence with the Mayenne along lateral canals running parallel to it. The countryside through which it flows consists of woodland alternating with meadows and fields of cereals, potatoes and early vegetables.

▷ Leave Le Mans on N 23 heading SW.

Spay

10km/6mi on N 23 and D 51 via Arnage.
Spay is bordered by the Sarthe. Note the 12C **church,** and **Spaycific'Zoo** 👤👤 (🕐*Apr–Sept daily 10am–6pm; Oct–Nov Wed–Sun 1.30–6pm;* ⊜€12 *(child 13–16 years €10; 3–12 years €8).* ☎02 43 21 33 02; *www.spayciczoo.com/),* which features 700 animals of 180 species.

▷ Take D 51 to Fillé.

Fillé

The village lies on the north bank of the Sarthe; its **church** contains a large painted statue of the Virgin Mary (late 16C), glazed somewhat by the fire of August 1944.

La Suze-sur-Sarthe

The bridge over the Sarthe provides a good view of the river, the remains of the castle (15C) and the church.

▷ Leave La Suze on D 79 going W through woods towards Fercé.

Fercé-sur-Sarthe

Attractive views from the bridge and from the road up to the church.

▷ Return across the river and turn right to St-Jean-du-Bois.

The road (D 229) passes the troubadour-style castle of La Houssaye and provides several glimpses of the Sarthe before reaching Noyen.

Noyen-sur-Sarthe

The village is built in terraces on the sloping north bank overlooking the canal, which at this point runs parallel to the broad Sarthe.

Pirmil

4km/2.5mi N of Noyen along D 69.
The **church**, a Romanesque building with buttresses, dates from 1165.

Malicorne-sur-Sarthe

Malicorne is pleasantly situated at the water's edge. From the bridge there is a pretty view of a mill and the poplars along the bank.
Downstream, set back from the south bank of the river in a park, stands the 17C **château** where Mme de Sévigné liked to stay, which belonged to the Marquise de Lavardin. It has turrets and mansard roofs and is surrounded by a moat that is spanned by a humpback bridge.

Malicorne Espace faïence

r. Victor Hugo. 🏃🕐*Tue–Sun 10am–12.30pm, 2–6pm (7pm in Jun–Aug).* ⊜€5. ☎02 43 48 07 17. *https://musee-faience.fr*
This interactive museum, devoted to the local speciality, is housed in the renovated buildings of a former factory. Workshops help to illustrate the process of making and firing earthen-

ware, its uses and the art of potters. On the eastern side of the town, there is a working **pottery** (&.☞*guided tours Apr–Sept Tue–Sat 11am, 2pm, 3pm.* ○*Shop open Mon 2–6pm, Tue–Sat 9am–noon, 2–6pm, and also Sun 2–6pm during Apr–Sept.* ✆*02 43 94 81 18; www. faiencerie-malicorne.com),* which produces pieces in the Malicorne style, as well as reproductions of period pieces.

▷ Take D 8 W towards Parcé, making a detour along a small country track (V 1) to the right via Dureil, which provides attractive glimpses of the River Sarthe before rejoining D 8.

Parcé-sur-Sarthe

Parcé is a charming little village grouped round a Romanesque tower with a mill on the river. The cypress-girted cemetery at the entrance to the village makes a peaceful setting for the chapel with its gable-belfry.

▷ After crossing the river and the canal, turn left onto D 57.

On leaving Avoise note, on the left, La Perrigne de Cry (☞*private property),* a 16C manor overlooking the river.

▷ Bear left to Juigné.

Juigné-sur-Sarthe

Juigné is a pleasant village set on a promontory that juts south across the valley. There are 16C and 17C houses and the 18C château that belonged to the Marquis of Juigné. From the church square there is a view of the river below and of Solesmes Abbey downstream.

Solesmes★
&*See SABLÉ-SUR-SARTHE*

▷ Take D 22 alongside the canal and the old marble quarries to Sablé.

ADDRESSES

🏨 STAY

😊😊 **Hôtel-Motel Papéa** – *RN 314, Bener, 72530 Yvré-l'Evêque.* ✆*02 43 89 64 09. www.hotellemanspapea.fr. 21 rooms.* 🅿 A budget-pleasing cross between camping and a motel of chalets.

😊😊 **Hôtel Charleston** – *18-20 r. Gastelier.* ✆*02 43 24 87 46. www. lecharlestonhotel.com. 31 rooms.* 🅿 A modern hotel near the station with sleek, contemporary rooms. Buffet breakfast served in the flower-decked courtyard in fine weather. Bikes gratis.

😊😊 **Chambre d'hôte La Ferme Chauvet** – *72430 Chantennay-Villedieu. 3km/2mi E of village.* ✆*02 43 95 77 57. www.fermechauvet.com. 5 rooms, 2 caravans* (😊😊). 🅿. All modern comforts at a reasonable price at this working farm.

😊😊 **Chambre d'hôte Le Fresne** – *72300 Solesmes.* ✆*02 43 95 92 55. www. lefresne.com. 3 rooms.* 🅿🍽. Discover the delights of a 130ha working farm; rooms are in an annex. Nice pool.

😊😊 **Chambre d'hôte Mme Bordeau Marie-Claire** – *Le Monet, 72190 Coulaines. 5km/3mi N of Le Mans.* ✆*06 85 04 08 34. levaldumonet.midiblogs.com. 2 rooms.* 🅿🍽. This restored typical regional house in the country, not far from town, has retained its original character.

😊😊 **Chambre d'hôte Le Petit Pont** – *3 r. du Petit-Pont, 72230 Moncé-en- Belin. 11km/6.8mi S of Le Mans on D 147 towards Arnage, then D 307.* ✆*02 43 42 03 32.* &🅿 *Evening meal* 😊😊. Situated on a working farm, the guest rooms are simply decorated and well equipped.

😊😊 **Hôtel Mercure Le Mans Batignolles** – *17 r. Pointe.* ✆*02 43 72 27 20. www.accorhotels.com. 66 rooms.* 🅿. Modern, practical and well-kept rooms; those to the rear are quieter. Garden with mini-golf. Restaurant (😊😊) serves traditional repertory.

😊😊😊 **Chambre d'hôte La Demeure de Laclais** – *4 bis pl. du Cardinal-Grente.* ✆*02 43 81 91 78. www.lademeuredelaclais.fr. 3 rooms.* Located in Le Mans' old town, opposite the cathedral, this 17C mansion is a haven of beauty and calm. Terrace garden and views of the city.

♈/EAT

⊖ **L'Épicerie du Pré** – 31 r. du Pré. ℘02 43 23 52 51. www.epiceriedupre.fr. Closed Sun–Mon. This Bohemian coffee house in a 16C building in Le Mans is a cultural hub for concerts, lectures, debates.

⊖ **Le Pré-Carré** – 2 r. Claude Blondeau. ℘09 53 61 83 73. Closed Sun–Mon. The friendly café at Carré Plantagenêt serves affordable regional fare, sandwiches and the like.

⊖⊜ **La Botte d'Asperges** – 49 r. Nationale, 72230 Guécelard. 18km/11mi S of Le Mans on N 23. ℘02 43 87 29 61. www.la-botte-dasperges.fr. Closed Sun eve, Mon except public holidays. This restaurant in a former staging inn in the village centre serves the famous local asparagus.

⊖⊜⊜ **Auberge du Rallye** – 13 r. des Gesleries, 72210 Fillé-sur-Sarthe. 12km/7.4mi S of Le Mans on D 147E, D 23 towards Allones, then D 51. ♿🅿. ℘02 43 87 40 40. www.laubergedurallye.com. Closed Sun–Tue eve, Wed. It's good to get away from the noise of the city and eat in a country setting in the Sarthe, on a shaded terrace.

⊖⊜⊜ **Le Beaulieu** – 34 bis pl. de la République. ℘02 43 87 78 37. Closed Sat, Sun. This restaurant offers an inviting modern setting for gourmet dishes featuring beef or fish, veal or lamb.

⊖⊜⊜ **La Ciboulette** – 14 r. Vieill-Porte. ℘02 43 24 65 67. www.laciboulettelemans. com. Located in a medieval house in Old Le Mans, this modern restaurant emits a bistro-like atmosphere. Traditional dishes. Chef's menu changes daily.

⊖⊜⊜ **Le Grenier à sel** – 26 pl. de l'Eperon. ℘02 43 23 26 30. www.restaurant-le-grenier-a-sel.fr. Closed Sat lunch, Sun. Situated right in the town centre, this former salt store now houses a pleasant restaurant serving modern cuisine.

NIGHTLIFE

Le Saint-Flaceau – 9 r. St-Flaceau. ℘02 43 23 24 93. This cocktail bar is something really different: the setting is an 18C apartment in the old town, complete with parquet floors and mouldings, and furnished with old sofas and chairs. Wide choice of drinks, and a wonderful terrace on the old Roman walls overlooking the town. Get there early.

La Péniche Excelsior – ZA La Raterie - Allones. ℘02 43 83 45 15. http://lexcelsior.fr. Moored on the banks of the Sarthe, the houseboat Excelsior was transformed into a concert hall in 1993. Today it's a venue for contemporary music (rock, hip hop, electro, etc.) at reasonable ticket prices.

ENTERTAINMENT

Les Quinconces L'Espal – 60–62 r. de l'Estérel. ♿℘02 43 50 21 50. http://quinconces-espal.com. Open Tue–Sat. The Espal is both a community arts centre and a cultural venue. It organises workshops and courses (dance, lithography) as well as performances.

LEISURE ACTIVITIES

Cheval en Belinois – La Gourdinière - Moncé-en-Belin. ℘02 4342 56 92. www. chevalenbelinois72.com. Horse rides in a pine forest (€20/45min, €110/1 day). Pony rides for young ones (3-10 years €13/30min, €18/1hr).

SHOPPING

À la Rouelle de Veau – 15 r. du Dr-Leroy. ℘02 43 28 30 45. Open Tue–Fri 8am–12.45pm, 3–7pm, Sat 8am–1pm, 3–7pm, Mon 8am–12.30pm. Traditional home- cooked meats prepared as rillettes are on offer: sausage, black pudding, beef tongue, pork crackling.

Maison Reignier – 19 r. Bolton. ℘02 43 24 02 15. http://maisonreignier.com. Mon 9.30am–6pm, Tue–Thu 9.30am–7pm, Fri–Sat 9am–7.30pm. This epicerie has been purveying delicacies to the public since 1885. Browse over two floors of high-quality wines, Reignier's own-brand top-class tea and coffee, delicatessen and regional specialities.

TAKING A BREAK

La Panetière – 32 av. François-Mitterrand. ℘02 43 24 93 90. Closed Sun. Breads are baked throughout the day at this bakery/café. The apricot bread and the rye are especially popular with patrons.

EVENTS

Europa Jazz Festival – May. Inter-national jazz festival. http://europajazz.fr.

Le Mans Classic – Jul (even years). Car races from 1923-1979.

24 Hours of Mans – Autos: Jun; motorcycles: Sept; trucks: Oct. 🛈Tourist Office.

Sablé-sur-Sarthe

Situated at a point where two tributaries, the Vaige and the Erve, flow into the Sarthe, Sablé is dominated by the austere façade of its château, which once belonged to the Colbert family. Famous for its shortbread biscuits *(sablés)*, the town is the second largest economic centre in the Sarthe region. A favourable environment and pronounced dynamism have helped develop the foodstuff industry and diversify the local economy. Nearby, art lovers will discover the fascinating Benedictine abbey of Solesmes and the church of Asnières-sur-Vègre, superbly decorated with Gothic murals.

▶ **Population:** 13 126.
🕭 **Michelin Map:** 310: G-7
🛈 **Info:** Impasse du Château, 72305 Sablé-sur-Sarthe. ℘02 43 95 00 60. www.sabletourisme.fr.
▶ **Location:** Midway between Le Mans and Angers.
☺ **Don't Miss:** Gregorian chant at Abbaye St-Pierre.
🕓 **Timing:** Half a day for the town and its surrounds.

VISIT

In the 17C, the fief belonged to Laval-Bois-Dauphin, Marquis de Sablé. In 1711 Colbert de Torcy, the nephew of the great Jean-Baptiste Colbert, Louis XIV's Minister, rebuilt the château and radically changed the appearance of the town; many houses and the hospital date from this period. Today **Château des Colbert** (○—*closed to the public*) houses the National Library's restoration and book binding workshops.

Development has highlighted a fine group of 19C buildings in rue Carnot. The small **port** on the canalised part of the Sarthe used to receive sand-laden barges from the Loire. Now it harbours about 20 craft for hire *(pénichettes)* as well as Le Sablésien, a **tourist boat** (*see Leisure Activities*) offering leisurely rides and luncheon-cruises along the Sarthe.

EXCURSIONS

Auvers-le-Hamon

8.5km/5.3mi N along D 24.
The chuch's nave has 15C–16C murals paintings depicting local saints and religious scenes.

Abbaye St-Pierre on the Sarthe, Solesmes

© Julian Elliott/agefotostock

Solesmes★

3km/2mi NE along the picturesque D 22.
A few miles upstream from Sablé lies Solesmes, which has won renown through its association with the Benedictine Order. From the north bank of the Sarthe and from the bridge there is an impressive **view★** of the north front of the abbey, a dark wall built at the end of the 19C in the Romanesque-Gothic style. The abbey buildings are reflected in the river, next to a less imposing, but rather more inviting-looking 18C priory. It expanded rapidly and by the early 16C had become very wealthy. The Revolution brought ruin, but a new community was established in 1833 by a priest from Sablé, Dom Guéranger, and in 1837 the abbey became the headquarters of the Benedictine Order in France.

The abbey **services**, to which visitors are admitted, demonstrate the beauty of the liturgy celebrated in Benedictine monasteries.

Abbaye St-Pierre★

Only the abbey church is open to the public (in the main courtyard).
The **church** comprises the nave and transept which date from the 11C and 15C and the domical-vaulted chancel which was added in 1865. The famous sculpture groups, which are known as the **Saints of Solesmes★★**, are in the transept. Note in the south transept a monumental Entombment (1496) with a representation of Mary Magdalene at prayer; on the left, a terra-cotta Pietà from an earlier period, and in the north transept, a remarkable composition of scenes from the Virgin's life.

Asnières-sur-Vègre★

10km/6mi NE along D 4 and D 190.
Asnières lies in an attractive setting, deep in the picturesque Vègre valley. The road *(D 190)* from Poillé gives a pretty view over the old houses with their steeply pitched roofs, the church and the Cour d'Asnières mansion.

Bridge – This medieval humpback structure provides a **view★** of the river, the old mill (still operational) and the elegant mansion with its turret and dormer windows on the right bank. Close to the mill stands a château known as the Moulin Vie dating from the 17C and 18C.

Church – The interior is decorated with Gothic **wall paintings★**: 13C in the nave and 15C in the chancel. The most famous, on the inside wall of the main façade, depicts Hell. On the left Christ is preparing to release the souls trapped in Limbo by attacking the three-headed dog, Cerberus, with a lance; in the centre Leviathan is swallowing up the Damned; finally, canine-headed demons are stirring a cauldron of the Damned in which the wimple of the lady of the manor and the bishop's mitre can be seen. The scenes on the north wall of the nave portray the Adoration of the Magi, the Presentation of Jesus in the Temple and the Flight into Egypt.

Cour d'Asnières – Just south of the church is an elongated Gothic building. It was here that the canons of Le Mans, the one-time lords of Asnières, exercised their seigneurial rights, hence the name *cour* meaning court.

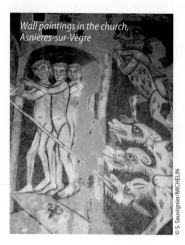

Wall paintings in the church, Asnières-sur-Vègre

© S. Sauvignier/MICHELIN

Jardin Mosaïque

At the N end of the village, along the D 190. La Salle, route de Poillé. ◐*Mid-Apr–mid-Oct Wed–Sun and public holidays 10am–noon, 2–7pm, Mon–Tue by appointment.* ☞€6. ✆02 43 92 52 35. www.lejardinmosaique.com.
This ecofriendly 2.5ha garden offers a bucolic scene. Butterflies flit among

hundreds of perennials. The collection of antique roses is especially fine.

St-Denis-d'Anjou

10.5km/6.5mi SW along D 309.
Guided tours may be arranged with the tourist office: *02 43 70 69 09. www.saintdenisdanjou.com.*
This village, with pretty gardens, has a 12C **fortified church** with keel vaulting and 12C and 15C frescoes that were discovered in 1947. Opposite the church, which belonged to the Chapter of Angers, stands the 15C canons' house (now the town hall), and the 16C wine market.

Chapelle de Varennes-Bourreau

10km/6mi S along D 159. *Guided tours by appointment. Contact tourist office:* *02 43 70 69 09.*
This chapel nestles in the lush vegetation beside the River Sarthe; it is decorated with 12C and 15C frescoes: a mandorla surrounds Christ, whose hand is raised. The village of Varennes was formerly a small port engaged in the transport of wine to Angers.

Miré

16km/10mi SW via D 309 and D 27.
In this small village, the church is roofed with wooden keel vaulting decorated with 43 late-15C painted panels depicting the Four Evangelists, Angels bearing the Instruments of the Passion and the Apostles presenting the Creed.

Château de Vaux

3.5km/2mi NW of Miré on D 29 towards Bierné. Visit of exterior free daily 10am–5pm. *Guided tours possible on request.* *02 41 76 10 60. www.chateaudevaux-anjou.com.*
The picturesque château stands well back from the road to the right. The ruined curtain wall enclosed an elegant building with a stair turret and mullioned windows. This manor house was built in late-15C by **Jean Bourré**, Lord of Miré, who introduced *bon-chrétien* pears to the Angevin orchards.

ADDRESSES

STAY

Hôtel Aster – *rte. de la Flèche, Vion.* *02 43 92 28 96. www.hotelaster.fr. 30 rooms.* An independent hotel close to the centre of Sablé. Bedrooms are functional with well-equipped bathrooms. The restaurant () offers provençal décor and traditional cooking at wallet-friendly prices.

Village Vacances nature et jardin – *53290 Bouère.* *02 43 06 08 56. www.vacances-nature-jardin.fr. 11 chalets for 7 pers.* A village of 11 wooden chalets (one adapted for those with reduced mobility) within a flowery village next to a 2ha lake. Each has a fireplace and a private storage area for bicycles and fishing tackle.

EAT

Restaurant Ricordeau – *13 r. de la Libération, Loué.* *02 43 88 40 03. www.hotel-ricordeau.fr. Closed Sun eve, Mon, Tue.* This former coaching inn along the Vègre has been transformed to an luxurious inn and restaurant. Terrace dining in fine weather. 13 pleasant rooms () for overnight guests. Pool.

SHOPPING

La Maison du Sablé – *38 pl. Raphaël-Elizé.* *02 43 95 01 72. Open daily 9am–7pm (Sun 1pm).* The world of the sablé biscuit lies within this pleasant boutique with an Art Deco-style façade. The round golden biscuits are still hand-made according to the house's 1932 recipe. Try a Croq'Amours – a light chocolate, coffee or vanilla-flavoured meringue made with whole almonds and hazelnuts.

LEISURE ACTIVITIES

Croisières Saboliennes – *quai National.* *02 43 95 93 13. www.bateau-sablesien.fr.* Cruises on the Sablesien II (74 pers max) can be combined with a meal. Various itineraries of varying duration available.

EVENTS

Fête Rock Ici Mômes – *Late Jul in the grounds of the château.* *02 43 62 22 22.* This child-oriented music festival brings together more than 10 000 youngsters between the ages of 3 and 12.

Saint-Calais

Situated on the border between Maine and the Vendôme region, St-Calais is a market town dominated by the ruins of a medieval château. A few old gables still look down on the narrow streets.

SIGHTS

The **quais de l'Anille** offer pleasant views of the riverside wash-houses, now overgrown with moss, and gardens of flowers against a background of picturesque roofs.

The district on the west bank developed round the Benedictine abbey, which was founded in the reign of Childebert (6C) by Karilefus, an anchorite from Auvergne. The monastery was destroyed during the Revolution, but the few 17C buildings that survived are now occupied by the library, the theatre and the museum.

Église Notre-Dame

Construction of the church began in 1425 with the chancel; the building is a mixture of the Flamboyant Gothic and Renaissance styles. The Italianate **façade★** was finished in 1549 and is typical of the second Renaissance. The carved panels of the twin doors portray scenes from the Life of the Virgin Mary. The first three bays of the interior are Renaissance; the vaulting with pendentives springs from majestic columns with Ionic capitals. The 17C loft came from the abbey, and the organ itself is of the same date. Restored in 1974, it is the pride and joy of the church's organists.

EXCURSION

Château de Courtanvaux

12km/7.4mi S along D 303 to Bessé-sur-Braye; from Bessé, follow the signposting. ⟳*Guided tours only May–Jun and Sept Tue–Sun, 3pm, 4pm and 5pm (Jul–Aug 11am, 3pm, 4pm, 5pm).* ⬤€5. ℘02 43 35 34 43. *www.chateaudecourtanvaux.com.*

The château, a Gothic building sheltering in the valley, was the seat of a marquisate held successively by the Louvois

- ▶ **Population:** 3 558.
- ⬤ **Michelin Map:** 310: N-7
- ▤ **Info:** pl. de l'Hôtel-de-Ville, 72120 St-Calais. ℘02 43 35 82 95. www.officedetourisme-payscalaisien.fr.
- ▶ **Location:** 44km/27mi SE of Le Mans and 95km/59mi W of Orléans.
- ✿ **Don't Miss:** The Apple Turnover Festival – the **Fête du Chausson aux Pommes** has taken place every year since 1581 *(first weekend in Sept)* to commemorate the end of the plague.
- ◷ **Timing:** Allow yourself 1–2 hours for the town. Take half day for the château.

and Montesquiou families; one of the owners was Michel Le Tellier, **Marquis de Louvois** (1639–91) and Louis XIV's Minister for War. In 1815, when Napoleon fell from power, the château came to life again after 150 years of neglect; it became the residence of the **Countess of Montesquiou**, who had been the governess to the King of Rome, Napoleon's son by Marie-Louise.

An avenue of plane trees leads to the charming Renaissance gatehouse. The buildings have typical 15C and 16C features: tall roofs, mullioned windows and pointed dormer pediments. The courtyard is overlooked by two terraces. The main block, called the Grand Château, has four rooms (47m long) on the first floor that were redecorated in 1882.

ADDRESSES

🛏 STAY

😊😊 **Chambre d'hôte Les Ganeries** – *Les Ganeries, Sargé-sur-Braye.* ℘02 54 72 78 44. *lesganeries.free.fr. 4 rooms.* Swim, walk and relax at this B&B with a rustic dining room. Above-ground pool.

Mondoubleau

Approached from the west, Mondoubleau can be seen clustered on the east bank of the River Grenne. Perched at a precarious angle on a bluff to the south of the road to Cormenon, the ruins of a keep overlook the village where remains of the curtain wall are partly hidden among the houses and trees. Several graceful churches and properties that once belonged to the Knights Templar can be seen in the surrounding area.

> ▶ **Population:** 1 541.
> ⚙ **Michelin Map:** 318: C-4
> ▮ **Info:** 2 r. Brizieux, 41170 Mondoubleau. ☏02 54 80 77 08. www.maison-tourisme.fr.
> ◐ **Location:** Between La Ferté-Bernard (30km/19mi to the NW) and Vendôme (25km/15.5mi to the SE).
> ◔ **Timing:** Allow about half a day.

FORTRESS

🕭*Visit by guided tour Jun–Aug (departing from the Maison du Perche, pl. du Marché) Call for hours and prices.* ☏02 54 80 77 08.

At the end of the 10C, Hugues Doubleau, from whom the town has taken its name, built a red-sandstone fortress over which towered a 33m-high keep. All that remains of this imposing stronghold are half a keep, the governor's house, known as the Maison Courcillon (15C), and the baronial building (16C).

🚗 DRIVING TOURS

1 NORTH OF MONDOUBLEAU

Round trip of 26km/16mi on D 921. About 1h.

Château de St-Agil

🕭*Guided tours of the outside only: call for details.* ☏02 54 80 94 02.

This interesting château is encircled by a moat. The part of the building dating from the 13C was altered in 1720. The early-16C gatehouse is flanked by two towers decorated with a diaper pattern in red and black bricks. The machicolations guard the sentry walk and the pepper-pot roofs. The main building has a dormer window with a medallion of the lord of the manor, Antoine de la Vove. The park was landscaped by Jules Hardouin-Mansart and transformed in 1872 in the English style complete with a fine ice house from the 16C.

Commanderie d'Arville★

◔*Apr–Aug daily 10am–6.30pm; Feb–Mar and Sept–Nov daily 10am–12.30pm, 1.30–5.30pm.* ⊙€8 *(audioguide +€2).* ☏02 54 80 75 41. www.commanderie-arville.com.

The road D 921 running south from Le Gault-Perche offers a good view of the Templar Commandery, which later passed to the Knights of St John of Jerusalem (⚙*see box next page*). This assembly of ironstone buildings in its rural setting makes an attractive picture. The 12C **chapel** housing the Commandery is crowned by a gable belfry that is linked to a flint tower, once part of the former ramparts. The town **gateway** (late 15C) is decorated with two brick turrets with unusual conical roofs made of chestnut.

The handsome tithe **barn** and dovecote have been restored and an information centre about military religious orders has been set up to retrace the history of the crusades and re-create the crusaders' life with the help of pictures, sounds and even smells (badian, anise, etc.).

Souday

The village of Souday has a **church** whose nave is extended by an interesting 16C two-storey chancel. Two flights of stairs have wrought-iron railings that date from 1838, lead to the upper floor which is lit by Renaissance stained glass depicting the Passion and the Resurrection of Christ. The elegant ogive vaulting in the 11C crypt springs from columns

The Templars

The Order, which was both military and monastic, was founded in 1119 in Jerusalem. The members took vows to defend the Holy City from the Muslims and protect all Christians making a pilgrimage to Jerusalem. They built fortified commanderies along the routes to serve as banks in the 13C: pilgrims deposited money at their local commandery then drew it out on arrival in the Holy Land.

The Templars thus grew rich and powerful. Early in the 14C, the Order of Templars numbered 15 000 knights and 9 000 commanderies. It had its own judicial system, paid no tax and took its authority directly from the Pope. Such wealth and independence earned it many enemies and brought the Order's downfall.

In 1307, Philip the Fair persuaded the Pope that the Templars should be brought to trial; he had every single member of the Order in France arrested on the same day. The Grand Master, Jacques de Molay, and 140 knights were imprisoned in Chinon castle; the following year they were brought to Paris on trumped-up charges. Fifty-four of them, including Jacques de Molay, were burned at the stake on one of the islets in the Seine.

without capitals. The south transept is decorated with 16C paintings of St Joseph, St Joachim and four scenes from the Life of John the Baptist.

② SOUTH OF MONDOUBLEAU
Round trip of 24km/15mi. About 1h.

Le Temple
All that is left of the Templar commandery is a 13C church with a squat bell-tower and a square chevet nestling pleasantly by a pool.

▶ Turn right onto D 56.

Sargé-sur-Braye
The town's church of St-Martin was built in the 11C and 15C. The painted wainscots date from 1549. The murals discovered in the nave are 16C (*Pietà*, *St Martin*) and in the chancel 14C (*Christ in Majesty* and *Labours of the Months*; note the three faces of Janus symbolising January).

Baillou
The little village is attractively clustered below a great 16C–17C **château**. The early-16C **church** stands alone on a mount. The Renaissance doorway is flanked by scrolled pilasters, surmounted by figures of Adam and Eve.

▶ Take D 86 back to Mondoubleau. Fine view of the town on arrival.

ADDRESSES

🍽 STAY

◻◻ **Chambre d'hôte Peyron-Gaubert** – *Carrefour de l'Ormeau. ℘02 54 80 93 76. www.carrefour-de-lormeau. com. 5 rooms. Evening meal ◻◻◻.* All of the furniture in this strangely seductive 17C property was made by the owner, a cabinetmaker and artist. Meals incorporate organic vegetables from the on-site garden, whenever possible.

SHOPPING

Medieval market – *rte. des Templiers, 41170 Arville. ℘02 54 80 75 41. www. commanderie-arville.com.* This Middle Ages-themed market takes place at the Commanderie-Arville each Sun from Whitsun onwards. Lively and hugely entertaining, it features local craftspeople, sword fighting, jugglers, fire eaters, dancers, and **👥 activities for children**. Great for local produce and brushing up on your French.

La Ferté-Bernard ★

The Renaissance houses of the town cluster round the church of Notre-Dame-des-Marais. The lush pastures of the Huisne valley are watered by the Huisne river, its tributary the Même and the Sarthe. La Ferté-Bernard was the birthplace of the poet **Robert Garnier** (1544–90), whose best-known tragedy, *The Jews*, echoes Corneille and foreshadows Racine.

A BIT OF HISTORY

The old fortified town that grew up round the castle *(ferté)* was erected on stilts in the middle of the marshes. It was distinguished by the name of the first feudal lord, Bernard, whose descendants held the domain until the 14C.

Under Louis XI it was the property of the Guise family; in the 16C economic prosperity gave rise to some fine buildings that enhance the town. After siding with the Catholic League and being defeated by the troops of Henri IV, La Ferté was sold to Cardinal de Richelieu in 1642; and held by his heirs until the Revolution.

Today **electric boat rides (Bateaux électriques)** 👫 explore the town *(depart from r. Alfred-Marchand 2.30–6.30pm: Jul–Aug daily; May–Jun and Sept Sat–Sun and public holidays; ⊜ €5.10, under 17 years €3.60).*

SIGHTS

Porte St-Julien

This gate, which is protected by two round towers and machicolations, was built in the 15C under Louis XI; the moat was fed by the River Huisne. There was a postern and a double gate guarded by a portcullis and a drawbridge.

Old houses

East of the Porte St-Julien in r. de l'Huisne are a few Renaissance houses. There are several old houses in rue Carnot including a pilgrim inn (15C) on the road to Santiago de Compostela and a house (butcher's shop) decorated with a figure representing a pilgrim (ground floor).

▶ **Population:** 9 452.
◔ **Michelin Map:** 310: M-5
🏢 **Info:** 15 pl. de la Lice, 72400 La Ferté-Bernard. ☎02 43 71 21 21. www.tourisme-lafertebernard.fr.
◑ **Location:** 40km/25mi NE of Le Mans, 90km/56mi SW of Chartres, and 5km/3mi from autoroute A 11.
🅿 **Parking:** There are town centre car parks as well as on-street parking around the church.
◉ **Don't Miss:** The St Julien gate.
◑ **Timing:** Allow 1–2 hours to explore the town and have a coffee.
👫 **Kids:** Explore the town by canoe or electric-powered boat.

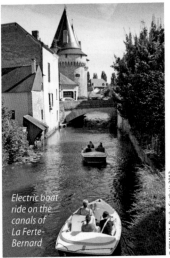

Electric boat ride on the canals of La Ferte-Bernard

© CEMJIKA, Perche Sarthois 2012

Halles

The market hall *(restored)* on place de la Lice and in rue Carnot was built in 1535. The façade overlooking the square is decorated with Guise lions on each gable and an extensive tile roof pierced by dormers and supported by a splendid timber frame.

Halles

© CEMJIKA, Perche Sarthois 2012

Fountain

pl. Carnot.

The granite fountain (15C–16C) is fed by a spring in the Guillottières district that is channelled beneath the Huisne.

Chapelle St-Lyphard

Thorough restoration work has revealed the chapel of an 11C feudal castle. The outbuildings (⊶ *private property*) also remain. The chapel, which was originally built against the main body of the castle and given a small side oratory, is decorated with modern stained-glass windows portraying Louis, Duke of Orléans, and his wife, Valentina Visconti, lord and lady of La Ferté-Bernard to whom the castle was endowed in 1392.

ADDITIONAL SIGHT

Église Notre-Dame-des-Marais★★

🕐 *Daily 8am–noon, 2–5.30pm.*

This magnificent church is a fine example of the Flamboyant Gothic style with early touches of the Renaissance. The nave, the transept and the square tower were built between 1450 and 1500; from 1535 to 1544 Mathurin Delaborde worked on the church, and between 1550 and 1590 the Viet brothers were in charge of the construction of the spacious chancel (completed in 1596). Don't miss the three **absidal chapels★**.

🚗 DRIVING TOUR

LE PERCHE-GOUËT★

87km/54mi round tour.
Allow half a day.

▷ Take D 153 via Cherreau and then the D 136 towards Ceton.

Le Perche-Gouet, which is sometimes known as Lower Perche, was named in the 11C after **William Gouet**, who owned five baronies within the jurisdiction of the Bishop of Chartres.

Le Perche-Gouët lies between the Loir and the Huisne. Much of the immense forest that once covered the land has been replaced by fields and orchards. The eastern part of Le Perche-Gouët is very similar to the Beauce, but is distinguished from it by its scattered farms and the abundance of hedges and trees. The farms hidden in the deep lanes were originally built of wattle and daub or within a brick framework. Their owners raise cattle, particularly dairy herds, which have replaced the breeding of the **Percheron draught horses**, their coats dappled grey, roan or black.

Ceton

In Ceton, the **church of St-Pierre** derives its importance from the Cluniac priory to which it belonged from 1090.

The tower is Romanesque, the Gothic nave and chancel were built in the 13C-16C. Each bay in the side aisles has its own roof at right angles to the nave in the Percheron manner.

▶ Continue along D 637 towards Coudray-au-Perche.

Les Étilleux

South of the village on the D 13, take the marked path that climbs to the summit of the hillock (270m high, with a radio-relay station) for fine views across the Ozanne valley, the Perche hills and the Huisne valley.

▶ Return to Coudray-au-Perche (D 124) then go on to Authon-du-Perche (D 9) to arrive at St-Ulphace on the D 13, which becomes the D 7.

St-Ulphace

Half way up the slope, the 15-16C church has an imposing façade leaning against a tower, and a Renaissance portal.

▶ Continue along D 14.

Montmirail

This attractive little town, once strongly fortified, was built on a site with excellent natural defences.

Castle – *guided tours: enquire at tourist office for current information.* Built in the 15C on top of a medieval mound, it was altered in the 18C by the Princesse de Conti. It still has the original underground works (11C and 14C).

In 1169, the castle was the scene of a memorable encounter between the kings of England and France during which the exiled Archbishop of Canterbury, **Thomas à Becket**, reaffirmed the primacy of the Church.

The apartments of the Princess (the daughter of Louis XIV and Louise de La Vallière) are open to the public, as are the dungeons and armouries. The Classical west façade, contrasting with the medieval south and east fronts, can be viewed from the terrace, which also provides a vast **panorama★** over the countryside of Le Perche-Gouet.

Église Notre-Dame-des-Marais

© CEMJIKA, Perche Sarthois 2012

▶ Go towards La Vibraye.
The D 302, the D72 cut through part off the Vibraye forest.

Semur-en-Vallon

This attractive village lies by a man-made lake. In the valley on the western edge of Vibraye Forest stands a 15C moated and turreted **castle**. The entrance façade, flanked by round towers with lanterns, was altered in the 17C.
A **tourist train** (*Jul–Aug daily; Jun and Sept Sun and holidays; €6, 2–12 years, €4.50; 02 43 93 67 86; www.lepetittraindesemur.com*) runs on a 1.5km/1mi long circuit.

▶ Take D 98 towards Lavaré. At Bois Guinant slow down to enjoy the view to the left and take first left.

Bouër

Don't miss this tiny village lost among the hills dominating the Huisne Valley. Its arrow-shaped slate steeple is attached to the tower by spiral volute scrolls.

▶ Take D 29 towards Montmirail until it meets the D 1. Go left here. At Lamnay, go right onto D 125.

Château de Courtangis

Among the tall trees in an idyllically isolated valley are the turrets, dormers and steeply pitched mansard roofs of a graceful early-16C manor house.

▷ Leave Courtangis towards Courtenard on D 36.

Courgenard

In this small village with its pretty gardens, the door of the **church** is carved with low-relief statues in the Renaissance style.

ADDRESSES

♀/EAT

⊖⊜–⊖⊜⊜ **Restaurant du Dauphin** – *3 r. d'Huisne.* ♿ *₰02 43 93 00 39. www.restaurant-du-dauphin.com. Thu eve, Sun eve, Mon.* This restaurant near the Porte St-Julien serves traditional and regional cuisine with an inventive twist amid warm tones and modern furnishings.

⊖⊜–⊖⊜⊜ **Auberge de la Forêt** – *38 r. Gabriel-Goussault, 72320 Vibraye. 16km/10mi S of La Ferté-Bernard, towards St Calais then D 211.* 🅿 *₰02 43 93 60 07. www.restaurant-auberge-de-la-foret.fr. Closed Sun eve, Mon.* "Content" describes how you will come away from this auberge after sampling its local dishes. Outdoor terrace in summer and 7 modern bedrooms (⊖⊜⊜) for a stopover.

Brou

Although Brou was once a barony in Le Perche-Gouet, it is more characteristic of the rich and fertile agricultural region of Beauce; it's a town centred on its market place where poultry and eggs are the main commerce. Many old street names here have remained unchanged since the Middle Ages.

THE TOWN

Place des Halles

On the corner of rue de la Tête-Noire stands an old house with projecting upper storeys, which dates from the early 16C; the timberwork is decorated with carved motifs.

In rue des Changes near the market place there is another 16C house with a curved façade; the corner post bears the figures of St James and a pilgrim, since Brou lies on the old pilgrimage route from Chartres to Santiago de Compostela in Spain.

Église de Yèvres

1.5km/0.9mi E.

The **church** dates mainly from the 15C and 16C, its Renaissance doorway

▶ **Population:** 3 480.
◉ **Michelin Map:** 311: C-6
🏢 **Info:** r. de la Chevalerie, 28160 Brou. *₰02 37 47 01 12. http://brou28.com.*
◐ **Location:** 22km/14mi NW of Châteaudun, 40km/25mi S of Chartres and 45km/28mi E of La Ferté-Bernard.
◷ **Timing:** Arrive Wednesday morning for the food market in the pl. des Halles.
👪 **Kids:** Let off steam in Brou's **Parc de loisirs**.

framed by carved pilasters and surmounted by a double pediment.

The interior contains remarkable classical **woodwork★**: the pulpit, which is decorated with effigies of the Virtues; the retable on the high altar; the altars in the side chapels; and an eagle lectern. The door into the baptismal chapel (fine carved wood ceiling) is beautifully carved with scenes of the Martyrdom of St Barbara and the Baptism of Christ.

EXCURSIONS
Illiers-Combray
Illiers, on the upper reaches of the Loire, 24km/15mi southwest of Chartres and 28km/17mi northwest of Châteaudun, is a market town serving both the Beauce and Perche regions.

It was under the name of Combray that French writer **Marcel Proust** (1871–1922) portrayed Illiers in his famous novel *Remembrance of Things Past*. Proust spent his holidays in Illiers where his father was born; the impressions young Marcel experienced here were later to become "that great edifice of memories".

Musée Marcel-Proust - Maison de tante Léonie
Place Lemoine. Guided tours daily except Mon: mid-Jan–Jun and Sept–mid-Dec 2.30, and 4pm; Jul–Aug 11am, 2.30pm, and 4pm. €7. Mid-Dec–mid-Jan, 1 May, 1 and 11 Nov. 02 37 24 30 97.
Some of the rooms, such as the kitchen and dining room, in this house belonging to Proust's uncle, Jules Amiot, are still as they were in the novel. The bedrooms have been arranged to match Proust's descriptions of them.
The **museum** evokes the writer's life, work and relationships. Portraits and mementoes as well as a number of early photographs taken by Paul Nadar are on display.

Le Pré Catelan
Just S of Illiers-Combray on D 149. Rte. de Transonville. Daily: May–Aug 9am–8pm; Sept–Apr 9am–5.30pm. Free. 02 37 24 00 05. www.illiers-combray.com.
Designed by Proust's uncle, Jules Amiot, these lovely gardens are also named The Garden of Marcel Proust as well as Swan Park. The peaceful grounds include a serpentine, a dovecote, a pavilion and some fine trees; they make a pleasant place for a walk beside the Loir.

DRIVING TOUR

LE FAUX-PERCHE
65km/40mi. Allow half a day.

Although it also borders the Beauce region, the western part of le Perche-Gouët, known also as **Faux-Perche**, differs from le Bas-Perche due to its varied habitats – abundant hedgerows, trees and rolling landscapes. Farms are known locally as "borderies", and rely mainly on cattle breeding, particularly dairy herds, which have taken the place of breeding dapple-grey, black or chestnut percheron draf1t horses. The waterways of the Ozanne, Yerre and Braye flow towards the Loir; only the Rhône meets the Huisne at Nogent-le-Rotrou.

Take the D 921 via Chapelle-Royale to La Bazoche-Gouët, the gateway to the Perche Regional Natural Park.

Le Bazoche-Gouët
The 12C–13C **church** in this town was modified at the start of the 16C by adding flamboyant window bays and side aisles. Note the portal with spiral columns of the south bay. Inside is a square 16C belfry; the Renaissance stained glass in the chancel depicts the Passion of Christ as seen in German engravings that were a gift from the local Lords, the Bourbon-Conti family. Note the realism of expression and details.

Take D 9 towards Nogent-le-Rotrou, then approx 5km/3mi after Authon-du-Perche, go right onto D 371 towards Vichères where you turn off to La Gaudaine.

Ferme de Rougemont
From D 371 at this high farmstead enjoy a sweeping **view** over the Ozanne basin.

Thiron-Gardais
This village has developed on the south bank of the Thironne, which flows out of the Étang des Moines (Monks' Pool) near the abbey founded by St Bernard in 1114 and dedicated to the Holy Trinity. Tiron abbey (written without the "h" in

Abbey church, Thiron-Gardais

those days) was especially prosperous in the 12C and 13C. The **abbey church** is still a huge building even though the chancel collapsed in 1817.

▶ Continue along D 922 towards Brou via Chassant.

Frazé

Frazé is a small village nestled beside the River Foussarde. Its origins are Gallo-Roman; later it was fortified and surrounded by water. The village square provides a charming view of both the church and the château.

The **château★** was first built to a square ground plan in 1493 and protected by a moat and a pool; it was completed in the 16C and 17C with the outbuildings that form an entrance porch. The surviving buildings include a watchtower; two towers, of which one stands alone and is decorated with machicolations and a moulding; a fort flanked by towers and ornamented with sculpted corbels; and an interesting chapel with historiated ornaments.

An old well, gardens, canals and terraces enhance the courtyard and the park (&⊙*only the château grounds are open to the public: early Apr–Oct Sun 3–6pm; ℰ02 37 29 56 76).*

ADDRESSES

🛏 STAY

⊜⊜ **Hôtel le Plat d'Étain** – *15 pl. des Halles, 28160 Brou. ℰ09 70 35 03 00. www.leplatdetain.com. 20 rooms. Restaurant (⊜⊜).* This hotel in the town centre offers comfortable, modern rooms, and terrace dining in summer. Breakfast is buffet-style.

🍴 EAT

⊜⊜ **L'Ascalier** – *9 pl. Dauphin, 28160 Brou. ℰ02 37 96 05 52. www.lascalier.com. Closed Mon eve, Tue.* Near Brou's market hall, this restaurant features simple cooking, reasonable prices, and a lovely 16C staircase. Outdoor dining seasonally.

LEISURE ACTIVITIES

Parc de loisirs – *rte. des Moulins, 28160 Brou. Jul–Aug daily 10am–7pm; Jun Sat–Sun 2pm–7pm. €5.80 (children €3.75). ℰ02 37 47 02 17. www.brou28.com.* This 28ha park offers a lake, beach, watersports, tennis, fishing. Camping, mobile homes and chalets welcome.

Although Le Loir cannot offer the architectural splendours of La Loire, it has a more rustic charm that many find more seductive than its stately big sister, as visitors dawdle gently through a lushly verdant, lightly wooded landscape with little bridges straddling the waters at each village. The confusingly named tributary runs more than 300km/186mi from south of Chartres to Angers, and is at its most attractive between Vendôme and Trôo, where a maze of troglodyte dwellings marks the land.

A Breath of Fresh Air

The Loir offers churches, châteaux and historic towns, as well as fishing, boating, walking and cycling, and wine-tasting. In its upper reaches, the river winds its way through hills, meadows, well-heeled towns and pretty villages. At the busy market town of Châteaudun, the Château de Dunois soars dramatically from a bluff above the river banks. The next major port of call heading south is Vendôme, a captivating town built on islands in the river. Pilgrims heading for Santiago de Compostela once stopped here; now it is a chic place to live within commuting distance of Paris, with trendy waterside restaurants to cater to an affluent clientele. Continuing west along a lovely wooded stretch of the Loir, you arrive at quaint Lavardin, a small village of restored houses and a romantically ruined château. Then comes Montoire, where Pétain and Hitler met in 1940, and the poet Ronsard was prior of the frescoed Chapelle St-Gilles.

Wine and History

After a trip around troglodyte houses and Romanesque frescoes in the church

of St-Jacques-des-Guérets in Trôo, wine buffs might want to explore the vineyards on the slopes around Poncé and La Chartre-sur-le-Loir, where Côteaux du Vendômois and the unique Vin Gris wine is produced.

North of the river, a foray among the oak of the Forêt de Bercé awaits. Rejoining the Loir, the parkland and formal gardens of the Renaissance Château du Lude are a must. Finish at La Flèche, where the Prytanée, a military academy set up originally as a Jesuit college in the 17C by Henri IV, can be visited.

Highlights

1 **Châteaudun** and its imposing castle (p322)

2 **Old Vendôme** and la Trinité (p328)

3 **Lavardin**'s ruined château (p338)

4 The **Bercé** forest for a walk (p343)

5 Magnificent park of **Château du Lude** (p347)

Château du Lude

© Arnaud Chicurel/hemis.fr

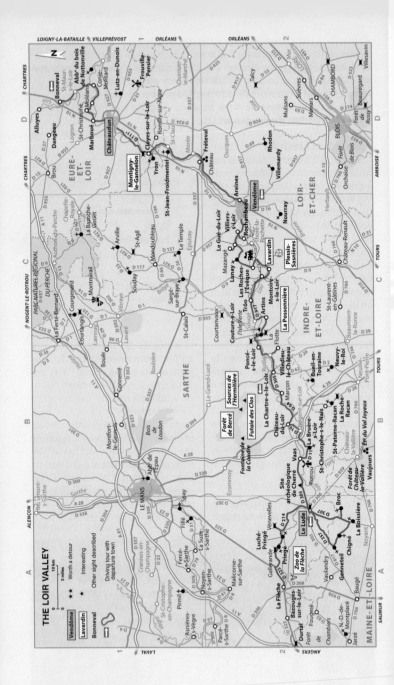

THE LOIR VALLEY

Vendôme ★★ Worth a detour
Lavardin ★ Interesting
Bonneval ☐ Other sight described

Driving tour with departure town

10 km
5 miles

Bonneval

Bonneval developed in the Middle Ages around the 9C Benedictine monastery of St-Florentin on the River Loir. The old town walls are reflected in the waters of the surrounding moat. With its small attractive churches, often decorated with frescoes, and shaded riverbanks, the Bonneval region is an angler's paradise and a walker's dream. Its network of canals have earned it the nickname "Little Venice of the Beauce".

- ▶ **Population:** 4,986.
- **Michelin Map:** 311: E-6
- **Info:** 2 pl. Westerham, 28800 Bonneval. https://otdubonnevalais.com ☎ 09 63 60 34 33.
- **Location:** Along the N 10, between Chartres (28km/17.4mi to the N) and Châteaudun (15km/9mi to the S).
- **Don't Miss:** The Loir Valley is well worth exploring; very scenic.
- **Timing:** You can explore Bonneval in 1 hour, but take a day and get to know the surrounding area.
- **Kids:** A boat trip on the canals (☎ see box p320).

SIGHTS

Ancienne Abbaye de St-Florentin

A specialist hospital centre now occupies the former abbey buildings. The handsome 13C **fortified gateway★** with its pointed archway was integrated into the abbot's lodging, which was built for the Bishop of Chartres in the late 15C. The lodge is an attractive building of chequered stonework, flanked by two machicolated towers and capped with pinnacled gables over the dormer windows. In front of the abbey stretches the **Grève**, a large shaded promenade beside the moat.

For an attractive view of the old towers and the church spire, go to the end of r. des Fossés-St-Jacques to the west of the town.

Église Notre-Dame

The early-13C church was built in the pure Gothic style: a fine rose window above the flat chevet, an elegant triforium in the nave, fine woodwork behind the font and a 17C figure of Christ. From the nearby bridge there is a picturesque view of the fortifications and of the moat lined with washhouses.

Porte St-Roch and Tour du Roi

Several pointed arches mark the old houses that line rue St-Roch, the street that leads to St-Roch Gate with its two round towers. Beside it stands the King's Tower, the old keep, pierced by loopholes and capped with a pepper-pot roof.

Porte Boisville and Pont du Moulin

To the west of town, between the railway and the bypass, stands the Boisville Gate (13C); the only remaining part of the first town wall, it was reduced in size in the 15C.

EXCURSIONS

Alluyes

7km/4.3mi NW on D 144.

All that is left of the old **castle** is the great round tower of the keep and a fortified gate spanning the moat. On the riverside, the 15C–16C **church** has two fascinating murals.

Dangeau

9km/5.6mi W on D 27.

The village square is bordered by old houses of brick and timber construction (15C). The **Église St-Pierre**, which was built in the early 12C by monks from Marmoutier, is a vast, well-balanced structure in pure Romanesque style. The buttresses and facings are in ironstone. The door in the south porch is embellished with scrolls and strange symbols carved on the lintel: the Cross appears between the Sun and the Moon, which have been given human faces. Avarice is shown as a demon holding a purse, whereas Lust is portrayed as a female figure.

The wooden ceiling in the nave is supported on archaic pillars. There are several statues in the aisles: the two figures on horseback are typical of popular 15C–17C sacred art. The baptistery contains a marble triptych of the Passion and the Resurrection, dated 1536.

🚗 DRIVING TOUR

UPPER REACHES OF THE LOIR
77km/48mi. Allow one day.

The Loir wends its leisurely way through a peaceful landscape defined by rolling hills, green meadows, smart towns and charming villages that have earned the region the name *La Douce France* (Gentle France). Originally the river was navigable up to Château-du-Loir, but now the only boats are occupied by fishermen who appreciate the variety and abundance of the fish and the beauty of the poplars and silvery willows at the water's edge.

▶ Leave Bonneval to the S.

There are uninterrupted views of the surrounding countryside as the road cuts through the plateau. Before **Conie**, the road crosses the river of the same name and follows it (D 110) downstream to **Moléans** with its 17C castle.

In the pretty village of **St-Christophe** the road rejoins the slow waters of the Loir, which it follows (D 361) to Marboué.

Marboué
Once a Gallo-Roman settlement, the village is known for its tall 15C bell-tower and crocketed spire as well as for its bathing beach on the river.

Châteaudun★★
⌖See CHÂTEAUDUN.

Montigny-le-Gannelon★
The castle, rising on the north bank of the Loir, can be seen from afar. The name Montigny comes from Mons-Igny meaning Signal Hill; Gannelon evokes either the traitor who betrayed Roland to his enemies, or more likely the priest of St-Avit abbey in Châteaudun who inherited the fortress in the 11C. The **church**, dedicated to St Gilles and St-Sauveur, houses the shrine of Ste Félicité.

Château★
av. du Marquis de Lévis.
♿🚶‍♂️*By guided tour only: Easter to September, 10am–5.30pm, closed Mon.*
⌖*Park and château €9; park only €4.*
☎*02 37 98 30 03.*
www.domainedemontigny.com.
The château is approached through the park, in full view of the highly composite west façade. The combination of brick and stonework is striking. Two towers – Tour des Dames and Tour de l'Horloge – are the only remains of the Renaissance château that was rebuilt from 1475 to 1495 by Jacques de Renty.

The interior contains interesting information on the illustrious **Lévis-Mirepoix** family. To the right of a large Renaissance staircase adorned with portraits of Marshals of Lévis in medallions are the Gothic cloisters with a fine collection of 16C Italian faïence plates. The richly furnished rooms that follow contain numerous portraits and mementoes of the Montmorency and Lévis-Mirepoix families. They are the Salon des Colonnes, Salon des Dames, Grand Salon (portrait of Gilles de Montmorency-Laval, Sire of Rais, said to have

Mural paintings, Chapelle d'Yron

© Philippe Blanchot/hemis.fr

inspired Charles Perrault for his character Bluebeard) and the Salle à Manger Montmorency (portraits of Louis XVIII and Charles X by the Baron Gérard).

On the grounds, ostrich, emu, nandu (a South American ostrich), waterfowl and pheasant roam beneath 150-year-old trees.

Hidden behind a screen of greenery stand the former riding school and stables, a vast shed on a frame of steel girders built at the same time as the Eiffel Tower in Paris. Today it contains old farm implements, carriages and stuffed animals.

Cloyes-sur-le-Loir

Once a fortified town and staging post on the pilgrim road to Santiago de Compostela, Cloyes straddles a bend in the Loir on the southern edge of the Beauce region. It is a welcoming town with several picturesque old houses and a church with a 15C belfry. In 1883 **Émile Zola** stayed in Cloyes to study the local customs for his novel *The Earth,* which is set in Cloyes and **Romilly-sur-Aigre**.

▷ Leave Cloyes on D 81 E to Bouche-d'Aigre. Drive 1km/0.6mi S on D 35 (towards Vendôme), then turn right onto D 81; the entrance is in the garden of the home for the elderly.

Chapelle d'Yron

This Romanesque chapel is decorated with well-preserved **mural paintings** in red and ochre tones.

Those in the nave are 12C and depict the *Flagellation* and the *Offering of the Magi (left),* the *Kiss of Judas* and an abbot (St Bernard) *(right)* and the *Apostles (apse)* below a gentle-featured *Christ in Majesty* (14C) on the oven vault of the apse.

▷ Return to Cloyes and take the D 8 toward Bouche-d'Aigre. The D 145 follows the Loir and crosses St-Claude.

St-Jean-Froidmentel

On the west bank is the village of St-Jean-Froidmentel. Its church has an attractive Gothic Renaissance doorway.

▷ Return to the east bank.

A row of poplars separates the road from the river. Between Morée and Fréteval fishing huts line the bank as do one or two pretty riverside houses with flat-bottomed boats moored nearby.

Fréteval

The ruins of a **medieval** castle *(15min round trip on foot)* look down from their bluff on the east bank to Fréteval on the far bank, a favourite meeting place for fishermen. Soon after, the signed tourist road leaves the river bank.

Areines

Lying in the Loir plain, this village was an important town in the Roman era. The 12C **church** bears a plain façade, adorned by a 14C Madonna.

Châteaudun★★

Châteaudun is the first of the Loire châteaux to come into sight on the road from Paris. The town of Châteaudun and its castle stand on a bluff, indented by narrow valleys called *cavées,* on the south bank of the Loir at the point where the Perche region joins the Beauce. The château's circular keep, built by Thibaud V, dates to the 12C.

A BIT OF HISTORY

Dunois, the Bastard of Orléans (1402–68) – Handsome **Jean de Dunois**, the faithful companion of Joan of Arc, was the illegitimate son of Louis I of Orléans and Mariette d'Enghien. He was brought up by **Valentina Visconti**, Louis' wife, who loved him as much as her own children. From the age of 15, Dunois fought the English for several decades. In 1429 he rallied the army to the defence of Orléans and delivered Montargis. He took part in all the great events of Joan of Arc's career. Towards the end of his life, having won all the honours it is possible for one man to win, he retired to Châteaudun in 1457.

Dunois was buried in the church of Notre-Dame at Cléry. He was well educated and well read: Jean Cartier, the chronicler, described him as "one of the best speakers of the French language."

A heroic defence – On 18 October 1870 the Prussians attacked Châteaudun with 24 cannons and 12,000 men. Confronting them were only 300 local members of the national guard and 600 free fighters, who managed to hold out all day behind their barricades, despite heavy bombing that lasted from noon to 6.30pm. Finally, they had to admit they were outnumbered and consented to retreat. The Prussians promptly set fire to the town and 263 houses were razed. In recognition of services rendered to France, Châteaudun received the Legion of Honour and adopted the motto *Extincta revivisco* ("I rise again from the ashes"). *See EXCURSIONS, Musée de la Guerre 1870.*

- ▶ **Population:** 12,980.
- **Michelin Map:** 311: D-7
- **Info:** 1 r. de Luynes, 28200 Châteaudun &02 37 45 22 46. www. chateaudun-tourisme.fr.
- **Location:** 130km/80mi SW of Paris, between Chartres (45km/28mi to the N) and Vendôme (40km/25mi to the SW).
- **Don't Miss:** The dungeon, and the Musée des Beaux-Arts et d'Histoire naturelle.
- **Kids:** Explore the Loir by canoe or horseback. Visit the Foulon caves.
- **Timing:** Allow 2 hours to explore the town, and at least 1 day for Excursions.

WALKING TOUR

OLD TOWN★

Rue du Château, which is lined by overhanging houses, opens onto a charming little square with two old houses: the one with pilasters, beams and carved medallions dates from the 16C; the other, heavily restored, is a corner house with a carved corner post showing the Virgin and St Anne *(badly damaged).* It is prolonged by rue de la Cuirasserie (fine 16C house with a corner turret), which opens onto a square named after **Cap-de-la-Madeleine**, a town in the province of Quebec in Canada founded in the 17C by a priest from Châteaudun. On the right sits the Hôtel-Dieu, founded in 1092 and modernised in 1762; on the left rises the Palais de Justice (Law Court), housed in a former Augustinian abbey built in the Classical style.

The **Église de la Madeleine★** is built into the ramparts; its north façade is topped by pointed gables. The church was built in the 12C, but never completed due to insufficient funds.

▶ Continue down rue des Huileries to rue de la Porte-d'Abas.

Château de Châteaudun

On the left, near the ruins of a Roman gate, stands the 16C Loge aux Portiers (Porters' Lodge) decorated with a carefully restored statue of the Virgin Mary.

◗ Walk up rue St-Lubin, lined with impressive houses (Nos. 2 and 12), to return to the front of the château. Go through the arch at the beginning of rue de Luynes and onto impasse du Cloître-St-Roch, then turn right onto a narrow, winding street, venelle des Ribaudes, which opens onto a small square on the edge of the bluff.

From here there is a pleasant **view** of the Loir and its valley. On the right of

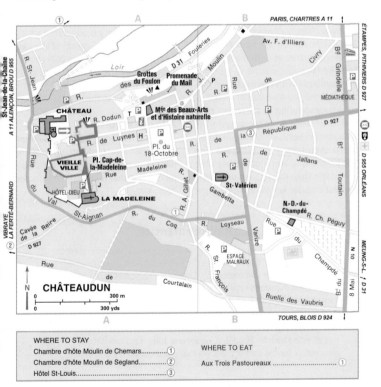

WHERE TO STAY

Chambre d'hôte Moulin de Chemars .... ①
Chambre d'hôte Moulin de Segland .... ②
Hôtel St-Louis .... ③

WHERE TO EAT

Aux Trois Pastoureaux .... ①

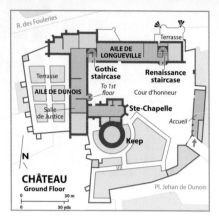

R. des Fouleries

Terrasse

AILE DE LONGUEVILLE

Gothic staircase

Terrasse

To 1st floor

AILE DE DUNOIS

Renaissance staircase

Cour d'honneur

Salle de Justice

Ste-Chapelle

Accueil

Keep

N

CHÂTEAU
Ground Floor

0   30 m
0   30 yds

Pl. Jehan de Dunois

the square stands a 15C house with a Flamboyant door and mullion windows.

▶ Take rue Dodun back to the château.

CHÂTEAU★★

Pl. Jean-Dunois. ○*Daily: May–Jun 10am–1pm, 2–6pm; Jul–early Sept 10am–1pm, 2–6.15pm; early Sept–Apr 10am–12.30pm, 2–5.30pm.* ◉€6. ○*1 Jan, 1 May, 25 Dec.* ✆*02 37 94 02 90. www.chateau-chateaudun.fr.*

The castle combines the majesty of medieval fortresses with the luxury of early Renaissance mansions. It blends harmoniously with the medicinal garden and the town's maze of medieval streets descending to the river. Crude and fortress-like from the outside, the structures resemble a stately mansion when seen from the courtyard. The **keep**, which is 31m high without the roof, dates from the 12C; it is one of the earliest circular keeps, as well as one of the most impressive and best preserved.

The **basement rooms** extend into the Dunois wing *(entrance at the bottom of the Gothic staircase)*. Two of these rooms, handsomely decorated with intersecting ribbed vaulting, housed the kitchens, each with a double fireplace running the whole width of the room. The small rooms on the north side were occupied by the guards in charge of the cramped prison cells, some of which feature ogee vaulting.

Sainte-Chapelle

Dunois was responsible for this elegant 15C building; it is flanked by a square belfry and two oratories and the chancel ends in a three-sided apse.

The upper chapel, which was provided for the servants, has a panelled wooden ceiling; the lower chapel has ogee vaulting.

The south oratory is decorated with a well-preserved 15C mural of the Last Judgement. The charming collection of 15 **statues**★★ is an excellent example of the work produced in the workshops in the Loire Valley in the late 15C.

Aile de Dunois

This wing was begun c.1460 and is built in the true Gothic tradition, although the interior furnishings suggest the desire for comfort that followed the Hundred Years War.

A Wise Financier

A local man called **Dodun** gradually worked his way up from nothing to become Financial Controller under the Régence of Philippe d'Orléans. In 1724, his portrait was painted by Rigaud; in 1727 Bullet built him a magnificent mansion in rue de Richelieu in Paris; the château and the marquisate of Herbault also came into his possession.

Dodun showed loyalty to his region by finding the money to rebuild Châteaudun after the town had burnt down in 1723. Reconstruction work was directed by Jules Hardouin, nephew of Jules Hardouin-Mansart; he was responsible for the part of the town that is laid out on the grid system.

The huge living rooms have massive overhead beams and are hung with tapestries, including, on the first floor, a superb series from Brussels depicting the Life of Moses. Visitors then come to the Salle de Justice (Court Room), where the Lord of the Manor passed judgement and which was panelled in the 17C and painted with the arms of Louis XIV for an occasion when the King visited Châteaudun. This room served as a Revolutionary tribunal in 1793.

Aile de Longueville

In completing his father's work, François I de Longueville had a **staircase★** built in the Flamboyant Gothic style. The design echoes the transition between the medieval turreted staircase of the Dunois wing and the Renaissance at the east end of the wing. The Longueville wing was built between 1510 and 1520 by François II de Longueville and then by his brother the Cardinal on foundations that date from the preceding century, but it was never completed. At roof level an Italian cornice supports a Flamboyant balustrade.

The Renaissance **staircase★** at the east end is richly decorated with Italian motifs set in a Gothic setting. The ground floor rooms, including the Renaissance gallery, are hung with 17C Paris and Amiens tapestries. In the Grand Salon *(first floor)* are carved 16C chests and facing each other, two monumental chimney-pieces, one in the Gothic and one in the Renaissance style.

Medieval Gardens

At the foot of the keep, the herb garden contains useful plants grown in the Middle Ages for cooking and medicine. Roses and lilies grace the Mary garden.

ADDITIONAL SIGHTS

Musée des Beaux-Arts et d'Histoire naturelle

3 r. Toufaire. ◐Sep–Jun Mon, Wed–Fri 9am–noon, 1.30–5pm, Sat–Sun and public holidays 1.30–5pm; Jul–Aug 9.30am–noon, 1.30–6pm. ◉€4.30. ℘02 37 45 55 36.

Birth of the Alexandrine Metre

It was at Châteaudun in the 12C that the poet **Lambert le Tort** was born. He was one of the authors of the *Story of Alexander*, a heroic poem inspired by the legend of Alexander the Great that was popular in the Middle Ages. Its 22,000 lines were written in the heroic metre, with 12 feet or syllables to the line, which subsequently came to be known as the Alexandrine metre.

This Fine Art and Natural History Museum has a remarkable **collection of stuffed birds★** (2,500) from countries all over the world.

The **Egyptian archaeology** room contains funerary objects from the early Dynastic Period (3100–2700 BC) discovered at Abydos, and **mummies** and sarcophagi from Roman Antiquity. Local history is evoked by the reconstitution of a typical Beauce domestic interior and artefacts excavated in the Châteaudun area.

The **Asian art** collection features French East India Company porcelain, and pieces belonging to the Wahl-Offroy collection: weapons from the Middle and Far East, Chinese jewellery, Buddhist statuary and Islamic miniatures. The **Painting Gallery** displays local landscapes of the 19C.

≛ Grottes du Foulon

35 r. des Fouleries. ☞Guided visits at 2pm, 3pm, 4pm: Jan–Mar and mid-Sept–mid-Dec Sat–Sun and public holidays; Apr–Jun and 1–mid-Sept daily except Tue–Wed; Jul–Aug daily except Mon morning, tours also at 10am, 11am, 5pm; mid-end Dec Sat–Sun and public holidays. ◐1, 8 and 25 May. ◉€9 (child 6–10, €5, 11–17, €7. ℘02 37 45 19 60. www.grottesdufoulon.sitew.com.

Lining the roadside, and clearly visible, these caves owe their name to the fullers

Grottes du Foulon

© Grottes du Foulon

(*fouleurs*) who worked here. Hollowed out in Senonian limestone by the waters of the Loir, the cave roofs have flinty concretions that, in places, have been transformed into geodes of chalcedony or quartz by the effects of crystallisation.

Promenade du Mail
The mall walk along the bluff above the river has been turned into a public garden. The **view★** stretches westward across the two branches of the Loir, the suburb of St-Jean and beyond to the hillsides of the Perche region.

Église St-Valérien
The 12C building is topped by a tall belfry with a 15C stone spire. On the southern flank, admire the fine poly-lobed romanesque portal.

Chapelle Notre-Dame-du-Champdé
All that remains of this funerary chapel, destroyed at the end of the 19C, is a Flamboyant façade with finely worked ornamentation; a delicate balustrade is supported by sculpted consoles at the base of the gable that holds an effigy of the Virgin Mary, to whom the chapel is dedicated.

Église St-Jean-de-la-Chaîne
Exit the town via r. St-Jean across the river (see map p323).
In the suburb of St-Jean on the north bank of the Loir stands an early-16C ogee-arched gate at the entrance to the churchyard. The **church of St-Jean** was built mainly in the 15C but the apses date from the 11C and 12C.

EXCURSIONS
Lutz-en-Dunois
7km/4mi E along D 955.
Lutz has a Romanesque **church** with a low bell-tower crowned by a saddleback roof. The interior is decorated with 13C **murals** in red and yellow ochre: those on the oven-vault above the apse depict the Apostles and Bishop Saints; on the walls of the nave are Christ's Entry into Jerusalem, the Entombment, the Resurrection and the Descent into Limbo.

👥 Moulin de Frouville Pensier
10km/6mi SE. Take D 31 towards Ozoir-le-Breuil, then go left on D 144 towards St-Cloud-en-Dunois.
🐌 *By guided tour: contact for details.* ℘*06 86 84 80 19. http://moulin.frouville.free.fr.*
This is the only surviving stone wind-mill of the Beauce region. It dates from 1274, but was rebuilt after a fire in 1826.

See it in action and the impressive mill-stones (1.9m and 1.3m in diameter), its 21m wingspan and the roof that pivots with a rudder tail.

Abbaye du Bois de Nottonville

18km/11mi E; take D 927 to Varize and then follow the signs. ☞Guided tours only by 2-day advance request May–mid-Oct. ✆02 37 96 91 64.

The 11C priory (restored in the 15C) belonged to Benedictine monks from Marmoutier. Note, in particular, the fortified doorway, the barn with a roof shaped like an inverted ship's hull, and the dovecot.

Musée de la Guerre 1870

In Loigny-la-Bataille, 34km/21mi W along the D 927 towards Janville and Pithiviers. At the Orgères-en-Beauce exit, turn right on to the D 39. ⏱Apr–May and Sept–Oct Tue–Fri, Sun and public holidays, 2.30–6.30pm; Jun–Aug Tue–Fri 10am–noon, 2.30–6.30pm, Sat–Sun, and public holidays 2.30–6.30pm. ⊛€5.50. ✆02 37 36 13 25. www.museedelaguerre1870.fr.

The village's name and neo-Roman-esque memorial church next to the museum honour 9,000 men who died in the battle of 2 Dec 1870. The crypt holds the tombs of Generals Charette and Sonis; in the nave, paintings by Lionel Royer depict the night of the bat-tle with the Prussian army. The soldiers' bones (1,200 French and 60 Prussians) lie in an ossuary. The recently renovated museum holds a unique collection of objects, weapons and uniforms from the war of 1870.

Château de Villeprévost

At Tillay-le-Péneux 34km/21mi W on D 927. 3km/1.8mi after Orgères-en-Beauce go right onto the D 118 via Tanon. ⏱Jul–mid-Aug Wed–Sat 1–7pm. ⊛€5. ✆02 37 99 45 17.

Surrounded by French-style gar-dens, this 17C–18C manor house once belonged to Amand-François Fougeron, a King's counsellor and Justice of the Peace for Orgères. Thanks to his efforts

the 'Orgères scorchers' were arrested – a dreaded gang of more than 300 criminals who terrorised the region by burning their victims' feet. Their trial was held in Villeprévost in the reception lounge of the château. The 16C dovecote contains the horrific death masks of the condemned men.

ADDRESSES

⌂ STAY

⊛ **Le Saint Louis** – *41 r. de la Républ.* ✆*02 37 45 00 01. 36 rooms.* 🅿 The hotel, 1km from the chateau, has a restaurant/bar. Simply furnished rooms include private bath (shower). Continental breakfast.

⊛⊛ **Chambre d'hôte Moulin de Segland** – *54 r. de Segland, Saint-Denis-les-Ponts, 3km/1.8mi W of Châteaudun.* ✆*02 37 45 22 02. http://segland-chambres dhotes.wifeo.com. 4 rooms.* The B&B in this old mill offers riverside tranquillity and countryside greenery. Simply furnished rooms and a kitchen for guests, and a village just 1km away.

♟/EAT

⊛⊛⊛ **Aux Trois Pastoureaux** – *31 r. André-Gillet.* ✆*02 37 45 74 40. www.aux-trois-pastoureaux.fr. Closed Sun, Mon, and Tue lunch.* Wood panelling and local art add a Provençal air to this inviting restaurant. Traditional and medieval menus and a selection of wines by the glass.

LEISURE ACTIVITIES

Centre Équestre Dunois – *chemin de St-Martin.* ✆*02 37 66 00 00. www. centreequestredunois.ffe.com. Closed Sun.* Horse-related activities on-site, and horse or pony rides in the area. Itineraries of several days, staying in gîtes, farms or campsites.

Club Canoë Kayak Dunois – *4 r. des Fouleries.* ✆*06 33 32 53 64. http://canoe-kayak-chateaudun.fr. Daily Apr–Oct Sat–Sun and public holidays; Jul–Aug daily 9am–noon, 2–6pm.* Canoe or kayak the Loir river. The gently-flowing river means that all ages can enjoy a calm journey downstream.

Vendôme★★

At the foot of a steep bluff, which is crowned by a castle, the River Loir branches out into several channels that flow slowly under a number of bridges. Vendôme stands on a group of islands dotted with timber-framed houses, gables and slate roofs, the haunt of the poet Ronsard.

▶ **Population:** 16,716.
◔ **Michelin Map:** 318: D-5
▤ **Info:** Hôtel du Saillant, 47-49 r. de la Poterie, 41100 Vendôme. ✆02 54 77 05 07. www.vendome-tourisme.fr.
▶ **Location:** 30 km/18.6mi NW of Blois, between Tours (56km/35mi to the SW) and Châteaudun (40km/25mi to the NE). By TGV, Vendôme is just 45min from Paris.
▣ **Parking:** Large car park at pl. de la Liberté.
◉ **Don't Miss:** The older parts of town.
♟ **Kids:** Water sports at Pland d'Eau de Villiers-sur-Loir.
◔ **Timing:** A guided tour of the town is 2 hours, but allow half a day to get the most from your visit.

A BIT OF HISTORY

Although its origins of can be traced back to Neolithic periods, before the town received its name, Vindocenum, in the Gallo-Roman period, Vendôme only began to acquire importance under the counts, first the Bouchard family, who were faithful supporters of the Capet dynasty, and particularly under the son of Fulk Nerra, **Geoffrey Martel** (11C), who founded La Trinité abbey.

Vendôme was given to César de Bourbon, the eldest son of Henri IV and Gabrielle d'Estrées as a royal prerogative. César de Vendôme was often resident on his feudal estate while he involved himself with conspiracies, first during the minority of Louis XIII and then against Richelieu. He was imprisoned at Vincennes for four years before being exiled. He eventually lent his support to Mazarin's cause, before dying in 1665.

SIGHTS
Jardin public
Cascading down to the riverside, the public garden affords a good view over the town, the abbey and the 13C–14C gateway, **Porte d'Eau** and Arche des Grands Prés.

From the open space on the opposite bank, place de la Liberté, there are views of the Porte d'Eau from a different angle as well as of the 13C **Tour de l'Islette**. Together with the Porte St-Georges, these structures are all that is left of the old ramparts.

Parc Ronsard
Round this shaded park are the Lycée Ronsard (originally the Collège des Oratoriens, where Balzac was a pupil and now occupied by the offices of the town hall), the late-15C Hôtel de Saillant (now the tourist information centre) and the municipal library with its important collection of old books. A 16C two-storeyed washhouse is sited on the arm of the river running through the park.

Chapelle St-Jacques
Rebuilt in the 15C, and subsequently attached to the Collège des Oratoriens in the 16C, the chapel once served the pilgrims on their way to Santiago de Compostela.

Église de la Madeleine
Dating from 1474, the church belfry is topped by an elegant bracketed spire.

Place St-Martin
Until the 19C, St-Martin's church (15C–16C) stood here; only the bell-tower remains. There is also a fine 16C timber-framed house called the Grand St-Martin; it is ornamented with figures and coats of arms and has a statue of Maréchal de **Rochambeau** (◔see DRIVING TOURS).

Vendôme with Ancienne Abbaye de la Trinité viewed from the castle gardens

Porte St-Georges

St-Georges gateway was the entrance to the town from the Loir; it is flanked by towers largely built in the 14C, although the front facing the bridge is decorated with machicolations and carvings of dolphins and Renaissance medallions that were added early in the 16C by Marie de Luxembourg, Duchess of Vendôme.

Château

Access on foot by the garden, by car via Faubourg St-Lubin. ◑*Grounds open 9am–5pm.* ✆*02 54 77 01 33.*

The ruined castle is set on the top of an outcrop, La Montagne, which overlooks the Loir. It consists of an earth wall and ramparts with 13C and 14C machicolated round towers at intervals; the great Poitiers Tower on the east side was reconstructed in the 15C. The early-17C Beauce gate leads into the precinct that is now a huge garden. There are traces

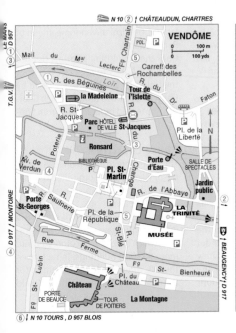

WHERE TO STAY

Chambre d'hôte Ferme
de Crislaine.................................①

Chambre d'hôte La Borde...........②

Chambre d'hôte Le Moulin
d'Échoiseau.................................③

Hôtel Le St-Georges....................④

Hôtel Le Vendôme.......................⑤

Mercator......................................⑥

WHERE TO EAT

Auberge de la Madeleine............①

La Vallée......................................②

Le Moulin du Loir........................③

Le Terre à TR...............................④

Restaurant Pertica......................⑤

Honoré de Balzac (1799–1850)

On 22 June 1807, the Collège des Oratoriens in Vendôme registered the entry of an eight-year-old boy, Honoré de Balzac. The future historical novelist was an absent-minded and undisciplined pupil. Balzac was to recall the severity of school discipline of those days in his writing. His general clumsiness and ineptitude at standard children's pursuits made him the frequent butt of his fellow pupils' jokes. He regularly got himself put into detention in order to read in peace. The harshness of the school regime eventually undermined his health and his parents had to take him away.

Balzac's early efforts at writing met with minimal success, so he embarked on a career in printing. However, the firm in which he was joint partner went bankrupt, leaving him with debts at the age of 30, which he was to spend the rest of his life attempting to pay off. He returned to writing and over the next 20 years produced a phenomenal number of novels (about 90), a vast collection which constitutes a richly detailed record of contemporary society, covering all walks of life and reflecting what he saw as people's overriding motivations at that time, chiefly money and ambition. Typically, Balzac's novels contain keenly observed settings, peopled by characters exaggerated almost to the point of caricature by their creator's vivid imagination. Balzac's fascination with the contrast between life in the provinces and that in the glittering French capital is also reflected in his work.

Balzac retrospectively attached the label **La Comédie Humaine** to his life's work, giving some indication of the breadth of scope of the world he had tried to evoke – an ambitious project formulated after he had already written many of his most famous novels, but which was to remain incomplete on his untimely death from overwork, just months after he had finally married Eveline Hanska, the Polish countess with whom he had passionately corresponded for more than 18 years.

of the collegiate church of St-Georges, which was founded by Agnès of Burgundy: the counts of Vendôme were buried here. Antoine de Bourbon and Jeanne d'Albret, the parents of Henri IV, were also buried here.

Promenade de la Montagne
From the terraces there are fine **views★** of Vendôme and the Loir Valley.

ANCIENNE ABBAYE DE LA TRINITÉ★
One summer night, Geoffrey Martel, Count of Anjou, saw three fiery spears plunge into a fountain and decided to found a monastery, dedicated to the Holy Trinity on 31 May 1040. Under the Benedictine Order the abbey grew considerably, becoming one of the most powerful religious foundations in France, to the extent that eventually the abbot was made a cardinal. In the late 11C this office was held by the famous Geoffroi of Vendôme, friend of Pope Urban II.

Until the Revolution pilgrims flocked to Trinité Abbey to venerate a relic of the Holy Tear (Sainte Larme) – shed by Christ on Lazarus's tomb – which Geoffrey Martel had brought back from Constantinople.

Abbey Church★★
The abbey church is a remarkable example of Flamboyant Gothic architecture. The entrance to the abbey precinct is in rue de l'Abbaye.

On either side of the wall stand the Romanesque bays of the abbey granary, which have been incorporated into more modern buildings. In fact, from the 14C onwards, it was common for the monks to allow tradesmen to build their shops against the abbey walls.

Exterior

To the right of the west front and set apart from it stands the 12C **bell-tower**. An interesting feature is the manner in which the windows and arcades, which are blind at ground level, grow larger as the embrasures also increase in size. The transition from a square to an octagonal tower is made by means of openwork, mini bell-towers at the corners. The Flamboyant **west front**, accentuated by a great carved gable, is thought to have been built in the early 16C by Jean de Beauce, who designed the bell-tower of Chartres Cathedral. The decorative openwork, so delicate it looks like a piece of lace, contrasts with the plainer Romanesque tower.

Interior

The nave, started at the transept end in the middle of the 14C, was not completed until the early 16C; the transept, all that is left of the 11C building, leads to the chancel and ambulatory with its five radiating chapels.

The baptismal chapel **(1)** in the north aisle contains a Renaissance font in white marble supported by a carved pedestal from the gardens of Blois Château.

The primitive capitals of the transept crossing are surmounted by statues (13C) of the Virgin Mary with the Archangel Gabriel, St Peter and St Eutropius, who was venerated in the abbey church. The transept vaulting was altered in the 14C in the Angevin style.

The 14C chancel, which is lit through windows from the same period, is decorated with beautiful late-15C **stalls★ (2)**. The misericords are decorated with naïve scenes illustrating daily life with various trades and zodiac signs. The choir screen **(3)** enclosing the chancel bears the influence of the first Renaissance. To the left of the high altar is the base of the famous monument of the Holy Tear, decorated with tears, with a small aperture through which the relic was displayed to the faithful by one of the monks.

The chapels radiating from the ambulatory are decorated with 14C and 16C stained glass that has been extensively restored: the best section, which depicts

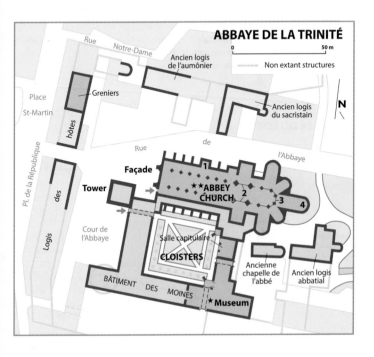

the meal in Simon's house, taken from a German engraving, is in the first chapel to the left of the axial chapel. It also contains a **window** dating from 1140 depicting the Virgin and Child **(4)**.

Conventual buildings
Only the east side of the 16C cloisters exists in its entirety. In the 14C **chapter house** (⊙ *Apr–Oct daily 10am–6pm, rest of year Mon–Sat 10am–6pm;* ⊙ *1 Jan, 1 May and 25 Dec; ℘02 54 77 26 13)* a number of **wall paintings★** have been uncovered, depicting episodes from the Life of Christ. The Classical-style buildings now house a museum. Take the passage through the south range of buildings to admire the monumental south front that was built between 1732 and 1742; the pediments bear the royal fleur-de-lis, the motto (Pax) and the emblem (Lamb) of the Order of St Benedict.

Museum★
⊙ *Apr–Oct daily 10am – noon, 2–6pm; Nov–Feb Mon–Sat 10am–noon, 1.30–5.30pm.* ⊙ *1 Jan, 1 May, 25 Dec.* ⊛*Free. ℘02 54 77 05 07.*
The museum collections are displayed in the abbey's monastic buildings, which are reached by a majestic stairway. Rooms on the ground floor are devoted to **mural painting★** in the Loire valley and to **religious art★** in the Vendôme area from the Middle Ages to the Renaissance. On the upper floors are sections on archaeology and natural history. Certain rooms are devoted to 16C–19C paintings and furniture and to earthenware; there is a superb late-18C **harp★**, the work of Nadermann, Marie-Antoinette's instrument maker, together with contemporary sculptures by the artist **Louis Leygue** (1905–92).

EXCURSIONS
Nourray
12km/7.4mi S on D 16, then right onto D 64 in Crucheray.
The little **church** that stands alone in the square has a row of Romanesque arcades beneath carved corbels. Inside, the oven-vaulted apse is surrounded by arcading with carved capitals.

Villemardy
14km/9mi SE on D 957; turn left to Périgny and bear right to Villemardy.
The **church** dating from the 12C has a simple nave ending in a Gothic chancel. The interior decoration in carved oak is remarkably uniform; the high altar and tabernacle, which are surmounted by an altarpiece, are in the Classical style, as are the two small symmetrical altars in the nave.

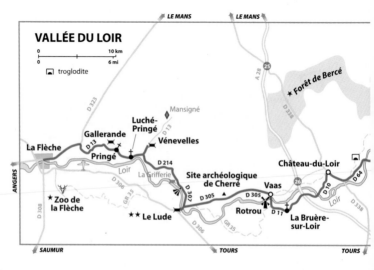

Rhodon

20km/12.4mi SE on D 917 (towards Beaugency), then turn right in Noyers.
The internal walls and Gothic vaulting of the church bear traces of 14C and 15C mural paintings: Christ in Majesty in the apse and the Months of the Year on one of the transverse arches of the nave.

🚗 DRIVING TOURS

MIDDLE REACHES OF THE LOIR★

1 FROM VENDÔME TO LA CHARTRE

78km/48.4mi. Allow one day.

Villiers-sur-Loir

The village overlooks the sloping vineyards opposite Rochambeau Castle. Numerous outdoor activities are available: swimming, rambling, fishing, volleyball, boules, table tennis, sailing, archery and more. In Riotte, special courses offer an introduction to the local fauna and flora.

▶ Take the road towards Thoré. Immediately after crossing the Loir turn left.

Rochambeau

The road runs along the foot of the cliff through the semi-troglodyte village up to the castle in which **Maréchal de Rochambeau** (1725–1807) was born; he commanded the French expeditionary force in the American War of Independence and was buried in Thoré.

▶ Return to the west bank of the river and turn left onto D 5.

Le Gué-du-Loir

The hamlet was built where the Boulon joins the Loir amid lush meadows and islands ringed by reed-beds, willows, alders and poplars.

On leaving the hamlet the road (D 5) skirts the wall of **Manoir de Bonaventure**, which was probably named after a chapel dedicated to St Bonaventure. In the 16C the manor house belonged to Henri IV's father, Antoine de Bourbon-Vendôme, who entertained his friends there, including some members of the Pléiade, a group of 16C French poets which included Ronsard and du Bellay. Later Bonaventure came into the possession of the De Musset family.

The poet, **Alfred de Musset**, whose father was born at the manor, used to spend his holidays as a child with his godfather, Louis de Musset, at the Château de Cogners, since the manor had by then been sold.

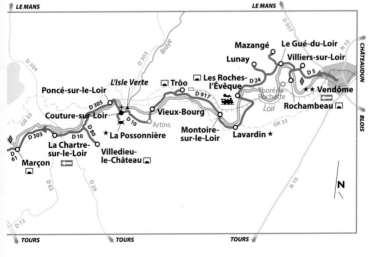

333

The Princely Poet

In 1524 **Pierre de Ronsard** was born at Possonnière. Promised a military or diplomatic career, he became, at age 12, a page in the court of François I. But at 15, an illness greatly weakened him. He studied poetry and the ancient poets and soon excelled at sonnets. *Odes* was published in 1550, *Les Amours* in 1552. In 1558 Ronsard became Poet Laureate. Beset by gout, he retired to the Ste-Madeleine-de-Croixval priory *(6km SW of Possonnière)*; in 1585 he died at St-Cosme-lès-Tours.

▶ Continue W on D 5 towards Savigny; then take the second turning to the right (C 13) at a wayside cross.

A wooded valley leads to the village of **Mazangé** clustered round its church.

▶ Return to Gué-du-Loir; turn right onto D 24 towards Montoire-sur-le-Loir, then right again onto D 82.

Lunay
Lunay is clustered in a valley round the main square, where a few old houses have survived. The huge, Flamboyant Gothic **church** of St-Martin presents an attractive doorway.

Les Roches-l'Évêque
The village occupies a long narrow site between the river and the cliff. The troglodyte dwellings are a well-known feature of the region, their hen houses and sheds half-concealed by festoons of wisteria and lilac in season.

▶ Cross the Loir (D 917 – follow the signposts); turn right to Lavardin.

Lavardin★
See LAVARDIN.

▶ Take the pretty minor road along the south bank of the river to Montoire.

Montoire-sur-le-Loir
See MONTOIRE-SUR-LE-LOIR.

▶ Soon Trôo and its church appear on the skyline. Continue to Sougé where you turn left onto the signposted tourist road to Artins.

Vieux-Bourg d'Artins
The village is situated right on the river bank. The **church** has Romanesque walls with Flamboyant Gothic windows and a pointed-arched doorway.

▶ From Artins take D 10 E; then turn right to L'Isle Verte; shortly turn left onto a road that runs in front of the Château du Pin.

From the bridge opposite the château **L'Isle Verte** (Green Island) can be seen a little way upstream where the Braye joins the Loir. It was here, where the row of poplars sway in the breeze and the willows mark the edges of the meadows, that the poet Ronsard wanted to be buried; nowhere is more evocative of his genius.

Couture-sur-Loir
The **church** has a Gothic chancel with Angevin vaulting and 17C woodwork in the Rosary Chapel.

▶ In Couture-sur-Loir take D 57 S to La Possonnière.

Manoir de la Possonnière★
Mid-Jun–mid Sept daily 10am–6pm; Apr–early Jun and late Sept–Oct Thu–Sun 2–6pm. €5.50. ℘02 54 72 40 05. *www.val-de-loire-41.com.*
When Louis de Ronsard, soldier and man of letters, returned from Italy in the early 16C he undertook to rebuild his country seat in the new Italian style. The result was La Possonnière, characterised by

the profusion of mottoes engraved on the walls.

The name comes from the word *posson* (*poinçon*, a measure of volume) and has sometimes been altered to Poissonnière under the influence of the Ronsard family coat of arms – three silver fishes (*poisson*) on a blue ground – which can be seen on the pediment of the carved dormer window at the top of the turret.

The **manor house** is built against the hillside on the northern fringes of Gâtines Forest and enclosed with a wall. The main façade has mullioned windows in the style of Louis XII on the ground floor but the windows on the first floor are flanked by pilasters with medallions, in the Renaissance style. Projecting from the rear façade is a graceful staircase turret adorned with an elegant doorway capped by a pediment decorated with a bust.

The **rose garden** is filled with lovely antique and modern varieties, including a pale pink rose named for Pierre Ronsard. From the vegetable garden, a view of the valley unfolds.

▶ Return to Couture and continue N (D 57), crossing the Loir at the foot of the wooded hill on which Château de la Flotte stands.

Poncé-sur-le-Loir
In Poncé (exit E), you'll find a Renaissance castle.

Château
🕐*May–early Jul and mid-Sep, Sat–Sun 10am–noon, 2–6.30pm, Jul–Aug, Thu–Sun 10am–noon, 2–6.30pm.* ⌾€6.50. 𝒥*02 43 44 24 02.*
http://chateaudeponce.com.
The castle originally had two pavilions flanking a central staircase tower, one of which was destroyed in the 18C and replaced by a more austere wing.

The stone **Renaissance staircase★★** is one of the most remarkable in France; in front of it are the remains of a loggia. The coffered, white-stone ceilings of the six straight flights are sumptuously sculpted, executed with refinement, fluidity and a mastery of the art

Château de Poncé
© Christian Guy/hemis.fr

of perspective rarely found. More than 160 decorative motifs portray real-life, allegorical and mythological subjects.

The well-tended **gardens**, with their symmetrical layout, are a pleasant place for a stroll: beyond the flower beds edged with boxwood, the arbour leads to several clearings where leafy branches meet overhead to form a ceiling of foliage, a maze and a long vaulted path.

The **dovecote** with its 1,800 nesting holes and revolving ladders for gathering the eggs is still intact. The outbuildings house the local folklore museum, the **Musée départemental du Folklore sarthois.**

▶ In Ruillé turn left onto D 80, which crosses the Loir.

Villedieu-le-Château
This village has a pleasant **setting** in a valley with troglodyte dwellings. Houses, gardens, crumbling remnants of the old town wall and the ruins of the belfry of St-Jean priory all add to its charm.

▶ Return to Tréhet and left onto D 10.

La Chartre-sur-le-Loir

On the north bank of the river, opposite this village, are the Bercé forest and the Jasnières vineyard, which produces a white dessert wine that ages well.

LOWER REACHES OF THE LOIR★

② FROM LA CHARTRE TO LA FLÈCHE
75km/46.6mi. Allow one day.

The road from La Chartre to **Marçon** passes through peaceful countryside.

▷ In Marçon turn right onto D 61. Turn left onto D 64, which skirts the hillside with its numerous troglodyte dwellings.

Château-du-Loir

The keep in the public gardens is all that remains of the medieval castle, to which this town owes its name. Underneath it are the old cells occupied briefly by convicts who passed through here bound for the penal colony of Cayenne. The **St-Guingalois church** preserves a monumental 17C *Pietà*, and two wood panels of the Flemish Mannerist school.

▷ Leave Château-du-Loir on D 10 going S towards Château-la-Vallière. After crossing the bridge in Nogent turn right immediately onto C 2.

La Bruère-sur-Loir

The **church** here contains elegant chancel vaulting in the Renaissance style and 16C stained-glass windows.

▷ Leave La Bruère on D 11 towards Vaas and turn right onto D 30.

Vaas

On the left, just before the bridge, stands an old corn mill, the **Moulin de Rotrou** (☞ 90min guided tours Jul–Aug daily 2.30–5.30pm; Apr–Jun and Sept–Oct Sun and public holidays 2.30–5.30pm; €5; ℘02 43 79 36 81, www.lemoulinderotrou. com). The riverside, with its houses, tiny gardens and church makes a delightful scene.

▷ Follow D 305, then turn right to Cherré archaeological site.

Site archéologique de Cherré

The Gallo-Roman settlement comprises a temple, baths, two other buildings and a theatre of pointed reddish sandstone, which has been completely excavated. During the digs a necropolis from 8C–5C BCE was discovered under the *cavea* (the seating area).

▷ Carry on towards Le Lude along the north bank of the Loir.

Château du Lude★★
See Château du Lude.

▷ Take D 307 towards Pontvallain, then first left towards Mansigné. Bear left onto D 214 to Luché-Pringé. After the bridge over the Aune, quit for a moment the signed route and turn left on D 13 to reach the manor.

Manoir de Vénevelles
No public access.
This 15C–17C manor with a wide moat sits in the hollow of a sleepy small valley. Before reaching the Château de la Grifferie there is a view of the valley laid out in fruit orchards, asparagus beds, potato fields and maize plantations.

▷ Take D 214 again to Luché-Pringé.

Luché-Pringé

The exterior of the **church** (13C–16C) is unusual, with many gables decorated with crockets and the row of tiny musician figures sitting on the edge of the roof on either side of the façade.
The interior contains an early-16C *Pietà* (right) carved in walnut. The wide chancel (13C) ends in a square chevet; the Angevin vaulting is supported on tall slim columns in the Plantagenet style.

Pringé

An arched Romanesque portal opens through the façade of the small **church**. Inside are 16C murals depicting Saint Hubert, Saint George and Saint Christopher.

Château de Gallerande

☞ *No public access.*

The D 13 skirts the moats around the grounds where cedars, lime trees and oaks border sweeping lawns. Walk to the gateway of the courtyard for a view of the northeast façade, which is divided by round towers with machicolations and an octagonal keep.

ADDRESSES

🏨 STAY

⊖⊖ **Chambre d'hôte Ferme de Crislaine** – *41100 Azé. 11km/7mi NW of Vendôme.* 🖉*02 54 72 14 09. www.crislaine. com. 3 rooms.* 🅿. This organic farm is ideal for families and walkers. Bikes, BBQ, kitchenette and **pool** ⌇ for guests' use.

⊖⊖ **Chambre d'hôte La Borde** – *41100 Danzé. 2km/1mi N of Danzé.* 🖉*06 33 22 62 92. www.la-borde.com. 5 rooms.* 🅿⤢. Situated in the middle of a 10ha park, this manor house dates from the 19C. **Heated pool** ⌇. ⌧No pets allowed.

⊖⊖🛏 **Chambre d'hôte le Moulin d'Echoiseau** – *Le Gué-du-Loir, 41100 Mazangé. 1km/0.6mi S of Mazangé.* 🖉*02 54 72 19 34. 4 rooms.* 🅿⤢. You will long remember the calm atmosphere staying at this former mill, full of character, with a library and **swimming pool** ⌇.

⊖⊖🛏 **Hôtel-Restaurant Mercator** – *rte. de Blois.* 🖉*02 54 89 08 08. www. hotelmercator.fr. 56 rooms.* 🅿. Close by a roundabout but surrounded by greenery, this family-run hotel up-to-date rooms. The restaurant (⊖⊖) serves traditional dishes.

⊖⊖🛏 **Hôtel le Vendôme** – *15 faubourg Chartrain.* 🖉*02 54 77 02 88. www. hotelvendomefrance.com. 35 rooms.* 🅿. Inviting hotel in the town centre, with modern bedrooms. Buffet breakfast. Cosy lounge with piano.

⊖⊖🛏–⊖⊖🛏🛏**Hôtel le St-Georges** – *14 r. Poterie.* 🖉*02 54 67 42 10. www.hotel-saint-georges-vendome.com. 27 rooms.* ♿🅿. Located in the centre of town, this hotel offers modern, stylish rooms, with spa tubs in some. The restaurant (⊖⊖🛏) serves continental dishes.

🍽 EAT

⊖🛏 **Auberge de la Madeleine** – *pl. de la Madeleine.* 🖉*02 54 77 20 79. Closed Wed.* Regional inn, with split-level dining room and terrace on the Loir. Also has 8 small rooms (⊖) in neo-rustic style for overnight stays.

⊖⊖🛏 **Le Moulin du Loir** – *21-23 r. du Change.* 🖉*02 54 67 13 51. www.le-moulin-du-loir.com. Closed Wed.* Housed in an old mill in the old part of town, this bar-restaurant serves traditional cuisine in a bright, charming setting. The large pleasant terrace overlooks the river.

⊖⊖🛏 **La Vallée** – *34 r. Barré-St-Venant.* 🖉*02 54 77 29 93. www.restaurant-la-vallee.com.* ♿🅿. *Closed Mon, Tue (except holidays).* A splendid find with exposed beams in the pleasant dining room. Seasonal cuisine is served; the cheese plate is noteworthy.

⊖⊖🛏–⊖⊖🛏🛏 **Restaurant Pertica** *15 de la Républic.* 🖉*02 54 23 72 02. www. restaurantpertica.com. Closed Sun, Mon, Wed lunch.* The creative, Asian-influenced cuisine in this fine-dining restaurant is heavy on fresh vegetables and fruits locally sourced. The kitchen is state-of-the-art and the setting modern.

LEISURE ACTIVITIES

Plan d'Eau de Villiers-sur-Loir – *41100 Villiers-sur-Loir.* 🖉*02 54 23 04 84. www.neovent.org. Open Jun and Sept Sun 3–7pm; Jul–Aug daily 3–7pm.* Swim, fish, sail, hire a pedal boat or a mountain bike. Archery and boules on-site too.

SHOPPING

Verrerie des Côteaux – *27 r. des Côteaux, 72340 Poncé-sur-Loir.* 🖉*02 43 79 05 69. www.verreriedescoteaux.com. Open Tue–Sat 9am–12.30pm, 2–6pm, Sun 2–6pm. Closed Mon.* In the workshop beneath the château in Poncé-sur-Loir, visitors can watch the traditional art of the glassmaker.

Cave Coopérative du Vendômois – *60 av du Petit Thouars, 41100 Villiers sur Loir, 6km/3.7mi west of Vendôme.* 🖉*02 43 72 90 69. www.caveduvendomois.com. Open Tue–Thu 9am–noon, 2–6pm, Fri–Sat 9am–noon, 2–7pm. Closed Sun (except May–Aug, 10am–noon, 3.30–6pm), and Mon.* Here, find the famous Pineau d'Aunis and other wines.

Lavardin★

The crumbling ruins of Lavardin fortress occupy a rocky pinnacle towering above the village and the Loir, which is spanned by a Gothic bridge, forming a picturesque scene. Far from the tumult of its past, the hamlet flourishes today around the ruins; in fact, it is ranked as one of the most beautiful villages in France.

▶ **Population:** 749.
   Michelin Map: 318: C-5
▯ **Info:** 16 pl. Clemenceau, 41800 Montoire-sur-le-Loir. ℘02 54 77 05 07. www.vendome-tourisme.fr.
▶ **Location:** 22km/14mi SW of Vendôme (via the D 917 or N 10 and then the D 108).
◷ **Timing:** Allow 1hour, or more if you take a guided tour.

A BIT OF HISTORY

The principal stronghold of the counts of Vendôme in the Middle Ages, Lavardin's strategic importance greatly increased in the 12C owing to its location half way between the kingdom of France under the Capets and the possessions of the Angevin Kings. In 1188 Henry II of England and his son Richard the Lionheart besieged the castle, but in vain.

In 1589 the troops of the Catholic League captured the castle, but the following year it was besieged by Henri IV's soldiers under the Prince de Conti and surrendered. The King ordered the castle to be demolished.

SIGHTS

Mansions anciennes

Of the two **old houses**, one is 15C and half-timbered; the other is Renaissance with an overhanging oratory, pilastered, mullioned dormer windows and a loggia overlooking the courtyard.

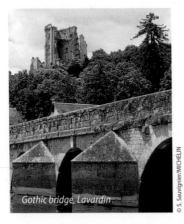
Gothic bridge, Lavardin
© S. Sauvignier/MICHELIN

The **mairie** (town hall, *2 passage St-Genest; ℘02 43 27 71 87; www.lavardin.net*) contains two 11C rooms with handsome 15C vaulted ceilings.

The 13C **bridge** offers an attractive view of the lush green river banks.

🚶 *A lane behind the church climbs up to a group of cave dwellings.*

Château

◷*Jun–late Sept Tue–Sun 11am–noon, 2–6pm; May Sat–Sun and public holidays 11am–noon, 2–6pm.* ⊚€5. ℘06 81 86 12 80.

Although well worn by the weather and the passage of time, the ruins are still impressive. They give a good idea of the three lines of fortified walls, the gatehouse (12C–15C) and the rectangular 11C keep, or **donjon** (26m high), which was reinforced in the next century with towers of the same height. The innermost defensive wall is best preserved.

Église St-Genest★

The priory was built in an archaic Romanesque style with a square belfry-porch. Low-relief sculptures have been reused in the structure; those in the apse represent the signs of the zodiac.

Interior – The church is divided into three parts by square piers capped by delicately carved early 12C imposts. The chancel, which is entered through a triumphal arch, ends in an oven-vaulted apse where curious Romanesque pil-

© Hervé Lenain/hemis.fr

Château de Lavardin

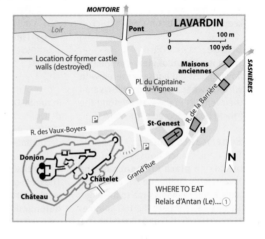

lars (probably part of an earlier building) support roughly hewn capitals. The windows in the north aisle are framed by twisted Romanesque colonnettes.

The **mural paintings★** date from the 12C to 16C. The oldest, most stylised and majestic ones are on the pillar at the entrance to the left apsidal chapel, depicting the *Baptism of Christ* and a *Tree of Jesse*. The well-conserved group in the chancel and apse shows scenes from the *Passion (on the right)* and the *Washing of the Feet (on the left)* on either side of a *Christ in Majesty* surrounded by the symbols of the *Evangelists*. In the right apsidal chapel, note the *St Christopher* and *Last Judgement* (15C) where *Paradise (above)* and *Hell* are colourfully portrayed. On the pillars in the nave and aisles are 16C figures of saints that are venerated locally.

Note also the *Martyrdom of St Margaret* on the wall of the south aisle and the *Crucifixion of St Peter* on a pillar on the north side of the nave.

EXCURSION
Jardin du Plessis Sasnières

6km/3.7mi SE by D 108. ⏱*Apr–Oct Thu–Mon and public holidays 10am–6pm.* ⊘*€10.* ℰ*02 54 82 92 34. www.jardin-plessis-sasnieres.fr.*

This attractive 3.5ha English-style garden, enhanced by clumps of trees and shrubs, surrounds a pretty lake laid out at the foot of a hill. It presents a wide range of plants belonging to many different species. The garden is particularly appealing in spring and summer when its roses and magnolias are in bloom. The autumn season is a feast for the eyes as well, when the foliage takes on superb shades of russet.

Montoire-sur-le-Loir

This charming riverside town developed round the priory of St-Gilles founded in the 7C. In the 9C, Charles the Bald had a fort built to protect the country from Viking incursions. Pilgrims heading for Tours to pray at the tomb of St Martin used to stay the night in Montoire, which was on the route to Santiago de Compostela in Spain. During this period leper houses were set up in Montoire and Trôo.

SIGHTS

Castle

A stone fortified wall encloses the 11C keep, which stands on a spur of rock.

Bridge

There is a beautiful **view★** of the Loir flowing past old houses covered with wisteria where weeping willows trail their tendrils in the water among the fishing boats moored to the banks.

Renaissance houses

Two Renaissance houses stand side by side on **place Clemenceau**; the larger, with mullioned windows and high dormer windows, is also the older. There are two others: the 16C Antoine-Moreau Hospital in **rue St-Laurent** and,

▶ **Population:** 3,808.
- **Michelin Map:** 318: C-5
- **Info:** 3 pl. Clemenceau, 41800 Montoire-sur-le-Loir, ℰ02 54 77 05 07. www.vendome-tourisme.fr.
- **Location:** 20km/12.4mi to the W of Vendôme and 19km/12mi N of Château-Renault. Try to approach along the D 108 and the minor road from Lavardin, which runs alongside the river.
- **Parking:** You will find only on-street parking.
- **Timing:** Allow 1 hour to explore the village.

in **rue St-Oustrille**, the Maison du Jeu de Quilles, which owes its name, the "Skittle-game house", to the columns decorating the façade.

Chapelle St-Gilles★

The main gate opens on to the apse of an elegant Romanesque chapel, which belonged to a Benedictine priory founded in the 7C. The chapel and the

Frescos, Chapelle St-Gilles

© Hervé Lenain/hemis.fr

The Meeting at Montoire

In mid-October 1940, convoys of German soldiers swarmed into the region and set up anti-aircraft batteries on the hills. Patrols searched houses in Montoire and barricaded the roads. Electricity and phones were cut off. French SNCF railway workers were replaced by Germans, and people whose houses overlooked the railway were ordered to close the shutters and stay indoors. A Messerschmitt squadron scared cattle in the fields, and two armoured trains bristling with cannons criss-crossed the line from Vendôme to Tours, Bordeaux and Hendaye.

On 22 October, Hitler met up with Pierre Laval at Montoire station; in case of emergency his train could shelter in the tunnel near to St-Rimay. Two days later, the infamous meeting between the Führer and Marshall Pétain took place, a black day during which the German word *zusammenarbeit* (cooperation) was translated as collaboration.

prior's lodging are set against a pleasant backdrop of lawns and yew trees.

In the 9C an envoy of Charles the Bald oversaw the building of a fort on the hilltop to defend against Norman raids. The poet **Pierre de Ronsard** set off from St-Gilles in October 1585 to visit the priories of Ste-Madeleine-de-Croixval and St-Cosme, where he died two months later (☉ *see box p334*).

Frescoes★★ decorate the three apses laid out in a cloverleaf shape with the chancel and transept. The spherical vaults each diplay a Christ from a different era. The oldest, dating from the early 12C, is to be found in the main apse: seated on a rainbow, he holds the Book of the Seven Seals surrounded by four angels and four animals symbolising the evangelists. In the southern transept arm, a Byzantine-influenced Christ in majesty (1180) passes keys to St Peter (*now effaced*). In the northern transept arm, a 13C Christ sits with the apostles. the tormented attitudes, whites, ochres and sky blues show the nascent style of the local school of artists.

Gare Historique – Musée de la Seconde Guerre Mondiale

av. de la République. &☉*Apr–Jun and Sept 10am–12.30pm, 2–5pm; Jul–Aug 6pm.* ☞€4.50. ℘*02 54 85 33 42. www.mairie-montoire.fr.*
Occupying the site of the famous meeting of 24 October 1940 (☉*see box above),*

the musée portrays the event by means of a large-scale model, photographs and period film footage.

Musikenfête

Espace de l'Europe, quartier Marescot. ☜*By guided tour only, Tue–Sun Mar–Sept 10am–noon, 2–6pm; Oct–Dec 2–6pm.* ☉*25–26 Dec.* ☞€7. ℘*02 54 85 28 95. www.musikenfete.fr.*
In this show-museum of traditional music from all across the globe, many instruments – often left by musicians who have performed at festivals in Montoire – are brought to life.

☺ **Summer street music** – The second week in July, the music of violins, double basses and other instruments is heard in Montoire's streets; then from mid-August for 8 days, the **International Folklore Festival** takes over (℘*02 54 85 35 16; www.festival-montoire.com*).

ADDRESSES

�!/EAT

◌☺☺ **Le Manoir de St-Quentin** – *Bourg de St-Quentin, between Montoire and Trôo.* ℘*02 54 77 54 96. www. lemanoirdesaintquentin.com.* ☷. Housed in a handsome manor house behind the church, this restaurant offers fine cuisine.

Trôo

A 900-year-old picture book, yet still extraordinarily fresh, awaits on the walls of the delightful church of St-Jacques-des-Guérets. Make sure to explore Trôo thoroughly (it is pronounced "tro") and discover a tangle of tiny streets with tiered houses, staircases and mysterious underground passageways. On summer weekends a tourist train stops at Troo on its 36km/22mi trip through the Loir valley (*departs from Thoré-la-Rochette mid-May–Sept; 02 54 72 95 03; www.ttvl.fr*).

▶ **Population:** 312.
🕐 **Michelin Map:** 318 B-5
▮ **Info:** 39 r. Auguste-Arnault, 41800 Trôo. ℰ02 54 73 55 00. www.troo.fr.
◖ **Location:** 26km/16mi W of Vendôme and 16km/10mi SW of St-Calais.
🚹 **Kids:** The petrified caves.
🕐 **Timing:** About an hour to see the village.

SIGHTS

The Mound★

From the top of this feudal hillock, an excellent **panorama** stretches across the coiling Loir and its valley. Look for the little church of St-Jacques-des-Guérets, opposite Trôo.

Ancienne collégiale St-Martin

Founded in 1050, and remodelled a century later, the church is dominated by a remarkable square tower pierced by Angevin-style window bays. The interior features convex vaulting, historied Romanesque capitals, and 15C stalls and communion table; also note the 16C statue of St Mamès, whose name is invoked to cure stomach pains.

Grands Puits

The Great Well is also known as the Talking Well, thanks to its 45m/148ft depth, which provides an excellent echo.

Maladrerie Ste-Catherine

Located on D 917 at the far end of town, this quarantine hospital for pilgrims on the routes to St-Martin de Tours and

Trôo with the mound and Ancienne collégiale St-Martin

© Trôo Tourisme

Santiago de Compostela features lovely Romanesque arcatures. A leper hospital used to exist outside the walls, to the west of Trôo.

👥 Grotte pétrifiante

39 r. Auguste-Arnault. 🕐*Jan–Mar 10am-12.15pm (plus 2-4.15pm Tue and Fri) closed Sun–Mon; Apr–Sept Sat, Sun, Mon 10am–noon, 2–6pm (Mon until 5pm), Tue–Fri 2–6pm.* 👓*€1 (under 12 years free).* 📞*02 54 72 87 50. https://trootourisme.jimdo.com.* Water streams abundantly into the cave to form stalactites and petrified shapes.

Église St-Jacques-des-Guérets

On the left bank of the Loir.

The splendid **murals★** in this church, painted between 1130 and 1170, were influenced by Byzantine art. They have preserved an amazing freshness of colour. The most remarkable are to be found in the apse, and show the Crucifixion, Day of Judgement, Christ in Majesty and the Last Supper.

Forêt de Bercé★

Bercé Forest is all that remains of the great Le Mans forest that once reached from the Sarthe to the Loir. The magnificent sessile oaks mixed with chestnuts and beeches, provide cover for a herd of deer. The forest is now carefully exploited for high quality oak.

SIGHTS

🔊*Guided tours (2h) weekly mid-Jul– Aug (depart from Carnuta). For information* 📞*02 43 38 10 31. Several waymarked mountain bike itineraries of varying lengths criss-cross the forest, many of which are ideal for beginners.*

- 🚴 **Michelin Map:** 310 L-8
- 🅿 **Info:** 20 bd de Montréal, 72200 La Flèche. 📞02 43 38 16 60. www.vallee-du-loir.com.
- ▶ **Location:** The vast forested region of 5 377ha lies 30km/19mi SE of Le Mans, and 11km/7mi N of Château-du-Loir.
- 👥 **Kids:** There's a special children's mountain bike trail.
- 🕐 **Timing:** Allow a whole day for outdoors action, walking and biking in the forest.

An historic destiny

The remaining tracts of the ancient forest of the Carnutes, where the annual gathering of the Druids of Celtic Gaul once took place in the 1C BCE, acquired the name of Burçay under the rule of the Counts of Anjou.

The forest came under the ownership of the Crown in the 16C and supplied oaks for shipbuilding for many years, while its beeches were in great demand for making clogs. Nowadays, the Bercé forest is managed by the ONF (Office Nationale des Fôrets) – the French Forestry Commission – and produces top-quality oak. The trees are felled when they are between 200 and 240 years old to produce pale yellow, fine-grained timber that is prized as a veneer by cabinet makers, and exported widely throughout Europe.

Forêt de Bercé

© Office de Tourisme de la Vallée du Loir

♣♣ Fontaine de la Coudre

The spring, which is the source of the River Dinan, a tributary of the Loir, flows slowly under the tall oaks known as the Futaie des Forges. An **educational trail** explains the workings of the forest to children, including "hammering", the system whereby trees due to be felled are carefully marked and numbered.

Sources de l'Hermitière★

A deep valley thick with towering oaks and beeches hides the pure waters of these springs.

Futaie des Clos★

This is the finest stand of oaks in the forest. Two violent storms in 1967 caused gaps among the trees. While some of the giant oaks (300 to 350 years old) are decrepit, others are splendid specimens. 🚶 A path leads to the Boppe oak, or rather to its stump, protected by a roof, since the ancient tree was struck by lightning in 1934 at the age of 262. Its neighbour, Roulleau de la Roussière, is still flourishing after more than 350 years.

♣♣ Carnuta – Maison de l'Homme et de la Forêt

2 r. du Bourg Ancien, 72500 Jupilles. Carnuta is in the village of Jupilles, approx 35min drive SE of Le Mans. Take exit No. 25 or 26 on A 28. 🕐*Mid-Jun–*

mid-Sept daily 10am–6pm; rest of the year check website. ⊜*€6, under 18 years* ⊜*€3.50.* 📞*02 43 38 10 31. www.carnuta.fr.*

The Carnuta centre is a cross between an interpretation centre and a place for children to learn, in an informative and fun way, about the Bercé Forest and the men and women who have lived and worked with it for centuries. Using pictures, sounds, slide shows and games, it brings to life the forest experience in a modern and engaging manner.

ADDRESSES

♈/ EAT

⊜⊜ **Chez Miton** – *15 pl. de l'Église, Chahaignes.* 📞*02 43 44 62 62. www. chezmiton.com. Closed Sun and Thu eves, Mon.* Atmospheric street-side café-restaurant serving inspired regional fare coupled with a wine bar offering the wines of the valley.

SPORT

Mountain biking – 📞*02 43 38 16 60. www.vallee-du-loir.com.* A total of 315km/197mi of marked trails between 8km/5mi and 41km/26mi in length. No climbs above 100m. Good for beginners as well as experienced bikers. Ask for map of trails.

St-Paterne-Racan

The village of St-Paterne stretches out along the Escotais River, which is bordered by riverside washhouses and weeping willows.

CHURCH

The church contains interesting works of art, some from the **abbey of La Clarté-Dieu** (*1.5km/1mi NW of the village; ℘02 47 29 39 91; www.amis-abbaye-clartedieu. fr*). The 16C terra-cotta group to the left of the high altar portrays the *Adoration of the Magi*; at the centre is a charming **Virgin and Child★**. In the nave, note the polychrome statues of the figures of church authority, dating from the 18C.

EXCURSIONS

Château de la Roche-Racan

2km/1mi SE on D 28. 🔎Guided tours (45min) Jul–mid-Aug 9.30am–12.30pm, 2.30–5.30pm. ⬤€6. ℘02 47 29 20 02.
The Château de la Roche-Racan stands perched on a rock overlooking the Escotais Valley which, together with the Loir, was a constant source of inspiration to the first owner and poet, **Racan**.
Born at Champmarin near Aubigné, Honorat de Bueil, Marquis de Racan (1589–1670), was a member of the well-known local family, the Bueils.

> ▶ **Population:** 1,695.
> Ⓖ **Michelin Map:** 317 L-3
> ▣ **Info:** 30 Rue de la Gare 37370 Saint Paterne Racan. ℘02 47 29 30 87. www.stpaterneracan.fr.
> ◐ **Location:** Between Le Mans (60km/37mi NE) and Tours (30km/18.6mi SW).
> ◉ **Don't miss:** The polychrome statues in the church.
> ♟ **Kids:** Outdoors activities by the Val Joyeux lake.
> ◷ **Timing:** Allow 2–3 hours for the village and surrounds.

Not really cut out for the life of a soldier and following a number of unlucky love affairs, Racan retired to his country seat for the last 40 years of his life, a period described in his work, *Stances à la retraite*.
There he was quite content to stroll by his fountains or hunt game or visit Denis de la Grelière, the Abbé de la Clarté-Dieu, who invited him to put the Psalms

Château de la Roche-Racan

into verse. He brought up his children, pursued his lawsuits, grew beans and rebuilt his château.

In 1635, Racan commissioned a local master mason, Jacques Gabriel, a member of a long-established family of architects, to build this château. The main building was originally flanked by two pavilions, only one of which remains, pedimented and adorned with a corner turret and caryatids.

Long balustered terraces, above arcades decorated with masks, overlook the park and Escotais valley.

St-Christophe-sur-le-Nais

2.5km/1.5mi N on D 6.

Also lying in the Escotais valley, this village is the scene of a pilgrimage in honour of St Christopher. The **church** is composed of two separate buildings, an old 11C–14C priory chapel and the parish church with its 16C nave and belfry. On the threshold of the nave a gigantic St Christopher welcomes you. To the right is a reliquary bust of the saint. To the left of the chancel, the door leading to the prior's oratory is surmounted by a fine 14C statue of the Virgin and Child. Two Renaissance medallions adorn the church's timber roof.

Neuvy-le-Roi

9km/5.6mi E on D 54.

The **St-Vincent church**, which dates from the 12C and 16C, has a Romanesque chancel and a nave covered with Angevin vaulting.

Bueil-en-Touraine

8km/5mi NE along D 72 and D 5.

Set above the valley of the River Long, this village is the cradle of the Bueil family which has supplied France with an admiral, two marshals and a poet, Honorat de Bueil, **Lord of Racan**.

At the top of the hill stands a group of buildings formed by the juxtaposition of the church of **St-Pierre-aux-Liens** *(left)* and the collegiate church of **St-Michel** *(both churches are open during restoration)* founded in the 14C. In St-Pierre-aux-Liens is a remarkable Renaissance baptistry (1521) decorated with statuettes of Christ and the apostles. St-Michel was built as a sepulcre for the Bueil family, whose recumbant stone effigies are in the crypt.

Château de Vaujours

17km/11mi SW. www. chateaudevaujours.fr.

The fortified barbican is visible among the remains of more romantic round towers and a chapel of this 15C château, which welcomed Louis XI on several ocassions. Reopened to the public after a 20-year restoration.

👥 Étang du Val Joyeux

17km/11mi SW.

A vast expanse of water at the foot of a pleasant wooded hillside offers the possibility of swimming and even sailing.

👥 Forêt de Château-la-Vallière

17km/11mi SW.

Vast woodlands of pine and oak dotted with marshes extend for some 3,000ha around Château-la-Vallière. Come in autumn and you may hear the sounds of a hunting horn and the barking of the pack.

ADDRESSES

🏠 STAY

😊😊 **Chambre d'hôte Le Clos de Launay** – *rte. de Tours, 37330 Souvigné.* ☎*02 47 24 58 91. www.chambres-touraine.fr.* 🅿. *5 rooms.* Nothing disturbs the peace in this lovely modern house set in 7ha of gardens. The cosy set-up includes a comfortable guests' lounge and a fish pond for pleasant walks.

😊😊😊 **Chambre d'hôte Domaine de la Bergerie** – *On D 959, 37330 Braye-sur-Maulne.* ☎*02 47 24 90 88. www. domaine-bergerie.fr.* ♿🅿📷. *5 rooms. Closed Jan–mid-Feb.* This 19C château is set in immense grounds with ponds and woodland. Romantically rustic rooms and independent gîtes. Warm welcome with a glass of wine, and table d'hôte dining available (😊😊😊) in the restaurant.

Château du Lude

Château du Lude★★

This magnificent château, on the south bank of the Loir and surrounded by a lovely park, offers a mixture of Gothic, Renaissance and Louis XVI styles. The 11C fortress of the counts of Anjou was replaced in the 13C–14C by a castle that withstood several assaults by the English before it fell in 1425; it was recaptured two years later by Ambroise de Loré, Beaumanoir and Gilles de Rais.

A BIT OF HISTORY

In 1457 the castle was acquired by Jean de Daillon, a childhood friend of Louis XI. His son built the present château on the foundations of the earlier fortress: it kept the traditional square layout with a massive tower at each corner, but the large windows and the delicate decoration make it a country house of its age.

VISIT

Gardens

Created in the 17C, the gardens were transformed in the late 19C by landscape architect Edward André, who developed the English garden.

Exterior

Facing the park is the François I wing. Its façade is a combination of the fortress style, with its round medieval towers, and Renaissance refinement. Overlook-

- **Michelin Map:** 310: J-9
- **Info:** *Apr–Sept daily 11am–12.30pm, 2.30–6pm; Oct Sat–Sun 2–6pm. Wed Mar and Sept. Château and gardens €9. Gardens only €6. ℘02 43 94 60 09. www.lelude.com.*
- **Location:** In a wooded area midway between La Flèche and Château-la-Vallière along the D 959.
- **Don't miss:** Fête des Jardins held in the grounds.
- **Timing:** You will need 2 hours to visit the château and explore the grounds, but up to half a day if you want to explore more widely.

ing the river, the Louis XVI wing exemplifies the Classical style; it is sober and symmetrical, its façade broken only by a central projecting section topped by a carved pediment.

Interior

The Louis XII wing houses a large 19C library with 4,000 books, the oldest dating back to the 16C. The 18C building

A Thousand Years of History

The 11C fortress of the Counts of Anjou was replaced by a fortified château in the 13C and 14C, which stood up to several assaults by the English before it was taken in 1425, then re-conquered two years later by Ambroise de Loré, Beaumanoir and Gilles de Rais.

Jean de Daillon, a childhood friend of Louis XI acquired the château in 1457, and his son built the current edifice on the foundations of the old fortress. It was further modified during the Renaissance period and in the 18C. It has stayed in the same family until today. Unusually, most of its furniture survived the Revolution. Famous guests include Henri IV, Louis XIII and Madame de Sévigné.

contains a fine suite of rooms including a splendid oval salon in pure Louis XVI. One room, decorated with 15C wall murals, is a unique example of an Italian *studiolo* in a French château. In the François I wing a small library contains a 17C Gobelins tapestry; in the dining room, where the window recesses reveal the thickness of the medieval walls, there is a vast chimney-piece with a carved salamander and ermine.

EXCURSION
Maison des Architectes

3 r. du Marché-au-Fil, near the château entrance. ⌖ *No public access.*
Built in the 16C by the architects who designed the château, this house displays Renaissance features such as transom windows, pilasters with corinthian capitals decorated with circles and lozenges, and a frieze underlining the first floor.

🚗 DRIVING TOUR

THE QUEST FOR THE CROSS OF ANJOU
Round trip of 28km/17.4mi. About 1hr 30min. Drive S out of Le Lude on D 257.

Genneteil
The Romanesque **church** has a 13C bell tower with a stair turret and a 11C doorway; note the arch stones, which are carved with the signs of the zodiac and human faces.

▶ Take D 138 E to Chigné.

Chigné
The **church** (12C–15C) features an interesting façade flanked by a round tower.

▶ Continue via Les Quatre-Chemins to La Boissière.

La Boissière
This 12C abbey was partially burned and rebuilt in the 15C and again in the 18C. Its name is linked with a precious relic: the **Cross of Anjou** (⌖ *see BAUGÉ*). The cross was brought from the Middle East in the 13C, and during the Hundred Years War was kept in Angers. It was returned to La Boissière in about 1456 and remained there until 1790, when it was transferred to Baugé.

▶ Drive back towards Le Lude on D 767; in La Croix-Beauchêne turn right onto D 138.

Broc
The **church** has a Romanesque tower and apse decorated with 13C frescoes.

▶ Return to Le Lude via La Croix-Beauchêne then turn right onto D 307.

ADDRESSES

🛏 STAY AND 🍽 EAT

⌂⌂ **La Renaissance** – *2 av. de la Libération.* ☎*02 43 94 63 10. www. renaissancelelude.com. Closed Sun eve, Mon. 8 rooms.* ♿🅿. Stay by the château in this hotel-restaurant serving modern cuisine. Dining room and terrace.

La Flèche★

Situated on the banks of the Loir, this charming Angevin town is renowned for its Prytanée, a military school that has trained generations of officers. Today its students tend to congregate around the Henri IV fountain (on the square of the same name). A stroll along boulevard Latouche and Carmes gardens is a pleasant way to orient yourself.

A BIT OF HISTORY

Henri IV – La Flèche was given as part of a dowry to Charles de Bourbon-Vendôme, grandfather to Henri IV of Navarre. It was here that the young Prince Henri spent a happy childhood, and here in 1604 he founded a college.

A breeding-ground for officers – The Jesuit college grew rapidly; by 1625 there were 1 500 pupils. Over the years it has produced a great many celebrities who have distinguished themselves in the service of their country: Charles Borda, René Descartes, Marshalls Bertrand, Clarke, Pelissier, Gallieni and, more recently, astronauts Patrick Baudry and Jean-François Clervoy and the actor Jean-Claude Brialy – not to mention more than 2 000 generals and a number of government ministers.

Missionaries in Canada – **Jérôme le Royer de la Dauversière**, a native of La Flèche, was one of the founders of Montreal. Another old pupil of the college in La Flèche, **François de Montmorency-Laval**, became the first bishop of Nouvelle-France in 1674.

Unhappy exile – Under the monarchy La Flèche was a peaceful town with nothing to offer by way of entertainment but a hairdresser's, two billiard halls and a café. The witty poet **Jean-Baptiste Gresset** (1709–77) composed the heroic-comic masterpiece on the adventures of the parrot Ver-Vert, for which he is famous, while in exile in La Flèche for the indiscreet use of his tongue and his pen.

▶ **Population:** 15,185.
Ⓖ **Michelin Map:** 310: I-8
🄸 **Info:** 20 bd. de Montréal, 72200 La Flèche. ℘02 43 38 16 60. www.vallee-du-loir.com.
◗ **Location:** Two major roads feed into the city: D 323, a tourist route linking Le Mans (55km/34mi NE) and Angers (50km/31mi SW); and the D 938 to Saumur (77km/48mi S).
👪 **Kids:** Zoo's sea-lion show.

SIGHTS

Prytanée National Militaire★

22 r. du Collège. ◷*Jul–mid-Aug 10am–noon, 2–6pm.* ℘*02 43 48 59 91.* *https://prytanee-national-militaire.e-lyco.fr*

This military academy educates more than 900 male and female students, housed in two pavilions, named respectively after Henri IV and Gallieni. This State establishment offers an all-round education, and is open to any French youths wishing to prepare for entrance to the national service academies *(grandes écoles militaires)* such as the École Polytechnique, the École Spéciale Militaire in Coëtquidan, the École Navale in Brest, the École de l'Air at Salon-de-Provence and academies specialised in engineering. The school boasts an excellent library containing around 45,000 volumes, some of which date back to the 15C.

Église St-Louis★

Within the Prytanée National Militaire. The layout is typical of the Jesuits with its single well-lit nave. This is a remarkable example of Baroque decoration, from the main altarpiece to the magnificent **organ casing★**. Tucked away in the left transept, the gilded heart-shaped urn contains the ashes of the hearts of Henri IV and Marie de' Medici.

Zoo de la Flèche

© Zoo de la Flèche/Office de Tourisme de la Vallée du Loir

Chapelle Notre-Dame-des-Vertus

In av. Rhin-et-Danube in the direction of Laval, go right into Impasse des Vertus.
This delightful romanesque edifice has a semicircular archway above the portico. Note the wooden vaulting entirely covered with 17C painting and superb Renaissance **panelling★** taken from the château du Verger. Don't miss the so-called **Muslim warrior★** carved into the leaved door.

Château des Carmes

The 17C buildings erected on the ruins of a 15C fortress now house the town hall. The façade facing the Loir consists of a steep gable flanked by two machicolated turrets.

The **Parc des Carmes**, which is open to the public, stretches down to the river; from the bridge there is a fine view of the calm water reflecting the garden and the château.

EXCURSIONS

👤👤 Zoo de la Flèche★

5km/3mi E. Leave La Flèche on D 306, toward Le Lude, and turn right onto D 104; the zoo is 1km/0.6mi after the third-level crossing (Le Tertre Rouge).
♿🕐*Jul–Aug daily 9.30am–7.30pm; Sept Mon–Fri 9.30am–6pm, Sat–Sun and public holidays 9.30am–7pm;*
Oct daily 9.30-6pm; Nov-early Apr Mon-Fri 10.30am-5.30pm, Sat-Sun 10am-5.30pm; mid-Apr-Jun 9.30am-7pm. ⚭€24 (child 3–11, €19). ✆*02 43 48 19 19.*
www.zoo-la-fleche.com.
The zoo covers 14ha in a forest setting. There are mammals (big game, monkeys, deer, elephants, etc.), many birds and numerous reptiles housed in two vivariums (pythons, crocodiles, boas, tortoises, etc.). Sea-lions appear at scheduled performances.

Bazouges-sur-le-Loir

7km/4.3mi. Drive W out of La Flèche and follow D 323.
From the bridge there is a charming **view★** of the river with its wash-houses and river gate, of the castle and the mill, of the church and its tower in the square and of the gardens climbing towards the roofs of Bazouges.

Château de Bazouges-sur-le-Loir

👣*By guided tour Mid-Jul–Aug daily 3-6pm. Call for other dates earlier in the year.* ⚭€6. ✆*02 43 45 36 85.*
The Château de Bazouges, together with its watermill, was built on an attractive site on the banks of the Loir in the 15C and 16C by the Champagne family, one of whom, Baudoin (Baldwin), was chamberlain to Louis XII and François I.

The entrance is flanked by two massive towers, with machicolations and pepper-pot turrets; one of them contains the 15C chapel decorated with Angevin vaulting and two old statues portraying St Barbara and St John. The guard room over the gateway leads to the sentry walk. Another more imposing guard room, with a stone chimney-piece, is on view as well as the 18C State Rooms. The formal French park is planted with cypress and yew trees and circled by water.

Chambiers Forest

🏃 A former hunting ground of royalty, this forest on the southern edge of the town provides 1,300ha/5sq mi of walking trails among oak and pine trees; broad paths radiate from a clearing where the Table au Roy ("King's Table"), a stone on a pedestal that resembles a small table, stands in the centre.

Château Royal de Durtal

15 pl. des Terrasses, Durtal 49430.
🍽 *Guided tours at 10.30am, 11.30am, 2.30pm, 3.30pm, 4.30pm, 5.30pm: Jun–late Sept Wed–Mon. From Easter to All Saints' Day, open Weekends and public holidays.* ✆€9. *☎02 41 69 92 60. www.chateau-durtal.com.*

This grand stronghold on the Loir belonged to François de Scépeaux, Marshal of Vieilleville, who was host to Henri II, Charles IX and Catherine de' Medici. It came through the Revolution relatively unscathed.

The 15C wing is flanked by round towers with machicolations and pepper-pot roofs. The highest one (five storeys) affords a good view of the Loir valley. The Renaissance Gallery, lavishly decorated with paintings, overlooks the river. The Schömberg Pavilion, characterised by string courses, cordons and cornerstones with vermiculated bossage, prefigures the Classical period.

A tour of the interior takes in the guard room, the kitchen quarters, the dungeons, the Renaissance Gallery and the Great Tower *(Grande Tour)*.

Porte Verron

This 15C gate flanked by two turrets is part of the original curtain wall of the castle.

Vieux Pont

This old bridge commands a nice **view** of the River Loir, the watermills, the pointed roofs of the town and a medieval round tower upstream.

ADDRESSES

🛏STAY

⌂ **Camping municipal de la Route d'Or** – *Allée du Camping. ☎02 43 94 55 90. www.camping-lafleche.com. Open mid-Mar–mid-Oct. 190 pitches. Reservation advised.* ♿⚒. This well-run campground offers tent sites, sanitary blocks and mobile homes. Playground, 2 swimming pools (one heated) and, next door, a canoe centre. Bakery service (am).

⌂🍽🍽 **Chambre d'hôte Le Grand Moulin** – *8 r. de Syke, La Chartre-sur-le-Loir. ☎02 43 44 65 78. 4 rooms.* 🅿. Rooms are in a substantially built 18C mill in the heart of the village. In warm weather, breakfast by the Loir.

⌂🍽🍽 **Le Vert Galant** – *70 Grande-Rue. ☎02 43 94 00 51. www.vghotel.com. 25 rooms.* ♿🅿. This former 18C post station in town, not far from the Prytanée, offers traditional and contemporary rooms. Breakfast is served on the veranda when the weather is fine.

🍴EAT

⌂🍽🍽 **Auberge du Port des Roches** – *Port des Roches, Luché-Pringé,14km/8.6mi E of La Flèche by D 54.* 🅿 *☎02 43 45 44 48. Closed Sun, Mon.* Garden terrace over the water. Warm, pleasant dining room serving good, traditional cuisine. 12 pretty rooms (⌂🍽) are on-site for overnight guests.

⌂🍽🍽 **Le Moulin des Quatre Saisons** – *r. du Maréchal Gallieni. ☎02 43 45 12 12. www.camilleconstantin.com. Closed Wed and Sun eves, Mon.* Your first impression upon arriving at this 17C watermill in summer will be the scent of wisteria that overhangs the front path. The restaurant overlooks the Loir and features cooking from the south of France.

INDEX

INDEX

INDEX

INDEX

🏠 STAY

🍷 EAT

MAPS AND PLANS

THEMATIC MAPS

MAPS AND PLANS

MAP LEGEND

★★★   **Worth a special journey**

★★   **Worth a detour**

★   **Interesting**

Tourism

Sightseeing route with departure point indicated

Ecclesiastical building

Synagogue – Mosque

Building (with main entrance)

Statue, small building

Wayside cross

Fountain

Fortified walls – Tower – Gate

AZ B   Map co-ordinates locating sights

Tourist information

Historic house, castle – Ruins

Dam – Factory or power station

Fort – Cave

Prehistoric site

Viewing table – View

Miscellaneous sight

Recreation

Racecourse

Skating rink

Outdoor, indoor swimming pool

Marina, moorings

Mountain refuge hut

Overhead cable-car

Tourist or steam railway

Waymarked footpath

Outdoor leisure park/centre

Theme/Amusement park

Wildlife/Safari park, zoo

Gardens, park, arboretum

Aviary, bird sanctuary

Additional symbols

Motorway (unclassified)

Junction: complete, limited

Pedestrian street

Unsuitable for traffic, street subject to restrictions

Steps – Footpath

Railway – Coach station

Funicular – Rack-railway

Tram – Metro, underground

Bert (R.)...   Main shopping street

Post office – Telephone centre

Covered market

Barracks

Swing bridge

Quarry – Mine

Ferry (river and lake crossings)

Ferry services: Passengers and cars

Foot passengers only

Access route number common to MICHELIN maps and town plans

Abbreviations and special symbols

A   Agricultural office (Chambre d'agriculture)

C   Chamber of commerce (Chambre de commerce)

H   Town hall (Hôtel de ville)

J   Law courts (Palais de justice)

M   Museum (Musée)

P   Local authority offices (Préfecture, sous-préfecture)

POL.   Police station (Police)

Police station (Gendarmerie)

T   Theatre (Théâtre)

U   University (Université)

Hotel

Park and Ride

COMPANION PUBLICATIONS

travelguide.michelin.com
www.viamichelin.com

MAPS

Regional and local maps

To make the most of your journey, travel with Michelin **Regional maps nos 513, 518 and 519**, and also with the new local maps which are illustrated on the map of France below.

And remember to travel with the latest edition of the **national map of France no 721**, which gives an overall view of the region of the Châteaux of the Loire, and the main access roads which connect it to the rest of France. The entire country is mapped at a 1:1,000,000 scale and clearly shows the main road network. Convenient Atlas formats (spiral, hard cover and "mini") are also available.

ROUTE PLANNING

Michelin is pleased to offer a route planning service at **www.viamichelin.com**.

Personalised route plans, comprehensive maps, addresses of hotels and restaurants featured in *The Red Guides* and practical and tourist information.

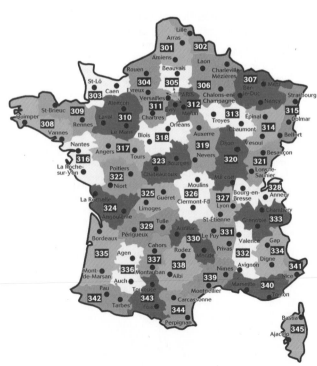

HARLEQUIN®
Presents

Welcome to a month of fantastic reading, brought to you by Harlequin Presents! Continuing our magnificent series THE ROYAL HOUSE OF NIROLI is Melanie Milburne with *Surgeon Prince, Ordinary Wife*. With the first heir excluded from the throne of Niroli, missing prince and brilliant surgeon Dr. Alex Hunter is torn between duty and his passion for a woman who can never be his queen.... Don't miss out!

Also for your reading pleasure is the first book of Sandra Marton's new THE BILLIONAIRES' BRIDES trilogy, *The Italian Prince's Pregnant Bride,* where Prince Nicolo Barbieri acquires Aimee Black, who, it seems, is pregnant with Nicolo's baby! Then favorite author Lynne Graham brings you a gorgeous Greek in *The Petrakos Bride,* where Maddie comes face-to-face again with her tycoon idol....

In *His Private Mistress* by Chantelle Shaw, Italian racing driver Rafael is determined to make Eden his mistress once more...while in *One-Night Baby* by Susan Stephens, another Italian knows nothing of the secret Kate is hiding from their one night together. If a sheikh is what gets your heart thumping, Annie West brings you *For the Sheikh's Pleasure,* where Sheikh Arik is determined to get Rosalie to open up to receive the loving that only *he* can give her! In *The Brazilian's Blackmail Bargain* by Abby Green, Caleb makes Maggie an offer she just can't refuse. And finally Lindsay Armstrong's *The Rich Man's Virgin* tells the story of a fiercely independent woman who finds she's pregnant by a powerful millionaire. Look out for more brilliant books next month!

EXPECTING!

She's sexy, successful... and PREGNANT!

Relax and enjoy our fabulous series about couples whose passion results in pregnancies... sometimes unexpected!

Share the surprises, emotions, drama and suspense as our parents-to-be come to terms with the prospect of bringing a new life into the world. All will discover that the business of making babies brings with it the most special love of all....

Our next arrival will be coming soon!

Lindsay Armstrong

THE RICH MAN'S VIRGIN

EXPECTING!

HARLEQUIN®

TORONTO • NEW YORK • LONDON
AMSTERDAM • PARIS • SYDNEY • HAMBURG
STOCKHOLM • ATHENS • TOKYO • MILAN • MADRID
PRAGUE • WARSAW • BUDAPEST • AUCKLAND

ISBN-13: 978-0-373-12658-3
ISBN-10:   0-373-12658-1

THE RICH MAN'S VIRGIN

First North American Publication 2007.

This edition published by arrangement with Harlequin Books S.A.

® and TM are trademarks of the publisher. Trademarks indicated with ® are registered in the United States Patent and Trademark Office, the Canadian Trade Marks Office and in other countries.

www.eHarlequin.com

Printed in U.S.A.

All about the author…
Lindsay Armstrong

I was born in South Africa, but I'm an Australian citizen now, with a New Zealand-born husband. We had an epic introduction to Australia. We landed in Perth, then drove around the "top end" with four kids under the age of eight. There were some marvelous times and wonderful sights and ever since, we've been fascinated by wild Australia. We've done quite a bit of exploring the coastline by boat, including one amazing trip to the Kimberley.

We've also farmed and trained racehorses, and after our fifth child was born I started to write. It was something I'd always wanted to do but never seemed to know how to start. Then one day I sat down at the kitchen table with an abandoned exercise book, suddenly convinced the time had come to stop dreaming about it and start doing it. That book never got published, but it certainly opened the floodgates!

PROLOGUE

MAGGIE TRENT and Jack McKinnon conducted rather unreal conversations at times.

Why this should be so had something to do with the unreal nature of their relationship, Maggie felt. Nothing ever went according to plan in their lives. Their first meeting had been sheer coincidence, their second meeting sheer disaster, their third meeting should have had labels stuck all over it shouting, 'Spoilt, little rich girl determined to get her own way'—according, at first anyway, to Jack.

They'd parted after that extended meeting, not well, and determined never wittingly to come together again.

Yet just under a year later Maggie began one of her unreal conversations with Jack McKinnon on the subject of their two-month-old son who had started out life known as Trent/McKinnon—it had been written on his wrist band and on the label on his cot. They'd dispensed with the stroke after a week but stuck with the Trent McKinnon.

The gist of their conversation was this.

'This is a very proper baby,' Maggie said seriously one evening.

'I never thought he was a porcelain doll.'

'No. I mean, he's very well organized. He does everything by the book.'

Jack frowned. 'He's only eight weeks old. How can you say that?'

7

Maggie was attractively dressed in slim white trousers and a floral seersucker jacket trimmed with green. Her dark gold hair was tied back with a green scrunchie; her green eyes were clear and she was sitting beside a cot.

Trent McKinnon was asleep in the cot.

'I'll tell you. He adapted himself to a four-hourly schedule right from the start under extremely difficult circumstances. He burps beautifully and he mostly sleeps between feeds just as the book says he should. He has one wakeful period, after his two p.m. feed, where he'll accept conversation and he quite appreciates being carried around for a bit. He now sleeps through the eight hours from ten p.m. to six a.m.'

'Is there anything he doesn't do by the book?' Jack asked with a grin. 'He sounds almost too good to be true.'

Maggie considered. 'He hates having his hair washed. He gets extremely upset, but even that isn't going against the book exactly. They do warn that some babies hate it.'

'Screams blue murder?'

'Yes. Otherwise—' she shrugged '—there's nothing he doesn't do very correctly.'

'What are you worried about, then?'

Maggie stared down at her sleeping son with her heart in her eyes. 'I can't help thinking he would be horrified if he knew how—irregular—his situation was.'

She looked up and their gazes clashed.

'Born out of wedlock, you mean?' he said, and for a fleeting moment his mouth hardened. 'That was your choice, Maggie.'

She inclined her head. 'That was before—all sorts

of things happened,' she said quietly and ran her fingers along the arm of her chair. 'That was definitely before I came to appreciate the reality of having a baby and what a baby deserves.'

CHAPTER ONE

Maggie Trent sold real estate.

None of her family or friends particularly appreciated her job, although her mother was supportive, until Mary Donaldson of Tasmania got engaged to Crown Prince Frederik of Denmark and it was revealed that she had worked in a real estate office.

From then on, everyone looked at Maggie Trent with renewed interest, even a little spark of 'the world could be your oyster too'!

In fact, the world could have been Maggie's oyster anyway, had she wanted it. She came from a very wealthy background. At twenty-three she was a golden blonde, attractive, always stylish and well groomed.

Nevertheless, she also had a well-developed commercial instinct and a flair for her job in the form of matching the right people to the right properties plus a very real 'eye' for the potential in houses that many missed.

This came from the Bachelor of Arts degree she'd done at university along with courses in architecture and draughting, as well as her natural interest in people and her ability to get along with them. She'd been born with great taste.

If she had a creed it was that nothing was unsaleable.

She was enjoying her life and her career far too much, especially with the property boom going the

10

way it was, to contemplate marriage, although there was at least one man in her life who wished she would—not a prince of any designation, however.

But Maggie had two goals. One was to prove that she was a highly successful businesswoman in her own right. She had visions of opening her own agency one day. The other was to allow no man to make her feel inferior because she was a woman. Both these ambitions had been nurtured by a difficult relationship with her father, a powerful, wealthy, often arrogant man who believed she was wasting her time working at all and equated real-estate agents with used-car salesmen.

It was undoubtedly—she didn't try to hide it from herself—this mindset that saw her take such exception to Jack McKinnon, wealthy property developer, with such disastrous results—not that she'd ever intended to deprive him of his liberty!

She couldn't deny that was how it had turned out, though. Nor had the fact that she'd been deprived of *her* liberty at the same time seemed to hold much weight with him at all. In fact, he'd ascribed some really weird motives to it all that still annoyed her to think of…

Anyway, it all started one sunny Sunday afternoon.

She and Tim Mitchell were sipping coffee and listening to an excellent jazz band amongst a lively crowd on a marina boardwalk. Her relationship with Tim was fairly casual. They did a lot of things together, but Maggie always drew the line at getting further involved. Truth be told this was placing undue strain on Tim, but he did a good job of hiding it.

'Who's that?' Maggie asked idly. She was feeling relaxed and content. She'd sold a house that morning that was going to earn her a rather nice, fat commission.

Tim glanced over his shoulder at the new arrivals that had caught Maggie's attention and drew an excited breath.

'Jack McKinnon,' he said. 'You know—the property developer.'

Maggie stared at the man. She did know the name and the man, but only by reputation.

Jack McKinnon was a millionaire many times over and amongst other things he headed the company that was developing new housing estates in what Maggie thought of as 'her patch', the Gold Coast hinterland.

If she was honest, and she was, Maggie disapproved of the kind of housing estates Jack McKinnon developed. She saw it as tearing up of the rural land that had always been the Coast's buffer zone. The area where you could own a few acres, run a few horses, breed llamas or whatever took your fancy; the green zone that was a retreat for many from the high-rise and suburbia of the rest of the Coast.

Now, thanks to Jack McKinnon and others, part of that green zone was disappearing and thousands of cheek-by-jowl 'little boxes' were taking its place.

Unfortunately, the reality of it was that the Coast's population was burgeoning. Not only did it offer a good climate and great beaches, but its proximity to Brisbane, the state's capital, also made it desirable and future urban development was inevitable.

Doesn't mean to say I have to like the people involved in doing it and making a fortune out of it at the same time, she mused.

'Do you know him?' she asked Tim as Jack

McKinnon and his party, two women and another man, selected a table not far away and sat down.

'I went to school with him, but he's a few years older. Bumped into him a couple of times since. He's a Coast boy who really made good,' Tim said with pride.

Maggie opened her mouth to demolish the likes of Jack McKinnon, then decided to hold her peace. Tim was sweet and good company. At twenty-nine he was a dentist with his own practice. With his engaging ways and a passion for all things orthodontic, and the prices dentists charged these days, she had no doubt he would 'really make good' as well, although perhaps not on the scale of Jack McKinnon.

It was on the tip of her tongue to ask Tim what the man was like, but she realized suddenly that she couldn't fathom why she wanted to know, and she puzzled over that instead.

It came to her there was definitely an aura to him that she found a little surprising.

His dark fair hair streaked lighter by the sun fell in his eyes. He would be over six feet, she judged, slim but broad-shouldered and he looked lithe and light on his feet.

Unlike many of the 'white shoe' brigade, Gold Coast identities, particularly entrepreneurs, who had over the years earned the sobriquet because of their penchant for flashy dressing, Jack McKinnon was very casually dressed with not a gold chain in sight.

He wore jeans, brown deck shoes, a white T-shirt and a navy pullover slung over his shoulders.

There was also a pent-up dynamism about him that easily led you to imagine him flying a plane through the sound barrier, crewing a racing yacht, climbing

Mount Everest, hunting wild animals and testing himself to the limit—rather than developing housing estates.

As these thoughts chased through her mind, perhaps the power of her concentration on him seeped
through to him because he turned abruptly and their
gazes clashed.

A little flare of colour entered Maggie's cheeks and
Jack McKinnon raised an ironic eyebrow. Even then
she was unable to tear her gaze away. Somehow or
other he had her trapped, she thought chaotically as
more colour poured into her cheeks. Then he noticed
Tim and instant recognition came to him.

That was how Tim and Maggie came to join Jack's
party.

She tried to resist, but Tim's obvious delight made
it difficult. Nor was there any real reason for her to
feel uneasy amongst Jack McKinnon's party, at first.

Her slim black linen dress and high-heeled black
patent sandals were the essence of chic. Her thick
dark gold hair fell to her shoulders when loose, but
was tied back with a velvet ribbon today. Her golden
skin was smooth and luminous.

She was, in other words, as presentable as the other
two women. Nor were they unfriendly, although they
were both the essence of sophistication. One, a flash-
ing brunette, was introduced as Lia Montalba, the
other, Nordic fair, as Bridget Pearson. The second
man, Paul Wheaton, was a lawyer who acted for the
McKinnon Corporation, but who was paired with
whom was hard to say.

The conversation was light-hearted. They discussed
the music. The McKinnon party had spent the night
out on Jack's boat cruising the Broadwater, and had

some fishy tales to tell, mainly about the ones that got away.

The man himself—why did Maggie think of him thus? she wondered—had a deep, pleasant voice, a lurking grin and a wicked sense of humour.

All the same, Maggie did feel uneasy and it was all to do with Jack McKinnon, she divined. Not that he paid her much attention, so was she still stinging inwardly from that ironically raised eyebrow and her curious inability to tear her gaze from his?

Well, if he thought her scrutiny was the prelude to her making a pass at him, if that was why he was now virtually ignoring her, he was mistaken and she was perfectly content to be ignored.

Or was she?

It occurred to her that what he was doing was a deliberate insult and before much longer everyone was going to realize it, to her humiliation. Her blood began to boil. Who did he think he was?

Then he trained his grey gaze on her and said musingly, 'Maggie Trent. David Trent's daughter, by any chance?'

She hesitated. 'Yes,' she replied briefly.

'*The* David Trent?' Lia asked, her big dark eyes wide. 'Ultra-wealthy, from a long line of distinguished judges and politicians, grazier, racehorse owner, champion yachtsman?'

Maggie shrugged.

'Maggie doesn't like to trade on her father,' Tim murmured.

What an understatement, Maggie marvelled, considering how stormy their father/daughter relationship had sometimes been.

'Lucky you, Maggie,' Paul commented.

'Yes,' Jack McKinnon agreed. 'Do you actually do anything useful, Maggie? Not that one could blame you if you didn't.'

Even Tim, obviously a fan of Jack McKinnon, did a double take.

As for Maggie, she stared at Jack out of sparkling green eyes—green eyes sparkling with rage, that was.

'I knew there was one good reason not to like you,' she said huskily. 'I detest the little boxes you build and the way you destroy the landscape to do so. Now I have another reason. Wealthy, powerful men who are completely in love with themselves mean absolutely nothing to me, Mr McKinnon.'

She got up and walked away.

She had a rostered day off on Monday, and she spent the morning with her mother.

In contrast to her sometimes stormy relationship with her father, Maggie adored her mother.

In her middle forties, Belle Trent looked years younger. Her straight dark hair was streaked with grey, but it was so glossy and beautifully cut many younger women envied it. With her fine dark eyes and slim figure she was essentially elegant. She was also a busy person; she did a great deal of charity work.

Yet there were times when Maggie sensed a current of sadness in her mother, but it was an enigmatic kind of sadness Maggie couldn't really fathom. She knew it had to do with her father, that at times their marriage was strained, but for no real reason Maggie could put her finger on.

Belle never complained and there was never any suggestion that it might break up, although, with a certain cynicism, Maggie sometimes wondered whether neither her mother nor her father could face the Herculean task of sorting out a divorce settlement.

But that Monday morning as she had coffee with her mother at a chic Sanctuary Cove pavement café, Maggie had something else on her mind.

'Do you know anything about the McKinnon Corporation and Jack McKinnon, Mum?'

Belle stirred sugar into her latte. 'Uh—I believe he's a bit of a whizkid. He started with nothing, I heard. Somehow or other he persuaded a bank to finance his first development and he hasn't looked back since. He now not only develops the estate but he has a construction company that builds many of the houses. Of course housing estates are not the only string to his bow.'

'No?'

Belle shook her head. 'No,' she said. 'Once he made his first few millions he diversified into boat-building. McKinnon Catamarans have taken off. If you looked through this marina—' she waved a hand towards the forest of masts and all sorts of boats moored in the Sanctuary Cove marina just across the road from the shopping and restaurant precinct '—you'd probably find quite a few.'

'So, if he started with nothing, he must be—clever,' Maggie hazarded.

'I believe he's one of *those*.' Belle wrinkled her nose. 'You know, the kind of gifted person with a lot of foresight and a lot of drive who is always going to make good. I don't believe he's at all ostentatious about it, though.'

'Hmm…'

Belle raised an eyebrow. 'Do you know him?'

'I met him. Yesterday, as it happens. He was rather rude to me.'

Her mother blinked. 'Why?'

'I have no idea.' Maggie frowned. 'How come you know so much about him?'

'Your aunt Elena has decided to put him on her list of eligible bachelors,' Belle said ruefully.

They stared at each other, then started to laugh. Elena Chadwick was actually Belle's cousin. She'd never married yet she wrote a column in a weekly magazine dispensing advice on all sorts of marital problems. When anyone took issue with her lack of experience on the subject, she protested that it was her unbiased views that were invaluable. She was a great promoter of innovative methods for 'holding onto your man'.

She also kept and updated quarterly, to the delight of her readers, a ten most eligible bachelors' list; the other noteworthy thing about Elena Chadwick was her talent for unearthing all sorts of unusual facts about people.

'If I didn't dislike him so much,' Maggie said, still gurgling with laughter, 'I'd feel sorry for him with Elena in hot pursuit! On the other hand, I have no doubt that he can look after himself.'

'What's he like?'

Maggie considered. 'I don't know, but he could be the kind of man women ride off with into the sunset without giving it a great deal of thought. Some women.'

'Hmm…' Belle said, echoing her daughter's earlier *Hmm* of doubt and reservation, but accompanied by a searching little look that Maggie missed.

*   *   *

When she got home later, Maggie closed her front door and took her usual few deep breaths of sheer appreciation of her home.

It was a two-storeyed villa overlooking a lovely golf course on Hope Island. It had a small garden, a conservatory dining room overlooking a fountain and she'd inherited it from her paternal grandmother. She'd also inherited some of the lovely pieces that furnished and decorated it.

She'd been very fond of her father's mother. Everyone told her she took after Leila Trent, not only in looks but personality although, curiously, this was the one area where they'd failed to agree. Leila had always insisted that if Margaret Leila Trent took after anyone, it was her father, David Trent.

'But we never do anything but fight!' Maggie protested, more than once. 'Well, not always, but you know what I mean.'

'That's because, underneath, you're so much alike,' Leila insisted. 'Oh, you've got your mother's more gentle genes to balance it, darling, but essentially you're a Trent and, whatever else you might like to say about your father, that means you have a lot of drive and a lot of nerve. Your grandfather was much the same.'

Once, Maggie voiced the opinion that she should have been a boy—to gain her father's approval anyway.

Leila looked at her piercingly. 'Don't go down that road, Maggie. Your mother has and—' She stopped, then added slowly, 'You just be yourself.'

Leila would never elaborate on what she'd been about to say and six months ago she'd died peacefully in her sleep.

Maggie tossed her bag onto the settee and slipped off her shoes.

She'd managed to avoid Tim, although she'd spoken to him on the phone and accepted his apologies for what had happened. What she hadn't been able to accept was his complete bafflement over the incident.

'Jack's just—normally—not *like* that,' he said several times.

Oh, yes? she thought cynically, but she told Tim it wasn't his fault and said simply that she'd be in touch shortly.

'I hope that's not a 'don't call us, we'll call you' message, Maggie?'

Maggie said no, of course not, but now, as she padded out to water her garden in her bare feet, she frowned, because the fact was that since Sunday afternoon's incident she'd been curiously at odds with herself. She just couldn't put her finger on why this was so. Why her smooth, successful life she'd been enjoying so much was suddenly not so appealing to her any more.

It couldn't have anything to do with Jack McKinnon's insulting manner and words, surely?

After all, he'd completely misread her. He'd taken her for an idle little rich girl, a daddy's pet, so how on earth could that start her thinking along some strange lines?

Strange lines such as a sudden dissatisfaction to do with her relationship with Tim?

Not that you could call it much of a relationship, but there was the fact that Tim dearly wanted to make it into something more while she didn't, and she was suddenly feeling guilty about it.

It wasn't only that, though. To be tarred with the same brush as her father was extremely annoying. She might, according to her grandmother, have inherited some of her father's genes, but not, she devoutly hoped, his arrogance. She might have a fairly well-developed commercial instinct when it came to the property market, but a lot of people thought of her father as a ruthless businessman—she certainly wasn't ruthless.

As usual, her garden soothed her. She'd had no idea she possessed green fingers until she'd inherited her villa. In six months she'd transformed the small garden into a colourful showpiece. She grew roses and camellias, impatiens, petunias and daisies, yellow, pink and white. Her lawn was like green velvet and her herb garden provided basil, mint, coriander, rosemary, sage, parsley, thyme and oregano.

So she watered and pottered and pruned dead heads until both Tim Mitchell and Jack McKinnon faded from her mind, quite unaware that Jack 'the man' would raise his undeniably attractive head in the most unexpected way when she went back to work the following morning.

Maggie was the only agent not engaged with clients when an elderly couple walked into the office on Tuesday morning, so she took them under her wing and set about making her usual assessment of what kind of a property they wanted to buy. This could often be a tricky business, but with Sophie and Ernest Smith it proved to be more—it proved to be a marital war zone.

It transpired that they had sold their previous prop-

erty, a house and eight acres, to a developer. Sophie
had not been in favour of doing this at all and claimed
she wasn't going to be happy anywhere else, anyway.

Ernest, with a lack of patience that indicated this
battle had been fought many a time before, detailed
to Maggie why he'd thought it was such a good idea
at the time.

They were getting on and eight acres were quite a
handful. Once developers got their eye on an area
what option did you have but to sell out unless you
relished the thought of being hemmed in by hundreds
of houses? The price they'd been offered would as-
sure a comfortable retirement...

'Yes,' Sophie Smith said grimly, 'but if you'd hung
on as I suggested, we would have got a lot more for
it!'

Ernest bristled. 'We weren't to know that, woman,
and a bird in the hand is worth two in the bush!'

Maggie spent a few moments calming them down,
then asked for more details. The Smiths were the first
to be approached in their road by the developer, and
the ones to sell out cheapest. Others in the road who
had held out over a period of time had received better
offers.

It was obvious to Maggie that, not only had Sophie
really loved her property and not wanted to sell anyway, but that the higher prices some of her neighbours
had attained were going to be a thorn in her flesh and
a cause for discontent between her and her husband
for the rest of their lives.

'Who was the developer?' she asked.

Ernest heaved a sigh. 'The McKinnon Corporation.'

As Maggie surveyed the two unhappy people before her once again her blood boiled directly on account of Jack McKinnon.

All the same, she might never have done anything about it had fate not intervened.

A few days later, she was doing a property assessment.

The owners had relocated to Melbourne over a year ago. They'd contacted her by phone with instructions to value the property with a view to putting it on the market and they'd posted her the keys.

The house, she discovered, showed every sign of not having been lived in for quite a time—it was distinctly unloved and it was a crying shame because it had obviously once been a beautiful home with loads of character. But the acreage was green and rolling, there were lovely trees on it and a delightful, secretive creek ran through it. A creek, she felt sure, you would find platypus playing in.

There was also a large brick shed. She left it to last to inspect and finally tore herself away from the creek to do so. The shed had two means of access: a set of double doors you could drive a vehicle through, but they were heavily barred and padlocked, and a stout wooden single door with a deadlock. She unlocked it and walked into the cavernous gloom of the building.

One corner of it had been converted into a rudimentary dwelling, she found, complete with kitchenette, bathroom and toilet. The kitchenette had a small two-burner stove. There were an old kettle and a couple of pots as well as some mismatched china and cutlery. The kitchen cupboard held some tinned food and dry goods, but there was little furniture, only a sagging settee and a Formica-topped table with four chairs. But there were, as she clicked a light switch then ran a tap, both electricity and water connected.

She made some notes and looked around again, but it was bare except for a large mound covered with tarpaulins in one corner. She was just about to investigate when the scamper of mice in the rafters caused her to grimace and decide against it.

That was when she heard a vehicle pull up outside. To her amazement, as she watched through the doorway, who should step out of the late-model Range Rover but Jack McKinnon?

She stared through the door wide-eyed, but there was no mistaking him as he stretched and looked around. He wore buff chinos and a dark green long-sleeved shirt with patch pockets, casually dressed again in other words, but still—how to put it?—a very compelling presence? Yes.

All the same— *Oh, no! No, you don't!* were her next sentiments. No way are you going to turn this little piece of heaven into a housing estate, Jack McKinnon.

She emerged from the shadows of the shed with an ominous expression on her face.

'Well, well,' he drawled as they came face to face, 'if it isn't little Miss Trent, green crusader and man-hater.'

He looked her up and down and decided, somewhat to his surprise, that if she were anyone but David Trent's daughter he would find her rather peachy despite her grim expression.

Peachy? he thought with an ironic twist of his lips. Where did that come from? You wouldn't exactly call—he dredged his mind for an example—Lia Montalba peachy. Svelte, stunning, sexy, sophisticated—yes, definitely that, but peachy? No. So why apply it to this girl? Did it indicate a succulent, fresh and rather innocent quality he detected in Maggie Trent alongside the expensive grooming and the stunning green eyes?

He shook his head, mainly to dislodge an image of her without her clothes—she was David Trent's daughter, after all—and reminded himself that she could certainly stand up for herself.

But that produced another inclination in him. As well as speculating on her figure, he discovered a desire to indulge in more verbal fencing with her.

Hell, Jack, he thought, isn't that a little immature? Not to mention a dead-end street with this particular girl?

In the meantime, Maggie discovered she was clutching her mobile phone as tightly as if she wished to crush it, so she put it, together with her notes, carefully on the roof of her car and planted her hands on her hips as she delivered her reply.

'At this moment, yes to all of those names, Mr McKinnon,' she said through her teeth. 'But since I'm here at the express instructions of the owner in my capacity as a real-estate agent, you *can't* be here legitimately so would you mind moving on?'

He smiled fleetingly, thought, Immature? Maybe, but what do they say? Men will be men! And he took his time about summing her up from head to toe again.

With a rural inspection to do, Maggie wore jeans, short boots and a pink blouse. Her hair was fish-plaited and she wore the minimum of make-up, only lip gloss, in fact. It was also her last assignment of

the day so she'd gone home to change into something
suitable for tramping round a paddock.

None of that hid the fact that she was long-legged,
high-breasted and had a particularly lithe way of
walking that was an invitation to imagine that supple,
golden body in your arms, in your bed…

Nor, he noted, did his scrutiny of her breasts, hips
and legs, her smooth, silky skin, indeed his systematic
stripping of her, go unnoticed.

Once again, bright colour flooded her cheeks, but
at the same time her eyes started to sparkle with rage.

He observed the wrathful turmoil he was exciting
in her with another smile, this time dry.

'So that's what you do for a—shall we say hobby?
But it so happens you're wrong, Miss Trent,' he said.
'I was also contacted by the owners. They want to
know if this property has development potential.'

Maggie closed her eyes in sheer frustration. 'They
didn't say a word about that to me!'

He shrugged. 'You're welcome to check back with
them.'

She reached for her phone, but put it down on the
roof of her car again as her emotions ran away with
her. 'You can't—you wouldn't! It's so lovely. It
would be a crying shame.'

'To destroy it and cover it with little boxes?' he
suggested, and strolled into the shed.

Maggie followed him. 'Yes!'

'Listen.' he turned on his heel towards her and she
nearly ran into him. 'A lot of you do-gooders amaze
me.'

She backed away a step.

It was impossible not to be slightly intimidated by
Jack McKinnon. He was tall, for one thing, and he

moved with superb co-ordination. His grey gaze was boring right into her and the lines and angles of his face were set arrogantly beneath that dark fair hair. The arrogance was compounded by a beaky nose and a well-cut but hard mouth and—at such close quarters there was even more to contend with.

He was so essentially masculine it was impossible to be in his company without a sense of man versus woman coming into the equation.

That translated, she realized, to a competitive form of self-awareness that took her by surprise. An 'I can be just as judgmental of you, Jack McKinnon, because I can be just as alluring, sexy and damned attractive as—as Lia and Bridget are!'

She blinked as it shot through her mind. Could she? She doubted it. She had never mentally stripped a man the way he had stripped her and she was quite sure she couldn't render him as hot and bothered—and stirred up, she acknowledged honestly—as his lazy, sensual summing-up of her had. Not to mention—how dared he do that to her? Who did he think he was?

There was also, if all that weren't bad enough—and she wondered why she hadn't taken this into account before because even her mother had mentioned it!—the distinct impression that he was diabolically clever, as he proceeded to demonstrate.

'If you have real concerns about the environment and the impact of urban sprawl, take them to the city council. If you object to rural zonings being overturned do something positive about it,' he said contemptuously.

'Something?' she echoed unwisely.

'Yes. Campaign against it. Stand for council yourself. Use your ballot power to vote for a 'greener' council. It can be done. But don't rail against me in a virtually uneducated fashion, because I'm not breaking any laws at all.'

'What about moral and philosophical laws?' she challenged. 'What about enriching yourself at the expense of the environment and people like the Smiths?'

'I have no idea who the Smiths are but...' he paused and once again that grey gaze roamed over her, although this time clinically and coldly '...it's often the wealthy, the old money entrenched in their ivory towers and open green spaces, who lack concern and understanding for the less fortunate majority of the population.'

Maggie gasped. 'That's not true, of me anyway!'

'No?' He raised a sardonic eyebrow. 'You should try being one of that majority, Miss Trent. You should experiment with existing as a couple and raising a family on a single income because the kids are too small to leave, or child-care is too expensive—and see what it means to you to have your own roof over your head.'

'I—'

But he continued scathingly, 'You may think they're little boxes, but they're *affordable* and they're part of the great Australian dream, owning your own home. Come to that, it's a vast continent but inhospitable, so suburbia and the fact that we cling to the coast is another fact of life.'

He paused and eyed her. 'How much does your privileged background stop you from understanding some basic facts of life?' he asked her then. 'How many acres does your father own all green, untouched and lovely?'

That was when Maggie completely lost her temper. One innuendo, one insult too many, she raged inwardly, and looked around for some way to relieve the pressure of it all—she grabbed the door and banged it closed.

'I hope,' he said as the echoes of it slammed around the shed, 'this isn't what I think it is.'

'And I hope it demonstrates to you the force of my emotions about the likes of you,' she returned icily.

He looked around with a gathering frown and mentally castigated himself for playing verbal war games with this girl. 'Are your emotions savage enough to want to kidnap me?'

'Savage enough to make me want to scream and shout, throw things and slam things—' Maggie stopped abruptly. 'Kidnap you? What on earth are you talking about? The last thing—'

'One wonders if your antipathy is towards my housing estates or the kind of man you think I am?' His grey glance brushed over her insolently. 'So you have a key in your pocket?'

Maggie looked bewildered. 'What do you mean? A key? No. Why?'

He walked past her to the closed shed door and turned the handle. Nothing happened. 'This door is now deadlocked. From memory, you had a key in this lock but on the outside, didn't you?'

'Yes.' Maggie stopped and her lips parted as understanding of what she'd done started to seep through. 'Yes.' She cleared her throat. 'But there must be other ways out.'

'Show me,' he commanded. 'As far as I can see the only two windows have burglar bars fitted and both doors are locked now.'

'Oh, my...' Maggie breathed. 'I don't believe this! What about your keys? You must have had some.'

'No. I wasn't really interested in the house or the shed.'

'Well, well—phones,' she gabbled, and was hit by the memory of her mobile sitting on the roof of her car. She closed her eyes. 'Please tell me you've got your mobile phone on you?' she begged.

'I don't. I left it on its mounting in my car. This is all very affecting, Ms Trent,' he said with utter contempt, 'but whatever you *don't* like to call it, and for whatever reason you decided to deprive me of my liberty—' his gaze was cold enough to slice right through her '—you're going to pay for this.'

'Hang on, hang on.' Maggie took some deep breaths. 'It was an accident. Yes, OK, maybe I got a bit carried away, but I have every right to, on the Smiths' behalf if nothing else! There is no reason in the world, however,' she said emphatically, 'that would make me want to kidnap you!'

'The ubiquitous Smiths again,' he murmured, then said trenchantly, 'Lady, you were bestowing enough attention on me last Sunday to make the hairs on the back of my neck stand up.'

Maggie sucked in her cheeks in the effort she made not to blush. 'That was the power of my disapproval,' she offered stiffly.

'Oh, yeah?' He said it softly, but the two words contained a world of disbelief.

'Yes!' she insisted at the same time as a most treacherous little thought slipped into her mind— So why hadn't she been the same since?

But that spurred her on to say hotly. 'You can't

have it both ways, Mr McKinnon. Either I'm a man-hater or I'm not!'

He lifted an eyebrow. 'Perhaps I should qualify that—a hater of wealthy, powerful men completely in love with themselves.'

'Bingo! Now you've got it right.'

'I wonder,' he mused. 'There could be two sides to that coin, but anyway—' he looked briefly amused '—I don't agree that I'm in love with myself so you mightn't have to hate me totally, or the opposite,' he added softly.

Maggie stared at him. 'I have no idea what you're talking about!'

He rubbed his chin and narrowed his eyes.

'Look…' She hesitated as she tried to gather her thoughts, then she threw up her hands. 'If I'd *lured* you here then locked you in, that would be a different matter, but it's a supreme coincidence the two of us being here today!'

'You could be a quick thinker for all I know,' he countered. 'And there are women who take the most amazing liberties and—opportunities.'

She studied the harsh lines of his face. She thought of the pent-up dynamism she'd sensed in him. She had to acknowledge that he would be extremely attractive to most women and when you added his wealth to his looks and his aura, you had also to acknowledge there could be some women, gold-diggers, fortune-hunters, who would take what opportunities they could.

'You forget,' she said quietly, 'I probably have as much money in my own right as you do.'

He said, with a flash of irritation, as if he was suddenly heartily sick of her, 'I don't really give a damn for your motivation. I'd much rather you worked out how to get us out of here. I have a plane to catch in a couple of hours.'

Maggie looked around helplessly, then upwards. 'Maybe—maybe we can go through the roof?'

He swore comprehensively and pointed out just how high the roof was and that there was no ceiling. There was also no sign of so much as a set of steps, let alone a decent ladder, or…

Maggie finally stemmed the tide. She planted her hands on her hips again. 'You're a man, aren't you? Surely you can think of something?'

He folded his arms and looked sardonic. 'Even wealthy, powerful men have their uses? Isn't that a double standard?'

Maggie opened and closed her mouth a couple of times.

'Cat got your tongue, Miss Trent?' he drawled. 'Never mind, here's what I suggest. Since you got us into this—*you* get us out.'

CHAPTER TWO

'THAT'S...that's ridiculous,' Maggie stammered.

'Why?'

'I thought you had a plane to catch.'

'I get the feeling even my best efforts won't catch me that plane.'

She gazed around in serious alarm. 'That doesn't entitle you to twiddle your thumbs!'

He looked her over sardonically, but she was entirely unprepared for what he said next.

'Let's try and clear the decks here. If you're not trying to make some stupid statement about the kind of housing estates I develop, what are you after, Maggie Trent? My body?'

She went scarlet, instantly and—it felt—all over, and could have killed herself. 'In your dreams, mister,' she said through her teeth.

'Why so hot, then?' he taunted and ran his gaze up and down her. 'We might suit rather well. In bed.'

Her tongue seemed to tie itself in knots as all her mental sensors seemed to attune themselves to this proposition in the form of a picture in her mind's eye of just that—Jack McKinnon running his hands over her naked body.

What was particularly surprising about it was the fact that she didn't often fantasize about men. In fact she'd sometimes wondered if there was something wrong with her. The other surprise she got was the realization that this man had got under her skin from the very beginning in this very way, and succeeded in unsettling her even when she'd been telling herself she hoped never to lay eyes on him again.

Perhaps, but that didn't mean she had to like it, or him, she thought.

'Look—' she ignored his assessing gaze; she ignored her burning cheeks '—don't push me any further with this kind of—cheap rubbish!'

He smiled slightly as he took in the imperious tilt of her chin. 'Ever tried a real man, Maggie, as opposed to a good-mannered, docile boy like Tim Mitchell?'

Her lips parted.

'You might find your stance on men somewhat changed if you did,' he drawled, and went on before she could draw breath. 'And if you're not making a statement on housing estates, what's left?'

'You tell me,' she suggested dangerously.

This time he smiled quite charmingly, although it didn't take the sting out of what he said. 'A flighty, spoilt little rich bitch who hates not getting her own way?' he mused. 'A right chip off the old block,' he added with that lethal smile disappearing to be replaced by a cold, hard glance of contempt. Then he turned away.

'Hang on! What's that supposed to mean? Do you…do you know my father?' she demanded.

He turned back casually. 'Everyone knows about your father. His high-handed reputation precedes him by a country mile.'

Maggie bit her lip, but she soldiered on. 'I told you—well, no, Tim told you, but all the same—I don't trade on my father.'

'Your kind generally stick together in the long run,' he observed and shrugged his wide shoulders.

'What "kind", exactly, is that?' she queried with awful forbearance.

He looked at her indifferently. 'Old money, class, breeding—whatever you like to call it.'

'People who make those kinds of statements generally have none of those advantages—but wish they did,' she shot back.

He grinned. 'You're right about one thing, I have no breeding or class, but you're wrong about the other—I have no desire to acquire them. Well, now that we've thoroughly dissected each other, not to mention insulted each other, should we get down to brass tacks?'

'And what might they be?'

'How to get out of here. Is anyone expecting to see you this afternoon or this evening? Does anyone know you're here?'

Maggie pulled out a chair and sat down at the table at the same time as, with an effort, she withdrew her mind from the indignity of being tarred with the same brush as her father again or, if not that, being classed as a flighty little rich bitch.

That one really stung, she discovered. True, she could be hot-tempered, as she'd so disastrously demonstrated, but it had no connection with being spoilt or rich. How to make Jack McKinnon see it that way—she shot him a fiery little glance—was another matter. Then again, why should she even bother?

She frowned and addressed herself to his question. 'The office knew I was going to do a property valuation, but I wasn't planning to go back to work this afternoon so they won't miss me until tomorrow morning, oh, damn,' she said hollowly.

He raised an eyebrow at her.

'I've just remembered. I wasn't planning to go into the office at all tomorrow.'

'Why not?'

'I have a doctor's appointment in the morning and I was going to spend the afternoon—' She broke off and grimaced a shade embarrassedly.

'Let me guess,' he murmured. 'Getting your hair done, a facial, a manicure, a dress fitting, perhaps a little shopping in the afternoon?'

Maggie's cheeks started to burn because most of the things he'd suggested were on her agenda for tomorrow afternoon. But she ignored her hot cheeks and beamed him a scathing green glance.

'Listen,' she said tersely, 'yes, my hours can be elastic. On the other hand sometimes they're extremely long and I have a day off this week, two actually, because I'm working *all* next weekend. I do not have any more time off than anyone else in the office!'

He shrugged.

Prompting her to continue angrily, 'And if I'm the only woman you know who gets her hair cut now and then, has a manicure occasionally and shops from time to time, you must mix with some strange types, Mr McKinnon.'

He studied her hair and her nails. 'They look fine to me,' he said smoothly, but with an ironic little glint. 'Be that as it may, only your doctor and your beautician are likely to miss you tomorrow I take it?'

Maggie sat back with her expression a mixture of frustration and ire. 'Yes!'

'Anything serious with the doctor?'

'No.'

'So they're hardly likely to mount a search and rescue mission.'

'Hardly.'

'You live alone?'

'I live alone,' she agreed. 'How about you?'

'Yep.'

'What about this plane you're supposed to catch?'

He looked thoughtful. 'It could be a day or two before I'm missed. I'm—I was—on my way to a conference in Melbourne, but I planned to call in on my mother tomorrow in Sydney on the way.'

Maggie sat up. 'Surely she'll miss you?'

'She didn't know I was coming. It was to be a surprise.'

'That's asking for trouble!' Maggie said. 'You could have missed *her*.'

'Apart from complicating our situation?' He waited until she looked slightly embarrassed. Then he added, 'Not much chance of missing her as she's not fit enough to go out.'

This time Maggie looked mortified. 'I beg your pardon,' she said stiffly.

His lips twisted. 'As it happens I'm in agreement with your first sentiment.'

She looked startled. 'Why?'

'I'm sorry now I didn't let her know, but the reason I don't usually is because if I don't turn up exactly at the appointed time, she gets all anxious and unsettled.'

'Oh.' Maggie found she had to smile. 'My mother's a bit like that.'

They said nothing for a few moments, both locked

into their thoughts about their respective mothers, then he shrugged and strolled over to the pile of tarpaulins in the corner and started to pull them off.

Maggie confidently expected an old utility vehicle or tractor to be revealed, so she sucked in an incredulous breath when a shiny black vintage car in superb condition and a Harley Davidson motor bike, both worth a small fortune, were exposed.

'They didn't—the owners didn't say a word about these!'

'No? It does explain the security, however,' he said. 'This shed is like a fortress.'

Maggie frowned. 'It doesn't make sense. They haven't lived here for over a year, they told me. They don't have a caretaker. The house is a shambles but, well, who in their right minds would—sort of—abandon these?' She got up and walked over to the car and stroked the bonnet.

'You would have thought they'd put them up on blocks at least,' Jack said. He opened the car door and they both looked in.

The interior was as beautifully restored as the rest of it with plump, gleaming leather seats and the keys were dangling in the ignition. Jack slid into the driver's seat and switched it on. The motor purred to life.

He let it run for a few minutes, then switched it off and got out of the car. 'They must know they're here,' he said. 'Someone has to be starting this car regularly or the battery would be flat.'

'What did they say to you?' she asked. 'The owners.'

'I didn't speak to them, but...' he paused '...same as you; they gave my PA to understand that no one had lived here for over a year. They certainly didn't mention any vintage cars and bikes to her, but I wasn't planning to come into the shed so...' He stopped.

Maggie turned on her heel and ran across to the kitchen cupboard. 'These tins,' she said, pulling out a can of baked beans, 'don't look over a year old. Nor—' she reached for an open packet of cornflakes and peered inside '—would these have survived the mice I happen to know are here. But they're fine.'

She proffered the packet to him.

He didn't look inside. 'I believe you. Are you saying someone has taken over this shed?'

'It's quite possible! The nearest neighbours are miles away on a different road. The driveway in here is virtually concealed. You could come and go and no one would be any the wiser!'

'If it's true it's not much help to us unless they actually live here and come home every night.'

'Maybe they do!' Maggie said with a tinge of excitement.

He walked round the car and opened the boot. 'Well, that's something, in case they don't.'

'What?' She went to have a look.

'A tool kit.' He hefted a wooden box out of the boot, put it on the floor and opened it. 'Of sorts,' he added and lifted out an electric key saw. 'We may just be able to cut our way out of here somehow.'

Maggie heaved a huge sigh of relief. 'Oh, thank heavens!'

He glanced across at her. 'Hear, hear.'

'In time to catch your plane?'

'No. This is more a hobby saw; it's going to be a long, slow process.'

'Why don't you get straight to work?' she suggested. 'I'll make us a cup of tea.'

The look he tossed her was full of irony.

'I've never used one of those,' she said, 'but if you'd like to show me how, you could make the tea and I could do the sawing. Would you prefer that?' she queried innocently.

'No, I would not. We could be here for a year,' he returned shortly.

Maggie hid a smile.

'But what you could do is scout around for an extension cord. The nearest power point is too far from the door—' He stopped abruptly and looked frustrated.

'There's power!' she assured him. 'And water. I checked.'

He looked relieved this time, but in no better humour. 'OK. Start looking for a cord.'

Maggie resisted the temptation to salute and say, Yes, sir! And she toned down her triumph when she found an extension cord on top of the kitchen cupboard.

An hour later, his mood was even worse. There were no spare blades for the saw and the one in it was blunt.

'This thing wouldn't cut butter,' he said, having succeeded in cutting no more than a shallow, six-inch-long groove in the door. He threw it aside in disgust.

It was dark by now and the only light was from a single bulb suspended from the rafters. Its thin glow didn't reach the corners of the shed, and the mice, having decided they weren't under threat from the humans who had invaded their space, were on the move again.

Maggie had made tea an hour ago, then coffee a few minutes previously. She now stared down into the dark depths of her cup, and shivered. 'We're not going to get out of here tonight, are we?'

He came over to the table and pulled out a chair. 'No, Miss Trent, we are not. Not unless whoever is moonlighting in this shed comes home.'

'So you agree someone *is* doing that?'

'Was there power connected to the house?'

Maggie thought swiftly. 'No. That's strange, isn't it? On here but not up there.'

'Whoever they are, they may have found a way to tap into the grid illegally.' He suddenly slammed his fist onto the table in a gesture of frustration.

'I...' she looked at him fleetingly '...I do apologize.'

'So you bloody well should.'

He had wood shavings in his hair and he brushed them off his shirt. There were streaks of dust on his trousers.

'You don't have to swear.'

'Yes, I do,' he contradicted. He looked at his hands. They were filthy and several knuckles were grazed. 'Would you like to know what I'd be doing now if I wasn't incarcerated here? I'll tell you.'

He glanced at his watch. 'I'd just be arriving at my hotel in Sydney where I'd shout myself a sundowner and have a shower. Then I'd order a medium-rare pepper steak with Idaho potatoes, maybe some rock oysters to start with and a cheese platter to follow. I feel sure I'd wash it all down with...' he stared at her reflectively '...a couple of glasses of a decent red, then maybe some Blue Mountain coffee.'

Maggie flinched inwardly and couldn't think of a thing to say.

'How about you?' he queried.

She thought for a moment. 'Toasted cheese with a salad and an early night,' she said briefly.

He lifted an eyebrow. 'That sounds very bachelor girl.'

'I am a bachelor girl.'

'A very well-heeled one by the same token,' he murmured.

Maggie started to feel less embarrassed and guilty. 'Don't start on all that again,' she warned.

'Why shouldn't I? If you were an ordinary girl rather than ultra-privileged, and if you were without strong, unreasonable prejudices, I wouldn't be here.'

'Listen, mate, you offered the first insult!'

'Ah, yes, so I did.' He grinned reminiscently. 'I take nothing back.'

'Neither do I. But you,' she accused, 'went on doing it.'

He shrugged. 'You have to admit it was a rather bizarre situation to find myself in.'

Maggie frowned. 'What did you mean there being two sides to that coin? The one about me hating powerful, arrogant men or words to that effect?'

'Sometimes,' he said reflectively, 'girls are secretly attracted to power and arrogance in men even if they don't like to admit it.'

'I am not one of those, assuming they exist and are not a figment of your imagination,' Maggie stated.

He grinned. 'Very well, ma'am. And it doesn't

make you at all nervous to be locked in here with me in our current state of discord?'

Maggie hesitated. 'I know it must have looked rather strange, what I did,' she said slowly, 'and I suppose I can't blame you for wondering what on earth was going on. Therefore everything you said, even although I found it offensive—'

'All that cheap rubbish?' he interrupted gravely, although with an inward grin.

'Yes.' She eyed him briefly and sternly. 'Therefore everything you said was—understandable, perhaps, so—'

'I see.'

'Will you stop interrupting?' she commanded. 'This is hard enough as it is.'

'My lips are sealed,' he murmured.

She eyed him dangerously this time. 'Put plainly, I'd much rather you disliked me and were irritated by me than any other ideas you might have had, all the same!'

He laughed softly, then he watched her intently for a long moment. 'Are you really that naïve, Maggie Trent?'

'What's naïve about it? Well,' she hastened to say, 'perhaps I am, in a general sense. I did have a very sheltered—' She broke off and bit her lip.

'Upbringing?' he suggested.

'My father—' She stopped again. She might have her problems with her father—she did!—but broadcasting them to strangers was another matter.

'Saw to that, did he?' Jack McKinnon eyed her reflectively. 'I'm surprised he let you out of his sight.'

Maggie drew a deep breath, but discovered she couldn't let this go. 'The fact that I actually have a job and live on my own is testimony to a battle for independence that you might find quite surprising.'

He said nothing, but the way he stared at her led her to believe he might be reviewing all the facts he now had at his disposal, and changing his opinions somewhat. Good, she thought, and, with a toss of her head, stood up.

She would have died if she'd known that he was actually contemplating the—pleasure?—yes, of having her as his dinner companion at his mythical dinner in Sydney, then disposing of her clothes article by article in a way that drove her wild with desire even if she didn't like him particularly...

'You know,' she said blandly, 'it's just occurred to me that I could alleviate at least one of your discomforts.'

He looked supremely quizzical. 'You could?' And wondered what she'd say if he told her at least one of his discomforts sprang from the way he kept thinking how she'd look without her clothes...

She went over and rummaged in the kitchen cupboard. What she produced was half a bottle of Scotch. She gathered two glasses and a jug from below the sink. She rinsed them all out, filled the jug with water and placed everything on the table.

'It may be tinned food rather than steak, oysters and cheese but at least we can have a drink—we may even find it puts us in a better mood.'

He studied her offerings, then studied her expression. 'Miss Trent, you are a peach.' He reached for the bottle.

She was right.

After a Scotch and a meal of a heated-up Fray

Bentos steak pie and baked beans, Jack McKinnon was rather more mellow.

'Tell me about the Smiths,' he said as she prepared to wash the dishes.

Maggie looked rueful and did so as she found a small bottle of dish detergent and squirted some green liquid into the sink. 'The thing is—' she turned on a tap '—is it ethical?'

'To offer people who hold out more money?' he mused. 'There's no law against it.'

Maggie eyed the mound of bubbles building in the sink. 'It's going to drive Sophie and Ernest mad for the rest of their lives.' She switched off the tap.

'Don't you think the heart of this dilemma might lie elsewhere?'

She turned to him. 'Elsewhere?'

'Such as…' he paused '…Ernest jumping at the chance to get out of a property he was finding too much for him—and even the original price was a very fair one, believe me—while Sophie wanted to stay? A marital lifestyle dilemma, in other words.'

Maggie started to wash the dishes in silence. 'Perhaps,' she said eventually.

'And did you know, Maggie, that I always exceed the town planning regulations regarding open spaces, sports fields and community centres like kindergartens? They may appear to you like little boxes, the houses I build, but they're always well provided with those facilities. And while my houses may not be mansions, they are not shonky.'

'I'll…I'll have to take your word for it, Jack.' She rinsed the last dish, then turned to face him. 'On the other hand, I could not but regret *this* property, for example, being scraped bare and built on.'

He was sitting back looking relaxed, even amused, although she wasn't sure why.

'What?' she asked with a frown.

'I'm in agreement with you, that's all.'

She blinked. 'But you said—'

'I said I was contacted about it with a view to urban development. As you probably know that would mean applying for a re-zoning that I doubt I'd get, but that's not why I came to look at it personally.'

'It isn't?'

He shook his head. 'I'm interested in providing a buffer zone now.' He ruffled his hair. 'So I'm looking for the right properties to provide it. I'm also looking for one that I might live on. This could be it.'

Maggie stared at him with her mouth open and all sorts of expressions chasing through her eyes.

'I felt sure the irony of that would appeal to you,' he drawled. 'Why don't you sit down and have another drink with me before you explode?'

'I…you…this…I will,' Maggie said. 'Of all the…' She couldn't find the words and she dropped into a chair and accepted the glass he handed her.

'Double standards?' he suggested.

'Yes! Well…'

He laughed softly. 'But at the same time preserving the rural environment? That is a tricky one.'

'I was thinking about you joining the "ivory tower" club after all you said on the subject,' she returned arctically.

'Oh, I don't think there's any chance of that,' he drawled.

Maggie sipped some Scotch gratefully. It was getting cold. As she felt the warmth of it go down she watched him covertly.

He had his hands shoved in his pockets, he was sprawled back and he appeared to be lost in thought.

It suddenly struck Maggie with a peculiar little pang that Jack McKinnon was actually in a class of his own. Much as she would like to, she couldn't deny his ivory-tower-club theory, although she'd certainly fought her own battles against being drawn into the socialite/debutante kind of society he meant: the polo, the races, fashion shows, winter skiing/summer cruise followers.

She'd always longed for a broader canvas. She wanted to work; she wanted to travel, but a different circuit from the one her father and his friends travelled from one exclusive resort to another.

She wanted, she realized, to know people like this man and overcome his basic contempt for her kind. Yet, it struck her with some irony, only hours ago she'd been so angry with him, her thoughtless expression of it had reinforced everything he disliked about her 'kind'.

The mystery of it all, though, was why did it matter so much to her? There was a whole world of unusual, interesting people out there…

'So what do you suggest?'

She came out of her reverie at his question to find him watching her narrowly, as if he'd got the vibes that her preoccupation was to do with him, and she moved a little uncomfortably.

'Uh—what do you mean?'

He shot her a last lingering look, then got up and stretched. 'Where do we sleep, Miss Trent?'

'That's not a problem. I've already worked it out,' she told him as her mind moved like lightning. 'I'll

use the back seat of the car. You can—' she gestured
'—use the settee.'

He grimaced. 'Quick thinking, that.'

'You're too long for the car,' she pointed out reasonably.

'I'm too long for the settee and it looks filthy.' He
crossed over and tested it, then looked down at it
critically. 'On the other hand, if this is what I think
it is,' he said slowly, 'I might not be so hardly done
by after all.'

'What do you mean?'

He pulled off the cushion seats, pulled up a bar and
the settee converted itself into a sofa bed. What was
more, it was made up with fairly clean-looking sheets,
a thin blanket and two flat pillows.

'Diagonally, I might just fit if I bend my knees.'

'Lucky you,' she said rather tartly.

He cocked his head at her. 'While you're left without a blanket or any covering—is that what you're
suggesting?'

She shrugged.

'The penalty for such quick thinking,' he murmured, and laughed at her expression. 'Here's what
we'll do. Did you happen to see a pair of scissors in
the kitchen cupboards or drawers?'

Maggie went to check and came back with a rusty
pair. 'Only these.'

'They'll do.'

'What are you going to do?'

'This. Not our property obviously, but desperate
circumstances call for desperate measures and we can
replace them.'

He made several cuts then, using both hands, he
ripped the double blanket and two sheets in half. He

handed her hers ceremonially along with one of the pillows. 'There you go. I may never belong to the ivory tower club, but I can be a gentleman of sorts.'

She knew from the wicked look in his grey eyes that the joke was on her, but not what the joke was. She suspected it could be more than the ivory tower club, but…?

'Don't worry about it, Maggie Trent,' he said softly, but with more humour apparent in his eyes. 'Go to bed.'

Maggie turned away slowly. Before she did go to bed, she removed her boots, released her hair and paid a visit to the bathroom. Then she climbed into the back seat of the car, only to climb out again.

'What?' He was seated on the sofa bed taking his shoes off.

'I think it would be a good idea to leave the light on.' She gestured widely. 'Might deter the mice from getting too friendly.'

'You're scared of mice?'

'Not *scared*,' she denied. 'I just don't like the idea of close contact with them. Do you?'

'Not particularly. OK. It can stay on.'

'Thank you.' She hesitated as she was struck by an amazing thought—that her arbitrary organization of the sleeping choices might have been a miscalculation. Or, put it this way, she would feel much safer and more comfortable if she were to share the sofa bed with him, purely platonically of course.

Her eyes widened as she combed her fingers through her hair and posed a question to herself— You're not serious?

'Maggie?'

'Uh—' some colour came to her cheeks '—noth-

ing. It's nothing. Goodnight,' she said and could have
shot herself for sounding uncertain.

'Sure?'

'Mmm…' She marched over to the car and got in
again.

Jack McKinnon waited until she'd closed the door,
wound down a window and disappeared from view.
Then he lay back, pulled his half of the thin blanket
up and examined his very mixed feelings on the subject of Maggie Trent.

Something of a firebrand, undoubtedly, he wouldn't
be here otherwise—he grimaced. Plenty of hauteur,
as well, a good dose of her father's genes, in other
words, yet her personality was curiously appealing in
a way her father's could never be, not to him anyway.

How so? he asked himself. She'd exhibited just
about every failing you might expect from a spoilt
little rich girl, even to ordering him to sleep on the
sofa.

Perhaps it was the power of her emotions, then, he
mused. Even if misguidedly, she was passionate about
the environment. She felt deeply about the plight of
the Smiths—he grimaced again. But there was something else…

Her *peachiness*? That damned word again… OK,
then, she was lovely. About five feet four, he judged,
her figure was trim, almost slight, but he got the feeling it might be delightful: delicately curved, velvety
nipples, small, peachy hips—yes, the word did fit
somewhere!—satiny skin and all that tawny hair, not
to mention stunning eyes to set it off. But what was
it that puzzled him about her—an aura of sensual un-
awareness?

Maybe, he thought, then amended the thought to—

sometimes… When he'd mentally stripped her she'd got all hot and bothered as well as angry. Now, though, being trapped in a shed with a strange man, virtually, who *had* mentally stripped her, appeared not to faze her. Why not?

Had a habit of command kicked in that didn't allow her even to contemplate things getting out of hand? Whatever, he concluded with an inward smile, it was rather intriguing and refreshing. Not that he'd do anything about it…

So why—he posed the question to himself—was he not more…absolutely furious about the current state of affairs? True, he'd been frustrated and irritable when trying to saw through the door, he'd been incredulous and angry when it had first happened, but…

He shrugged. All the same, he was going to have to come up with something tomorrow. He stared upwards. If he could figure out a way to get up to the roof, that might be his best shot after all.

Maggie arranged herself as best she could on the back seat of the car, only to discover that sleep suddenly seemed to be the furthest thing from her mind.

She was confused, she realized. Confused, tense and annoyed with herself. What an incredibly stupid thing to do! Would she ever grow out of these rash, hot-headed impulses that plagued her from time to time? When *would* they get out of this wretched shed?

Well, that explained the tension and the annoyance, she reasoned, but what was she confused about?

Jack McKinnon, it came to her. It seemed to be impossible to tear her thoughts away from him! Because she didn't understand him? Was that so surprising? She barely knew him, but, going on what she did know of him, his reactions *had* been rather surprising.

Yes, there was still that underlying contempt, there had been open contempt, but he *could* have made things much more uncomfortable for her. He could have treated her far more severely and scathingly... Had she misjudged him? Well, no, he had offered the first insult. Then again, that had obviously been based on her father's reputation.

All the same, she hadn't expected to end up liking him...

She sighed exasperatedly and closed her eyes.

Jack woke up at three o'clock.

As he glanced at his watch he was amazed that he'd slept so long; he didn't need much sleep. What also amazed him was the sight of Maggie Trent asleep at the table with her head pillowed on her arms.

He sat up abruptly and the rusty springs of the sofa bed squeaked in protest.

Maggie started up, wide-eyed and alarmed. 'Who...what...?'

'Only me,' he said reassuringly. 'What's the matter?'

'I...just couldn't sleep. It was like being in a coffin, no, a hearse,' she corrected herself. 'I felt seriously claustrophobic.'

'You should have told me earlier!'

She eyed him, then smiled, a faint little smile of pure self-mockery. 'I do sometimes find it hard to admit I could be wrong about—things.'

He grimaced, then had to laugh. 'OK.' He got up. 'That admission earns you a spell on the bed.'

'Oh, you definitely wouldn't fit into the car, so—'

'Don't argue, Maggie,' he ordered. 'I have no intention of trying the car anyway.'

'But it's only three o'clock,' she pointed out. 'What will you do?'

'Seriously apply myself to getting us out of here. Come on, do as you're told.'

Maggie got up reluctantly, but she sank down onto the sofa bed with a sigh of relief. Then she frowned. 'Does that mean you haven't been serious about getting us out of here until now?'

He glanced at her. Her hair was spread across the pillow and even in the feeble light her eyes were discernibly green—he couldn't remember knowing anyone with those colour eyes, he thought, then remembered her father. Of course. His mouth hardened.

'Let's just say I don't like being thwarted.' He turned away.

'Did that annoy you,' she asked, 'me saying you weren't serious?'

He shrugged. 'It reminded me that I've been in this damn shed for long enough.'

'You've been—for the most part—you've been pretty good about it. I do appreciate that.'

'Yes, well, why don't you go to sleep?'

She didn't answer immediately, then, 'The more I think about it, the roof is the only way to go. I hate to say I told you so, but if we could get up there somehow, it is only an old tin roof and maybe we could prise one of the sheets open or apart or something. I'm actually quite good at climbing.'

He was stretching and he turned to her with his arms above his head.

Maggie took a strange little breath as the full impact of his beautiful physique hit her.

'Climbing?' he said.

'I used to do gymnastics, seriously, and I've done an abseiling course. I'm not afraid of heights and I have good balance.' She looked upwards. 'I wouldn't have any trouble balancing on those beams.'

He studied her thoughtfully, then stared around. 'If I got onto the roof of the car and you got onto my shoulders, you might just reach a beam.'

Maggie sat up. 'Yes!' She subsided. 'But what to use to attack the roof with?' she asked whimsically.

The toolbox he'd got the saw out of was lying on the floor next to the table. He bent over and pulled out a short chrome bar. 'Heaven alone knows what this is for, but it might do, although—' he grimaced '—whether you'd have the strength—'

She cast aside the blanket and got up. 'I could try!'

He hesitated a moment longer, then shrugged. 'We'll give it a go.'

Five minutes later they were both on the roof of the car.

'Just as well they built them solidly in those days,' he commented with a fleeting grin, and squinted upwards. 'OK, here's what we'll do.'

He had both halves of the blanket. 'I'm going to try and throw these over the beam. That should give you something to work with. Look—' he stripped off his shirt '—take this up with you. Once you get up there, if you do, you'll need as much protection from splinters as you can get and I'll also tie the bar into one sleeve. You sit down while I throw.'

This time she did say it—'Yes, sir!'—but good-naturedly and even with something akin to excitement in her voice.

He looked down at her. 'You're a strange girl, Maggie Trent.'

'I know,' she agreed.

He opened his mouth as if to say more as they gazed at each other, but changed his mind.

Maggie sat down cross-legged and tied his shirt around her waist. It took him several attempts, but he finally got both bits of blanket dangling over the beam.

'Now for the tricky bit.' He knelt down. 'Climb onto my shoulders. Don't worry, I won't drop you and I won't fall myself—I also have good balance.'

'Are you a gymnast too?' Maggie asked.

'No, but I did some martial arts training in my misguided youth.'

Maggie climbed onto his shoulders. 'Well, I'm happy to know I wasn't completely wrong about you.'

'Oh?'

'I took you for a much more physical guy who'd prefer to be climbing Mount Everest rather than building housing estates.'

'Really.' He grinned. 'That should provide an interesting discussion at another time. Are you comfortable, Miss Trent? If at any stage you would rather not be doing this, for heaven's sake tell me. I won't hold it against you and we can all be wrong at times.'

Maggie looked down at the top of his head and placed her hands lightly upon it. 'Up you get—I was going to say Samson, but your hair's not long enough. I'm fine.'

'Here's hoping you don't have any Delilah tenden-

cies,' he commented wryly and brought his hands up
to wrap them around her waist. 'Here goes.'

He got to his feet slowly and steadily. At no time
did Maggie feel insecure and at all times she had to
appreciate his strength and co-ordination.

When he was upright, she carefully lifted her hands
until she was able to grasp the blankets.

'All right?' he queried, his breath rasping in his
throat.

'I've got them.' She tied the ends together and
wrapped her hands in them. 'If I could stand up, I
could reach the beam. It would be just above waist-
height and easier to vault onto. I'd also have the blanket as a sort of safety strap.'

'Are you very sure, Maggie?'

'Yep. Can you handle it, though?'

'No problem. Easy does it.'

Putting her weight on the blankets, Maggie levered
herself up onto her feet. 'I'm not hurting you, am I?'
she asked anxiously as she felt his hands close round
her ankles.

'What do you think I am?' he countered.

'Very strong. Well…' she swallowed '…here goes
again.' A moment later as he rocked beneath her but
stayed upright she was straddling the rafter.

'Well done, Maggie!'

She beamed down at him. 'Piece of cake. I did win
a state title, you know.'

'I believe you. So. If you can crawl along it towards the wall, where the roof is at its lowest you
could do a recce. Still got the bar?'

She untied his shirt from her waist and felt the
sleeve. 'Yes. Yuck, it is full of splinters and nails,
this beam, as well as cobwebs!'

'Be very careful.'

'Care is my middle name. Actually Leila is my middle name, after my grandmother—why am I babbling?' she asked at large as she started to crawl along the beam.

'Exhilaration? Stress? I don't mind. I don't have a middle name,' he said as he watched her inch her way forward.

'How come?' Maggie stopped moving and stared down at him.

He shrugged. 'I was adopted as a baby, although that may not have a thing to do with it.'

'You're joking!' she said incredulously. 'But you were talking about your mother!'

'She's my adoptive mother. Why am I babbling?' he asked humorously.

'Well, I'll be…' Maggie shook her head and started to inch forward again. 'Then you have done tremendously well for yourself! But it must have had some effect. Are you full of neuroses and so on?'

'Oh, definitely,' he said with a straight face, but a world of devilry in his eyes.

'I'm not sure I should believe that—ouch!'

'What?' he queried.

'A nail. I seem to have got my blouse hooked on it. Damn.' She struggled upright to the tune of tearing material as the front of her blouse ripped from the neckline to the waist.

'Take it off,' he suggested, 'and put my shirt on instead. The material might be tougher. Then use yours and a blanket to protect yourself.'

'Roger wilco!' She wrestled her blouse off, sitting easily enough on the beam with her feet hooked together beneath it. But just as she was about to put his shirt on they both froze at a loud noise outside the shed—a motor revving then being shut off followed by a car door slamming.

'Maggie, come down,' Jack said softly but urgently.

'Of course. We're about to be rescued!'

'Perhaps. But if this shed has been hijacked and there's something fishy going on, we may not be too welcome and I can't look after you up there.'

'OK, OK, I'm coming,' she whispered and backed along the beam until she was above him. 'Now!'

She slithered down the blankets and into his arms, leaving his shirt and her blouse dangling on the beam. At the same time the door was thrown open from the outside, a powerful searchlight was shone in and a string of expletives in a harsh male voice was uttered.

Maggie gasped and clutched Jack, completely dazzled by the light. He put his arms around her.

'Bloody hell!' the same harsh voice said. 'What is this—some sort of kinky sex set-up?' And to Maggie's utter disbelief the searchlight moved away revealing, not one, but two men, and some flash bulbs went off.

Jack growled in his throat, then he said into her ear, 'One, two, let's get down, Maggie.'

'OK,' she whispered back, and on his call of two they slithered down to the boot, then hit the floor together. He held her in his arms only until she was steady on her feet, then he strode forward to confront the two men.

Things happened so quickly after that, she couldn't believe her eyes. Both men backed away from him until one of them, the man with the camera, tripped and fell over a chair. He dropped the camera and Jack swooped onto it.

'I am sorry about this,' he said quite politely as he opened the back of it and exposed the film, 'but you wouldn't want to be responsible for some highly misleading pictures, now would you?'

The man got up nervously and dusted himself off. 'Not if you say so, mate,' he agreed.

'Good! Why don't you both sit down and tell me who you are? Sophie,' Jack added over his shoulder, 'you might be better off waiting in your car.'

It took a moment for Maggie to twig that he was talking to her, but as soon as she did she accepted the suggestion gratefully. It was still one of the hardest things she'd ever done—to achieve a dignified exit wearing only her socks, jeans and her bra. She did resist the temptation to run, however, until she was out of the shed, then she spurted to her car, climbed in with a sigh of sheer relief, and reached over into the back seat for the denim jacket she'd tossed there the day before.

It was fifteen minutes before Jack came out to her and he stopped on his way to retrieve his mobile phone and bag from his Range Rover and then to lock it.

He got into the passenger seat, glinted her a daredevil little smile and said, 'Home, James, I think.'

'What about your—?'

'Maggie, just go,' he commanded. 'I've done my level best to protect your fair name, let's not hang around.'

She switched the motor on and nosed the car forward. Two minutes later, she turned out of the concealed driveway onto the road and turned to him. 'I'm dying of curiosity! Who were they? What did you tell them? Do they still think we were…we were…?' She stopped and coloured painfully.

He was fishing around in his bag and he dragged a T-shirt out and shrugged into it with difficulty. 'Hang on,' he said as he began to punch numbers into his phone. 'What's your address?'

She told him.

It was someone called Maisie he rang—a Maisie who didn't object to being woken at four-thirty in the morning and given all sorts of instructions.

To wit, someone was to retrieve his Range Rover at the farm address, using his spare keys; someone was to pick him up at Maggie's address in about half an hour; a new flight to Melbourne was to be booked for him later in the day, no, he wouldn't be stopping in Sydney this time—what had happened to him?

'I was kidnapped by a girl, locked in a shed and— maybe I'll tell you the rest of it one day, Maisie, just be a love and sort all that out for me, pronto.'

He ended the call.

Maggie looked over at him. 'That's not funny!'

'No? I have to tell you it has been one of the funnier days of my life, Maggie Trent,' he said with his eyes glinting. His hair was standing up from his struggles with his T-shirt, and he ran his fingers through it.

She bit her lip and concentrated on her driving for a bit until he dropped his hand on her knee. 'All right. I apologize. Who were they? A private investigator and a journalist.'

Maggie's eyes widened. 'Oh, no!'

'As you say,' he agreed dryly, and told her the whole story.

The owners of the property had had a farm machinery hire business, now defunct. All the equipment had been stored in the shed, which explained why it was built like Fort Knox. They also had a wayward son, apparently, who'd stolen the vintage car and the bike on a whim and as a bit of a lark, and decided there was no better place to keep them under wraps than his parents' shed—he'd contrived to get copies of the keys made.

But he was also a garrulous young man when under the influence of liquor and drugs and the journalist, who wrote a motoring column and was a vintage-car freak himself, had got wind of the heist. He was also aware that the owner of the car and bike had hired a private investigator to look for them when the police had failed to trace them, so they'd decided to pool their resources.

'I see!' Maggie said at this point in the story.

'Yes,' Jack agreed. 'It all falls into place. How much more interesting to find Jack McKinnon and Margaret Leila Trent engaged in what could have looked like weird practices, though?'

She flinched. 'Do you think they believed our story? What did you tell them?' She pulled up at a traffic light on the Oxenford overpass.

'The truth, mostly. That the property was about to come onto the market and we were interested in it.'

'Perfectly true!'

'Yep.' He shot her an amused look. 'But I had to tamper with the truth a bit then. I told them the wind banged the shed door shut on us, locking us in.'

Maggie flinched again. 'That's a very small white lie,' she said, although uncertainly. 'Isn't it?'

'Almost miniature,' he agreed gravely. 'Uh—the light has changed, Maggie.'

She changed gear and moved forward a little jerkily. 'I know you're laughing at me,' she accused at the same time.

He did laugh outright then. 'Perhaps you should bear this incident in mind the next time you're moved to scream, shout and slam things,' he suggested and sobered suddenly. 'Because it wouldn't have been funny to be splashed across some newspaper because of who we are, *you* are particularly, and because it did look very strange.'

Maggie cruised to a stop at the next set of lights on the overpass. 'I never get these damn lights,' she said tautly, then sighed. 'You're right. I will.'

'Good girl. Anyway, I had to tell some more white lies. They think your name is Sophie Smith—'

'That was inspired,' she said gratefully and shivered suddenly.

He looked over at her and raised an eyebrow.

'I just thought of what my father would say if I got splashed across some newspaper in—those circumstances. He'd kill me! No, he wouldn't,' she corrected herself immediately, 'but he'd be furious!'

'He'd be more liable to want to kill me,' Jack said prosaically. 'However, although I suppose there always may be a question mark in their minds, those two have nothing to go on other than your car registration, and I don't think I gave them time to get it, in the dark.'

'It's not registered in my name. It's the firm's car,' she told him.

'Even better.'

'But—' she turned to him '—what about you? Do they know who you are?'

'They know and they're not likely to forget it.'

Maggie stared at him and shivered again. 'You can be very scary at times, you know.'

He shrugged. 'You've got a green light again, Maggie.'

She drove off. 'Not that I'm complaining,' she added. 'I'm very grateful to you for handling it all so well. Even my father would be grateful.'

'I wouldn't bet your bottom dollar on it.'

She drove in silence across Hope Island for a while, then as she turned into her street she said, 'What will we do now?'

He stirred. 'If I were you, Maggie, I'd go away for a while. Just in case they decide to snoop around a bit.'

'I can't just go away! I'm a working girl,' she objected, and pulled into her driveway.

Jack McKinnon looked through the window at her lovely villa and shrugged.

'Don't tell me we're back to all that nonsense!' she accused. 'What a spoilt little rich girl I am.'

His lips twisted as he transferred his gaze to her. 'Not entirely,' he said. 'Actually, I think you're one of a kind, Maggie Trent. On the other hand...' he paused and searched her eyes '...on the other hand you do bear some responsibility to your name and your family so it would be a good idea to take out some—' he gestured '—extra insurance. I'm sure that's what your father would advise and rightly so.'

He turned to look over the back of his seat as a car pulled up across the driveway. 'My lift has arrived.'

'Maisie?' she said.

'Not Maisie.'

'So…so that's it?' Her voice was slightly unsteady.

He grinned. 'A better outcome than it might have been, in more ways than one. You could still be balancing on a splintery beam trying to force open a tin roof.'

'Will you buy it? That property?'

'Don't know. Listen, you take care, Miss Trent.' He leaned forward and kissed her lightly, then he opened the door and slid out of the car, pulling his bag after him.

Maggie was still sitting exactly as he'd left her, with her fingers on her lips, when the other car drove off, taking Jack McKinnon out of her life.

Later in the day, a huge bouquet of flowers arrived for her with a simple message—'All's well that ends well, Jack.'

In the event, Maggie's mother was of exactly the same opinion as Jack McKinnon when she heard all about her daughter's ordeal. Not only did she insist that Maggie should go away for a while, taking a month's unpaid leave, but she also accompanied her for the first week.

CHAPTER THREE

THE ocean stretched forever beyond the arms of the bay. It was slate-blue and wrinkled. A layer of cloud rimmed the horizon, but the sun had risen above it and was pouring a path of tinsel light over the water. Long, lazy lines of swell were rolling in to crash onto the beach in a froth of sand patched white that looked like crazy paving until it slipped away.

To the south, the green, rock-fringed dome of Point Cartwright with its white observation tower stood guard over the mouth of the Mooloolah River.

To the north and much further away, the monolithic bulk of Mount Coolum stood out as well as Noosa Head, insubstantial in the distance. Closer to home Mudjimba Island lay in the bay like a beached whale complete with a tree or rock on its head to resemble a water spout. The whole area was known as the Sunshine Coast. It was an hour's drive north of Brisbane and it competed with the Gold Coast as a holiday destination.

Maggie withdrew her gaze from the distance and studied the beach. She was on the ninth floor of an apartment block in Mooloolaba, just across the road from it, a lovely beach, long and curved and protected from the dominant south-easterly trade winds. The road itself was lined with Norfolk pines, some as tall as the floor she was on.

There weren't many people on the beach although it was crisscrossed with footprints—the lull between the serious early-morning walkers and the beach frol-ickers.

It was an interesting spot, Mooloolaba. Its river was home to a trawling fleet and wonderful fresh seafood abounded. There were often huge container ships and tankers anchored off Point Cartwright awaiting clear-ance and pilots for their journey into Moreton Bay and Brisbane, services that originated in Mooloolaba together with an active Coastguard.

It was also a haven for many recreational mariners on their voyages north or south. Mooloolaba was the last stop before the Wide Bay bar, a treacherous wa-terway between the mainland and Fraser Island, or the first stop after it. Many a mariner had heaved a sigh of relief to be safely inside the Mooloolah River after a scary bar crossing and a sea-tossed trip south after it. If you were sailing north, it was like a last frontier.

Is that what I'm facing? Maggie wondered sud-denly. A last frontier...

She sat down at the small table and contemplated her breakfast of fresh fruit and muesli, coffee and croissants. She'd been in the luxury apartment for ten days. It belonged to a friend of her mother's and had no connection with the Trent name. Her mother had spent the last week with her before having to go to Sydney for a charity engagement she was unable to break.

Her father, thankfully, was overseas on business and she and her mother had agreed that he needn't ever know about the episode in the shed.

She'd enjoyed the days with her mother—they'd window-shopped, sunbathed, swum, walked, been to the movies and read—but she was now bored and ready to go back to work although she had two and half weeks of leave left, well...

She ate some muesli, then pushed the bowl away unfinished and poured her coffee. To be honest, she didn't know what she was ready for, but more of the same wasn't it and at the heart of the matter lay one man—Jack McKinnon.

She'd heard nothing more from him although she'd arranged to have her mail checked and all her phone calls rerouted to her mobile.

I wonder what he would think, she mused several times, if he knew how much I've changed my stance on him? If he knew I can't stop thinking about him, if he knew...come on, Maggie, be honest!...I seem to have fallen a little in love with him?

It was the strangest feeling, she reflected. While she'd been doing her 'trapeze act' she'd been a little nervous, but mostly fired with enthusiasm. She hadn't been aware of him as a man, only as a partner she could more than rely on. Now, the close contact with him invaded her dreams and made her go hot and cold in her waking hours when she thought about it.

Not only that, she might have felt annoyed by him at times—here she always paused and looked a bit guilty—but his company had *energized* her. It must have or why else would she be feeling as flat as a tack? Why else would she have this feeling she was at a last frontier in her life with nowhere she wanted to go?

Nor had her mother failed to notice her abstraction.

'Darling...' Belle regarded her seriously once '...did Jack McKinnon get you in just a little bit? Is that why you're so quiet sometimes?'

Maggie chose her words with care. 'If you have to get locked in a shed with a guy, he was all right.'

She got up abruptly, her coffee untasted. No good sitting around moping, she decided. Action was called for. She'd go for an invigorating swim.

The water was glorious. She swam out, caught a wave and surfed in expertly and she laughed at the sheer bliss of it as she lay on the sand with the water ebbing over her. That was when it came to her. If the mountain wouldn't come to her, she would go to it.

She packed her bags that morning and drove home.

Two days later, two very low-key days in case anyone was snooping about looking for her, she'd exhausted every avenue she could think of to get in touch with Jack McKinnon to no avail.

Either she was on a hit list of people to be kept away from him or he had the most zealous staff who kept *everyone* away from him. She couldn't even reach Maisie—no one seemed to have heard of a Maisie.

She'd even sat outside the headquarters of the McKinnon Corporation's head offices in her own car, not her firm's car, hiding behind dark glasses and a floppy linen hat, but she'd sighted neither the man himself nor his Range Rover.

She lay in bed that night, wide awake and with very mixed feelings as she listened to the mournful cries of the curlews on the golf course.

What had seemed so clear and simple to her in the surf at Mooloolaba was now assuming different proportions.

The polite spiels she got from a secretary saying

he was currently unavailable, but she'd be happy to take a message although she had no idea if, or when, Mr McKinnon would return it, were an embarrassment to her. Sitting outside his headquarters was the same—both were entirely out of character and she was finding it hard to live with the almost constant churning of her stomach and nervous tension involved.

Was she doing the right thing? It was all very well to tell herself that she didn't deserve to be brushed off like this, but if Jack McKinnon didn't want to be tracked down, should she respect his wishes?

Why, though? she asked herself passionately. Why was she such a *persona non grata* for him? Had she completely misread their, if nothing else, spirit of camaraderie in those last hours in the shed?

I guess, she thought forlornly, I really want an explanation from him, but that could be as embarrassing, if not to say as demoralizing, as what I'm going through now.

She turned over and punched her pillow, but still sleep didn't come. She got up and made herself a cup of tea. As she drank it and dawn started to rim the horizon it came to her that she would let it all drop. For one thing, she had no idea how to proceed now. For another, she wasn't feeling completely happy with herself.

She stared at the rim of light on the horizon and blinked away a sudden tear but when she went back to bed she slept until nine o'clock in the morning.

And it was a relief, although a sad one, the next morning, to have made the decision to stop her search.

Then her aunt Elena came to call, as she did fairly

regularly. Maggie invited her in and since it was that time of day asked her to stay to lunch—Elena was always good company.

She prepared open smoked salmon sandwiches drizzled with lemon juice and dusted with cracked pepper and she opened a bottle of chilled chardonnay to add to her lunch.

'How nice!' Elena approved.

'Let's sit outside,' Maggie suggested.

When they were comfortably installed on her terrace with a sail umbrella protecting them from the sun, they chatted about this and that until Elena said out of the blue, 'Your mother mentioned a while back that you'd met Jack McKinnon.'

Maggie went still and swallowed. 'What did she say?'

'That he was rather rude to you, so I'm thinking of taking him off my list of eligible bachelors.'

Maggie relaxed. Not that she had any qualms about Elena broadcasting the shed debacle, but she couldn't help feeling that the fewer people to know about it, the better. 'Oh, you don't have to do that on my behalf,' she said.

Elena settled herself more comfortably and sipped her wine. 'It's not only that, he's extremely elusive.'

Maggie eyed her humorously. 'That must be irritating for you.'

Elena grimaced. 'I've got *some* background on him. It's his love life that's the problem.'

Maggie hesitated, then she couldn't help herself. 'Background?'

Elena elucidated.

Jack McKinnon had been adopted as a baby by a loving but very average family. From an early age he'd exhibited above-average intelligence; he'd won scholarships to private schools and university, where he'd studied civil engineering and marine design.

Despite something of a mania for protecting his privacy, he appeared to be very normal considering his difficult start in life. He certainly wasn't ostentatious..no particularly fancy homes, no Lear Jets, et cetera.

'As for the women in his life—' Elena sighed '—he doesn't flaunt them and they don't talk once it's over.'

'What about...' Maggie thought briefly '...Lia Montalba and Bridget Pearson?'

'Both models, both Melbourne girls.' Elena frowned. 'I wouldn't class either of them as one of "his women". They were hired to advertise his catamarans. There's a big promotion coming out shortly, but both girls are back in Melbourne now.'

'Is there anyone at the moment?' Once again Maggie couldn't help herself.

'Not as far as I know. He does,' Elena said thoughtfully, 'have a hideaway. Maybe that's where he conducts his affairs.' She shrugged.

Maggie frowned. 'How do you know that?'

Elena tapped her nose. 'My sources are always classified, but he has a holiday home at Cape Gloucester—keep that to yourself please, Maggie! So, you reckon I should leave him on my list?'

'I...' Maggie paused as she tried to think straight. 'It doesn't matter one way or the other to me. Where...where is Cape Gloucester?'

'North Queensland. Up in the tropics near Bowen. I believe you have to drive through a cattle station to get to it, that's all I know.'

*   *   *

After Elena left, Maggie sat for a long time staring at the lengthening shadows on the golf course.

Was this fate? she wondered.

Everything she wanted to know including, perhaps, Jack's whereabouts, literally dropped into her lap?

Of course, she cautioned herself, he could also be in Sydney, New York or Kathmandu, but if he was at Cape Gloucester and she went up there, might that be the only way she would ever get the explanation she so badly wanted?

Working on the theory that what her mother didn't know about she couldn't worry about, Maggie left her a vague message and she packed her bags again and drove north. At least, she thought as she set off, she would be off the local scene, should a certain P.I. and journalist be looking for the mystery girl found in a shed in compromising circumstances with Jack McKinnon.

Or what might have looked like compromising circumstances, she reminded herself.

The Gloucester passage flowed between the mainland and Gloucester Island, a regal green island with several peaks. The passage, at the northern end of the Whitsunday Islands, was the gateway to Bowen and Edgecumbe Bay. It was a narrow strip of water and you could visualize the tide flowing swiftly through it. There were several sand banks and patches of reef guarded by markers.

It was remote and beautiful and, although you did have to drive through a cattle station to get to it, this was an improvement upon, until recent times, only being able to approach by sea.

There were two small beach resorts nestled into the tree-lined shores of the mainland, one overlooking Gloucester Island and Passage Islet, one overlooking Edgecumbe Bay. Maggie chose the one overlooking Gloucester Island; there was something about the island that intrigued her.

Her accommodation in a cabin was spacious and spotless and it was right on the beach. There was a coconut palm outside her veranda, there were casuarinas and poincianas, some laced with bougainvillea. Many of the trees had orchids growing from their bark; many of them were rather exotic natives like pandanus palms and Burdekin plums.

The coarse, dark crystals of the beach reminded Maggie of brown sugar, but the water lapping the beach was calm, crystal-clear and immensely inviting, especially at high tide. She spent an hour on her first evening sitting on the beach, watching fascinated as ripple after little silvery ripple raced along, tiny imitations of waves breaking on the beach.

Then she caught her breath in amazement as two strange ducks skimmed the water's edge—ducks that looked as if they were wearing leather yokes when in fact it was a strip of dark feathers on their creamy necks and chests. Burdekin Ducks, she was told, when she enquired.

There was only one other couple at the resort and she ate dinner with them before using a long drive as an excuse for an early night. In fact it was nervous tension making her yawn, she thought as she strolled back to her cabin. Had she done the right thing? Was he even here in his beach house tucked away amongst the trees beyond the resort? Why hadn't she gone to find out straight away?

'I'll be better in the morning,' she told herself. 'More composed. Less conscious of the fact that this is a man I'd pegged for the kind women rode off with into the sunset because they couldn't help themselves—and what's going to make me any different?'

She shook her head and went to bed.

The sun came up at six-fifteen. Maggie was walking along the beach at the time.

Gloucester Island was dark with its southern outline illuminated in gold; trees, beach and rocks were dark shapes pasted on a gold background as the sun hovered below the horizon. Then it emerged and light, landscape and seascape fell into place and fled away from her—and the tall figure walking along the beach towards her carrying a fishing rod was unmistakably Jack McKinnon.

Maggie took a great gulp of air into her lungs and forced herself to walk forward steadily, although he stopped abruptly.

When she was up to him she held out her hand. 'Dr Livingstone, I presume?'

He didn't reciprocate.

'OK, not funny—' Maggie dropped her hand '—but I nearly didn't find you, which brought to mind the Livingstone/Stanley connection, I guess. Are you not going to say anything?'

He took in her bare legs and feet, her white shorts, her candy-striped top and her pony-tail, and spoke at last. 'How did you find me?'

'That's classified. But if you were to offer me a cup of coffee, say, I'll tell you why I went to all the trouble I did.'

'Are you staying here?' He indicated the resort down the beach.

'Yep, although I've told no one why. Your secret is safe with me, Mr McKinnon.'

'Maggie,' he said roughly, then seemed to change tack. 'All right, since you've come this far the least I can do is a cup of coffee, I guess. Follow me.'

His house was only a five-minute walk away and from the beach you'd hardly know it was there. It was wooden, weathered to a silvery grey, two-storeyed, surrounded by trees and covered with creepers. A smart, fast-looking yacht under a tarpaulin was drawn up the beach on rails.

She followed him up the outside steps to the second storey and gasped at the view from his top veranda. Not only the Gloucester Passage lay before her, but also Edgecumbe Bay towards the mainland and Bowen, with its rim of mountains tinged with pink and soft blues as the sun got higher.

'You sure know how to pick a spot,' she said with genuine admiration. 'This is so beautiful.'

'It also used to be a lot further from the madding crowd before the road was opened,' he said.

'Including me?' She swung round to face him. 'What exactly is so maddening about me?' she asked tautly. 'Correct me if I'm wrong, but I thought a lot of our differences and misapprehensions about each other got sorted when we were trying to get out of the shed?'

He put the fishing line down and checked that the colourful lure with its three-pronged hook was tucked into a roundel on the rod out of harm's way. 'There are other differences you don't even know about, Maggie.'

He straightened and pushed his fingers through his hair. He wore khaki shorts and an old football Guernsey with the sleeves cut off above the elbows. He was brown, as if he'd spent quite a bit of time in the sun, and his hair was streaked lighter by it, and was longer, as if he'd forgotten to get it cut.

'If there are, why can't I know about them?' she countered. 'Believe me, I am not the spoilt little rich girl you mistake me for and I don't take kindly to being treated as such.'

His lips twisted and he folded his arms. 'So you don't think this exercise has labels stuck all over it shouting ''Maggie Trent has to get her own way''?'

Her nostrils flared. 'No. If anything it shouts, ''Maggie Trent deserves better''.'

'Better,' he repeated.

'Yes, better. As in—why on earth can't we get to know each other better? For example, I wouldn't dream of judging you on your father.' She stopped and bit her lip, then soldiered on, 'You know what I mean!'

'Men,' he said slowly, 'and their grievances don't always work that way.'

'Then perhaps you should take more notice of women,' Maggie suggested tartly. 'Come to that, the whole world might be a better place if people did.'

A reluctant smile chased across his mouth and he seemed about to say something, but he merely shrugged and walked inside.

Maggie hesitated, then she shrugged herself, and followed him.

*   *   *

His house was simple and open plan, but there was nothing rough and ready about it.

The floors were gleaming polished wood throughout. There was a low double bed covered with a faux mink throw and several European pillows covered in dusky pink linen. One bedside table was stacked with books, the other bore a beautiful beaten-copper lamp.

Two corner leather couches sat about a vast wooden coffee-table bearing more books and some model ships, one in a bottle. A big cabinet housed a television, stereo and DVD player. Brown wooden and raffia blade fans were suspended from the ceiling and louvre blinds protected the windows.

The kitchen was all wood and chrome and state-of-the-art with black marble bench tops. There were several cane baskets with flourishing indoor plants dotted about and on the wall facing the front door there was a huge, lovely painting of two gaudy elephants in soft greens, matt gold and dusky pink.

'Yes!' Maggie stared at it enchanted. 'The perfect touch.'

'Thank you.' He pulled a plunger coffee-pot out of a cupboard and switched on the kettle.

She watched him assemble ground coffee, mugs, sugar crystals and milk. 'Where did you get it?'

'What?'

'The painting?'

He glanced over his shoulder. 'Thailand.'

Maggie pulled a stool out from the breakfast bar and perched herself on it. 'Is there anything I can say to make this easier?'

'You don't appear to be having much difficulty as it is.' He spooned coffee grounds into the plunger and poured boiling water over them.

Maggie inhaled luxuriously. 'Believe me, never having done this before, I'm a basket case inside,' she said, however.

He stopped what he was doing and regarded her expressionlessly. 'Done what?'

She laced her fingers together on the counter. 'Well, changed my stance on a man rather drastically to begin with. Not,' she assured him, 'that I had much to do with that. It just—happened. Unfortunately there's a whole lot of baggage I carry that makes it—'

'You're talking about locking me in a shed first of all, then cornering me here?' he suggested dryly.

A hot sensation behind her eyes alerted Maggie to the fact that it would be quite easy to burst into tears of frustration—to her absolute mortification should she allow it to happen. It was obviously going to be much harder than she'd anticipated to get through to Jack McKinnon.

'It's not that I'm only after your body, nor do I have any agenda to do with forcing you round to my way of thinking on housing estates,' she said quietly.

He smiled with so much irony, she flinched. 'That's just as well,' he commented, and poured a mug of coffee and pushed it towards her. 'Because while *your* body is perfectly delightful, and has even deprived me of my sleep on the odd occasion, I don't intend to do anything about it.'

Maggie's eyes nearly fell out on stalks. 'Say that again!'

He hooked a stool towards him with his foot and sat down on the other side of the counter from her. 'You heard.'

'I may have heard, but it doesn't make sense.'

'No?' He shrugged and sipped his coffee. 'I thought if I removed the thorn from your flesh of me not appearing to return your physical interest, you might feel better about things. You might even go away.'

Maggie stared at him as he put his mug down. Then she stood up on a rung of her stool and slapped his face.

His coffee-mug overturned as he moved abruptly and a brown puddle stretched between them. Then the mug rolled off the counter in slow motion and smashed on the floor. It was the only sound although the thwack of her palm connecting with his cheek-bone seemed to linger on the air.

There was something utterly terrifying in the way his narrowed grey gaze captured hers as she sank back onto the stool; it was still and menacing and full of unconcealed contempt. It was also as impossible to tear her gaze away as it had been the day they'd first laid eyes on each other, until he moved again and snaked out a hand to capture her wrist.

Maggie panicked then. She tore her wrist away and slipped off the stool all set to run away as fast as she could. Two things impeded her: she slipped on the wet floor and yelped in pain. By the time she'd righted herself and realized she'd got a sliver of china in her foot, he'd come round the breakfast bar, grabbed her by the waist and lifted her into his arms.

Forgetting everything but the awful insult she'd received, she launched into speech. 'Yes, yes, yes!' she said, her green eyes blazing. 'Yes, OK, it has been a thorn in my flesh! I went from hating and despising you to liking you and—and—feeling as flat as a tack because all I meant to you was a *bunch of flowers*, obviously, but there's a singular difference between what you're implying and the facts of the matter— what are you *doing*?'

He strode over to a leather couch and sat down with her in his lap. 'This.'

Maggie struggled to free herself, but he resisted with ease. 'Just keep still, Maggie,' he advised. 'You can't go anywhere with a splinter in your foot and I don't know if you make a habit of slapping men—'

'I don't!' she protested fiercely

'That explains it, then. You failed to realize it's just asking for some comeuppance.' He released her waist and put one arm around her shoulders.

'Come whatance…?' she said with a lot less certainty.

His lips twisted into a wry smile as he looked down into her eyes. 'This, Miss Trent—much pleasanter actually.' He bent his head and teased her lips apart.

It had occurred to Maggie that he was going to kiss her. What hadn't occurred to her was that through her rage and disappointment she could feel any spark of physical attraction, so her confusion was boundless on discovering herself pitched forward into a hot-house of sensual awareness; a sudden, wide open appreciation of Jack McKinnon, the feel of him, the taste of him, the sheer pleasure of him.

This can't be happening to me, she thought, but she was unable to resist the lovely sensations he was arousing in her as he kissed her lips, then her neck and throat, and it was all so warm and close and— most curiously—entirely appropriate.

So appropriate, she didn't protest when he slipped his hand beneath her top and cupped her breasts in their flimsy layer of silk and lace.

She even voiced her approval. 'Mmm...mmm.'

'Nice?' he murmured.

'Very.'

'How about this?' He circled her waist with his arm and started to kiss her deeply.

She clung to him and moved against him, loving the hard strength of his body against hers and becoming extremely aroused, so much so, she doubted her ability to withstand any kind of closure between them other than the final one between a man and a woman.

He was the one who brought them back to earth, slowly, until she was lying in his arms, her eyes dark, her mouth red, her hair gorgeously mussed and her breathing highly erratic.

She blinked several times, her eyes were very green and quite bewildered. 'Where did that come from?'

He smiled and kissed the tip of her nose. 'Powerful emotion often has its other side.'

'You mean being so angry with you made me—I don't know—vulnerable to that?'

'Perhaps.'

'How about you?'

'I—' he paused '—have wanted to do it before. Why don't you finish what you were saying?'

She shook her head. 'I've lost the thread—'

'No, you haven't,' he contradicted. 'You were all set to be extremely passionate about the ''singular difference'' between the facts and what I was implying.'

He was so close she could see the fine laugh lines beside his mouth, a little nick in one of his eyebrows, she could smell soap on his skin and there was a patch of stubble on his jaw his razor had missed.

It came to her with a punch that she'd never looked so closely at a man before, never been interested enough to wonder, for example, how he'd cut his eyebrow and what it would be like to wake up in his arms…

'I…' She tried to collect her thoughts. '*You* seemed to be completely confident I'm one of those predatory girls who won't rest until she gets her man, *plus*—' she looked at him challengingly '—the hoary old spoilt-little-rich-bitch-who-has-to-get-her-own-way bit. That couldn't be further from the way it really is.'

'Which is?' He arched the split eyebrow at her.

'It's never happened to me before,' she said slowly. 'I've always had to fend men off. I've never before been…really, *really* interested. Oh, there've been a few flirtations and I've had some nice friends—Tim is one of them—but you could truthfully say I'm a bit of a novice who's been quite happy…' she sighed and shrugged '…doing my own thing, I guess.'

'Go on.'

'For some…' she paused '…mysterious reason that changed overnight when I was locked in the shed with you. Suddenly I was interested and no one,' she said with emphasis, 'seems to be able to give me one good reason why I shouldn't be, not even *you*, although you dropped me like a hot potato.'

'Maggie—'

'Look.' She laid her hand on his arm. 'Perhaps you are right about me. Perhaps I don't take no for an answer easily, but it's pretty important for me at least to be able to assess what this change means to me.'

He put his finger under her chin and tipped her face up to his.

'In other words...' she smiled fleetingly '...give me one good reason to say to myself, Maggie Trent, you came of age over the wrong man because there's absolutely nothing you can offer him—or there's someone else in his life—and I will go away.'

He stared into her eyes, fingered her chin lightly, then laid his head back with a sigh. 'Your father and I will never see eye to eye—'

'Forget about my father. It so happens I have the same problem with him. And I have taken quite some pains, believe me, to live my life the way I want to rather than the way he wants me to. Yes,' she added intensely, 'it may still be a pretty privileged life compared—perhaps—to how you grew up, if *that's* what you hold against me!'

He smiled slightly. 'No. There's not a lot I have against you, personally.'

'And there's no one else?' she asked seriously.

He watched her for a long moment, then shook his head.

'Well, then.' She gestured. 'Would it be such a bad idea if we got to know each other better?'

'Taking into consideration the fact that I have wanted to kiss you and you don't seem to mind being kissed by me?' he queried.

A glint of laughter shone in her eyes. 'I wasn't going to say that, although I suppose it is fairly pertinent, but there's a lot more to getting to know someone, isn't there?'

If I had any sense, Jack McKinnon mused as he studied the lovely crumpled length of her across his lap, I would end this now, for once and for all.

On the other hand, I did walk away from her and she was the one who wouldn't accept it. Does that absolve me? Not in her father's eyes, I have no doubt. Whichever way I travel with her, to the altar or simply an affair, David Trent is going to hate like hell me knowing his daughter in a biblical sense. But will it be revenge? Only if she falls in love and I don't…

What if I'm right and there's a genuine naivety— and all she's said so far bears that out—that would make it child's play to have her fall in love with me and want to marry me? Talk of revenge or poetic justice, if you like, and there's no doubt the bastard deserves it, but…

'Maggie…' he paused '…what if it doesn't lead towards wedding bells or a relationship, at least?'

She shrugged. 'I don't know—how can I? But the really important thing to me is to know that I didn't sit back and let something I judged special to me just pass me by.'

He grinned suddenly and bent his head to kiss her lightly. 'You're…I don't know, pretty special yourself, I guess.'

'So we could be friends, at least?'

'We could be friends, at least,' he agreed wryly. 'There is a proviso, however.'

'You're not the marrying kind?' she hazarded. She said it perfectly seriously, but there was a glint he was coming to know in her eyes.

'I—'

'I don't know if I am yet,' she interposed. 'Because—and not that this has anything to do with being rich, spoilt and privileged; I'm quite sure I would have been the same if I'd been born in a poorhouse— I can be very dictatorial, I'm told.'

'I wonder why I find that quite easy to believe?' he murmured.

'Some of my actions to date may have led you to suspect it?' she suggested with deep, suspicious gravity.

'One or two.' He circled the outline of her mouth with his finger. 'So how long did you plan to spend up here at the Cape?'

'I booked in for a week, but I have another week's leave up my sleeve. It seemed like a great place, especially for someone dodging journalists and P.I.s, even if you weren't here.'

He narrowed his eyes. 'How *did* you find out about this place?'

'I can't tell you that.' She hesitated. 'But don't worry, it won't go any further.'

He frowned.

'How long are you here for?' she queried.

'Same. Another week,' he said abstractedly.

'When did you arrive?'

'A couple of days ago.'

'Oh, good!' She sat up. 'That gives us plenty of time.'

He removed his arms and folded them across his chest. 'Are you planning to move in with me?'

She thought for a moment, then glinted him an impish glance. 'No. That *would* look as if all I was after was your body.'

'Perish the thought,' he murmured and drew her back into his arms.

'If you're going to kiss me again…' she began.

'I am. You have a problem there?'

'Not *per se*—'

'I'm glad to hear it,' he commented, and ran his fingers down her thigh.

'There is only the fact that—' She stopped and shivered as he stroked her neck and the soft skin just below the neck of her top. 'Uh—the fact that...'

'Go on,' he invited.

'Things could get out of hand rather easily.' She grimaced. 'For me, at least.'

'Then you'll have to rely on me to exert the will-power.'

She eyed him suspiciously. 'Are you laughing at me, Jack?'

'No. Yes,' he corrected himself.

'Am I so—laughable?'

He did kiss her, lightly, his grey eyes gleaming with amusement. 'No. You're unique, that's all.'

She lay back in his arms. 'That's one of the things I like about you.'

He raised an eyebrow.

'I feel safe with you,' she said.

He paused and lifted his head to stare into the distance.

Maggie waited but he didn't enlighten her about whatever he was seeing in his mind's eye. Then, with a strange little sound in his throat, he gathered her very close and kissed her deeply.

Once again it was a sublime experience for Maggie. She felt comforted and cradled but very alive at the same time, and supremely conscious of him, and she uttered a blissful sigh at the end of it that made him laugh.

'The next bit might not be quite as pleasant,' he said, still grinning.

'The next bit?'

'Mmm…' He moved her off his lap and sat her in the corner of the settee. 'Getting rid of the sliver of china in your foot.'

'Oh, that.' She waved a hand. 'I'd forgotten all about it.'

But although he was quick and decisive with his tweezers, she had to sniff back a tear or two as the sliver came out.

'I should have done that the other way around,' he said with a keen glance at her as he bathed her foot in a disinfectant solution.

She raised her eyebrows questioningly.

'Taken it out first and kissed you afterwards,' he elucidated as he peeled open a plaster.

She leant forward and cupped his cheek. 'Kiss me now, quick—and I'll be fine.'

But as his lips rested on hers briefly and they were cool and he smelt of disinfectant she had to resist an almost overwhelming urge to ask for more…

CHAPTER FOUR

THEY had five wonderful days.

They went sailing on his boat, *The Shiralee*, and fishing.

Maggie was in her element on a boat. One thing she did share with her father was a love of the sea and as she was growing up she'd crewed for him.

'I see you know what you're doing,' Jack said to her on their first sail.

'Aye, aye, skipper!' she responded as she turned the boat smartly into the wind so he could set the sails.

He climbed back into the cockpit and put his hands on her waist from behind as she stood at the wheel, and the jib ballooned out in the breeze. 'OK, cut the motor.'

The silence after the motor died was lovely, to be replaced by the equally lovely whoosh of wind in the sails and the rush of water against the hull.

Maggie leant back against him as they braced themselves against the tilt as *The Shiralee* heeled and sped along. 'She sails well,' she said.

He slid his arms around her. 'So she should, I designed her myself.'

Maggie smiled. 'No false modesty about you, Mr McKinnon.'

He turned her around in his arms. 'Not, at least, about boats. You're looking very trim, Miss Trent.'

Maggie glanced down at her short navy shorts and

blinding white T-shirt. She also wore a peaked navy cap with her hair pulled through at the back, and sunglasses. 'A suitably nautical presence for your boat, I hope?' she queried gravely.

'I would say so.' He removed her sunglasses.

Maggie raised her eyebrows.

'Your eyes are amazing. And it is a pleasure to see them not blazing or looking absolute daggers at me,' he said.

A gurgle of laughter rose in her throat. 'That feels like another lifetime ago.'

'On the contrary, it's only a day ago that you slapped my face.'

She coloured and he watched the tide of pink stain the smooth skin of her cheeks. All the same, she said, with an attempt at insouciance, 'Ah—just heat of the moment, I guess.'

'Isn't it always?' he murmured.

Maggie stilled. 'What are you trying to say, Jack?'

His gaze lingered on her face, then he grimaced. 'I'm not sure—'

'That I might be highly impulsive, if not to say irrationally so?'

'As a matter of fact—' he paused '—there is only one "highly" I'm conscious of at the moment in association with you and that's—kissable. How say you, Maggie?'

The growing frown in her eyes was replaced by something quite different. 'Actually, I love the sound of that!'

He laughed and started to kiss her thoroughly until the wind changed and the sails started to flap and they had to draw apart and concentrate on their sailing.

'Goodness, we did come close to those rocks!' Maggie called.

He was reeling in the jib. 'I suspected there was a touch of Delilah in you, now I'm wondering about a siren,' he called back.

Maggie watched him. He was precise and economical in his movements and his physique was breathtaking in khaki shorts and nothing else as he reached up to free a rope.

I knew it, she thought with a sense of satisfaction. There's definitely an action man in there.

There was also, she discovered, an inspired cook within the man.

He'd produced a divine chicken stir-fry served with saffron rice on their first evening together. He grilled fish to perfection. He had a marinade for steak that was to die for. A lot of the food he produced was seafood he'd caught himself—fish, crabs, oysters and painted lobsters.

They explored Bona Bay on Gloucester Island and Breakfast Bay. Once they sailed east through the passage and south to Double and Woodwark Bays and they fished off Edwin Rocks. Maggie caught a Spanish mackerel that day to her intense excitement.

'I've hooked a very large fish, Jack,' she told him as the trolling line she was manning sang out.

'You've probably hooked a rock,' he said prosaically.

'Don't be silly!' She was highly indignant. 'That's no rock! Will you please slow this boat down so I can reel him in?'

Fortunately they were motoring, not sailing, so he was able to stop and drop the anchor and Maggie was able to get the rod out of its holder and start winding in.

'Here, you better let me do it.' He came over to take the rod from her. 'I think it is a fish.'

'I told you so, but it's my fish. Stand aside!'

'Maggie—' he was laughing at her '—you'll never handle it.'

'Oh, yes, I will!'

She nearly didn't. She wound until her arms and shoulders were screaming in pain, and her face grew scarlet.

'Don't bust a gut,' he warned.

'It's nearly in,' she panted. 'Oh, there it is—glory be!' she enthused as the fish leapt out of the water. 'What a beauty!'

'Steady on, now.' He leant over the side of the boat with the gaff in his hands. 'OK! I've got it. Well done!'

Maggie collapsed in a heap and burst into tears.

Jack looked heavenwards, then secured the fish and bent down to scoop her into his arms. He sat down on the padded cockpit seat with her, holding her close. 'You're the most stubborn girl I know,' he said ruefully, 'but I do admire you. Don't cry.' He smoothed the tangle of her hair out of her eyes. 'You won!'

'I know.' She licked some tears from her upper lip and wiped her nose on the back of her hand. 'I just felt very sorry for it all of a sudden. It put up a great fight. I would have liked to let it go.'

'Too late now, but it won't be wasted. Is there any difference between buying fish to eat in a fish shop and catching it yourself?'

She considered. 'No. No, you're right. So you'll cook it?'

'I won't waste a scrap of it,' he promised. 'Even the carcass will be used for the crab pots and I'll reserve some for bouillabaisse.'

'You're a real hunter-gatherer—aren't you?'

'In certain circumstances,' he agreed.

'Good. I like that. Ouch.' She looked at her winding hand. 'This could be a bit sore for a couple of days.'

'I have two temporary solutions.' He picked up her hand and kissed the back of it, then her palm, and gave it back to her. 'The second solution is probably even more efficacious in the short term.'

'Oh, I don't know,' she began. But he sat her on the cushions and disappeared down below. Two minutes later he emerged with a bottle of champagne and two glasses.

He popped the cork ceremonially and poured the champagne. He handed her her glass and raised his to propose a toast. 'To a magnificent fighter!' he said, in the direction of the fish.

'Hear, hear!' Maggie agreed and dissolved, this time, into laughter.

He sat down and put his arm around her shoulders. 'I should have said—to two magnificent fighters.'

She laid her head on his shoulder, feeling more content than she could ever remember.

True to her word, she didn't move in with him, but apart from the hours she slept in her cabin at the resort, often restless hours, the rest of her time was all spent with him.

When they weren't walking, sailing, swimming or

fishing they puttered around his house, they read, they listened to music, they watched DVDs. Her current choice of reading material amused him.

'Don't laugh—I like Harry Potter! And the kids next door are fanatical fans so I have to keep up with the books and we always watch the movies together!'

'Did I say anything?'

'You looked—' She paused. She was snuggled into a corner of one of his settees wearing a long cotton shift, a charcoal background patterned with creamy frangipani flowers. 'You looked *askance*. But I read all sorts of books—crime, romance, adventure, although not science fiction generally.'

'Good.' He returned her gaze with a perfectly straight face.

'Is your taste in literature particularly highbrow?' she queried.

He held up his book cover.

'*Master and Commander*,' she read. 'Surprise, surprise!'

He grinned. 'I like sea stories.'

'That's an understatement. I'd say you have a passion for all things maritime!'

'I do have a couple of other passions,' he objected, and eyed the twisted grace of the way she was sitting with her feet tucked under her.

'Women in general or me in particular?' she asked gravely.

'That's a leading question.' His grey eyes glinted. 'Put it this way, I am enjoying getting to know you better.'

'Same here,' she said. 'I just have this *feeling* that women may come second in your life.'

He shrugged. 'A lot of my design work takes women very much into account,' he said.

'How so?'

'I'll show you.'

First of all he showed her the designs of his catamarans, then he showed her some of his house designs, and she was struck by certain similarities.

'There's absolutely no wasted space,' she said slowly as she studied the floorplan of two admittedly small, compact homes that even had nautical names, The Islander and Greenwich. 'It's all rather shipshape.'

He looked rueful. 'My main ambition was always to design boats.'

'But some of these space-saving ideas are really good. That, plus the fact that they are not shonky…' she paused, then glinted him a wicked little smile '…do take your houses out of the realm of little boxes.'

His lips twitched. 'Thanks, but they still don't fall into the category of your house.'

'For my sins I inherited my house from my grandmother. Where do you live when you're at home?'

'In an apartment at Runaway Bay.'

'A penthouse?' she suggested.

'No.' He grimaced. 'A sub-penthouse.'

'Could we be as bad as each other in the matter of our living arrangements, Mr McKinnon?' she said impishly. 'Incidentally, I don't have a marvellous hideaway on Cape Gloucester.'

'On the other hand, you're likely to inherit a cattle station and more very desirable Gold Coast property, amongst other things.'

Maggie blinked. 'How do you know all that?'

He paused. 'It's fairly common knowledge.'

'I suppose so.' But she frowned, then shrugged. 'I get the very strong feeling my father would dearly love to have a son to bequeath it all to rather than me. He's petrified I'm going to be taken for a ride by a man on the make or I'm going to fritter it all away somehow.'

Jack McKinnon gazed at her so intently, she said, with a comically alarmed expression, 'What have I done now?'

'Nothing.' He rolled up the house plan. As he did so he dislodged a book from the pile on the coffee-table and a photo fell out of it.

Maggie picked it up. 'Who is this?' she asked as she studied the fair, tall woman on board, by the look of it, *The Shiralee*.

'My sister Sylvia,' he said after what seemed to be an unusually long hesitation.

Maggie's eyes widened. 'Your real—'

'No. We're no relation. We were both adopted by the same family as babies. She's a couple of years older but we grew up together as brother and sister. She still lives with our adoptive mother in Sydney, who has motor-neuron disease now. Our adoptive father died a few years ago.'

'That must be why she looks sad,' Maggie commented. 'Lovely but sad. Has she never married?'

'No.' He picked up the ship in a bottle. 'Ever wondered how this is done?'

Maggie blinked at the rather abrupt change of subject, but she said, 'Yes! Don't tell me you did that?'

'I did. I'll show you.'

Cape Gloucester wasn't entirely reserved for relaxation, Maggie found over those days. He kept in touch with his office by phone and twice a day he spent some time on his laptop checking out all sorts of markets: stock, commodity, futures and the like. At these times he was oblivious to anything that went on around him.

He was also rather surprised, when she let fall an idle remark on the subject, to find that she knew her way around the stock market.

'I'm not just a pretty face, Mr McKinnon,' she assured him with mock gravity, then went on quite seriously to tell him about the portfolio of shares she was building on her own.

'So it's not only property you dabble—correct that—you're interested in?' he said.

She directed a cool little glance at him and told him exactly how much she'd earned in commission over the past twelve months. 'I do seem to have a flair for it,' she said with simple honesty.

'You do.' He frowned. 'You also seem to know your way around these rather well.' He gestured to the house and boat blueprints he'd shown her.

She told him about the courses she'd done at university.

'All of which,' he said, and smiled suddenly, 'leaves me with egg on my face, I guess.'

Maggie gazed at him, then she said, 'I told you it was a good idea to get to know me better.'

He laughed. 'You were right.'

She thought, after this conversation, that there was a subtle shift in their relationship, as if the playing field had been levelled a little between them, intellectually.

She caught him watching her thoughtfully sometimes, then he invited her to participate when he checked the stock market and some of their discussions on all sorts of things—life, politics, religion—became quite deep.

'Where did you learn to cook like this?' she asked once, halfway through an absolutely delicious seafood crêpe they were having for lunch.

'I grew up in a household where food was important.'

'Your adoptive family?' she queried.

'Yes.'

'Do you…have you…do you know anything about your own family?' she asked tentatively.

'No.' He helped himself to salad and held the salad servers poised above the bowl for a moment. 'I decided—' he lowered the servers gently '—to take the road they took.'

'Which was?' she queried, feeling a little chilled, but not sure why.

'If I wasn't good enough for them, the same applied in reverse.'

He said it quite casually, but she thought she detected a glint of steel in his eyes.

'But,' she heard herself object even although she had the feeling she was trampling on dangerous ground, 'there could have been any number of reasons…I mean, maybe your mother *had* to give you up, for example. I don't think it was as easy to be a single parent thirty-two years ago as it is now. I don't think it's easy *now*, come to that, but there is a lot more support and social security available.'

He sat back with his food untouched and something about him reminded her of the man she'd first met at a jazz concert on a marina boardwalk, very sure of himself, controlled and contained and—as he'd proved then—lethal.

'What would you know about it, Maggie?'

'I—well, nothing, I guess. Look, I'm sorry.' She took a sip of her wine in a bid to hide her discomfort, her discomfort on two fronts. The feeling she'd rushed in where angels feared to tread and her concern for him, she realized with a little rush of amazement. 'I shouldn't pry.' She half smiled. 'Or give gratuitous advice. But—'

'Listen—' he ruffled his hair and pulled his plate towards him '—it's all water under the bridge. It was water under the bridge when I was far too young to understand anything other than the presence of a loving family in my life even if they weren't my own. And that's all that counts really.'

The smile he cast her as he cut into his crêpe was completely serene, and she would have believed him if she hadn't seen that steely, scary glint in his eyes.

He was also quite a handyman, she discovered, and that he set himself an improvement project every time he visited Cape Gloucester.

His current project fitted in with one of Maggie's enthusiasms—gardening. His garden was quite wild and in need of taming, he said. There wasn't much more he could do for it since water was a problem. There was only tank water or extremely salty bore water.

But Maggie was more than happy to pitch in and help him prune and clear away the worst of the tangled overgrowth.

He had a book on the local flora and she also took it upon herself to identify as many of the shrubs as she could. To her delight, she found, amongst the native elms and Burdekin plums, some small trees she identified as *Guettarda Speciosa* that produced sweet-smelling night flowers.

'Listen to this,' she said to him one evening. They were relaxing on the veranda after a divine swim in the high-tide waters only a stone's throw away. The sun had set and he'd lit a candle in a glass and poured them each a gin and tonic in long frosted glasses garnished with slices of bush lemon harvested from a tree in his garden.

'"In India *Guettarda Speciosa* is used for perfume,"' she read from the book.

'How so?'

'Amazingly simply! You throw a muslin cloth over the bush at night so it comes into contact with the flowers. The dew dampens the cloth and it absorbs the perfume from the flowers, then it's wrung out of the muslin in the morning and bingo! You've captured the essence of the perfume.'

'Bingo,' he repeated and watched her idly. She wore a pink bikini beneath a gauzy sarong tied between her breasts. Her golden skin was glowing and her green eyes were sparkling with enthusiasm. 'Let's see if I can anticipate your next question—no, I don't have any muslin cloths.'

Maggie dissolved into laughter. 'How did you know?'

'You're that kind of girl. You like to get out and do things and, the more exotic they are, the better you like it. But despite the absence of muslin...' he leant over the veranda railing and plucked a creamy flower just starting to open '...you could wear a *Guettarda*

Speciosa in your hair.' He leant forward and handed her the flower.

Maggie smelt it. 'Lovely,' she pronounced. 'Thank you.' And she threaded the stem into the damp mass of her hair. 'They do also use it for garlands and hair ornaments in India.'

He smiled and sipped his drink.

'You've read this book, haven't you?' she accused. 'I wasn't telling you anything you didn't know!'

'No. But I've never had a girl to do the honours for before. You look very fetching,' he added.

She studied him. He was sprawled out in a canvas director's chair wearing only a pair of colourful board shorts, and his body was brown, sleek and strong. Coupled with how he was watching her, lazily yet in a curiously heavy-lidded way, the impact on her was one she was becoming very familiar with.

It was as if he could light a spark in her that caused her heart to race, her skin to break out in goose-bumps and a sensual flame to flicker within her just by looking at her. It was also a prelude, she knew, to an intimate moment between them.

Trying to fight it was useless, she'd discovered, although she didn't really understand why she would want to. He'd been as good as his word. He'd taken her to the brink several times, then brought her back, as if he knew she wasn't quite ready to cross that Rubicon. So it had been five days of loving every minute of his company and the things they did, five days of growing intimacy between them—and now this, she thought.

The sudden knowledge that the time was right?

She took a sip of her drink and saw that her hand

wasn't quite steady as it hit her. He hadn't moved at all. How, though, to transmit that knowledge to him?

'I know you think I'm impetuous,' she said huskily, 'and maybe I am, but not over this. I also take full responsibility for my actions. There won't ever be any recriminations.'

He stirred, but said nothing as his gaze played over her.

'Only if *you* want it, of course,' she added, and stumbled up suddenly in a fever of embarrassment—what if he had no idea what she was talking about?

'Maggie…' he got up swiftly and caught her in his arms '…*of course* I want it,' he said roughly, 'but—'

'Oh, thank heavens,' she breathed. 'I've never propositioned a man before—do you mind?' she asked anxiously.

A smile chased through his eyes, but it left them.. bleak? she wondered. Why would that be?

'It's just that some things can never be reversed.' He circled her mouth with his thumb as her lips parted.

'I know that,' she said. 'It doesn't seem to make the slightest difference to how I feel. And if you're trying to say you may not be a marrying man, I may do my darndest to change that, knowing me, but that's…in the future, and what will be will be. Just don't turn your back on me now; I couldn't bear it.'

He stared down into her eyes. They were glimmering with unshed tears like drowned emeralds, but her gaze was very direct and very honest. All the same he held back for some moments longer.

Moments where he thought back over the past days and how he'd had to rein in a growing desire for this girl. Days during which he'd questioned his motives time and again. Times when he'd told himself firmly that she was just another girl, rather touchingly innocent at times, yes, then exceedingly determined at others, but all the same, he could take her or leave her...

He had to doubt that now, in the face of her.. what was the word for it? Gallantry? Yes, and honesty. And what his body most ardently desired. The truth of the matter was, he reflected with a streak of self-directed irony, he could no longer keep his hands off Maggie Trent, or any longer deny himself the final satisfaction of taking her.

'Turn my back on you,' he repeated and released her to cup her face in his hands. 'I couldn't bear it either.' He lowered his head and kissed her.

Maggie clung to him and kissed him back in a fever of relief this time. Then he untied the knot of her sarong and it floated away. Her bikini top suffered the same fate shortly afterwards.

'The perfect gymnast's body,' he murmured as he cupped her high, small breasts peaked with velvety little nipples.

'Thank you.' She drew her hands down his chest and trembled because it felt like a rock wall. Then he was kissing her breasts and sliding his hands beneath her bikini briefs to cup her hips and cradle them against him.

Maggie shivered with delight and she stood on her toes and slid her arms around his neck. 'You do the most amazing things to me,' she said against the corner of his mouth.

He lifted her off her feet and she curled her legs around him. 'If we're not careful this could be over

in a matter of seconds,' he replied with a wry little
smile and walked inside with her, 'on account of what
you do to me.' He nuzzled her neck, then lowered
her to the bed.

He turned away and opened a drawer of the bedside
table.

'If that's what I think it is,' she said softly, 'you
don't need to worry. I'm on the pill—to correct a
slight gynaecological problem I have but, according
to my doctor, I'm protected against—as he put it—
all eventualities.'

Jack looked down at her. 'Is that what you were
going to the doctor for the day after we got locked in
the shed?'

'Mmm... It's not serious, just a bit debilitating
sometimes.'

He lay down beside her and said no more or, she
thought dreamily, he let his hands and lips do the
talking. He held her and caressed her until she became
aware that areas of her body she'd never given much
thought to before could become seriously erotic zones
beneath his hands and mouth. The nape of her neck,
the soft, supple flesh of the inside of her arms, the
base of her throat and that pathway that led down to
her breasts, her thighs...

She became aware that she could make him catch
his breath by moulding herself to him and sliding one
leg between his. She discovered that his touch on her
nipples sent a thrilling, tantalizing message to the
very core of her femininity.

She marvelled at his clean, strong lines and the feel
of sleek, hard muscles, and she buried her face in his
shoulder with a gasp as he parted her thighs and a
rush of warmth and rapture claimed her.

'I just hope you're experiencing what I am,' she breathed as she started to move against him in a rhythm that seemed to come naturally to her. 'It's gorgeous.'

He laughed softly, then kissed her hard. 'To put it mildly, I'm about to die. Ready?'

'Yes, please!'

He claimed her and they rode the waves of their mutual desire to a peak of ecstasy.

They came down from the peak slowly. Their bodies were dewed with sweat and Maggie clung to him as if she were drowning and he was her rock.

'That was...that was...' she said hoarsely, but couldn't go on.

'You're right,' he agreed and kissed her eyelids. 'That was something else. No...' he pushed himself up on his elbow '...pain?'

Her lips trembled into a smile. 'Only the opposite, thanks to you.'

He considered. 'Well, maybe the gymnastics had something to do with it. It's very active.'

'No,' she said firmly, 'it was—*always you*, like the song.'

He grinned. 'OK, I won't argue with you. But if you have any plans to get up and go back to the resort tonight, forget 'em.'

'It was the furthest thing from my mind,' she said dreamily and snuggled up to him.

They slept for a while, then got up and showered, and he made a light supper.

They ate it on the veranda and watched the moon. Then he was struck by an idea. 'Muslin,' he said musingly and picked up her sarong still lying on the veranda floor. 'Anything like this?'

Maggie sat up alertly. 'That's voile and silk, but it's very fine, like muslin—it might just do the trick.'

He looked from the sarong in his hands to the *Guettarda Speciosa* just beyond the veranda railing with the perfume of its night flowers wafting over them in a light breeze. 'How do we anchor it?'

'Clothes pegs?' she suggested.

He nodded and disappeared inside to get them and between them they spread the sarong over the top of the tree.

'Morning will tell,' he commented as he applied the last peg.

'The morning after the night before,' she said with a humorous little glint in her eyes.

'There is that too,' he agreed. 'In the meantime—' he put his hands on her shoulders and drew her against him '—how about back to bed?'

'That sounds like a fine idea to me,' she whispered.

He tilted her chin and looked into her eyes. 'You know what's going to happen, though, don't you?'

She licked her lips. 'Another fine idea by me,' she said softly.

'But what you may not realize,' he temporized, 'is that I suddenly feel like a starving person deprived of a feast.'

She slid her hands around his waist and up his back and pressed her breasts against his chest. 'Who's depriving you of anything?'

He groaned and picked her up.

This time their lovemaking was swift and tempestuous, as if he had felt truly starved of her, but Maggie matched him every inch of the way as the barrier of never having done it before lay behind her and she could express her need of him with a new sureness of touch.

The bed was a tangled mess when they came down from the heights this time, but Maggie was laughing as she caught her breath. 'Wow! I see what you mean.'

He buried his head between her breasts. 'Sorry.'

'Don't be.' She ran her fingers through his hair. 'Let's just call it our epiphany.'

He looked up with something in his eyes she couldn't immediately translate. A tinge of surprise coupled with admiration, she realized suddenly, and it gave her a lovely sense of being on equal terms with him that carried her on to sleep serenely in his arms, once they'd reorganized the bed.

But the next morning it all caught up with Maggie in an embarrassing way.

All her life she'd suffered from a digestive system that took exception to too much excitement and too much rich food.

She woke up feeling pale and shaken and distinctly nauseous. Then she was as sick as a dog.

At first Jack was determined to drive her into the nearest doctor at Proserpine, but she explained between painful bouts of nausea and other complications what the problem was. 'On top of everything else I should have gone easy on the wonderful Mornay sauces and marinades,' she gasped.

He was sitting on the side of the bed watching her with concern. 'Are you sure? You may have picked up a gastric bug.'

'I'm quite sure! A bit of rest, just liquids and plain food for a while and I'll be fine.'

She saw some indecision chase through his eyes and she put her hand over his. 'Really. And I have a remedy I always carry but it's in my luggage back at the resort.'

He came to a decision. 'All right. Do you think you can talk on the phone long enough to tell the resort it's OK to release your vehicle and your luggage to me?'

'Yes.'

Several hours later, she was starting to feel better and Jack McKinnon couldn't have been a better nurse to add to all the other things she admired about him.

He'd made her as comfortable as he could with clean sheets on the bed and a clean nightgown from her luggage. He'd darkened the bedroom section. He'd made up an electrolyte drink for her to replace the minerals she might have lost, and some clear, plain chicken soup. He was as quiet as possible so she could sleep.

And by four o'clock in the afternoon Maggie felt quite human again.

He brought her a cup of black tea and sat on the bed while she drank it.

'I'm too excitable,' she said ruefully. 'That's what my mother puts it down to.'

He gazed at her. She was still pale, but her eyes were clear and she'd brushed her hair into two pony-tails tied with green bobbles.

She could have been about sixteen, he thought, a lovely, volatile child. Yet a brave one who'd matched his ardour in anything but a childlike way until she'd made herself sick.

'I may have been at fault,' he began.

'No. Well—' she smiled faintly '—you could be too good a cook.'

He grimaced. 'What about the rest of it?'

'The way we made love?' She breathed deeply. 'I could never regret a moment of that.'

'Neither could I, but—'

'You're wondering if this is going to happen every time you make love to me? It won't,' she assured him. 'These last few weeks have been—' she gestured '—quite turbulent for me. It was probably bound to happen sooner or later, but I'm feeling—' she chewed her lip '—much more tranquil now.'

He shook his head as if trying to sort through it all.

'But—lonely,' she added softly, 'in this vast bed all on my own.'

'Maggie—'

'If you could just put your arms around me, that would be the best thing that's happened to me today.'

He stared at her and she thought he was going to knock back her suggestion, then he changed his mind.

She sighed with sheer pleasure as he lay down beside her and gathered her close.

'How did the perfume go?' she asked drowsily.

'Your sarong smells lovely, but there was nothing to wring out of it—not enough dew.'

She chuckled. 'We may have to move to India.'

He stroked her hair.

But although they slept in the same bed that night, and although she drew strength and comfort from his arms and it was a magic experience on its own, that was all that happened until the next day when she could demonstrate she was as fit as a fiddle again.

The day after that, on what should have been their last day at Cape Gloucester but they'd made a mutual decision to stay on for a few days more, it all fell apart.

She had no intimation of the drama about to unfold when they swam very early that morning, naked and joyfully.

'This adds another dimension,' she told him as he lifted her aloft out of the sea. She put her hands on his shoulders with her arms straight and her hair dripped over his head. Her skin was covered with goose-bumps and her nipples peaked in the chill of it all.

'Know what?' He tasted each nipple in turn. 'If we hadn't just made love, guess what we'd be doing as soon as we got back? You taste salty,' he added.

She flipped backwards over his encircling arms and wound her legs around him. 'No idea at all!' she said as she floated on her back and her hair spread out on the water like seaweed. 'This water is so buoyant.'

'And you're particularly buoyant this morning, Miss Trent,' he teased. 'Not to mention full of cheek.'

She arched her body, then flipped upright, laughing down at him. 'I wonder why?' She sobered and stroked his broad shoulders. 'What is the masculine equivalent of a siren?'

'There isn't one.'

'There should be,' she told him. 'Anyway, you're it, Mr McKinnon. Enough to make any girl feel very buoyant, not to mention—wonderful!'

He stared into her eyes, as green as the sea at that

moment, with her eyelashes clumped together and beaded with moisture, and at the freshness of her skin. And he said with an odd little smile, as if there was something in the air she wasn't aware of, 'I haven't felt quite so wonderful myself for a while.'

She insisted on cooking breakfast, saying it was about time she earned her keep.

They'd showered together and she'd put on a short denim skirt with a green blouse that matched her eyes. Her hair was loose as it dried and she frequently looped it behind her ears as she cooked—grilled bacon and banana with chopped, fried tomato and onion and French toast.

'There,' she said proudly as she set it out on the veranda table. 'I may not be in your gourmet class, but I'm not useless in the kitchen either.'

'Did I say you were?' he drawled.

She pulled out a chair and wrinkled her nose at him. 'You've carefully avoided any mention of it, which led me to wonder if you'd simply assumed my privileged background had left me fit only to rely on someone else to provide my meals—what a mouthful, Maggie,' she accused herself with a gurgle of laughter.

He grinned. 'I did wonder.'

'Well, now you know. I'm actually quite domesticated.' She picked up her knife and fork, then paused and frowned. 'Was that a car in the driveway I heard?'

He cocked his head. 'I'm not expecting anyone.'

A moment later they heard a door bang, then footsteps crunching on the gravel path around the side of the house.

'Anyone home?' a voice called at the same time as a tall fair woman appeared at the bottom of the steps, then, 'Oh, Jack! I'm so glad I caught you. Maisie did say you'd decided to stay on for a couple more days, but one never quite knows with you!'

To Maggie's surprise, Jack McKinnon went quite still for a long moment, still and tense and as dangerously alert as a big jungle cat. Then he relaxed deliberately and stood up. 'Sylvia,' he said. 'This is a surprise.'

Maggie blinked and Sylvia, his adoptive sister, arrived on the veranda. She was as lovely as her photo and there was no trace of sadness about her as she greeted Jack, full of laughing explanations.

'I really needed a bit of time off—Mum and I were getting to the stage of wanting to shoot each other! So I flew up to Proserpine yesterday, hired a car and took off before dawn hoping to catch you and surprise you—oh!' Her gaze fell on Maggie. 'Oh, I'm so sorry. Maisie didn't say anything about…' She trailed off awkwardly.

'Don't be silly, Syl,' Jack said quietly. 'I'm always happy to see you. This is Maggie.'

Maggie got up and came round the table, holding out her hand. 'Maggie Trent, actually. How do you do?'

Sylvia's mouth fell open, as if she was completely floored, and she appeared not to notice Maggie's proffered hand. Instead, her gaze was riveted on Maggie's tawny hair and green eyes. Then she closed her mouth with a click. 'Not—Margaret Leila Trent?'

'Why, yes!' Maggie beamed at her. 'I don't know how you know that, but that's me.'

'Jack,' Sylvia said hollowly, and turned to him,

'don't tell me this is what I think it is. He'd…' she swallowed visibly '…he'd kill you if he knew…'

'Who?' Maggie said into the sudden deathly silence.

'Your father,' Sylvia whispered. Then she put a hand to her mouth and turned around to run down the steps.

'You stay here, Maggie,' Jack ordered. 'I'll be back as soon as I can.' He followed Sylvia.

CHAPTER FIVE

IT WAS an hour before he came back, a tense, highly uncomfortable hour for Maggie.

She got rid of their uneaten breakfasts and tidied up, but there was a dreadful feeling of apprehension at the pit of her stomach and all her movements were jerky and unco-ordinated.

As far as she was aware he'd never met her father, so what could be involved? Then her mind fastened on something he'd said the day she'd found him here. Something about men and their grievances not being parted lightly.

She'd assumed when he'd said that, and something else she remembered about never seeing eye to eye with her father, that her father's arrogant, high-handed reputation and the ruthless businessman he could be, also by repute, were the things Jack McKinnon took exception to...

Then she remembered his reluctance—she put her hands to her suddenly hot cheeks—to have anything more to do with her after the shed incident. What had she precipitated?

When he came back she was sipping coffee, but sheer nerves made her rush into speech. 'What's going on? How is she? Where is she?'

There was a plunger pot on the veranda table and another mug. He poured coffee for himself in a completely unsmiling way that terrified Maggie all the more.

'She's booked into the resort for the time being. Maggie, believe me…' he pulled out a chair and sank into it '…I would rather—climb Mount Everest—than be the one to tell you this, but since you're here, and this has happened, I don't seem to have any choice.'

'No, you *don't*,' she agreed. 'You obviously *know* my father!'

'Not well,' he said rather grimly. 'Sylvia is the one who knows him, or knew him. They had an affair—' He stopped abruptly at the shocked little sound she made.

'It's common enough,' he said then.

'Well, yes.' She paused and laced her fingers together. 'And my parents haven't—it doesn't exactly seem to be a joyful marriage at times, but they are together so—' She broke off and looked at him with a painful query in her eyes.

'Your father desperately wanted a son and your mother couldn't have any more children.'

A bell rang in the recesses of Maggie's mind. Something her grandmother had said to her, then never explained. Something in response to *her* saying she should have been a boy. *Don't go down that road, Maggie. Your mother has and…* But Leila Trent had never completed the statement.

She blinked several times as she looked back down the years, and it all fell into place. The growing tension between her parents, her mother's anguish, carefully concealed so that her growing daughter would not be affected, but now it came back to Maggie in a hundred little ways… How could she have been so blind? she wondered.

She cleared her throat. 'Go on.'

'Your father met Sylvia about six years ago. They fell in love—at least Sylvia assures me they did. She…' he paused and looked out over the glittering sea with his eyes hard and his mouth set '…fell for him in a big way despite his being married.'

'Did…did he offer to leave my mother and marry her?'

'He certainly led her to expect it. Then things changed dramatically.' He turned back to her. 'Talking of gynaecological problems, Sylvia has had more than her fair share of them and the net result is that she's unable to have children. When your father discovered that, the terms of his proposition changed somewhat. There was no more talk of marriage.'

Maggie went pale.

'I guess,' he said slowly, 'I need to fill you in on a bit of background here. Possibly because we were both adopted—there was never any secret made of it—we had more common ground than many siblings have, Sylvia and I. We looked out for each other as we were growing up. There were times when we almost seemed to be on the same wavelength like twins. So I knew exactly how Sylvia was going through the mill with your father. And I knew she was too loving, too special to be any man's mistress.'

'Did she agree with you?' Maggie asked.

He shrugged. 'Pertinent question. Did I rush in and sort out her life as *I saw fit*?'

'Did you?'

'No. To give your father his due, he was infatuated. Sylvia took the first steps to break it off herself, but he wouldn't hear of it. She finally came to me and begged for help. She said she doubted she would ever love anyone quite like that again, but the sense of inadequacy she felt—your mother may have had the same problem—over this inability to provide sons was crippling her and she had to get out.'

'You...you confronted him?' Maggie hazarded.

He smiled unamusedly. 'Yes.'

'How did you make him see sense?'

Jack stared at her. 'I threatened him with exposure to his wife and his, at the time, seventeen-year-old daughter. You may not realize this, Margaret Leila Trent, but your father, for all his sins and his thirst for a son, loves you dearly. He often talked to Sylvia about you with a great deal of pride.'

There were tears running down Maggie's cheeks. 'I didn't know,' she whispered. She stood up and walked to the veranda railing. 'It's all so sad!' She dashed her cheeks. 'My mother *still* loves him, I'm sure. Sylvia...?' She turned back with a question in her eyes.

'Sylvia went to hell and back.'

Maggie sniffed. 'And that's all you had to do to get him to stop seeing her?'

He folded his arms. 'Yes, but it didn't end there. We've been playing a game of tit for tat ever since.'

Her eyes widened. 'How so?'

'He tried to ruin me financially.' This time his smile was pure tiger. 'But two can play that game, as he's found to his cost several times.'

Maggie sank back into her chair and dropped her face into her hands. 'That's horrible.' She swallowed, then looked up. 'Of course. That explains the revenge element.'

He didn't deny it. He was silent for so long, Maggie found it difficult to breathe as she wondered what was coming.

'It crossed my mind,' he said and grimaced. 'More than once. That is why, Maggie,' he said slowly, 'I dropped you like a hot potato, or tried to.'

She bit her lip and coloured. 'You could have told me this a lot sooner.'

'It was hard enough to tell you now.' He gestured. 'But in the end revenge didn't come into it.' His lips twisted. 'You may be a right chip off the old block in some respects, but in others you're very sweet and lovely and refreshing and I...' he paused '...I just couldn't resist you even although I knew damn well I should.'

'I didn't give you much choice,' she said bravely. 'I...was just like the women who ride off into the sunset with you because they can't help themselves.'

He looked comically confused. 'What women?'

She waved a hand. 'Doesn't matter—'

'I've never ridden off into the sunset with a woman against her better judgement,' he protested. 'I've never "ridden" off with anyone.'

A spark of irritation lit Maggie's eyes. 'Will you leave it? It's just something I thought to myself once, in relation to you, that's all.'

A trickle of understanding came to his eyes. 'I see. Sorry, that was a bit dense.'

'Yes, it was. So, what are we going to do now?'

He finished his coffee and sat back, then, 'You may like to think the responsibility is yours, but it isn't, it's mine, and only I can redeem things. Go back to your family, Maggie, and forget me, otherwise you'll be torn to pieces,' he said very quietly.

'I...my father...' She couldn't go on and her throat worked.

'In a sense I'm as bad as he is,' he pointed out.

'He's also a man to whom sons may legitimately mean a lot, it is quite an empire and a very old name. Mid-life crises can happen to the best of married men and Sylvia is gorgeous. He—'

'Don't,' Maggie begged. 'Don't make any more excuses for him for *my* sake and if you don't mean them. Do you really think any better of him?'

He watched her impassively, then shook his head.

'The other thing is, only—' she pointed to sea where they'd swum '—a couple of hours ago we...we were...' Once again tears started to roll down her cheeks.

'You may never know how hard this is, Maggie,' he said abruptly, 'but one day you'll be grateful. Can you imagine having to tell your mother why your father hates me the way he does?'

That stopped Maggie in her tracks. 'Maybe she knew but decided to live with it?' she whispered.

He shook his head. 'From his reaction when I delivered my threat I could see that neither of you knew.'

Maggie made one last effort. 'What if Sylvia hadn't turned up or found out about me for, well, ages?'

He ran his hand through his hair and sighed. 'No doubt I'd have come to my senses before that.'

'Has this—has ''us'' meant anything to you at all, Jack?'

Her hands were lying helplessly on the table and he reached over to cover one of them with his own. 'Yes, it has, but I'm not the right man for you.'

'Why not? Apart from everything else.'

'You can't separate them, Maggie.' He hesitated, then shrugged. 'I just don't think I'd take well to domesticity.'

'A loner?'

He narrowed his eyes and looked past her. 'That's how I started out in this life. But—' he withdrew his gaze from the past and concentrated on her again '—for the *right* man,' he stressed, 'you're going to be a wonderful wife. A bit of a handful, prone to some excesses like locking people in sheds and—'

She pulled her hand away and stood up as his words acted like a catalyst. She wiped her face with her fingers, but although the tears subsided her heart felt as if it were breaking and all the fight drained out of her.

If he could even *think* of her with another man after what had passed between them, she had to believe that all he felt for her was a passing attraction.

Yes, maybe there was affection too, but not the conviction she held. The conviction that she'd fallen deeply in love with him. Not the pain at the prospect of being parted from him, nor the sheer agony of thinking of him with another woman...

No, she had to believe it hadn't happened for him as it had happened for her and—talk about being torn between him and her family—that would really tear her apart, going on with him under those circumstances.

And she remembered her original proposition—she would take full responsibility for her actions and there would be no recriminations. But how to act on those brave words? something within her cried.

She drew a trembling breath. 'What do they say? You live and learn.' She smiled, but she couldn't eradicate the bitterness from it. 'I'll go now,' she added simply.

He stood up and watched her like a hawk for a moment. 'Will you be all right?'

She cast him a look tinged with irony.

'Look, I know—'

'This will take a bit of getting over?' she suggested. 'Of course.' And she squared her shoulders and tilted her chin at him with further, this time patent irony. 'But I am a Trent, after all.'

'Maggie,' he said exasperatedly, 'I meant will you be all right physically? I long since stopped classing you with your father.'

'Perhaps you shouldn't have, Jack. Physically? Oh, you mean...? Well, I should be fine on both those fronts. I am on the pill and I've been careful about what I ate after the other day. No, I'll be fine.'

She stopped and stared at him. 'Provided I do this very quickly,' she said barely audibly and stood on her toes to kiss him briefly. 'You were...you were everything a girl could pray for. Take care.' She turned away and went inside. He moved, then stilled.

It took her all of five minutes to stuff her possessions into her bag and he carried it to her car.

She said goodbye unemotionally and he did the same. She even drove off with a wave. Two miles down the road she pulled up and was overcome by a storm of weeping and disbelief—how could it have ended like this?

To coin a phrase, she returned to the bosom of her family for a few days despite the new ambivalence of her feelings for her father, but some things had changed, she discovered.

Something in her mother's voice, when she rang her to say she was home, alerted her to it. A new lightness, a younger-sounding voice—I must be imagining it, Maggie thought—but when Belle suggested a family reunion on the cattle station, Maggie gave it some thought. The fact that her father was home had her in two minds, though.

Would she find herself unable to hide her hatred for his actions and the misery they'd caused her and Sylvia McKinnon? Was there any way she could heal the breach between David Trent and Jack McKinnon so there need not be this misery, for her, anyway? Come to that, could she hide her misery and despair from her mother?

In the end her curiosity got the better of her and she used the last few days of her leave to drive up to Kingaroy and the sprawling old wooden homestead, over a hundred years old but now extensively modernized, that had been the birthplace of the Trent dynasty.

She needn't have worried about hiding anything from her parents. By some miracle the breach had been healed. They were in love again and, despite observing the usual courtesies, there might have been only the two of them on the planet.

I don't believe this, Maggie thought. What has happened?

She watched them carefully, especially her father. The tawny hair was a little grey, he was close to fifty now, but even so he was attractive—it was not hard to see how he would have appealed to Sylvia six years ago despite a twenty-year age gap. And as always, when he set himself to be pleasant, he was more than that. He was vital, funny—entirely engaging, in fact, until you ran into the brick wall of the other side of his personality, the high-handed, arrogant side she had clashed with frequently down the years.

To her confusion, however, the weight of Jack's revelations didn't add a black hatred to her difficult feelings for her father.

Because she was so happy to see him making her mother happy again? she wondered.

Because a certain streak of common sense told her there were always two sides to a story such as— Sylvia had known her father was a married man and should have thought twice about breaking up any-one's marriage?

Because David Trent had conveyed enough admi-ration of her, his daughter, to someone else even al-though his thirst for a son had driven him to betraying her mother?

I don't know what to think, she acknowledged. I'm all at sea. What would happen if I told him about Jack and tried to smooth things between them? In this new mood he's in, maybe I could?

But something held her back. Would Jack McKinnon want her permanently in his life under any circumstances? She had strenuously to doubt it. As for her feelings for Jack, she just didn't know where she stood there at all.

Her mother did come down from her cloud nine briefly as Maggie was leaving.

'Darling, are you all right?' she asked anxiously as they were walking to the car. Maggie had taken leave of her father earlier. 'You still seem a little quiet.'

'I'm fine.' Maggie gestured to take in the wide blue sky and the vast dusty paddocks, and artfully changed the subject. 'I don't know how this happened.' She turned to Belle and put her arms around her. 'But I'm very happy for you, Mum. You're looking so beautiful.'

Belle trembled in her daughter's arms. 'You can tell?'

'See those steers in the paddock? They could tell,' Maggie said humorously but lovingly. She disengaged and got into her car. 'Take care of each other,' she added with a wave, and drove off.

She went back to work.

A month after her stay at Cape Gloucester, she went to see her doctor with an incredulous question.

'I thought you told me I was covered against all eventualities?'

'Sit down, Maggie,' he invited. 'What do you mean?'

'I'm pregnant! It's the only explanation I can think of, but I never once forgot to take my pills.'

The doctor digested this and said slowly, 'It was a low-dose pill. Sometimes they're not infallible, as I'm sure I told you—not that we were discussing them so much as a contraceptive at the time, but as a means of helping you with difficult periods. Have you had any cataclysmic upsets?'

Maggie closed her eyes and thought of explaining that she'd fallen in love overnight, she'd pursued her man relentlessly and given him little choice about taking her to bed—events that had gone around and around in her mind and pointed an accusing finger at her each and every time.

'Gastric upsets or the like?' the doctor added.

Her lashes flew up.

'I did mention how they could interfere with the pill,' he said gently.

Maggie put a hand to her mouth. 'I forgot all about that. I...I...was so carried away I didn't even think of it,' she admitted. 'Oh, what a fool I've been!'

'Tell me all about it,' he invited.

Half an hour later, still in a state of shock, she drove home.

The doctor's advice had been copious. Termination was her choice, but even the thought of it was horrific. If she didn't go ahead with that, the father of the child she was carrying deserved to know about it and no child should be completely deprived of its father even if circumstances prevented its parents from living together. And in that event, she should seek moral support from her family.

'If only you knew,' she murmured as she unlocked her front door. 'If only you knew! On the other hand, termination is out of the question, so...'

Three weeks later she was still grappling with her problems on her own when fate took a hand.

The property that had started it all was now officially on the market. It had been advertised and there'd been quite a bit of interest—none from the McKinnon organization or anyone bearing that name, however.

Maggie had been happy to be able to distance herself from it. As the agent who'd received the initial enquiries from the owners it should have been her 'baby'. In other words, even if another on their team sold it, she would still be entitled to some of the commission, but she'd waived that right when she'd taken four weeks' unexpected leave.

But there came a day when a woman rang in requesting an inspection and Maggie was the only one available to do it. Very conscious of the strain she'd put on the team with her unexpected leave, she temporized, then knew she should do it.

She arranged to meet the woman on the property at four in the afternoon and made a note of her name—a Ms Mary Kelly.

It wasn't as beautiful a day as the day she'd met Jack McKinnon on this little bit of heaven, Maggie thought as she pulled her car up behind a smart blue BMW. There were dark clouds chasing across the sky and a threat of rain, but it was still lovely.

She got out and went to meet Ms Kelly, a smartly groomed woman in her forties who also sparkled with intelligence and had a decisive air about her.

As they began their inspection Maggie said, 'Do you intend to live here, Mary?' They'd quickly got onto first-name terms.

'No. I'm doing this inspection on behalf of a— friend,' Mary replied. 'A second opinion is always helpful, isn't it?'

Maggie agreed, but realized suddenly that her usual 'selling persona' wasn't quite in place because she wasn't feeling very well. She struggled on, however. She dredged up several ideas she had for the house, she enthused about the creek, she was just about to suggest a tour of the shed when a violent bout of nausea overtook her and she had to run for a clump of trees where she proceeded to lose her lunch and afternoon tea.

Mary was most concerned and helpful. She dipped

her scarf in the creek, wrung it out and offered it to Maggie to wipe her face and hands.

'Thank you,' Maggie breathed and patted her face with the cool cloth gratefully.

'Something you ate?' Mary Kelly suggested.

'No.' Maggie shook her head, and for some reason, maybe because she'd told no one but her doctor, it all came tumbling out. 'I'm pregnant and this is, so I'm told, morning sickness in the afternoon.' She grimaced ruefully.

'You poor thing,' Mary said slowly and with a gathering frown.

'Oh, it hasn't been too bad! It just.. catches me unawares at times. There.' She rinsed the scarf thoroughly and handed it back. 'Thanks so much—unless you'd rather I kept it and sent it back to you properly laundered? Oh, by the way, no one at the office knows about it yet so—'

'I won't tell them,' Mary promised. 'Are you sure you're all right now?'

'Fine! Would you like to see the shed?'

'No, thank you, I think I've seen enough. Uh…' Mary hesitated as if she had her mind on other matters, then she said, 'Is there much interest in the property?'

'Quite a lot, I believe, although there've been no offers yet.'

'Do you think the owners have much up their sleeve—are prepared to negotiate, in other words?'

'Look, I'm not sure about that. I did have it originally, but Mike Davies is now the agent in charge, so to speak, only he wasn't available this afternoon. What say I get him to give you a call?'

'That would be fine, Maggie. Now you take care! How far along are you?'

'Roughly two months.' Maggie held out her hand. 'Nice to meet you, Mary.'

They parted and Maggie drove home slowly. Although she hadn't got to the shed, the whole exercise had woken all sorts of memories in her and reactivated all sorts of heartaches to fierce and hurtful from the dull pain they'd coagulated into.

She also knew she would have to make some kind of a decision very shortly. Follow her doctor's advice or go into hiding and cope with it all on her own?

In fact, there was only one lessening of the tension for her, and that was her growing curiosity about the baby. And the thought that it might fill the gap in her life Jack McKinnon had created.

She showered and changed into loose long cotton trousers and a long white shirt as the threat of rain earlier became a reality and thrummed on the roof in a series of heavy showers.

She made herself an early dinner, a snack really, of toasted cheese and a salad. She was just sitting down to eat it when her doorbell rang.

Her eyes widened in shock as she opened the door and Jack stood there.

'You!' she breathed and clutched her throat.

'Yes,' he agreed dryly. 'Let me in, Maggie. It's wet out here.'

'Of course.' She stood aside. 'But what are you doing here?'

'Come to see you,' he said briefly. 'Brrr… It's not only wet, there's a distinct tinge of winter in the air.'

'Come into the lounge. It's warm in there.'

He followed her through, then eyed her snack on the coffee-table next to the TV remote.

'I'm not very hungry,' she said defensively.

He looked around the lovely room, then his gaze came back to her and he looked her up and down comprehensively. 'How are you?' he asked abruptly.

She moved and pushed her hands behind her back because they were shaking. Nothing had changed about him, although he was more formally dressed than she'd ever seen him in a beautiful charcoal suit with a pale grey shirt and a bottle-green tie with anchors on it.

But his clothes didn't change him. They added a kind of 'high boardroom flyer' touch, but they didn't disguise the perfection of his physique. His streaky fair hair was shorter and tamed, but he still had a tan, and she could see him in her mind's eyes, aboard *The Shiralee* wearing only shorts...

She couldn't read his grey eyes at all—why had he come? Was it to say—*I made a mistake, Maggie. I can't live without you...?*

'Maggie?'

'I'm fine,' she said jerkily. 'Sit down. Would you like something?'

'No, thanks. Don't let your supper get cold.'

'Oh, that's all right.' She sat down and pushed the plate away.

He sat down opposite and studied her penetratingly. Then he said quietly, 'Any news?'

Foolishly, her mind went quite blank. What's he asking me? she wondered. How can there be any news? He was the one who sent me away... 'No,' she said bewilderedly.

His mouth hardened for some reason. 'I'd more or

less made up my mind to buy that property, you know.'

Maggie blinked. 'The one…?'

'The one with the shed that was hijacked to house a stolen vintage car and bike; the one you locked us into,' he said deliberately.

She blushed.

'But I decided to get a second opinion,' he went on, 'from someone whose judgement I value.'

'A second opinion,' Maggie repeated as the words struck a chord in her mind and it started to race.

'Yes,' he agreed. 'I think Maisie's name has cropped up between us before. She's my right-hand man. I rely on her extensively.'

Maggie blinked furiously. 'But there's no Maisie at the McKinnon Corporation, I checked,' she blurted out, then her cheeks burnt even more fierily. 'I mean—'

'That's because I'm the only one at the office who calls her Maisie. Her real name…' he paused and their gazes clashed '…is Mary Kelly.'

Maggie froze. 'She…she told you?' she breathed.

'Yes.'

'But that's not fair! I had no idea who she was. I would *never* have—' She stopped abruptly.

'Told her you were pregnant otherwise? How about telling me? I gather you hadn't planned to do that either.'

Maggie got up and paced around in deep agitation with the bottom line being—*So much for the I can't live without you, Maggie, bit.*

Then she turned to him incredulously. 'How would she know it was your baby?'

'She didn't. But she did know about what happened

in the shed because I alerted her to be on the lookout for any unforeseen complications while I was away. When she came back to me with her report this afternoon, she told me it was you who'd shown her around—and the rest of it.'

Silence stretched between them until he added, 'I was the one left to put two and two together—although Maisie is very adroit at reading between the lines.'

Maggie sat down again suddenly. 'When I said there was no news, I think I must have been still in shock at seeing you again. My mind just went blank.'

'OK, reasonable enough. What about the two months prior to tonight?'

Maggie rubbed her face, then she laced her fingers and said urgently, 'I just haven't known what to do!'

'How did it happen?' he queried grimly. 'You seemed so certain you were safe; you *told* me you were on the pill.'

'I was,' she said hollowly and explained what must have happened.

'Do your parents know?'

'No.'

He stared at her, taking in the faint shadows beneath her eyes and her slender figure beneath the long white shirt and flimsy trousers. There was no sign of any changes in her as yet—or, yes, there was, he thought suddenly. There was a new air of vulnerability about her.

'There's only one thing to do,' he said. 'The sooner you marry me, the better.'

CHAPTER SIX

MAGGIE reached towards her plate and took a carrot stick out of the salad, a purely reflex action as the impact of what Jack had said hit her.

Then she stared at him with the wand of carrot in one hand and her mouth open.

A glint of humour lit his eyes. 'A curious reaction. I can't read it at all.'

She closed her eyes. 'That's because I can't read my emotions at the moment at all.' Her lashes lifted. 'You're not serious?'

'Oh, yes, I am.'

'But, apart from all the complications you so carefully pointed out to me at Cape Gloucester, you don't particularly want to marry anyone, do you? Unless that was a sop to my sensibilities, but that's even worse because it means you particularly didn't want to marry me!'

'Eat the carrot or put it down, Maggie,' he suggested.

She stared at him, then threw it down on the plate because a moment or so ago she might have been shell-shocked and unable to get in touch with her emotions—that could have been true of her for the last two months, she realized—but she was no longer.

Jack McKinnon had hurt her almost unbearably, she now knew. Yes, a lot of it was her own fault, but that didn't alter her vulnerability to this man, and to let him marry her only because of their baby—was that asking for *more* hurt than she could bear?

'I got myself into this,' she said. 'I will handle it.'

This time it was a glint of anger that lit his eyes. 'Don't go all proud "Trent" on me, Maggie,' he warned. 'If you think that I, of all people, would allow you to wander off into the sunset with a child of mine, think again.'

Her eyes widened as she realized what he was saying, but there was more.

'If you think I would allow a child of mine to be swallowed up in the midst of *your* family—that is also simply not on the cards.'

She swallowed a couple of times. 'Look, I know that as an adoptee yourself you…you must feel pretty strongly about this, but I would never deny you access to your child—'

'And do you think you're strong enough to hold out against your father, Maggie, if he sees things differently? I don't. So we'll both be there for it, whether you like it or not.'

She stood up tensely. 'It's not a question of liking it or not! What I'm talking about is a shotgun marriage—'

'That is another possibility.' He lay back in his chair and steepled his fingers. 'You could find your father does come after me with a shotgun.'

'Nonsense!'

'I'm speaking metaphorically, but marriage, even to me, may be his preferred option for his only daughter rather than single motherhood.'

It came to Maggie in a blinding flash that perhaps even her sanity and therefore the welfare of her baby could be at risk if she allowed herself to become a pawn between these two powerful, arrogant men. Yes, two—I was right about you in the first place, Jack McKinnon! she said to him in her mind.

She put her hand on her flat stomach, thought of the life within her, and breathed deeply. Then she picked up the cordless phone on the coffee-table, and she dialled the Kingaroy homestead number, where she knew her parents were still holidaying.

She suffered a moment of anguish while the phone rang at the thought of their, particularly her mother's, new happiness, but how happy would either of them be if she ran away?

'Dad?' she said when her father answered. 'It's Maggie. Will you please just listen to me? I happened to meet and have an affair with a man you detest, Jack McKinnon. I know what all the bad blood is about, but I will *never* let Mum know. Unfortunately—'

She paused and listened for a while, then, 'Dad, please, if you love me at all, just listen. I was the one who did the chasing, not Jack. Unfortunately, and this was also my own fault entirely, I'm pregnant. Jack has decided I should marry him although our affair was—completely over before I realized I was pregnant. But while I'm immensely concerned about this baby's welfare, I don't think a loveless marriage is the solution—'

Once again she broke off and listened, then, 'No, Dad, I won't be doing that either. I appreciate your concern but this is the point I need to make you both understand—neither of you can make me do anything. In fact, if you continue this feud and—' she raised her eyes to Jack's '—either of you make my life unbearable, I'll go away where neither of you can find me.'

Her eyes didn't leave Jack's face while she listened again, then she looked away and said into the phone, 'I'm *sorry*, Dad, I know this must have come as a shock. Please break it gently to Mum. I love you both, but I meant every word I said.' She put the phone down.

Jack stirred at last. 'Was that slamming the shed door well and truly, Maggie?'

She shrugged. 'I've been living in a terrible vacuum since I found out. How to tell you? How to tell them? What to do? Until it suddenly came to me I'm no one's hostage and what I'll be doing is staying right here and continuing my job as long as I'm able, and letting this baby grow in peace. Yes, I was angry,' she conceded.

'Who's to say it would be a loveless marriage?' he queried.

'Jack—' she rubbed her face wearily '—you have given me absolutely no indication to the contrary—'

'Because I didn't burst in on you and sweep you into my arms?' he asked. 'Your father isn't the only one to get a shock today.'

She rubbed her knuckles on her chin. 'I know. I'm sorry.' She gestured helplessly.

'As a matter of fact, the thought of my own child has had a rather startling effect on me.'

'Me too,' she conceded. 'I mean, it could probably be quite an interesting child.' A ghost of a smile touched her lips.

'It would certainly give us a lot of common ground.'

His words hung in the air, but Maggie was too tired

and emotionally wrung out to continue the contest. She simply stared at him with deeper shadows etched beneath her eyes and her face very pale.

He frowned, then he got up and came round to her. He took her hand and drew her to her feet.

'You're extraordinarily brave and feisty, Maggie, but you don't have to bear this burden on your own. No,' he said as her lips parted, 'don't say anything now. But I do have your welfare, just as much as the baby's, very much at heart. Think that over, but, in the meantime, get a good night's sleep.'

His lips twisted, then he went on, 'It may have been equivalent to slamming the shed door, but you certainly cleared the air.' He kissed her gently. 'I'll see myself out. By the way, don't forget to eat. It's important now.'

Maggie inhaled deeply as he walked away from her, and closed her eyes. The brush of his lips on hers had taken her right back to Cape Gloucester and the times she'd spent in his arms and his bed.

'I really loved you, Jack McKinnon, but I don't believe you will ever really love me because if it hadn't been for—fate—you would never have come back to me,' she whispered. 'That is so sad.'

Despite the deep well of sadness she felt, after taking the phone off the hook, she went to bed and slept like a top, the first time for ages. This was just as well since her mother and father arrived on her doorstep early the next morning.

Over the next days Maggie continued resolutely along the course she'd set for herself.

She told Jack that she still couldn't see her way clear to marrying him because—apart from anything else and there was plenty of that!—if he hadn't seen himself as the right man for her before, a baby wasn't going to change things.

He took it with surprising equanimity, although she intercepted one tiger-like little glance from him that seemed to say, We'll see about that. But she didn't see it again and she decided she'd imagined it.

She told her parents that they had to accept the fact that she'd come of age in her own way and she'd made her own mistakes. She told them that Jack would always be a part of her life now because of their child and would they please, please make the best of it.

It was her mother who surprised her. To her intense relief none of the new closeness between her parents seemed to have been lost beneath the weight of her news. But while her father's face changed and hardened at every mention of Jack's name, Belle, if she felt any animosity towards the man responsible for this contretemps, didn't show it.

Then she took Maggie aside and said to her quietly, 'I know all about it now.'

Maggie stared at her. 'You mean…you mean…?'

'Sylvia McKinnon?' Belle nodded. 'Your father, well, we'd been at odds for some time before it happened. I felt inadequate and angry because I knew how much he longed for a son, he felt guilty and defensive and it coloured our whole relationship. I knew he was restless and unhappy six years ago and that there was probably another woman in his life although I didn't know—I didn't want to know who it was.'

Belle paused and Maggie spoke. 'You're making it

sound as if Dad—as if *you* were the one at fault; that's crazy!'

'Darling…' Belle smiled a little painfully '…I know that, but sometimes these urges are so powerful in men you can't fight them. The important thing is, your father finally fought it himself and he's come back to me. In many ways we're happier now than we've ever been.'

Maggie stared down at her hands a trifle forlornly.

'There is still,' Belle said, 'the problem of Jack McKinnon.'

'I know. Men don't part with their grievances towards each other lightly.'

'You're not wrong!' Belle looked humorous. 'Tell me about him? By the way, I may not get your father to do this yet, but I intend to meet him.'

Maggie hesitated, then she told her mother everything. 'Of course this is only between you, me and the gatepost,' she finished.

'Of course. So you fell in love but he didn't?'

Maggie got up and wandered over to the window. They were in her bedroom on the second floor and she looked down over her colourful garden. 'Yes,' she said at last. 'That's why I can't accept second-best from him.'

A week later her mother did meet Jack and, although it had to be inherently awkward and there was a certain reserve that Maggie detected in Belle, it went well. Jack was quiet but courteous.

He was the first to leave and Maggie found her mother staring at her—well, staring right through her, actually.

'What?' she queried.

'Nothing,' her mother replied absently.

'What did you think of him?' The question came out before Maggie could guard against it and she bit her lip.

'They could be two of a kind.'

Maggie's eyes widened. 'Jack and Dad? That's exactly what I thought in the beginning!'

'Yes, well…' Belle seemed to come to a decision, and she imparted some surprising news to Maggie. Her father had bid successfully on three cattle stations and for the next few months they would be spending most of their time on them in Central Queensland.

'That's quite a coup,' Maggie said dazedly.

Belle agreed. 'Will you come with us? We'd love to have you.'

'No. No… I'm fine here.' But would she be, she wondered, without her mother's moral support?

'Of course I'll come and see you frequently, darling,' Belle assured her, 'and I'll only ever be a phone call and a short flight away.'

It wasn't until months later that Maggie realized what a clever strategy of her mother's this was…

Three months went by and at last Maggie started to show some signs of her pregnancy.

They went surprisingly swiftly, those months. She made all the difficult explanations—much less difficult than the ones to her parents and Jack, but not easy either. It was one thing to announce you were pregnant and to produce a partner even if he wasn't a husband, quite another to have to explain you were doing it on your own.

Her boss was clearly concerned for her, but he did

agree it made no difference to her work and she could continue for as long as she wanted to.

'You have a real flair for it, Maggie,' he said to her. 'A born natural, you are.' Then he frowned and seemed about to say more, but he obviously changed his mind.

Tim Mitchell was the hardest of all to tell. He was horrified, he was mystified and he offered to marry her himself there and then.

She thanked him with real gratitude, but declined. And she gradually withdrew herself from the crowd they both moved in.

'You don't have to do that, Maggie,' Tim said reproachfully. 'You need friends at least!'

'Yes, but I'm a different person now. I guess I have different priorities. Tim…' she hesitated but knew she had to do it '…I'm a lost cause, but there's got to be the *right* girl for you out there and you should forget about me—like that, anyway.' She stopped rather painfully as her words raised echoes in her mind she'd rather forget. But after that, she always found an excuse not to see Tim.

The one person apart from her family she couldn't seem to withdraw from was Jack.

He came to see her frequently in those months, although he never repeated his offer of marriage. It puzzled her that he should do this—at least as frequently as he did. It made it harder for her because of all the memories it brought back, but every time she thought of refusing to see him, she also thought of her promise never to separate him from his child.

She knew that she *could* never do that and, not only because he simply wouldn't have it, but also because he'd let her glimpse the pain and trauma of being abandoned by your natural parents.

She told herself that it was going to be a fact of her life from now on, his platonic presence in it, and she might as well get used to it. And it was platonic. He didn't try to touch her; he didn't refer to Cape Gloucester.

It was as if the desire he'd once felt for her had been turned off at the main switch and that caused her a lot of soul-searching. Had it been *such* a light-hearted affair for him? Had he achieved his revenge with spectacular success? Was there another woman in his life now? Was he turned off by pregnancy?

Perhaps I should check that out with Aunt Elena, she thought once, with dry humour.

The same couldn't be said for her. Yes, she'd suffered a couple of months of numbness after leaving him. In contrast now she was visited acutely at times by cameos from their past, like the one when they'd dragged an inflatable mattress out onto the veranda under a full, golden moon...

'We could be anywhere,' she said dreamily as they lay side by side on a cool linen sheet and the dusky pink pillows from his bed. 'On a raft up the Nile.'

'What made you think of that?'

'Well, you can hear the water, it is a wooden floor. Gloucester Island could be a pyramid sailing past.' She turned on her front and propped her chin on her hands so she could watch him. 'Have you ever been up the Nile?'

'Yes, I have.' He had one arm bent behind his head and he cupped her shoulder with his free hand and slid his finger beneath the broad lacy strap of her sleepwear. 'Have you?'

'Mmm… With my parents when I was sixteen. I loved it. Sadly, however, the whole experience was so momentous, I made myself sick.'

A smile flickered across his lips. 'That could have been the Egyptian version of Delhi belly.'

She bent her knees and crossed her ankles in the air. 'I think Africa would suit you,' she told him reflectively, 'or would have in times gone past.'

'I do remind you of Dr Livingstone? How?' he queried amusedly.

'No. But maybe Denys Finch-Hatton. I've seen his grave in the Ngong Hills, you know.'

'Same trip?'

She nodded. 'And Karen Blixen's house. It's preserved in her memory. The Danish government gave it to the Kenyan government on independence. She's a bit of a hero of mine.'

He turned his head towards her. 'Are you trying to tell me I'm a disappointment to you because I'm no Denys Finch-Hatton?' he queried gravely.

She denied this seriously. 'Not at all.'

'You did say something about taking me for a more physical guy.'

Maggie curled her toes. 'I just got that impression—well, yes, it presented itself to me in the form of hunting wild animals, crewing racing yachts et cetera, but translated it seemed to me that you liked to test yourself to the limit.'

He was silent for an age, just stroking her shoulder, then, 'In lots of ways I do—and did. When I started out, using the bank's money, not mine, I took some

huge gambles. I often had to strain every nerve just
to keep my head above water.'

'Did you enjoy that?'

He grinned fleetingly. 'There were times when I
was scared to death, but on the whole, I guess I did.'

'So I was right about you all along,' she said with
deep satisfaction.

'Wise as well as beautiful…' He drew the strap of
her top down. 'Striking as this outfit is, I've got the
feeling it's going to get in my way.'

Maggie flipped over onto her back and sat upright.
'This outfit' was a camisole pyjama top in topaz silk
edged with ivory lace and a matching pair of boxer
shorts.

'That could be remedied.' She slipped the top off
over her head.

He watched her as she sat straight-backed with her
legs crossed, like a naked ivory statue in the moonlight, slim, beautifully curved, grave, young and gorgeous. Her hair was tied up loosely with wavy tendrils
escaping down her neck.

He sat up abruptly. 'If we changed the location
slightly, moved this raft east across the desert sands,
say, I could be the Sheik of Araby and you could be
a candidate for my harem.'

Maggie's lashes fluttered and she turned to him
with an incredulous look, but a little pulse beating
rather rapidly at the base of her throat.

'Jack! That's very—fanciful.'

He grimaced. 'Surprised you?'

'Uh—' she licked her lips '—yes.'

He shook his head wryly. 'I've surprised myself,
but that's how you make me feel at this moment and

you were the one who put us in another spot in the first place.'

She thought for a moment, then bowed her head. 'Do I qualify?'

'Oh, yes, fiery little one,' he drawled. 'You do.'

'Fiery?' She lifted her head.

He touched one nipple, then the other, then he trailed his fingers down her spine towards her bottom. 'Fiery, delicious, peachy—definitely peachy. I knew I was right about that even if I couldn't understand it at the time.'

'Right?' She looked confused. 'What do you mean?'

He laughed softly. 'Don't worry about it. Come here.'

She moved into his arms and not much later he made exquisite love to her in the moonlight, on their raft anchored in the sands of Araby.

Two things Jack touched on during his visits were rather surprising. His latest development project, a retirement village, and the property he'd bought.

'Not the one with a shed hijacked to hide some vintage vehicles, the one I locked us into?' she said, her eyes wide with surprise as she unconsciously repeated how he'd described it the last time it had been mentioned between them. 'I happen to know it's been sold to a company, Hanson Limited, or something like that.'

'It's one of my companies.'

It was a Sunday morning and he'd arrived just as she was starting a late breakfast. He wore a navy tracksuit and running shoes, his hair was windblown and he was glowing with vim and vigour.

'Good,' he added as he sat down at her breakfast table. 'I'm starving.'

'What have you been doing?' Maggie asked as she got out more plates and cutlery.

'A two-mile jog down Main Beach.'

'Then you might need something more substantial.. like steak and eggs.' She looked at him humorously.

He scanned the table. There was yoghurt and fruit, rolls and jam and, striking a slightly discordant note, a steaming bowl of chicken noodle soup.

He eyed it. 'Going for oriental cuisine, Maggie?'

She shrugged. 'I just get this incredible craving for chicken noodle soup. It can happen to me at any time of the day or night.'

'Out of a packet?'

'Oh, no. I make it myself so I can keep the level of salt down and there are no preservatives. I'm taking very good care of your unborn baby, Jack.'

He laughed. 'I wasn't suggesting otherwise. Well, don't let it get cold, I'll look after myself.'

'There's some leg ham and a nice piece of Cheddar in the fridge.' Maggie lifted a spoonful of soup to her mouth and blew on it gently. 'Help yourself if you like.'

He raised a wry eyebrow. 'A continental breakfast? I will, thanks.'

'So you bought it after all,' she said when he'd assembled a much larger breakfast and was tucking into it.

'Mmm… I thought you might be interested. Maisie said you had some good ideas for the house.'

'I'm sure you could afford to pull it down and start again.'

'I know you may still cherish the opinion that I delight in destroying landscapes and pulling things down to put up new ones, but in this case I don't,' he said mildly. 'That house has a lot of character and potential.'

Maggie drank her soup, having had the wind somewhat taken out of her sails. Nor was it that that she had against Jack McKinnon any longer, she reminded herself. It was the fact that he could arrive uninvited at her breakfast table, make himself completely at home—well, she had suggested that, but all the same—and, treacherously, it reminded her of all the breakfasts they'd shared at Cape Gloucester.

One particularly came to mind…

'What will we do today?'

He eyed her seriously. They'd had an early morning swim and she wore her pink bikini with her sarong knotted between her breasts. They were drinking coffee at the breakfast bar.

'Nothing,' he said.

'Nothing?' She wrinkled her nose at him. 'How idle!'

'I didn't plan to be completely idle. Perhaps decadent would be a better word for it—starting now.' He put his mug down and carefully untied the knot between her breasts to release her sarong, then he reached round and undid her bikini top.

Maggie looked downwards, entranced and feeling her heart start to beat heavily at the sight of his lean brown hands on her breasts.

'It doesn't feel decadent to me,' she said softly and bit her lip as her nipples flowered and a wash of sensuousness ran through her body.

'Actually—' he looked up briefly '—I can't think of anything more lovely and fresh and entirely the opposite from decadent than you, Ms Trent.'

'So?' Maggie queried with difficulty.

'I was referring to the time of day, that's all. Eight o'clock in the morning is not renowned for its romantic properties. Moonlit evenings, starry, starry nights, dawn, perhaps?' He looked into her eyes and shook his head. 'However…'

She put her hands on his shoulders and rested her forehead against his. 'Eight o'clock in the morning feels very romantic to me.'

He lifted her off her stool to sit across his lap, and slid his hands beneath her bikini bottom to cup her hips. 'You are a siren, you know,' he said against the corner of her mouth.

'Not Delilah?'

'Her too… Come to bed.'

She came out of her reverie feeling hot and cold, aroused and with her senses clamouring for that touch on her body again as she remembered the slow, perfectly lovely way he'd made love to her despite it being eight o'clock in the morning.

I thought I had it all sorted out, she reflected bitterly. I was no one's hostage; I was this independent, mature—recently matured but all the same—person in charge of my own destiny. So why can't I forget Cape Gloucester and all the things he did to me?

'I did have some ideas,' she said abruptly, anything to banish those images from her mind. 'But they wouldn't—' she wrinkled her nose as she forced herself to concentrate '—come cheap.'

'Spoken like a true Trent,' he murmured, and

grinned at her expression. 'That's fine with me. If I'm going to do it I want to do it properly. Tell me your thoughts.'

She did. And she couldn't fight the quickening of interest she felt.

CHAPTER SEVEN

THE next time Jack came to see Maggie, as usual unannounced, he dumped a heap of blueprints on her coffee-table.

'What on earth…?' She stared at him.

'I'm planning a retirement village. I do not want it to resemble a bloody chicken coop, but it has to stay affordable. What do you think of these?'

She took her time as she paged through the designs. 'Ghastly,' she pronounced at last. 'They're so poky!'

'That's what I told the architect. He's withdrawn from the project. On the other hand, they are retirement homes, not vast mansions.'

Maggie pulled some cushions behind her back, which ached occasionally nowadays, and considered the matter. 'I think it would be a help if they were more open plan. Separate bedrooms, yes, but not separate boxy little kitchens, dining rooms and lounges, so you got a more spacious feel even if it isn't necessarily so.'

He waited alertly as she thought some more.

'And since they don't have gardens—'

'Retirees are generally longing to get away from being slaves to lawnmowers and the like,' he put in.

'Perhaps,' she conceded, 'but a decent veranda so they can grow some nice pot plants and herbs if they want to would be…would be a priority of mine.'

'There are going to be plenty of landscaped gardens,' he murmured. 'All taken care of for them.'

'It's not the same as suddenly being cut off from growing anything of your *own*,' she countered. 'In fact, if I were planning a retirement village, I'd set aside a section where those interested could have their own little plots to grow their own vegetables or whatever they liked.'

'You are a gardening fanatic, Maggie,' he pointed out and glanced at the riot of colour outside.

She shrugged. 'Those are my ideas!'

'OK. I'll come back to you on it.'

'Why me?' she asked.

'I think you might have a feel for these things which could be helpful to me, Ms Trent. I've never done a retirement village before. I've been more concerned with kids and families.'

'Oh.'

He looked amused. 'If you feel like doing some designing, some doodles even, I'd be very appreciative.'

Maggie blinked, but she allowed the matter to drop.

For some reason, she'd recently begun to feel as if she'd walked into a brick wall and nothing was of more than passing interest to her.

Or rather, one reason for it was loud and clear. Added to her memories, added to her growing desire to drop all her defences and say simply to Jack, Marry me, please, I need you and I can't do this on my own, was her growing curiosity about other women in his life. It haunted her. There were times when it made her hate him and be prickly and uncommunicative with him. It sapped her energy. It was entirely unreasonable, she tried to tell herself.

You wouldn't marry him when the offer was open. Perhaps the best thing for you *is* to hate him...

On the other hand, when she wasn't being cross and out of sorts with him, she had to admit that his presence in her life was a bit like a rock she was coming to rely on.

What a mess you are, Maggie, she thought frequently.

She was five and a half months pregnant when he called in one chilly evening after dinner time.

They talked about nothing very much for a while, then he fell silent as his grey gaze flickered over her. She wore a loose ivory wool sweater over dark green tartan stretch pants. The sleeves of the sweater were a fraction too long for her and sometimes she folded them back, but they always unrolled.

Was it that, he wondered, that gave her a waif-like air? The exposure of her fragile wrists? Her loose hair tucked behind her ears? Her cream flat shoes that reminded him of ballet shoes?

Or her secretive eyes?

Grave and secretive now, when they'd been like windows of her soul only a few months ago. Capable of teasing him, querying him or laughing at him in a swift green glance, expressing honest desire. Expressing joy or, of course, sparkling with anger. But that had been longer ago, the anger, and what crazy voice in him told him he'd prefer that to this secretiveness?

'How are you feeling?' he asked abruptly.

'Fine,' she replied automatically.

'No, tell me.' He'd come straight from a business dinner and hadn't discarded his jacket, although he'd loosened his tie.

Maggie pushed a cushion behind the small of her

back. 'Apart from a bit of backache I do feel fine.
The morning—afternoon sickness has gone and I'm
told this middle trimester, before you get too heavy
and slow, is when you should really glow.' She grimaced.

'But you're not glowing, are you?' he said quietly.

She shrugged and stood up suddenly. 'According
to my doctor every pregnancy can be different. Would
you like a cup of tea? Or a drink? I'm dying for a
cuppa.'

'Thanks, I'll have one too.'

She turned away, but not before he noted some
differences in her figure. Her wrists might look fragile, but those high, firm little gymnast's breasts were
ripening and her waist was no longer reed-slim...

When she brought the tea tray back, he studied it
rather than her figure.

He knew she liked Earl Grey tea so he wasn't surprised at the subtle fragrance of citrus oil of Bergamot
that rose above the lovely china cups as she poured
boiling water into them.

He knew she drank hers black and sugarless, but
she hadn't forgotten that he took milk. He knew she
always deposited the tea bags into an antique silver
dish decorated with griffins rampant.

'All the same, why is that, do you think?' he queried as he accepted his cup and took a shortbread
biscuit from the salver she offered.

'Why is what?'

'Is it the strain of being a single mother? Is that
why you're not glowing, since there aren't any other
problems?' he said deliberately.

She sat down and tucked her legs up. 'You'd be
the last person I'd confess that to—if it were true.'

'In case I repeated my offer of marriage? I'm not.'

She pushed her sleeves back and wrapped her hands around her cup. 'No, it wouldn't make any difference. It's still no one's fault but my own that I find myself a bit daunted at times, but especially not yours, that's why I wouldn't admit it to you.' She hesitated. 'It's probably only because it's such new territory and many a new mum might feel a bit daunted anyway.'

'Have you made any preparations for the baby?'

A glint of humour beamed his way. 'Jack, whenever my mother comes to visit me, which is frequently, we do nothing else. That's not quite true— we go to the movies, concerts and so on and every few weeks she insists I spend a weekend on the cattle stations with them. But this baby will have everything that opens and shuts; more clothes than any single baby could wear, many of them exquisitely hand stitched. She loves doing that kind of delicate sewing.'

'OK.' He finished his tea and thought for a bit. 'What about your other social life?'

She wrinkled her nose. 'What social life?'

'Well, girlfriends, then?'

Maggie sighed unexpectedly. 'One or two, but I think I may have been a bit—I don't know—I think I may have given off pretty strong vibes that I would rather be alone.'

'And Tim Mitchell?'

She flinched.

'Did he drop you like the proverbial hot potato?'

'Oh, no. He offered to marry me.'

'I hope you turned him down flat,' he said and was rewarded by a definitely hostile green glance.

'Tim would make a fine husband,' she said tersely.

'Come on, Maggie,' he drawled, knowing full well he was out to hurt and anger her further, as if he had the devil himself riding him, 'that would have been a recipe for disaster. At least you loved going to bed with me.'

'Don't say—'

'Another word? Why not? It's true. You certainly made love to me as if you loved every minute of it. You tracked me down where no outsider has ever been able to find me to do so, come to that,' he said lazily, then added, 'And all the while you had Tim Mitchell virtually sitting in your lap.'

Maggie gasped. 'That's…that's—'

But he broke in before she could go on. 'If you're contemplating a loveless marriage to anyone, Maggie, I fail to see what Tim Mitchell has over me. Then again, I did think that's what you were expressly holding out against.'

'I am. If you'd allowed me to finish you would have heard me say that Tim would make a fine husband for the right person who was not *me*.'

'Bravo,' he applauded. 'I'm all in favour of sticking to your guns. Did that ring a bell with you, though?'

'It gave me a distinct sense of *déjà vu*,' she replied through her teeth. 'Why are you being so—horrible?'

He shrugged. 'I thought you needed taking out of yourself a bit.' He ignored her incredulous expression. 'How's the job going?'

Maggie opened her mouth to dispose of this query summarily, but something stopped her. Did she need taking out of herself? Was she floundering in a slough of despond?

'I'm giving it up in a fortnight.' She sniffed suddenly. 'I seem to have lost my edge. It's become a bit of a chore rather than a pleasure. Besides which…' she looked down at herself ruefully '…I've got the feeling I'm about to burst out all over and driving around a lot and getting in and out of cars may not be too comfortable.'

He smiled, and it was almost as if he'd gone from tiger mode to gentle mode in the blink of an eye. 'You could be right. How about working from home? For me, I mean, or as an associate?'

Maggie stared at him.

'I adapted the retirement village to your ideas, but now I need an interior decorator.' He paused and looked around. 'You have some wonderful ideas and taste.'

Maggie stared at him with her lips parted this time.

'You seem to have pretty strong convictions about retirement homes,' he said into the silence with a tinge of irony.

'Are you furnishing them?' she queried.

'Not all of them. There are several levels of accommodation. The ones I will be furnishing are for single occupants, widows and widowers mostly, I guess. I'd like them to be—cheerful and comfortable. But even the ones I don't furnish will need colour schemes, carpets, curtains, kitchen and bathroom finishes, et cetera.'

'And…' she licked her lips '…you…you think I could do all that from home?'

'I don't see why not. Of course you can check out the site as often as you like, but Maisie could organize all the samples—fabrics, carpet, paint—to be sent here.'

She stared at him again, transfixed.

He waited for a moment, then added, 'I've also set aside some land that can be divided into plots for keen gardeners.'

Why that did it, she wasn't sure, but all of a sudden, although it was a huge project, it beckoned her in a way that lifted her spirits immediately.

She opened her mouth to say the first thing that popped into her mind—*What a pity you don't love me, Jack*—but at the last moment she amended it to, 'Why are you doing this?'

'I told you. Your welfare is important to me, as well as the kid's.'

She fell asleep with tears on her cheeks that night because that unbidden, out-of-context thought—*what a pity you don't love me, Jack*—had revealed to her that she still hungered for his love; perhaps she always would. Why it had popped into her mind, she wasn't sure. Because he'd taken her advice to heart on garden plots for retirees? That didn't make much sense. Or did it? Could they become quite a team in every respect but the one that mattered most and it broke her heart to think of it?

Her life changed, her outlook in most respects changed from then on, however. During the last few months of her pregnancy she became very busy and found it fulfilling. She did pop out in some directions, but she did also glow, at times, at last.

She also got closer to Jack and the McKinnon empire. She accepted an advisory position on his board, although she demurred at first on the grounds of the speculation it might produce along the lines of whose baby she was carrying.

'That's no one's business but our own, Maggie,' he said decidedly. 'Anyway, no one knows of our connection. I haven't told anyone.'

'Not even Maisie?'

'Not even Maisie, although she may suspect, but she's the soul of discretion. Have you told anyone?'

'Who the father is? No.'

They eyed each other until he said, 'Well, then? It could be the start of a new, more suitable career for you as a single mother.'

Maggie opened her mouth, but, much as she would have loved to refute this for reasons not at all clear to her, she couldn't deny it was something she should give thought to.

'You could be right,' she said eventually.

She got to know his sub-penthouse, which was where he did his business entertaining. It was elegant but restrained and she got the feeling that if he felt really at home anywhere, it was Cape Gloucester.

She experienced the dynamic businessman he was at firsthand and knew that she and her mother had been right: he could be as arrogant and ruthless as her father, but he did temper it so that all his employees were devoted to him and his partners in any ventures respected him highly.

Sylvia came to see her out of the blue one day.

'I got Jack's permission to do this,' she said as she stood on the doorstep.

Still blinking with surprise, Maggie said, 'You

didn't need his permission! Uh—come in. I didn't know you knew…'

'I didn't until a couple of days ago when I came up to tell him some news of my own. I do find,' Sylvia said wryly when they were settled in the lounge, 'that it's not a good idea to cross Jack these days. Actually, it never was, because even as a kid he had an infuriating habit of being right about most things.'

'I know the kind.' Maggie looked heavenwards.

'I suppose you do. You got sandwiched between two such men, didn't you?'

The reference to her father chilled Maggie a little and perhaps Sylvia sensed it because she went on in a sudden rush. 'I was as much to blame as your father was. I knew he was married. I should never have got involved.'

Maggie thawed, she couldn't help it, but she also said honestly, 'I wondered about that. Still, these things happen, I guess.'

'Something else has happened to me. I've fallen in love again when I thought it could never happen to me.'

'Not a married man?'

'Not a married man, but he will be married to me shortly.'

On an impulse Maggie got up and crossed over to Sylvia to hug her with some difficulty that caused them both to laugh.

'I'm so happy for you,' Maggie said, with a genuine feeling of warmth.

'Would there be—any possibility your mother and father have—have…?' Sylvia hesitated.

'Got together again?' Maggie supplied. 'Yes! They have and it's wonderful to see.'

Sylvia breathed deeply. 'That's an enormous relief. But has he forgiven you for Jack, and this?'

'This?' Maggie patted her stomach affectionately. 'He's putting a good face on it. I don't think they'll ever be friends, but somehow or other I made them see that they had to be civilized at least. Not that they've met yet.'

'Maggie, why won't you marry Jack?'

'Sylvia...' Maggie paused and searched Sylvia's blue eyes '...you could be the one person who knows how hard it is to pin the real Jack McKinnon down. I think there's a core in him that will always shy away...' she stopped to think carefully '...from any true attachment and it goes right back to being put up for adoption as a baby.'

Sylvia heaved a sigh. 'Even under a loving adoption arrangement, it can be like a thorn in your flesh or you can secretly hold the belief that your mother was this wonderful, wonderful person who is always tied to you by an invisible string. That's the path I opted for. Jack went the other way. You could be right but—'

'The thing is,' Maggie interrupted quietly, 'I'm an all-or-nothing kind of person.' She raised her eyebrows. 'In lots of respects I've come to see I might be a chip off the old block, after all.'

'He, Jack, I mean—'

Again Maggie interrupted. 'He's been wonderful in lots of ways.'

'He was wonderful to me when I—when your father—without Jack to pick up the pieces, I don't know where I'd be.'

'Yes, he is rather good at picking up the pieces, isn't he?' Maggie said slowly.

Sylvia looked awkward. 'I didn't mean you.'

Maggie grimaced and decided to change the subject completely. 'Tell me about your new man? And would you like to see the nursery?'

'Well, well, kiddo.' Maggie patted her stomach after Sylvia had left—she'd taken to talking to her baby ever since she'd come out of her slough of despond. 'That was your aunt. Come to think of it, that's yet another difficult situation resolved. Which only leaves us but, hey, between the two of us we can conquer anything!'

A couple of days later, she got an even greater surprise.

Jack held a dinner party to celebrate the retirement village foundations being dug.

Actually, it was Maisie who organized it all down to the caterers, the flowers and guest list.

Maggie received her invitation in the mail. Jack was overseas until the afternoon of the dinner, but she didn't RSVP until the last moment. She was in two minds.

Then she thought, What the heck? She was part of the team and although, at eight months, sitting for any length of time was uncomfortable, she felt absolutely fine.

She also went out of her way to look absolutely fine. She chose a long French navy dress in a silk georgette that, despite being a maternity dress, was the essence of chic. It was round-necked, sleeveless and spring-like in tune with the new season. The fine pintucking on the bodice was stitched with silver thread.

She got her hair and her nails done; her tawny hair was loose and lightly curled so that it looked gorgeously windswept as only an expert hairdresser could achieve.

Her shoes were a complete folly, she knew—high, strappy silver sandals she couldn't have resisted if she'd tried. She covered the few patches of pregnancy pigment on her cheeks with a glowing foundation and her lipstick matched her nail polish.

She stared at herself in her beautiful rosewood cheval-mirror and addressed her unborn child again...

'You couldn't say we were *hugely* pregnant, honey-child. I've been very careful dietary-wise and I've been pretty active. Incidentally, *you're* pretty active these days, a right little gymnast! But I am more, well, rounded, even in the less obvious areas, although it doesn't seem to look too bad. Not tonight anyway.'

She turned away from the mirror ruefully and swept her silver mesh purse off the bed.

Maisie was more positive about it when she met Maggie at the door of the sub-penthouse.

'Maggie,' she said affectionately—they'd become good friends, 'you look fantastic!'

'I second that.' Jack loomed up behind Maisie and Maggie took an unexpected little breath.

She hadn't seen him for a week, but it was more than that. He wore a dinner suit and the beautifully tailored black suit and white shirt highlighted his tall, strong lines and broad shoulders. It shot through her mind that she loved him however he looked.

Windblown and with blue shadows on his jaw,

wearing an old football jersey with the sleeves cut off as he'd often been at Cape Gloucester—but this Jack was electrifying.

She swallowed something in her throat. 'Thanks, you two! You sure know how to make a very pregnant lady feel better.'

It was a buffet dinner for about twenty people and because it was a calm, warm night there were tables set out on the veranda high above Runaway Bay and overlooking the Broadwater and the ocean beyond.

The food was inspired and fine wine flowed although Maggie didn't partake of the wine and she ate sparingly. But the company was pleasant, she knew everyone and she enjoyed herself.

All the same, she attempted to leave a little early. She was making her explanations to Maisie when Jack's hand closed round her wrist. 'Stay a bit longer,' he said quietly. 'It won't be long before the party breaks up. Then I can drive you home.'

'But I drove myself here,' she objected.

'Doesn't matter. You shouldn't be out and about on your own at this time of night.'

'That's true,' Maisie agreed.

'I am a little tired, though,' Maggie said and stifled a yawn.

'How about I settle you in the den where you can put your feet up and bring you a cuppa?' Maisie offered.

'Oh, thank you!' Maggie said gratefully. 'My shoes are killing me.'

Maggie had never seen the den and it brought a slight smile to her lips. There was definitely a nautical flavour to it.

There were gold-framed ships on the walls; there was a wonderful antique globe of the world and a polished brass sextant on the coffee-table. There were also deep, inviting buttoned leather armchairs…

'And this one,' said Maisie triumphantly as she pushed a lever on the side of the chair, 'is a recliner chair.'

'Just what I need!' Maggie slipped off her shoes and sank down into it gratefully.

'Tea's on the way!'

Maggie had her tea, then she stretched out in the chair, to find she couldn't keep her eyes open.

Half an hour later something woke her from the gentle slumber she'd fallen into. Her lashes lifted, and Jack was standing beside the chair looking down at her, Jack looking austere but divine with his streaky fair hair tamed tonight and that wonderful physique highlighted by his dinner suit.

Her lips parted as their gazes caught and held, then she struggled upright.

He held out his hand and helped her to her feet.

She opened her mouth to thank him, but the words died on her lips because he was studying her—in a way she knew well, a way that was anything but austere—from top to toe. The sleep-flushed curves of her face, the glorious disarray of her hair, her mouth and throat, her full, rich breasts beneath the fine navy georgette, the mound of his child…

His gaze was intent and heavy-lidded and the pressure of his fingers on hers grew.

He still wants me, Maggie thought chaotically as

her colour fluctuated and her breathing grew ragged. That's how he used to look at me before he made love to me, just like this... So that the power of his gaze was almost like having his hands on me.

Have I not been the only one to suffer from the unassuaged ache of being physically deprived of him? Not the only one plagued by so many memories of our lovemaking? she wondered wildly. But what does it mean? I was so sure that he'd stopped wanting me.

She was destined not to know what it meant. A phone rang softly on the desk.

He turned his head at last to look at it, a hard, irritable look, then as it rang on he shrugged and walked over to it.

'Maisie,' he growled down the line, 'what the hell—?' He stopped.

From then on he answered in monosyllables until he said, 'All right. Will you drive Maggie home?'

She looked a question at him as he put the phone down.

'Sylvia rang. Our mother is critically ill now and not likely to survive for more than a day or so.'

'I'm sorry,' she said quietly. 'Don't worry about me—but will you get a flight at this time of night?'

'No, and the earliest flights tomorrow are booked out so I'll drive. If I start off now, I'll get there early tomorrow morning, anyway. I'm sorry.'

'That's all right! Just—take care. On the road.'

'I will.' He picked up her hand. 'You take care too.'

The baby moved at that moment and she put her hand on her stomach with his over it.

He blinked as he felt the movement. 'How often does that happen?'

'Quite a lot nowadays.' A smile trembled on her lips. 'He or she loves doing cartwheels so we could have another gymnast on our hands.'

Maisie coughed discreetly from the doorway, and the moment was lost. 'Sylvia again,' she said apologetically.

For the next few days Maggie felt as if she were on cloud nine.

Don't equate wanting you with loving you and not being able to live without you, she warned herself, but it made no difference. The long months of unhappiness, of blaming herself for her situation, of feeling that she hadn't lived up to what he needed in a woman melted away behind her.

If he could still want her when she was eight months pregnant, maybe he always would? Had she been proud and foolish all that time?

But I didn't know, she thought dazedly. He hid it so well. Why?

This thought occurred to her as she was walking down a busy pavement in Southport on the way to her doctor. She didn't even notice the man who passed her, then turned round and came back to her.

Until he said, 'Hang on—don't I know you?'

Maggie blinked and stared at him uncomprehendingly.

'You weren't pregnant then and all you were wearing was a bra and jeans while you and Jack McKinnon were—supposedly, although I had my doubts—trying to get out of the roof of a shed.'

Maggie suffered a surge of sheer revulsion at the

hateful way the man's eyes gleamed, and recognition came to her. It was the journalist who'd been with the private detective when she and Jack had been locked in the shed.

When he put his hand on her arm to detain her, she wrenched it free. 'Go away,' she ordered and made a dash for her doctor's surgery only a few doors away.

She heaved a huge sigh of relief as she passed through the doors and no one followed her, although she supposed it was always possible he would hang around until she came out.

Maisie, she thought. I'll ring Maisie and ask her to pick me up. Maisie will know how to handle it.

She got out her mobile phone and did just that.

But the first question she asked Maisie was if she'd heard from Jack.

'I just got the call. Mrs McKinnon passed away this morning. I believe it was a blessed relief.'

'Oh, that's still so sad. Please pass on my deepest sympathy.' Maggie paused, then went on to explain her current situation.

'I'll come and get you,' Maisie said immediately. 'Just tell me where and stay put in your doctor's rooms.'

When Maggie ended the call, she looked around and discovered she was in the wrong corridor.

She turned back just as a little boy, looking gleefully over his shoulder at his mother who was in hot pursuit, raced towards her.

They collided.

The child fell over, but bounced up. Maggie, robbed of her usual agility, toppled over with one ankle twisted beneath her. She fell on her back and hit her head on the floor. She passed out like a light.

CHAPTER EIGHT

SHE swam up slowly out of a deep, dreamless sleep. She opened her eyes a couple of times, but it was too much of an effort to keep them open. The third time she did it, though, she moved her head slightly and something swam into her line of vision that caused her to keep them open—a crib.

She froze as jumbled, painful memories tumbled through her mind, some memories of labour and the enormous effort and concentration it had required, memories of all sorts of people attending to her and X-raying her, but no memories of a birth.

She clutched her stomach and found it flat but floppy rather than hard and round. She froze again and realized her deep sleep since then must have been sedative-assisted because someone had put her into a fresh nightgown and a crisply made bed in a strange room she'd never seen before. And someone had put a crib beside the bed.

She moved convulsively but found her lower limbs wouldn't move at all.. and Jack said quietly, 'Take it easy, Maggie.'

Her astonished gaze fell on him, sitting on a chair beside the crib. 'Jack!'

'Yes. How do you feel?'

'I have no idea.' She blinked rapidly. 'Is this—us?'

He looked briefly amused. 'A good way to put it. Uh—it says on the crib—Trent stroke McKinnon—

so I guess it must be.' He tilted the crib so Maggie could see into it.

There was a baby fast asleep in it.

'So it's all right? It's...*all right*?' she asked urgently.

'Fine. Quite perfect, in fact, so they tell me.'

Maggie fell back against the pillows with a gasp of relief. 'Girl or boy?'

'Boy. He's a little premature and he's spent a bit of time in a humidicrib but they reckon he's coping very well on his own.'

She studied the baby, not that she could see much more than the curve of a cheek, one tiny fist and a fuzz of brown hair. Then he moved and more of his features came into view—and Maggie held her breath. But with great seriousness, the infant Trent stroke McKinnon yawned, opened his hand, then slept on.

'He seems to be...very composed,' Maggie said in some confusion.

'Yeah.' Jack shoved a hand through his hair, then rubbed his unshaven jaw. 'A lot more composed than I feel.'

'How can that be so?' she queried seriously. 'After what he's been through?'

'You were the one who went through the worst.'

'I don't seem to remember a lot about it,' she confessed. 'Well, some parts of it, but it's all confused and fuzzy.'

'Just as well and not surprising—you had concussion on top of everything else.'

Jack paused, then reached for her hand. 'What happened was, you sprained your ankle when you fell, you have a bump on your head and they think you may have slipped a disc or done something to your back. Then you went into labour. Fortunately, Maisie arrived not long after it all happened and she was able to identify you and get your own doctor—they'd called out another doctor who has consulting rooms in the same building.'

'Why can't I move my legs?' she asked.

'You've had a couple of epidurals. The birth itself was quite straightforward so they chose not to inter-vene—seems this young man had decided not to muck around!' He smiled at her. 'But you were in a lot of pain from your back as well as your ankle so it was for your sake and it may take a while to wear off.'

She blinked dazedly. 'How long ago did this all happen?'

He looked at his watch. 'About eight hours ago. I got here just after he was born.' He smiled again and released her hand to stroke her hair for a moment. 'I've had my first cuddle.'

Maggie closed her eyes. 'Can I?' she said with ab-solute longing in her voice.

'Sure. Your parents are also here, incidentally. They went to have a cup of coffee.'

Maggie's lashes swept up. 'You—you and my fa-ther have met?'

He nodded. 'No fireworks, no hard words. We're all too concerned about you. And too taken with the baby.'

Maggie breathed very deeply. 'That's—I can't tell you how happy that makes me.'

He said nothing, just stroked her hair again.

'And my back?' she asked after a while.

'They're not sure. What with everything else going on—' he gestured ruefully '—they haven't been able to assess it properly. But they have taken X-rays. We're waiting on the results now. Your ankle just needs time.'

'Will you please give me my baby, Jack?' she begged. 'You see, I've been talking to it, to him,' she corrected herself, 'for weeks and weeks and I'm sure he can't understand why he hasn't heard my voice since he was born.'

'Of course.' He got up and picked Trent stroke McKinnon up gingerly. In the moment before he placed the bundle in Maggie's arms, he looked down at the child in a way that made Maggie catch her breath—with sheer pride and tenderness.

It shot through her mind that even if she never achieved a breakthrough to the real Jack McKinnon, this child would.

Then she accepted the bundle and her own attachment began. Her breasts tightened and she put a finger into her son's open palm and his tiny hand closed around it.

'Well, well, honey-child,' she breathed, 'we get to meet at last. How do you do? Oh, look,' she said to Jack, 'I think he's got your nose!'

Jack grimaced and felt his nose. 'If there's anyone he looks like,' he said ruefully, 'it's a Trent.'

They laughed together—and that was how her parents found them.

But when the injections wore off a couple of hours later, Maggie was once again in great pain, although at least the cause of it had been diagnosed. She'd broken a transverse process, a small bone running off the spine, in her lower back.

It would heal, she was told, of its own accord, but

many movements would be painful for her until it did so. All they could do was manage the pain for her until it became bearable, in about a week they estimated, but even then it would probably be quite a few weeks before she regained full mobility.

Unfortunately, they told her, all this would interfere with her ability to breast-feed her baby.

'No, it won't,' she said.

'Maggie,' her mother began.

'Mum, there has to be a way. Dad—' she turned her head to her father '—why don't you take Jack out for a drink while we work this out? He looks as if he could do with it.'

'Maggie,' David Trent warned, 'darling, it's not the end of the world if you can't breast-feed and it's just as important for the baby for you to recover well and quickly.'

'I will,' she promised, 'but I will also do this, *somehow*.'

It occurred to her a moment later that she never, ever thought she'd see what she saw then—her father and Jack exchange identical helpless glances.

Belle also saw it and she exchanged a laughing glance with Maggie before she shooed both men out. Then she sobered and turned back to her daughter. 'How?'

'I've read a lot about it and there's great support for breast-feeding mums. What we need is an expert, but I don't see why my milk can't be expressed for the next few days so I don't lose it, until I come off the painkillers—and I intend to do that as soon as possible.'

'But what about the baby?'

'We need to find someone with loads of milk who

wouldn't mind suckling him so he gets the hang of it, and they will have to feed him a supplement. Mum, please help me here,' Maggie said urgently, then looked exhausted. 'I want to do this!'

Belle eyed her daughter, then sighed. 'All right. All right.'

It was a traumatic and painful week for Maggie. Expressing breast milk might sound fine in theory, but in practice it could be excruciating. Transverse processes might be little bones, but they hurt like the devil when you broke them.

On the plus side, however, Bev Janson, who'd had her third baby the same day as Maggie's, had more milk than she knew what to do with and was grateful for the relief she gained from feeding another baby. Not only that, she and Maggie became firm friends.

And Trent stroke McKinnon throve through it all.

Then came the day when Maggie could sit up properly and she was given the go-ahead to feed her baby herself.

Her sense of triumph was huge. So was her joy.

'See?' she said to Jack. 'I knew there had to be a way.'

'Maggie…' He stopped, then shook his head at her. 'You're a bloody marvel. I don't think I've ever seen such guts.'

'The doctor said I could probably go home in three or four days.'

He hesitated. 'Have you had any thoughts about that?'

'No!' She grimaced. 'Too much on my mind.'

'We have.'

She eyed him. Apart from a couple of days when

he'd gone south for his mother's funeral, he'd spent time with her every day.

He'd taken the nursing staff by storm.

He'd brought her a DVD machine and lots of movies, including all the Harry Potter movies; he'd brought her books. He'd sent Bev a magnificent floral tribute and got friendly with her husband. On discovering the Jansons would dearly love to move into a bigger house than the one they were renting but couldn't afford to, he'd organized one at the same rent for them on one of his estates.

But he'd said nothing about marriage, although, when he was with her in her painful times, Maggie could have been forgiven for thinking he cared deeply about her.

Now, it was a Sunday, he wore jeans, deck shoes and a white polo T-shirt. He looked casual, big and…

Maggie paused in her summary of him. And what…?

'We have?' she repeated suspiciously. 'Who are we?'

'Your parents and I. We came to the conclusion it would be a good idea if you moved in with me.'

'Jack—'

'I have so much space and it's all on one level whereas your house is double-storeyed—'

'I know that!'

He half smiled. 'Then you'll agree that since you'll need a wheelchair for a while it makes sense not to have stairs to negotiate.'

She was silent as she stared at him fixedly.

'Your mother has offered to stay with us for as long as you need her,' he went on. 'There's also a gymnasium in the building and a swimming pool. Your doctors have recommended a programme of exercise under a physiotherapist's care to get your back and your ankle strong again.'

'I see,' she said at last.

'What do you see, Maggie?' he asked with his lips quirking.

'Something I never thought I would live to see,' she said. 'You and my parents ganging up on me.'

He opened his mouth to reply, but a nurse walked in with their baby in her arms. 'Feed time! Now listen up, you two.' She gave the baby to Maggie. 'We, the nursing staff, have decided it's about time this baby got a name. You can't go on calling him Trent stroke McKinnon for the rest of his life!'

'How about,' Jack suggested, 'Trent McKinnon?'

'Trent McKinnon,' Maggie said slowly. 'Do you approve, sweetheart?' she asked the baby.

Their child wrinkled his face and began to wave his fists, a prelude, Maggie was coming to know well, to a very vocal infant conniption. 'Call me what you like; just feed me!' Maggie said rapidly and started to unbutton her nightgown.

They all laughed.

'Yes, I like that,' she added, 'but he needs a middle name—can be very helpful in certain circumstances, kiddo! So, let's make it Trent Jack McKinnon.'

'Agreed.' Jack got up and kissed her briefly. 'I've got to go, but I'll be back this evening. Shall I set it all up?'

Maggie looked up from her baby with a tinge of confusion, then she nodded helplessly and turned her concentration back to Trent Jack McKinnon.

It all went according to plan.

Maggie grew stronger and used the motorized

wheelchair less and less, but it was still invaluable by
the time Trent was two months old because it allowed
her to do everything for him without placing the burden of his weight on her back and ankle.

One of the bedrooms in the sub-penthouse had been
converted to his nursery cum her bedroom and, with
his flair for good design, Jack had had all the surfaces,
change table and so on, made to a height Maggie
could cope with sitting down.

He'd also taken advantage of her mother's presence
to catch up with business trips he'd put on hold while
Maggie had been in hospital. So they hadn't seen a
great deal of him—for which Maggie had been curiously grateful.

She tried desperately to analyze not only her feelings, but the whole situation as her strength returned,
but all she could come up with was the fact that she
only seemed to be able to take each day as it came
with a sense of what will be will be.

Then her mother decided to go back to the cattle
stations. She left the day Jack was due to return after
a week in New Zealand.

For some reason, although Maggie was perfectly
confident with Trent now, although she experienced
no pain now and wasn't afraid to be left alone, the
quiet, empty apartment acted as a catalyst for her.

She started to think of the future. She started to
question Jack's feelings for her, and hers for him.

There had been no repeat of what had taken place
in the den a few nights before Trent was born, but
that wasn't so surprising in the circumstances, and she
might have been partly responsible for it anyway. She
had been preoccupied with her baby and getting herself fit again for him. Jack, apparently, had had a lot

of work to catch up on. And her mother had been with them all the time.

Yet, lately, little things about him had started to catch her unawares.

She'd been talking to him over breakfast one morning when she'd found herself breaking off and watching the way he was drumming his fingers on the table. It was a habit she'd first noticed at Cape Gloucester and it suddenly reminded her of his fingers on her skin, exploring, tantalizing her until she was weak with desire…

She'd had to get up without finishing what she was saying on the pretext of hearing Trent.

He'd come back from one trip, but had only been able to spend half an hour with them before going off to a meeting. She'd unpacked his bag for him and she'd suddenly buried her face in one of his unlaundered shirts, feeling a little dizzy with longing for his tall, strong body on hers.

So not a lot has changed there, she thought, while she waited for Jack to come back from New Zealand. I still don't know where he stands, though, but I do know he's been wonderful in every other way.

She was sitting on her bed as she thought these thoughts, with Trent lying beside her obviously deeply interested in his teddy bear.

She leant over and tickled him under the chin. He made a trilling little sound, then grabbed her hand and started to nuzzle it.

'But in the end, honey-child,' she said to him, 'what it boils down to is this—if your mama thought only of herself in times gone by, that has to change. OK, I know! You're hungry.'

*   *   *

Jack got home just after Maggie had given Trent his six p.m. feed and was settling him.

She was still in the nursery when she heard him arrive and called out to him. 'In here, Jack!'

He came through a few minutes later looking rather tired. He wore khaki trousers and a round-necked T-shirt under a tweed sports jacket.

'A busy trip?' she queried.

'Yep.' He stretched. 'How's my son and heir?'

'He's fine. He was talking to his teddy bear today. Jack.' Maggie hesitated, then knew there was only one way to do what she had to do and that was to plunge right in. 'This is a very proper baby.'

Jack stared at his now-sleeping son for a long moment, then sat down on the end of her bed. 'I never thought he was a porcelain doll.'

'No. I mean, he's very well organized. He does everything by the book.'

Jack frowned. 'He's only eight weeks old. How can you say that?'

Maggie was still sitting in her wheelchair, attractively dressed in slim white trousers and a floral seersucker jacket trimmed with green. Her dark gold hair was tied back with a scrunchie; her green eyes were clear and free of pain.

'I'll tell you. He adapted himself to a four-hourly schedule right from the start under extremely difficult circumstances. He burps beautifully and he mostly sleeps between feeds just as the book says he should. He has one wakeful period, after his two p.m. feed, where he'll accept conversation and he quite appreciates being carried around for a bit. He now sleeps through the eight hours from ten p.m. to six a.m.'

'Is there anything he doesn't do by the book?' Jack asked with a grin. 'He sounds almost too good to be true.'

Maggie considered. 'He hates having his hair washed. He gets extremely upset, but even that isn't going against the book exactly. They do warn that some babies hate it.'

'Screams blue murder?'

'Yes. Otherwise—' she shrugged '—there's nothing he doesn't do very correctly.'

'What are you worried about, then?'

Maggie stared down at her sleeping son with her heart in her eyes. 'I can't help thinking he would be horrified if he knew how—irregular—his situation was.'

She looked up and their gazes clashed.

'Born out of wedlock, you mean?' he said, and for a fleeting moment his mouth hardened. 'That was your choice, Maggie.'

She inclined her head. 'That was before—all sorts of things happened,' she said quietly and ran her fingers along the arm of her wheelchair. 'That was definitely before I came to appreciate the reality of having a baby and what a baby deserves.'

Jack stared at her for a long moment, then he got up and started to push the wheelchair towards the door.

'I can walk or do this myself,' Maggie said.

'Stay put. I need a drink.'

She didn't protest any further and he wheeled her out onto the veranda, and left her to get their drinks. The sun had set, leaving a fiery pattern of cloud and sky to reflect in the calm waters below them.

He came back with a Scotch for himself and a tall

glass of lemon, lime and bitters for her with a sprig of mint in it.

Then he leant back against the railing and studied her. 'What are you suggesting, Maggie?'

She sipped her drink. 'Will you marry me, Jack?'

The silence lengthened between them until he stirred and said, 'Is that what you *really* want?'

What did I expect? she wondered. That he would leap at the idea? That he would declare his undying love for me?

She put her glass down on the veranda table and stumbled up out of her chair.

He caught her on the threshold to the lounge. 'Whoa! Why are you running away?'

'Because you haven't changed one bit,' she flashed at him. 'You never did understand me and you never will.'

He looked down into her anguished eyes, her scarlet face as she tried to pull away. 'Oh, yes, I do.'

'Then why say that, as if—as if it's just another of my mad, impetuous whims?'

'Blame your mother if you want to blame anyone for a desire on my part to be sure of your feelings,' he said harshly.

'My mother!' she gasped. 'What has she got to do with this?'

'A lot. She came to see me after we'd first met at your house.'

Maggie sagged in his arms with disbelief and confusion written large in her expression as she remembered her conversation with her mother about Jack and how she loved him... 'What did she tell you?' she whispered.

He led her towards a settee and they sat down side

by side. 'She told me that you could lead a horse to water but you couldn't make it drink.'

Maggie's mouth fell open.

He smiled briefly. 'She didn't use those words, but that was the gist of it. She told me there was no way I'd get you to marry me unless it was what you yourself had decided to do.'

'She…she really said that?'

He nodded. 'I told her that I had already received that impression and was prepared to bide my time. She then offered me some assistance. Under normal circumstances, she said she would never have dreamt of deserting you in any way, but it would provide *me* the opportunity to provide *you* with some moral support at least and who knew what might come of that?'

'I wondered about that,' Maggie confessed. 'Her going away like that. I put it down to, well, their reconciliation, Mum and Dad's, but I was a bit surprised. I put *that* down to selfishness on my part.'

He lay back and shoved his hands in his pockets. 'I also made a promise to your mother. She can be…' he smiled fleetingly '…a hard woman.'

'I wouldn't have thought that!' Maggie objected.

'Believe me, on the subject of her only daughter, she exhibited some—almost—tigress tendencies.'

Maggie blinked in sheer surprise. 'What did she say?'

'First of all she pointed out the error of my ways to me. To use someone like you as a tool for revenge against your father was diabolical.'

Maggie gulped a breath of astonished air. 'Did you tell her…did you tell her how I followed you and—?'

'No.' He put a hand over hers. 'And it made no

difference; she was *right*. With things the way they were between me and your father, with a girl like you, I was—inexcusable.'

'Was it only revenge?' she asked barely audibly.

He turned his head to her at last. 'Did it feel like it?'

'Not until you sent me away,' she whispered.

His hand tightened on hers until she made a small sound.

'Sorry.' He released her and sat up. 'She then explained that to turn up out of the blue and propose marriage because there was a baby on the way was the height of arrogance even if I still wanted you. And the promise she extracted was that I would stand by you in every other way until, if ever, you discovered I was the one *you* wanted.'

'Oh my,' Maggie breathed. 'Does that mean to say you did still want me? I thought so once, but that was just before Trent was born and it was only once...'

'Maggie—' he rubbed his jaw almost savagely '—I never stopped wanting you. I couldn't get you out of my mind even if I couldn't reconcile—I honestly didn't think I could bring the commitment to a marriage that was needed. There has always been a small part of me that—I don't know—was closed off to that particular traffic. The last nine months have changed all that,' he added.

She was silent, her lips parted, her eyes huge.

'You see,' he went on, 'yes, I cared about my adopted family and Sylvia will always be special to me, but no one has ever walked into my heart and taken it over the way you have.

'No one,' he said quietly, 'brings me the joy and pleasure just in their company you do. And that's one of the reasons I took what turned out to be an increasingly long, hard road these past months. Then there was what you did for Trent. I have never seen anyone battle such painful odds as you did for our son. So you not only have my whole-hearted love, but my utmost admiration, Maggie Trent.'

She wiped her eyes. 'If only you'd told me this sooner—'

He took her hand again, gently this time, but shook his head. 'If there was one thing that finally made me see how much I loved you, it was when your welfare became more important than mine.

'Maggie...' he paused '...sometimes, often, your first love turns out not to be what you think it is at the time. It can be powerful but fleeting, a crush maybe. Also, I had no way of knowing—you possibly had no way of knowing yourself—if you could ever forgive me, or—'

'If it hadn't all been a Maggie Trent, heat-of-the-moment whim?' she suggested gravely.

'I wasn't going to say that.'

'I couldn't blame you if you did.' She gestured.

'What I was going to say was,' he continued, 'there were so many complications it would have been perfectly natural for you to feel dreadfully confused. All I could hope for was that.. time might be on my side. But if it's Trent that's made you come to this decision—'

She put her hand to his lips. 'Jack, I've had my own revelations. I'm a lot more like my father than I dreamt. I'm an all-or-nothing kind of person and that's why I thought it wouldn't work for me with you.'

She hesitated as he kissed her fingers. 'Yes, I

thought I was asking you to marry me for Trent's sake because I didn't know how you felt. But the truth is there's a plus side to the all-or-nothing person I am. I fell in love with you overnight. I will always love you—it may even be a bit of a trial to you at times, but that's me, and it was *always you*, for me.'

'A bit of a trial?' He pulled her into his arms and held her extremely hard as he buried his face in her hair. 'If you only knew how many times I've wanted to do this,' he said on an edge of desperation. 'If you knew how close I came to lowering my guard the night Sylvia rang.'

He lifted his head and looked into her eyes.

She placed a fingertip on the little scar on his eyebrow. 'If you knew what that did to me. Suddenly I was on cloud nine; nothing else mattered!'

'Then…' He hesitated. 'Your back?'

'It's fine, if I take care. Why don't you unplug the phone?'

'Good idea.'

But they didn't go straight to bed. They finished their drinks, he with his arm around her, and they talked.

He told her how he'd manufactured some of his business trips in the last few weeks because actually living in the same place with her had become more of a test of his endurance than he could bear.

She asked him how he felt about her mother now.

He rested his chin on the top of her head for a moment. 'What I said just now was a throwback to earlier times. I may have agreed with her, but there's a certain natural reluctance to think too blackly of oneself.'

She looked up in time to disturb a rueful expression in his eyes.

'I know the feeling,' she agreed.

He kissed her forehead. 'I've made my peace with your mother. To be honest, Trent has to take a lot of the credit for the new state of goodwill between the House of McKinnon and the House of Trent.'

'It's amazing what a baby can do.'

'Mmm… It's just as amazing what his mother has achieved.'

Maggie laid her head on his shoulder. 'I've missed this so much,' she whispered.

He put his other arm around her. 'Me too.'

They sat like that for an age, feeling warm and content, then it grew into more and he started to kiss her.

'The Nile? Or the sands of Araby?'

Maggie looked around Jack's bedroom. It was large, luxurious, but quite impersonal and they were lying on a vast bed, renewing their intimate acquaintance. 'Ah,' she said, 'this is going to take a bit of imagination.'

He looked up. 'I know what you mean. I bought it like this, this place, but it reminds me of a hotel. I haven't got around to changing anything but the den.'

'I could change it for you,' she offered.

'I've had a better idea, I'll tell you about it tomorrow. But talking of change—'

'I know.' She ran her fingers through his hair. 'I've changed a bit.'

He kissed the soft underside of her arm. 'You're still gorgeous. Actually—' he swept his hand down her body and returned it to her breasts '—apart from these, there's not much change at all.'

'All the swimming, gym work and physio has helped enormously,' she told him. 'But you've—lost a bit of weight.'

'I had the feeling I was fading away beneath all that longing for you, Maggie Trent.'

Maggie smiled and kissed the corner of his mouth. 'Well, now you've got me, what do you want to do with me, Jack McKinnon?'

He showed her. He visited all her most erotic spots with his usual care and attention until she was quivering and on fire, and her responses became just as intimate.

'This is going to be quite a ride,' he said with the breath rasping in his throat.

They were lying facing each other. She was in his arms with one of her legs riding high on his thigh.

'It always was,' she murmured.

He brought one hand up to cup her cheek and it was so exquisitely gentle a gesture and there was so much tenderness in his grey eyes, Maggie caught her breath and felt as if her heart could burst with love.

'Now?' he queried.

'Now,' she agreed. 'Yes, please.'

'I thought of a way to do this with the least strain on your back.'

'Oh?'

He rolled onto his back, taking her with him on top of him. 'Not only easy on your back, but you're in total control now, Maggie.'

'Jack,' she gasped as he entered her, 'I'm in no position to... You told me once you were about to die. I'm in the same situation!'

'Hold hard there for a moment, sweetheart,' he commanded, and clamped his hands on her hips. 'We might as well die together. How's that?' he asked as their rhythm co-ordinated.

'Well,' she conceded with a faint smile chasing across her lips, 'that's perfect.'

They said no more until they climaxed together, not only in physical unity but mentally transported as well.

'I love you, I love you, I love you,' she said huskily when she could talk again, with sheer sensual rapture still sweeping her body.

'Me too. I mean I love you, Maggie. When did you plan to marry me?'

She had to laugh, and slowly they came back to earth together. 'Uh—tomorrow?'

Of course it wasn't possible to arrange it that soon, but she got another lovely surprise the next day.

'I'd like to show you and Trent something,' he said the next morning after breakfast. 'We'll take his pram.'

'What is it?'

He studied her. She was feeding Trent and she looked voluptuous, languorous and completely serene. As if she had most satisfactorily been made love to recently, which, indeed, she had.

As have I, he reflected, and I will never let her go again.

'Wait and see.'

'There's a surprise in the air, honey-child,' she told Trent, and Jack grinned.

But her astonishment at his surprise was huge.

'Jack,' she said uncertainly as they stood in the

house on the property that had first brought them together, 'how did this happen?'

The house was no longer neglected. It wasn't furnished, but it had been renovated exactly as Maggie had suggested. It was clean and sparkling and the smell of new paint lingered on the air.

'You told me what you wanted,' he reminded her.

'Yes, but you never mentioned it again!'

'I wanted to do it as a surprise. I thought it might be the perfect place for Trent to grow up.' He took her hand and led her to a window. 'The garden has been cleared and is all ready and waiting for you. I thought you might even like to see if you could grow some *Guettarda Speciosa* here and harvest their perfume.'

'Oh, Jack.' She stood on her toes and kissed him. 'Thank you, from the bottom of my heart.'

He held her close. 'Happy?'

'Yes, very happy. Almost happier than I can bear.' They turned as Trent made a protesting sound from his pram, as if he was taking exception to being ignored.

They linked hands and walked over to the pram.

'We're here, kiddo!' Jack said and they both bent over the pram.

Trent wriggled ecstatically, then he smiled a blinding, toothless smile at them.

Maggie gasped. 'Did you see that—did you see *that*? Do you agree that was a smile and not wind?'

'Sure do. What's wrong with it?'

'He's only two months old! I didn't think it was supposed to happen so early.'

'Maggie—' Jack tossed her a laughing look '—perhaps he's divined that we've got the message and are doing everything by the book now, so he can relax and please himself occasionally?'

BILLIONAIRES' BRIDES

Pregnant by their princes...

Take three incredibly wealthy European princes
and match them with three beautiful, spirited women.
Add large helpings of intense emotion and passionate
attraction. Result: three unexpected pregnancies—and
three possible princesses—if those princes have their way....

Coming in September:

THE GREEK PRINCE'S CHOSEN WIFE
by Sandra Marton

Ivy Madison is pregnant with Prince Damian's baby—
as a surrogate mother! Now Damian won't let Ivy go—after
all, he didn't have the pleasure of taking her to bed before....

Available in August:

THE ITALIAN PRINCE'S PREGNANT BRIDE

Coming in October:

THE SPANISH PRINCE'S VIRGIN BRIDE

IN Bed WITH THE Boss

Chosen by him for business,
taken by him for pleasure…
A classic collection of office romances from
Harlequin Presents, by your favorite authors.

Coming in September:

THE BRAZILIAN BOSS'S INNOCENT MISTRESS
by Sarah Morgan

Innocent Grace Thacker has ten minutes to persuade
ruthless Brazilian Rafael Cordeiro to help her.
Ten minutes to decide whether to leave and lose—
or settle her debts in his bed!

Also from this miniseries, coming in October:

THE BOSS'S WIFE FOR A WEEK
by Anne McAllister

REQUEST YOUR FREE BOOKS!

 HARLEQUIN® *Presents*

PASSION GUARANTEED SEDUCTION

2 FREE NOVELS PLUS 2 FREE GIFTS!

YES! Please send me 2 FREE Harlequin Presents® novels and my 2 FREE gifts. After receiving them, if I don't wish to receive any more books, I can return the shipping statement marked "cancel." If I don't cancel, I will receive 6 brand-new novels every month and be billed just $3.80 per book in the U.S., or $4.47 per book in Canada, plus 25¢ shipping and handling per book and applicable taxes, if any*. That's a savings of close to 15% off the cover price! I understand that accepting the 2 free books and gifts places me under no obligation to buy anything. I can always return a shipment and cancel at any time. Even if I never buy another book from Harlequin, the two free books and gifts are mine to keep forever.

106 HDN EEXK 306 HDN EEXV

Name _____ (PLEASE PRINT)

Address _____ Apt. #

City _____ State/Prov. _____ Zip/Postal Code

Signature (if under 18, a parent or guardian must sign)

Mail to the Harlequin Reader Service®:

IN U.S.A.: P.O. Box 1867, Buffalo, NY 14240-1867
IN CANADA: P.O. Box 609, Fort Erie, Ontario L2A 5X3

Not valid to current Harlequin Presents subscribers.

Want to try two free books from another line?
Call 1-800-873-8635 or visit www.morefreebooks.com.

* Terms and prices subject to change without notice. NY residents add applicable sales tax. Canadian residents will be charged applicable provincial taxes and GST. This offer is limited to one order per household. All orders subject to approval. Credit or debit balances in a customer's account(s) may be offset by any other outstanding balance owed by or to the customer. Please allow 4 to 6 weeks for delivery.

Your Privacy: Harlequin is committed to protecting your privacy. Our Privacy Policy is available online at www.eHarlequin.com or upon request from the Reader Service. From time to time we make our lists of customers available to reputable firms who may have a product or service of interest to you. If you would prefer we not share your name and address, please check here. ☐

HP07